RIGHT PLACE – RIGHT TIME

C000164630

Right Place – Right Time

by

C<small>HRISTOPHER</small> A<small>UDLAND</small>

The Memoir Club

© Christopher Audland 2004

First published in 2004 by
The Memoir Club
Stanhope Old Hall
Stanhope
Weardale
County Durham

All rights reserved.
Unauthorised duplication
contravenes existing laws.

British Library Cataloguing in
Publication Data.
A catalogue record for this book
is available from the
British Library.

ISBN: 1 84104 091 6

Typeset by George Wishart & Associates, Whitley Bay.
Printed by CPI Bath.

For Maura, Rupert,
Claire and William

Contents

List of Illustrations

Foreword

by Sir Franklin Berman, KCMG, QC

Legal Adviser to the Foreign and Commonwealth Office, 1991-99

I AM FLATTERED to have been asked to write this foreword. My closest working contacts with Christopher Audland were during his Foreign Office period, when he was Head of its Science & Technology Department, and later when I had the good fortune of a double tour in Germany, first in Berlin and then at the Embassy in Bonn, while he was Head of Chancery there. During his lengthy period in Europe after that, our paths, I'm sad to say, hardly crossed. But that made more enthralling the opportunity to catch up, as it were, in all the vivid detail the book purveys. After his retirement, though, we were able to pick up the threads, many of them golden ones, notably Brantwood and the quite wonderful Ruskin Library at Lancaster University, and the early excitement of Opera Europe; and to spend time together in his beloved Cumbria.

As the book was taking shape, we talked about its title. I was pleased when he settled on *Right Place, Right Time*, for the reasons explained in his Preface. They are not, of course, unique to him. But what matters is to spot the opportunities for what they are, and seize them. That must surely be ranked as one of Christopher's great talents: right place, right time, right person.

His own modest account comes, however, with a strain of justified pride. An overriding theme does emerge from the whole course of his life, and that is Europe. More precisely, building a Europe fitted for the demands of the future and permanently freed from the murderous rivalries of the past. He would have hated 'my part in building a modern Europe', yet that is in effect what the book does describe, and the role was a notable one which deserves to be recognized (as it was) and recorded (which it now has been).

My principal recollection of working in close harness with Christopher is his tactical adroitness. He had that rare gift of being able to picture the steps a negotiation would have to move through to arrive at a satisfactory conclusion. He always seemed to be one step ahead of the game – or even one step ahead of those who were already one step ahead. Nor was he ever thrown when something unexpected happened; his mental framework seemed to make an instantaneous adjustment, to come up, like a well programmed computer, with a clear notion of what to do next.

Allied to this was another quality; Christopher knew how to use every member of his team. It was not however a matter of manipulation, but rather of deploying to best advantage all the resources at his disposal; in other words, a rather military quality of leadership, which again his full life story puts into focus. For 'resources', read 'assets': because we were all made to feel valued for what we were and could do, even as we were expected and required to do it. For me, as the lawyer, and therefore standing at a little remove from the main team, it was an especially exhilarating experience, one which taught me a great deal about negotiating, and about how you help shape the policy you are negotiating to achieve.

All this goes to make up Christopher Audland's style, whether in official service, or in his fascinating array of public-spirited activities after retirement. People matter to him. Morale mattered to him also, not just because it improved efficiency, but because morale is about people, and people matter. Nobody reading this book will be surprised to see that said about someone to whom family, and family life, mean as much as they evidently do.

This brings me in turn to my only complaint about the book. There is too little in it about Christopher's wife, Maura. I can readily imagine, though, the sternness of the prohibition under which he laboured! But that, as my fellow lawyers would say, is *res inter alios acta*, and can't prevent me, as a long-standing admirer, from saying my own word on the subject.

To do so I have to digress. The excitement and occasional glamour of official life abroad are not hard to imagine; the harsh practicalities of constantly re-making a home are much less readily grasped. Even less so does the outside world take proper stock of what it's like to keep the family together with the children away; or with the children at home, but their father away. It used to be common for retiring Ambassadors to end their valedictory despatches with a paragraph of affectionate tribute to their wives. These were often genuinely moving. Had Christopher Audland retired ambassadorially, he would surely have found the words to describe the grace and sweetness with which Maura had done all these things, and in doing them had made possible the life which the book describes.

I come back finally to the question of Europe. It is hardly surprising that this is the chosen subject of Christopher's epilogue. Nor his twin themes: the absolute need for European unity, coupled with the need for Britain to recognize its proper place in Europe and throw in its lot wholeheartedly. Even if expected, this dual message comes with added weight on the back of his unrivalled inside experience of making the EU work. Could one perhaps have hoped for something more unbridled still? For example, an equally incisive insider's view of whether the original Six had always done their best to draw Britain in, not punish her for having been out. Or a hard-headed assessment of what the recipe is and will now have to be for handling the United States. Or some frank comments on how the 'Union' itself can set about becoming one in the face of its expanded membership, and what sort of union that could reasonably be.

Material for someone else's book perhaps? In the meanwhile, it is a great satisfaction to add, most warmly, my recommendation to this one.

The why of the book

IN 1997, I embarked on an activity quite new for me – the writing of a book. For what reason? Probably none of us really know why we do any particular thing. Our decisions result from many inputs, conscious and unconscious. But it may be worth recording the conscious considerations which led me to begin: the more particularly because my inclination had, always before, been to leave authorship to others. Once started, I was gradually led to reflect more deeply about my career, both professional and otherwise.

The seed of authorship was sown by my godfather, Herbert Bryson. Not long after he died, my wife and I visited his widow. In casual conversation Rosemary remarked that Herbert had dealt with a certain matter in his book. She explained that, in his latter years, he had written a short autobiography, not for publication, but for his children. I read it in a few hours, with real pleasure. It shed new light on Herbert; and made me reflect that here was a pattern I might one day follow. When his children told me how much they treasured their father's little volume, that reflection was fortified. It was further strengthened by the thought that my own father, after retirement, had devoted so much time to researching and writing up the history of his own and my mother's families; and that the resultant Family History had proved of real and continuing interest, not only to my parents' descendants, but to many of their other relations as well.

For a decade after retirement from the European Commission, life was filled with many activities, which left no time for such an enterprise. I had always meant to wind these down on reaching the age of seventy, inspired by the sight of people who *had* been effective, but had carried on with responsibilities long after they were capable of doing them justice, to the distress of those around them. In 1996, our Christmas newsletter to friends recorded that Maura and I had embarked on what consultants [then] called down-shifting, in other words doing less. In response, a wise Belgian friend chided me for appearing to see old age negatively. The third age, he wrote, should be devoted to reflection about one's life; to being in touch with one's grand-children; and to prayer. The shaft struck home: I am a second league performer in terms of prayer; at that time I had no grand-children, though now happily there are two; but I *could* reflect. So the idea of a book returned, with renewed force, and was taken up. To fortify my resolve, I told family and friends that I would embark on the process once my term of duty as Pro-Chancellor of Lancaster University ended, in July, 1997.

Although initially I followed the Bryson model – autobiographical, and written for my children – this exercise led me to reflect that I had had a life of enormous variety. I have lived in five continents – Europe, Asia, Africa, and North and South America. I have performed – whether professionally or pro bono – at least twenty-five different jobs in the most varied fields. Some of these have been of real importance – as for example my involvement with international affairs in Europe and the Americas, the development of the European Union, the conservation of the built and natural heritage at local and international level, the creation of the Ruskin Library and Foundation at Lancaster University, and the establishment of the European Opera Centre at Manchester. On top of that I have enjoyed a home life, full of family, friends, country pursuits, art and culture.

The book therefore developed into something considerably more structured. While it remains essentially personal, some of its chapters contain fullish accounts of my more interesting involvements, which might appeal to a rather wider public. It is based essentially on memory and personal papers, and there has been little serious external research or meticulous checking of details. The personal papers are nevertheless extensive, as explained in the introductory section of 'Notes to the Text' at the end of the book. This approach means that I have relied primarily on reflection and analysis – life-long tools of my various trades. Maura wanted very little to be written about her, a wish reluctantly respected. I have also tried not to embarrass other family members.

I hope the meaning of my Title will progressively become clear to the reader. My life has been much influenced by being often at the right place, at the right time – a matter entirely outside my control – which enabled me to deploy and develop effectively such talents as I have. Of course, it was not always the case!

Given the range and complexity of subjects covered, I have turned to literally dozens of individuals for advice. It has always been forthcoming. Any attempt to list such contributions would lead to inadvertent omissions. Instead, I would like to close this preface with a very warm thank you to all who have helped me in so many ways.

The Old House, Ackenthwaite, Cumbria   **Christopher Audland**
31 December, 2002

Chapter 1

Family origins and parents

Although my father's professional career meant he moved around the world, he never for one moment forgot his Cumbrian – he would have said Westmorland – roots. Audlands had by then been living at Ackenthwaite for nine generations – and quite possibly the preceding three as well. 'Johnes Aydland', born in 1547, is known for certain to have resided there by 1575. The House passed from him, in direct male succession, to my grandfather. At first, the Audlands were substantial, yeomen farmers; in the eighteenth century, they were blacksmiths, and then whitesmiths; in the nineteenth, following educations at Kendal Grammar School and various Colleges, they embarked on liberal professions, as academics, doctors of medicine and clergymen. At this stage they began to move around. But all came back to Ackenthwaite in retirement. The sole exception was my grandfather, who nonetheless died there! These events were meticulously recorded by my father, after his retirement, and some further details are given in the notes to this Chapter.[1]

What sort of people were my parents – Edward Gordon Audland (always known as Gordon); and Violet Mary Shepherd-Cross (who hated the name Violet and, from infancy, refused to answer to anything but Mary)? There follow a few facts, and some reflections by myself.

Gordon was born at Wellingborough in 1896, the son of Edward and Laura Audland. He had been preceded by two sisters, Freda and Marie; and was followed by a third, Joan. He went to Lindley Lodge, a private preparatory school at Higham on-the-Hill in Staffordshire, and then to Winchester College (Trant's House) from 1910 to 1914. Surprisingly, considering his later career, he did not reach 'Sixth Book' (The VIth Form). He was initially expected to become a General Practitioner, following his father's example. But the First World War intervened.

Like so many young men, my father volunteered for military service at the earliest possible date, and was given a temporary commission in the Royal Artillery Reserve on his 18th birthday, 30 December 1914. (A year later he became a regular officer.) He served continuously in France, from April 1915 until the end of the war, in the 16th Battery, Royal Field Artillery, which he commanded from the summer of 1917 onwards. The guns were horse-drawn, and the conditions in which they had to operate, often appalling. My father would have divided his time between the gun position and the observation post, the latter being in or near the front line. His War Diary – the original is in the Imperial War Museum – records his impressions. The major battles in which he participated included those of Loos, Vimy Ridge, the Somme, Passchendaele, Cambrai, and the final advance into Germany.

He was remarkably lucky to receive only three splinter wounds. By the end of the war, he had been awarded the Military Cross, and been mentioned in despatches; he was the longest-serving surviving officer in his Division; and also one of the only five survivors of the 38 boys he had known in Trant's in 1914. Photos taken at the front nevertheless show a man with a sunny disposition.

After the war he was posted to Britain, serving in various Gunner Batteries (1919-1922). He was able to resume fox-hunting, a sport his father – known as 'The Doctor of the Pytchley Hunt' – had taught him as a boy. Whilst stationed at Brighton, he met my mother, also a fox-hunter. The couple married in 1922. By then he had moved to the Riding Troop at St John's Wood – now renamed 'The King's Troop' – participating in the musical drive at the Royal Tournament. A year later, he was posted to the British Army of the Rhine, to serve in administrative jobs at Cologne and then Wiesbaden (1923-1927). Next, he went to the Staff College, Camberley.

Then came a long period of service with the British Army in India (1930-36). My parents had to decide whether or not to take with them the three young children who had meanwhile been born: Michael, myself and Elizabeth. They went alone. Their service included a spell at Quetta. They were there when, in 1936, the great earthquake struck, leaving 50,000 dead in 60 seconds. My father was responsible for feeding the 40,000 Indian survivors in a refugee camp on the race-course. My mother worked as a volunteer in the Indian emergency hospital. Returning to Britain in 1936, my father soon joined Southern Command Headquarters in Salisbury, where my parents rented a house.

With the outbreak of the Second World War, my father joined the British Expeditionary Force in France; his lease on Malmesbury House was terminated; and my mother took care of the children – when not in boarding school. My father was a Staff Officer throughout the War. Called back to Britain, some months before the end of 'the phoney war' and the fall of France, he held various posts before becoming Brigadier (DA and QMG)[2] in the new Fifth Corps: this was the first British Corps to arrive in Algeria during 'Operation Torch', the Allied invasion of North Africa, in November 1942. When, next year, the German forces in North Africa surrendered, he found himself initially in charge of the 250,000 German prisoners captured. Subsequently, he remained in the same job, as the Corps fought its way through Italy, from Taranto to Rimini.

Then, in November 1944, he was sent to Athens as Second-in Command to General Scobie at Headquarters Land Forces, Greece. (Brigadier Teddy Tryon-Wilson, of Dallam Tower, also in Milnthorpe, who by chance had earlier been his Deputy in Fifth Corps, took over from him in Italy.) In Greece, the British forces, in the months to come, defeated the massive Communist insurrection against the Government. For his part in this operation my father was made a Commander of the Order of George I with Swords (Greece): during the Second World War he was also made a Commander of the Order of the British Empire (CBE) and three times mentioned in despatches.

A short spell in England (1946-1948) saw him as Commander of the Liverpool Garrison, and of Gunner Regiments of the still large Territorial Army, living in a rented house in Southport. Then, he went abroad again, this time to be Commander, Cyrenaica District, with Headquarters at Benghazi (1948-1951). Initially, the idea was that the substantial British Garrison in Egypt would be moved – lock, stock and barrel – to Cyrenaica; but this project was abandoned, and my father's life was quieter than it might have been. My mother and Elizabeth were with him. This was the job from which he retired, and went to live at the family house at Ackenthwaite, which he had inherited on his father's death, a year earlier. He was now awarded a CB.

A quarter of a century of life remained to him. He spent much of it performing voluntary, public duties of many kinds[3]. A heart attack, at the age of 64, may have been a blessing in disguise. He slowed down and gave up smoking (he had been consuming 70 cigarettes a day). For the rest, his health was generally good until his last months. My father also did much to improve the family's property in and around Ackenthwaite, a cause to which he was devoted[4]. He died there in 1976, at the age of nearly 80.

What sort of person was he? He had a strong intelligence, and formidable powers of analysis. He was not an intellectual, but used his brain as a man of action. He was quiet, calm, reserved, modest, thoughtful, considerate, generous and utterly dependable. He had a strong Christian commitment

My father – Brigadier Gordon Audland.

and a stern sense of duty. He had administrative skills which were seen as outstanding by fellow officers best placed to know. He had a quiet but strong sense of humour, and enjoyed teasing those close to him. With his family he was deeply affectionate, but wore his affection lightly. In short, he was someone whom everybody loved to know: after his death, my mother took comfort from the multitude of tributes received from many local people.

His main private interests included riding, shooting and travel, for which his upbringing and career gave him many opportunities. He was also deeply interested in our family history from an early age. After retirement he devoted enormous efforts to research and analysis in this domain (mainly between 1955 and 1973). In the process he became an authority on local life and lore, and enjoyed answering questions on these fields from his many friends. The Family History he wrote bears eloquent testimony to his labours.

Mary Shepherd-Cross, whom my father married in 1922, had been born into a different world. Her father's family were industrialists, bankers and businessmen, and her father was an MP for many years. Oddly, we know

My mother – Mary Audland.

little of the early life of her mother, Herbert's second wife, Patty Penelope Hortor, whom he married in 1895, except that she was the daughter of James Hortor, described as being 'of Edinburgh'; that she was born in Peterborough in 1856; and that she had been governess to Herbert's children by his first wife.

Born in 1900, at her father's London house at 19 Queen's Gate Gardens, Mary spent the first 16 years of her life at Hamels, Herbert's country house in Hertfordshire, with a 600-acre park. There would have been a large indoor and outdoor domestic staff. Mary was the last of her father's six children – three by each wife – and he was 53 when she was born. Given a gap of 18 years between the two groups, it was with the second that she was brought up: Arthur (always known as Jack) and Helen. Considered a tomboy, she related closely to Jack. But there was always – and there still is – a strong family bond between all branches of the Shepherd-Cross family.

Educated at home to age 16, Helen and Mary had a governess, who stayed with them for the last eight of these years. When her father died in 1916, Mary insisted on going to Public School, following the example set by Jack;

and spent two years at Cheltenham Ladies College, characteristically ending as Senior Prefect. After a year as a VAD at a war hospital near Preston, she went to live with her widowed mother, now established at Offham House (sometimes called Offham Place), near Lewes, Sussex, a smaller, but substantial, Georgian country house.

Helen and Mary were both pretty girls. They liked dressing up. And they frequented the Southdown Hunt, which met at least once at Offham House. This gave them opportunities for encountering eligible young men. There were also tennis and swimming parties. Helen's future husband is first photographed with her in 1920; and Mary's, in 1921. Both were then serving in the 56th Battery, Royal Field Artillery, stationed at Brighton. Helen's wedding to Lieutenant (Jack) Winterton at Offham Parish Church, when Gordon was best man, was spectacular. There was a military escort, and the couple went off in a landau at a canter. Jack Winterton, my favourite and much-loved uncle, had begun married life the way he meant to go on – with *panache*! He was to end his career as British High Commissioner in Austria, and then Military Governor and Commander of the British/US Territory of Trieste (1951-54)[5].

My mother's own romance pursued its course. It was not all smooth going. Her mother initially refused my father's request for Mary's hand in marriage, saying they should wait a year to see if they felt the same. However, Gordon's Battery Commander at Preston Barracks, Major Gibbon, took up his cause; called on my grandmother; and persuaded her that my father – whom he had nick-named 'Sunny' – was a fine and serious officer, and the wedding should not be delayed. Thereafter all went well, and my mother visited the Audland family in Wellingborough and at Ackenthwaite in 1922. Meanwhile my grandmother, during that summer, had moved to 27, Fourth Avenue, Hove, a nineteenth century, red-sandstone, three-storey town house, with domestic offices in a basement and servants' quarters on the top floor. From there, Mary went to Hove Parish Church, on 8 February 1923, to marry my father. The first marital home was in St John's Wood. But later that year my father was posted to the British Army of the Rhine, to serve in Cologne, and they moved into a substantial town house at Georgsplatz 16. My older brother, Michael, was born there. I was born later, when they had moved to Wiesbaden: and my sister Elizabeth followed after their return to England.

At no time was my mother a quiet, stay-at-home wife. Like my father, she loved riding and travelling. She did a lot of voluntary hospital and medical missionary work in India. This included visiting, with a British lady doctor, un-escorted, remote villages on the Afghan frontier, where reputedly no white man had been, except to fight wars. At Salisbury, she was Commandant of the Local Branch of the St John's Ambulance Brigade. She also entertained extensively. At Ackenthwaite, where the family was based throughout the Second World War, besides looking after her house, garden and smallholding – we shall come to this – she took a prominent part in women's voluntary activities and Church work. Later, in Cyrenaica, she supported her husband by entertaining, and by social work of many kinds with the armed forces and their families. On returning to Ackenthwaite in 1951, she resumed her voluntary activities, besides steadily improving the garden.

And how does one think of her now? Like my father, she had a Christian commitment and a strong sense of duty; but in other respects she was a very different and more complex person. She was tough, determined, not in the least intellectual, courageous, energetic and indefatigable. She could never relax, but must always be doing something. She was well turned-out – she would have said 'tidy'. She was something of a puritan, and never touched alcohol. She was not naturally sensitive to the feelings of others. Her views were formed more by personal background, intuition and impulse than by analysis and reflection. But, once formed, she usually held to them strongly, and did not care to be crossed.

My mother had an aura of authority which attracted respect. She liked to organise and to lead: whether parties, social or charitable events, or voluntary organisations. If she took on any task, she would commit herself fully to it. She went at things with a rush, which worked sometimes, but not always.

If she could have chosen, she would have been a boy; so she did not take easily to motherhood. She privileged boys against girls. Nevertheless, she was devoted to the well-being of her family, and nurtured it through very difficult times, especially in the Second World War when her husband's prolonged foreign postings often left her without real marital support. She loved her children, but un-emotionally. She was stern, and there was never a lot of maternal warmth. She was not easy to live with: either for her husband – who was at times hectored, but knew how to avoid trouble without surrendering anything he valued – or for her children.

All this gives a picture of a rather tough cookie: and so she was. But there were surprising sides to her character. Once, in her later years, when she was with my Aunts Freda and Marie, the former asked her bluntly why she had married their brother: *'we never could understand what you saw in Gordon!'*. My mother replied: *'simply because he was the kindest man I ever met'*. It was a fair statement, but not one to be expected from her. Like most of us, she had no doubt mellowed with the passage of years. For my part, I learnt a lot from her better qualities; and largely kept out of the way when the less positive were in evidence.

People can only be fairly judged in the context of their time. So perhaps some paragraphs should be devoted to wider events during my parents' lives. These were dominated, first and foremost, by the two World Wars, and their own involvement in them (my father served right through both of them and my mother lost her half-brother, Cecil, at Ypres in 1917). The quarter century between the Wars was a period when hopes of a better world soon disappeared, and people began again to live in the expectation of further disaster. In the 1930s, my parents were strongly opposed to any kind of appeasement of Germany. They lived through, and saw all too clearly, the incredible horrors and inhumanities of Hitler and Stalin. For a long time after the Second World War, they found it hard to accept Jean Monnet's view that the Western Allies had helped Hitler fuel German nationalism by their Versailles policies of keeping the Germans down, instead of trying to bring about reconciliation, and integrate them into a civilised international framework.

It therefore came as a shock for them when, in 1958, my brother, serving as a Regular Army Officer in Germany, decided to marry a German girl, Renate Weber. But the marriage in the end helped my parents to think differently about Germany, and about Europe; and my own heavy and continuing interest in both Germany and European unity likewise played a part. They came to favour strongly the European idea. And I remember how deeply moved my mother was, as she sat quite alone in the House with my father's coffin, waiting for the hearse to come, when she answered the door and received a wreath inscribed by Emile Noël, Secretary-General of the European Commission.

There were other huge international changes. When they were born, the British Empire was at its zenith; vast areas of the world were coloured pink on the atlases; and most people in the United Kingdom saw their country as the world's greatest power. Although in fact Britain's decline gathered momentum after the First World War, it did not suit politicians to say so, and what was already an illusion was therefore still perceived by the general public as the reality. For my parents, service in India, where a few tens of thousands of British troops kept control for so long over hundreds of millions of Indians, would have strengthened the illusion.

The Second World War helped to maintain it. Britain fought a remarkable war. But historians agree that the lion's share of the Western war effort came from the United States. This too was something British politicians did not like to say. So people here were again given an exaggerated idea of their country's place in the world. The dramatic withdrawal from India in 1947 was not perceived – even at high levels in Whitehall and Westminster – for what it was: namely the end of Britain's Imperial period, and the moment of progressive relegation to the World Second League. All this explains why people like my parents continued to think of Britain, during the 1950s to 1980s, as a great power which could defend its own interests successfully in a tough world outside the growing European Community. Many still do.

My parents also witnessed huge domestic political change: the vote for women; massive recession and un-employment in the 1930s; the emergence of the Labour Party as a serious political force; the invention of the Welfare State; the thrust of feminism; ever-widening access to education at all levels; the growth in the instrumentarium and power of the media; a revolution in attitudes to sex, and to the family as an institution; the loss of respect for authority of all kinds; ever more rapid technological change; and much else besides.

Moreover, there was vast change in the structure of society. My parents were brought up in a class dominated world, which only began to break up in the First World War. They would have perceived the aristocracy, the landed gentry and even the older moneyed classes as upper class; the professionals as upper-middle class; tradesmen, shopkeepers and white-collar workers as lower-middle class; with blue-collar workers and domestic servants as lower class. Movement between the classes was difficult, but not impossible: money and/or education were the keys. My parents had domestic servants most of their lives. Yet, by the time of their deaths, the class system had effectively disappeared; and living-in servants were almost unknown, having been replaced by machines and 'dailies'.

This broad-brush review seeks to show some of the external influences which played, directly or indirectly, on my parents' lives. Merely writing it down has confirmed me in the respect I always had for their ability to adapt; and to maintain, despite so much change around them, for themselves and for their children, a strong sense of tradition and continuity, in the best sense of both words. It did us a world of good.

CHAPTER 2

Childhood and Twyford School

I WAS BORN ON 7 July 1926, in an undistinguished nineteenth century house at 12 Lessingstrasse, Wiesbaden, Germany. Less than two years later my father moved to the Staff College at Camberley, so I have no contemporary personal memories of my birth-place, though I saw it later.

In Camberley, we lived for some two years at 'The Bourne', a red-brick, detached, house in Connaught Avenue, with a garden at front and rear. Elizabeth was born there. Neither Michael nor I recall much of life at 'The Bourne'. We were often taken for outings and picnics to the Royal Military College grounds, where the lake offered bathing possibilities. My Uncle Jack was also at the Staff College, and he and his family were living round the corner. With them was Jill, our Shepherd-Cross first cousin, whose mother had deserted her father soon after she was born.

When I was four, after my parents went to India, and for six years, contact between parents and children was limited. My father returned to England on home leave every other year, and my mother came every year. In between, there were only letters. And, to begin with, there was no airmail, so the answer to any question took seven weeks to arrive. (The telephone was not used for such long distances, then; and the telegraph was expensive.) My paternal grandfather, and my Aunts Freda and Marie, acted lovingly *in loco parentis*.

Our first move was to a cottage in Camberley. We were placed in the care of Nanny Hoyle – who came from Bolton, where my maternal grandfather had so long dwelt – and a nursemaid. This was another red-brick, detached, but much smaller, dwelling. Again there was a small garden at front and rear, with sand-pit. Michael and I went to a nearby kindergarten, 'The Brocas', where there were more girls than boys, and net-ball was played. There were occasional childrens' parties, when we looked for sweets hidden in the bushes. But otherwise we saw little of other children.

From 1930 onwards, summer holidays were usually taken at Ackenthwaite: other holidays were often at my paternal grandfather's house, 'Nurton' in Davenant Road, Oxford; and sometimes at Coldash, Newbury, in a pre-prep school where my Winterton cousins were also parked, and where Elizabeth was to be sent from 1934-36. Nurton was the house in Oxford to which my grandfather had retired, after selling his medical practice in Wellingborough. He had wisely bought a 'double plot', giving room for a tennis court. My Aunts Freda and Marie originally benefited from this to lead a fairly social life; but my grandmother's health problems became increasingly severe, and this was curtailed.

In summer, beginning in 1930, we three must have been taken to Ackenthwaite from Oxford by train, to Milnthorpe Station, by Nanny Hoyle, or by one of my Aunts, probably Freda. We usually stayed as paying guests in Crosby Lodge, with John and Annie Wilson. The former would have met us at the Station with the milk-float.

I can recall going from the farm to visit our great-uncle John, who had retired to what was then called 'The Green House' at Ackenthwaite, and who died in 1931. He had been for many years Vicar of Dinton (Wilts). At Ackenthwaite, he employed a housekeeper, Mrs Ross. He impressed us all with his long white beard, and old-world manner. It sticks for some reason in my mind that he always pronounced the word 'medicine' with its full three syllables, equally weighted, instead of with two ('med-sinn'), like everybody else. In those days I supposed that 'The Green House' was so called, because the paintwork was that colour. Now, we have realised that it was really 'Ackenthwaite Green House'. Had we done so earlier, we would no doubt have re-used this name, on retiring here in 1986, instead of calling it 'The Old House'.

After great-uncle John died, my grandfather took to staying at Ackenthwaite (otherwise vacant) in the summers, until 1940. He would have motored up, with my grandmother and my Aunt Marie. (My grandmother died in 1937.)

In the 1930s, the House was primitive, and remained so until my parents retired in the 1950s and enlarged and modernised it. There were then only three 'bays' to it. On the ground floor, a front south-facing door, and two windows, were shaded by a Victorian veranda with tiled floor. From the kitchen, the back door led to the street; or, by turning right along the back wall, one came to the old peat-house, later removed by my parents so they could add to the House. It was used for coal and wood, but no longer peat: upstairs, reached by a ladder, was a rather dangerous glory hole, where of course we loved to play. More details are in the notes[1].

There was no 'phone or electricity. (These only came in the 1950s.) The Milnthorpe Gas Company supplied town gas, which lit the downstairs rooms, the stairs, and the principal bedroom; and fuelled a gas stove in the kitchen. Gas supplies were always unreliable. In other parts of the house, lighting was by candles, which by day were kept on a shelf above the kitchen door. I recall occasions, later, in the war, when the bathroom candle fell into the huge bath, often shared by me with either Michael or my cousin, Tim Winterton. The hot water, and much of the cooking, was provided by an open kitchen range, which in war-time I cleaned and 'blacked' regularly, before breakfast.

Life at Ackenthwaite was a joy. In particular, Crosby Lodge farm was an inexhaustible resource. In those days, there was very little mechanisation, though milking machines came in shortly before the Second World War. Everything depended on horse-power. The farm had two cart horses; and the pony, Jess, used mainly for pulling the milk float. This beloved vehicle appears often in photographs: it had a tarpaulin, under which children joyously disappeared when it rained.

There must have been about 100 acres of land with the farm. It was considered large by the scale of the times: nowadays, with heavy mechanisation and investment, the typical local farm is three or four times as big. There was quite a lot of arable land, mainly growing oats. (Later, in the war, farms here were required to sow at least one-third of their acreage to corn.) At the same period, Ackenthwaite Farm (the Garnetts next door), with also around 100 acres, had only 26 milking cows. But the present Wilson Garnett's father was an expert breeder of cart-horses, and owned up to 62 horses of different ages, though some would have been kept on rented land. Nowadays, on 350 acres, Wilson Garnett has upwards of 350 cattle, but no horses.

The farmhouse at Crosby Lodge had a thoroughly warm and friendly atmosphere. Annie Wilson was a motherly figure. The Wilsons, senior, had three daughters (Annie, Elsie and Edith), then in their late teens or early twenties, none as yet married, and all very kind to us; and there were two living-in hired hands. Annie looked after the poultry; Elsie worked in the house; and Edith dealt with the milking and dairy (including delivering the milk). We children 'helped' Annie and Edith. We also did a lot of playing in the hay; feeding of cows, calves and horses; and joining in the fun of hay-making, harvesting, sheep-dipping and threshing (for which latter a great steam engine arrived, huffing and puffing, and friends of the Wilsons from all around came to help for the day). All these events required un-ending provision of cups of tea; apple and currant pasties; and gingerbread. These delicacies were all home-baked, and everything was carried out in baskets and aluminium milk-cans to the scene of action, usually the fields.

Special pleasures were rides on carts or cart-horses; journeys in the milk-float to the Station to take the milk in churns to the train for Preston (the Milnthorpe milk factory was only built in 1934), or to other farms like Wath Sudden to make into butter; collecting the eggs (the free-range hens laid them in haystacks, hedgerows, feeding troughs, sheds and all over the place); petting motherless lambs; making tunnels in the hay in the top and bottom shippens (stone barns); and generally being surrounded by kind country people. Some milk was also delivered by the milk-float to the then Mental Home on Workhouse Lane – now Kirkgate Lane. And some was taken round Ackenthwaite, by hand with us helping, and measured out, on the doorstep, by the pint or the gill. On these milk rounds, there was no lack of conversation.

The flavour of life on the farm may be conveyed by recalling elements from the youth of the youngest Wilson daughter, Edith, of whom I have specially warm memories. She married Leslie Powell, a Milnthorpe solicitor, and thereafter lived at Ackenthwaite until her death in the Millennium Year at the age of 88. She was the most extrovert and affectionate of the three sisters, and outlived her siblings. Her father, Johnny Wilson, was at first a tenant at Crosby Lodge, and bought the farm in 1925. There he, and his extended family of seven – including the two hired hands – lived a simple but happy life. Before beginning to farm, Johnny Wilson had been a schoolteacher. He and his wife made sure their girls got a good education. This meant travelling daily to Kendal High School. In those times, the girls probably walked across the meadows, and through the lane, to catch the steam train, drawn by 'Kendal Tommy', at Heversham Station – later abolished by Dr Beeching's reforms!

There were usually some two dozen cows to be milked, at that time by hand. In those days, all were shorthorns. Edith would start milking at 5 a.m., for most of the year by lantern light. In the shippen, her father would bring her a cup of tea. But breakfast had to wait until milking was done. It was taken in the great kitchen, then running up through two floor levels to the rafters. Sides of bacon hung above one's head: the old kitchen range glowed alongside, blacked and shining. Breakfast was a social occasion for the whole family. In the Wilson-Inman family at Crosby Lodge, there was a warm, cultivated, friendly atmosphere.

A feature of Ackenthwaite then, and indeed for some years after the war, was the 'Mental Home' (modern idiom: psychiatric hospital), which had long since been housed in the former Victorian Workhouse. The patients were non-violent, and went for walks in and around Ackenthwaite, under

With my sister in the Crosby Lodge Farm milk-float, with Johnny Wilson, 1933.

supervision. They also played cricket, on a part of the meadow behind what is now Crosby House. Edith recalled two escapes. One inmate got out at night; quietly stole the Crosby Lodge pony; and was later recovered grazing her two miles away. Another got clean away for a fortnight, and then walked into the Royal Albert Mental Hospital at Lancaster, tired and hungry, asking to be *'sent home to matron'*.

The Ackenthwaite garden was a great delight. There was a regular gardener, Mr Chamley from Heversham. Below the ha-ha, there were only three vegetable patches. We were much in the orchard. I recall, in summer, thatching with hay a large semi-circular tree-guard, to make a house. I was devoted to climbing trees, and in 1934 duly fell out of one, breaking my arm.

In 1932, my mother returned from India on leave. Michael was sent to Twyford School. Elizabeth and I were placed with a Miss Peggy Munn, a middle-aged spinster living at Bury House in the charming Wiltshire village of Codford St Mary. This was a fair-sized, square, Edwardian-style house, built of a mellow, creamy brick. We were not the only children, but there were few others: I can recall only Tony. Photos show up to six. Miss Munn was helped by an older spinster lady, called 'Ferdie'. We were given some lessons. There was a big garden, which I loved. Part was bounded by a beech hedge, beyond which there were meadows with a stream running through. I specially recall the orchard, where Tony and I constructed wattle huts, using the apple prunings. There were also enjoyable walks on the downs and in the water meadows.

And so life went on, until I was sent to Twyford School in September 1934, where I was to remain for five years, apart of course from holidays. (Elizabeth was sent to Ridge House, another pre-prep boarding school, near Newbury.) Besides my own memories of Twyford, the following paragraphs draw on material in a book about the School written by the Reverend R G Wickham, to whom we shall return, entitled *Shades of the Prison-House*[2]; on 'Memories of Twyford School 1932-36'[3], an unpublished monograph written by my brother Michael, who had preceded me there; and on photographs.

The School had corresponded to the present concept of a preparatory school from at least the beginning of the nineteenth century; but there had been predecessor schools on the same site. Its *alumni* had included Thomas Hughes, the author of *Tom Brown's School Days*; Sir Hubert Parry, the composer; and Dick Crossman, the Labour politician. *Alumni* from my time and after included Douglas Hurd, a long-serving Foreign Secretary; Brian Trubshaw, Concorde's first Chief Test Pilot; and Mark Tully, for so long the BBC's remarkable correspondent in India.

My time at Twyford fell into two quite distinct periods. Both were happy, but the second was the happier. In the first (1934-36), when Michael had not yet gone on to Winchester, the School was run by an elderly and ante-deluvian bachelor Headmaster, Mr Harold McDonell, known to the boys as 'Doni', assisted by his spinster sister, Daisy (or 'Miss Doni'). The academic side was good, as could be seen by the places obtained by *alumni* in top public schools, notably Winchester; and we were encouraged to think for ourselves. The masters were excellent, and stayed faithful to the School over very long periods. But Doni, who had been Headmaster since 1910, was old-fashioned. The accommodation was for the most part Victorian in character. The lavatories were equipped with earth closets. There was no electric light. There was gas lighting, but only on the ground floor. Elsewhere, notably in the dormitories, we had oil lamps.

One prospective parent, being taken round the school by Daisy, ventured to ask why there was no gas in the gymnasium, which was at the end of a long passage on the ground floor. There are two versions of the reply: either, *'do you think it would reach so far'*; or, *'but surely it can't turn corners'*. Either testifies to the McDonells' knowledge of current technology! Personally

The author, in prep-school suit, 1934.

I was not very bothered by these things, perhaps because the sanitary and lighting arrangements were very similar to those at Crosby Lodge! Food was not appetising. Our school uniform was as *démodé* as the sanitation: knickerbocker tweed suits in winter, and Eton collars. There were, however, some very good things about the school. It was at the edge of open country – the Hampshire Downs and the water-meadows of the River Itchen – where we were taken for walks on Sundays. The playing grounds were excellent and extensive, and there were lovely trees around them (especially vast beeches). I suspect it was at Twyford that I began to acquire that love of landscape which has inspired and uplifted me throughout life. There was a small golf-course, operational as early as 1890, for use by boys as well as staff, adjacent to the school grounds; and a heated indoor swimming pool – completed in 1914: both were remarkable features for a preparatory school in the 1930s. The gym was well equipped, as was the carpentry shop. There were courts for hand-fives and bat-fives (a local speciality).

Moreover, there was an outstandingly good Library, built as a War Memorial after the First World War. It was there that I first learnt the

Bob Wickham, Headmaster of Twyford School, ca. 1939.

pleasure to be had from serious literature: and Doni, in his regular and well-delivered Sunday evening readings to the boys from great literary works (his favourites were Scott and Dickens), helped me along that road. Looking back, it seems remarkable that all this was available, alongside a good academic grounding, for fees which remained at £125 a year from the end of World War I to the end of World War II.

There was quite a lot of corporal punishment under Doni, though I personally evaded it. I was always good at evasive action, and even got away without detection when from time to time sneaking into the school's kitchen garden and stealing strawberries, on summer evenings when the 'late beds' (older boys) were in chapel, and the 'early beds' (younger ones) were meant to be asleep. In the end, none of us were sorry to see Doni go. He was not a loveable person.

Shades of the Prison-House offers a marvellous description of the two McDonells, which deserves quotation[4]. '*They were in many respects a peculiarly inhibited couple, who had probably grown up in an extremely correct and strict home. Neither had any real sense of humour. Daisy was long and thin from her face downwards, generally dressed in black, and practically never seen without a hat. Her smile was wintry. At the daily staff tea parties she presided at one side of the fireplace, with Harold on the other, and the whole teaching staff seated along the far side of the drawing room. Cosy conversation was hardly the order of the day.'*

My second period in the school was totally different. The out-dated McDonells were replaced by nice, young, and thoroughly modern, Bob and Betty Wickham (the former was 32 when he took over the School in 1937). Bob, who had by then taken Holy Orders, was as good a headmaster as a prep-school could hope to have. Himself once a pupil at the School under Doni, a descendant of the family which had founded it, and by now its owner, he was later to assure its long-term future by handing it over to a Trust. He also became, in due course, the Chairman of the Incorporated Association of Preparatory Schools. His own view of a prep-school speaks volumes about his personality: he wrote that '*...a good modern preparatory school (is one) in which everyone is regarded as part of a large family, devoted to the society to which he belongs, and realising the importance of the contribution he can make to it'.*

He was a natural teacher, a natural leader, and a man able to get the best out of both his staff and the boys. By the latter he was greatly liked, and at the same time respected for being firm but fair. Under him, corporal punishment became rare. Betty was equally popular, and very kind to the boys. There was immediate and massive modernisation. In the first summer holidays after the hand-over, main drains and electricity came in. Long-needed repairs were done. The food went from poor to good. Eton collars, knickerbockers and straw hats were out: grey shirts and shorts, and caps, were in. But, above all, the atmosphere of the place was humanised overnight.

Even in Doni's day, but much more under Bob Wickham, most boys enjoyed themselves. There was so much to do. When not in class, or in compulsory sport, we could roam as we liked in the huge grounds, climb trees, build brushwood houses and so forth. Sports always included soccer, cricket, swimming, gymnastics, athletics and golf. When Bob arrived, an old Marlburian, hockey was added, and this turned out to be the team game I was to love and play best. Special fun were the annual cricket matches between the School First XI and the Parents; and also between the same XI and the 'Club and Ground' (i.e. the Staff). We had a much-loved porter, Fred, with a stiffened leg. He had to have a 'runner' but was the star performer for the Staff. The whole school would gather, when he batted, to see him hit sixes all round the boundaries. (Like the masters, he stayed and stayed with the school, completing 58 years of service.) There were less formal outdoor games, too. One, whose name escapes me, was a complicated team game, in which each team was a 'fleet', and each player was a ship (cruiser, destroyer, submarine etc.). The goodies' 'fleet' would convoy their merchant ships around a set course, while the baddies' 'fleet' tried to sink them.

In our spare time we could receive music lessons. My mother arranged for me to learn the piano – I think because it was the done thing. But I got impatient with it, and asked permission to stop. My mother, no musician, for once let me have my way, remarking that it would save money. I have regretted giving up ever since!

In summer, there were small garden plots for boys to tend, which one could share with a friend when sufficiently senior. It was here that my love of gardening was awakened. My gardening friend was a certain John White – whose parents were also in India, but who had a kind aunt at nearby Compton, Mrs Kathleen Longhurst, whom we visited for tea on Saturdays. John and I regularly won the school's gardening prize. In summer, too, the boys could and did rear caterpillars, and keep stag-beetles, in glass-sided boxes behind the cricket pavilion! Another great feature of the summer term was that, when the weather warmed up, we always took lunch and tea in a huge marquee, with sides that raised: to us it seemed like a permanent picnic. On Guy Fawkes' Day we had a marvellous fireworks display, and after that a huge bonfire was lit in one of the fields. It must have been three metres high – huge to a small boy. Four tunnels penetrated from edge to centre. The four youngest boys – including me once – were sent down the tunnels with a taper, to light the paper at the heart of the fire. A staff member stood behind each – ready to pull the boys out by the heels, if need be!

All year round, we attended chapel once a day: twice for the older boys. The school was rather musical, and the singing was good. If very lucky, one had the honour of hand-blowing the organ. Although I had always, from infancy, attended church every week, and been taught to pray before going to bed, this increased religious observance had an effect, especially after Bob Wickham, who was a good preacher, took over that duty from the indifferent cleric whom Doni had hired for the purpose on Sundays! The beautiful language of the Authorised Version of the Bible, and of the Book of Common Prayer, heard every day, gradually became embedded in my heart and mind, where they have had a life-long influence. (Winchester College was to fortify the process.)

While Michael hated the whole of his time at Twyford, I enjoyed life there throughout. Perhaps my years at Codford had made me more self-reliant and adaptable than he had been, since he went to Twyford straight from being a 'nanny's boy'. Nevertheless, for me, Michael played the role of path-finder: I was happy to look to him for advice. I made friends easily, and kept them.

School reports, whether by Doni or Bob Wickham, reveal much about my character at the time. From the start, my teachers[5] reported that I had good potential, but did not try hard enough! Here are some of their recurrent phrases: has a good brain but is careful not to overtax it; apt to lose concentration; needs more perseverance; tries to work too fast. One master wrote: *'When he thinks for himself he is quite sensible; but he still prefers to ask questions…to try…(and) save himself the trouble of doing so'*. Clearly, I was seen as smug and self-satisfied! Despite these criticisms, I ended by getting good results in the Winchester College entrance exam. My explanation of the discordance is simple. I had a healthy respect for my parents, and wished not to let them down. But they did not see me as being of scholarship grade, so their expectations were not high. There was no need for me to work very hard in order to remain where I wanted, somewhere in the top layer of any class entered. So I tended to coast along until the Winchester exam loomed, and then accelerate rapidly.

Doni's letters to my parents and to Nurton covering the reports were sometimes more direct than the reports themselves. He could be scathing about one's social or spiritual graces – or lack of them. When I was nine, he wrote: *'I have thought seriously of getting Christopher a bib to wear at meals…it might encourage him not to slobber so much'*. A year later he wrote of both Michael and myself: *'they are both dreadfully badly behaved in chapel, especially during the non-choral parts of the service…they ought to be capable of following the service reverently, without having to fidget and stare out and disturb other people'!*

In 1936, my parents came home from India, and my father, after a very short posting in Norwich, where for a few months we lived at George House, Old Catton, settled down as a Deputy Assistant Quarter-Master General (DAQMG) at Headquarters, Southern Command, Salisbury. So for three years (1936-39), until the Second World War broke out, we had a family home to go to in the holidays. And what a home! By some stroke of good fortune, my father had managed to rent from the Dean and Chapter of Salisbury Cathedral one of the most beautiful houses in the Cathedral Close. There can be few more attractive and emotive places to live in than the Salisbury Close, with its superb Gothic Cathedral, Cloister and Chapter

House, encompassed as they are by a vast expanse of grass, itself surrounded by a ribbon of seventy-five lovely houses, many of them backing onto the River Avon, the whole enclosed in a fourteenth century wall, pierced by only three Close gates, which were locked at night. In those days, traffic was not a problem: even today the Cathedral authorities have found means of containing it.

Our address was 'No 15, The Close'; but our then home was previously – and now again is – called Malmesbury House. King Charles II stayed there. Handel used to stay, to compose, and to play in the Chapel. The House has developed over many centuries, beginning in the 13th. The back part – the kitchen and service areas, and above them some of the bedrooms – incorporates a section of the Close wall. The main front rooms and the façade – by Christopher Wren – are eighteenth century, though the pure line of the latter was then broken by an undistinguished Victorian porch (since happily removed). On the south wall is painted a sundial, a well-known feature of the Close. Abutting the House to the south, and then forming part of it, is St Anne's Gate. Above the gate is the former Gothic chapel, long since de-consecrated, and used by us as a table-tennis room: it was ideally suited for this because of its size, and big windows at each end.

The House stood in a large, and completely walled garden. From the bow-window of the drawing room, a lavender-lined walk led first to a circular rose garden, and – beyond that – to a classical Orangery, which concealed a genuine priest's hidey hole. The rest of the garden incorporated a tennis court, flowerbeds, garages and a mass of out-houses. As to the garages, we had become – something very rare at the time – a two-car family, with a Morris 25 and an old Austin 7. (Two were evidently needed while the family was at Norwich – my father having gone ahead of us to Salisbury: later, no doubt, it seemed convenient to keep both on.)

Entering through the front door, one found oneself in a beautiful hall, running up through two floors, with a fine staircase rising round three sides of it (there was another hidey hole beneath it.). The main rooms were very fine. Michael and I had an oak-panelled bedroom, and a dressing room, on the Close wall side. We came to an arrangement with the newsagent and confectioner over the road that, when we waved to attract attention, one of the staff would cross the road; collect our order (usually of sweets, or of the new weekly magazine *Picture Post*) from a basket we let down, together with the money; and then place the ordered goods in the basket.

The second floor was given over to maids' quarters, except for one largish room which was our second playroom. There still <u>were</u> living-in

Malmesbury House, our home in the Salisbury Close, 1936-39 (as it now appears).

maids in those days. We had three: a cook, a house-maid and a parlour-maid (Rose, Flo and Madge). They were all young, and we got on famously. My parents still maintained a firm social division between themselves and the maids. They expected us to do likewise; and in their presence we and the maids acted the part. However, when the parents went out for the evening, as they quite often did, it was another matter. The social barriers disappeared; and the maids enjoyed, as much as we did, riotous pillow-fights and other larks. (My parents never guessed this was going on; and my mother was shocked and indignant when, over a quarter of a century later, we told her!)

We attended services in the Cathedral on Sundays, and got to know the Cathedral people. The Bishop had a grandson, Timmy Maroney, who often stayed with him, and was my age. So we had the run of the Bishop's garden as well as our own.

We also knew the Clerk of the Works, Mr Messenger, who let us wander rather freely behind the scenes, and around the clerestory of the Cathedral. More than once he took us up to look out of the little window, 20 feet below the top of the 404 foot spire, from which lumberjacks would occasionally have to climb up to the orb and cross, to inspect them. Considering that, when you reached the top of the tower at 200 feet, the remaining ascent of the spire was entirely by long wooden ladders, with no safety measures, I am amazed by Mr Messenger's courage – or foolhardiness!

Looking back, I am surprised that my parents, both of whom were by nature careful with their money, should have chosen to live in such a style. It was certainly grander than would have been expected of an army major at the time. It is true that they were not entirely reliant on army pay, since my mother received income from a Trust set up by her father. But that was never a huge amount. I believe they were influenced by a number of factors. They had probably saved money whilst in India. They certainly, from as early as 1936, saw the danger of a Second World War breaking out; and so felt that life should be lived to the full meanwhile (they told Michael this). They may also have felt that they and their children had for six years had no family life; and that it was time to compensate for that.

Certainly, their behaviour towards the children conformed to the last consideration. They did a lot <u>with</u> us, and they did a lot <u>for</u> us. We were taken to see historical sites. Old Sarum, Stonehenge, Wilton, and the New Forest, were on our doorstep. But we were also shown places a lot further afield, like Raglan and Chepstow Castles, and Wells. And we were taken, every now and then, to London. Visits there included sites like the Tower of London or Westminster Abbey; but also, in accordance with my parents' taste, to the latest 1930s musical. We usually lunched at 'The Rag' – the Army and Navy Club – at No.1, King Street, to which my father belonged. This was still an elegant mid-nineteenth century building, very different from the characterless structure with which its members replaced it in the early 1960s.

At home, my father, who always enjoyed sawing and chopping, taught us to help in those activities: my mother did the same for gardening. My father had a gun in a shooting syndicate, so there were shooting parties. When older, I would have been upset by the slaughter of so many birds; but at that age I could join to some extent in the enthusiasm of my elders, and the picnic lunches were fun. My parents played golf with us, and took us swimming, either at a nearby prep-school pool or sometimes on the south coast. We had a dog and a cat. The first dog was a delightful border collie, imported from Ackenthwaite, and named Rob. Sadly, he could not be contained within the garden, leaping too easily over the gate, and did not long survive in urban traffic. He was succeeded by a small cairn, Patsy. The cat was a Siamese, which happily shared Patsy's basket. We also had black and white rabbits, which multiplied rapidly, and in due course went into the pot. The keeping of these cuddly animals might have been a means of giving the children some education about sex. But my mother did not see it that way, simply telling us not to ask silly questions if we enquired about our furry friends' antics!

There were tennis parties at home. These required some preparation, since the old stone walls of the garden had many cracks, within which lurked incredible quantities of toads. They seemed to know when tennis was at hand, and to emerge in large numbers to sun themselves on the tennis court, up to 70 at a time! The would-be players had to devote some minutes to clearing them off, and lowering nets to prevent their re-joining us on court! The same interstices harboured huge numbers of snails, whose depredations on her plants enraged my mother. She once offered a shilling a hundred for any we caught, and drowned in a bucket of brine. Welcoming the chance of a quick buck, I spent a whole day on the job, collecting 700. My mother cheated by reducing the reward to a penny a hundred – with retrospective effect! I was not amused.

My mother did a lot of entertainment, including for us children. For the grown-ups, there were dinner parties, when Michael and I would be allowed sometimes to attend the early part of the evening. For the children's parties my mother exercised a lot of imagination, and invested much effort. They usually included the ever popular 'hide and seek' or 'sardines', when the rambling shape of the house, and the hidey holes, were a great asset. But there were many other party games too, often invented or developed by my mother, and several using many balls of string. In return for her hospitality, we children got invited out to many of the other houses in The Close.

My mother's love of dressing-up found ample expression. Many of the parties, whether for grown-ups, children, or both, were of the fancy dress and 'Lambeth Walk' varieties. There was a huge dressing-up box. My parents had brought back Indian clothes, so that sometimes all five of us – parents and children – went as a complete Indian family, with carefully darkened faces. In the summer of 1938 my mother had an even better opportunity for dressing-up, when a fourteenth century pageant was held in the grounds of nearby Longford Castle in aid of charity, with 300 participants. My mother was cast as a noblewoman, in the train of King Edward III (Lord David Cecil) and Queen Philippa (Lady Pansy Lang), and in the photo albums looks elegant in a tall conical hat, with wimple, and a long gown with puffed sleeves.

Each year, my parents took us to the Tidworth Tattoo. It was a true outdoor spectacular. The concept was the same as at the Royal Tournament: a mix of massed bands, mock battles, musical rides and drives, drills, marching, motor-cycle displays, gymnastics, and so forth. There was always a good turn-out; and the event traditionally ended in a moving way, with the entire cast of armed forces personnel, and the whole audience, rising to sing *'The day Thou gavest, Lord, is ended'*, accompanied by the massed bands.

During holiday times we were now taken to Ackenthwaite by my parents. There were no motorways then. So, although we had a powerful car (a Morris 25 h.p.), and there was little traffic by today's standards, the average speed for the whole drive from Salisbury was a little below 30 m.p.h.

There were of course no air pollution controls. We had to switch on head-lights passing through the potteries area. The same was true in the old County of Lancashire (i.e. starting at the Manchester Ship Canal), as far north as Preston. Until the 1950s, this area was a <u>mass</u> of coal-mines, slag-heaps, cotton-mills and other industrial plants. In 1996 the last coal-mine in Lancashire was closed; the slag-heaps have today largely been removed or landscaped; and the fumes and effluents from other industrial plants – themselves generally smaller – have been greatly reduced. It has been a quiet and welcome revolution.

At Ackenthwaite my father did a lot of overdue heavy work, notably indulging his penchant for cutting down or lopping trees; and we children were expected to help. But there was time for golf, on the nine-hole course on Heversham Head, which existed until after the Second World War. We were also taken for walking excursions to the Lakeland Fells. It was then that my love affair with them began. A 1937 photo shows me with my parents for the first time on a summit – the Langdale Pikes. Many other peaks were to follow. My parents used to be mildly irritated by my usually reaching the top before them!

Another great feature of our time at Salisbury was that it brought us children, for the first time, into direct contact with continental Europe. It was not that my parents took us there: our family summer holidays were still in England. But they seemed to conclude that we should be more exposed to the French language. Michael tells me he had been struggling with it at school, and having to take lessons during holidays at Nurton. Somehow, arrangements were made for a young French girl, Odile de la Varende, who had been teaching at a convent school in Kent, to come and stay in the holidays, and give us conversational practice (1936-38).

Odile was charming, and we stayed in touch until she died. During the War, she acted as Secretary to the Comtesse de Kéranflech, known to Odile as *'Tante Simone'*, at the Château de Quelenec in Brittany. The Countess started hiding American airmen who had been shot down, as early as 1943. Then, in 1944, she had many Allied parachutists staying with her: they and their supplies could be hidden in nearby woods. Unfortunately a local Frenchman denounced them to the Gestapo. They were due to be arrested. The American Army arrived just in time. The traitor escaped, but left his papers behind, with all their secrets. The rest of her life was more peaceful. She married a Royal Air Force Officer; lived in Brussels; and worked in NATO. It was through Odile that first Michael (in 1937), and later myself, were sent, on an exchange basis, to stay in the summer with a French family, the Forest-Divonnes, who lived at Pomiers, a thirteenth century Château, on the edge of the small village of St Martin-du-Mont, in the Department of the Ain.

My own visit was seminal. Despite gathering war-clouds, I was taken by my mother to Waterloo Station in early August 1939, and put on a train for Paris. Wagon-Lit Cook's agents oversaw my journey by train and boat from there to Paris; and from the Gare du Nord to the Gare de Lyons, where I was put on a train for Bourg-en-Bresse. There I was met by Madame de la Forest-Divonne, and driven to Pomiers, where I was to spend a month.

The Forest-Divonnes were (and are) a charming family. The father was a retired French Naval Officer. The mother was a member of the Lur-Saluce family, until recently the proprietors of Château D'Yquem. There were five children: Louis, Emmanuel, Eugène, Anne-Marie (Mimi) and Amédée. I must have been a little younger than Eugène (who changed places with me). I had already met, and liked, Louis, when he had stayed with us at Salisbury in 1937; I soon came to like them all. From the start I was treated, and felt like, a member of the family. We still remain in touch, so that now I have met four generations of Forest-Divonnes, over more than 60 years. Of course, I ate and drank what their children did, which included wine with main meals, usually 'coupé' with water. The Admiral had some kind of property in the Beaujolais, whilst of course Madame had her Château D'Yquem! (If we were allowed a sip of the latter wine, it was not 'coupé'!) It did not seem necessary, on return to England, to mention wine-drinking to my parents: my mother would have been shocked.

Pomiers is delightful. The house stands on the east side of the Rhône valley, and about 100 metres above it. Its grounds are small, and informal, but delightful. The foothills of the Jura rise behind, to the east. There is a beautiful western prospect, looking down over the Château's own vineyard, and across the Rhône valley. From the start, there was total linguistic immersion, although members of the family would help out with some English if essential. French was well-taught at Twyford, and had never been difficult for me. But this was the first time I had had to use it in practice.

Because everybody was kind, and I enjoyed life with the family, speaking French became easy and natural. The experience brought home to me, for the first time, that speaking a foreign language is not just an intellectual exercise; but rather the opening of a door to understand and enjoy the life, culture and literature of other peoples. From then on, I focused my education deliberately on languages, and by the age of eighteen could understand, write and speak French, Italian, Spanish and German. (The Italian was subsequently submerged, because I operated diplomatically for four years in a Hispanic country, and only used Italian occasionally.)

Towards the end of my month with the Forest-Divonnes, Hitler's actions made it clear that war was only days away. My hostess and my parents agreed I must leave at once. Madame de la Forest-Divonne took me to Paris, and set me on the train to London. This family had a very tough war.

When I got back to Salisbury, events were moving fast. My mother, who had played a leading part in the local St John Ambulance Brigade, was soon heavily engaged at the Railway Station, where teams of volunteers were handing out drinking water to the masses of evacuees, whose special trains would pause on their way to the west country. Michael and I were roped in to help. And thus it was that, on 3 September 1939, in the waiting room of Salisbury Station, we heard Neville Chamberlain announce that Britain was at war with Germany. As it turned out, many of the evacuees went back to London during the long period of the 'phoney war'; and had to be re-evacuated when the Blitz on London began.

My father was at once immersed in the despatch of the British Expeditionary Force to the continent, and was rapidly sent to France with Headquarters Second Corps. We children were dispersed to boarding schools: Michael went back to Winchester, where I now joined him; and Elizabeth became a boarder at Overstone, a girls' school in Northampton-shire. The lease on the house in Salisbury was brought to an end. My mother moved our family belongings into store, and then for a time revolved between her in-laws' house at Oxford, and her mother's at Hove. Thus ended the only three years of my life, between the ages of 4 and 18, in which we three children were to be at home with the full and continuing attention of <u>both</u> our parents.

CHAPTER 3

Winchester College

WHEN I ENTERED Winchester College, in September 1939, it had much the same reputation as today. The oldest public school in the country, founded by William of Wykeham in 1384, its academic standing was of the highest. It did not have the social cachet of Eton or Harrow; but was not bothered. Its relatively small size – about 450 boys – gave it a human scale, and meant that everybody, teachers and taught, to some extent knew everybody else. This is a great help in creating and maintaining a sense of solidarity, and of loyalty to an Institution.

The key unit was the House. There were ten, each with 40 or less boys – once again a human scale. These commoner Houses had been added, over the previous two centuries, to the original foundation of 70 scholars. The latter lived in the fourteenth century College buildings, and were usually known as 'College-men'. The Houses were mostly of nineteenth or twentieth century vintage. The boys all came together – scholars and commoners – for lessons, chapel services, sport and much else.

The school felt itself unique, and indeed cultivated that impression. It had its own words and phrases, known collectively as 'notions', which meant the boys could converse openly amongst themselves while outsiders could not understand them. These notions had to be learnt on arrival, and one was examined on them after a fortnight! One notion was that boys were never referred to as such, but always as 'men': to a 13-year-old neophyte, fresh from prep-school, this was a strange concept, but also challenging.

My House – to which my father and Michael had preceded me, and my son William was to follow – was known informally as Trant's, after its founder, or officially as H House. Houses each have their own character, which alters over time in response to the personality of the House-master, the current cohort of boys and social trends. The first of these three influences is the most important, so the personality of my House-master needs description. I arrived in the same term as a new one – the Reverend John d'Ewes Evelyn Firth – officially 'Mr Firth' to us, but always known as 'Budge'. He was corpulent, and we were told that his nickname derived

Budge Firth, my House-master.
By kind permission of the Warden and Fellows of Winchester College.

from some wag asking: *'Who can budge Firth?'* He had recently married; and his wife, Priscilla, was a kind, gentle, conscientious and quiet person, reassuring for new arrivals.

Budge, himself a Wykehamist and a College-man, is even now the only man to have taken all 10 Eton wickets in an innings at that great sporting fixture – the Eton and Winchester match. This got him off to a good start with the young men. And, although he did not excel at other sports, he followed with enthusiasm the progress of his boys in them all. He was the butt of jokes because of his very high-pitched voice. He, like Priscilla, had a quiet manner, and kept a low profile; and many boys, including myself, only came to a full appreciation of the great and positive influence he had exercised on their lives after they had left school. He would do anything for them.

Budge was a considerable scholar of history and languages – the classics, French and Spanish – and an intellectual. He adored mimicry and acting, and would keep language and history students in stitches, during lessons, by acting to perfection the part of any famous person under discussion. History was brought very effectively to life. He was a very good teacher. He would also take part with enthusiasm in amateur dramatics. And, on Sunday evenings in Trant's, there were often play-readings. His high-pitched voice allowed him to do justice to female parts as well as male: by common consent his rendering of Lady Bracknell was on a par with that of the late Dame Edith Evans. Budge, though not an active musician, enjoyed and encouraged music. The House, in my time, responded to his personality. The expectation of Trantites, to generalise, was that they would work hard academically; give lower priority to sport, but still do their best; and be musical, artistic and interested in theatre.

Life was tough. A full week-day routine went something like this: the details may not be perfect, but the substance is true. Rise at 0630; obligatory cold bath; one lesson of 45 minutes before breakfast (morning lines); after that a chapel service, and then four more lessons; lunch; the afternoon for sport; shower and change; three more lessons; high tea; 100 minutes of Toyetime (prep); a cup of tea; house prayers; up to bed soon after nine, but with many older boys putting in an hour or more of private study before retiring. So, on full week-days, all were doing at least seven hours and forty minutes of study. There were however three half-holidays a week (Tuesdays, Thursdays, Saturdays), when either two or three evening lessons fell away; and on Sunday, apart from two chapel services, there was only the evening's Toyetime. So we studied for at least 40 hours a week.

The Winchester entrance exam was set to a high standard. The boys who passed were usually able to cope with the exacting schedule. The parents of those who could not were advised to remove their boy to a less demanding establishment, and usually did. Certainly, although the pace was now a lot faster than at Twyford, I did not find the change of gear too hard, and indeed enjoyed the challenge, determining to remain in the top third of any class I joined. It is clear, however, that once again I did not exert myself unduly. To the end, School reports contained phrases like 'He has ability, but has still to learn how to be more than superficial [German]…He has all the gifts of ear and fluency necessary to a linguist, but he will skate over the surface [French]'. Be that as it may, I ended with good School Certificate results; and two full years in Sixth Book (the Sixth Form, as non-Wykehamists would say) with modern languages as my main field. Much of this time was spent in the 'div' (division, or class) taught by my House-master.

There must now be a digression, to consider the effect of the War on the pattern of our life. At Winchester College, every House had its own shelter, equipped with enough bunks for both boys and resident staff. For nearly a year, however, the War seemed remote. It was not until Hitler's forces rolled westwards in the summer of 1940, conquering the Low Countries and France, and forcing the evacuation of the British Expeditionary Force (BEF) from Dunkirk and other French ports, that British perceptions of what was in store for them became more realistic.

That summer, the threat of an imminent German invasion seemed so real that my parents withdrew Elizabeth and me from our schools well before the end of term, though Michael was left at Winchester because he was taking exams. My mother took the two of us – joined later by Michael – to spend the rest of the summer in a cottage, belonging to Major Pugh, an old friend, on his beautiful estate at Cymmerau, high above the mouth of the River Dovey in West Central Wales. The contrast between what was happening in southern England – where the Battle of Britain was being fought out day after day – and the remoteness and peace of our mountain retreat – could not have been greater. In the south, RAF fighter pilots, pitted against vastly superior numbers of German aircraft, but greatly helped by Britain's secret weapon of Radar, were giving their lives to save the country. With us, little happened to disturb the rural beauty and calm. Each day, to the dismay of the RAF, dawned clear and sunny. The postman rode up the valley with the mail, riding a grey pony. We children were free to roam the fells, or swim in the Pughs' pool, to our hearts' content.

After Dunkirk the Government decided to establish 'Local Defence Volunteers' (LDV), later re-named the 'Home Guard' by Churchill, and later still immortalised as 'Dad's Army' on TV. Our local platoon was commanded by Major Pugh, who suffered two disadvantages: he was paralysed from the waist down; and he spoke no Welsh, while many of his men spoke little or no English! Michael was too young to be enrolled. However, LDV units were desperately short of rifles or other fire-arms. Michael had an air-rifle and was therefore 'co-opted'! The best shot in the platoon was a one-armed former poacher! One sees that the TV series had elements of truth!

By September, the threat of immediate invasion appeared less, and we children went back to school. Hitler was coming to the conclusion that he could not wipe out the RAF and should switch to bombing of major cities in order to break the British resistance. Before the War ended he had killed 30,000 civilians in London and 11,000 elsewhere. The *Blitz* was resisted by all means possible. So far as we in Winchester College were concerned, boys of 16 or even younger went on fire-watching duty at night, by rota. Only occasional bombs fell on the City. But nearby Portsmouth, Southampton and Eastleigh were major targets. During heavy raids, the light from explosions of bombs, and the anti-aircraft tracer shells, were clearly visible and audible from Winchester. It could be a nervous affair, for a young teenager, on duty for two hours in the small hours, to make a round of our City block with a small torch in the total black-out. Our tasks were to spot any incendiary bombs, report them to the local HQ, and be prepared to try and put them out with shovels of sand.

If the air-raid sirens went off, the entire House would repair to the shelter, carrying blankets and pillows. This happened sometimes night after night, until the Allied invasion of France in 1944 made it difficult for the Germans to mount conventional air-raids. Later, however, the V1 and V2 raids took their place. There was a rule in the College that, if the all-clear siren did not sound before a certain time (I think midnight), then 'morning lines' (the pre-breakfast lesson) was cancelled for the next day: a cheer used to ring through the shelter!

The Junior Training Corps (JTC) took on more importance during the war, as a training ground for future soldiers, and almost all boys joined at age 15: those who did not, had to join the Boy Scouts. One afternoon a week was devoted to it. The older boys (from their 17th birthday) were also formed into Home Guard platoons, which trained on Sundays. Both bodies undertook small arms training, with live ammunition, and 'live' tests of gas masks. Very realistic exercises were organised. In the latter years of the war, the College Home Guard would have been able to put up a fair resistance to enemy infantry, if any had landed. For me, all this was 'playing at soldiers' at its best, and good fun. It was, moreover, a valuable preparation for Army service.

Also valuable, in that sense, was the fact that we were frequently addressed by 'Monty' (General, later Field Marshal, Montgomery). His son was in the School. So Monty came and lectured after each campaign: Alamein, Tunis, Sicily, Salerno and Anzio – are words that spring to mind. We felt privileged: we were hearing about key moments of the war 'straight from the horse's mouth'. But we were offended by his taking all the credit for British or Allied successes so personally. The picture was always presented in the first person singular: *'I decided to make a left hook; I sent in the .. Division and told them to punch their way through; then I ordered the .. Division to exploit the gap; I told the RAF to give close support; and…'* Young though we were, we felt somebody else must have done something towards the successful outcome. Perhaps Monty sensed this. He always wound up by saying that

Winchester College Chapel.
By kind permission of the Warden and Fellows of Winchester College.

the Headmaster had agreed to his request for an extra half-holiday, which ensured hearty applause.

Another aspect of the war which affected the College was the 'Dig for Victory' campaign, in which the Government encouraged everybody to grow food. Each House was allotted a field, and expected to cultivate potatoes on it. In Trant's we drew the short straw: our field was at the top of Sleeper's Hill, a big hill so steep that we had to push our bikes up it (a very long haul) before digging!

Winchester College made an enormous input to my development. It gave me a very solid secondary education, with a focus on modern languages, but also a broad understanding of many other subjects in both the humanities and science fields. It taught me the value of taking good advice before reaching decisions; the benefits of keeping fit; the importance of team-work and of keeping in with all around one; and the need to stand on one's own feet. My House-master, moreover, was good at broadening his flock's horizons and social skills.

Finally, it was at Winchester that my insatiable intellectual curiosity was most strongly nurtured. At home, my parents thought I asked far too many questions. But that was not a complaint likely to be made in a place as intellectual as Winchester. So the habit was formed of not being afraid to ask 'idiot child' questions – in other words those which others do not ask for fear of revealing their ignorance. It is a habit I have maintained throughout my life, and it has stood me in good stead.

Living, as one did, immersed in a way of life that had grown up in an unbroken process over nearly 600 years, surrounded by beautiful buildings and countryside, with manifold opportunities to experience marvellous music (in the College, in the Cathedral and in the City of Winchester), with amateur drama of high quality available, my time at Winchester broadened immensely my understanding of the British cultural heritage, and made me realise that it was part of a wider European one. As at Twyford, there was a constant exposure to Christian thinking and Christian attitudes. The words of the Authorised Version, and of the Book of Common Prayer, continued to sound in my ears. I have never been a specially religious person, in the accepted sense. But my Christian faith has never been in doubt. None of these thoughts, naturally, were in my mind at the time. My school diary for 1942 records what I did, but reveals nothing of my reflections. I was always a down-to-earth person, who believed in getting on quietly with the job in hand – whether it was preparing for School Certificate Exams, playing squash or digging potatoes.

My choice of career fell out in this way. For reasons not entirely clear to Michael or me, we had been brought up from earliest years to believe that there was an Audland family tradition of soldiering, and left in no doubt that we were both expected to follow it. There was in fact no such family tradition. Indeed, my father's later genealogical researches were to show that he was the first Audland ever to join the Services – and that was because of the accident of war! But, as we can see from the persistence of Euromyths today, long after they have been shown to be without substance, the dispelling of myths is far harder than their creation.

Michael accepted that soldiering would be his career, without enthusiasm perhaps, but without demur. So did I at first, when the problem was not actual. But, in September 1943, when I had turned 17, Budge suggested the army was a career which might not fit my temperament. He presented it as one where there was a system for everything, and original thought was not greatly encouraged. He probably exaggerated, to make his point; but he made me think, and ask about alternatives. When he suggested diplomacy,

I was at a loss, having no idea what diplomats did. He explained, at the same time pointing out that modern languages, my *forte*, constituted a key tool of the trade. I was convinced, and wrote to my mother, saying that I wished not to be a regular soldier, but go into the Foreign Office. She kept a meticulous and detailed diary throughout the war, which I now have. And the following passage reflects what it revealed.

My mother felt that such a course raised big questions. She couldn't see me *'fulfilling a happy life shut up in an office'*. She assumed a University Degree would be necessary. This was not something in prospect for Michael or Elizabeth: was it fair to finance it just for me? She decided to find someone to look after the house and the animals whilst she went to Winchester to talk things over. Her journey took place early in November. When the interview with Budge and me took place, after dinner that evening, she could not have been feeling her best. She had passed a sleepless night; caught an early train to London; done a lot of shopping; caught a train on to Winchester; and dined with me and two school friends.

The interview lasted an hour. My mother took the offensive. She told Budge *'there was no doubt the general public thought all the duds would do for the army, and trusted he had never let me [sic] think it was his opinion'*. I felt my mother was hectoring both Budge and me. It was very uncomfortable. However, it has never been my habit to resile from a decision I think right, unless convinced to the contrary. A weakness in my position was that I had then little knowledge of family history, and certainly not enough to refute the military myth. So I simply maintained my view, and left it to Budge to play the hand. He did so with skill, giving me a free lesson in diplomacy. He remained calm, courteous and logical, but firm.

In the end, my mother effectively struck her colours. I would join the Artillery in the following year *'without prejudice as to the future regular commission'*. Meanwhile I would be entered at Caius College, Cambridge – where my uncle was Bursar – to take a degree after the war, ahead of trying for the Foreign Office. (This inscription was later done.) But I was to realise that this University education would be a great financial strain on my parents, and *'must be for work, work, work'*.

It will be noticed that my father is not mentioned in this context. He was, for military reasons, inaccessible; and he anyway had a habit of leaving parental guidance largely to my mother. He did, however, make clear that he thought my decision was a mistake. And both parents continued to hope I would later *'see sense'*. Michael has remarked that they must have lived to wonder about the merits of the decisions they were pressing on their sons.

In his case, the contraction of the army in 1960 led to his being retired when it was very difficult for a 37-year-old retired army officer to make a new career. (Ageism was the norm.) In my case, diplomacy suited me well, and I retired voluntarily at 60, after 38 years in the career.

This chapter concludes with some account of my wartime holidays from Winchester. Beginning at Christmas 1940, my grandfather lent the House at Ackenthwaite to my parents until the end of the war, to serve as a permanent base for my mother; as a holiday base for the three children; and as an occasional base for my father, when able to get away for weekends or leaves – as he did quite frequently when in the UK between 1940 and 1942. It was an area with little risk of bombing or of invasion. But it was difficult of access, in wartime travel conditions, especially from Winchester; and also from Northamptonshire, where Elizabeth was at School.

What were these wartime travel conditions? After the early months, our family had no car. The Austin 7 had been sold. Petrol rationing came in soon: if memory serves, the ration enabled one to drive 300 miles a month. Our Morris 25 was soon laid up. We were dependent on trains, buses, taxis and bicycles. The railway system was a prime target for air-raids. It was also over-loaded, because of the need to transport servicemen and war supplies for us and our Allies; and badly maintained, because of other demands on the economy. It was therefore unreliable. To illustrate this, a description is now given of a typical journey, on an occasion when we three children were making for Ackenthwaite from the south, at the end of, say, an autumn term.

My parents sensibly considered it would be folly to pass through blitzed London. So Michael and I were routed from Winchester via Oxford and Bletchley, where we would pick up the main line trains north. It had to be a two-day affair. As far as Oxford, a section we covered in daylight, the delays were seldom serious, since these cross-country lines were not normally disrupted. There, we spent the night at Nurton. Next day, at Bletchley, the troubles began. The trains from London were usually overcrowded, and we often sat on suitcases in the corridor all the way home. They were also subject to long delays and to cancellations. One would climb on to the first that was going the right way. We had, however, to wait for one stopping at Blisworth, where Elizabeth would be on the platform. Thereafter, we often had to change at intermediate stations like Crewe or Preston. Such changes were not eased by the fact that we had with us suitcases, and also bicycles in the Guard's van (which latter were needed at both ends). We were spared the burden of trunks and tuck-boxes, which in those days could be sent separately. Over and above these difficulties, one could easily make a mistake about where to change, because station names (like road signposts) had been removed in case they might help any German parachutists! Trains went more slowly in those days: in wartime, moreover, there were endless stops and starts; and station stops were often long-drawn-out. It was not unusual for us to arrive home several hours late. There was no telephone at home, so my mother spent some anxious evenings. I even recall an occasion (after Michael had left for the army in 1941) when, due to these delays, my train arrived at Preston <u>after</u> the departure of the last train for Milnthorpe (then a main-line station). I spent the night in the Preston waiting-room, catching the first train home next morning, the journey from Oxford having been completed in a total of some 22 hours!

The trains themselves were in a bad state. Since there were no resources for re-furbishment, the rolling stock got steadily scruffier. Blacking-out made carriages gloomy after dusk. There were blinds, which had to be kept down; and the lights were hooded, so as to leave most of the compartment in the dark. One carried one's own rations, as there was no food or drink on sale in trains. Stations were blacked out too. Refreshment rooms, where they existed, had little to offer. They and the waiting rooms were heated inadequately or not at all.

One might think that, in these circumstances, there would be moaning and groaning. But there never was. Why? Because we were living in an atmosphere of <u>total</u> <u>national</u> <u>commitment</u> to winning the war, often described as 'the Dunkirk Spirit'. With that, went an absolute acceptance of the consequences – the loss of near and dear (whether military or civilian), air-raids with consequent destruction of homes and personal possessions, other disruptions and difficulties of daily and family life, rationing, shortages, the need to undertake voluntary duties to aid the war effort, and much else besides. With this acceptance of the consequences, was coupled in turn a determination to 'keep smiling', a phrase one heard time and time again; and a readiness to help others.

So the sort of travel problems mentioned above were treated as minor, and young people travelling could count on a helping hand. One would never have wished for the <u>cause</u> of all this to arise – the most lethal war of all time. But one can be deeply thankful – and I am – for having lived for nearly six years in a marvellous atmosphere of national dedication to a great purpose, of co-operation and of self-sacrifice. The contrast with the selfish and materialistic national atmosphere of today needs no comment.

These journeys, of course, all ended at the Old House. Our world there consisted of what we could reach by the local train network (Lancaster to Oxenholme and Windermere, plus the old rail link from Grange through Arnside and Heversham Station to Oxenholme); or by bus or bicycle; or on foot.

A large part of our time was necessarily spent outdoors. There was daily dog-walking duty. At first, after that, we would often set off to Crosby Lodge, once again to play in the two barns – then filled with hay – or help feed the chickens and collect the eggs. But progressively the garden and (old) paddock became a small-holding. Below the ha-ha were three vegetable beds, which needed much attention. The orchard was fenced off from them completely. My mother acquired hens (up to two dozen, for eggs and eating); a couple of ducks (for eggs – and to keep down slugs); bees (up to three hives); geese (up to eight before Christmas); and finally a pony, Nancy (which of course had to be exercised daily, after being bought in 1944). All were kept in the orchard, except the geese (usually in the paddock) and Nancy (in the peat-house or paddock, when not out to livery). By the time the small-holding was well established, Michael had gone off to the army. It then fell to me, as the only available male, to wring the chickens' necks, when their time came. Fortunately, not even my mother, though herself un-squeamish, thought me physically capable of coping with geese (this is a much more gory business), and James Melling of Crosby Lodge used to 'oblige' shortly before Christmas. We, however, were left to pluck the great birds (as many as six, of which we ate one and sold the rest). This was a time-consuming affair since it then had to be done by hand.

Feeding so many birds was not easy. One got a ration of 'balancer meal', which was mixed with potatoes or other household waste. But one could not buy grain for them, and the birds did not lay well without. So we went into the Crosby Lodge or Garnett fields, after the summer harvest, with permission to glean any grain left on the ground by the harvesters. There was plenty, but collecting sacks full of grain was slow work. To get around this to some extent, we would often drive the geese to a stubble field, and leave them there for a few hours to do their own gleaning. The fowls gave us a lot of work; but they added hugely to our diet. War-time rationing was severe. It extended to almost all foods, even bread. To be able to supplement the rations with practically limitless chicken meat and eggs was a big plus. We also shot rabbits. And fish, which was not rationed, could be bought in Westmorland, though in many other places it was not available.

Apart from the animals, there were also household chores. Coal was in short supply, and we burnt mostly wood from garden and paddock in the kitchen range and the fireplaces (no central heating then!). The wood was cut with a two-handed saw; and split with axes and wedges. In the house, the task of cleaning out the fires and 'blacking' the kitchen range and grates was chiefly mine. Given these activities, it may not be altogether surprising that my mother saw fit to dress all three of us for six months of the year in corduroy breeches: we felt rather out of date!

Besides helping look after our own livestock, my mother arranged for me to work on local farms in the summer holidays. One was at Lower Rowell. But my real joy was the beautiful, mediaeval, Hincaster Hall, then farmed by the Pricketts, who in August, 1943, took me very much into the family. It consisted of Mr and Mrs Henry Prickett and their three children – Thomas, Emmie and Elsie. They had no other male help, and an energetic and willing boy of 17 could make himself very useful, in those un-mechanised days, and get huge pleasure and satisfaction from it. The scene in the fields was like a Victorian water-colour. One was occupied in minding and leading the great cart-horses; turning the hay; stooking up the sheaves as they fell from the binder; throwing up the sheaves (or the hay) on to the carts or the stacks; fetching in the cows; helping to milk them; and so forth.

Though there was much work like this to do, there was also time for play. In the summer, the fells were reachable for walks, though it was hard work. We would put our bicycles on the train, at Milnthorpe or Heversham stations; train to Windermere; cycle to, say, Dungeon Ghyll; climb the Langdale Pikes; and then return by the same means. We swam at Grange or Sandside. Wartime winters tended to be cold: when they were, we skated and tobogganed. After our pony, Nancy, arrived, we rode regularly.

By the end of busy days outdoors, one was ready for early bed. This was just as well, because the public entertainment resources were limited. We went to the cinema quite often: there was one in the village, as well as in Kendal. And there were some amateur dramatics or concerts, though my mother, no musician, was not keen on the latter. We played a lot of card-, board- or table-games in the winter evenings.

To complete the picture of war-time life in Ackenthwaite, I need to mention one important aspect which arose after my own departure for the Army. In September, 1944 my mother voluntarily accepted that a whole family from London should be billeted on us; and they stayed for seven months. (Her only legal obligation was to take in a single refugee.) The family's name was Cunnell; and there was a mother, daughter and son (Gill and Derick). Mrs Cunnell was pregnant, and was soon delivered of a boy (Michael). In the House as it then was, this produced a considerable squash in the holiday periods. The solution was to give the Cunnells the (then) 'boys' room as their bedroom, and the dining room for overflow and play. Mr Cunnell joined the party on some weekends. Fortunately, they were easy to get on with, and a happy relationship persisted throughout their longish stay. Indeed, photos show them visiting Ackenthwaite socially in 1946. Be that as it may, I was most impressed with my mother's generosity.

It was during these many months at Ackenthwaite, spread regularly over three and a half years, from Christmas 1940 until I joined the army in July 1944, that I first came to understand fully the strength of my family's roots in this part of the world. At this stage, I knew little of our family history: my father's researches followed much later. The realisation came rather from living in a House which I soon realised to have been home to a long line of ancestors; going to Church at Heversham and reading inscriptions on so many Audland memorials – including seven on a single grave(!); coming across farms named Audland at the end of a long ride; and being recognised as a true 'local' by all those around me (despite my public school accent!). They were happy days.

CHAPTER 4

Army Service in Britain and the Middle East (1944-48)

I LEFT WINCHESTER shortly after my eighteenth birthday in July 1944. My studies had kept me busy, and preparations for packing had been low priority. I ended by doing the job in the House Hall, between 2200 and 0200 on my last night. Characteristically, Budge Firth spent most of those hours with me, as he was cleaning the shoes of the whole House – a task he performed when staff was short, and which he never mentioned to others! Early next morning I left for home, there to repack for my first army posting.

Although I had been accepted by the Royal Artillery on voluntary enlistment in Salisbury, in December 1943, there was a requirement for all recruits to begin with eight weeks of basic training under the aegis of the General Service Corps. Mine took place at the 5th Primary Training Centre in barracks at Lanark (a mile or so out of town), to which I reported on 2nd August 1944. The training staff were supplied by the Argyll and Sutherland Highlanders. We benefited from the presence, in the same camp, of the Pipe Band of the Royal Scots.

Up to now, I had lived a sheltered life. My contacts had been limited to those at boarding schools with me, both staff and pupils, and those I met in my home environment. There was a big culture shock on finding myself in an intake of some 25 or 30 recruits from every walk of life. Few were well educated. Some were very rough. The language was typical of army 'Other Ranks' – known as 'O.R's'. Every second word was a swear-word, many of them coarse and never heard by me before.

There springs to mind a man who had until then been a professional bruiser at fairs, challenging all comers at fisticuffs. Though ignorant, he adopted strong views on everything, which he never changed. Being disputatious, I at first questioned some of his opinions. He never argued. He simply said: 'You shut up, or I'll knock your block off'. The threat was real: I learnt that life was easier if one never took issue with him.

Our first night at Lanark is also easy to recall. We had been issued with our regulation four Army blankets, and made our beds. There were of course no sheets. When the time of 'lights-out' approached, and we were preparing for bed, I started to put on my pyjamas. At once, a boot was hurled at me. Looking round, it was apparent that everybody else was getting into bed wearing underclothes. This was a novel concept to me, but the message was clear.

The training course was demanding. Discipline was strong. A key aim was to raise our standards of physical fitness sharply in the eight weeks. There was much 'square-bashing' and physical training. And there were frequent route marches, always in full battle order: with rifle, 20 or 30 rounds of bullets, tin-hat, gas-mask, knapsack and water bottle. The knapsack contained two bricks. The water bottle was full, but one was not allowed to drink from it. From time to time we had to march a mile or more wearing gas-masks. By the end of the course we were doing route marches of up to ten miles in these conditions (and it was August); but the build-up was so progressive I do not recall any recruit giving up on a march.

Sometimes, the final stage of a march would take us through the streets of Lanark. We would 'be fallen out' at the outskirts of the town, and given ten minutes to rest and smarten up. The pipe band would be waiting, and play us back to camp. The effect of the pipes is amazing. As no other military music does, they stir the blood: in our case they turned a group of footsore recruits into a well-drilled platoon, whose marching and morale did credit to our instructors and impressed the townspeople. At Lanark we learnt the basic skills of infantry soldiers, including the use of rifles, Bren-guns, mortars and hand-grenades. Lessons usually began with that indispensable Sergeant-Major's phrase: *'Right, what we are going on about now is…'*.

The eight weeks over, we were posted to our Regiments. I went to the 4th Royal Artillery Training Regiment at Larkhill, arriving in September 1944. There I was to spend a number of months (eight I think) training as a 'Driver-Operator', in other words as a driver of vehicles, properly qualified also to operate a radio transmitter-receiver. It was commanded by Colonel Gibbon (known as 'Gibboon'), who as a Major had assisted my father's romance[1], and who had been called out of retirement. Nobody else was aware of the connection between the Colonel and my family, and I took care not to mention it!

My squad was again of about 25 men. We were now called 'Gunners', not 'Privates'. We were in the charge of a Bombardier (Gunner equivalent of a Corporal). We were taught, not only the obvious Driver-Operator skills, but also basic Gunnery skills. These were concentrated on the 25-pounder gun, by now the Field Artillery's standard weapon; but we were given experience of firing the 17-pounder anti-tank gun, and the much larger 5.5 inch medium gun. Once, when we were working with a troop of 5.5s, the shoot was being controlled by an 'Air OP' [air observation post]: in other words, the officer observing the target and giving the orders to the guns was not on the ground, but flying round in an Auster spotter plane. Sadly he forgot where he was. Having issued instructions to align the ranging gun, he flew forward to see the shell fall; ordered 'fire'; and thereby blew himself to smithereens.

The radio side of things came easily to me. The key requirement was to be able to cope with the Morse code: to tap out messages at 10 words a minute and receive them at 15. Morse soon became second nature; and even now – though I have never used it since Army days – I can still reel off the code from A to Z without a moment's hesitation.

On driving, I was a slow learner. We were given instruction on every kind of vehicle: from tanks and Bren-gun carriers; down through 3-ton and 30-hundred-weight lorries; to 15-hundred-weight trucks. We had to take our tests on the lorries, in my case of the 3-ton variety. I distinguished myself by damaging three *other* army lorries in the space of a mile during my first test. This happened on a narrow road near Tidworth. The other lorries were part of a long, very spread-out column proceeding in the opposite direction; and I consistently misjudged the distances between us. The side of the first oncoming lorry was slightly grazed; the second lorry lost its mirror; and the third lost its canvas canopy! After an exchange of appropriate language between the commander of the oncoming column and my instructor, the latter took over the wheel and placed me on a charge for damaging army property! Next morning I was brought before Colonel Gibbon. He heard the case; pronounced me guilty; and sentenced me to a period of 'CB' [confined to barracks]. Then he dismissed the Sergeant-Major, telling me to stay behind. Soon after, I was sent away with my tail between my legs, having been told that I was disgracing my father!

Being CB was not very terrible. It meant reporting to the guardroom during off-duty hours and until lights-out. One would be given menial tasks. If lucky, one would merely have to clean the guardroom or the latrines, or brew up 'char' for those of the guard who were off duty. If unlucky, one might find oneself engaged on that proverbial military employment – white-washing heaps of coal – supposedly so that no-one would fall into them in the dark!

As at Lanark, there was much square-bashing. The worst was for compulsory Church Parade on a Sunday in the depth of winter. The Larkhill barrack-square can be incredibly cold. It stands high on Salisbury Plain: vicious winds often sweep across it. We used to form up on parade well before Church; and then had to stand still whilst every Gunner was meticulously inspected (and placed on a charge if at all scruffy!), before being marched to the Garrison Church. Many fainted on their feet; crashed to the ground; and were carried off to the Medical Centre! At Larkhill we lived in wooden barrack rooms. These had been condemned early in the 20th century as unfit for continued occupation. The arrival of the First World War saved them from destruction; their condemnation was forgotten in the inter-war years; so they were still there for us!

Getting a place in a course like this flowed from some kind of selection process by higher authorities. How it worked remains for me a mystery: IQ tests probably had something to do with it. But the authorities clearly felt it pointless to accept people unless they had a reasonable level of education. We were still a very mixed bunch; but there was more homogeneity in the squad than at Lanark. Because we were together much longer, we also got to know each other better. But there was no-one with whom I sought to establish a close friendship. The vocabulary was the same as before. Off-duty, many of my companions told tales of their sexual exploits: even then, ignorant though I was on the subject of sex, I felt that hope was often being confused with reality.

Fortunately, it was not difficult to find entertainment. Larkhill, Bulford and Tidworth, at that time, contained a vast population of soldiers. There were NAAFI clubs galore, where food and drink were cheap. There were plenty of cinemas. At Larkhill, we even had a Garrison Theatre. As part of their war effort, great stars of the stage came to entertain us. Those I saw personally included the youthful Peter Ustinov, Jack Hulbert, Edith Evans, Arthur Askey and others of that quality.

In April 1945, whilst at Larkhill, I passed a War Office Selection Board, with the result that, when my course there ended in May, I was posted to No 123 Officer Cadet Training Unit [OCTU] at Catterick, for training as a Gunner Officer over another six month period. At once, life improved. The barracks were of inter-war vintage, and built of brick. But the main improvement was psychological. One knew one had passed a threshold, and that a higher level of responsibility could be obtained through success at OCTU. Much more was expected, and the intellectual effort involved was substantially greater. One was no longer learning simply how to fire guns on the orders of others, but rather how to deploy them; how to control their fire; and how to relate the Artillery to other arms of the service – infantry,

The author as a Royal Artillery Officer Cadet, 1945.

engineers and so forth. We learnt also how to ride 250 and 500cc motor-bikes cross-country. (The reason for this piece of our training was unclear, since in my experience as a Gunner Officer I never used a motor-cycle; but it was entertaining!) The training staff were of higher quality. Moreover, one was treated as an Officer Cadet, in other words as a person half way to being an officer. This meant that, for example, a Drill Sergeant or Sergeant-Major might address sharply critical words to you; but he would then, after a pause for dramatic effect, add '...*Sir*' at the end! We were very much on our mettle. By no means all would pass the course.

Still higher standards of fitness were promoted. *Inter alia*, we had a week's battle-camp at Bannerdale, east of Ullswater, the last day of which was gruelling. It was mid-summer, and very hot. Up early, we were transported by lorry to Glenridding, in full battle order. From there, we were required to <u>race</u> to the top of Helvellyn (950 metres) and down again. After a sandwich lunch, we were sent off again, still racing, over the fells direct to Bannerdale. On arrival at the camp, we had to get through a rigorous assault course, with directing staff throwing thunder-flashes under our feet (some brave spirits threw them back again before they went off!); and to end the proceedings by firing 10 rounds at a target with our rifles. By now, after a year in the army, I had achieved a standard of fitness which permitted me to get through that day, not only without exhaustion, but even with satisfaction.

It was to my great surprise that, at the end of the course, I was named as Senior Under-Officer, in other words top of the class. As such, I marched at the head of the passing out parade; and, to mark the occasion, received a leather-covered swagger stick at the hands of the officer taking the salute. This was General Ambrose Pratt, the Master Gunner. By the same token, I was selected as one of the two Officer Cadets to participate in the wreath-laying ceremony at the Gunner Memorial in front of Apsley House next day, 11th November 1945, alongside Field-Marshal Ironside.

General Pratt, as it turned out, was a good friend of my father, having served as Commander, Corps Royal Artillery, at Vth Corps. He gave me a lift to London in his Humber staff car, when we talked a lot; and put me up for the night in his own home. Later he wrote very nicely to both my parents, who received all this news with astonishment and pleasure. No doubt they hoped this success would swing my mind in favour of a permanent Army career!

Soon after, on 8 December, I was commissioned as a 2nd Lieutenant; given an embarkation leave which enabled me to spend Christmas of 1945 at Ackenthwaite; and required to report at the Royal Artillery barracks in Woolwich for posting abroad. From there I went to the Suez Canal Zone. Nearly sixty years later, it may seem surprising that, although VE Day and VJ Day had both taken place in the summer of 1945, six months later young officers were still being sent in large numbers to the Middle East or other theatres of the Second World War. But it did not seem strange at the time. Britain was governing, whether as imperial or occupying power, huge areas of Europe (jointly with her Western Allies), of Africa and of Asia.

In many cases, governance was not easy. The Indian sub-continent, where the War had vastly increased the pressure for independence, is an obvious example. But it was not so very different in the Middle East. To give but a few illustrations: in Greece, Communist groups had been fighting to try and take over the Government of the country; in Palestine, the end of the British mandate was in sight, and Jews and Arabs were preparing to fight each other; and in Egypt, nationalism was taking firmer root. The British military presence abroad could not be run down fast; yet the soldiers, sailors and airmen who had fought through all or most of the War expected to get home to their families; so replacements had to be found and despatched.

One travelled by troopship to Alexandria. Just before leaving England I noticed an article in the 'Evening Standard' headed *'Whips out in Suleiman Pasha Street'*. It reported a riot in Cairo, which the Egyptian police had quelled by the energetic use of rhinoceros hide whips! Clearly, violence formed part of the local culture. This was soon to be dramatically demonstrated. When our train from Alexandria to Cairo stopped at Zagazig, we were besieged by street-vendors, most of them in the 'feelthy picture' trade. Bargaining between vendors and soldiers was brisk, and on the whole satisfactory to both sides. However, as we pulled out of the station, a soldier who tried to retain something for which he had not paid was stabbed in the stomach by a vendor; commotion ensued; and the soldier was carried away to hospital. It was a salutary lesson to be prudent in the Middle East!

My own arrival at Alexandria had not been without incident. When the ship docked, and before we landed, myself and others were idly watching from an upper deck the process of baggage being unloaded from the hold. In those days, every officer had a regulation black tin trunk, with his name stencilled in large white letters on the top. Nets full of these were being hoisted out of the hold. Suddenly a net broke, and its entire contents started to fall from a height back into the hold. We onlookers roared with laughter; but my mirth was cut short when a colleague pointed to the name 'Audland' on one of the trunks in mid-flight! It bears a huge dent to this day.

At Cairo we spent a few days in a Transit Camp in Heliopolis. I shared a tent with a more senior officer who had been some years in the Middle East, and liked to drown his sorrows in drink. He moved in one night, when I was asleep. Next morning, when I looked across at around 0600 hours, he was already drinking gin straight out of a bottle, and offered me a swig! I soon found that he consumed a steady two bottles a day, single-handed. I preferred to use my time seeing some of Egypt's treasures: the pyramids of Giza and Sakkara, and the Cairo Museum.

Before long I was posted to the 2nd Field Regiment, Royal Artillery, then serving in a tented camp on the west bank of the Suez Canal, somewhere between the Great Salt Lake at Ismailia and Port Said. (Like so many others, I was impressed by my first sight of the Canal: the appearance of a large ship, apparently sailing gently through a sea of sand.) A Field Regiment, at that time, consisted of three batteries, each in turn divided into two troops of four 25-pounder guns each. As a subaltern, I was second in command of a troop. Each gun was drawn by a 'quad', a 4-wheel drive vehicle, with a limber between quad and gun. (This doubly articulated unit was very hard to back!) Each gun had a crew of six men.

We had no active duties: we were simply part of Britain's Suez Canal Garrison. Our official hours were not long. Off-duty, we indulged in much organised sport. The hockey skills acquired at Twyford came into their own. In the Middle East, hockey was much favoured by the Army. Grass pitches were unknown: instead we used compacted sand or tarmac. Both produce a very fast game, especially tarmac. And we often played six-a-side, in considerable heat. In these conditions, passes must be very accurate, and physical fitness is tested to the limit! The game gave me pleasure throughout my Middle-Eastern career.

Otherwise, time off was spent either in Ismailia, relaxing in the Officers' Club on the Great Bitter Lake, or in Port Said. In the latter, street-vendors seemed to make up at least a quarter of the population, and were very pressing. There was a story told of a British soldier who bought a watch from one of this fraternity. He returned to camp mightily pleased, and boasted of the enormous reduction in price he had obtained by haggling. Sadly, after a few days, the watch stopped. The soldier took it back to the vendor and complained. The vendor opened the back, and shook the watch. Out fell an earwig. At this, the vendor handed back the watch with the words: *'ow you expect watch to work, mister – engine-driver dead'!* Apocryphal, certainly, but reflecting the resourcefulness these people always displayed in plying their trade!

This relaxed life did not last. In early 1946 the Regiment was ordered to move to Palestine (still under mandate), to serve as part of the First Division. We crossed the Sinai Desert – a forbidding experience – and travelled on north to our tented camp at Benyamina, some 30 kilometres south of Haifa.

The political situation in the country was difficult. World Jewry was pressing for a 'national home' for the Jews in Palestine, which the Arabs were vigorously opposing. The British Government cut a sorry figure because, having first promised Palestine to the Arabs as a reward for their help in driving out the Turks during the First World War (Lawrence of Arabia), it had later gone along with the idea of a national home for the Jews (The Balfour Declaration). Though the Mandate had left Britain as the civil power, the maintenance of law and order was as difficult then as it was to become in Northern Ireland in the 1980s and 1990s. Both Jews and Arabs were building up illegal underground armies. Those of the Jews turned out to be far the more impressive when the British moved out in 1948; but this was not yet apparent. The Jews were also re-inforcing their presence by bringing in thousands of illegal immigrants from Europe, in addition to the official quota established by Britain. The soldiers' thankless job was to assist the Civil Power, and especially the Palestine Police, in keeping the peace. In practical terms this meant that we were called out, for example, to man road-blocks or patrol streets; to search villages for illegal arms or wanted persons; and to prevent the landing of illegal immigrants on the coast, or round them up if they got on shore.

We were natural targets for terrorists – or, as they would have said, 'underground fighters' – on both sides. So we were never allowed out of barracks except with side-arms; and we had to be at least two together by day, or four by night. Although we could go to dances, in Officers' Clubs or even in civil establishments, these rules still applied – and of course somewhat reduced the enjoyment!

Life at Benyamina reflected these realities. Our camp lay in the Palestinian plain, a few kilometres east of the sea, in a valley with hills to north, south and east. It was scenically beautiful, and the scent of orange-blossom was all-pervading. The camp was surrounded by barbed wire; and had a single entrance, guarded day and night. When the sun went down, it was never quiet. Frogs, cicadas and jackals – and also, at irregular intervals and distances, bursts of small arms fire, whether rifles or machine-guns – saw to that. Living in our tents, we had no protection from stray bullets, so were never very relaxed.

Sentries patrolled the perimeter wire throughout the night. The duty officer had to do the rounds, making sure they were alert. The ground was rough, and most officers lit their way with a torch. One night, when on duty, I indulged in what the French would call 'un excès de zèle'. I walked round without use of torch. I was punished by falling fair and square, in a particularly dark corner, into the sump to which our camp drains all ran! It took me hours, with the help of my disgusted batman, to wash the stink out of my hair; and most of my clothes had to be replaced!

To illustrate the kind of work we were called on to do at that time, two memories will suffice. The first was the organisation, in the middle of one night, and over a vast area of the country, of a sweep leading to the arrest of no less than 6,000 Jews, suspected of illegal immigration or terrorism; their incarceration; and their detention for some days while the Civil Power carried out interrogations. On a separate occasion another unit in our Division was sent to a Jewish settlement with instructions to search for a suspected arms cache. The search went on most of the day, and yielded nothing. The troops were then called together, to be transported away. One of the soldiers dropped his rifle against the slanting, stone, retaining wall at the base of some agricultural buildings. It rang hollow. Suspicions were aroused. Re-inforcements were brought in. Engineers came with metal detectors and specialised equipment. A more thorough and intrusive search was mounted. By the end of it, in this one small settlement, the searchers had found, cleverly concealed, much of the stuff being under a bull's pen, something like 300 rifles, many mortars and grenades, a few machine guns, and masses of small arms ammunition. The discovery was interesting, not only intrinsically, but also because it showed that Jewish settlers had prepared to hide materials in this way from the moment the settlement was built, and it suggested that, in the country as a whole, the Jews must have cached arms on a huge scale.

When not needed by the Civil Power, our way of life was similar to that in Egypt. There was a pleasant beach nearby, at the old Roman port of Tantura: but, when time allowed, we preferred to drive a bit farther north to the great bay at Athlit, well protected from swells by the rocky headlands which almost closed its mouth, on one of which the spectacular ruins of the great crusader castle still stood.

Another common diversion was to travel around the length and breadth of the Holy Land, from the Heights of Golan and the Lebanese border in the north; to the River Jordan in the east; and to the Negev and the Sinai Desert in the south, visiting the main biblical sites, including Galilee, Nazareth, Jerusalem, Bethlehem and Beer-Sheba. My regular companion on these visits was a fellow officer some three years older than myself, Ian Edwards-Jones, who became a life-long friend. We shared many interests. Moreover, he was an excellent photographer, and inspired me to practise the hobby.

In the Palestine of those days, the ever-present threat of terrorist ambush lent a certain spice to this tourism: in other respects it was much enhanced by the fact that there were <u>no</u> civilian tourists. One had places like the Church of the Nativity, the Garden of Gethsemane, or the Way of the Cross, almost to oneself.

All this was too agreeable to last! In July 1946, after promotion to Lieutenant, I was unexpectedly posted to another Regiment, in Greece (the 81st Field Regiment). This saddened me, as I had been so few months with the 2nd Field, had made good friends, and felt I was beginning to pull my weight. When I made representations on these lines to my superiors, they were amazed. They thought they had been doing me a good turn. They knew my father was at that time Second-in-Command to General Scobie at Headquarters, Land Forces, Greece, in Athens. And they had supposed that by posting me to Greece, they would give pleasure to both him and me. They were right, though I did not see it that way at the outset.

Travelling by troopship from Egypt, I arrived in the Port of Peiraeus very early one morning. Waking, I lay still in my bunk, and listened in amazement. Voices were calling – of dockers, of stevedores and of men with wares to sell. The language was Greek and no longer Arabic. But the sounds were no less those of the Middle East. It was borne in on me that Greeks are Levantines: neither wholly European nor wholly Asian. When I joined the 81st Field Regiment, it was in a tented camp at Voula, 10 kilometres south of Athens, with the beach just across the coastal road from our tents. Later, we moved to a camp at Glyfadha, nearer the capital but still on the coast.

The political situation in Greece was by now settling down. The British Army had moved into the country in September 1944. In October, Churchill had agreed in Moscow with Stalin on a formula for spheres of influence in the Balkans. It included that *'In Greece, Great Britain (in accord with the USA)'* was to have *'90% predominance; Russia 10%'*. The British intention was therefore that – as the Germans withdrew – the British should move in behind them; secure the Athens area; facilitate the establishment of the *emigré* Greek Government; and make possible the distribution of relief supplies.

The British Government had, however, badly misjudged the local situation. Communist partisans – whom the British had encouraged, in the belief they would fight the Germans – had instead made a secret pact with the latter. The Germans had agreed that, if not harried, they would leave substantial military supplies – including dozens of field guns – for the partisans to collect. The Communist partisans – known as ELAS – with this help gained control of most of Greece, outside of Athens and Salonika. In so doing they committed appalling atrocities against thousands of fellow Greeks who would not join them. This did not prevent the left-wing of the Labour Party in the UK, and many in the USA, from seeing ELAS as left-wing heroes. Fortunately Churchill was not put off by this nonsense.

In December 1944, ELAS had proclaimed itself the 'Guard of the People's Freedom', which amounted to rejection of the returning *emigré* Government's authority. On 4 December, Civil War broke out, and 50,000 ELAS guerillas soon began an all-out attempt to drive the small British forces out of Athens. The British-held area of Athens was rapidly reduced to an area round Syntagma (the central Square) with a radius of only 500 metres. Survival was touch and go. Large re-inforcements arrived from Italy, and the British counter-attacked; but it was not till the end of the year that ELAS were driven out of the City. Later, too, they were driven out of all other major towns and villages. However, they continued to hold out as partisans in the mountains. And their continued presence, long after the British forces had left the country, with the Greek Government in apparently firm control, caused President Truman, in 1947, to authorise US military intervention to destroy them.

My father never personally told me anything about his involvement in this urban guerilla war. But he was very much in the thick of it. His War Diary reported, *inter alia,* that, on Christmas Day, 1945, *'I was relieved not to know until after it had happened that three quarters of a ton of dynamite was removed from the sewer just below my bedroom window this morning – and only just in time too. A very cleverly laid on scheme as we had the sewers wired, and patrolled every hour or two. There is quite a lot of sewer warfare going on'.*

Recently I had occasion to compare my father's Diary with a book about the uprising by Henry Maule, entitled *Scobie, Hero of Greece*[2], and I have written up the result. It was a fascinating and educative experience.

Thus, I arrived in Greece only some 18 months after a Communist takeover had been very narrowly avoided. By now, however, except in the mountains, all was pretty quiet, and the civilian Government was in control. The British Army was effectively in a deterrent role, and was helping to train the re-formed Greek Army. This meant that life, for us, was very relaxed: far more than in Palestine. When I arrived we were on a delightful summer schedule: up at 0545; parades, drills and training before and after breakfast; lunch around 1300; then completely free for the rest of the day. The afternoons we usually spent on the beach in the blazing sun (nobody thought of skin cancer in those days, which is perhaps why I suffer from it now!); and the evenings playing bridge in the mess or visiting Athens. Recreational transport was supplied by the Army: as an Officer I recall having the use of a Jeep whenever I wanted.

Agreeable though it was to swim in the warm sea daily, there was one drawback: a plague of sea-urchins such as I have never encountered before or since. These prickly beasts, black or red, with their myriads of poisonous spines, clung to the coastal rocks, and also to the submerged parts of the stony shore, in a continuous band from sea level to about 30 centimetres below. There was nothing for it but to wear plimsolls at all times. I assume the plague was caused by man-made pollution of the sea. When I resumed visits to Greece, some 30 years later, after pollution control had become a major political issue, the sea-urchins had disappeared.

Visits to Athens were a delight. Rationing had long since ceased in Greece, if indeed there had ever been such an institution amongst these undisciplined people! After 1941, the front-line war had passed the country by, though partisans of all political persuasions harassed the German occupying forces. There was not a lot of destruction, but much dilapidation.

The place had become a honey-pot for top-class cabaret artistes, for whom conditions elsewhere in Europe remained austere. So their services came amazingly cheap. It was a huge delight to young officers like me to watch these cabaret turns, though they were no doubt staid by modern standards. They were all the nicer for being performed on outdoor dance-floors, under pine trees, by moonlight, on endless warm evenings, and to the sound of traditional Greek music. Pleasure was compounded when one could find a girl to entertain, whether from the female staff of the Army or from the Greek population. My father had introduced me to a nice and very attractive Greek girl, Sophie Soutzis. It was all very romantic!

The Army created a slight technical problem – by requiring all troops to be back in their camps by midnight. This accorded ill with the Greek timetable, since supper is virtually unobtainable before 2130 hours, and cabaret turns therefore began very late! We ignored the rule, and generally aimed to get to bed by 0200! On one occasion I thought my number was up. Going home in the early hours, I was pursued and stopped by an Army Provost Marshal (Military Policeman). However, when he spoke, it was to inform me politely – and with a twinkle in his eye – that one of my rear lights was not working!

Looking back on that period, it amazes me that we managed to keep up this sort of routine for week after week! Often I had no more than three hours' sleep a night. Some officers made up with an afternoon siesta: I swam or walked.

The summer routine also meant I saw a lot of my father (until he was posted home a few weeks after my arrival). He would pick me up in the afternoon, in his big Humber staff car, with his attractive Secretary Jane Carte often completing the party; drive off somewhere, for example to Sunium (Sunion) or Marathon; and have a swim. Sometimes there would be weekend expeditions. The places I visited with my father in this way included Corinth, Nauplia, Epidaurus and Mycenae. On the trips into the Peloponnese or Central Greece, where the partisans were active, we went armed, and there had to be four in a group. Later, after my father left, I made similar tours with Alec Catto, our Regimental Medical Officer. Travel conditions were hazardous. Communist revolutionaries and straightforward bandits abounded in the mountain areas (i.e. much of Greece!). Outside big towns, British military vehicles travelled in pairs. Few country people had radios or read newspapers. On a tour of the Peloponnese, we were several times taken for German soldiers – though it was nearly two years since the last German troops had left the country! The roads in Greece had been virtually un-maintained for years, because of War and then Civil War.

A charming event comes to mind. Alec and I were doing a one-week tour of the Pelopponese in November 1946. Approaching Olympia from Nauplea, and rounding a corner of the wooded mountain road, we came across a group of about ten woodcutters, who had just finished a day's work. They asked for a lift to the town. We allowed them to hang on where they could, on the jeeps and trailers, or just clinging to the jeeps' sides! As we drove, they started singing opera choruses, and kept it up all the way to town. We made an unforgettable entry into Olympia!

In the autumn of that year, my Battery was moved to Megalo Pefco, on the Athens-Corinth road, to serve as the Range Battery of the Greek School of Artillery. Fortunately this was not a tented camp. We were in Nissen huts. But Greek winters are far colder than most people would expect for a country of the eastern Mediterranean. The north wind blows down on to Attica, bringing icy air from the Parnassus range. We had wooden stoves, but the wood to fill them was in short supply. I recall lying in bed, with thirteen layers of thick Army blanket on top of me, still shivering.

My Regiment decided to search for supplies of fuel. A so-called wood merchant came into our Headquarters camp at Glyfhada one day, and offered our Adjutant a few lorry-loads at an attractive price if we would send the lorries to a village in the Island of Euboia. I was detailed to lead a convoy. The journey was appalling. Much of our road was 30 centimetres deep in mud. The lorries frequently got stuck, and had to be winched out. It got later and later. Then it began snowing steadily. Finally, exhausted, we reached the village, in a remote part of Euboia, around 2200 hours.

We wanted to collect the wood quickly and return. But our wood-merchant would not move from the Taverna. He said his supplier had still to come, which he did around midnight! We all set off to a clearing, and there picked up the wood. The Greeks were urging us to hurry the loading. I began to suspect all was not as it should be. However, we paid the money and removed the goods. Only later did I realise, by piecing together bits of evidence, that we had taken the wood from the estate of Mr Philip Noel-Baker, then a British Cabinet Minister. It seemed unlikely that he had authorised the transactions, or received the money. I am afraid we kept quiet!

Providing the Range Battery for the Greek School of Artillery was an extra-ordinary experience. Before describing a typical day's firing, some background is needed. Modern guns are normally deployed well behind one's own lines: out of sight of the enemy's lines, and *a fortiori* of the target. (The maximum range of a 25-pounder was some 12,300 metres.) They are controlled on the ground by a Gun Position Officer (GPO). But his firing orders are received from an Officer in an Observation Post (OP), who can see the target and is usually at or near the front line. The OP Officer works out the relative positions of guns and target. He issues orders for a single gun to fire ranging rounds. He notes where the first shell falls; issues new orders to take account of his observation; and another round is fired. And so it goes on, until the OP Officer is content that the shell is falling close enough to the target. Then he orders the whole troop (or battery, or regiment) to start firing in earnest.

At Megalo Pefco, the lie of the land produced a very artificial situation. The whole range sloped gently uphill from the Gun Position, so that any possible target could be seen from the guns. Chaos was inevitable. When a shoot was to be conducted, the Greek Chief Instructor [CI] of Gunnery, a Colonel, positioned himself at the OP, well ahead of the guns but visible from them. A Greek Cadet was then told to conduct the shoot, and the Instructor pointed out a suitable target, such as a ruined farmhouse. Meanwhile, at the Gun Position, the British soldiers withdrew from their posts and Greek Cadets took their places. The British GPO nevertheless remained responsible for safety, i.e. for ensuring that no shell fell outside the range! To assist him, he placed a British Sergeant behind each gun.

At first all would go well. The Cadet's Orders would be passed, by 'phone or radio, to the GPO. The latter would call them out to the guns, and the ranging gun would fire. Soon, however, the Cadets at the Gun Position started to guess, from where the rounds were falling, what the target was.

The scenario changed! Greeks are great individualists! The OP would issue an order. The GPO would tell the OP that his order was mistaken, and/or that the correction should be of greater (or less) range, and/or that the change of line should be different. After a while, some accommodation would be reached, at which stage the GPO would issue his own orders to the Cadets in charge of each gun (the No. 1s). Each No. 1 would then argue vociferously with the GPO. Usually they did not agree with him (or with each other). Each No.1 would then issue to his gun crew the order he thought best (sometimes all were completely different). One gun would swing left and up; another left and down; another right and up; and so forth. There was nothing for the British GPO and his sergeants to do except shout '**STOP**' with the full force of their lungs. This meant that nobody and nothing could move again till order was restored!

The scene at the OP was likewise very Greek. The CI would install himself comfortably in a canvas folding chair. The Cadet conducting the shoot sat at his feet, while the others waited their turn. After naming a target, the CI left the Cadet to get on with the shoot. But, whenever the hapless Cadet issued an order the CI thought erroneous, the latter simply hit the Cadet hard on the head with his swagger stick. It was as well that they were made to wear Officers' peaked caps when conducting shoots, or a fair number would have become casualties.

One thing which puzzled me was how the Greek private soldier made ends meet, and indeed seemed to live rather comfortably. I knew pay rates ranged from the equivalent of one and a half old pennies a day to a maximum of five. (The British Tommies were getting perhaps four shillings a day – 32 times as much as the bottom of that range.) I was told that each Greek soldier organised some kind of personal racket. A driver, for example, would offer lifts to people going his way, and then charge them a fare. He would always charge less than a bus – by a small margin. Another soldier would go into town; exchange all his new army clothes for old ones (at a profit); return to barracks; and then get the quartermaster to change the old clothes into new ones again. Such was life in the Greek Army of that time!

Home leave had by now been re-instituted; and I was able to go back to the UK for a few weeks in the spring of 1947, having been promoted Captain in January. I went to stay with my parents. They were living at Southport, as my father had been made Garrison Commander at Liverpool. Whilst in Transit Camp in Egypt, I contracted amoebic dysentery. I did not see the Medical Officer, for fear of missing my ship. As a result, I had raging dysentery on board all the way to Toulon; then on the (very cold) troop train, which took nearly two days, in the post-war condition of French railways, to reach the Channel Ports, following a circuitous route via Carcassonne and Bordeaux; and finally on the trains from the Channel to Southport. I arrived a physical wreck, and spent most of my leave recovering.

Much of my recuperation took place in a deck-chair in my parents' garden. From there I witnessed something deeply impressive. It was a time of year for migration of wild geese. Day after day they used to pass over my head in thousands, flying in their customary V formation, and honking as they went. Geese are easy to count, and I had nothing more urgent to do. One first counts the geese in a single V. It is simple, after that, to assess the number of geese in each further V with sufficient accuracy for statistical purposes. In a single afternoon I counted no less than 20,000 geese!

My Troop of the 81st Field Regiment, RA, in the last King's Birthday Parade ever held in Jerusalem, 1947.

On returning to the Middle East, I learnt, in Port Said, that my Regiment (the 81st Field) would be moving from Greece to Isdud (ancient Ashdod), near Gaza. Soon after, however, my Battery was sent to Acre, to become once again a Range Battery, this time of the British Middle East School of Artillery. This was excellent news. First, we had a comfortable camp, on the Mediterranean shore. Second we were freed of all operations in support of the Civil Power. And third, we were doing a lot of what we had been trained to do: firing our guns. The range itself, near the Lebanon border, was a 'real' one, where the targets were <u>not</u> visible from the Gun Position! And the countryside was beautiful.

The range had one drawback – an abundance of scorpions! One became very aware of these creatures if one had to spend a night there. When dry, the clay-based soil of the range fissured deeply, and the scorpions retreated into the cracks to hide, or perhaps to escape the heat of the day. At night they felt the cold, and liked nothing better than to cuddle up to a warm, slumbering human body: when it stirred, they were frightened and they stung. One took precautions. We slept under mosquito nets, which were tucked in under the edge of the blankets. And Officers had further protection, being on camp beds, raised above the ground. But it was too easy, by turning in one's sleep, to disturb these defences. Mosquito nets could work free; and blankets could fall over the side of the bed, providing a tempting ladder for the scorpions. Scorpion bites were not frequent, but nor were they rare. Their effect on individuals varied. In Palestine they were seldom if ever fatal; but they often meant a spell in hospital. I was fortunate in escaping a bite.

At some stage it was decided that the three Artillery Regiments of our Division should spend a few days together at the edge of the Sinai Desert to 'calibrate' our 72 guns, something which must be done regularly if guns are to maintain accuracy. Because my Battery had so much experience, we were told to organise the calibration shoot and the task was given to me. It was an exciting moment, and I was determined to make a good impression on the Gunner Brigadier in Charge: the 'Commander, Royal Artillery', or CRA. The Regiments now moved to a place called Bir Asluj, where there was the last substantial water supply before the road to Egypt snakes westwards across the Sinai Desert. Here, as it turned out, I was to hold my 21st Birthday Party. Nothing less romantic could be imagined. There was some kind of NAAFI establishment where one could buy a drink. The choice was limited: beer or egg-nog. Misguidedly I chose the latter, not because I knew and liked it, but because it was different. It made me sick.

Next day, I had to choose a suitable target area in the desert, and set out markers for the calibration. The idea was that, after fixing a range in yards, and taking as an axis a line from the Gun Position to the target, one would set out markers at regular intervals before and behind it, and also at regular intervals on a line crossing it at right angles. When the time came for calibration, the calibrating officer would first, with the aid of these markers, 'range' a master gun for the Regiment; and then, using the data for elevation and line thus produced, apply it to each other gun in turn, and adjust it so that, when fired, it too hit the target. The essence of the matter was to set up markers which were easily visible from the OP. Having chosen the target area, I sent out my Gunners to collect very large boulders; to set them up on the 'cross' pattern described; and then, since they were the same sandy colour as the rest of the desert, to white-wash them for easy observation. When all was done, we returned well pleased to our camp.

Next morning, all three Regiments were to be ready to fire at first light. Long before dawn I reported to the CRA at the OP, and told him what we had done. The dawn came slowly, and we waited for my white boulders to appear through the dark, so that the day's work could begin. They never did! Bedouin, who had seen us setting them out the night before, had concluded that, if stones had to be whitewashed, they must be valuable. In the night, they simply came and stole them! My notion of being the CRA's blue-eyed boy went out of the window!

That summer, our Regiment took part in the last King's Birthday Parade to be held in Jerusalem before the end of the British mandate.

As the end of the Mandate approached, Jews and Arabs stepped up their clandestine preparations for the war both wished to see following our withdrawal, and which both thought they would win. (The Arabs were soon to prove mistaken.) The British were increasingly caught in the cross-fire, and the need for good security by the troops became ever greater. But security is tedious, especially when it has to be maintained over many years. The British soldiery did not take it too seriously. The Military Police decided on an experiment. A jeep-load of them were dressed in semi-military garb of khaki hue, though definitely not in official uniforms. Thus clad, and bearing a variety of side-arms, they drove up to each British camp and demanded admittance. Some sentries just waved them in. Others, more conscientious, demanded to see their 'work ticket' (the document carried by drivers of all Army vehicles, giving details of the driver and his business). The work ticket shown in each case stated that the driver was Colonel Stern (a well-known Jewish terrorist); that his unit was the IZL (a well-known Jewish terrorist group); and that the purpose of the journey was sabotage! In every case the sentry cast a rapid eye over the work ticket; and then waved the jeep through!

With my Regiment, I spent a few weeks, towards the end of 1947 and therefore of my active army career, at a practice camp near Zerqa in Trans-Jordan [now Jordan]. The country was then ruled by the Emir Abdullah; and the legendary Colonel Glubb (Glubb Pasha) was still in command of his Army (the Arab Legion). In Trans-Jordan more sight-seeing was possible. It included Jerash and Amman.

But now my 'Age and Service Group' for demobilisation came up. I sailed to England, disembarking in early December; was 'processed' at York Barracks next day; issued with my 'demob suit'; and given 77 days 'demob leave'. My actual release from the Army took effect on 24 February 1948; but I spent the intervening time at home in Southport. My Army service had entitled me to wear the General Service Medal (Palestine) and the War Medal 1939/45.

Thus ended my military career. If one excludes a preparatory phase, in the Junior Training Corps and the Home Guard at Winchester, I had started in July 1944 as a very green Private in Lanark Barracks. I had finished, three years and five months later, as a Temporary Captain, and Troop Commander in a Field Regiment of the Royal Artillery in Jordan, quite capable of controlling the fire of three Regiments with 72 guns and a field strength of 3,000 men. Over the whole period, my pay had progressively risen from three to twenty-three shillings a day: it was not munificent, but pounds went a lot farther then than now!

What did this experience teach me? Many things. It had fallen into two very different parts: the first 16 months, training in Britain prior to being commissioned; and the remaining 24, serving as an Officer in the Middle East and Greece.

During the first part, I had to leave behind me the protective cocoon of my middle-class youth, and get along with people from every walk of life. This meant finding out what made different kinds of people tick; learning to live and let live; and knowing how to keep one's head down when there was nothing to be gained by raising it above the parapet. The lessons were sometimes hard, but invaluable. For some people, national service was seen as a pain, and a waste of time. For me it was a vital ingredient of my education.

I also came to appreciate the value of organisation, training and man management. One could not experience the way in which the British Army took in huge numbers of recruits – many of them resenting the restrictions of Army life, many also of low education, and most very unfit – and turned them rapidly into tough and efficient soldiers operating in well-disciplined units – without being deeply impressed. There was indeed, as Budge Firth had earlier suggested to me, a system for everything. But no system can cover all eventualities. There is always room for initiative; and, in my experience, initiative often got recognition and reward. The professionalism of the British Army had been diluted by the recruitment of literally millions of conscripts, who joined a pre-war force of under a quarter of a million. But the habits and traditions of the regular Army were strong enough to bear the burden.

It was certainly during the course of my army career that I moved from the comfortable approach to life, criticised by my schoolmasters at Twyford and Winchester, of not exerting myself more than necessary; and adopted one in which I was guided by the notion that 'if a job's worth doing at all, it's worth doing well'. Ever since, I have sought to follow this principle. It is one to which my father certainly subscribed, so genes may have played a part!

My time in the Middle East also started me, in an unconscious and painless way, on the long process of learning to see things with a broader and more international perspective. It is one of my constant complaints against the British educational system, in all its forms, that it tends to be very insular and introvert.

I was myself the product of a privileged branch of that system – the top-class preparatory and public school route. Our minds were more open to thinking about the world at large, and Britain's place in it, than those of the less privileged. Even so, we were brought up in something of an imaginary setting, in which Britain was seen as the leading nation, whereas in fact the Empire had peaked at least half a century earlier and was in sharp and continuing decline (camouflaged only by the onset of World War II, in which Britain was, almost perforce, to 'punch well above its weight'). Perhaps we were not actually told that British is always best; but it was something we were given to understand. Britain was presented to us as a role model; foreigners as somehow inferior. I had already had one small opportunity to check these impressions against reality, through my 1939 stay in a French family, when I had felt that the differences between France and Britain were less than I had been led to expect. Now, I had been able to see at first hand something of life in four or five other, very different countries. It had helped to open my mind.

Certainly my knowledge was limited. I never learnt Arabic or modern Greek, so could not read the local newspapers, listen to the local radio (much less important then than now), or even talk to the people, except where English would serve. But eyes need no language, and there was much to see. My feel for things political was inevitably awakened by direct experience of the Suez Canal Zone, of Palestine, of the burgeoning East-West tensions which underlay the political situation in Greece, and of terrorism in various manifestations. At that age, I did not think deeply or continuously about any of these matters; but they had an impact on my subconscious. At another level, I was brought face to face with the achievements of the great civilisations and cultures of the Mediterranean and the Middle East: in particular those of Egypt, of Greece, of Rome, of Judaism, and of Islam. Wherever I was, for two years of my life, I had only to look around me to see the impact they had made on their world. This unconscious indoctrination was gratuitously re-inforced by my growing interest in what one would now call cultural tourism. I began to see these civilisations, no longer as history book concepts, but as things with real meaning for me personally. I began to see the connections between those civilisations, and between them and the civilisation of modern Western Europe. It was the beginning of a life-long learning process.

As a footnote to my military career, and on a less intellectual level, it is perhaps worth noting that it established my attitude on two issues: nicotine and alcohol. There was, at that time, strong peer pressure to indulge excessively in both. Fortunately, I soon found I disliked both the taste and the after-taste of smoking: on this front it was easy to follow my instinct and resist the pressure.

On alcohol, whilst I was in the ranks, almost everybody drank beer; beer-drinking was the standard method of socialising; and many, perhaps most, of the soldiers regarded getting drunk as a *macho* virtue. The bitter taste of most beers did not appeal. So I never became an addict, and certainly never got drunk on it. Once commissioned, the picture changed. In an officers' mess, whilst beer was drunk, the officers could better afford gin and whisky, and these were popular. I found gin agreeable. Just once, I drank sufficient to become decidedly drunk. It was a valuable inoculation. I so disliked losing control of my limbs and my speech, vomiting, and the resultant hangover, that I never succumbed again.

CHAPTER 5

Entering the British Diplomatic Service

Recruitment

THUS, IN EARLY 1948, I was living in my parents' home, at Southport, and considering how best to reach my aim of becoming a British diplomat. During the early post-war period there were two methods of entry to the Administrative Branch of the Civil Service (including the Diplomatic Service), both run by the Civil Service Commissioners. The traditional method involved first obtaining a University Degree and then taking a written competition. But the authorities felt that young people who had spent in the Armed Forces the years when they might normally have gone to University should have an alternative entry method, not involving University. So a 'reconstruction method' was devised, open to those who had spent a certain period in the Services. This took place in three stages. First, there was a relatively simple written examination, testing basic skills of English, mathematics, etc. Then, if one got over that hurdle, came a weekend at a 'Country House', where the candidates were observed closely for three days non-stop; and generally put through their paces. Those who passed that second test went forward to a final interview board.

Both options were open to me, but I had little idea of the relative advantages and disadvantages. My father was able to help. He arranged for me to call at the Foreign Office to see Harold Caccia (later Lord Caccia), who had been the British Minister in Greece during my father's time in Athens, and who had now become Chief Clerk (the most senior administrative officer) in the Foreign Office. He wasted no words. A University education was important, if I was to have the intellectual equipment and maturity needed to get ahead in the Diplomatic Service. This was not what I had wanted to hear. Now well past my 21st birthday, and used both to being financially independent and to holding positions of responsibility, I was not keen either to 'go back to school' or to ask my parents to finance me through three years or more of University (though they were willing to do so). I wanted to stand on my own feet, and get on with my chosen career. I quickly decided to go for the 'reconstruction method'. Often, afterwards, I wondered how things would have turned out if the University route had been followed. On the one hand, my education would have been broader and more thorough. As against that, practical experience on the job is probably the best training for diplomacy; so there is much to be said for an early start. Certainly, I benefited from a very wide range of different experiences, and enjoyed them all.

It was one thing to decide on the route: another to reach the end successfully. Competition was fierce. I think only about 10% of applicants got into the Diplomatic Service. And I knew that, whilst the Army had taught me a lot about man-management and problem-solving, my brain had not been tackling more intellectual tasks for nearly four years. The written part of the competition was a few short months ahead. The nose needed to be put to the grindstone.

For the only time in my life, I enrolled for a correspondence course, designed to prepare candidates, in three months, for the written examination. The course was impressive. One had to write essays, or deal with practice papers, against the clock; and send in the results. The test papers, like the exam for which they were preparing the candidates, dealt heavily in current affairs; so there was a lot of systematic newspaper reading to be undertaken. The marked papers came back quickly, with comments which were to the point. The proof of the pudding came in the eating: the exam was passed, and I was summoned to the 'Country House', a red-brick early 20th century pile at Stoke d'Abernon near Cobham.

The humorous author, the late Sir Alan Herbert, has written a funny book about the experiences of a candidate at one of these long weekends. His son was there, on the same weekend as me, in July, 1948: the book, published in 1951, is based on the son's experience. It was called *Number Nine*, with 'The mind-sweepers' as an alternative title. Almost everything it describes about the official proceedings could in practice have occurred, though not all of the strange experiences could really have happened to a single individual on a single weekend. And Alan Herbert enlivened reality by a sub-plot about a fictional Admiral.

In practice, things went more or less as follows. There were 21 candidates, divided into syndicates of seven for all group exercises. We were each given a number, for identification purposes: hence the title of the Herbert book. Each group was monitored by a team of three: a chairman, often a senior civil servant; a psychiatrist, who was meant to consider one's personal history and background; and a third person, drawn from some other walk of life, who was known as an observer, and was meant to focus on intellectual quality. Besides directing the group exercises, they watched us throughout the day, including taking meals with us. They also each had a 'one-on-one' interview with us, taking as a starting point the 'interest forms' we had each filled in on arrival. (I vividly recall the psychiatrist's interview. He began it by saying '*Now, tell me about your life.*' Then, when he could see me wondering how much detail he wanted, he added: '*...for about 20 minutes*'!)

We had to take the chair in group discussions; give a ten-minute talk on a subject chosen from a list proposed by oneself; and recount something humorous. We did many problem-solving exercises, both written and oral. Most of these were based on events in 'The Island Story', a factual memorandum covering aspects of an imaginary British Dependent Territory. There were also debates on current affairs. There were five or more hours of psychological and intelligence tests. There was also an unpleasant 'self-analysis test', in which one was required to write two pen-portraits of oneself: one from the point of view of a close friend; and the other from that of one's worst enemy. At another moment, one was unexpectedly asked to place the other members of one's group in the order in which one would like to see them as Civil Servants, and also the order in which one would like to have them as companions on a holiday.

One felt under pressure the whole time. I was glad when it was over: gladder still when I heard I was to go on to final interview. Some time later, when a friend going to Stoke d'Abernon sought my advice, I told him that for me the most striking feature of the whole course was the way in which any endeavour on the part of the candidate to 'put on an act', was almost sure to be found out. Discovery would be fatal: it would lead to a suspicion that the candidate had something to hide!

The final interview took place in London some three weeks after the Country House. I remember feeling bullied. The main idea, presumably, was to see if one could 'take it'. One was ushered in to a large room, alone, to face eight examiners round a table. They were drawn from very different walks of life, and saw one's reactions from different perspectives. Questions were snapped out by each of them, at speed. One was tempted to reply at the same rate. I resisted that temptation, for fear of saying something stupid; and found that a pause of 10 or 15 seconds to reflect about difficult questions was acceptable. One question was whether I would accept a position in a Government Department other than the Foreign Office: I indicated that the Commonwealth Relations or Colonial Offices appeared to me to be possibilities; but that my very clear preference was the Foreign Office. The interview was one of those occasions when one can only do one's best, and hope it is good enough: happily it was. I was recruited to join the Administrative Branch of the Diplomatic Service, in the Ninth (bottom) Grade, with effect from 6 September 1948, and told to report then to the Foreign Office. (My starting salary was £400 a year.) My new career had begun. In those days, all officers of the Administrative Branch received a formal Commission, signed by the Monarch and by the Secretary-of-State for Foreign Affairs. I had to wait a while for mine: no doubt the Monarch had more urgent things to do. But it came in the end, dated 22 July 1950, and signed by King George VI and Ernest Bevin. It is written in a charmingly old-world style.

This description of the recruitment process is fore-shortened. There were intervals between the three phases, and I did not just sit at home between each. Indeed that would have been impossible, because, in the spring of 1948, my father was posted to Cyrenaica, packed up the house at Southport; and went off to his new home in Benghazi with my mother and Elizabeth. Between their departure and my own entry into the Foreign Office, I was homeless, and there was a good deal of time to be passed.

Part of it was devoted to a holiday in Southern France, with Ian Edwards-Jones. Currency restrictions continued in Britain for long after the war, and at that time one was entitled to only £35 of foreign currency a year, although boat and rail tickets did not count against that figure. Money was worth much more then, but it still surprises me how much one could do. We stayed abroad for two weeks; lodging in cheap but adequate 'pensions' and ate in simple restaurants. But we never slept rough or went without food.

It was on this journey that I was able to re-establish contact with the Forest-Divonne family, when Ian and I spent a night or two as their guests at Pomiers[1]. The family had had a traumatic war, succinctly documented in a letter which Madame de la Forest-Divonne had written to my mother in February 1945, soon after the German occupation of France was over.

In her letter, Madame described how she and her husband had spent the war at Pomiers; how the eldest son, Louis, had been conscripted into the 'Chantiers de Jeunesse', a kind of obligatory civilian service set up by the Vichy Puppet Government, and used by them for various types of work (Vichy was not permitted to have an army on the French mainland), but had also worked actively for the Resistance and eventually gone into hiding from the Gestapo; how the second, Emmanuel, had served with the Free French Forces in North Africa (where indeed he had met my father); how the third, Eugène, had been forced by the Germans to witness 120 men of a French town being taken at random and hanged in a reprisal operation in July 1944

The Château de Pomiers, St Martin-du-Mont, 1948.

(he never came to terms with this, suffered nervous disorders throughout life, and died relatively young); how the two other children (Mimi and Amédée) had stayed with relatives in quieter regions and survived unhurt; and how Pomiers itself had been the scene of fierce hand-to-hand fighting between Americans and Germans in the liberation, whilst the father and Amédée were both present. That all this should happen to a single French family brought home to me starkly that the sufferings of the British people were not of the same order as those of the peoples of the German-occupied countries. It gave me a perspective on Europe's sufferings which helped me understand the move for European integration.

Much of the remaining time before I joined the Foreign Office was spent with my half-cousin, Mike Shepherd-Cross, and his family, at their charming house in Yorkshire – The Old Rectory at Brandsby. Mike and Mollie were an immensely warm-hearted couple. They treated me as an additional member of their own family, which consisted of Giles, June and James, with ages ranging between 10 and 5. I spent with them a thoroughly enjoyable, outdoor oriented, summer; and tried to repay some of their kindness by helping to keep the children entertained. They rejoiced with me when the news of my having passed into the Foreign Office arrived, and it was from their house that I went forth to my new career.

The Forest-Divonne Family, 1948[2].

Early days in the Foreign Office

It was Diplomatic Service practice to post new recruits, for their first job, to a Department in the Foreign Office, and give them a year or so to learn the ropes, before sending them abroad. I found myself sent to the Commonwealth Liaison Department (CLD), and reported for duty in early September, 1948. In those days, a dark suit was obligatory. A short, black coat, with striped trousers, was favoured, and I soon acquired these.

CLD was a small Department, with only three Administrative or Executive Class Officers including myself. Its Head, Geoffrey Furlonge, was an Arabist, who later rose to be Ambassador to Ethiopia. Shy and gloomy, he usually kept aloof. Was he perhaps suffering the after effects of some tropical disease? He taught me nothing.

The rest of us sat together in the 'Third Room', the name traditionally given in the Office to the room containing the 'desk-officers', or work-horses, of a Department, as opposed to the Head and the Assistant. In our case, because we were so small, the Assistant was also in the Third Room. This post was fairly soon taken by Micky Joy, who became a first and much-valued mentor in the Service, and a good friend for the rest of his life. We shared the room with Michael Starkie, nearest to me in age, and a middle-aged Clerical Officer, known to us only as Stingemore, who looked after our documentation.

The Department's main duty was to keep the Commonwealth informed. Before the War the Dominions, or – as we were now calling them – the countries of the 'Old Commonwealth' (Australia, Canada, New Zealand and South Africa), had largely relied on the 'mother country' to keep them abreast of international affairs, and had not developed sophisticated Diplomatic Services of their own. Later, following Indian independence in 1947, the 'New Commonwealth' emerged. And those countries too (India, Pakistan and Sri Lanka in the first instance), at first looked to the United Kingdom to keep them in the picture. This was done by our Department, principally through the circulation to the Commonwealth Governments of 'INTELS', or circular information telegrams. The more sensitive ones went to the Old Commonwealth countries only: the rest went to all.

To inform others, we had to be well informed. So our Department received a vast number of the often lengthy telegrams passing between the Foreign Office and its posts overseas, perhaps 300 daily, and many other official papers besides. After studying this mass of material we considered, each day, on what subjects the Commonwealth should be updated. On each, an INTEL would then be prepared, involving careful analysis and synthesis. The INTEL had to be cleared in draft with the Foreign Office officials having operational responsibility for the subject matter, and also checked over with the Commonwealth Relations Department.

In this way, one rapidly acquired drafting skills, and also came to meet a huge range of people. (Guy Burgess – the famous Soviet 'mole' – was just one of those I saw frequently. He was habitually scruffy, and struck me as not specially bright. But perhaps that was because of drink, or because it was part of his 'cover', or both. Certainly none of us suspected his true role.) Quality of drafting has always been a Foreign Office strength; and new recruits had to come up rapidly to demanding standards. We used to be told:

'draft telegrams as if they were to be read by an idiot and paid for by yourself'
(telegrams were expensive to send). We were also instructed that, after
completing a draft of any kind, we should re-read it and eliminate every
adjective and adverb that was not essential to the meaning.

Although this information task was our bread and butter, we would
occasionally be called on to advise Foreign Office Ministers on issues
affecting the Commonwealth which were under consideration in Cabinet.
One such was the drafting of a new British Nationality Act. Many of the
details escape me, but a key point was this. A new Act was needed to take
account of great changes in the Commonwealth, which included Ireland
preparing to leave it and become a Republic. (Since 1921 it had remained in
the Commonwealth as the 'Irish Free State'.)

Before this new change in the country's status, Irish citizens had
automatically held British nationality. Employment being tight in Ireland, a
very large number of Irish citizens were officials of the British Civil Service.
Many Civil Service posts could be held only by British nationals, so there
was clearly a problem. The London Irish mandarins put their heads
together, and rapidly came up with a solution which the British Government
in the end approved. The new Nationality Act had been drafted so as to
recognise only two categories of person: 'British' and 'Foreign'. The solution
was to provide for a third category: 'Non-Foreign'. Persons in this Category
would be entitled to hold British Civil Service positions. The only country
whose citizens would in fact be in it would be Ireland! 'Sir Humphrey', of
'Yes Minister' fame, would have felt at home!

Ernie Bevin, the Labour Minister and former miner, was Foreign
Secretary. His straightforward way of doing business, the fact that he
behaved always naturally, never putting on any side, and the strong authority
he had within the Cabinet, combined to make him perhaps the most
popular Foreign Secretary, within the Office, of all time. Delightful stories
used to circulate about him: here are some of the best I heard.

A Foreign Secretary has to deal with a vast range of problems. Every day,
he receives numerous submissions from the different Departments of the
Office. These usually make a recommendation to the Foreign Secretary for
action. The latter is expected to approve, or react in a different sense. Ernie's
responses tended to be brief and direct. On one occasion, confronted with
some important recommendation he did not like, he simply told his Private
Secretary: *'I won't 'ave it'*.

Things became more difficult when Ernie took a box of submissions
home, to work overnight. He would then have to comment in writing, and

his hand-writing was awful. Next morning, his Private Office staff had the task of decyphering it. Having done so, the official would write or type, below Ernie's scrawl on a submission, a few neat lines beginning: *'the Foreign Secretary has minuted as follows:...'.* The file would then return to the Department concerned for follow-up. This put the Private Office in a position of strength. Sometimes, when a submission returned, the originating Department would see that Ernie had scribbled a single line on it; but that the Private Secretary had 'interpreted' this to the tune of several lines of well-turned prose! One wondered!

Some years later, Sir Roderick Barclay, who was Ernie's Principal Private Secretary from 1949 to 1951, told me a couple of delightful tales. To appreciate the flavour it may help to explain that Roddie, while charming and very kind, with a nice, dry sense of humour, was a thoroughly traditional Diplomat of the old school, and a typical product of the Harrow and Cambridge of those days. The first story had to do with one of the frequent, long-drawn-out Conferences of the Foreign Ministers of the Four Great Powers (Britain, France, the USA and the USSR), which at that time were still seeking to agree on the post-war fate of Germany. This one was at the Château de Saint Cloud. Day after day, Ernie and Roddie would drive from the Paris Embassy to the Conference, and back again. Ernie always pronounced the name of the Conference venue with a strong cockney accent, and exactly as though it was an English word (rhyming with the way in which Ted Heath was later to pronounce the name of his yacht *'Morning Cloud')!*

Though this greatly offended Roddie's sensitivities, he bore with it for a long time. But finally, one day in the car, he plucked up his courage and said: *'Secretary-of-State, please tell me why you insist on mis-pronouncing the name of the place we're going to?'* Ernie looked at him in genuine astonishment, and replied: *'I don't <u>mis</u>-pronounce it, Roddie – I just don't know '<u>ow</u> to pronounce it!'*

On another occasion Ernie had for the first time to host a State dinner for a visiting foreign dignitary at Greenwich. He had no experience of this sort of thing, and it worried him. He got a full briefing from Roddie about all the details: how to greet the guests; when to go into dinner; when toasts should be proposed; when smoking should be allowed; and so forth. At the dinner, Roddie had himself placed well away from the Foreign Secretary, but in a position where the latter could easily have eye contact. All went swimmingly, right to the end of the meal. Then Roddie observed the Foreign Secretary casting agonised glances at him. He sidled discreetly round the table to a point behind Ernie; lent forward; and asked whether there was a problem. '*Yes, Roddie,*' came the answer, '*I've forgotten 'ow to get out of 'ere!*'

This period of just under a year in CLD was ideal as an introduction to the Foreign Office and its ways. It offered a marvellous opportunity to gain an overview of British Foreign Policy, and be brought into contact with countless individuals throughout the Foreign Office. Moreover the Department was not under pressure. One had time to reflect, and to absorb things quietly.

This was the first time I had had to organise my own off-duty life, and to explore London. Initially, I joined a fellow bachelor Ian Edwards-Jones, by then at the beginning of his distinguished career as a barrister, in a boarding-house at 10 Westbourne Terrace. We shared a largish room on the top floor, with access to a communal bathroom. We had breakfast and supper with the other denizens of the boarding-house, and the food was quite good. All this cost us only two guineas a week – £2.10 in today's terminology – out of my net take-home pay of around £7.00 a week.

Times have changed, and perhaps nowadays two bachelors living in this way would be suspected of homosexuality. But in that era, it was a common arrangement, and suspicions – rightly! – did not arise. Living at such close quarters required friendship, tolerance and understanding on both sides. This had existed when we soldiered together in Palestine, had further developed on our shared holiday in France, and was now deepened and strengthened by our months together in London. Our friendship remained just as close up to the time of Ian's death in the mid-90s. Although, because of my career pattern, we often went for years without seeing each other, whenever we did, we found our friendship as fresh and rock solid as ever. It was a sad duty, but also a privilege, to recall his great qualities and achievements in an address at the funeral.

Both of us, however, always saw the cramped conditions of the boarding-house as temporary, and intended to find something more comfortable when finance allowed. Thus, after a few months, I made an arrangement to be a 'paying-guest' with Cecil and Christian de Sausmarez, who had a delightful house at 50 York Terrace East, on the edge of Regent's Park. Cecil had served in the Foreign Office during the war, which made it easy for us to relate; and he was an excellent conversationalist. He was later to become the Seigneur of Guernsey. The arrangement was that I had a nice room of my own, where my privacy was always respected; that I had all meals except weekday lunches with the De Sausmarez; and that I could join them in their drawing room whenever I wished. In other words, the De Sausmarez treated me as family, which was delightful. It was a period of my life when, within my modest means, I probably enjoyed more in the way of concerts, plays and museums than at any other.

So, living in London had major attractions. There was also one important drawback – smog – which was at its worst. The use of coal was maximal. Pollution control had not begun. They said there were occasions when, if you stretched out your arm in front of you, you could not see your hand. Perhaps there was some exaggeration. But certainly I can recall times when you could not see a person approaching until he or she was within two metres. Traffic became almost motionless. From this angle, it was a relief when, in September 1949, the Foreign Office Personnel Department informed me that I was being seconded to the staff of the Political Division of then Control Commission for Germany (British Element) at Berlin.

CHAPTER 6

Berlin and Bonn: the Federal Repulic joins the Free World (1949-52)

Berlin

THUS, IN OCTOBER OF 1949, I left London for my first foreign posting. The British Element of the Control Commission for Germany (CCG) relied on the Army for administrative support. After a rail and boat trip via Harwich to the Hook of Holland, the journey from there to Berlin was completed by British troop trains. It took place some weeks after the end of the blockade of the Western Sectors of Berlin (WSB) and of the successful US/British airlift to supply the City[1]. Our train was allowed by the Russians to pass through the Soviet Zone. But there was a lot of formality. At the Helmstedt crossing point, east of Braunschweig, which we reached after dark, the Russians had somehow to be satisfied that our train contained only military (or CCG) personnel. Then, we were required to pull down the blinds, and not raise them again until we had passed through the checkpoint at the entry to the WSB. It was claustrophobic and sinister.

After settling into a billet in the British Sector in Caspar Theysstrase, I was taken to meet Kit Steel (later Sir Christopher Steel), Political Adviser to the British Military Governor and C-in-C, Germany, and as such my new boss. He was tall, bluff and had a military bearing. His first words, uttered with evident irritation, were: *'What on earth are you doing here?'* When I replied that Personnel Department had said additional staff were urgently needed, he commented *'blithering idiots'*. By now, however, he had realised I found his attitude alarming. He more patiently explained that he had indeed asked for more staff, but some time ago. Now, the situation was different. The three Western Allies had recently approved the merger of their Occupation Zones to form the Federal Republic of Germany (FRG), with Konrad Adenauer as the first Chancellor; the Occupation Statute[2], under which the three Allies devolved most of their powers to the Republic, had entered into force; the Basic Law (or Constitution of the FRG) had been promulgated on 8th May, 1949, four years to the day after the end of the War; the new Republic had established its capital at Bonn; and the Allies were shifting their respective Headquarters to the Bonn area. The British would be moving in three weeks. In this situation it was a positive nuisance to have a new boy on the scene. Kit then told me that I was welcome to stay, so long as I did not come into the office! I should use my time thoroughly to explore the City!

I followed his advice with enthusiasm. Mainly I stayed in the Western Sectors. But military and CCG staff could and did move around the Soviet Sector too. There was no possibility of visiting the Soviet Zone, beyond the City Boundary, except for Army personnel in the British Mission accredited to the Soviet military occupation authorities (known as Brixmis).

For a while after the war, the Commanders-in-Chief of the four Occupying Powers (Britain, France, the USA and the USSR), sitting as the Control Council, had attempted to govern Berlin as a single entity. But Soviet ideas on how to treat the defeated Germans were so different from those of the West, that this attempt soon had to be abandoned. Soviet withdrawal from the Council divided Germany *de facto* in two. By 1949, the Western Allies were governing their Sectors of Berlin largely as one City, and devolving more and more of the civil power to the elected Governing Mayor, at that time Willi Brandt: the Soviets ran their Sector as they wished. The blockade had of course hardened the divide.

Berlin had been the scene of incredible devastation during the war, due to repeated bombing and then the final struggle to defend Hitler in his last stand. By 1948, there had been some tidying up. But the blockade of the City by the USSR, which lasted nearly a year, brought reconstruction to a halt in the WSB. So, when I arrived, mountains of rubble still lay everywhere. It was an amazing sight, even for those who had seen the worst that Hitler's bombs had done to London.

This was the city in which I wandered, foot-loose and fancy free. I roamed everywhere, enjoying especially the Tegelsee, Havelsee and Wannsee lakes; the Grünewald and Spandau forests; and the busy heart of West Berlin, centred on the Charlottenburg-Tiergarten-Kurfürstendamm area. I loved my very first experience of grand opera, when I saw *Tosca* at the Staatsoper. I was not to know that, 21 years later, this detailed knowledge and understanding of Berlin would stand me in good stead during my participation in the next meaningful negotiations between the Western Allies and the Russians, which led to the Berlin Agreement of 1972.

Many were the tales told about Berlin in those strange days. Two of them, very different in kind, have stuck in memory.

One had to do with the British Army, ever inventive in amusing themselves. The famous Volkswagen Beetle car had just begun rolling off the production lines. No sooner had the first few appeared in the WSB, than the soldiers started a competition to see who could pack the largest number of men into one of them. It was won by a team which drove down the Kurfürstendamm, with 21 men crammed into or onto a single Beetle car, shouting loudly as they went – *'Ein Reich, Ein Volk, Ein Volkswagen'*. (Half a century later, it is perhaps necessary to explain that this was a parody of Hitler's famous Nüremberg cry of *'Ein Reich, Ein Volk, Ein Führer'*.)

The other story concerned the then French Military Governor, who was in fact a civilian, Ambassador André François-Poncet[3], and relates to the airlift period, before my appearance. At that time, the three Military Governors were General Lucius Clay (US), General Sir Brian Robertson (Britain), and François-Poncet.

They had Headquarters not only in Berlin but also in their respective Zones. The Americans and British had, some time before, merged the economies of their Zones, and brought them under the authority of a Bizonal Economic Council based in Frankfurt. Now, the next step towards the uniting of all three Zones to form the Federal Republic had been taken. The three Military Governors were constantly flying along the air corridors. On one particular day, they had to be in Berlin for a morning meeting, and in Frankfurt for another in the afternoon. Arrangements had been made for François-Poncet to fly to Frankfurt with Clay in the latter's plane. The French Ambassador arrived in good time at Tempelhof Airport; and sat in the waiting room. Clay was late; suddenly the doors burst open; Clay and his entourage rushed through to the tarmac and leapt into the waiting plane; the doors slammed shut; and the plane took off. Clay had not been adequately briefed.

François-Poncet was a French Diplomat of the old school: well-informed, shrewd, correct, but taking offence easily. In addition, the French in Germany then always felt, rightly I fear, that they were regarded by the Americans and the British as the junior partner. Perhaps this was inevitable, given the relative contributions of the Three Allies to the war effort (and later the airlift), and the fact that Russia, the USA and Britain had originally carved Germany into three Zones, and the Americans and British had then re-divided their two Zones to make three, and thus enable France to be an occupying Power.

François-Poncet suspected a deliberate insult, and flew into a rage. American officials did their best to calm him, saying that they would accommodate him on another US plane which would leave for Frankfurt shortly. The Ambassador waited. Then came further confusion. An American Master-Sergeant marched through the lounge calling out, in ringing tones and a broad American accent, the immortal words: 'Paging Pónsett, Fráncis'. He was out of the lounge long before the Ambassador realised it was him they were paging. Offended by the form of address he rose and spluttered 'Qui? Moi? L'Ambassadeur de France?'. After this inauspicious beginning, the Ambassador soon emplaned; and the trip was accomplished. However, the chapter of misfortunes was not over. The small party who had assembled on the tarmac at Frankfurt to do the honours, were mortified to see the Ambassador, by now apoplectic, descend from the aircraft, black from head to foot. It turned out that he had been put in a plane whose normal duty had been to carry coal to Berlin as part of the airlift. The partitioning could not keep the coal-dust at bay. Clay was never forgiven!

Bonn

At the end of my three weeks exploring Berlin, the British Headquarters moved to its new home: the barracks at Wahnerheide, the Luftwaffe air-base which was later to become Köln-Bonn International Airport. The barrack blocks themselves were pleasant-looking and comfortable, laid out amongst woods west of the airfield. This time my journey from Berlin to the British Zone was made in a CCG car down the autobahn to Helmstedt. Once one had left West Berlin at the Drewitz checkpoint, one was not allowed to stop at all in the Soviet Zone, and there were Russian soldiers and East German Police on patrol all the way to Helmstedt, to ensure the rule was obeyed. It was again eerie and uneasy.

Travelling to the Federal Republic was a shift from one world to another. In West Berlin, though the occupation staff could move around locally with a high degree of freedom, one was in reality a prisoner of the Russians, in a remote enclave of liberty behind the Iron Curtain. They could take control of the city by military force at any time: that they did not, was no doubt because they feared Allied military counter-moves, with the danger of events getting out of hand and leading to a Third World War and a nuclear holocaust. In addition, as already remarked, the devastation of war was still ever-present, and life was tough.

In the Federal Republic, we were in the free world. Although there was still a large military occupation force, its actions were discreet, and subject to sharp constraints laid down in the Occupation Statute. The Federal Government was in charge of the country for all internal purposes, although it was not permitted any armed force, and its external relations were a matter for the Western Allies. There had been a highly successful currency reform in 1948, when the worthless Reichsmark was replaced by the now stable Deutschemark. The reconstruction of cities, towns, villages and communications had for some time been proceeding apace. And the Germans, led by Chancellor Adenauer, and by Ludwig Erhard as Minister for Economics and Finance, were launched on the path which was soon to produce the German economic miracle. Although rationing continued in Britain till 1954, five years earlier it was already a thing of the past in the FRG.

Some explanation is needed about the political set-up in which I was to operate for the next three years. The Western Allies had agreed to exercise their important residual powers in the FRG through an Allied High Commission (AHC), whose Headquarters and international staff were established at what is now the Petersberg Hotel. It is a spectacular location, atop one of the beautiful, thickly wooded Siebengebirge hills, overlooking the Rhine as it flows out from its long and deep gorge into the flat plain around Köln. Symbolically, the Petersberg overlooked the quiet University town of Bonn, now adapting to its new status of Federal Capital, a status which it owed to being as close as one could conveniently get to the point at which the US, British and French Zones met.

The three High Commissioners came together here regularly, often with Chancellor Adenauer; and there were meetings of their professional advisers in various Committees. A major side benefit was that the Petersberg restaurant was run by the French: the food and wine was excellent, and all was duty-free and subsidised. Each High Commissioner also had his national Headquarters. The location of the British HQ has already been mentioned. Jack McCloy, a banker who had succeeded Clay as the top American, had offices in Mehlem, across the Rhine, while the French were at nearby Bad Godesberg. Each High Commissioner also had a grand Residence, in his own Zone. General Robertson, who was soon succeeded by Sir Ivone Kirkpatrick, was at Schloss Röttgen, near Wahnerheide, an elegant nineteenth century house nestling in woods, belonging to the owners of the 4-7-11 *Eau de Cologne* business. McCloy was in a Schloss near Wiesbaden. Ambassador François-Poncet was at Schloss Ernich, superbly positioned on a bluff west of one of the narrowest parts of the Rhine gorge, a few kilometres south of Godesberg.

Sitting on that bluff, to the west of the river, a great thrumming of sound comes up from below – a combination of the noise of the great Rhine barges, and of main roads and railtracks on each side of the river: to me it always felt like listening to the heart-beats of the industrial German giant.

The local costs of the armed forces and civilian staff of the Allied Powers were borne by the FRG. They lived comfortably, and at times excessive expenses were condoned. Our furnished housing came free; and German cleaning staff were also available without charge. To begin with, the married staff arrived without families. But, as new accommodation was built by the Germans for the Allied personnel, their wives and children joined them. Single staff were initially housed in the unattractive industrial village of Troisdorf, but later relocated to Friesdorf, between Bonn and Bad Godesberg. (They were known as *'single elements',* in the strange para-military jargon of the CCG. There was a CCG regulation which stated that *'female single elements will not normally be allowed maternity leave more than once'.* One fall from grace was excusable: a second not!) The dispersal of the British staff between Köln, Bonn, Godesberg and Honnef, with office work divided between the Petersberg, Bonn and Wahnerheide, meant much time was wasted in travel. But there was a good (CCG) bus service, and official cars could be used for other business journeys, or hired cheaply for leisure. It was during months of daily bus journeys between Friesdorf and Wahn, when the bumpy, post-war German *pflaster [pavé]* roads made reading impossible, that I learnt to knit. My male colleagues thought this eccentric: the females thought it sensible and were most helpful at picking up stitches!

I now found myself in the Political Division of the British Element of the Control Commission for Germany, or CCG (BE). I was at the bottom of a chain of command in which every higher rung was occupied by a star performer: Ivone Kirkpatrick as High Commissioner; Kit Steel as his Deputy; Con O'Neill as Head of the Political Division; Terence Garvey as Head of its External Relations Section; and Peter Male as the latter's deputy. Of these, every one was later to become British Ambassador in a key post; Kirkpatrick became Permanent Under-Secretary of the Foreign Office; and O'Neill ended his diplomatic career as the official Head of the Delegation, under the political control of Geoffrey Rippon, which negotiated British entry into the European Community in 1972. (Con had the remarkable distinction of leaving the Service three times – the first time in protest at the Munich Agreement – and then each time being asked to return.) For me, this set-up was an extra-ordinary stroke of fortune: it was a tremendous stimulus to the mind and imagination to be kept up to the mark by such a brilliant and demanding group.

As my post was new, I started with no clearly defined area of activity. My superiors threw me problems one-by-one. The Divisional Clerks also saw me as a convenient repository for incoming mail which nobody more senior seemed to want. I took everything that came. Before long I was responsible for a wide range of different kinds of work.

One experience amused me. In the Political Division in Berlin I had met a middle-ranking Foreign Office official, named Dugald Malcolm, who had not come on to Bonn, but been posted elsewhere. I soon noticed that many of the bits and pieces the clerks sent me represented business he had handled. I made enquiries. He was known as an eccentric; and also as one who did things well if they interested him, but otherwise tried to have them forgotten. He had a lockable filing cabinet in his office. Papers he found tiresome to deal with, were consigned to it. Sometimes, they would be needed by another staff member. Dugald would be approached; go to the cabinet, of which he alone had a key; open it a crack, with his back to the enquirer; pull out the required file; hand it over; and then at once lock the cabinet again. When the move from Berlin took place, he had already left for his new post, taking the key with him. The staff took the cabinet to Wahnerheide; opened it with a jemmy; and found it full of unfinished business. This now fell like rain on my desk.

For a few months I went on steadily learning my trade. But then the press of world events led to a change in tempo. The Cold War, which effectively started in 1948, when the Russians invaded Czechoslovakia to ensure a Communist régime, and then blockaded Berlin, was hotting up. South Korea was invaded by the Communist North in June, 1950. And an aggressive and monolithic Communist Bloc, with China then closely tied to Russia, menaced the free world at every point. The West Europeans felt exposed.

That autumn, Dean Acheson, the American Secretary-of-State, told his British and French counterparts that the US, which had run down its forces in Europe rapidly after the War, was ready to send re-inforcements, but only if the Europeans raised their own military strength to 60 well-armed divisions, of which 10 should be German. (Later the 10 became 12.) The time had come to accelerate the bringing of the FRG fully into the European family. The process had two main prongs: to develop the European Community system – as proposed by Robert Schuman (the European Coal and Steel Community) and later by René Pléven (the European Defence Community); and to give the FRG full sovereign status by means of international agreements between it and the three Western Allies (later to become known as 'The Bonn Conventions'). With the second of these prongs I was soon involved.

A digression is again in order. After the war the Allied authorities had initially frowned strongly on any 'fraternisation' between the occupation forces and the local population. In the British Zone, not only the armed forces, but also the CCG staff, had been guided by this policy. With the altered political climate, it had to change. Guidance went out that fraternisation was no longer bad, but on the contrary very good! The British forces were in general happy enough, and a rash of Anglo-German marriages followed. But the civilian staff of the CCG was another matter.

It had been found necessary, when recruiting to the CCG, to engage good German speakers. However, the German language had been little taught in Britain before the War. So inevitably a high proportion of CCG recruits were naturalised Germans, who had left Germany before the war to escape from Hitler's persecution. Many of these people were upset by the new turn of events.

A stronghold of resistance was the network of CCG Clubs throughout the Zone – social establishments run on the lines of an army mess. The High Commissioner therefore wrote a circular to all Club Chairmen. He explained that, while he could not order them to admit Germans to their Clubs, he could and did instruct them to hold a General Meeting to consider the matter. Soon after, a British-born friend of mine, travelling in the Zone, and wanting a drink, called at the local CCG Club, only to find such a meeting in progress. He sat down quietly, and waited for it to finish. One by one, the members rose to say, with no variations of substance: 'vee cannot 'ave zeese chairmans in our clobs'. My friend, feeling this one-sided, wanted to intervene. He asked his neighbour the name of the Club Chairman. Shocked, the latter replied: 'vee are non of us chairmans here – vee are all Breetish'!

To return to the narrative, and more particularly to the negotiations for the Bonn Conventions[4], the decision to launch these must have been taken at one of the then frequent meetings of the Allied/FRG Foreign Ministers. (NB. The word 'quadripartite' is used amongst Germanists uniquely to denote the US/UK/French/Soviet combination.) The negotiators were the three Allied High Commissioners in Bonn and the Federal Chancellor, Konrad Adenauer, who was his own Foreign Minister. Throughout the negotiations they met regularly, normally weekly. Their meetings were usually at the Petersberg. At a fairly early stage of the talks, it was decided that the legal instruments would take the form of a number of Conventions and some associated documents. The Conventions were six in number.

The cornerstone was to be a 'Convention on Relations between the Three Powers and the Federal Republic of Germany', establishing broad principles: the termination of the occupation; the attainment by the FRG of 'the full *authority of a sovereign State over its internal and external affairs';* the retaining by the Three Powers of certain rights and responsibilities relating to Berlin and Germany as a whole; the stationing of armed forces of other countries in the FRG [but now for the defence of the Free World, and no longer as occupiers]; and a statement of the *'common aim of a re-unified Germany enjoying a liberal-democratic constitution like that of the Federal Republic, and integrated within the European community'.* This last point, which was reiterated time and time again by the Allies and the FRG in official statements over the following 40 years, was sadly ignored by Prime Minister Margaret Thatcher when, in 1989, she reacted negatively and very publicly to the prospect of German reunification taking place on precisely the terms envisaged in the Convention: her reaction cost Britain dear in terms of her relationship with Germany.

Four other Conventions were to deal, in more detail, with the stationing of foreign forces in the FRG. And there was to be a sixth Convention 'on the Settlement of Matters arising out of the War and the Occupation'.

The High Commissioners and the Chancellor set up groups to handle the detailed negotiations on each of these Conventions: each group had an Allied Chairman, a member from each of the other two Allied Powers, and a German member. The Allied representatives to each group prepared each round of negotiations with the Germans in Three Power meetings of their own.

To my amazement, I found myself appointed by Kirkpatrick to be the British negotiator for the sixth Convention. The Allied Chairman was Whitney Debevoise, a leading Wall Street lawyer who had been recruited by Jack McCloy as Legal Adviser in the US High Commission, and a delightful person. The name of the thoughtful, quiet diplomat who represented France sadly escapes me[5]. The leading German negotiator was Dr Heinz Trütschler von Falkenstein.

To give an idea of the range and political importance of the subjects in 'our' Convention, here is a slightly edited list of its Chapter Headings: the treatment of legislation of the former Occupying Powers; the de-cartelisation and de-concentration of German industry; the restitution of property to victims of Nazi oppression; compensation for victims of Nazi persecution; the treatment of foreign claims against Germany, of claims by German nationals against foreign countries, and of foreign interests in Germany; reparations by Germany; the treatment of displaced persons and refugees; facilities for Allied Embassies and Consulates in Germany; and the re-establishment of German Civil Aviation.

Of course I could not deal with this vast range of subjects without much expert help and advice. Most of this came from other Divisions of the High Commission, such as the Economic, Financial, Transport and Legal Divisions, while some was from the Foreign Office. Experts from those same Divisions considered the matters coming up for negotiation, and supplied briefing. Often they accompanied me to Allied or Allied/FRG meetings, and did follow-up work. But it was nevertheless <u>my</u> responsibility to ensure that the preparation was done; to be titular representative of Britain at the meetings; and to report on them to my High Commission superiors and the Foreign Office.

Difficult issues arising in the various groups had to be referred to the weekly meetings between the High Commissioners and the Chancellor; and I was in attendance whenever these came from our group. Given the huge range of our subjects, this meant attendance at most such meetings. They were conducted in a friendly and informal way. Adenauer had a dry, but strong, sense of humour. The British and American High Commissioners also had a light touch. François-Poncet was relatively stiff.

An occasion sticks in mind when a sensitive issue was de-fused by that informality. One of the difficult questions connected with the stationing of troops in the FRG was the number of duty-free cigarettes they should be allowed to import. After much discussion at Group level, the matter was referred up. Kirkpatrick was the High Commissioner chairing the meeting. The four principals began by speaking from their respective briefs. McCloy argued for 40 cigarettes per person per day; Adenauer for 7; while Kirkpatrick and François-Poncet gave quiet support to McCloy (knowing that they could live with anything which satisfied the Americans). There was *impasse*.

Suddenly, Kirkpatrick asked for silence. Then he said to Adenauer: *'Herr Bundeskanzler, I see that General Heusinger[6] has just entered the room ready for the next item on our agenda. You know and I know that he has not been involved at all in the negotiations on what we have been discussing. Would you allow me to ask him a question?'* The Chancellor assented. *'Herr General',* said Kirkpatrick to Heusinger, *'if, during the war, German soldiers under your command could have smoked every day as many cigarettes as they wished, what would the figure have been?'* Without a moment's thought, Heusinger replied *'forty';* everybody roared with laughter (not least the Chancellor); and the matter was settled accordingly!

The negotiations for the Bonn Conventions must have lasted for over a year. They were signed on 26 May 1952 by Dean Acheson, Anthony Eden,

At the signature of the Bonn Conventions, 26 September, 1952.
L to R: Anthony Eden, Robert Schuman, Dean Acheson and Konrad Adenauer.
By courtesy of the Bundesbildstelle Berlin.

Robert Schuman and Konrad Adenauer. The original idea was that they would be ratified soon after, alongside of the Treaty establishing the European Defence Community. The failure of the latter to secure the approval of the French National Assembly, in August 1954, caused a change of plan. It was agreed that the Brussels Treaty Organisation (Britain, France and the Benelux countries) would be expanded to include Germany and Italy; this cleared the path for the requisite German Divisions to be created; and the Allies/FRG signed a Protocol in October 1954 whose ratification in the following year enabled the Bonn Conventions finally to enter into force.

From the moment when this negotiating role came my way, it was obvious that a big challenge lay ahead. I had certain advantages. Almost (though not quite all) of the matters dealt with in our Convention were ones for which I had haphazardly acquired responsibility within the Political Division in the preceding months. One might say that my rag-bag of subjects had turned to riches. My experience in CLD had given me a broad view of British Foreign Policy, and taught me to see individual issues in the wider context, very important in this case. It had also taught me the arts of keeping many balls simultaneously in the air, of clear reporting, and of grasping essentials. I had by now developed good written and spoken German. As against this, I was an unsophisticated and immature 23 year old, with no previous experience of negotiating. My superiors deliberately took the risk of my falling short, and decided that I should be given a chance. They must have felt that I responded adequately, since I was left as the British negotiator for the whole period. I have never ceased to be grateful, especially to Con O'Neill and Terence Garvey. I learned by practical experience the key skills of multilateral diplomacy and of handling complex negotiations. They stood me in good stead for the rest of my life. By the time I left Bonn, I had begun to find my niche in the Service.

The impression should not be gained that Bonn was all work and no play. My work was fascinating, but could after a while usually be accommodated within normal hours (a 5-day week, from 0900 to 1730 or thereabouts). So I had much leisure time, as well as 6 weeks holiday a year. My main leisure activities were gliding and repairing gliders; ski-ing; party-going; friends; and listening to music.

Working at the edge of Wahn airfield, flying was an obvious draw. Wahn was an RAF base, the home for a squadron of Meteor jet fighters. At weekends there was almost no military activity, and Germans were still banned from all forms of flying. CCG enthusiasts soon set up a gliding club, under RAF supervision; I saw a notice advertising it; and immediately joined. The Club Chairman, Henry Waugh, was also the Vickers Aircraft representative in Germany, preparing to sell the Germans some Viscount Aircraft once they were again allowed to operate a civil airline. That was, for me, the beginning of a love-affair with aviation.

This is not the place for a technical discourse on gliding: the aim is simply to give an impression of the part it played in my life in Bonn. Our aircraft had originally been the property of the Luftwaffe, or in some cases of private German owners. Because of the rule that Germans could not fly (part of the post-war de-militarisation process), all aircraft in German ownership had been impounded by the Allies, and either used by the latter, destroyed or stored. Our Club tracked down gliders and sail-planes in store all over the British Zone; begged them off the British authorities concerned; brought them back to Wahn air-field; and restored them in one of the hangars placed at our disposal by the RAF. Expert advice and assistance was given by a former Luftwaffe technician named Schmitz, and several of our members had relevant experience. I had none, beyond having learnt carpentry at Twyford School and Winchester College. But we were all enthusiastic; devoted long hours to the work; and were rewarded by ending up with a fine stock of aircraft at very little cost. It included Kranich I and II two-seaters; and, Minimoa, Rhön Bussard, Grunau Baby, and SG 38 single-seaters.

To begin with, we had only single-seaters, and I learnt to fly in that way. (The SG 38, a string-bag reminiscent of the Wright Brothers' aircraft, was the glider on which all beginners started.) Later, we acquired two-seaters as well, and *ab initio* training was sometimes given in them. But it seemed to me better to go solo from scratch. There was little risk, because you were winched up to a low altitude (say 10 metres) initially, and then gradually moved further up, flight by flight, to the maximum winching height of about 400 metres, doing a little more flying each time. There was no horrible moment of truth such as you have in the two-seater training mode, when suddenly the instructor gets out and you are left to take off all alone. Later, when an instructor myself, I always trained people on the single-seaters, using the two-seaters only for improvement once the basic skills were solid.

Most of my gliding took place from Wahn, using the big thermals which built up above quarries and Rhineland factories. They could be amazingly strong: sometimes they would lift a half-ton sail-plane upwards at more than 10 metres a second. One could make triangular flights to Köln, Bonn, and back to Wahn, in a couple of hours, meeting on the way only a few soaring buzzards, competing with us for the use of the thermals. But the time came when I was trying to get my Silver C Certificate, which involved, amongst other things, staying in the air for five hours at a stretch: this is not easy on thermals alone. So we used to go and spend a few days at a time at a gliding establishment run by the RAF in the Weserbergland, near Hameln. It was situated on top of a big ridge, running roughly north and south, adjacent to Scharfoldendorf. So long as the prevailing westerly wind blew, one could stay aloft indefinitely.

On 24 March, 1951, as my log-book shows, I was trying for my five hours. It was the last chance before returning to Bonn. All went well for two hours. Then a storm-front came through, with the clouds well below the ridge-top. Clearly we were going to be ordered down. Preferring not to know, I flew north along the ridge; got out of sight of the directing staff; waited till I saw a rift in the cloud; flew through it; emerged in clear air behind the front; and resumed soaring on the face of the ridge. I saw that everybody else had obeyed orders and landed; and felt cocky.

Pride comes before a fall. An hour later, another front came through; the pattern was repeated, up to the point when I again saw a rift in the cloud.

But this time, when I flew into it, the cloud closed round me and all was swirling fog. Instantly, I realised the folly of a decision taken earlier. At take-off, something had blocked my Grunau's pitot head, which measures air-flow and thus enables the air-speed-indicator to work: I had decided not to descend and clear it, thinking the time lost might represent the difference between getting the 5 hours and not.

So now I was left with only three working instruments: an altimeter; a compass, and a variometer (or rise and fall indicator). The aircraft had no artificial horizon. The compass worked only when the plane was flying horizontally. But, in nil visibility and with the instrumentation described, it could not be kept that way. In seconds, the aircraft was out of control. Impossible to tell whether one was diving, climbing or in level flight; or whether one was banked at a steep angle, or not at all, or in a spin. All I could be sure of was my altitude; and the fact that I was not completely upside down, since in that case I would have been hanging from my straps.

The danger was extreme. I might go into a spin, or a steep dive, without the instrumentation which would allow me to right the fault, and hit a ridge before emerging from the cloud. The only comfort came from my altimeter and variometer: the former told me I was still comfortably above the highest hills around; the latter that the lift in the cloud was taking me still higher. Even this was limited comfort, because of another complication. My ridge was only 40 kilometres west of the Soviet Zone, and a strong westerly wind was blowing me straight towards it.

It was terrifying. How long I remained out of control and helpless, buffeted this way and that in the impenetrable cloud, I do not know. It can only have been minutes, but felt much longer. Suddenly the cloud cleared. I saw that I was in a near vertical dive; and that I was a long way down-wind from my ridge. I must have been doing about 200 kms an hour – far more than the recommended maximum for the plane. I pulled the stick back very gently, fearful of tearing off the wings. On attaining an acceptably slower speed, I made for the top of the ridge, and cleared it by a matter of metres.

That was the end of the adventure. I completed my 5 hours. The directing staff gave me a colossal dressing-down, but surprisingly did not disallow the flight. I obtained my Silver C Certificate, and was by then also a gliding instructor, Class B (i.e. authorised to instruct in solo or dual mode). But it was the closest I had ever been to death. And I had learnt, the hard way, not to take risks when flying.

Whilst in Bonn I first learnt to ski. A number of friendly enthusiasts inducted me. The nearest practicable ski-ing area was Winterberg, some distance to the east. It wasn't very good, but there was a makeshift tow. The first day I went, a number of British soldiers were, like me, on skis for the first time. They would take the tow up; launch themselves down the slopes with enthusiasm; reach the bottom after a series of punishing falls; repair briefly to an army truck; and then re-start the process. I was impressed by their courage until I inspected the truck. The courage was Dutch: a generous nip of gin was taken between each go! Nevermind: I had been thoroughly bitten by the ski-ing bug.

In the winter I set off on a proper ski-ing holiday, being recommended to find a hotel at Mittelberg, in the Austrian part of the Allgäuer Alpen. Arriving there on the last Postbus from Oberstdorf, I watched it disappear down the valley and then enquired for my hotel. The travel agent had boobed. I was booked at a hotel in Mittelberg-Oy, some 40 kilometres away in Germany, not in Mittelberg, Klein Walsertal, at all; and there were no hotel rooms available in the latter! A kindly German couple helped me find a room in a farm, where the grandmother spent all day toasting herself on top of the tiled stove in the living room! Some days later, my wallet fell out of my anorak un-noticed, when I fell in a snow drift: all my money was lost. Another German couple, who had no personal knowledge of me, bailed me out with enough money to finish my holiday!

In Bonn there were parties galore, perhaps because for many it was the first opportunity for real party going since before the war. Some CCG people consorted only with Allied personnel. Fortunately the opportunity came my way to go mostly to parties where there was a mix of Allies and Germans.

The smartest parties, of course, were those given by the High Commissioners at their different Schlösser. There were also many parties offered by rather less senior people. On the British side, Kit and Kate Steel were particularly charming hosts. They had a delightful house at Bad Honnef – the Berghaus, Heckenfels, Bonndorferstrasse – on one of the foothills of the Siebengebirge overlooking the Rhine. (On one occasion, when they were away, they lent it to me for a fortnight!) Their parties, and those of other British hosts, were usually enlivened by John Killick[7] and Lance Pope, two members of the UK High Commission staff, singing a range of songs to the accompaniment of their own guitar and concertina. Both, for different reasons, spoke fluent German. They would sing old favourites, or witty, satirical, topical songs of their own devising, in both German and English. The political songs, which were set to some well-known tune, so that all could join in the choruses, became the talk of the town. Killick and Pope sent up everything and everybody, both Allied and German. Chancellor Adenauer, if he knew there had been such a party, would next morning ask to be told of the latest songs! Many of them poked fun at him personally, but he took it all in very good part.

One song was so catchy that the first verse sticks in my mind, over 50 years later. It had to do with the rather grand way in which the British Land Commissioners lived: these were the senior British officials in each Land (Federal State) in the British Zone. It was sung to the tune of McNamara's Band, and ran thus:

Verse
We are the Land Commissioners,
We're a shocking idle crew,
We live in the lap of luxury,
We've nothing at all to do.

Chorus
Oh, some are redundant, and some retire,
And some of drink do die,
But we'll go on for ever,
Or we'll know the reason why!

This was followed by a separate – and cheeky – verse about each individual Land Commissioner, the chorus then being repeated. (The author on this occasion was Terence Garvey.)

A favourite memory is of a dinner in a British home, when I found myself at a long table seated opposite Carlo Schmid, the SPD leader, who was very stout indeed, a German Cyril Smith. Half way through the meal, came the sound of wood creaking and cracking. Schmid knew his chair was collapsing. His first reaction was to reach out on either side for help; but he saw neither of his two lady neighbours had the physical strength to assist. His next thought was to grab the cloth that covered the whole table, for support; but then he realised he was beginning to pull it, and everything on it, onto himself. Despair and resignation took over. Slowly the chair gave way, and Schmid simply disappeared from view beneath the table. It was something one had seen in light-hearted comedies, but had never expected to witness in real life.

One of the nicest features of Diplomatic Service life is that all members of a well-run Embassy feel they are part of an extended family. This is particularly true of the UK based members, who know they may meet each other again in future postings, or perhaps already have. Of course, the Political Division of the CCG (BE) was not a normal Embassy. It was part of a wider body whose members mostly came from outside the service. Nevertheless, the extended family concept applied in our Division, and I made many friends, with some of whom I am still in touch. My Gliding Club activities – another field where the clan concept strongly applies – broadened the field.

Of course, not all of them can be mentioned. But two had special influence on me. First was Michael Warr and his family. Michael had recently married a war widow, Gillian Addis. There was a son by her first marriage, and their own first child soon arrived. They lived in a nice house at Honnef, and frequently had me to stay. I have always liked children, and got on well with theirs. Twice I was invited to join the family on summer holidays, in Germany and Austria, which were enormous fun. The Warrs' cultural interests broadened my own. They exposed me to German architectural masterpieces. And they developed my interest in world-class opera, by taking me to the Salzburg Festival. From now on my enthusiasm for opera grew and grew. Another British friend further encouraged it by taking me to the Wagner Festival at Bayreuth. Michael, being not a part of my chain of command, would also offer me disinterested but invaluable reflections about the Diplomatic Service as a career.

The other friend to be mentioned was an American lass, who was working in the US High Commission. She became a girl-friend in the then sense of the term: that is, she was a girl and a friend, but to me not more. We saw a lot of each other because she joined the gliding club; and she had a snazzy MG in which she often gave me a lift to the airfield. (My own first car was bought just before leaving Bonn.) She was good fun, and we did a lot together. But it came as a shock when she gave me a gold watch for Christmas. I realised she had read more into our association than I had, and moved (tactfully I hope) into reverse. The experience made me cautious with girls.

In November, 1952, three years after my arrival in Germany, and with all work on the Bonn Conventions complete, I was given my next Foreign Office posting. This was to Strasbourg. Since I had been living in fully furnished accommodation, there was little packing to be done. I piled all my belongings into my newly acquired Ford Consul and drove up the Rhine Valley to my destination.

CHAPTER 7

Strasbourg: Maura and the Council of Europe (1952-55)

Maura

I FIRST SAW HER, facing me by chance across a set, at a Scottish country dancing session, in the old building of the Council of Europe. Instantly and instinctively, I liked what I observed: a beautiful girl, attractively turned out, with a lovely smile and a warm, gentle and open face. Maura wore a kilt and a white, three-quarter-length sleeved, top. I soon found her to be intelligent, perceptive, rather reserved but not shy, possessed of a warm sense of humour, and a good linguist; also that we had many common interests, including music (in my case only as a listener), art, architecture, landscape, walking, tennis, swimming and ski-ing. I was looking at the girl who was to marry me three years later, and through so doing was to change my life completely, and incomparably for the better.

Strasbourg was propitious for romance: the city has great charm; the Council of Europe staff, with which I was to work closely, were mostly young, because the organisation itself had started from nothing only three years before; many of them were very interesting and stimulating; there was plenty of socialising, and many diversions.

I soon began going around with Maura; but the progress of our romance was not rapid, no doubt through my own fault. After my mistake in Bonn, I was cautious. For some while I went out with more than one girl. Gradually Maura's attractions prevailed. We did more and more together – parties, concerts, operas, ski-ing, walking, exploration of Alsace and the Schwarzwald, and much else. I got to know her better and better, and became ever more attracted. There seemed to be a similar movement on Maura's side. I had always looked forward enormously to the prospect of getting married to the right girl, and later raising a family. So I began to think of proposing; but simultaneously felt myself not very mature and wondered whether I was yet ready for marriage. My mother, who visited me in September 1954, appears in photos with Maura at the Titisee (Schwarzwald); and told us later she was then convinced we should soon be engaged!

In fact, things went on for a while longer; but, in the spring of 1955, outside events excluded further delay. The Foreign Office posted me to Washington: I was not prepared to leave without first asking Maura to share her life with me. I reached that decision in May whilst on an official visit to the Saar, and wasted no more time. Driving quickly back to Strasbourg, and arriving late one evening, I called at Maura's flat; made my proposal; and was at once accepted. It was the most marvellous moment in my life. From the moment Maura said 'yes', I felt absolute conviction that the commitment made on both sides that evening was total, irrevocable, and for the whole of our lives; and that I had been fortunate enough to find a rock on which a happy family life could safely and surely rest. And so it has been, ever since.

My parents, who were told when they happened to pass through Strasbourg on holiday a few days later, were delighted, though of course they told me I should have proposed much earlier! Sadly, Maura's father had died of leukaemia whilst we were both at Strasbourg; but the rest of her family were equally enthusiastic. The engagement was at once announced; but, for reasons to be explained, I left for Washington still a bachelor, returning to England for our wedding at Fulmer, Buckinghamshire on 16 November 1955.

During the three years we had known each other, I had learnt much about Maura's background. Her father, Group-Captain John Sullivan, had a long career as an RAF Officer, and (like mine) had seen service in different parts of the world. This gave us further points in common. Although Maura had been born at Letchworth, on 6 April 1930, during a home posting, her parents were soon despatched to Cairo, and she has a clear memory of childhood days in Heliopolis. Returning to the UK in 1938, they settled in Rose Garden Cottage, the house in Layters' Way, Gerrards Cross, which was to remain the family's home until the death of Maura's mother, Dorothy [Dolly], in 1992. Maura attended a small private day-school there, Chalfont Lodge [now closed], until she was 16; and then became a day-girl for two years at Wycombe High School. After training at the London College of Secretaries, and then working briefly at the BBC Radio Times, she was employed at the British Institute of Management for a couple of years. In 1951, she was approached by Dunstan Curtis, Head of Committee Services of the Consultative Assembly of the Council of Europe, and asked to join the staff of the organisation. (Maura had been recommended to Dunstan by Tony Elton-Mayo – soon to be his wife – for whom she had worked.) Starting in Committee Services, she was, by the time I met her, Personal Assistant to Tony Lincoln, the Deputy Secretary-General of the Council of Europe.

The Council of Europe

Why had the Foreign Office sent me to Strasbourg? The posting was to the British Consulate-General, where I was to be Deputy to the UK Permanent Representative to the Council of Europe, and also Vice-Consul with special responsibility for the Saar. Both activities need explanation.

The Council of Europe, whose creation was a main consequence of the great Hague Conference of May 1948, had been set up a year later by the ten founding Member States: the three Benelux countries, Denmark, France, Ireland, Italy, Norway, Sweden and the UK. It operated at two levels: the Council of Ministers and the Consultative Assembly [now called the Parliamentary Assembly]. It was inter-governmental, and all Council decisions required unanimity. The Assembly had no real powers, but was to be, for a decade, the only authoritative forum for debates on the future of Europe amongst the continent's politicians.

The Ministers met infrequently. Between their meetings, preparatory work was done by their Deputies, otherwise known as the Permanent Representatives. The UK was represented at that level by Peter Scarlett[1], who was also the British Consul-General at Strasbourg. He had asked the Foreign Office for assistance, and my posting was the consequence.

The work of the Ministers and their Deputies had become tedious. By now, the European Convention on Human Rights had already been adopted. There were to be no further moves of that importance. The Ministers talked about many matters of general European interest. But, because of the unanimity rule, things moved slowly; and any Conventions or Agreements adopted had little substance, as they simply represented the highest common factor of consensus. My task was to prepare and report on all the meetings. As at Bonn, it meant keeping many balls in the air simultaneously; but the balls themselves were of little worth. I did the job properly; but it was dull.

Another part of my work, on the other hand, was of truly enormous interest, and was to have a profound impact on my career pattern. I had to follow, and report to the Foreign Office, the work of the Parliamentary Assembly of the Council of Europe; of the newly created Common Assembly of the European Coal and Steel Community; and of an expanded version of the latter, known as the 'Ad Hoc Assembly', which was set up soon after to develop and agree the draft of a 'Treaty Establishing the European Political Community'.

The original Council of Europe Building, 1952.

This meant that, for three years, I watched, from a privileged position on the touch-line, as all the 'Great Debates' on European issues unfolded before my eyes. (Maura watched too, because the Council of Europe wisely encouraged its staff to do so.) The key statesmen all came and spoke: Adenauer, Schuman, De Gasperi, Spaak, Luns, Mollet and many others. Jean Monnet was often in the corridors. I knew the first two already from my time in Bonn: I soon learned to know the others.

All the key issues were debated: the underlying disputes between Federalists and Functionalists; the concept of supra-nationalism and the sharing of national sovereignty; the proposals for a European Defence Community [EDC] and for the associated European Political Community; and, after the rejection of the EDC Treaty by the French National Assembly in August 1954, the Eden proposals for enlargement of the four-nation Brussels Treaty Organisation [BTO]. The latter was now to include Italy and the Federal Republic of Germany, and form the Western European Union [WEU]. The acceptance of these last proposals cleared the way for the entry into force of the Bonn Conventions; full independence for the Federal Republic; the creation of a West German Army; and West German entry into NATO.

I was allowed to go to Paris to attend the debate in The French National

Assembly concerning ratification of the EDC Treaty. It was one thing to get to Paris, and quite another to get into the Assembly hemi-cycle. At that time the diplomatic box at the Palais Bourbon was very small, seating about 30 persons. But there were over 100 Diplomatic Missions; each had one permanent ticket for the box; and all wanted to send one or more representatives to observe. There was clearly going to be a problem.

The British Embassy had promised to see I got in. But the Ambassador, Sir Gladwyn Jebb [later, Lord Gladwyn], and the First Secretary (Political) wanted to go too. So the First Secretary entered first, without the card, simply waving at the *huissiers* and muttering '*Vous me connaissez n'est-ce pas!*'. The Ambassador followed, also without the card, responding to the *huissiers'* requests for it with the words, spoken in a very stern and authoritative voice, '*Je suis l'Ambassadeur de la Grande Bretagne*'. Nobody dared stop him; so I was then able to enter legally, with the card! This was all very well. But the box was soon like the Black Hole of Calcutta, many other Embassies having played similar games. Dozens of diplomats were there. And it was very hot weather, into the bargain. If one left the hemi-cycle, one would not get back; so one stuck it out – all day long. It was obvious that, although the debate was to continue for four days, the first day's tricks would not work twice. Fortunately I knew Senateur Radius, the Senator for the Bas-Rhin, and he somehow fiddled me a place in the distinguished visitors' gallery. So I saw the whole debate. It was sustained and passionate. Everybody knew that the fate of the whole European package – EDC, European Political Community, and the Bonn Conventions – hung in the balance. And when, at the vote, the EDC was ultimately rejected, the whole construction of European unity was thrown into turmoil. Many grown men were in tears.

Diplomats are often thought to have no views of their own about great issues; but simply to express those of their Government. One must, of course, faithfully perform the latter duty, and do it to the best of one's ability. But one may have personal views which are different, so long as one is discreet. One may keep them to oneself; or there may be occasions when one can express them, so long as one makes sure that interlocutors understand they are personal, and at variance with those of one's Government. On the great issues under debate in Strasbourg, it was impossible not to form views of my own as to what was right for the UK.

On arrival at the Council of Europe I knew that the British Government was officially and strongly opposed to the UK becoming part of any supra-national or federalist international organisation. Officially, it was prepared to say that the Community concept might be a good idea for other countries; but most of the more senior officials in the Foreign Office not only <u>thought</u> the Six would fail to make the concept work, but even <u>hoped</u> they would, because that would mean Britain would not have to face up to a powerful grouping of Six Member States, united at the heart of Western Europe, while the UK was outside.

The British Government's position was described as being that of standing at the heart of three intersecting circles: the North Atlantic; the Commonwealth; and the West European. British Ministers and senior officials lived profoundly in the past. They exaggerated in their own minds the continuing significance of the UK/US 'Special Relationship', forgetting that the War was long since over and that the relative strength of the UK had greatly declined; they exaggerated also the importance of the Common-wealth, perhaps because it was a convenient way of justifying, to a British public brought up to revere its imperial past, the ongoing and rapid withdrawal from Empire; and they failed to perceive how quickly the other countries of Western Europe, so weakened by the War, were recovering their strength.

It did not take me long, as I listened to the Assembly debates, and heard the powerful arguments in favour of the Community approach, and the strong criticisms of Britain for its contrary stance, which appeared to conflict with many of the things Winston Churchill had publicly said about the need for a United Europe, to conclude that a strong Community system would be good for the peace and prosperity of the continent; that British participation would be good for the UK; and that standing aside would leave us on the European sidelines. By no means were these ideas kept private. Obviously they coloured my reporting to the Foreign Office. Moreover, when the UK Permanent Representative was called on to make policy recommendations to London, these were drafted by me, and reflected my beliefs. Peter Scarlett usually followed the line proposed.

With benefit of hindsight, I am inclined to wonder whether my former Housemaster, Budge Firth, had not sowed a seed in my mind. He was also the Chaplain of the College. True to Winchester tradition, his sermons were of a very adult and soul-searching kind. Preaching in Chapel in Armistice week, 1937, he had spoken strongly about the need for a new international order. His extraordinarily prescient sermon was printed in 1938[2], and Budge must have recalled it to the House. Below follows a key part.

'The paths of glory lead but to the mutual slaughter and the waste of the glorious. While, therefore, we rightly honour those who fell in the Great War, we must firmly

maintain the conviction that *"Patriotism is not enough"*. [These last four words were spoken by Edith Cavell on the day of her execution by the Germans in Brussels.] Budge went on as follows. *'Patriotism should not be simply depreciated, but it must be transcended, and the high qualities which the narrower cause has inspired must be taken over and consecrated to the service of a wider end. Armistice Day itself must gradually cease to lay its main emphasis upon commemoration, and become increasingly a day of dedication towards the construction of an international order, the only basis, quite obviously, for enduring peace. Enlarge your view or perish. That is the lesson which must be learned, unless we are to drift from humbug to humbug, from dodge to dodge, till the butcher's shop opens once more and we find that all we have been able to do is to provide the several butchers with sharper knives.'*

The Saar

My second task was to act as the British Vice-Consul to the Saar. (Once again I received a Commission, this time signed by Queen Elizabeth II and Anthony Eden. Thereafter, however, this agreeable tradition fell into desuetude.) The Saar Territory had been detached from Germany after the Second World War, and was being administered by France through a High Commissioner, responsible directly to Paris, and not through the French High Commissioner in Bonn. Its future status was uncertain. The French wanted it to remain independent of Germany, while the Germans wanted it to join the Federal Republic as one of the constituent *Länder*.

The French had therefore encouraged the formation of political parties in the Saar analogous to the three principal parties in the Federal Republic – the CDU, the SPD and the FDP – but statutorily quite independent. These were called the 'official parties', and the French authorities did not recognise the existence of any other. The CDU had a majority, and its leader was therefore Minister-President. His name was Johannes Hoffmann, invariably called *'Der Alte Jo-Ho'*. However, popular sentiment in the Saar was strongly in favour of re-integration with Germany. So three other parties existed *de facto*, corresponding in political colour to the official ones, and being known as 'the Pro-German Parties'.

My monthly one or two day visits to the Saar were therefore sensitive. On the one hand it was my duty to remain on good terms with the French High Commissioner, M Gilbert Grandval, and his staff. On the other, if I was to report usefully to the Foreign Office on the state of opinion in the Territory, I had to talk to the leaders of the pro-German parties; but to do so discreetly, and in a way which did not offend the French. It was a useful exercise in tact for a young diplomat. It proved possible, though not easy, to manage affairs satisfactorily.

There was, however, one awkward incident. I had arranged to call on the leader of the pro-German FDP, a lawyer by the name of Schneider, at his office in the Bahnhofstrasse – the main street of Saarbrücken – one summer evening at the end of his day's work. On my arrival, his Secretary said he was talking to a client. Soon after, she slipped into his office to announce that I was in the waiting room, and that she was leaving. I read a newspaper and waited for the client to leave. Next, I heard Schneider's door open, and the two men go downstairs (the offices were on the first floor). I assumed Schneider would escort his client to the street and then return. In fact, he had forgotten all about me; went out himself; and locked the door. At first I was not worried, feeling sure Schneider would remember and return. As time went by, this became less and less likely. I looked for a telephone, but the only offices so equipped were those of Schneider and his Secretary, both now locked. Next, I considered whether I could let myself out quietly. But all the windows were on the first floor, and gave directly on to the Bahnhofstrasse, where a Saarland policeman was on point duty at a busy intersection just beneath. The only practical way out would be to hail the policeman and ask for help; but of course explanations would be needed, the media would pick up the story, and Grandval would be affronted! Finally I decided, Micawberish, to wait half an hour and see whether anything turned up: if not, I would call the policeman.

Just twenty-nine minutes later, the key turned in the street door, and Schneider entered. Ironically, he had not remembered about me: he had simply come back for a paper left in the office by mistake. We had a good laugh; went off for a drink and a chat; and faces were saved all round!

Some time after I had settled into this work, the Consultative Assembly of the Council of Europe took the initiative with a view to resolving the future of the Saar. Its Political Affairs Committee was requested to submit proposals to the Assembly. A Rapporteur was appointed – M Van der Goes van Naters from the Netherlands. The preparation of the Report and proposals was in practice left to two Council officials of British nationality, both of them friends of mine: Noël Salter, the new Secretary of the Political Affairs Committee, and Uwe Kitzinger of the Secretariat of the Economic Affairs Committee. They in turn sought my advice, not officially and as a representative of the UK, but informally and confidentially as someone with expert knowledge of the situation in the Saar. The resultant Report, duly approved by the Assembly, recommended that the Saar should be internationalised, under a European Statute the draft of which was attached. It was later agreed by all the Governments concerned – some time after I had left Strasbourg – that this Statute should be placed before the Saarlanders in a referendum. It was rejected by a substantial majority, and France accepted the logic of the situation, which was to unite the Saar with the Federal Republic.

The domestic and social sides of life

Strasbourg was the only place in which I had a bachelor flat for a significant period. In Bonn I had shared with John Trout. In Washington, I was to be married soon after arrival. The flat was at La Meinau, a suburb on the road to Colmar. It was on the first floor of a white, square-looking house. It gave on to a tree-lined street on one side; and a little square on another. Both were very quiet; and there was a pleasant restaurant 50 metres away from my door. A *'bonne à tout faire',* Madame Maechlin, came in every weekday until after lunch. She looked after the flat, served my breakfast and lunch, and left something out for the evening meal. She was a good cook, so I was able to entertain in a modest but adequate way.

Strasbourg parties were varied, and good fun. Sometimes it was a matter of a group of friends meeting at a Restaurant in or near the city: it did not take long to find that Alsatian cuisine and wine are some of the best in France. Often there were drink parties or buffet suppers in friends' houses.

We were much given to 'expeditions' at weekends. Strasbourg is well placed. The Vosges and the Black Forest are close at hand. Paris, Switzerland, Baden-Würtemberg and Bavaria are not far. We went sight-seeing, walking, ski-ing, sailing – and wine-tasting! My new car was a great asset. Besides enabling me to organise expeditions, more surprisingly it helped in my continuing operatic education. I got to know Jani Strasser, the then Musical Director of Glyndebourne. He spent his winters working at the *Comédie de l'Est* at Strasbourg, and was well placed to visit continental opera houses and look for rising stars. I had a car and he didn't; so we made a natural team! He decided what we should hear, when and where; and then got excellent complimentary tickets. All I had to do was drive! Sometimes we were two in the party, sometimes four. In this way, we went in privileged conditions to Stuttgart, Karlsruhe, Freiburg, and on one occasion to La Scala at Milan. In summer, Jani and Irene Strasser also invited Maura and me to Glyndebourne, where we saw a lovely production of Rossini's *Le Comte Ory.*

I also struck gold, and furthered my education, in the wine department. Having tasted a nice Gewurtztraminer when lunching at Gérardmer one day, I noticed that the producer was Théo Faller, of the Clos des Capucins at Kaysersberg, and realised that we could call there on the way home. We did; were warmly welcomed to a tasting with Théo; and thus started a connection which was to last until his death. Only later did I learn that he was already the Vice-President of the Association des Viticulteurs d'Alsace: soon after, he became President! On one occasion when I was in his cellar, a bus-load of German tourists passed. One of them saw the Faller name; remembered knowing Théo when the latter was doing forced labour on a farm in Germany during the war; stopped the bus; and decanted all the passengers into the cellar, where there was a friendly re-union scene and a large-scale tasting. We all ended up singing popular German songs, with excellent resonance from the surrounding vats!

There was another occasion – though very different – when wine was also much in evidence. This was the wedding of Lucie Jehl, the charming local Secretary of the British Consulate-General. Lucie and I got on well, and she delighted me by having me as '*témoin*' at her wedding to a young Canadian. Her father was high up in the Strasbourg police: it was clear that no expense would be spared. After the ceremony, we all returned to Lucie's family home for a memorable celebration. It started around noon with champagne and *petits fours*. Then we sat down to a seven-course lunch. Each course was served twice, and with each course there was a different wine. There were also speeches. Nothing was hurried. At the end came coffee and liqueurs. After that, dancing began, with further refreshments served '*à volonté*'! As *témoin*, I could not be amongst the first to leave. When it was finally OK for me to do so, my watch showed 0200 hours! The bride and groom were still dancing. I marvelled at the stamina of the happy couple, and still more at that of their parents! Lucie and I were next to meet in Canada, about three years later.

At La Meinau, I was only a few hundred metres from the Polygone airfield, suitable for gliders and light planes only. My gliding activities therefore continued. And I also took a short conversion course – about 8 hours of dual – before obtaining my French pilot's licence, flying a Morane-Saulnier Stampe biplane (rather like the classic Tiger Moth). It authorised me to fly '*tous les types d'Avions de Tourisme*' (*Brevet d'aptitude… no. 33.643*, dated 18 November 1954). I did this because I felt such a licence might be of practical use one day, though in fact it never was. But my heart was always in the magic and romance of gliding, not in the mechanics of powered flight.

I had already done a little, gentle dinghy-sailing on Windermere, and was pleased to be asked by an English friend – Ian Dunlop – to have a go on Lake Constance: he gave me the impression that he was well experienced (which I was not). One April weekend we drove to Überlingen (on the north shore of the Lake), and hired a dinghy. It was fine, and there was a stiff breeze. We sped over the water. I was asked to get out our sandwiches; I was scrabbling in the bottom of the boat, when we heeled strongly; Ian said resignedly *'well I've let go of the tiller and the sheet';* and over we went. We clung to the boat and tried righting her: but this was difficult. When she was upside down, the heavy centre-board had fallen out. Twice we got the mast up: twice the wind blew us over again. We abandoned attempts to right the boat, as being exhausting and unlikely to succeed; and instead focused on survival until help came.

At first we thought we should be rescued soon; but after a while realised perhaps no-one had seen our accident. We were a kilometre from the nearest shore (on the Swiss side); the wind had whipped up quite a sea; and our hull was not visible to a chance lakeside observer. I suggested swimming ashore, only to learn that my friend could not swim: in those days life-jackets were not obligatory on hired craft and we had none. The water, fed by the melting snows of spring, was icy cold. Our teeth started chattering. Still no sign of help. It was so unpleasant that, after 45 minutes in the Lake, I began to think it might be less disagreeable to give up the fight; slide under the waves; and drown.

Just at that moment we saw a small motor-boat put out from the Swiss shore. There was one man in it. He reached us; we were pulled on board; and then our boat was towed to a jetty and we came ashore. We found that our rescuer was the engineer of a small electric power station on the Lakeside, which owned the jetty. We were take into the station's engine-room; told to strip; and stood in front of some kind of hot air blower until the warmth had come slowly back into our bodies. Later, as we ate cakes and drank cognac with the engineer's wife, we were introduced to the person who had really saved our lives: not the engineer, but his 3-year-old son! This little boy had seen us turn over; run to his father; and persuaded him to put to sea, even though at first we could not be seen. It was a close shave!

One last thing about Strasbourg sticks in my mind: for the only time in my life I was a member of a political debating club! Most of the junior Council of Europe officials had left University not long before, where many had belonged to such Clubs. I was invited to join seven other young men in forming one – which inevitably became known as *'Le Club des Huit'.* The other members included three Brits, Hugh Beesley, Uwe Kitzinger and

Noël Salter; two Germans, Per Fischer and Nicholas Sombart; Victor De Pange (French); and Rinaldo Petrignani (Italian). All were highly articulate. All went far in their careers later. We met about once a month, with one member invited to launch debate on a specific issue. Being required to explain and defend, before an intelligent and highly critical audience, the reasons for British policy towards European integration, was amongst the influences which led me to believe that it was wrong-headed!

CHAPTER 8

Washington and marriage (1955-58)

I HAVE ALREADY explained how, in 1955, the Foreign Office told me I was to move to Washington during the summer, and how that event led in May to my engagement to Maura. The Foreign Office also said I could not take more than a very short leave in the UK en route, because the Embassy needed me quickly. The leave was to start in early June. Maura was going home anyway at that time; and we arranged to stay with our two families. I assumed that, if I went to the Foreign Office at once, in the changed circumstances they would agree to an extension, enabling us to organise a proper wedding before taking up the new job. How wrong I was!

When I called on the Personnel Department, long faces were pulled. Much was made of the Washington Embassy's urgent need for re-inforcement. The Department did not have the nerve even to put to the Ambassador my request for an extension. I was asked why, on a recent 'post-preference form', I had told the Department I had no marital intentions. My explanation that it had been true at the time was treated as frivolous! This was very annoying. Plucking up my courage, I told the official concerned that, unless a leave extension was granted, or alternatively a promise was given in writing that the Foreign Office would pay for my travel home to be married as soon as the Ambassador would allow, I was not going to oblige! I would return a few hours later to hear the response. I went off gloomily: the Department had been categoric about non-extension, and it seemed highly unlikely they would contemplate my alternative suggestion, since there was a rule that one was entitled to home leave from posts like Washington only after two years' service!

On my return, all was sweetness and light. The Department <u>would</u> agree to my alternative; and set their agreement down in writing there and then! I was amazed, and asked how this could be reconciled with the two-year rule. Simple, they said. The files showed that, although I had been three years in Strasbourg, I had never officially claimed home leave. Gradually things became clear. I had taken leave in the UK more than once, but had always travelled by car, and had not thought about claiming mileage! So, officially, I had taken only 'local leave'. Since I had a balance of 'home leave', and since, because of the Foreign Office, it could not all be taken *en route* for Washington, it followed that I was entitled to a free journey home from the moment of arrival in the United States. From the Department's viewpoint, therefore, I could return and get married as soon as the Ambassador would spare me. On that basis I duly set off at the end of June for New York from Southampton, in RMS *Queen Mary*, taking my new, Ford Zephyr Convertible with me; landed in the New World on 5 July 1955; and went on to Washington. (Maura returned to Strasbourg to serve out her last few weeks with the Council of Europe.)

On reaching 'the Nation's Capital', I was taken to see my Ambassador – at that time Sir Roger Makins, who later became Lord Sherfield – and a conversation ensued which was very reminiscent of one in Berlin six years earlier. After welcoming me in a friendly way, the Ambassador enquired where I hoped to live. That was the cue to explain that I should be looking initially for a bachelor pad, to tide me over till my wedding; and to ask how soon I could be spared to return for the ceremony.

This was the first Roger had heard of the whole idea, and he naturally asked why on earth I had not got married before coming over. My report of the discussion with the Personnel Department caused an explosion. *'Blithering idiots'* he said, or something very like it. Of course he needed re-inforcement; but, if the FO had asked about an extension, he would have agreed at once. As things were: *'You'll think of nothing else until you're married, so fix the wedding for the earliest convenient date, and I'll give you leave!'*

The way was thus clear for fixing the date, and 16 November was chosen. My short summer leave in Britain had been spent partly at Ackenthwaite, and partly at Maura's home, Rose Garden Cottage at Gerrards Cross. Whilst there, we had agreed that the Parish Church was rather large and cold for anything but a big society wedding, and that St James's Church at Fulmer would be far nicer. The Vicar, Rex Lloyd, was at first allergic to marrying in his Church a couple who had no steady connection with Fulmer. But, when we told him that Maura would like first to confirmed there, he agreed. The confirmation took place after I had left for Washington, and my mother represented me.

The work menu

The Washington Embassy was very impressive. The location was striking: a large house standing in a big garden, near the top of Massachussetts Avenue, a beautiful, leafy and airy part of the City, near St Alban's Cathedral. The house itself was architecturally fine, built by Lutyens between the Wars, and comprised the Residence behind and the Chancery in front. The staff was enormous, some hundreds of people, if one includes the Military Missions: this reflected the fact that, even ten years after the Second World War, the British Establishment still saw the UK as a World Power and thought of the Special Relationship which Roosevelt and Churchill had built up in the war as being as strong as ever – an illusion which the Suez operation was soon to expose. For the same reason, staff quality was high. Once again, as in Bonn, I had a chain of command above me in which all the links were strong. Although I had moved up to Second Secretary in 1953 – and was to attain the rank of First Secretary whilst in Washington, I was still near the bottom rung.

In fact, the Embassy was a sort of mini-FO. Each of the Foreign Office Departments, whether geographical or horizontal, had one or more connected Officers in the Embassy, who were expected to keep in close touch with the development of American thinking on everything in their sector. By watching the flow of telegrams between the Embassy and the FO, one could follow world affairs from a very privileged position.

For most of the three years I was there, my tasks were twofold: I was in the Section which reported to the Ambassador, and to the American Department of the Foreign Office, about United States domestic politics; and I was Desk Officer for one or more geographic areas.

My work on the domestic front was fascinating. We had a set-up which sifted not only the newspapers and periodicals from Washington and New York, but also a good selection from right across the nation. I attended the regular press conferences at the White House and the State Department, where Dwight Eisenhower (Ike) and John Foster Dulles were the protagonists. I was encouraged to spend as much time as possible on Capitol Hill, listening to debates in Senate and House, and in Committees of both; talking to Senators, Congressmen and their respective aides; and also attending key public proceedings of the Supreme Court.

There was an extra-ordinary difference in style between Ike and his Secretary of State at press conferences. Ike would start a sentence; break it off part way through and start another; inject long parentheses on different subjects; and often not complete a sentence at all. Notwithstanding all these deviations of syntax, the intelligent listener usually felt that he or she knew exactly what Ike was driving at. The problem was for note-takers like me, who would start trying to distil a logical report out of what was said, and then realise that it was, if taken literally, absolute nonsense! Dulles was the exact opposite. A distinguished lawyer, he was the most precise and accurate speaker I ever heard. He would speak slowly but without notes, and never hesitate. The structure, logic and syntax of everything he said was faultless. Whether or not you agreed with the substance, you could not but admire Dulles's mastery of thought and expression.

As to the subjects of my study, Washington is always bubbling with stories, and I could not recall all the main themes of our three years of reporting. Suffice it perhaps to say that the period saw the high point of the segregation argument, with the start of implementation of the Supreme Court's historic ruling that *'separate but equal'* schooling arrangements for blacks and whites were un-constitutional, endless debates and filibusters in Congress on the issue, and the calling out of the National Guard on several occasions to keep order in the Southern States; and that McCarthy-ism, though by now on the wane, was still a major cause of controversy. Foreign affairs issues which excited Washington included the ongoing Korean War; in 1956 the Franco-British military intervention in Egypt to *'protect'* the Suez Canal, and the Soviet repression of the Hungarian up-rising; in 1957 the Soviet Union taking a lead over the United States in space by launching the first *'Sputnik'*; and the ongoing endeavours of the French to hold down the situation in Indo-China.

McCarthy-ism gave rise to a diplomatic incident worth recalling. Our Consul-General in San Francisco was a distinguished-looking, larger-than-life, Irishman, Sir Robert Hadow (known to colleagues as 'Shadow'). He found himself at a large lunch or dinner party in California, seated next to a strong McCarthy-ite, Senator Malone of Nevada. The latter, in a speech, made some disobliging remarks about the Commonwealth. The Consul-General rose to his full height of nearly two metres and said: *'if you don't take that back, I'll biff you on the nose!'*. The Senator refused to retract and was duly biffed. This was instantly red-hot news, nation-wide, on radio, TV and in the press.

The Foreign Office took fright. The Embassy was told to report full details and advise how to handle Sir Robert. They needn't have worried. The general line of media comment was that Malone had got what was coming to him: it was only a pity it had taken a Brit to meet out justice! The incident figured as *'picture of the week'* in Life Magazine. Sir Robert was, I believe, the only Brit to be awarded this honour twice, as some time before, he had figured in a picture taken at a major social event of the 'Daughters of the American Revolution' in San Francisco.

Now for a few words about my other task, as Embassy Desk Officer for certain geographic areas. One was the Far East and South-East Asia. I cannot

Portrait of the author, Washington, 1955.

say this interested me much, because (apart from Korea) it was not an area where Britain was likely to play an active role.

Another was Antarctica, which had much more appeal. At that time a number of nations had, over the preceding century or so, laid claim to 'cake-slices' of Antarctica principally on the grounds that the nation concerned was sovereign over the nearest land area to the north: Britain was one of them. Most other nations challenged these claims, whether explicitly or tacitly. Whilst I was in Washington the idea emerged of suspending all the claims, and devising a system of international management of the world's last uninhabited continent for the benefit of mankind as a whole. I was attracted by this attempt to escape from theoretical, prestige arguments about sovereignty; and try and perceive and advance the common good. I did my modest best – as a junior official – to encourage the idea in my reporting to the Foreign Office, and in my interpretation of their views to the Americans and other Embassies involved. I was delighted when, after we left America, the Antarctic Treaty was signed in Washington (on 1 December 1959) by twelve States,

Portrait of Maura Audland, Washington, 1955.

including all those with territorial claims. Each subsequently ratified: and the Treaty has worked well to this day.

In closing these remarks about my work, I should mention that, after I had been in Washington for a while, Sir Roger Makins was replaced as Ambassador by Sir Harold Caccia. I often wondered whether the latter recalled the advice he had given me, in 1948, to go to University before seeking to enter the FO, and had registered my non-compliance! My guess is that he had not, but I did not ask, and he never mentioned the matter!

Social life

On arrival in Washington, I was more than fortunate about finding somewhere to live. John and Marquita Wraight, Embassy colleagues, were due for home leave about the time I arrived, and kindly offered me the use of their flat in the Westchester Apartments, near the Cathedral. I settled in happily, and began to adapt to the American way of life; explore Washington and its surroundings; and make friends, both American and diplomatic.

Our first home, in Washington – 5171 Manning Place – 1956.

After the wedding arrangements had been made, my next task was to find a dwelling for Maura. I was determined our first home would be a nice one, a house rather than a flat, and have some kind of a garden. Here too, my luck held. I was able to arrange the lease of a colonial style white-painted house at 5171, Manning Place, a delightful quiet street between Spring Valley and the Potomac, near the Maryland State line.

The day before the wedding, I flew home by Boeing 'Double-Bubble' airliner. In those days air-travel was still rare for Europeans, so it was exciting. It was a lengthy flight, since jets had not yet entered airline service, and the trans-Atlantic routes were operated by lumbering, traditional, four-engined, piston-driven aircraft. In fact, sea-crossings were still the general rule for Embassy staff; however it had been agreed, since the Ambassador wanted my leave kept as short as reasonably possible, that I should fly home but bring Maura back by sea. There was to be just one week for the honeymoon.

The wedding was traditional. Formal dress was standard; and Maura was in white with a white bouquet. Fulmer Church is a charming, sixteenth century, Elizabethan structure, and quite small. So, although the number of guests was limited, they filled the nave. Afterwards, there was a cheerful reception at the Ethorpe Hotel in Gerrards Cross. Then Maura and I were driven off to spend our first night together at Brown's Hotel in London, before leaving next morning by train for our Padstow honeymoon. Maura's family had always loved sea-side holidays: no doubt that was why she chose Padstow. In mid-November, we had sun and blue sea. We spent our time walking and talking. Afterwards we always remembered how, over breakfast, conversation was often interrupted by a large gull, which tapped the window imperiously with its beak in hope of tit-bits.

For the return journey we travelled from Southampton on RMS *Queen Mary*. We found that the others on board included Peter and Pat Male, whom I had known well in Bonn; their four children; and their English Nanny. I had thought the sea-trip would be an extension of our honeymoon; but it turned out otherwise. Maura is a bad sailor, and we had force 8 to 10 gales for the whole five days of the journey. The stabilisation of ships was in its infancy, and the great liner rolled and pitched violently, without ceasing. Once out of the Channel, Maura virtually never left the cabin, and hardly ate anything. Pat Male and the Nanny were in similar condition. So Peter and I took over the children! We were also among the very small number of passengers who ate regular meals; and Maura recalls that I tactlessly gave her daily details of the excellent cuisine! She was mightily relieved when the skyscrapers of Manhattan came into view on 30 November.

We were to spend a night in New York with Whitney Debevoise, who had meanwhile returned from Bonn to his Wall Street legal practice, and his vivacious wife Babs, in their splendid apartment on Fifth Avenue, overlooking Central Park. Earlier in the year I had spent a weekend with them on Long Island. Now, Babs had decided to celebrate our arrival with a dinner party to which she invited a group of friends, some very distinguished.

This was a baptism of fire for Maura, being her first experience of the way Americans traditionally treat a 'bride'. (In the USA, this word is taken to mean any young lady in the first year of marriage.) The bride is always treated as the senior lady present, and seated on the immediate right of the host, no matter what the importance or seniority of the other guests. It is a charming and romantic habit, but gives a young beneficiary anxious moments. The anxiety would have been enhanced for Maura by the fact that, after five days of gales, she still felt as though the floor was moving under her feet!

Next day we travelled on to Washington by train. We were met at the Union Station, and driven to the house I had chosen. I carried Maura over the threshold, wondering whether she would approve my choice?

Fortunately she did. And we stayed in 5171 Manning Place until the lease fell in.

In those days, and for long afterwards, women's lib was not even a twinkle in the eye. The Foreign Office had a regulation which more or less ruled out a British Diplomat's wife having any paid employment while with her husband on a foreign posting. Indeed, the Office regarded a diplomatic couple as constituting a husband and wife team, though wives were not paid anything for their part in the operation! Maura had fully understood and accepted this before we got married. So now she adapted to being a housewife, and to diplomatic entertaining. Of course, a Second Secretary is not expected to entertain in a big way. It was more a question, at that stage in one's career, of gaining experience. Certainly we received far more hospitality than we gave. But we did our bit.

Maura spent much time in the house, often by herself. On her first evening, after dark, but before my return from the Embassy, the bell rang and she opened the door. All she could see was a pair of very white eyes staring at her, and a set of white teeth. Then a deep voice said: *'Aa'm Washin'ton ma'am: aa've come for de leopard-skin'*. Before she really knew what was going on, the owner of the voice, a large black man, had moved into the house and disappeared into the cellar. He re-emerged with a bundle, and departed. It later transpired that the owner of our house had remembered leaving a leopard-skin in a cupboard; given instructions to his retainer to collect it; but forgotten to warn us!

It was in Washington that we first became accustomed to TV. Television had been, until then, an expensive luxury in Europe. In the United States it was already the norm, though still in black and white. We had a set, and still recall watching the original broadcasts of such old faithfuls as 'Sergeant Bilko' and 'Bewitched'. We continued with B/W television when we returned to the UK. But the two postings which followed (Brussels and Buenos Aires, covering the period 1961-67) were 'TV-free'. After that, TV entered our lives for good.

There were many nice people in the Embassy. My work also brought me into contact with a wide range of Americans, many of whom joined our large circle of friends.

Travel in the USA

During our time in Washington, Maura and I seized every opportunity to move round and learn about this vast and varied country, mainly by car but sometimes by air. The excellent roads, empty by comparison with Europe, meant that long distances could be covered fast and in comfort. Maryland, Virginia, West Virginia, Pennsylvania, Delaware, New Jersey and New York City could be explored at weekends.

We also had good holidays. Both in the Foreign Office (when serving in normal overseas posts), and later in the European Community, we were entitled to six weeks leave a year. Often, superiors urged renunciation of part of one's entitlement due to pressure of work. Many colleagues succumbed, and claimed virtue for the renunciation. This seemed foolish. Private life was essential for us, and in short supply when actually at post; so getting time away from the office was vital. Pressure of work is often the result of bad organisation, and in any case usually exaggerated. Nobody is indispensable. When I returned to work after an absence, even a long one, I never found the situation desperate. So I always insisted on my leave, and later pressed my juniors to take theirs too. My boast is that, at the end of 38 years of service to the British Government and the European Commission, I had never lost a day of my entitlement.

From the start we decided that, since we might never live in the States again, we would use all our leave there, and not return to Europe until the end of our posting. On our first motoring tour, in the spring of 1956, we went south, exploring the Carolinas, Georgia, Alabama, the Great Smoky Mountains and the Blue Ridge. That summer, we motored northwards, to Niagara and the Great Lakes, following the St Lawrence River to Quebec, and returning via Maine and New England. Thanks to friends in the Canadian Embassy in Washington, we were given a day's tour of the construction works for the St Lawrence Seaway. The highlights in New England were the White Mountains, Sturbridge Village (a replica of an eighteenth century village), and lovely Nantucket Island, once a Headquarters of the whaling industry (where streets are cobbled and bicycles are the normal means of transport).

But our greatest ambition – as for most of our British colleagues – was to drive to the Pacific and back. We saved up leave; got approval, well in advance, for an absence of six weeks during the summer of 1957; and planned our journey accordingly. And then, at a late stage, it was announced that HM The Queen was to visit Washington and our leave was cut to only a month. Logically we should have reduced our itinerary in proportion; but of course we didn't. We feared we might never get across the States again. So we squashed everything into the time available. In what the Americans called our 'little car' – our ivory-coloured Convertible – we covered around 8,000 miles on a hot, tiring, but fascinating and unforgettable journey: it took us out through Chicago, Wisconsin, Minnesota, the Dakotas and Yellowstone; down the Snake and Columbia Rivers to the Oregon and Californian coasts; and then back through the Mojave Desert, the Grand Canyon, Mesa Verde, Colorado, the Great Plains, St Louis and Cincinnati. (In the desert, the mid-day heat was so fierce that we rose every day before daybreak, and covered all the mileage before lunch.) We returned to Washington exhausted but spiritually enriched.

Approaching the Grand Canyon, Maura fell foul of a streptococcal bug. At Billings, a medium-sized town, we looked for a doctor, and were not encouraged by the reply: *'They're mostly horse-doctors round here'.* We did eventually find one who wasn't, but he had been thrown off a horse a few days before, and was more interested in his own symptoms than other people's! The treatment prescribed was not a success; sadly, while I descended the canyon and explored its rim, Maura stayed abed.

Our last major trip, as it turned out, took us for two weeks, in March 1958, to the Deep South. This time we travelled partly by plane, partly by Greyhound bus, and partly by rented car. We loved Natchez (Mississippi), where we visited magnificent plantation houses, and heard moving negro spirituals. The old French quarter at New Orleans was a disappointment, very down at heel. In Florida, we stayed at Clearwater Beach, an unspoilt and lovely island; and got to see the Everglades and the Cypress Gardens, with its stunning water-ski show.

Something which enormously impressed, as we travelled through the United States, was the variety, scale and number of the National Parks. Europeans forget that it was the United States which had the imagination and courage to invent the whole concept of national parks, and then to give it flesh and blood; and they did this in the middle of the nineteenth century, long before the National Trust was invented in Britain, and when their own vast country was still in a process of consolidation. The fact that their initiative has since been copied throughout both Europe and the Russian Federation, is a great tribute to its inventors. During our residence in Washington, and on subsequent visits to the United States, we count ourselves fortunate in having seen all but one of the twelve major National Parks in the country.

Occasionally, there would also be travel on official business. The Embassy used to receive many requests for British speakers. As a junior official I was not inflicted on top level audiences; but I got used to addressing Rotary Clubs, Round Tables and so forth all over the place.

Usually, the topics requested were either concerned with the British domestic scene, or with British foreign policy: in my case the latter. The mid-1950s were, in terms of British policy towards the former Empire, an in-between period. In the late 1940s the post-war Labour Government had, by its decision to withdraw from India, started a process of de-colonisation. But then the process, instead of accelerating, was slowed down. It would take a historian to explain the reasons. I merely record what happened. And it was something which puzzled, and indeed irritated Americans. India's independence had led them to think that their former mother country had realised the error of its Imperial past; and they had applauded this. So now they were perplexed by what appeared to them as a reversion to bad habits! As a result I was constantly being asked to explain to varied, often critical, audiences why Britain was fighting 'colonial' wars with the indigenous peoples to defend its continued rule over countries like Malaya, North Borneo, Kenya and Cyprus. One had to marshal the arguments carefully, to have any hope of getting people to understand. The fact that my personal disposition was to favour a faster de-colonisation made it all the tougher! But duty is duty, and I did my best.

Always, however, I was on the look-out for an invitation to speak about the broad sweep of British foreign policy. In my two previous Foreign Office postings, I had got used to reflecting on big issues – such as the Cold War, Germany, and the future of Europe – and I found the smaller themes limiting! One day, my chance came. Bob Jones University [BJU] in Greenville, South Carolina, had decided to hold a 'World Information Day', to be attended by their entire 3,000 strong student body, and had invited six organisations to send speakers, including our Embassy. Each speaker was allotted an hour to talk and answer questions, and each was free to chose his own theme. I offered my favoured subject, which was accepted with alacrity. This was my big moment. Much time and effort was spent preparing a solid presentation.

And then, the very day before I was to fly to Greenville, the British and French launched their ill-starred Suez operation! I personally felt the whole thing was a great mistake. Only later did I learn that my brother Michael, still in the Army, was actually in charge of the Operations Room in Cyprus, which ran the British contribution to the invasion of Egypt. He could not see any game-plan for what would happen there if our operation was successful. He felt that Britain had been fooled into the war by a sick Prime Minister. The US Administration and most of the media were totally opposed and very angry! It was no surprise when the University telephoned to say they would now expect me to talk about Suez! For good measure they added that the other speakers included diplomats from the United Arab Republic (as Egypt was then called) and Israel, and a representative of the United States Information Services [USIS]! I buckled to; read the flood of guidance and information telegrams pouring in and out; talked to Embassy colleagues concerned; and prepared for battle! Then I flew to Greenville.

When the invitation to speak arrived I had known little of BJU. My enquiries revealed that it was a Christian fundamentalist establishment at the heart of the 'Bible Belt'; and that the Reverend Ian Paisley had obtained his Doctorate of Divinity there! On the second leg of the southbound flight, the Captain of our DC3 announced that he would be happy to receive a visit in the cockpit from any passenger. My modest flying experience encouraged me to take up the offer, and I spent most of the flight with the Captain. When he politely enquired about my business, I explained about the BJU event and expressed concern about a possibly hostile audience. He told me not to worry. The students would be polite. He concluded with the remark: *'If you have any trouble, just tell them that Captain Jones of Allegheny Airways is mighty surprised at them.'*!

My next impression of BJU came when, at about midnight of a pitch-dark night, I stepped onto the tarmac at Greenville, a place I had never visited. A microphone was pushed at me, and someone said: *'Welcome to Greenville, South Carolina, Mr Audland. I'm reporting for the BJU Radio Station. What do you think of our great City?'* I mumbled something about being delighted to be there. Then, when the mike was switched off, I asked for a bit of briefing about the University in return. In reply, the reporter pressed into my hand a copy of that day's issue of the campus newspaper, a thickish tabloid, adding that I would be given a whistle-stop tour of the campus next morning, before 'World Information Day' began.

The newspaper, read over breakfast, gave me a good first feel for the atmosphere. There was a strong bible-punching flavour to many articles. One, in particular, caught my attention. It was a highly favourable review of the first night of a new production of *Hamlet* in the University's Theatre *'with Dr Bob Jones Junior, as usual, in the title role'*. I already knew the latter had taken over as Principal of the University some time before, succeeding the founder, Dr Bob Jones Senior.

The Campus tour was both instructive and impressive. Plainly there was money in the Bible Belt to support a fundamentalist University in style. A large number of camels were wandering free, eating the grass. These turned out to be part of the 'cast' for a new film on Barabbas being made by the Cinematographic Department. The University was strong on drama. They also had a very large theatre, with a full revolving stage, bought off some closing Broadway establishment, which had of course been the venue for *Hamlet*, and was soon to accommodate 'World Information Day'. Thence we moved on for a brisk look at the Picture Gallery. I found that most Old Masters were represented in the Collection, which would have done credit to a City the size of Philadelphia!

Short though my tour had been, it had greatly helped prepare me for 'World Information Day', for which the student body had by now assembled in the Theatre. The six speakers sat in the front row. Dr Bob Jones Junior gave an introductory talk, full of biblical quotations. Then each speaker in turn mounted the platform for his appointed hour: three before the short lunch-break, and the rest after. It was to be a real endurance test for the audience! I do not recall the order of speakers, though I think I came after the Arab and the Israeli. But I do recall the flavour of the talks by me and by the representative of the USIS. I launched off by simply telling the audience of my conversation with Captain Jones: it amused them; they behaved politely; and the questions, though critical, were advanced in a friendly way.

My USIS friend had less luck. His chosen theme – 'The importance of telling the truth' – was well attuned to the mind-set of his audience: perhaps too well attuned. He had been going for quarter of an hour, and was well into his theme, when a small, fragile-looking, elderly gentleman climbed on to the stage, and politely asked if he might interject a few comments. I was surprised when this interruption was taken as a matter of course; but somebody whispered that the interrupter was Dr Bob Jones Senior! The latter began by saying he had been very impressed by the *'mighty fine sentiments'* just expressed, and wished briefly to elaborate on them. He then proceeded to deliver what amounted to a sermon. It lasted for 15 minutes, and moved steadily away from the speaker's train of argument. Suddenly, when it had got very far away indeed, Dr Bob Senior turned to the speaker; said *'do please carry on'*; and quietly walked off stage. The poor speaker was completely non-plussed; struggled for a while without success to get back into his swing; and then abandoned his talk prematurely. I felt very sorry for him; but, for the students, this was clearly par for the course! I had learned some tough lessons about public speaking, which proved valuable in later life!

Early in 1958, the Foreign Office Personnel Department had one of those sudden changes of heart for which it is renowned. In the previous year our lease on the Manning Place house had come to an end; I had asked whether I could expect to be at least another year in the USA and been told yes; and we had rented another house at No. 4901 Chesapeake Street. The owner had been reluctant to sign a lease with a classic 'diplomatic clause', namely a provision for termination without penalty in the event of a new posting; but had agreed to do so when told of the correspondence with London. A few weeks after moving in, I was now obliged to give notice! It was a pity, because we were happy in the house.

Impressions on leaving

What were our overall impressions after a three-year stint in the United States? It had been mind-expanding on many counts. After a life so far spent in European or Middle-Eastern scale countries, one found oneself in one with a truly continental dimension. The United States was not only the world's leading power, in economic, military and political terms. It was also – despite the temporary setback of Sputnik – a power which would soon take over leadership in space. Compared with Europe, America was incomparably wealthier: the gap was greater then than now. One was struck by the self-confidence of the people: this contrasted with the post-war weariness, and uncertainty about its post-imperial role, which gripped Britain. An American never asks whether something <u>can</u> be done, only whether it <u>needs</u> to be.

For upwards of a century before we went to Washington, the Americans and their Canadian neighbours had been debating whether a St Lawrence Seaway was needed. About the time of our arrival they decided to go ahead. It was an immense task, involving damming and diverting the great river, over a distance of 200 miles and through rocky terrain; creating a channel able to handle large ocean-going ships; and moving many villages for the purpose. Vast machines had to be custom-built: huge resources to be mobilised. Yet, during our short time in Washington, the whole job was virtually completed. (Only a few years later, President Kennedy was to decide that the United States should put a man on the moon, and set a time-scale of ten years, which the country duly respected.) This go-getting attitude was deeply impressive. One came to understand something Europeans easily forget: the main constraints on human achievement are scale of ambition and determination.

Another principal impression of Americans was the warmth of their hospitality. You meet someone casually at a Washington reception; you find they come from some very distant State, like New Mexico or North Dakota; they tell you to look them up if you ever get there; and it's for real. If you take them at their word, and simply turn up, you may be sure of being greeted like a long-lost friend, and treated accordingly.

It was not until we had left the United States that we realised how, despite all there was to enjoy and admire, the Americans largely lack something imbued in all the older civilisations, a deep sense for tradition and cultural heritage. In Europe, for example, you cannot move more than a few kilometres without seeing some historic monument or building, evocative of the past, which is often a thing of beauty besides. In the United States, by contrast, historical and cultural development is learnt, rather than being absorbed from the stones. There are, of course, some historic monuments, including the fine buildings on Washington's Capitol Hill, George Washington's home at Mount Vernon, Jefferson's at Monticello, Williamsburg, the whaling settlements on Nantucket Island, and the Catholic Mission Churches of California. But they are infinitely rarer, and never more than four centuries old. Relics of the earlier American Indian civilisations do exist, as in Mesa Verde National Park: but they are few in number and remote of access. A European in America misses that sense of ancient cultural heritage we are all brought up to feel (some of course more than others). But it is a European characteristic which carries with it one obvious disadvantage: Europeans are inclined to live in the past, while Americans live much more in the future, a future which they feel more confident to shape.

These were all valuable lessons to learn. We counted ourselves fortunate to have had three years in the United States. A quarter of a century later, we were determined to give our children at least a taste of the New World, so we took them on two camper holidays there, at an impressionable age: it was a delight to see their minds expanding, just as ours had done. In addition, my whole professional career gave me opportunities for brief visits to the country, and I never passed them up. The United States is a great country. Now, however, we were to leave all that behind. Soon, we were on RMS *Queen Elizabeth*, sailing for Southampton.

CHAPTER 9

The Foreign Office: African Department (1958-61)

O N REACHING ENGLAND, Maura and I stayed for a while with her mother in Gerrards Cross, and looked for somewhere to live. Soon we rented a small but comfortable maisonette – Ferndown Cottage. It was an adapted part of the servants' quarters of Fulmer House, a fine country house then owned by the Bill Wrightons. Two of our windows looked out on their great cedar tree, and beyond it over the park. The other windows overlooked the former coach-yard, which now made a small garden for us.

Until 1960 I was a member of the Foreign Office African Department. This was the only period of my professional life when I was to serve in what was then the standard kind of FO Department – a Unit responsible for a particular geographical area. It was organised on classic lines, with a Counsellor as Head of Department, a senior First Secretary as Assistant (or number two), and a number of more junior officials as Desk Officers, each one handling a defined group of countries. My own Desk covered the Horn of Africa: in those days this meant the Ethiopia of Emperor Haile Selassie, which included Eritrea; Somalia, a former Italian Colony then under UN Administration; Djibouti, a French Colony; and British Somaliland, still a British Colony. The last-named was of course administered by the Colonial Office: my responsibilities in respect of it consisted in advising the other Government Department on relevant international affairs.

In those days there were still many British Colonies in Africa. The countries now known as Kenya, Tanzania, Uganda and Zimbabwe were amongst them. Once again I found the British Establishment living in the past. Having moved out of the Indian sub-continent and the Suez Canal Zone, the Armed Services wanted to set up a new major Base east of Suez. Their preference was Kenya. When our Department advised that, on current political trends, all the countries mentioned above were likely to be independent fairly soon, the Ministry of Defence clearly thought we were talking nonsense. Fortunately, the debate kept going for years, and in the end the military came to accept the inevitable before untold millions had been spent on the Base!

In those days, air travel was still seen as expensive, and ordinary Desk Officers in African Department never got a chance to visit their respective bailiwicks. Nevertheless I enjoyed learning about a completely different part of the world.

One of the tasks of a Desk Officer is to look after dignitaries from the countries in one's area when they come to the United Kingdom on official visits. There is always pressure from the national authorities for the dignitary to meet HM The Queen, another member of the Royal Family, the Prime Minister, and/or other Ministers. One tries to help. The then Prime Minister, Harold Macmillan, was co-operative. Moreover, he was amusing and witty, so his guests could expect to leave No 10 Downing Street happy.

We sent him a number of dignitaries from Africa; and as a result heard some amusing stories about the Prime Minister. He was an excellent *raconteur*. On one occasion a visitor – I cannot recall who – asked him to explain a famous case then going through the Courts. It had to do with a certain Dr John Bodkin Adams, a General Practitioner in Eastbourne accused of murder. The substance of the case was that he seemed to specialise in attracting old ladies to become his patients; encouraging them to review their wills so as to include a legacy to their faithful medical adviser; and then *'helping them into the next world'* by the administration of very small doses of poison over a long period. (He was in the end found guilty.) Macmillan, after regaling his guest with a summary of the facts, added the following comment: *'The trouble with that fella was – what started as a kindness became a habit'*.

In African Department I again benefited from a solid chain of command: Adam Watson was the Head of Department; and Howard Smith the Assistant. As a team, they complemented each other. Adam was a quick thinker, and strong on imagination and initiative. In later years he was to write books and plays. He went on to become Ambassador in various African posts; retire early; work in industry for a while; and then lead a more academic life. Howard worked well with Adam, but was by nature more cautious; insisted on careful preparation of submissions; and was a master of drafting and presentation. He went on to be Deputy Secretary at the Cabinet Office, and then Ambassador in Moscow.

In summer 1959, I fell victim to infectious hepatitis, almost certainly contracted by drinking from an African Department tea-cup, as a colleague had succumbed a little before. The early stages are tedious, inflicting on the patient a hideous yellow complexion and much vomiting; but in my case diagnosis was immediate, and things were soon under control. After that I actually enjoyed the disease. Because of a relapse, it kept me off work for three whole months. For most of the recovery period, one had to keep quietly in bed. I used this unaccustomed free time to watch the whole of a Rod Laver Wimbledon; and to read a lot of serious literature. My reading included Thomas Mann's *Zauberberg*, in German. When later the family spent many holidays in Davos, where the *Zauberberg* story unfolds, I often came back to it. In the recuperation phase, Maura and I went off for a delightful visit to the Ligurian Coast. There was, however, a longer term disadvantage. It was several months before I could drink so much as a beer, or a glass of wine; white liqueurs took some years; and brandy was permanently off limits!

Then it was time to resume the African Department rhythm. Life went on without major change until Rupert was born, on 8 July, 1960, at the Royal Canadian Memorial Hospital, in the grounds of Cliveden. We were delighted to have started a family: and all the more because we had had to wait nearly five years. There had been two miscarriages in Washington. There was to be another, later, in Buenos Aires. Who knows whether, if all had been straightforward, we might have ended with the six children of which we had hopefully talked (or at least I had) when we were first married!

Late that summer, I was transferred, within the FO, from African Department to European Economic Organisations Department: a move which was to be another career turning-point.

CHAPTER 10

The Heath Negotiations for Accession to the European Communities (1961-63)

T HE EUROPEAN Economic Organisations Department (EEOD) was the Foreign Office Unit handling Britain's relations with the European Communities – and with other European Organisations also. My move into it coincided with a sea-change in attitude by the Whitehall Establishment, which was to lead to an application by the Conservative Government of Harold Macmillan for British membership of the three European Communities, and to the long negotiations with their Six Member States, ending with the breakdown occasioned by De Gaulle's veto in January, 1963. This chapter deals with my involvement, from start to finish, in this important process. If the style is serious, so also is the subject.

Five years had passed since my involvement in European affairs at Strasbourg. It is necessary to recall, briefly, the principal, intervening events in the move towards greater European unity. The Six had recovered, with extra-ordinary rapidity, from the shock of the French National Assembly's rejection of the EDC and EPC. In June 1955, meeting in Messina, their Heads of Government had agreed to begin a new process of integration, leading, in January, 1958, to the entry into force of the Treaties establishing both the European Economic Community [EEC] and the European Atomic Energy Community [the EAEC or Euratom].

As with the ECSC, the British were invited to join the negotiations. Anthony Eden's Government agreed to attend, but within months withdrew, when it was seen the Six were again committed to important elements of supra-nationality. They simultaneously made clear the British establishment's strongly held belief that the negotiations were doomed to failure; that no Treaties would emerge; that if unexpectedly they did, they would not be ratified; and that, if ratified, they would not work! On all counts they were proved wrong. No sooner was this clear, than they began to reflect on a situation in which the UK found itself excluded, by its own actions, from what was to become the only European organisation with real clout.

Their first reaction was to attempt creation of a wider Free Trade Area, of which the Communities would be just a part [the Maudling proposals]; but this got nowhere. Next, they decided to create, with six other non Community countries, the European Free Trade Association [EFTA], born in May 1960. By now, however, Harold Macmillan, who had replaced Eden as Prime Minister after the Suez fiasco, was already having serious doubts about the value of his brain-child, and reflecting seriously about seeking to join the Communities. In July, 1960, the Cabinet accepted the broad thrust of his thinking; and Macmillan re-shaped his Government. Alec [Lord] Home became Foreign Secretary; Ted Heath became Lord Privy Seal and was, as a Cabinet Minister, given responsibility within the Foreign Office for all questions of European Unity; Duncan Sandys became Secretary of State for Commonwealth Relations; and Christopher Soames became Minister for Agriculture, Fisheries and Food [MAFF]. All these men held pro-European views. Macmillan had also arranged the appointment of Frank Lee, another known pro-European, as Joint Permanent Secretary of the Treasury, a key post in Whitehall. The scene was set.

A few words about other world events. Three years after Stalin's death, Kruschew had felt strong enough, in 1956, to denounce his unbelievably evil deeds to the Central Committee of the Soviet Communist Party. The Soviet conspiracy of secrecy was ended. In the same year, however, uprisings in Poland and Hungary had been ruthlessly crushed. Kruschew, after a honeymoon period, had fallen out with Mao Tse Tung in China. De Gaulle had been elected President of France; and both that country and China had exploded atom bombs. The world was uneasy.

That was the context when I joined the EEOD. It was a small Department. Its Head was Ken Gallagher – hard-working but perhaps uninspired. Its human dynamo, at desk officer level, was John Robinson. Above Ken, there were two Deputy Under-Secretaries: Roddie Barclay, responsible for 'economic' affairs, and Evelyn Shuckburgh, responsible for European unity at the 'political' level. Above them again was Ted Heath, with his Private Secretary, Roger Lavelle from the Treasury. With the exception of Ken, all these men were of the highest calibre. Once again, I was surrounded by top quality operators.

In his brilliant book *This Blessed Plot* – about Britain and Europe from Churchill to Blair[1] – the late Hugo Young, writing in 1998, rightly devoted a whole chapter to John Robinson, and his personal contribution to British policy in Europe over a period of 15 years. I offered some thoughts to Hugo and believe the picture he paints of John is entirely fair. Many people were upset by the latter's dryness and very direct speech. Fortunately, since we were destined to be joint linchpins of the Heath negotiations, and to sit side by side for the next two and a half years, this was not my case. From start to finish, we saw every issue in the same way. We always knew what the other was thinking, and would always cover for each other. There was a quite remarkable – and most enjoyable – symbiosis.

From the moment I joined the Department, the tempo steadily increased. The pressures were intense. The Heath negotiations, their run-up, and their follow-up, were to occupy two and a half years of my life. The first year or so was spent in the Foreign Office: then, towards the end of 1961, John and I moved to Brussels.

I cannot, in the compass of this chapter, set out masses of facts. I shall concentrate instead on the political climate, and on the way things were done. Plenty of supporting data may be found in a contemporary and authoritative source. After the negotiations broke down, the British Delegation wrote, for the Foreign Office, a full Narrative Report of the negotiations, of over 200,000 words. It was covered by a substantial commentary, drawing conclusions, both strategic and tactical. This document[2] – from now on called 'the Narrative Report' – may be studied in the Public Records Office. Its structure was designed by John and me; unfortunately, during its preparation, John suffered a heart flutter, and was laid up. At that stage I became sole general editor.

Returning to 1960, although Macmillan now wanted to move towards membership, he had to prepare the ground in the Conservative Party and in Parliament. Both had for long been told that membership was a very unappetising option: now they had to be turned round. So Macmillan launched a review by officials of the whole involvement of Britain in Europe: its relationship with the European Community; whether we should seek association or membership; and what would be the implications of either. That summer, a questionnaire was sent round the Whitehall Departments, covering many pertinent matters. When I appeared on the scene, the answers were in preparation. It was typical of the times that our unit was called the European Economic Organisations Department, reflecting the establishment's desire to play down in public the essentially political character of the Rome Treaties.

The Report containing the answers to the questionnaire came down heavily in favour of the UK seeking membership of the three Communities. The political arguments were seen as decisive. British interests would suffer if we were not in the inner councils of Europe. On the economic side, short-term problems were foreseen; but held to be outweighed by long-term advantages. The key problem was considered to be whether arrangements could be made to 'continue or replace the existing régime of duty-free entry for Commonwealth products, particularly temperate agricultural products', in other words grains, meat and milk products from the old Dominions. The problems for domestic agriculture and EFTA were dismissed lightly. Those of the new Commonwealth countries, and the Dependent Territories, were scarcely touched on at all.

The Report did however make an important proviso. After the failure of the Maudling Plan, Ministers were advised not to launch another initiative likely to lead to a rebuff. The first step, therefore, must be to sound out the Six, and notably France, as to whether they would welcome us into the Community on terms we could accept. Whilst the soundings were taken, there would be talks with the Commonwealth and the EFTA countries. Officials assumed that, in parallel, Macmillan would quietly seek to move public opinion in the desired direction.

The talks with Germany, Italy and the Benelux countries, predictably showed support. The French were cautious. Clearly General de Gaulle was not keen on UK entry. This was attributed by some to his desire to see the common agricultural policy in full operation before Britain joined: by others to wider political reasons. But at that time there was definitely no threat of veto. Consultations with the Commonwealth countries – the new as well as the old – showed them to be very sensitive. The EFTA countries were not at all pleased. Meanwhile, at home, the National Union of Farmers became restive. Macmillan did not force the pace at all. But he did not change his underlying view. A year later he decided the moment had come to move. He proposed to Cabinet that a straightforward application for membership should be made; and this was announced to Parliament at the end of July, 1961. The British application – a simple document drafted by me – was handed to the Community Presidency on 9 August. Three of our EFTA partners – Denmark, Norway and Ireland – applied simultaneously. On that same day, John and I enlivened our usually abstemious sandwich lunch in a Whitehall pub with a bottle of Château Batailley.

During that summer, arrangements were made to establish the British negotiating Delegation. Ted Heath was of course to lead the Delegation at Ministerial level. Sir Pierson [Bob] Dixon, at that time Ambassador in Paris, was controversially appointed leader at official level, with Eric Roll (now Lord Roll) as his Deputy. These top people were to be supported by senior officials of different Whitehall Departments. The latter were to remain members of their Departments, and travel to and from the Conference venue – which turned out to be Brussels – for meetings. Most of them were titled, and they inevitably came to be described as 'the Flying Knights'. They spent about three days a week in Brussels, and the rest of their time in London.

Finally, there was to be a small resident element of the Delegation, permanently stationed at the Conference venue, whose essential tasks were to underpin the whole team; to gather intelligence within the Community Institutions and the other Delegations; and to ensure continuity and cohesion of the British action on the ground. This resident element was headed by a Counsellor, Henry Hainworth; but he focused mainly on the Euratom negotiations. On the crucial, EEC side, John Robinson and I moved from London to be the work-horses.

The Flying Knights included some remarkable and charming men, representing notably the Commonwealth Relations Office, the Colonial Office, the Board of Trade and the Treasury. It was a great advantage to have people like this commuting to and fro. They were long enough in London every week – as well as carrying sufficient personal authority – to be able to keep their Departments in line with the development of thinking in the Delegation as a whole and with the flow of the negotiations. It was one of Ted Heath's great achievements that he exploited very successfully this situation, in which the Flying Knights had a dual loyalty: to their Departments at home, but also to the Delegation as such. In all cases but one, Ted persuaded the members of the commuting team to be at least as much concerned with the success of the negotiations as with the defence of a perceived Departmental interest. The exception was that temple of arch-conservatism – the then MAFF.

MAFF, at all official levels, from the most senior down, systematically opposed all pressures to alter the British agricultural system. Although Christopher Soames was personally in favour of British accession – and was later a very good Commissioner in Brussels – his senior officials undermined him at every turn. It was they who insisted that – alone of the Departments principally concerned – MAFF's representative on the Delegation would not be a Deputy Under-Secretary like the others, but would instead be a middle-ranking official who, though intelligent and charming, carried little weight in his Department; and who resided permanently in Brussels. The result was to leave Freddie Bishop, the MAFF Deputy Under-Secretary in London – an anti-European of the first order – as Christopher Soames's unfettered adviser. It is no wonder that the British position on agricultural matters remained unchanged until the late autumn of 1962, when I and Soames's Private Secretary were present at a painful meeting of Heath and Soames in Brussels, when the former squeezed out the first signs of movement.

The enlargement negotiations started with a clean slate. At their outset, the EEC and Euratom were less than three years old. Fusion of the Executives of the three Communities was something for the future. The Community authorities were heavily engaged on other important issues. These included: completing the transitional phase established in the Rome Treaties; the development of a common agricultural policy [CAP]; the future arrangements for community finances; and the conduct of the important Dillon Round of tariff negotiations in the GATT[3], predecessor to the World Trade Organisation [WTO] of today.

There were no precedents for handling accession; and literally the <u>only</u> thing the Treaty had to say was that *'the conditions of admission, and the adjustments to this Treaty necessitated thereby, shall be the subject of an agreement between the Member States and the applicant State'*. Yet suddenly the fledgling Community had to cope with applications from four countries, including the very large and particular problems of the UK. It was not only a question of finding answers to the problems of substance: an entire negotiating procedure had to be mounted as one went along. These considerations alone, go far towards explaining the length of the negotiating process.

An early decision had to be taken on whether the negotiations should be between the Six Member States and the Four applicants <u>together</u>; or between the Six and each of the Four <u>separately</u>. The Six quickly opted for the second course, and also made it clear that they were going to keep the UK negotiations ahead of the others. In so doing they were influenced by the thought that, if the UK negotiations failed, early accession by the others was improbable.

Another early decision was needed, in relation to each of these four negotiations, on how the Six would behave *vis-à-vis* the applicant country. They agreed that they would, by unanimity, establish a Community position on every matter, before discussing it with us. This process had to be repeated if, on any point, the position was not acceptable to the applicant. The arrangement did not make for speed or flexibility in the negotiations, and it gave the French very great leverage. There were one or two occasions when something more like a genuine discussion between seven countries emerged; but <u>only</u> one or two.

There were four other preliminary questions on which the Six found it much harder to agree. They were: the venue for the negotiating Conference;

whether the Commission should participate in the Conference at all, a matter on which the Treaty was strangely silent; whether the Chair should rotate, as in the Council, or be held by the same person throughout the conference, as during the negotiations at Val Duchesse for the Rome Treaties; and how the Conference Secretariat should be provided. The solutions found to these four questions are well known. Each had a major influence on the negotiations. In the Community, agreements are inherently difficult to reach. The power of precedent is correspondingly great. All the organisational decisions about the conduct of enlargement negotiations just described, have been maintained ever since.

Britain was invited by the Six, in advance of the formal negotiations, to make an opening statement about the problems facing the UK and the solutions it envisaged for them. Constructing this statement so that it would support our claim to be genuine converts to the Community method, keep our non-Community friends reasonably calm, and yet not offer hostages to fortune in the negotiations, was no easy task. In the event, the opening statement largely met these aims, except that we opened our mouths far too wide on agriculture. In the final stage, the drafting fell to me. I was very pleased when, on seeing my draft late one night, Evelyn Shuckburgh took the responsibility of making a number of changes which underlined the political aspects of our approach, inserting passages which I had felt went beyond what the Whitehall machine would accept! At all events, the opening statement was made by Ted Heath, in the Hall of Mirrors in the Quai d'Orsai at Paris, on 10 October 1961. And it was generally very well received. The rest of the negotiations took place in Brussels.

Another tale attaches to the Opening Statement. Before it was made, there was a meeting of the EFTA Council in Geneva, to brief EFTA Member States. I arrived the evening before, and had made an arrangement with Mimi de la Forest-Divonne[4] that she would dine with me at a restaurant in Nyon, the town where she was then working. The Consul-General lent me a car to go there and back. I had with me a copy of the latest draft of the Opening Statement, then highly classified. I did not dare leave it in my hotel, so took it along in a valise, which I pushed under the dinner table. When I left, it was forgotten. Coming to my senses half way back to Geneva, I rushed back – all the while fearing that some enterprising journalist might have got hold of the draft and be planning to publish it next morning. Happily, no harm had been done. Mine host had found it, and kept it safe. Otherwise, my career would certainly not have benefited!

For dogmatic Community reasons, the negotiations were not held in a building of the Council, but in the Ministry of Foreign Affairs of Belgium, the host country. The British noted wryly that the Ministry was then situated in the Rue des Quatre Bras, remembering that Quatre Bras was the scene of a battle, on the eve of Waterloo, in which the British and their Allies were forced from the field by the French! We tried to take comfort from the fact that the then Headquarters of the European Commission was in the Rue de la Joyeuse Entrée! But history was to repeat itself.

The Ministry building had not been designed to house a Conference on this scale. All the meetings, whether of Ministers or of their Deputies, took place in a low-ceilinged room far too small to hold the Delegations of the Six, of the UK, and of the Commission – usually up to 80 people, plus perhaps 10 interpreters in their cabins – in any comfort. The room was not air-conditioned; the windows could not be opened because of the noise of the traffic below; and in the 1960s most Delegates smoked like chimneys, often cigars. My eyes frequently streamed as a result. The temperature was always excessive. When it was hot outdoors, the room closely resembled the Black Hole of Calcutta. International conferences in those days often suffered from such problems; but they did not usually continue for 15 months at a stretch. Those who have only met in the spacious, air-conditioned conference rooms of today, can have no conception of the tortures we suffered.

Naturally the Belgian Ministry did not want to give up too many rooms to the Conference; so the individual Delegation Rooms in the building were few and small. This was doubly unfortunate for the Brits, because of the way the Six chose to conduct business. As we have seen, there was to be no Conference of the Seven: rather, a Conference of the Six as a *bloc*, with the UK. On a negotiating day, the Six argued amongst themselves for hours what to say to the British, and were then unable to budge an inch from laboriously agreed positions. So, meetings with us were usually short. But one was never to know <u>when</u> the Six would summon us. So, on Conference days, the British Delegation would often spend hours and hours, cooped in their tiny offices, receiving a copious flow of information about progress among the Six (from Delegations of the Five), and waiting for the call!

A first, exploratory, phase of the negotiations lasted from November 1961 to Easter 1962. It consisted of the British developing in more detail their views on the issues they had identified in the Opening Statement as needing discussion, and of the Six deploying a response. It was soon clear that, while we could expect considerable derogations from the Rome Treaty rules <u>during</u> a <u>transitional</u> <u>period,</u> the Six would be extremely resistant to all proposals from our side for<u> permanent</u> <u>derogations</u>.

From as early as end-January, 1962, John Robinson and I felt able to forecast to our superiors the likely content of any eventual Accession Treaty. It was far removed from what the official briefs had defined as the British objectives. But those briefs had always been unrealistic. The Narrative Report recorded that, in all the hundreds of pages of Whitehall briefing, there was *'hardly a fall-back to be seen'*. After some reflection, Ted Heath agreed that the Delegation should (in March) put to London its assessment of what was likely to be obtainable over the whole field of the negotiations. Although this forecast was very close to the terms of the provisional agreements worked out with the Six by January 1963 – and was subsequently refined in July and again in September – it achieved little. The Narrative Report is again instructive. It read: *'In London…it was decided to limit circulation of the forecasts severely. Although they no doubt influenced a small number of those directly concerned, they appeared to have no impact on Ministerial opinion generally or on our instructions.'*

A second, analytical, phase lasted from Easter 1962 to the beginning of August. It was by now a British tactical objective to agree with the Six on the broad pattern of the accession arrangements in time for this to be explained to a Conference of Commonwealth Prime Ministers in London in September. We put to the Six the notion of reaching a *'Vue d'Ensemble'* by end-July, and it was accepted. Unfortunately, both the French <u>and</u> the British were dragging their feet on substance: the French, for obvious reasons; the British, because Ministers did not give a corresponding instruction to Whitehall Departments to provide the Delegation with the necessary negotiating latitude. The *Vue d'Ensemble* reached was, therefore, far from complete. But Ted Heath again knew, and certainly communicated to the Prime Minister, the Delegation's view of what was negotiable.

A third, negotiating, phase lasted from the end of September until the Christmas break in 1962. The Commonwealth Conference at Marlborough House of that summer was behind us. I had attended, and there was no doubt that the Commonwealth countries were now resigned to British accession. Macmillan had also won over the majority at the Conservative Party Conference. To the Delegation, the way seemed clear for us to be told to complete the negotiations rapidly, on the basis of our own forecasts. But the word did not come. The anti-Europeans within the Conservative Party, and amongst the popular press, began to say that Macmillan would now feel free to *'sell Britain down the river'*. His reaction, amazingly, was to slow down forward movement in order to prove his negotiating *machismo*!

Before moving to the culmination of the negotiations, let me say a few words about the content. In essence, the negotiations turned on the Commonwealth; on agriculture; and on the level of the common external tariff. There was no difficulty about UK acceptance of what we now call the *acquis communautaire*, in other words Community legislation which has been adopted under the Treaties. No blocking problems seemed likely with regard to the ECSC and Euratom Treaties.

I have not mentioned EFTA as an issue. It might have become one if the negotiations had looked like succeeding. The British Government had rashly agreed, in EFTA, that the organisation would continue to operate on the existing basis *'at least until satisfactory arrangements have been worked out in the negotiations to meet the various legitimate interests of all members of EFTA'*. This had the advantage that the non-applicant EFTA members were content to leave the UK a free hand to negotiate. But it could have been used by them to impede any final package they did not like.

Very little was said in the negotiations about Institutions. The British side stated from the outset that they accepted the existing institutional structure. They also made clear their assumptions that they would receive the same weight of votes in the Council as France, Germany or Italy, accepting corresponding financial implications; and that English would become an official language. The Six readily agreed. No further details were raised before the negotiations ended.

At the end of 1962, events occurred outside the negotiations which led to their termination. The United States Administration had cancelled the development of their Skybolt missile, on which the future of the British nuclear deterrent then rested. Macmillan decided to ask President Kennedy to supply Britain, instead, with Polaris (submarine-based) missiles. He warned De Gaulle of his intention at a meeting in Rambouillet in mid-December; to be told that Britain should abandon its special ties with the United States. A few days later, at Nassau, he put his request to Kennedy, and it was agreed. It was against this political background that the final part of the Conference began in January, 1963. The Five were by now pressing for the negotiations to be brought to an early and successful conclusion – and it had been settled in December that there would be two 'crunch' Ministerial four- or five-day meetings in the second and fourth weeks of the January. The Delegation's instructions had at last become realistic.

Ted Heath has famously recorded, in his book *The Story of my Life*[5] how he went to Paris, on 11 January, for a private preparatory talk with the French Foreign Minister, Couve de Murville, over lunch at the British Embassy, when the only others present were Bob Dixon, Eric Roll and Couve's

Deputy, Olivier Wormser; and how Couve told him that *'No power on earth can prevent these negotiations from being successful'*. Just three days later, whilst the first Ministerial meeting in Brussels was in course, De Gaulle held the famous Press Conference at which he made clear that he was imposing a veto on British entry into the Community. (Couve was at the Press Conference, not at Brussels.) The key reasons the General gave for considering Britain was not *'fit'* to enter, were all things which had been evident when he agreed to the opening of the negotiations some fifteen months earlier. Couve, much later, admitted in a TV interview that France's behaviour had been *'une sorte de trahison'*.

After that thunderbolt, various efforts were made by the Five to keep the negotiations going, but to no avail. The last Ministerial meeting, on 29 January, was simply the occasion for a high-class funeral, demonstrating that the Five and the British believed an agreement was to hand and held France solely responsible for the breakdown. I wrote Ted Heath's own concluding speech, with all the Flying Knights commenting and arguing around me as I dictated each word in the Delegation Office! Later in the day, he spoke to the Press Corps, at the Hotel Metropole-Monopole, in a similar vein. The media representatives, at the end of his statement, broke into uncharacteristic, spontaneous and prolonged applause for the man who – as they all knew – had been far more committed to the success of the negotiations than his Prime Minister, and who had throughout never himself put a foot wrong.

In closing these notes about the Heath negotiations, I express a few brief thoughts about what went wrong; and also about what was achieved, despite the failure to secure immediate British accession.

As to what went wrong, this was exhaustively discussed in the Narrative Report. In essence it seemed to the Delegation clear that the British Government set its priorities too late; that it could have struck a deal, despite General De Gaulle, if it had moved faster; that we initially over-estimated the extent to which we could obtain special arrangements of a more than transitional nature; and that our approach to the Six's Common Agricultural Policy, then in full formation, was unrealistic.

The one point in this list of mistakes which many would challenge is the notion that faster movement might have led to an agreement before De Gaulle was willing to take the blame for failure; and thereby hangs a quite amusing tale. It has to be remembered that, when we sought negotiations, France was trying to hold down rebellion in Algeria, still one of its Overseas Departments. De Gaulle declared Algeria independent in July,

1962. Once this dramatic move had been accepted by the French people, the General's standing at home rose fast.

After the negotiations ended, the British Embassy in Paris, and the British Delegation for the negotiations, carried out post-mortems. Both addressed the $ 64,000 question. The Paris Embassy came up first with their view: in a despatch to the Foreign Office, drafted by Michael Butler (later Sir Michael) and signed by Bob Dixon in his <u>Ambassadorial</u> capacity, the Embassy opined that De Gaulle would <u>never</u> in fact have let us in. This vexed the Delegation in Brussels, which was still in the process of drafting its own report and thought differently. In the end, the Brussels Delegation persuaded Bob Dixon that, <u>in his capacity as its Head</u>, he should sign a Report which said the opposite to what he had written from Paris! He was quite uncomfortable about this, but too loyal to the Delegation to refuse. We cannot of course say, objectively, which view was right!

As to what was achieved, despite the failure to secure immediate accession, Ted Heath himself has argued that the Macmillan Government's decision to apply for membership of the Community was seminal; and that it determined the direction, not only of British policy, but also of that of Europe and the Atlantic Alliance. He has written: *'It signalled the end of one glorious era, that of the British Empire, and the beginning of a whole new chapter of British history.'* I wish this were the whole picture: in fact, 40 years after the Brussels negotiations, there are still many politicians in Britain unwilling to recognise that the days of Empire are past! Nevertheless the broad thrust of Ted's judgement must be sound. The process he launched led almost inexorably to the success of the Rippon negotiations, a decade later, and Ted's own signature, as Prime Minister, on the final Accession Treaty. The Rippon negotiations, in fact, took for granted almost all of what had been agreed by 1963, and went on to resolve outstanding or new issues.

The Heath negotiations were fruitful in another way too. They set the pattern of all enlargement negotiations. Because the Rome Treaties had so little to say about enlargement, the British were the guinea pigs. The Six, through their negotiations with us, developed a complete methodology for enlargement. It was followed – always a shade later – in the parallel negotiations between the Six on the one hand, and Denmark, Ireland and Norway on the other. The methodology has been applied in every enlargement negotiation since then, and is indeed being applied for the countries with which the European Union is now in negotiations.

It only remains to summarise the nature of the actual work undertaken by John and myself <u>during</u> the negotiations. Much of this will be obvious: the preparation of meetings in Brussels of the Delegation, and with the Six; attendance at the meetings; and reporting back to London on anything and everything to do with the negotiations. Less obvious is the fact that, after every meeting with the Six, the Delegation had to give Commonwealth and EFTA Delegations in Brussels a full account of the outcome; and field their questions and comments. As in London, there was a lot of drafting to be done: for example I was usually the person who prepared Ted's statement to the House of Commons, made after each Ministerial meeting in Brussels. The resident element of the Delegation was under a lot of pressure: John and I worked particularly long hours, often staying in meeting rooms, or our offices, until very late at night; and also doing much weekend work.

Some weekends, Ted would elect to have a brain-storming session with the Delegation at the Foreign Office, to review progress and discuss next steps. John and I were always required to fly back for these. The meetings were lively and informal. The Flying Knights would speak their minds freely; and their juniors did not hesitate to argue! The normal pattern was that Ted would let the discussion run until he felt there was nothing useful left to be said. He did not normally draw specific conclusions, except perhaps on anodyne matters. Instead, he would thank all those present for their input; and undertake to let us know later what he had decided. Then the Flying Knights would be sent away. John and I, however, would have been told discreetly to return. We would sit with Ted, and his Private Secretary, Roger Lavelle, and the necessary decisions would be taken there and then. It was for Roger to let the Flying Knights know about them, and for John and me to initiate follow-up.

It will be obvious from the foregoing that I saw an enormous amount of Ted over a period of nearly three years; and have a very high regard for him. Most people who have not had close contact with Ted tend to see him as curmudgeonly, because of the ungracious way in which he treated Margaret Thatcher, after losing the Tory leadership contest to her. It is not, however, his normal nature to bear grudges. He has, for example, left on record the view that De Gaulle, who dealt him a very hard blow, was on balance good for France, because he gave the country back its self-respect; and Ted remained on good personal terms with the General until he died. Another reason for non-comprehension of Ted is that he is very shy and reserved, and does not unbend easily. But, to those who <u>do</u> have the opportunity to be in close contact, it soon becomes clear that, beneath the surface, there is a very warm and human person. Of the many British Ministers for whom I worked, he was the one best able to attract and hold the personal loyalty of civil servants. He always showed appreciation when people worked hard for him: he never criticised them unfairly.

Maura and I, in July 1998, had the immense pleasure of attending a party for Ted's 82nd Birthday, organised by his then Private Secretary, to which were invited all those who had served him over the years in a Private Secretary or similar capacity. Two things were very clear. The high proportion of acceptances, and of individuals who travelled far to attend, showed how much he was appreciated by those well placed to judge. And the two speeches in his honour, one by Sir Donald Maitland, and the other by a much younger person, had a common thread: Ted's humanity. They spoke also of his achievements. To me he is, quite simply, the only British politician of the post-war period – I count Churchill as 'war-time' in this context – who has been a world-class statesman[6].

When the negotiations collapsed, the Foreign Office wanted John Robinson or me to stay on, in our Permanent Delegation to the European Communities, and asked our preferences. There was no problem. I wanted to be posted elsewhere, because staying would be an anti-climax. John wanted to remain: partly I think because of children's schooling, but also because he wanted to continue working actively for British membership of the Community. Matters were settled accordingly. I was posted to Argentina; and never worked closely with John again, except for a brief spell in the London in 1967, although we always kept in very direct personal touch until his premature death through illness.

When the Delegation was finally disbanded, Roddie Barclay had the task of writing a confidential, personal report for the Foreign Office about each of the Administrative Branch staff involved. He told me mine was positive. His Personal Assistant, however, was more specific: Roddie had said I should reach at least Grade 2 in the Service. (Grade 9 was a Third Secretary. As a First Secretary I was then Grade 5. Ambassadors in key posts like Washington or Paris were Grade 1.) Until now, I had not thought seriously about how high I should aim: Roddie's assessment challenged me. I set Grade 1 as my career target. It was never an over-riding aim. Life, for me, must be many-faceted. In the office, the important thing was to know one had done the best one possibly could, which automatically gives job-satisfaction. Outside, a substantial intellectual and cultural content was always needed. More important than anything else, was to attain a happy family situation. That said, it is a fact that my career target was achieved only 10 years later, when I became Deputy Secretary-General of the Commission in their Administrative Grade A1. Although the nature of the work is different, my immodest but firm belief is that holding down my job in Brussels was just as tough as being a top British Ambassador, and in some ways tougher. Whether top British Ambassadors would agree is another matter!

The negotiations, and the run-in and follow-up to them, were thus the backdrop to our small family's life from summer 1960 until early spring 1963. Obviously, during the whole of that period, I had to struggle hard (and sleep little) to squeeze time for the family out of a schedule which became progressively heavier. During the actual negotiating period, things were at their worst. I was therefore able to appreciate the merit of one of the European Commission's well-established traditions: which is to work very hard for ten months of the year, but to treat August as sacrosanct for holidays, and to take some significant time out at Christmas and Easter. The Six could never operate without the full-time support of the Commission; so negotiations (and even pre-negotiations) came to a halt at those times.

Shortly after Ted's Opening Statement of October, 1961, and the subsequent decision that the negotiations would take place in Brussels, the resident element of the Delegation was despatched; an Office was chosen; and the members of the team were told to find their own domestic accommodation. Maura and I packed up Ferndown Cottage; left Rupert with his grand-mother at Gerrards Cross; and went to Brussels to look around. Michael and Gillian Warr[6] kindly invited us to stay; and we greatly enjoyed their hospitality at their comfortable house in the Avenue Winston Churchill. Michael was at that time Counsellor in the British 'national Embassy' in Brussels. The expression 'national Embassy' is a term of art in Brussels, and shows that one is referring to the Embassy accredited to the Belgian Court, and not to the ones accredited to the European Union, NATO or WEU.

We soon found a duplex flat which suited us well, on the first and second floors of a comfortable, post-war house at 109 Avenue Defré, in the suburb of Uccle, then regarded as the diplomatic area of the City. It stood high; had spacious living rooms; was marvellously light and airy; and looked out mainly on tall trees. We duly installed ourselves, with Rupert, and remained there for our whole posting in Brussels. Rupert, now aged just over one, was looked after mainly by Maura, but she had a mixed succession of *au pair* girls, German and British, to help. The British girl tried to run off with a circus boy.

The collapse of the negotiations, in January 1961, transformed our life-style. True, I was at once plunged into the writing of the Narrative

Report, wisely commissioned by Ted. But, although this was a big job, it required regular hours and steady application. An excess of hours was counter-productive: one's muse went dead. We took Saturdays and Sundays off; and I came home regularly for lunch (whereas before I had always eaten in or near the office). It was an unaccustomed joy.

To make matters even better, our release from slavery coincided with a great freeze. Snow fell, and the ground froze to a depth of half a metre, before Christmas of 1962: the freeze was continuing unbroken when we left Brussels in mid-March. In the Forêt de Soignes, all the lakes and ponds froze hard. We laboriously swept large areas of ice free of 30 centimetres of snow; and there we skated and skated. Rupert, who had a metal-framed car-seat, was strapped into it and pushed round the ice to his great satisfaction. Visiting Scheveningen, in the Netherlands, one weekend, we saw great ice-blocks lining the shore, perhaps seven metres high. Many sea-ports were closed. We had one very nasty moment. Driving on one of the long, straight, *pavé* roads through the Forêt de Soignes, we came over a slight rise and found ourselves at once on black ice. We went into a skid, and our Zephyr started turning across the road. I could not regain control. We continued turning, slowly, slowly. On the other side of the road another car was approaching. We completed a full 360 degree turn; came off the black ice; and missed the other car by centimetres!

It was time to leave Brussels. Rupert acquired his first passport (previously he had travelled on Maura's); and was returned to his grand-mother at Gerrards Cross. We packed up our belongings, ready for shipment to England and then Argentina, and closed the flat. We sold our old White Ford Zephyr to Reg Hibbert, then a First Secretary in the British (National) Embassy. (Later, when Reg was my superior in Bonn, we learnt that it had caught fire and gone up in smoke soon after. To his credit, Reg never complained about this; but I became wary of selling things to colleagues!) Finally, we booked a fortnight's holiday in Zermatt, along with Clifford Jupp, who had been the Delegation's Press Officer, and his wife Brenda.

There is a moving tale about our departure. Soon after the collapse of the negotiations, the General Manager of the Hotel Metropole-Monopole – which had played home to Ted Heath and the Flying Knights for 15 months – visited Henry Hainworth, the Head of the Resident Delegation. He said he was very sad, not about losing good business, but because he and most Belgians had been keen to welcome Britain into the European Communities. He realised the Delegation would now be disbanded; and its members leaving. Some might need temporary accommodation for a few days, after packing up their houses, prior to actual departure. He wished, as a token of sympathy, to offer free accommodation at the Hotel to <u>any</u> members of the Delegation so placed. Henry thanked him warmly, and circulated the information. The Jupps and we found a need for one night's accommodation before driving to Zermatt. Clifford and I called on the General Manager, and asked if we might benefit from his offer. His reaction was heart-warming. He showed obvious delight at being taken at his word; insisted on providing us with two <u>bridal</u> <u>suites;</u> and invited us to dine on the house, eating and drinking <u>any</u> <u>food</u> <u>or</u> <u>wine</u> we fancied on his *gourmet* menu and wine-list! We accepted, and were treated like royalty.

The Zermatt holiday, to which we had all so much looked forward, was a near-disaster. After driving to Visp, we parked the car and went on in the crowded mountain train to Zermatt. We all stood in the corridor, littered with luggage. Clifford and I were separated from our spouses, but could see them in animated conversation with a stranger. Soon, one of them struggled over: the stranger had reported a typhoid epidemic had been raging in Zermatt for weeks. Clifford and I pooh-poohed this. The Swiss were proverbial for their attention to hygiene. If an epidemic had indeed been so long rampant, the Swiss would have announced it and given appropriate advice to travellers. But we should certainly check on arrival. At Zermatt, we went straight to our Hotel, the old Victoria Palace, long-since replaced. We interviewed the Management. It was true, they said, that there had been a small number of cases. The cause was uncertain. Perhaps people had <u>arrived</u> ill. But the water-supply had been tested, and was completely clear. Travellers were being advised to be inoculated; but that was all. When we asked whether there had been any case in the Hotel, we were given a categoric negative.

The two wives (and mothers) remained dubious; but the husbands thought these assurances satisfactory. After some debate, we stayed, and went off for our inoculations. The Doctor said we ought to have two. The usual one for travellers would offer long-term protection. However, it was not immediately effective: we should therefore also have a second, giving short-term cover at once. The side-effects were instant and dramatic. We all retired to our respective bedrooms, where we suffered from sore arms, headaches and temperatures, for two days.

During this time, it progressively emerged that we had been told a pack of lies. The epidemic <u>had</u> been hushed up by the Swiss Authorities, because Zermatt had just been home to a ski-ing competition, and had wanted to avoid cancellation. The water-supply <u>was</u> the cause of the outbreak, which was by now extensive. There had been a direct leak from the main sewer into the main water-supply! As to our hotel, its chef was already <u>dead</u> of the disease! It so happened that our Hotel's tennis court – just in front of our bedroom – had been pressed into service as a helipad. Many times a day helicopters would land; and we would see well-wrapped bodies being placed on board. Some must have been dead, and some alive: there was no way of telling the difference. It was gruesome.

By remaining two days in a suspect Hotel, we had already placed ourselves at risk. We were either already infected; or we were not. Time would tell. But, since the double-injection, there seemed no risk of <u>new</u> infection. We again decided to stay. But many others left. The result was that, instead of queues, and standing on the Gornergratbahn, we could march straight on to the train and choose our seats: lifts were similarly uncrowded! We enjoyed fine weather and fine ski-ing. But, after a week, the Swiss Authorities closed the resort, announcing that it would not re-open till the water supply was 100% pure. We left, and spent our remaining few days in the more restricted ski-ing of the Feldberg (Schwarzwald). Then we dispersed. Maura and I went first to Gerrards Cross, to be re-united with Rupert, and then on to Ackenthwaite.

My mother had initially planned a party or two, to enable us to say our good-byes before leaving for distant Argentina. By now we were officially considered by the then Ministry of Health to be out of quarantine. However, being by nature pessimistic, my mother would have none of this; convinced herself that we were still incubating the dread disease; and cancelled everything. She was not alone in super-caution. The Treasury Medical Adviser, who also advised the Foreign Office, refused to be guided by his Ministry of Health colleagues; and said that our posting to Argentina could not be confirmed until two days before we were due to sail. This did not make planning easy! Altogether, this interlude of a month between leaving Brussels and departure for Buenos Aires was distinctly fraught.

CHAPTER 11

Argentina, the Falkland Islands, and completing the family (1963-67)

We arrive in Buenos Aires

THE WHOLE IDEA of our posting to Argentina had excited us. It was the first time Maura or I had been in the southern hemisphere. The country was vast and varied. It was part of the Hispanic world: I was pleased to go to a place where the Spanish language skill acquired at school would be of practical use. The Falkland Islands issue had lain dormant for many years. There was a strong tradition of Anglo-Argentine friendship, sustained moreover by a large Anglo-Argentine community. The country appeared to be in a phase of democracy and relative stability. We knew that living conditions in Buenos Aires were congenial. On the work side, this was a step up for me: not in terms of rank (I remained a First Secretary), but in terms of responsibility. I was to be Head of Chancery: in plain terms, Chief of Staff to the Ambassador, and Head of the Embassy's Political Section.

We realised that, in my new capacity, there would be far more social obligations than in Brussels. We also hoped that Rupert would soon have a sibling: indeed Maura was pregnant, though we did not know this. So we had recruited, for the first and last time, an English Nanny. Her name was Sylvia Cooke. She joined us at Tilbury docks, where we were to be seen off by Maura's family and hers.

We were to travel on RMS *Arlanza*, a ship of around 12,000 tons, and very comfortable. The voyage was to take just under three weeks, with stops in Vigo, Lisbon, the Canaries, Rio de Janeiro, Santos and Montevideo. Maura began to feel sea-sick as soon as we moved away from the quayside and the loudspeakers belted out 'A life on the Ocean Wave'! Her pregnancy was a contributory factor, the more so when she developed signs of possible miscarriage during the sea voyage. As a result she spent much of the time in our cabin; had to see a Doctor in Montevideo; and was removed to the British Hospital in Buenos Aires by ambulance, direct from the quayside, as soon as we landed on 18th May. So it was only Sylvia, Rupert and I who got full benefit from the charms of an ocean liner on a long voyage. The ship had a pool, in which Rupert began learning to swim; and there were the usual games, competitions and so forth.

At Buenos Aires, with Maura initially in hospital, we three were installed in a hotel whilst I looked for a house to rent. Meanwhile the Embassy *despachante* rescued our car from the clutches of the Argentine customs. A dark blue Wolseley 6/110, it was for us a luxury; but we had been told to bring a high quality car because the strange import regime enabled diplomats to sell a car every two years at a substantial profit! For the first time in our lives we experienced the joys of power steering and automatic transmission. We never reverted to anything else.

We took a lease on a charming villa at no. 1109, Calle J J Paso, in the delightful suburb of Martinez. It had a lovely garden, in which a swimming pool was soon installed. When Maura was well enough, we moved in, and were soon surrounded by a small domestic army, of which more anon. Our first few months were anxious, filled with doubts as to whether Maura would keep her baby. In the end, happily, she did. Claire announced her imminent arrival at 0600 hours on Christmas Day, 1963. But then she changed her mind. We waited and waited. Nothing happened. We ate a full Christmas lunch – in an ambient climate of 30 degrees centigrade and 90% humidity. We had Christmas tea. Rupert was put to bed. We had a light supper. We went to bed.

Almost at once, Maura's pains began. Off we rushed in the car, bound for the 'Little Company of Mary', a Catholic Hospital, which we would normally have reached in a quarter of an hour. But the evening of Christmas Day is when the Argentines really celebrate. Our route lay along a road, the verges of which were occupied by *asado* after *asado* (barbecue). The families spilled out onto the street. Progress was unbelievably slow. The journey took well over an hour. The pains came faster and faster. We had visions of the child being born in the car! We just made it to the Hospital. Claire arrived 15 minutes later, at 0015 hours. She would surely have been a Christmas baby if traffic had not slowed things down! After that we settled to a normal rhythm at home.

Setting the scene

Meanwhile we had been looking around and learning about the country where we were to live for nearly four years: its geography, history, culture, economy and politics. The writer George Pendle had published the third edition of his authoritative *Argentina* shortly before we left England. I found it invaluable, and now quote its first paragraph, which encapsulates

the country's geography. *'Few countries contain so many different kinds of land –
and so many climates – as Argentina. In the north are the sub-tropical scrub-forests of
the Chaco, on whose southern fringe lie plantations of oranges, yerba (Paraguay tea)
tobacco and sugar. To the west is the majestic Cordillera of the Andes with, amidst its
arid foothills, occasional oases and irrigated vineyards. In the south are mountain lakes
and pine-trees, wind-swept sheep ranches, Argentina's principal oil-fields and, finally,
the bleak near-Antarctic latitudes where the Andean range breaks up into rocky bays
and islets. But the heart of this great country is the fertile central plain, the pampa
(a Quechua Indian word meaning a flat area or steppe), which, from the wide east-
coast estuary of the Rio de la Plata, extends towards the northern plantations, the
Cordillera and the Patagonian plateaux in a huge semi-circle whose radius is 500 miles
[800 kilometres] or more.'*

The country is in fact 4,000 kilometres from north to south, and – at
its widest – 1,200 kilometres from east to west. The Andes rise to nearly
7,000 metres. Argentina is about 11 times the size of the United Kingdom;
and its population was then somewhat 20 million. (However, the Argentines
have a high rate of reproduction, and the figure is now over 35 million.)

Historically, South America was inhabited by indigenous peoples, of
whom the Incas are the best known, until the Spanish and Portuguese
invasions in the sixteenth century. After the fall of the Inca Empire, virtually
the whole continent (except for Portuguese dominated Brasil) was formed
into the Spanish Vice-Royalty of Peru. Later, the areas we now call
Argentina, Bolivia, Paraguay and Uruguay were hived off, to form the Vice-
Royalty of the Rio de la Plata, with Buenos Aires as the Capital.

In the first years of the nineteenth century, the Spanish Empire in South
America collapsed. Efforts by the British to take control of Buenos Aires by
force, were defeated by the *criollos* (local population) in 1806 (an event
known as *la Reconquista*) and again in 1807 (an event known as *la Defensa*).
The Argentine National Day – 25 May – recalls the date in 1810 when the
criollos formed their own Government. Six years later a Constitutional
Congress declared that the Vice-Royalty had become an independent State,
'The United Provinces of the Rio de la Plata', out of which Argentina eventually
emerged in its present shape. In the nineteenth and early twentieth
centuries, there was much immigration, notably of Spaniards, Italians and
British. The Italians stayed mainly in the cities, especially Buenos Aires. The
British fanned out over the country, developing the port, railway and
telegraph systems; the meat-packing stations which would enable fortunes
to be made from the export of chilled beef to the United Kingdom; and
many associated *estancias* (large farms). An Argentine *estancia* is always large:

in Patagonia they may run to 200,000 hectares. Owners of the bigger ones use a light aircraft to get around them: these are known as *estancieros*.

These immigrants added to the cocktail of cultures – till then Spanish and Indian – which prevails in Argentina today. But Argentines – I have always wondered why so many British people wrongly call them Argentinians – still, for the most part, refer to Spain as 'the mother country'. Argentina has an impressive level of culture. Education is good, the literacy rate very high, and the country well esteemed in the Hispanic world in terms of literature, art, dance and music.

Economically, Argentina, at the beginning of the twentieth century, was enormously rich: that was when the French invented the expression *'riche comme un Argentin'*. To the British, it was known as 'the Fifth Dominion' (alongside of Canada, Australia, New Zealand and South Africa). Argentina has all the potential to be very rich again. It is not lack of resources or of education which has held the country back, but rather the failure, during the twentieth century, to maintain a stable and efficient political system within which the economy could thrive. Just a few years ago Argentina reached an economic nadir: with an inflation rate of 4,500% a year, and falling GDP. In a recent phase, as a result of strong economic discipline under President Carlos Menem, growth was up to 5% and inflation was zero. If that situation had persisted, Argentina could have become a major economic power once more. Sadly, however, the economy has slipped back into its bad old ways.

The country's modern political history dates from 1916, when the first elections under universal suffrage were held. Between then and 1962, the Argentines went through four political cycles: each consisted of a period of elected Government, then a military *coup*, and then new elections under rules which more or less pre-determined the result. First the Radical Party, representing the middle classes, held power; then the Conservative Party, representing land-owners and property-owners; then the Peronistas (followers of Colonel Perón), representing the working classes; then a branch of the Radicals again, led by Arturo Frondizi. We arrived at the beginning of a fifth cycle: a different branch of the Radicals, led by Arturo Íllia, had just taken office. Three years later, Íllia was to suffer the same fate as his predecessors, chiefly because the military feared the Peronistas were likely to get in again, a development they would not accept. The *coup* against Íllia was followed by a Government led by Argentina's most distinguished soldier, General Onganía, a man of moderate and essentially democratic ideas, who remained in power till we departed. This was the domestic political context of the work of the British Embassy's Political Section.

The *coup* against Frondizi led to an amusing incident involving the Duke of Edinburgh. He was scheduled to make an official visit to Buenos Aires. The *coup* had cast its shadow ahead. As the date for the visit drew near, the Foreign Office asked the British Ambassador whether it was safe to proceed. The Ambassador approached the Argentine military at top level. Having ascertained the dates of the visit, they assured him that nothing untoward would occur. The visit proceeded, and all was quiet.

On leaving Buenos Aires the Duke went off for a private visit to an *estancia* up country, no doubt to play polo. No sooner was the *estancia* reached than the long-awaited *coup* occurred. The Ambassador realised, too late, that he should have given the military the dates of the private as well as of the official visit! The telephone system had been disturbed by the *coup* in some way, so he despatched a junior Embassy official to the *estancia* to advise the Duke to slip away quickly over the adjacent frontier into Uruguay. His response was characteristic. *'I'm certainly not leaving. All my life I've wondered what a South American coup d'état was like. Now I'm in the middle of one, and I find it fascinating.'* The hapless Second Secretary returned to Buenos Aires and reported. But The Queen had by now expressed concern. The Ambassador flew personally to the *estancia*; persuaded the Duke it was his duty to leave; and whisked him over the border.

In June 1966, we ourselves were to witness a *coup*: the one which deposed Arturo Íllia. It too had been brewing for weeks. In the Embassy we were well informed of developments in military thinking. At this time – though it was not always so – the Argentine Army carried the most clout amongst the Armed Forces. So our Military Attaché should theoretically have been our best informant. In fact, the Naval Attaché, Commander Val Bailey, filled that *rôle*. He was a keen polo player, whereas the Military Attaché did not play. Polo is Argentina's national sport, and was played every day by senior staff at the Campo de Mayo, the Army Headquarters. We encouraged Val to play a lot of polo, and his reports were invaluable. They told us that, once again, the military were becoming concerned about the Peronists: they feared that the elections (due in 1967) would lead to a Peronist victory. They determined to forestall any such development.

Though it was easy to see a *coup* was imminent, its precise timing was a closely guarded secret: not even Val was party. It happened at dead of night. There was no fuss: indeed, military *coups* in Argentina were usually like that, perhaps because people were so used to them. (The military tended to see themselves as ultimate guardians of Argentina's conscience, and as rooters-out of political corruption; and somehow this was accepted.) Troops were deployed in strategic places well before dawn. The President and others were arrested. We woke to hear the radio announce that General Onganía had taken power. And that was that. When I drove to my office in central Buenos Aires around 0900 hours, I was not even stopped. Life went on 100% as usual. And the troops were back in barracks almost at once.

The British Embassy

The Chancery (i.e. the Embassy office) was in a run-down building in the centre of town. It had around 100 staff, of whom two-thirds were locally engaged. I have already mentioned that, as Head of Chancery, I was Chief of Staff to the Ambassador (initially Sir George Middleton, later Sir Michael Creswell), and also Head of the Embassy's tiny Political Section. I was not, however, the Ambassador's Deputy: there was a Minister (initially Tom Rogers, later Desmond Pakenham). The first of these had a special responsibility for Economic Affairs.

As Head of Chancery, therefore, I had a number of specific tasks, and was also thrown into any area where the Ambassador wanted a close eye kept on developments. The specifics included overall co-ordination of the work of the different sections of the Chancery; and dealing with administrative and personnel matters. The co-ordination function needs little explaining. It often involved one in interesting situations, of which I give but one example. Late-ish during our time in Argentina, the World Polo Championships took place in Buenos Aires. As President, HRH The Duke of Edinburgh decided he should attend for the whole three weeks, and this implied staying in the Embassy. Any Royal visit places an Embassy under strain, but they seldom last more than a few days at most. Three weeks is almost unheard of. I was told by the Ambassador to organise matters.

Buenos Aires society was agog with expectation of meeting the Duke at social occasions. He, however, said he was coming, not as Royalty, but in a private capacity as President of the World Polo Association: he could not agree to attend any social, non-polo function at the Embassy. Argentine society would have been mortally affronted. We pleaded with the Palace. In the end, the Duke settled for one large reception and one dinner, both in the Embassy, the beautiful and imposing Madero House.

The reception posed big problems of selection. Thousands felt they should be asked, but something like 300 was the limit. Many, inevitably, were upset. However, the selection was made and the great day came. The Ambassador deputed me to accompany the Duke at all times, and to introduce each guest who approached. In theory I knew all the guests by sight. For a while, all went well. I was enormously impressed by the Duke's skill in charming all and sundry. He found something lively or amusing to say to each individual. And he took care never to get tied down, but to keep moving easily around.

Then disaster struck. At the far end of the room, a man entered. I knew him well; but his name slipped from my mind. He was plainly determined to shake the Duke's hand. A game ensued, in which I constantly encouraged the Duke to turn in another direction, whilst the guest as constantly manoeuvred to get back into his path. Finally he succeeded, and stuck out his hand. I had to say something. *'Señor Brrrr...'* I announced, mumbling deliberately. The Duke's reaction was immediate: *'Speak up man: I can't hear you'*. It was clear he had seen the whole affair out of the corner of his eye and was deliberately teasing me!

The dinner party was far more fraught. This time I was not on the very limited guest list: instead I was in town, attending a party political gathering, which went on late. On my return home, Maura told me the Minister had called from the Embassy dinner. There had been a serious incident. I must phone. When I did, Desmond Pakenham told me what had happened. Madero House stands in its own grounds on top of a hill. A public road winds up the hill, passing two sides of the building. Terrorists had driven up it at speed, firing a continuous hail of machine-gun bullets at the Embassy, many of which smashed through the windows. Fortunately the dining room is on the first floor. Nobody could have been hit directly, but ricochets could have proved fatal. Fate was kind: no-one was hurt. Desmond added that there was no longer a need for me. He had dealt with the police and other authorities, and taken any necessary immediate action. We would talk further next day.

Next morning I passed by the Embassy on my way to the Chancery. The Ambassador was seeing the Duke off for the day's polo. (For the rest of his stay HRH was infuriated by a massive police presence wherever he went!) The Ambassador told me in detail what had happened; showed me the bullet marks; and himself left for an appointment. Almost at once the 'phone rang. It was the Foreign Office, where it was by now lunchtime. The voice said: *'The Queen has heard on the radio about some shooting at the Embassy, and wishes to know how her husband is.'* Clearly, though amazingly, in the hustle and bustle of the night before, the need to report to London had been overlooked! Equally clearly, it would not help the Ambassador to say so. I told a white lie. *'Have you not received our reporting telegram? With the terrorist excitement, there may have been an interruption in the telegraph service (we did not have a radio transmitter in the Embassy). I'll tell you what it said.'* I followed that statement with a report based on the Ambassador's remarks to me; went to the Chancery; wrote a telegram in the same sense; and sent it off with a cover note saying we understood the original copy of the message had gone astray. Nobody detected the trick!

We had arrived in May – late autumn in the southern hemisphere. Six months later we were entering the Argentine summer. At the latitude of Buenos Aires, the summer climate is tough. For three months, temperatures rise into the upper 30's centigrade, with humidity often 90% or above. The pace of life slows. At that time, air-conditioning was rare: there was none in our offices. I found it surprising that the Embassy was operating a normal winter schedule. The workload did not require it; and people finished the day very tired. I made a proposal to work from 0800 to 1400 during the summer season, and then knock off. It was agreed; and the summer hours were warmly welcomed by the staff. The arrangement still persists.

One of my less agreeable duties as Head of Chancery was to decypher specially sensitive telegrams. These would be identified by certain code-words; meaning that the text must be decyphered by a fairly senior member of staff or by the Ambassador himself (DEYOU). In those days we were still using 'book cypher', where each letter had to be looked up in a cypher book, and transposed into a different one. This was appallingly tedious.

There is a story told of a Head of Chancery in another South American Post – let us call him 'X' – who had an unfortunate experience with DEYOU telegrams. His Ambassador had been behaving more and more oddly; and the time came when X believed him to be completely round the bend. The Ambassador went on an extended tour of distant Provinces. After he left, X sat down and en-cyphered a telegram to the Chief Clerk (senior administrative officer) of the Foreign Office, explaining the Ambassador's symptoms and asking what to do. The duration of the Ambassador's absence was known to the Foreign Office. However, for some reason, he returned sooner than expected. Almost at once a 'DEYOU' telegram arrived. The first words the Ambassador decyphered were: 'We regret to hear that your Ambassador has gone mad'! All hell was let loose!

Neither of my Ambassadors were eccentric; but they were very different. The staff loved the Middletons, but took a definite dislike to Michael Creswell and his wife. The Embassy, which until then had been a happy family of 100 souls, rapidly suffered a big loss of morale. Sadly, there was little I could do to improve things, except protest against any injustices and otherwise offer a sympathetic shoulder for people to cry on.

These events drove deep into my consciousness some obvious and simple, but oft-forgotten, rules about keeping staff happy: have a clear chain of command; develop clear strategy lines; delegate as much as possible; insist on knowledge sharing and full reporting back; see that each person has a clearly defined job to do, and does it; give credit instead of taking it; never expect of others more than you expect of yourself; listen carefully, especially when staff have problems; do your best to help them; watch for any signs of ill-health and strain, making sure these are remedied; and be absolutely honest with everybody. On the last point, it is all too easy, when a person is doing a poor job, just to put up with it and work round the resultant problems. That is unfair. If people are told their faults when they occur, they can usually improve. If they are not, they have no chance. This was brought home to me very clearly when I once told a staff member his work was unsatisfactory; explained carefully why; and said improvement must follow. Far from reacting badly, he told me what a relief it was, after many years in the Service, to be told the truth about himself. He <u>did</u> in fact improve.

The Falkland Islands question

From the moment of my arrival, it was clear that the only cause of friction in Anglo-Argentine relations was the dispute about sovereignty over the Falkland Islands. It had been a low-key affair for years; but there was reason for thinking this could change. As part of the general reduction of the British military presence abroad, the small garrison of marines on the Islands had been removed, and the last British naval vessel on permanent station in the South Atlantic was being withdrawn. The nearest British fighting ship would now be a frigate on the West Indies Station, some eight days' sailing away. The Falkland Islands boasted no airfield; and only a very light aircraft could land on the race-course!

The Embassy's file about the Islands had received little attention since the war. I studied it carefully; considered the issues; and drafted a confidential despatch which the Ambassador sent to the Foreign Secretary, 'Rab' Butler. I do not have a copy, since, despite the thirty year rule for the opening of the British Government's historic archives, it still remains classified (2002). However, as its author, I have been permitted to re-read the despatch, and can affirm with confidence that its contents are fairly reflected in what follows.

My study of the file led me first to examine the merits of the Argentine legal claim. In the eighteenth century, France, Spain and Britain had all laid claim to the Islands. Each had occupied them at different stages. But they are inhospitable, and at that time had little economic or perceived strategic value. By 1811, they were uninhabited. In the 1820's, the newly independent Province of Rio de la Plata – later transmuted into Argentina – hoisted a flag and established a settlement. In 1833, however, two British warships removed the Argentine garrison and settlers to the mainland; and took possession of the Islands. Thus, when I looked at the file, there had been continuous British occupation for 130 years. The papers showed, however, that the Argentine authorities had not only lodged a formal, diplomatic protest about the forceful occupation by the British when it occurred, but had reiterated this, formally and frequently, ever since: also that Britain had refused to submit the dispute to the International Court of Justice. The British legal case did not seem to us very solid. The file drew attention to the fact that the Islands had played an important strategic rôle in both World Wars: the battles of the Falkland Islands (First World War) and of the River Plate (Second World War) were both won by squadrons based on Port Stanley, the Islands' main settlement. But of course, Britain was currently ceasing to pretend to a world-wide military rôle.

The line of thinking we developed in the despatch to London went something like this. Every Argentine Government since independence from Spain had maintained the British had no legal right to be there. Until now, Argentina had made no move to use military means to enforce its claim. So long as Britain had kept a significant military presence in or near the area, there had been no need to expect change. But, now that none of HM Ships were permanently on the South America Station, things could sooner or later alter. Moreover it would be simple for the large and reasonably equipped Argentine armed forces to take control of the Islands, only 500 kilometres from their coast. Once established, they would not be easy to evict. The message must have been clear in London: leaving the Islands unguarded was a risky course to follow.

Although the despatch did not go further than that, the Embassy indulged in further exchanges of a less formal kind with officials of the Foreign Office. We put forward the view that, if Britain was not prepared to defend the Islands adequately, she should think of negotiating a deal, in which sovereignty would be conceded to Argentina in return for a special status for the Islands and their inhabitants. (At that time Argentina had a democratic Government; and anyone who knows the country is aware that Provinces distant from Buenos Aires always have a lot of autonomy.) We said that, in such a negotiation, there would be effectively no limit on the privileges which could be secured for the Islanders. We learnt later that the despatch was submitted to the Cabinet; that there was no readiness to reverse the military dispositions already made; that the Chief Whip advised 'the back-benchers would not like the idea of negotiating sovereignty away'; and that Ministers therefore decided to change nothing and hope for the best! I have been told that subsequent British Ambassadors in Buenos Aires proffered similar advice, regularly, to every new British Government, including Margaret Thatcher's, with similar results. This inertia and Micawberism, too typical of the United Kingdom's post-war Governments, led in 1982 to the successful Argentine invasion we had foreshadowed, and to the needless sacrifice of hundreds of young lives on both sides.

Some years later I chanced to mention this despatch to the late Lord Sherfield. He told me that he too, as a young Foreign Office official in the 1930s, had had to study the Argentine claim. He remembered writing a memorandum to his superiors concluding that it was stronger than the British one. When the Falklands War took place he had asked the Public Records Office for a sight of it, only to be told it had been withdrawn from public access on orders from the Prime Minister!

Our home and family

The house I had found in the suburb of Martinez was unpretentious, but ideal for our then needs. It belonged to Aurelio Peccei, then the top man in Fiat's Corporate Headquarters.

The garden was very special. Not large: a rectangular plot of perhaps 25 metres broad and 50 deep; but very cleverly designed, so that one had a feeling of space and variety. There was a big patio, where our young children spent much time in the nine warm or hot months of the year. The garden proper was a riot of sub-tropical trees and flora. It contained an *asado* area; a covered patio for playing and eating; a beautiful, small, fenced, swimming pool; and a little garden house the children had to themselves. As to trees and bushes, I remember the big oak, whose metre thick trunk snapped off in a hurricane; the tall avocado (*palta* in Argentine Spanish), with black fruits which had to be pulled off with a hook on the end of a very long bamboo, and caught before they hit the ground; a line of conifers shutting off the neighbours; a *palo borracho* (literally, drunken pole); poinsettias; hydrangeas; a tangerine (whose fruit absorbed chlorine from the pool overflow and could not be eaten); and some hibiscus (often alive with humming-birds). There was also a very pretty tree (name unknown), with scaly bark, whose leaves attracted huge, green caterpillars, which sometimes fell into unsuspecting cleavages! As to flowers, zinnias grew like weeds. There were masses of geraniums, sunflowers, cannas, gladioli, marigolds, bird of paradise, candytuft and antirrhinums. The place was a riot of colour, and a permanent delight to our eyes.

The surroundings of the house were delightful also. Our street, and many others, were planted with Seville oranges. Argentines do not care much for marmalade. We used to go out with a wheelbarrow and harvest all we needed. Other streets were lined with jacaranda, wild lilac and flame trees. We were within easy walking distance of the River Plate.

I remarked earlier that we were soon equipped with a small domestic army, some living in. This was the only time in our lives when we had so large a staff, and they were all very different characters. It is time to paint the picture.

Sylvia, our English Nanny, was well-trained and very efficient. But she wanted us to leave the children entirely in her care, with as little 'interference' as possible from their parents. This we were not prepared to do. Indeed, since my work-load was not heavy, by the standards I had known in Brussels and was to know again later, I wanted to spend a lot of time with them. Maura felt the same. When, after two years, we went back to the United Kingdom on home leave, Sylvia remained there, and we came to a very different arrangement.

Ofelia Gomez, our cook, was of South American Indian origin. She had a strong personality, and adored children. (Though she had only one son, she had thirteen grand-children.) Ofelia was a very good cook: *inter alia* she made all the pasta on the marble-topped table of our kitchen. She was very clean. She was also a fundamentally cheerful soul, and would often be found dancing to the radio in the kitchen. But she rather enjoyed, also, a bit of domestic drama. Every so often, Ofelia would tell Maura that there were big problems, and that they must be presented to *El Señor*! This usually meant she wanted a rise in wages: given the rate of inflation, it was hardly surprising! The three of us would then sit down solemnly in the living room, after dinner. Ofelia would expose the problems at some length. There would often be talk of having to give in her notice. Things would begin to look bleak. But soon, when she had got things out of her system, the mood would change. It was time to offer a raise of wages: usually it did not take long to agree. And then, Ofelia was her usual sunny self again! In the end, she stayed with us till we left Argentina. We were very happy she did. She loved the children, and they reciprocated. She would often sing to them. When we left, she begged to be taken to England to look after us. But we

Ofelia Gomez, our cook and our friend, with Rupert and Claire, 1965.

had to refuse, not for financial or other reasons of our own, but because we were sure that she would not be happy so far away from everybody and everything she knew. It was well that we did. Soon after, her son died very young, and she was a tower of strength to his children.

Our living-in house-maid was initially Anna, a Paraguayan whose mother tongue was Guaraní. She was pleasant but very quiet, partly no doubt because her Spanish was indifferent. Later she was replaced by an Argentine girl from Buenos Aires, Diana, a very different kettle of fish.

Diana was a great one for the boys. But Maura had a rule they should not come into our premises. One evening she had invited her current boy-friend to come and see her quietly in the garden after work. There, they were confronted by an armed robber. He demanded the house-key from Diana. Somehow, she convinced him that she was not allowed a key, and would have to knock. He made off; the lovers parted; and Diana, letting herself in with the key she'd had on her person all the time, went quietly to bed. (To have spoken would have meant revealing the illicit presence of the boy-friend!)

Next morning, police were guarding the next-door house. We knew the Leyro Diaz family well. Their children – Riccardo, Maria and Martín – were always playing with ours. Especially Martín, who was Rupert's exact contemporary; and from whom Rupert learnt fluent Spanish by imitation.

(Maura, and Martín's mother, were unable to tell which boy was speaking unless they could see!) It turned out that the father, a surgeon, had been shot by a burglar. It was, of course, the man who had been fooled by Diana. Somehow he had broken in to the ground floor of the house, and gone upstairs. The father, emerging from his bedroom, likewise armed, had a shoot-out with him, and was worsted. The burglar made off. The father was shot through the right shoulder, the bullet narrowly missing vital tendons and ligaments which would have put him out of surgery for good. Happily he made a full recovery.

The last member of our living-in staff, from 1965 to 1967, was a surprise. Having decided to part company with Sylvia, on returning from home leave we advertised in the Buenos Aires Herald, the English language newspaper, expecting to recruit an Anglo-Argentine girl. To our surprise, none applied. Instead, one morning, Maura's phone rang and a voice said: 'You like Japanese girl, yes?' She was invited for interview; we engaged her; and she stayed with us till we went home. The children loved her: she was good-natured; had endless patience; and would sit on the floor playing with them. She also amused them with beautiful paper cut-outs. And she could paint in both Japanese and European styles. She fitted easily into family life. Her name was Hideko Yahagi.

Hideko's life-story was extra-ordinary: I record what she told us. Her father had committed suicide: in Japan that was a disgrace. Hideko was brought up by her mother, but an uncle played a key rôle. When she was still in her teens, he decided to arrange a marriage for her. She disliked the whole idea, and played for time. She asked her uncle if she might first go to Tokyo and attend a course at the Imperial Doll-making School. This was agreed. She emerged as third prize-winner in the national competition for her year. Again, the idea of an arranged marriage was advanced. This time, while again not contesting the principle, she asked if she might go and visit some relations in Brasil before getting married. This too was accepted. Hideko was given a return ticket on a Dutch boat sailing to Brasil, with stop-overs in South Africa and Argentina. Whilst crossing the Indian Ocean she confided her life-story to one of the ship's officers. The latter suggested that she get off the ship in Buenos Aires; claim a refund for the unused portion of her ticket; and use the money to make a new start in life. She did, and that is how she came to us.

Sadly, things later went awry. When we left Argentina she decided to visit the United States, staying with American friends she'd met in Buenos Aires. She married an American, who turned out to be very possessive. He forbade her to have further contact with the American friends or us, and so we lost touch.

A final member of the domestic staff was the gardener: he did not live in, but came frequently and kept the garden beautifully. Agostino was Italian, but had been a long time in Buenos Aires. He too was good with the children: Rupert, in particular, followed him around like a shadow. Their conversation, given the latter's modest Spanish, was at first limited; but gave satisfaction to both sides. Here is a sample. (Rupert) *'Que es esto?'* ('What is this?'). (Agostino) *'Esto es un bicho.'* ('This is a bug'.) Gardening was very different in Argentina. There were frequent tropical storms, when up to 30 centimetres of rain would fall in a day, washing out all the seedlings planted the day before. There were frequent ant invasions. A huge column of ants would appear from some distant garden; march into ours; saw off sections of leaves in (say) a bed of zinnias; and then march back a hundred metres or more to their home, each bearing a green flag. A whole flowerbed might be cleared in this way overnight! However, in summer, a new bed of zinnias would grow at the rate of two or three centimetres a day.

We also had a so-called *sireno*, or night-watchman, though we never saw him except when he came to be paid. The theory was that security was poor; and that the *sireno* would increase it by patrolling the streets at night and keeping miscreants at bay. The practice was different. The *sireno* patrolled all right. But he kept up a constant cry of *'sireno'* as he went. Any self-respecting criminal would therefore know he was coming, and hide until he had gone by. It was really a protection racket. We paid up for fear that otherwise the *sireno* would encourage criminals to come our way!

Another member of our regular cast – though not on our domestic staff – was the plumber, who rejoiced in the name of Don Juan! How he had acquired the 'Don', a term of respect, was always a mystery to us. Whenever we reported that anything needed attention his reaction was always the same. He would inspect the problem area, and then announce with great gusto *'hay que romper **todo'** ('we must break up everything') Out would come a heavy hammer, and whole sections of wall would disappear under its blows as Don Juan sought to trace the offending pipe through the house!

Rupert was rising three when we arrived; Claire was born soon after; and William appeared a few months before we left Argentina. Both Claire and William were baptised at St Saviour's Anglican Church, Belgrano, a suburb of Buenos Aires: Claire in 1964 and William in 1966. Rupert and Claire learnt to swim in our pool there, and William to crawl. Rupert learnt to ski, and started school. He also became bi-lingual; and, although the Spanish language went underground for a while after we went home, his Argentine experience came into its own when, fifteen or so years later, he went to live for good in Spain.

The children had lots of friends. All enjoyed being in the multi-racial, extended family I have described. All led a very outdoor life, mainly in our garden or those of friends. They began to enjoy the exploring kind of holidays which were to become a recurrent feature of their childhood and adolescence. And all benefited from a period when, more than at any other time in their lives, their parents had hours and hours to spend with them.

On first arrival, when people politely enquired whether we had a family, we replied affirmatively, explaining that we had one son, and that a sibling was on the way. We noticed reactions of surprise and indeed pity. Why? We soon learnt. In Argentina children are numerous: our interlocutors felt some terrible misfortune must have befallen a couple who had been married for eight years and had achieved so few! If you ask an Argentine couple about their family, they will not claim to have one until five children have arrived. A large family *(famille nombreuse)* begins at 12! An *estancia* owner will always want to have at least 8 boys, so as to be able to field two polo teams!

The Argentine way of life

Predictably, the way of life in Argentina was very, very different from anything we'd experienced before. Key words were *mañana* and *trámites*.

Everybody knows that, in the Hispanic world, *mañana* is not meant to be taken literally. But in Argentina, and no doubt in other parts of Latin America, it must be taken with still more doses of salt than in the mother-land. We learnt that *mañana* really meant 'some time'; that '*enseguida*' (immediately) meant 'fairly soon'; and that '*enseguidita*' (its diminutive) meant 'very soon'. There was <u>no</u> word which really meant 'tomorrow', the notion of urgency being alien to the Argentine temperament!

A good illustration of how things were, may be a description of how we used to organise a typical dinner party for eighteen at our home. We would start a month before, sending out perfectly normal invitation cards, bearing the magic letters RSVP. These seldom produced any response. Two weeks before time, we would telephone with a follow-up enquiry. Some would say yes, some would say no, and some would say maybe. We would then try to replace the drop-outs by telephoned invites to others. Once we had (finally) extracted eighteen acceptances, that was not the end of the story. Prudence dictated that, on the day of the party, one found it 'necessary' to speak to each invitee (or couple) on the 'phone about some other matter; and then, before closing off, just add 'We're looking forward to seeing you this evening'. One could expect at least one couple to cry off at that stage!

For one party, having been through all these hoops, we had fourteen out of eighteen drop out in the last 24 hours; but managed to replace ten by desperate appeals to close friends before the party began! We came to wonder whether people simply disliked us or our parties! But friends re-assured us: they all had the same experience!

'*Trámites*' are, literally, procedures. But the word carries many more overtones. In Argentina there is a *trámite* for everything. It is usually highly bureaucratic and time-consuming. Often, the successful completion of a *trámite* implies the handing over of a bribe. Most people, if not poor, find *trámites* so tedious that they employ someone to take over the process on their behalf: this person is called a *despachante*. The Embassy was forced to retain a number of such people.

A good example of a *trámite* was the registration of the births of Claire and William. Any person then born in Argentina in principle acquired that country's citizenship, whilst any person born to a British father was entitled to claim British nationality at the Embassy. We wanted our children to have British but not Argentine citizenship. As far as William was concerned this was particularly important, because, if he had acquired Argentine citizenship, and had then visited the country after reaching majority, he would have been arrested and made to do Argentine military service. Children of diplomats, exceptionally, did not automatically acquire Argentine nationality. But it was necessary to have this confirmed on the Argentine birth certificate. And, to do this, the services of a *despachante* could not be invoked: I went in person to Argentina's Central Registration Office.

As it turned out, there was no problem about getting confirmation of the nationality position in either case. But Claire's registration raised another, quite different, question. Argentine law provides that the only forenames permitted on birth certificates are those of Catholic Saints, as spelt in the Spanish language. Here too, diplomats were allowed an exception if they insisted. When I refused the name Clara, the official asked me to spell Claire, which I did. '*This is really too much*' he said: '*I can understand that a Diplomat should insist on the use of his own language; but why should an Englishman insist on spelling his daughter's name in French?*' In the end, however, we got our way. And then, until she left Argentina three years later, our daughter was invariably called Clara or Clarita by almost everybody! By the time William was born the same official did not even suggest '*Guillermo*'! Taken together, the *mañana* and *trámites* syndromes meant that the normal rhythm of life is more or less reversed. In Europe I had been used to spending (say) one fifth of my time administering family affairs, leaving the rest for professional work or recreation. In Argentina, more like half of my time went on self-administration!

Looking back at Buenos Aires, one thing comes specially to mind. The Colón Opera House was to be, for Maura and me, a delight, an education and an alibi. Soon after our arrival we took an *abonnement* at the Colón. The Theatre was built some time around the end of the nineteenth century, when Argentina was very rich. It is one of Opera's grandest and most beautiful Houses. Constructed in a classical style, its stage and auditorium are huge, the latter surrounded by a vast and lofty ambulatory, with many bars and cafeterias leading off it. The seating is the most capacious and comfortable of any House I know. The Colón at once became Argentina's pride and joy, and still is. It matters not what Government is in power, or what policy of retrenchment it may be following. The Colón's huge Government subsidy is never in question. It naturally has its own orchestra, chorus and ballet. And singers of the highest international renown are hired.

It was the first time we had ever taken an *abonnement* for opera. The season at the Colón is long, and the programme of twenty or so operas varied. As a result we heard, for the first time, many operas we would not have gone to see otherwise. Over three seasons, we heard many marvellous performances. Our operatic experience was enormously broadened.

The Colón season is the hub of cultural life in Buenos Aires. As at Ascot, '*every one who's anyone is there*'. Each performance is a social event; and the evening is organised accordingly. Intervals usually last for 45 minutes, giving ample time for coffee, drinks and conversation. You get to know well, many of the people who share your *abonnement* evening. Moreover, the Colón is an alibi in terms of other duties. Even if the President of the Republic were to invite one to dinner – though of course we were not so invited! – this was still the case. One would just remark to the Private Secretary, in accepting, that one would be disposing of one's Colon tickets that night, and would be told on no account to do so; the President would not wish it; one would be invited on a different occasion! At our more humble level, in a city where there was a good deal of entertaining of diplomats, it was a joy to have a series of sacrosanct evenings throughout the season.

Getting out and around the Country

At the Embassy it was felt that, in such a huge country, UK based staff, to get any true feel for it, must get out and about in the Provinces: by meeting local officials, and by talking to all sorts of audiences, they could both learn a lot and also contribute to better understanding in Argentina of the UK and its rôle in the world. I encouraged staff to proceed accordingly, and did so myself, taking Maura with me whenever her maternal commitments and health allowed. During our nearly four years, I got to fifteen of the twenty-two Provinces: Maura to rather less. But the distances are huge; we travelled mainly by car; so we never got to the southern Provinces or the Territory of Tierra del Fuego. In all, I made four tours: to the north-west; to the north-east; to Córdoba Province in the Centre; and around Buenos Aires Province (which alone is much larger than the whole of the United Kingdom). They were all conducted in a broadly similar way.

To give the flavour, I describe just one: namely the trip to the north-west in May 1964. On it, I was accompanied by Maura; and we invited her Argentine teacher of Spanish, by now a friend, to come with us in the car. The trip took fifteen days, during which we covered 5,000 kilometres. No matter which way you travel from Buenos Aires, you must begin by crossing 700 kilometres of *pampa*. Before we saw it we imagined the *pampa* to be as flat as a pancake and covered with pampas grass; but in fact pampas grass is more likely to be found in the *sierras* (the foothills of the Andean chain). The *pampa* is monotonous, but not entirely featureless. It varies from the dead flat to the slightly rolling: and from tree-less to lightly treed. We travelled across it, more or less northwest, and on to the *sierras* at La Rioja. The very names of the places we visited from then on are sonorous and evocative. Turning north, we followed the *sierras*, to Catamarca, Tucumán, Salta and Jujuy; and finally we drove half way up the '*Quebrada de Humahuaca*' a great gorge in the Andes which rises to the Bolivian border, with 5,000 metre peaks on either side.

The scenery in the *Quebrada* reminds one of the Grand Canyon in the United States: steep, rocky slopes of every hue, from black, through purple, red and yellow to green. Down this gorge the Spanish *conquistadores* passed, when they first moved from Peru and Bolivia into Argentina in the sixteenth century. We saw the same sort of Indians, driving the same sort of mules, and bearing the same salt in their donkeys' paniers down to the Argentine plains. Leaving all this behind, we retraced our steps to Tucumán, and then returned to Buenos Aires via Santiago del Estero.

Four gauchos *near Salta [note* 'guardamontes'*], 1966.*

The programme included speeches by me on many aspects of British life and thinking, some in Spanish and some in English. The programme also included showing films about Britain with the aid of the Embassy's film van (whose operator had sometimes shown Indians the first film they ever saw); calling on authorities; visiting Universities; and talking to the press, and on TV and radio. We also visited several Anglo-Argentine *'Culturas Inglesas'* (Associations of English Culture). These Culturas are remarkable. They exist only in Latin America, and especially Argentina. Started in the 1920s, at first they had a variety of activities. But now they were focused mainly on English language teaching.

The programme was full, and most of the time we were rushing to keep up with it. But we had arranged to have a long weekend free in the loveliest region we visited: the Provinces of Salta and Jujuy. Maura's sister, Patsy, then on an IMF mission in Buenos Aires, flew up and joined us. In Salta itself, we were able to see the magnificent annual *gaucho* parade on the National Day (25 May), when some three hundred or more *gauchos* paraded in traditional costume, on lovely horses equipped with *guardamontes*, the wide leather flaps, a bit like elephants ears, which protect the legs from the many prickly bushes of the *sierras*.

Some incidents stick in the mind.

In the Catamarca Cultura, a lecture by me – yes, me – on *'Four hundred years of Shakespeare'* was followed by a delightful display, by the students, of local music and dancing. In Salta the Governor lent us an *'estanciero'* for an hour's flight to get a good view of the *Cordillera*. In Jujuy we arrived to call on the Governor only two hours after a motion of censure had been introduced into the Provincial Legislature and had led to immediate rioting in the streets. Moreover the wreath I was given to lay, in front of the Argentine flag, was so heavy the local press photographer snapped me literally staggering under the weight!

In the *Cultura* at Santiago del Estero there was more music. The young ladies of the *Cultura*, besides being dark-eyed beauties, seemed to have been born with golden voices, a natural gift for harmony, and a guitar in their hands. We and the film operator – a General Anders Pole – were constrained to sing Tipperary in response; but our voices remained singularly un-golden.

A colourful British diplomat

As we began to move around the Provinces people repeatedly said: *'So you're from the British Embassy – how is Sir Eugen'*. Initially my response was simply to say I had not met the gentleman; but I observed incredulity, or even suspicion, on the part of my interlocutors. I made enquiries, and realised that Sir Eugen Millington Drake (1889-1972), was a living legend, not only in Argentina and Uruguay, but throughout Latin America. Later, he came to Buenos Aires, where Maura and I enjoyed his company and found him one of the most colourful diplomats we ever met. Even now, he is still remembered there.

Educated at Eton, and at the Universities of Oxford and Berlin, he was a distinguished rower, tennis player and boxer. He joined the Diplomatic Service in 1912. For his first posting abroad, a year later, he was offered a choice of Berlin, Paris or St Petersburg, and chose the last. Soon the First World War broke out and the German Army approached the gates of the city: the Embassy was evacuated. Eugen escaped on a sledge over the ice, leaving his belongings behind. His next posting, in 1915, was to Buenos Aires, where he began a life-long love affair with the Spanish language and the River Plate. From Argentina he went to Paris, where he served on the British Delegation to the Versailles Peace Conference. He was to serve again in Argentina (1929-33); and to end his normal diplomatic career as Minister to Uruguay (1934-41): smaller posts did not have Ambassadors in those days.

Meanwhile he had married Lady Effie Mackay, a daughter of Lord

Inchcape, then the owner of the Cunard Shipping Company. With the help of her money, Eugen became a public benefactor wherever he went, and notably in Uruguay, a small country where everybody knows everybody and Britain is popular. (When Winston Churchill died, one person in every 1,000 of the entire Uruguayan population went to sign the book of condolence at the Embassy.) Eugen was in charge of the Legation (as it then was) when, in late 1939, the German Pocket Battleship *Graf Spee* limped into the harbour at Montevideo, damaged, and hotly pursued by three British cruisers. He marched at once to see the President, and famously said: *'Get that bloody thing out of here!'* The President gave the German Commander the order to go, with a tight time limit: the ship was scuttled, and the wreckage was still visible in the harbour 25 years later[1].

Three years later he was seconded by the Foreign Office to the British Council, to be its roving Chief Representative to Latin America. By now he was not only world famous, because of the *Graf Spee*; but he was also known and respected in Latin America for his literary accomplishments. At one time Vice-President of the British Poetry Society, he had edited a book in Spanish entitled *'Joyas de la Poesia Inglesa' ('Jewels of English Poetry');* and also an anthology of Argentine Provincial Poetry. He enjoyed nothing better than reciting, and giving talks about, both English and Argentine poetry.

A favourite story about this larger-than-life character relates to one of his poetry recitals, given in Buenos Aires to an audience consisting largely of elderly ladies. He was standing by a lectern, declaiming, with one hand resting on it. Absent-mindedly, he had not paid enough attention to fastening his braces. In mid-poem, his trousers fell to the ground. Without allowing this to affect his composure, or even to make him pause in reciting, he stepped calmly out of the trousers, moved behind the lectern, and continued to the end!

George Middleton told me another classic. On leave in London, he was invited to lunch at the Argentine Embassy, and was pleased to find Eugen placed opposite him. As the staff began to serve lunch, George watched fascinated as Eugen dipped into his capacious pockets; brought out what was clearly a pack of sandwiches; and started unwrapping it. Seeing George's surprise, Eugen then said to him, in a loud voice: *'Always do this, you know – can't trust the food in these foreign houses!'* The Ambassador was unperturbed: Eugen's eccentricities were well-known throughout the length and breadth of Latin America, and merely added to people's love and admiration of him!

Holiday travels

In those days, Foreign Office Diplomatic Bags were carried by air by a Queen's Messenger on a route which ran through Rio de Janeiro, Montevideo and Buenos Aires to Santiago de Chile. The Buenos Aires Embassy was responsible for receiving the bag for Paraguay and arranging its onward transmission. It had to be carried on by air to Asunción by hand of a UK based staff member from one of the two Embassies. I made two of these runs, which fell conveniently at weekends.

The first time, I limited myself to Asuncion itself. Though the country was still under the strong dictatorship of General Stroessner, this did not much affect ordinary life. Asuncion was a quiet and pleasant place to spend a weekend; and I enjoyed Paraguayan music as a change from Argentine. (The Paraguayan *conjunto* is based on harps and guitars: the Argentine, on guitars and a *bombo*, which is a deep-toned, hide-skin, drum.) I admired some pleasing Spanish colonial buildings, and was surprised to find amongst them a large Railway Station. Entering, I asked where the trains went. 'Everywhere', was the reply. 'Even to Buenos Aires?' 'Yes, Sir, the train to Buenos Aires leaves every day at 1730 hours.' 'How long does the journey take?' 'Three or four days, more or less!' This last answer did not surprise. The distance is over 1,000 kilometres. The train would cross and recross the great River Paraná, which had no bridges or tunnels, only unreliable ferries, and which is still 2 kilometres wide when it reaches Paraguay. The track was no doubt often washed away. And the rolling stock was antique.

For the second visit to Paraguay, we arranged a long weekend; and Maura flew up with me. Hiring a VW minibus, the only vehicle available, we set off to see the Falls of Iguaçú, on the Brasilian border. The distance was some 300 kilometres each way, of which only the first 100 were metalled, the rest being earth road. On either side of it was dense tropical forest. We saw few human habitations. The red clay surface was firm and dry: we made good progress and were not far from our goal when disaster struck.

Coming over a steep rise, we saw a mud-slick just ahead. I could not halt in time. We skidded through 90 degrees, and rolled onto our backs. Hardly had we done so when, still lying prone and breathless, I saw the bare brown legs of a dozen Paraguayan Guaraní Indians, who had appeared from nowhere and were trying to help. I was soon freed; but Maura was unconscious. By chance, a Paraguayan doctor in a light ambulance passed down the road within minutes, and stopped to help. He told us later he only came that way once a fortnight. He declared Maura concussed, took her on board, bade me follow in the mini-bus the Indians had righted, and took us back to the Capital. Meanwhile I had noted that the Indians had carefully collected all our belongings for us, including Maura's handbag. Nothing was missing, and we were later told that the Guaraní are remarkably honest. Maura was uncomfortable for a while after we got back to Buenos Aires, but happily no permanent damage was done. We never got to see the Falls!

By now, we had reached the point at which, progressively, our children became old enough to be taken away on family holidays. Our key destinations were the Chilean Andes, the United Kingdom (on home leave), and the Uruguayan beaches. Maura and I also had the interesting experience of a visit to an *estancia* west of Buenos Aires.

We ski-ed in Chile in August and September 1964. Rupert and Sylvia came with us. Claire was left with her kind-hearted godmother, Frances Beak, in Buenos Aires. We drove 1,000 kilometres to Mendoza in the eastern foothills of the Andes, and then flew on to Santiago. The flight was spectacular, passing Aconcagua (6,960 m) and several smoking volcanoes. The Andes range rises incredibly steeply, and the peaks are awe-inspiring. We had rented a chalet from the Lings, for a fortnight, at La Parva (3,000 metres). John Ling (then my opposite number in Chile, later an MEP) met us at the airport; and took us home to dinner. There, John and Jenny fed us, and kitted us out with any ski things we lacked; John drove us up to the chalet, where he left us, along with our rations. The latter had to cover all our needs of food and drink for a week, as we had been warned there were no shops in La Parva. John was to re-victual us the following Saturday.

We woke to find ourselves in a truly magnificent setting. Perched in the midst of the High Andes, the chalet – its real name was '*Refugio del Señor Don Enrique Valenzuela*' – looked down the steep and narrow gorge we had climbed at night. Framed in the cleft we could see Santiago and the plain around it; and, beyond that, the coastal range. It was over this breath-taking panorama that, each evening, we watched a blazing sun sink. La Parva was a place of perfect peace. In winter it was too cold for insects, so there were very few birds. Nobody used a car, except to come or leave. When the ski-lifts stopped, the world fell totally silent. There were no phones or electricity, and no radios blared. We had bottled gas for lighting, cooking and hot water; and paraffin for central heating.

Pistes were limited. There were only three ski-lifts and a nursery tow: but almost nobody on them. We ski-ed happily for a week. Rupert loved his first experience on skis: Sylvia hated hers, and gave up. There was a fly in the ointment: we had forgotten sun-cream, and at that altitude the sun burnt one mightily. There were no shops at all. When we asked where we could buy cream, or for that matter a boot-lace, the answer was '*abajo*', i.e. down in Santiago. There was only one bus a day each way: so a return journey took two days. We did without, and burned!

By Friday we were looking forward to the re-victualling; but overnight there was a colossal fall of snow. We assumed no-one would get through; and Maura considered how to stretch the rations. That evening, as we sat on our balcony, drinking a gin and tonic in the setting sun at the end of a perfect day, we perceived a small man, with a vast *rücksack* and carrying a pair of skis, struggling up towards us. He finally stopped below our balcony; looked up; and said: '*Colonel Ramsay, Queen's Messenger, carrying your mail*'.

This improbable statement was 100% true. The Colonel had been carrying the bag to Santiago, and received mail for us in Buenos Aires. Arriving in Chile on the Friday night he had asked John whether he could ski, in his three-day rest period. John had replied that he was bringing us supplies next day; that we would surely not mind having the Colonel stay for a couple of nights; and that he could then return *abajo* by bus. John was blissfully unaware, down in Santiago, of the heavy snow. Well before reaching La Parva he found his car could make no headway; stopped; and nonchalantly left the Colonel, with our supplies, by the roadside. A French family, passing in a Jeep, gave him a lift to a point 300 metres below us: then they too could get no further. He walked the rest of the way! The story had an unhappy ending. On his first run, next morning, the Colonel, ignoring my advice to wait a little until the sheet-ice at the top of the run had softened a little, fell, twisted his knee, and could ski no more! We did not see him again for a while. But in 1967, when I was working in the Foreign Office, I took Maura and Rupert to see the 'Trooping the Colour' from one of the Office windows looking over the Horseguards. They were overcrowded. I led my little party up a staircase to a lavatory I knew had a good view and was unlikely to be in use! On entering we found – yes, Colonel Ramsay – who had had the same idea and was already peering out! We shared the loo!

One was entitled to home leave after two years, so in July 1965 we flew back to the United Kingdom to have the longest holiday of my entire working life. Four months were due to us, and I 'earned' another two weeks whilst on leave! We did not return till late in November! It was, of course, a time for letting the two families see something of Rupert and Claire. So we moved around a lot. Rupert and Claire had their first real taste of the Lakeland fells, the former on his feet and Claire on my back.

Our third holiday destination whilst in Argentina was Uruguay. Already in 1964, Maura and I had spent a weekend with the Wallaces at Montevideo, where Charles was now First Secretary and where they had a delightful house and garden. They had shown us the coast as far as Punta del Este, and we had liked it. Early in 1966 – on the leave earned whilst on leave! – we set off for a holiday at Punta Ballena, where we had rented a house set back from a glorious, sandy unspoilt bay two or three kilometres long and almost deserted. Getting there, however, turned out to be a major adventure.

In theory it looked simple enough. We had planned to catch the ferry north across the River Plate from Buenos Aires to Colonia – the crossing is about the same distance as Dover-Calais – and then drive east to our destination, 500 kilometres away. But fate stepped in: some weeks before our departure the ferry workers went on strike for more pay. When we saw the ferry would not run, we switched plans. Maura and Claire were to fly to Montevideo, where the Wallaces would look after them. My rôle was to drive Rupert and Ofelia – she was to look after us in Uruguay – round the River Plate estuary; across the River Uruguay by a different ferry at Concepción; and on through Uruguay to pick up the others and reach Punta Ballena. It added 500 kilometres to the driving. My car party was to team up with a Bolivian friend, Juan Pinilla, and his son of about Rupert's age, also driving a car bound for the Uruguayan beaches.

The cars were to leave at dawn. Overnight there was an immense tropical storm, with more than 10 centimetres of rain. This was a complication. Our chosen route involved 200 kilometres of earth road. Plans changed again. Juan and I decided to add another 500 kilometres of metalled road, in order to reduce the earth-road section to under 100 kilometres. We set off at 0600. The drive was appalling. Lorry after lorry had crashed on (or off!) the metalled roads. Sometimes it was difficult to get by. The rain kept falling. We hit the earth section at 2200. We were up to our axles in mud. We literally ploughed on. Amazingly, we made it to Concepcion – arriving at 0200 hours. There was no hotel room to be had. We slept fitfully in the cars. Our ferry was due to leave around 0900 hours.

At dawn we looked for breakfast. Only one café was open. It was the most fly-blown place I've ever encountered: worse than anything in the Middle East, or anything described in Evelyn Waugh's books! The problem was to get any morsel of food into one's mouth without an army of flies going in with it. Our solution was to buy small packets of biscuits; clutch the packet shut; remove one biscuit at a time from the pack; and in a single motion whisk it into the mouth, slamming the lips behind!

Fortunately the flies seemed less keen on black coffee: and the boys had water from bottles.

Then off we went to clear Argentine customs. I had obtained a document – known as a *franquicia* – from the Headquarters of the Argentine Customs in Buenos Aires. At Concepcion the Customs Officer took one look at it and said: '*Con esto, Señor, no se puede pasar*'. ('With this, Sir, you cannot pass.') We argued the point at length. I explained that the Head of Customs had personally assured me I could enter or leave the country with the *franquicia* at any border crossing: and asked him to telephone for confirmation. He responded that the 'phone was out of action. Juan came up in support, and warned the Officer of dire consequences for his career if he maltreated a senior British Diplomat. Finally, I was waved on. Not before time: the ferry was due to leave. We drove towards it. The Uruguay is a large river, perhaps one and a half kilometres across at this point, and fast-flowing. The ferries are correspondingly big. Ours was waiting to load at the jetty. Suddenly and without warning a '*pampero*' (whirlwind) burst upon us. A line of large poplars near us bent almost to the ground, some snapping off. All the smaller boats in the river sank at their moorings. Our ferry cast off at once, and stood out in the river. We ourselves escaped unhurt.

The *pampero* was gone in minutes; the ferry returned to the jetty; we went aboard and were soon landing on the other side, in Uruguay. We queued for the Uruguayan Customs, my car some places ahead of Juan's. Again I produced my *franquicia*, which the Uruguayan Embassy in Buenos Aires had promised would enable me to enter their country. The reply was by now predictable: '*Con esto, Señor, no se puede pasar*'. Again, there were long arguments. By now I was very tired, and became angry. When the Officer saw this he turned on me a warm smile, and came out with a disarming statement: '*Sir, there is a problem; however, the problem is not for you but for us!*' I asked him how it could be solved. '*Well, Sir, this is embarrassing. We here cannot authorise you to enter; but the Governor could. He is at the Provincial Capital, some distance away. If you would like to see him, I can take you; but first I shall be obliged to arrest you.*' I told him to go ahead. Then I remembered Juan, who I knew was trying to smuggle a case of whisky into Uruguay to lubricate his summer holiday, and said: '*I have a friend from Buenos Aires who is travelling with me – may he come along too?*' I identified Juan. The officer marched straight up to him and said, in a firm voice: '*You have nothing to declare, have you?*' Juan untruthfully agreed, and was waved through! We proceeded in convoy to the Office of the Governor, who had received warning of our approach. He met us at the door; gave us coffee; apologised profusely for any inconvenience;

asked if he could help us; and then sent us on our way.

It was by now approaching mid-day. I had not slept properly for nearly thirty hours. I dozed at the wheel. A moment later I was woken sharply by Ofelia, and brought the car to a halt in the middle of a ploughed field! We went on, our route taking us through a suburb of Montevideo. The road crossed some twenty railway tracks, all leading to the main station. Traversing one of them, my car had a blow-out and came to a dead stop. We had to change the tyre. Whilst we did so, a whistle sounded. A train was approaching at a steady pace on our track! We <u>just</u> finished, and got clear, before it came through. We arrived at the Wallaces' in time for tea. I was so grey, with dust and fatigue, that Maura was seriously worried. But a shower worked wonders. And an hour or so later we safely reached Punta Ballena. Personally I found the journey traumatic: Juan also, though less so. Rupert and Juan's boy had enjoyed the excitement. And Ofelia – for whom this was the first trip abroad of her life – had been enchanted by the novelty and the thought of all the traveller's tales she'd have to tell when she got back!

I close these holiday reminiscences with a few lines about a long weekend visit Maura and I made to an *estancia* in May 1964. It was near Ameghino, in the westernmost part of the Province of Buenos Aires, about 400 kms from the Capital. Not large by local standards, it comprised about 4,500 hectares; ran 4,000 head of cattle; and had about half its land area given over to cereals. It was pretty modern, so could be run by twelve men. The trucks, the farm, and the nearest town, were all linked by radio. Crop-spraying was done by plane. They simply called the local aerodrome by radio; requested that *'field no…be sprayed'* with such and such a mixture, and the job was done.

Estancia life in those days had a nineteenth century flavour. There were plenty of horses, dogs and servants, and time did not matter. The cooking on this *estancia* was first-class. *Estancia* families were huge. For visitors, the main entertainments were riding and shooting. There was any amount of game. Most *estancias* rear and train polo ponies. We were immediately mounted on two of the latter and equipped with polo sticks – the first time we had ever touched one. The ponies were so good that they automatically positioned one for the stroke. I was surprised to find I could hit the chuck without much difficulty.

Time to go

Our stay in Argentina was memorable for many reasons. It was one of our only two diplomatic postings outside Europe – the other having been Washington. It was our longest posting until we joined the European

Commission in Brussels. It was our only experience of Latin America. It was the only truly traditional posting I ever had: leaving the Falklands issue out of account, this was straight-forward bilateral diplomacy, quite different from work with international organisations and from the special case Embassies of Bonn/Berlin and Washington. And it was very much a family post. I do not mean simply that two of our three children were born there. I mean also that the pressure of work was moderate. As a result, and because of the summer hours, I was able to spend more time with the family – holidays apart – than in any other posting. Given that, not long after, Rupert would start boarding school, this was more than timely. Finally, the Argentine people are friendly and welcoming. We have many reasons for remembering Argentina with great affection.

But it was time to leave. And so, on 24 February 1967, our family, now of five, sailed from Buenos Aires for Tilbury on RMS *Amazon*. It was a moment of sad partings, especially from Ofelia and Hideko, neither of whom we ever saw again, but also from many good friends, Argentine and British, in the Embassy and outside.

CHAPTER 12

The Foreign Office: Rhodesian Sanctions; Science and Technology Department (1967-70)

The family settles in to a new home

*A*MAZON WAS A sister-ship to *Arlanza* (on which we had sailed to Argentina nearly four years before). She was very comfortable, and this time Maura was able to benefit. William, aged six months, was too young to appreciate the opportunities; but Rupert and Claire, the only children on board, loved the whole thing. The journey was pleasant but uneventful.

Reaching Tilbury in mid-March, we stayed with Maura's mother at Gerrards Cross, and looked for a home of our own. Until now, we had always rented accommodation; but we knew I would be at the Foreign Office for quite a while, and it made sense to get our feet on the property ladder. We were lucky, and found what we wanted quite soon: a house called King's Walden on the Windsor Road. The agreed price of £12,500 seemed enormous to us; but in fact was not a lot for such a good property. We loved living in it for the next three years.

Our first 'own' house deserves brief description. It stood back from the road, with a protective belt of trees and shrubs shielding it largely from view. Well built in the 1930s, of red brick, with a steeply pitched tiled roof and a detached garage, it suited our needs. There were three reception and four bedrooms; and with my own hands, I converted the spacious un-floored loft into a large playroom. Each child had his/her own room. After paying for the house, we had little cash left: so, over a few months, I personally redecorated the whole place. It saved money. It also left me with a 'frozen' right shoulder: in spite of a painful manipulative operation, shoulder movement thereafter was never better than 90%. Golf, squash and tennis were now out. This was sad, as I had enjoyed them all – and especially the last two. Behind the house was a delightful garden, enclosed, and ideal for children. Rectangular, it ran back for 50 metres or more, ending at the seventeenth century brick wall of Bulstrode Park.

Soon it was time for the two older children to go to school. Rupert and

Claire went off together, each morning, to a small private establishment (Oakend School). In the autumn of 1968, however, Rupert set off to Winchester, as a boarder at the Pilgrims' Preparatory School. Five years later, he moved to Bradfield College. In this book, no systematic attempt is made to follow our children's careers after reaching the age of majority.

It seems worth saying, though it means anticipating the story, that over the years Maura and I gave much thought to what might be best for the children's schooling. One's personal background and circumstances are always major influences. We had been brought up differently. When I was small, it was normal for sons of the professional classes to be sent to boarding school around the age of eight: first to preparatory, and then on to public school. This had been my father's lot. The fact that my parents went to India for six years when I was four, and did not take their children with them, meant this precedent was followed for myself and my siblings. For Maura, things were otherwise. It was not nearly so common for girls to be sent to boarding schools, although, because of the lack of good local schools in Egypt, Maura's elder sister, Julie, had been sent home in the 1930s to a boarding school in England. Maura's parents gave her the choice of a Boarding Grammar School (Bedford High), or staying in Gerrards Cross. She chose the latter. As to our circumstances, the Diplomatic Service involved an essentially peripatetic life, with its members being sent to a new post every two to four years: some of these posts could be tough – notably in health or political terms. We felt it important to ensure continuity in our children's education nevertheless.

That was why we launched Rupert into the British boarding school system, despite our sense of loss when he left the family circle. Later, it became clear that he was not very academically inclined; that Claire was definitely more studious; and that William was more so again. Rupert, moreover, far more than the others, disliked leaving home: perhaps partly due to being the first of the brood!

When Claire reached the age of eight, we were at Bonn. She started at the French Lycée, at the end of our street. It didn't work, so we switched her to the British Embassy Preparatory School (BEPS). Thereafter, she began forming her own views about education. There were too many boys for her liking at BEPS: she asked to be sent to boarding school like her elder brother; and was found a place at Rookesbury Park, a girls' prep school near Wickham, Hampshire. She was well taught, and had a perhaps over-rigorously Christian Headmistress. When we were in Wickham, the evening before Claire's Confirmation, having an extended family dinner in our hotel, Claire was summoned back for prayers when the soup course had only just finished! Claire went on from there to the Godolphin Public School at Salisbury, at age thirteen; but after a while she was irritated by a certain spirit of conformism, and also by a House-mistress who thought watching TV with the other girls was preferable to reading alone! She also complained about excessive incense at the C of E Church where they went on Sundays. Her Housemistress said it was moderate. Maura and I attended, one day, *incognito*, and found the Priest literally disappeared in a cloud of the stuff. We tackled the Headmistress, and another solution was found! At this stage, Claire asked to be brought back home to take her 'A' levels. By now, we had moved to Brussels, and had also decided that I would remain with the Commission for the rest of my professional career. Claire went to the British School of Brussels [BSB] to finish her secondary education.

At Bonn, William started at an excellent infant school, run by the charming but elderly Mrs Day, an English lady. At age six he moved on to BEPS. When we went to Brussels, we tried the European School for him (he was then aged seven). But it was in rapid transition. Following British, Irish and Danish accession, it had just created a new English language section. Initially there was confusion. William was not moving forward as he should, notably because his continental classmates were behind him, having started school a year later. After four terms, we resolved that he too should go into the boarding school system, and sent him, in Rupert's footsteps, to the Pilgrims'. He probably found it easier than Rupert, because the latter and Claire had set a boarding school pattern in the family. Like Claire, he then started taking a hand in the pattern of his education. Encouraged by his friend, Ewan Haggar, he applied for, and – to his parents' amazement and delight – won, a scholarship to join the Winchester College Quiristers. He was encouraged to go on singing in the Choir, when he went on to the College, until his voice broke: his adult voice might have been better if he had stopped sooner, but the musical education was superb.

Our constant aim, in all this, was to do what was best for the children – even if it meant being ourselves often separated from them. We tried to compensate by making visits in term-time whenever possible: from Brussels, in particular, Maura was forever driving over to the UK on short trips. We also spent all the time we could with them on their holidays. Only they can say whether they would have been happier if we had handled things differently.

I was by now occupying positions of greater responsibility in the Foreign Office. Hours were far longer than in Buenos Aires. Moreover, commuting

Our three children at Gummer's Howe in Cumbria, 1967.

ate up two and a half hours each day. (The conditions on my train-tube-bus journeys were disagreeable: after three years I told Maura I would never commute like that again; and fortunately never had to.) So I did not see much of the family during the week. But, apart from Foreign Office missions abroad, my weekends were generally free, and we continued to ensure we had our full ration of leave.

Living so close to Rose Garden Cottage, we saw a lot of Maura's mother and Julie. We also visited Ackenthwaite for holidays or weekends. And, in the lovely August of 1968, we had a memorable family holiday staying with Elizabeth in Aikiehill, her delightful cottage near Gatehouse, Kirkcudbrightshire. Here, Rupert began his long love-affair with horse-riding. There was also a lot of mucking about in water – whether on the coast or in the streams and lakes.

Besides these distant forays, we took the children at weekends to attractions nearer home. Rupert still recalls a Royal Artillery Open Day at Larkhill. There were visits to the Royal Tournament, and to many London sights and museums. Maura and I also attended, with pleasure, the Garter Ceremony at Windsor, invited by Priscilla Firth[1], now widowed and living there, at a period when her brother was Dean.

But not all our memories of King's Walden were to be pleasant. In late-

July, 1969, Maura contracted meningitis. It was very worrying. Fortunately her illness was at once correctly diagnosed by our stand-in General Practitioner. Maura was removed to Wexham hospital. The infection was brought under control. But it was many weeks before she could cope with home life; months before her strength really began to return; and years before she fully recovered.

The timing was fortunate in one sense: my summer holiday was due. But it was impractical for me to look after three children under ten; cope with house and large garden; and also be at hand to see and help Maura. Our two families saved the day. William went off, with Maura's mother and Julie, for a holiday in the Highlands. My parents took charge of Rupert and Claire at Ackenthwaite. And things gradually settled back into place. We hoped the Foreign Office would leave us four years, rather than three, in the United Kingdom; but in this we were to be disappointed.

The Rhodesian Sanctions Unit

The Office had not said, when they told me to return home, what would be my specific appointment: soon after I reached Britain, this became clear. I was to have a big change of scene, becoming Head of the Rhodesian Sanctions Unit [RSU]). I remained a First Secretary, but this was promotion within the grade.

Some scene-setting about Southern Rhodesia (now Zimbabwe) is needed. De-colonisation in Africa was progressing fast. However, South Africa had been committed to Apartheid (permanent government by the minority white population) since 1948. Southern Rhodesia, though still British, had enjoyed internal self-government since 1923. The white population had held political control throughout. Now, the British were ready and anxious to concede full independence to the country, in line with what was happening in other British dependencies in Africa; but they wanted this linked to a one-man, one-vote constitution, ending white supremacy. The whites, led by Ian Smith, were strongly opposed, and of course encouraged by the example of South Africa. After endless negotiations, Ian Smith ('Smithie') lost patience: on 11 November, 1965, he made a 'Unilateral Declaration of Independence' [UDI] and defied the British Government. Prime Minister Harold Wilson rejected this. But he was not prepared to use military force to bring matters under control. He announced that economic sanctions would be imposed, and bring Southern Rhodesia to its knees. The Foreign Office was given responsibility for co-ordinating the sanctions, and the RSU, a mini-Department with four officers, was set up. By the time I took charge of the Unit, my predecessor, Robin Farquharson, had built up a substantial machinery. I took over a going concern.

My immediate task was to familiarise myself both with the strategy and with the instruments for its execution. Britain's aim was to starve Southern Rhodesia of supplies. But, although this policy had wide international support, its execution was never going to be easy, because of geography. To the north, Zambia could be relied on to help the UK. Namibia, to the west, was under South African control. Botswana, to the south-west, was newly independent, but under pressure from South Africa. The latter, to the south, was clearly going to help Southern Rhodesia. To the east lay Mozambique: the country was still a Portuguese colony; but in fact Portuguese authority was weak, and Portugal was not supporting sanctions. Mozambique's key port of Beira had a good rail link to Southern Rhodesia.

Our first instrument was intelligence. We needed to detect sanction-busting operations in advance. Then we needed to head them off, by diplomacy or by force. The diplomatic work was to forewarn friendly governments about operations being prepared in their territory, and ask them to intervene. As to force, Britain established a naval patrol off Mozambique – the Beira patrol – which was tasked to intercept and search ships reasonably suspected of carrying goods for South Rhodesia.

Our intelligence was extraordinary. This was the first time I had been in a position where secret intelligence was of key importance, and I had to have a much increased security clearance. The whole apparatus of Government had been mobilised. In those days officials were not allowed to refer publicly to the Security Service [MI5], or to the Secret Intelligence Service [MI6]. The very existence of Government Communications Headquarters [GCHQ] was still secret! But all three were feeding the RSU with information. The extent of what we knew was amazing. A huge range of people and firms were busy smuggling stuff to 'Smithie'. Many were British, including some well-known and supposedly respectable people. Often we could, by different initiatives, prevent them succeeding. One would have loved to see many of them prosecuted, especially those who were actively working against their own Government's policy. But it was almost always impossible: not because there was any doubt of guilt; but because proving it would have involved revealing sources we wanted to keep hidden!

However, we in the RSU, though we worked hard to implement Harold Wilson's strategy, never believed it could succeed. There were simply too many ways of getting round sanctions. We were right. It was not until 1979 that UDI was abandoned by its authors: in the following year a multi-racial Southern Rhodesia – renamed Zimbabwe – obtained independence. Sadly, the end-result has been the establishment of the appalling dictatorship of Robert Mugabe. Out of the frying pan, into the fire.

Common Market Department (Commonwealth Office)

Meanwhile another Harold Wilson initiative had taken me to fresh pastures. On 2 May, 1967, the Prime Minister had announced to Parliament a renewal of the British application for membership of the Communities. Although the chances of General De Gaulle agreeing to fresh negotiations were minimal, Wilson persuaded himself to the contrary. Whitehall was told to make preparations in double quick time.

Within days, I found myself pulled out of the RSU to join the team. John Robinson was firmly ensconced in the Foreign Office's European Economic Organisations Department [EEOD], and we had already resumed our wine-bar lunches. The Commonwealth Office (the old CRO had absorbed the former Colonial Office in 1966, and been renamed) needed reinforcement. Ken Gallagher, for whom I had earlier worked, was Head of its Common Market Department. I was appointed to be his Assistant (i.e. his no 2).

On joining my new Department, I felt that, more than four years after leaving Brussels, I was out of touch with official thinking, and asked colleagues how to get up to speed. There was no problem, they said. After the Heath negotiations *'someone in the Delegation had written an excellent narrative report'*. This, they said, was the starting point for all the new briefs they were preparing. I should read it. There was no need. It was the document of which, in early 1963, I had been Chief Editor. How gratifying to find that the bread John and I had cast upon the waters had returned to us after so many days!

And so, through that summer and autumn, and despite the expected negative noises from the General, Whitehall continued to prepare for the negotiations that would never be. It was not until, on 27 November 1967, the General gave a public *'non'* to Harold Wilson so clear that even the latter could no longer misunderstand, that the Whitehall machinery began, once again, to be unwound. I was freed for other duties.

Science and Technology Department

By January of 1968 I was Head of the Scientific Relations Department of the Foreign Office. (Later that year the Foreign Office absorbed the Commonwealth Office and was re-named the Foreign and Commonwealth Office, or FCO.) For me, this move meant promotion to the rank of Counsellor. It also meant taking charge of a Department which was rapidly growing in importance, which would keep me heavily involved in European affairs, and which would open my naturally enquiring mind to many new ideas and activities. I was working to two outstanding senior colleagues I knew from my Bonn days: Terence Garvey as Assistant Under-Secretary, and Con O'Neill as Deputy Under-Secretary.

An early initiative was to get the Department re-named as Science and Technology Department [STD], which seemed to correspond better both with what it was doing and with the spirit of the times. This was a period when Harold Wilson was making speeches about *'the white heat of the technological revolution'* and the importance of Britain being in the forefront of it; and Tony Benn, then still seen as a European, was the ambitious and energetic Minister of Technology. When I was next posted abroad, two years later, I wrote a brief about the Department's work to give to my successor, Ronald Arculus. By then the Department's staff consisted of two first-class Assistants, Jeremy Thomas and Mike Newington; six other good Administrative Class Officers; and appropriate support personnel. I was fortunate in having excellent PAs: first, Joyce Cooper, who later joined me in Bonn; and then May Gibson.

My brief for Ronald began by identifying the six areas of Departmental activity: general scientific and technological questions; the human environment; satellite telecommunications; peaceful uses of outer space; the sea-bed; and peaceful uses of atomic energy.

Here is an extract from what I wrote. *'I have evolved a Departmental philosophy…which appears to be regarded by others…in the FCO as generally reasonable. STD is essentially a Department concerned with scientific and technological [hereinafter S&T] innovation. As new S&T questions move into the area of international relations, some fit naturally…into the work of other FCO functional Departments, for example Defence Policy Department, Disarmament Department, and Aviation, Marine & Telecommunications Department. But for others there is no obvious home, and these come to STD. Experience of them over a period…shows whether they are likely to involve substantial and continuing work by the FCO. If they do, the work may continue to be done by STD; or it may gradually become evident that it should be transferred to another Department. If STD is to retain its…capacity to continue accepting, and dealing effectively with, the stream of S&T questions crowding on to the international scene, this process of load-shedding will have to be sustained. But it is necessary, in keeping a balance between the acceptance of new work and the off-loading of old, to ensure that the Department always has a reasonably homogeneous block of work to do and a strong feeling of general continuity in its activities. These factors have been successfully balanced in the past and I see no reason why they should not continue to be in the future...*

The Department's main contacts in London are with the Ministry of Technology, the Department of Education and Science, the Chief Scientific Adviser to Her Majesty's Government, the Council for Scientific Policy, the Research Councils, the [House of Commons] Select Committee for Science and Technology, the UK Atomic Energy Authority [UKAEA], and the two nuclear reactor design and construction companies... The Department already has, and – if it is to do its work properly – must maintain and expand, a wide range of contacts with unofficial bodies. These include universities, international lawyers specialising in the abstruse subjects with which we deal, industrialists and others... This is a fascinating Department. I have thoroughly enjoyed my two years in it.'

A challenging but entertaining part of my work consisted of shadowing, and sometimes frustrating, the many initiatives taken by Tony Benn which impinged on the foreign policy sphere. These were legion. The Foreign Secretary, Michael Stewart, had given me a specific instruction: *'Find out what Tony Benn is up to, and keep me informed'*. From the start Tony amused me, and we got on well on a personal level. He had a very direct and informal manner, and did not stand on ceremony or pull rank. He was of course a populist. He used to say that the role of a politician was not to lead but rather to follow public opinion (a viewpoint which I regard as an abnegation of responsibility). Tony well understood what both he and I were up to. At the Grosvenor House Hotel, where he had been invited as guest speaker at one of the regular lunches organised by the Scientific Attachés of London Embassies, and where he knew I was present, he openly told his audience that he was *'conducting British foreign policy on S&T matters insofar as Mr Audland allows'!*

From amongst the many activities I undertook as Head of STD, I comment in some detail on just four, which for different reasons came to be of particular interest: the handling of peaceful nuclear energy affairs generally; the negotiation of the *'Agreement between the UK, the Federal Republic of Germany and the Netherlands on Collaboration in the Development & Exploitation of the Gas Centrifuge Process for producing Enriched Uranium'* (known as the Almelo Agreement); Space Policy; and Policy on the Seabed and the Ocean Floor.

Peaceful nuclear energy was a topical, technical and politically sensitive subject, of which I knew nothing, but on which, within weeks of my appointment, I was to find myself acting as the FCO's policy adviser and spokesman, in some delicate contexts. The learning curve was fast. I started with little scientific knowledge. The only thing to do was to leave technicalities to scientists and technicians, but get them to explain to me, in simple layman's language, what they were doing and see where political problems had arisen or might arise.

By the end of February 1968, I had carried out visits to a number of key installations throughout the country, all of which, in those days, were owned and operated by the UKAEA. Much of the information gathered went right over my head. But this crash course nevertheless gave me a first insight into the workings of peaceful nuclear energy. In the following months I learnt a lot more, both through participation in various Whitehall Committees and through direct involvement in the development of the gas centrifuge method of uranium enrichment, to which we shall come. (At no stage, then or later, was I involved in any aspect of the British nuclear weapons programme. Within the Foreign Office, this was in the provinces of the Defence Department and of the Disarmament Department.) By September of 1968, I was able to play a reasonably informed and constructive role in the British Delegation to the Annual Conference of the International Atomic Energy Agency (IAEA) in Vienna. The Hofburg was a delightful venue. In Vienna there are always both music to hear, and pictures to look at, in any spare moments.

Long before that September, however, I had faced my nuclear baptism of fire. For some time, Whitehall had been looking at the possibility of Britain no longer seeking to develop by herself the gas centrifuge enrichment process, but instead of co-operating with the West Germans and the Dutch, whose research and development programmes were thought to be comparable. Very soon after my arrival, the matter came to a head.

The words 'were thought to' used above are deliberately chosen. One has to remember that, in Britain, the peaceful use of nuclear energy had been a spin-off from the weapons programme. The UKAEA had always run the latter; and, apart from the actual construction of commercial reactors, it was still responsible in this country for the whole civil nuclear fuel cycle. The two sides of the AEA's activities – warlike and peaceful – complemented each other technically. So it was natural that, within the AEA, there should be all-pervading culture of secrecy.

So far as the gas centrifuge was concerned, moreover, the technology being developed would be as valuable in making weapons-grade high-enriched uranium as in making low-enriched material for civil reactors. In this sector, therefore, security levels were exceptionally high. Though the West Germans and the Dutch, of course, never had nuclear weapons programmes, they were equally aware of the possible uses of the centrifuge; so they too applied very high security restrictions in this field. Our beliefs about their progress, and theirs about ours, were therefore based on an assortment of estimates and assumptions.

It was in these circumstances that British Ministers decided to attempt the path of tripartite co-operation. The United States authorities were so informed, and immediately raised difficulties. They said that part of the British centrifuge technology had originated in the United States, in the days of close nuclear co-operation between the two countries; that their consent to the tripartite co-operation was therefore required; and that it would not be given. On 10 April, the British Cabinet deliberated, taking into account the view of British officials that our technology was totally home-grown. (Six days previously, the Attorney-General had grilled me intensively, to be sure he knew all the facts before advising in Cabinet about the legal issues.) The Cabinet determined to try and clear the American objections aside. It was decided that I, as the senior FCO official with any personal understanding of the issues, should be sent to Washington that night, to talk to the Americans and try to sort things out.

Shortly before lunchtime, Michael Stewart, the Foreign Secretary, called me to his office, informed me of the decision, and showed me the hastily prepared draft Minutes of this part of the Cabinet meeting, which were meant to constitute my political brief. I did not like them: there were words in the text which might actually increase our difficulties with Washington. I told the Foreign Secretary changes were essential. He instructed me to propose amendments; he then read these to the Cabinet Secretary on the telephone; and the two men agreed that my text reflected better what Ministers had meant! Thus is Cabinet business done when needs must! From then on, it was all systems go. For some reason my passport was in the Office. It was quickly furnished with an American visa. I completed my technical briefing as best I could. Maura brought a suitcase to Heathrow. I was driven there direct from the FCO. And by around 1830 hours I had taken off for New York. We arrived at JFK Airport rather late. I missed the last flight to Washington; had five hours sleep at an Airport hotel; and flew on first thing in the morning.

It was a great advantage to have spent three years working in Washington, since it gave me a feel for the best way to approach American officials on this sensitive subject. I cannot recall any details of the conversations. But my presentation must have carried some degree of credibility. After my visit, the United States decided not to make an issue of the matter, and we moved ahead with our approach to the Germans and Dutch.

We had a good negotiating team. Mike Michaels led for the Ministry of Technology; the UKAEA was represented by its Secretary, David Peirson, whilst Ned Franklin was their centrifuge expert; I represented the FCO; and my Departmental Legal Adviser (a key position) was Frank Berman (now Sir Frank). We were also in frequent contact with the Government's Chief Scientific Adviser, Sir Solly (later Lord) Zuckerman: he chaired the Whitehall Committee of senior Officials constituted to advise and control the negotiators. Jumping forward a bit, I would add that the Germans and Dutch also fielded effective teams. On the German side I remember particularly Günter Schuster, Rainer Loosch and Werner Ungerer, with all of whom I was destined to work closely again later on. Formally starting in autumn, 1968, the negotiations were complex: not because any of the three countries was in any doubt about wishing for a successful outcome, but because of the genuine technical, commercial and legal problems involved, compounded by the security complication.

Security had to be tackled first. We each needed to know the truth about progress made by the other two. Whether we would reach an agreement at all would depend, to a substantial extent, on our assessment of our partners' achievements. But none of us wanted to get into a position where, having revealed all mutually, it would be found that a partner was unable to contribute a fair share of the collective input to the project! We devised a procedure to avoid this, which soon became known as *'the dance of the seven veils'*. There were to be progressive revelations of progress, which could be arrested by any party at any time. Experts first agreed on a particular part of the process to be opened for mutual inspection, and on the form in which data were to be exchanged. The exchange took place. If the result proved acceptable – which in the end it always did – then the experts agreed on the next part of the process. And so on to the end! It was laborious; but it worked. In parallel with the dance of the seven veils we were busy devising the structure of the proposed agreement. I need not recall its details since the resultant Treaty is in the public domain [Cmnd. 4793]. It provided for a tripartite pooling of every aspect of development of the centrifuge; for the creation of tripartite industrial enterprises, with a monopoly on the building and operation of enrichment plants in all three countries; and for the nature of non-proliferation safeguards to be applied to the operations.

Most of the work was done by officials. But of course Ministers took final responsibility, and there were very occasional meetings at Ministerial level. One of these remains indelibly fixed in the minds of all participants at official level. It took place in the Tulpenfeld complex in Bonn, in the summer of 1969, probably in June. By now, we had actually agreed, at official level, the whole of the draft Treaty. We could have decided simply to recommend it to Ministers in each of our capitals. But we felt they might be upset if they could not feel they had personally completed the work. So we changed tack. What fools we were!

We agreed amongst ourselves that Ministers should be told that three points in the negotiations remained to be settled, and invited to a 'crunch' meeting to deal with them. We chose which three points should be considered 'open'. We agreed that each Delegation would recommend its own Ministers to envisage a certain solution for each open point. We even agreed which Minister should be invited to propose the solution in each particular case! Alas, this elegant scheme proved a recipe for disaster! The weather was atrociously hot and uncomfortable. Unsurprisingly, none of the Ministers involved were very clear about the meaning of the highly technical draft Treaty before them. I do not recall who they all were. On the UK side, Tony Benn and Fred Mulley (FCO) were present. Far from following his brief, Benn scoffed at the work of officials and injected into the Ministerial meeting a whole lot of ideas, off the top of his head, which were inconsistent with the whole drift of the negotiations. His German and Dutch colleagues followed suit. By the end of the meeting, not only had the Ministers failed to solve the three 'open points', they had also called into question many points which had been settled long before! They themselves departed, convinced that they had done good work, putting the bureaucrats in their place!

Once the Ministers had gone, leaving the wreckage behind, the officials got together over lunch; bound up their wounds; agreed that they should not have involved Ministers at all; and swore a mighty oath. The oath required that, come what might, Ministers would never be allowed to look at the Treaty again until they came together to sign it! The pledge was kept. Officials went quietly back to the text they had always wanted; allowed some time to pass; and then sold it to their Ministers individually in capitals! On 4 March, 1970, six Ministers met in Almelo (Netherlands); and signed the Treaty. After ratification, it entered into force on 19 July 1971. It worked exactly as intended. The tripartite co-operation led to major commercial successes, which have continued to this day.

By the time of signature, I had already left STD, and was on leave prior to my next posting. So it was a bonus to be invited to the signing ceremony. The British Delegation, led by Tony Benn, flew from Northolt in a British Government HS 125 executive jet. Once airborne, Tony asked whether someone knew how to use the coffee machine. Unaccustomed to this mode of travel, none of us did. Tony's reaction was characteristic. *'Never mind'*, he said, *'I'll make it myself'*. He then proceeded to make the coffee, and hand it round. Most Ministers would consider this beneath their dignity: it is one of Tony's good qualities that such considerations never affect him at all.

When I took over STD, space policy was as active as the centrifuge. Space was a field into which the supranational European Communities had never entered. Instead, two 'functional' European organisations had been set up, operating on traditional inter-governmental lines. One was the European Launcher Development Organisation (ELDO): the other, the European Space Research Organisation (ESRO). Later, in 1975, the two organisations were to merge, and become the European Space Agency (ESA).

Britain was a member of both ELDO and ESRO: her role was important in the first, because she had developed the Blue Streak missile. Blue Streak had originally been designed as the first stage of a delivery system for the British nuclear deterrent. When, however, Prime Minister Macmillan in 1962 secured from President Kennedy a promise to supply submarine-based Polaris missiles, Britain had no further military need for Blue Streak. She had, however, offered her ELDO partners the use of it as the first stage of a European satellite launcher, the idea being – if memory serves – that the second stage would be designed by France and the third by the Federal Republic of Germany. Design of the ELDO launcher had been proceeding for some time on this basis. However, around the time of my arrival in STD, a Government drive to reduce public expenditure had led to a review of Blue Streak, and a Treasury-led proposal to abandon its development.

Any such decision would deeply offend our ELDO partners, most of whom were also Member States of the European Community which we still wanted to enter. I thought it sensible to alert our Embassies in ELDO countries to the likelihood of the Treasury proposal coming to Ministers shortly, and to advise them to report to the Foreign Office what might be the specific reaction of the Government to which they were accredited to any decision to abandon Blue Streak. Needless to say, the Embassies generally took the view that ELDO Governments would be seriously upset.

My initiative got me into hot water when the Treasury learnt of it. The Under-Secretary concerned complained to Terence Garvey[2] that I was sabotaging Whitehall. Terence interrogated me fiercely. I explained my view that – if the British Government were indeed about to decide to scrap Blue Streak – they should at least be fully informed of possible fall-out on relations with friendly countries. On this basis, Terence persuaded the Treasury not to pursue matters further. This was, I think, the nearest I came to a formal reprimand in the course of my career. On the substance, I remained impenitent. But the incident taught me to think still more carefully about how others would perceive my actions. It further strengthened my life-long habit of always trying to put myself in the place of prospective interlocutors, and anticipate their reactions, before taking initiatives. In due course, the Government did decide to junk Blue Streak. This did considerably offend our partners. In the longer term it contributed to a complete re-organisation of European space activities and the emergence of the ESA.

For the rest, there is nothing special to say about my involvement in space policy, except that it involved frequent trips to Paris, where ELDO and ESRO both had their Headquarters. On one of these, in May 1968, I was caught in street rioting by French students, then at their height. I was in a taxi making for the Air Terminal at the Invalides when we rounded a corner and found ourselves engulfed in a pitched battle between students and police. One felt completely powerless. We could not go forward or back, because of the crowd. We could only keep still and hope for the best, Fortunately, the battle flowed away from us, and we made our escape. But it was a nasty experience.

Just before Christmas of 1967 the United Nations General Assembly (UNGA) had decided to take a look at a new subject: *'the seabed and the ocean floor, and the sub-soil thereof, underlying the high seas beyond the limits of present national jurisdiction'* [hereinafter referred to simply as 'the seabed'] *'and the use of their resources in the interests of mankind'*. The General Assembly's Resolution [2340(XXII)] noted that developing technology was making the area accessible and exploitable for scientific, economic, military and other purposes; recognised the common interest of mankind in the seabed as constituting the major portion of the planet's area; and stressed the importance of preserving it from actions and uses which might be detrimental to the common interest of mankind.

The Resolution went on to establish an Ad Hoc Committee (AHC) to study the peaceful uses of the seabed, composed of 17 nations, including the USA, the USSR, Japan, Britain, Australia, Canada, and Chile. The Committee was instructed to report to the next session of the General Assembly. It met twice in New York, in March and in June/July, and once more thereafter, this time at Rio de Janeiro from 19-30 August. The first two meetings were organisational and preparatory: the crucial meeting was the third.

Although this was the first time the seabed was to be considered seriously in the United Nations, the high seas themselves had for long been the subject of extensive international law. In immediately preceding years, however, one important aspect of the law of the sea, namely the width of territorial waters, had been the subject of violent controversy. Views on this subject ranged from 3 miles to 200! It was only many years later that an international consensus emerged favouring a 12-mile limit, coupled with a 200-mile 'economic zone' in which exploitation of the seabed was regarded as a national prerogative of the coastal state. Industry had also begun taking a marked interest in the whole question of exploitation of the seabed. The then recent, enormous, increase of exploitation of off-shore oil and gas reserves had encouraged industry to consider whether there might not be other valuable resources 'out there'. There was particular interest in the possibility of exploiting large deposits of manganese nodules which lie on the seabed in various parts of the world. (Ironically, after much fuss, this was later found to be uneconomic.) Finally it was becoming known that the United States, and perhaps others, were depositing monitors on the seabed to track the movement of submarines.

A few weeks after my arrival in STD the file began to demand my serious attention. My diary records attendance at a seabed meeting in mid-May. Later, the UK Delegation to the United Nations asked the FCO for instructions about the composition of the British Delegation to the Rio meeting in August, and about the policy line it would be taking. STD was requested to prepare a reply. This proved a far more difficult task than might have been expected.

Usually, there is a Government Department which should clearly act as 'Chef de File'. But, because of the novelty of the subject, in this case there was none. We approached all likely candidates: the Admiralty, the Ministry of Transport; the Board of Trade; and so forth. Without exception they registered a wish to be fully involved in the formulation of policy, but declined to make the initial proposals. Time was short. I concluded that the FCO – in practice STD – must put its own proposals on the table, and invite others to react. Jeremy Thomas, one of my two Assistants at the time (now Sir Jeremy), has recalled his amazement when I walked into his office and asked him to draft – within days – a policy paper on the Seabed, for submission to the Cabinet.

It was a tough assignment; but also a very interesting one. We were not without building blocks. The different Government Departments had been inputting thoughts. The serious newspapers and periodicals had also been discussing the issues. Jeremy rose to the challenge; our policy paper was well received by the other Departments. After modification to accommodate their comments, it was submitted to Cabinet and approved. The Delegation for Rio had got its brief.

Given this background, I was not entirely surprised to be appointed as Delegation leader. The Conference venue was to be the Copacabana Palace Hotel. The FCO administration people told me to work out of the British Embassy. How fortunate I had twice visited Rio and knew this was impracticable! It would have meant crossing the town centre – always choked with traffic – every time one needed to move from Conference to office. I said it would be hard to accept responsibility for leadership of the Delegation on that basis! This produced some flexibility. I was to go out to Rio and check, on the spot, whether the Embassy was really an impossible solution: if I found it to be so, I might rent. On arrival in Rio, on 17 August, it did not take me long to confirm to London that things were as I had said. Then I sought temporary accommodation. I found it – in the shape of the bridal suite of a very nice hotel on the Copacabana Beach itself! The sitting room became the Delegation office. It was only five minutes walk from the Conference venue. The balcony and windows of the suite looked directly on to the Copacabana Beach! Maura – home in England, and looking after three children under eight on their summer holiday – was somewhat wistful when she heard!

The Conference began on the 19th, chaired by a very effective Diplomat from Sri Lanka, Ambassador Shirley Amerasinghe. There were useful Plenary Sessions that day and the next, with Delegations making their opening statements. At 0100 hours on the 21st, however, the news broke that the USSR had invaded Czechoslovakia, in response to the 'Prague Spring', the Czech people's attempt to break free from Soviet bondage. Thereafter, the conduct of the Conference became difficult.

Nobody wanted to close it down: this would have made preparation of the Report in time for the General Assembly virtually impossible. But the Free World countries were not prepared to be seen doing 'business as usual': this would have looked like condoning the Russian invasion. From then on, there were endless Group caucuses. I was elected Chairman of the West European Group, and was therefore in constant contact with both the Conference Chairman and with Ambassador Tuthill of the United States.

With Ambassador Amerasinghe, Chairman, UN Seabed Conference,
Rio de Janeiro, August 1968.

Eventually, things were arranged so that the Free World countries could first give adequate public expression to their indignation, but then permit the Plenary Sessions to recommence two days later.

Somehow we kept the show on the road. The Conference, in the following week, produced a Report which proved seminal [Document A/7230 (XXIII)]. It formed the basis of a very substantial Resolution adopted by the General Assembly, in December of the same year [Resn. 2467 (XXIII)]. A mandate was thereby given for further work. The mandate included many key, basic concepts: legal principles should be evolved to promote co-operation in the exploration and use of the seabed for the benefit of mankind generally; this should not lead to any marine pollution; there should be full exchange of scientific knowledge on the subject; and there should be study of the possibility of reserving the seabed exclusively for peaceful purposes. Only two years later, in December 1970, such a Declaration of Legal Principles was adopted by the General Assembly [Resn. 2749 (XXV)]. This included the concepts that the seabed and its resources are the common heritage of mankind; that no State may exercise sovereignty over them; that an international regime should be established to govern all exploration or exploitation (it now exists); and that the seabed should be open to use exclusively for peaceful purposes by all States. Looking back, I know that, when we started work in Whitehall in the summer of 1968, none of us expected so much to be achieved, in so complex and sensitive a sector, in so short a time. I am pleased and proud to have helped launch such developments.

The Czech imbroglio meant that, for a couple of days, we had time on our hands. When this happened, I enjoyed the Copacabana beach in the company of Nick Flemming, a scientist on the Delegation from the Institute of Oceanography: it was fascinating, as we sat looking at the great breakers rolling in, to hear how they had been formed off the coast of South Africa, and then grown steadily as they moved thousands of miles across the Atlantic. Nick also gave me a scientific explanation of undertows, and how to escape from them, which I have never forgotten and sometimes had to use! Sad to say, he soon after lost all movement below the waist as a result of a car-smash. But he was a man of great courage. He went on to become Deputy Director of the Institute of Oceanography, and never gave up Scuba diving!

Late in 1969, the Foreign Office told me they wanted me to take over as Head of Chancery in Bonn. For me, the job was ideal. The German political scene, as we shall see, was in a fascinating state of rapid movement. I knew the family would enjoy the tied house at 21 Im Etzental where, fifteen years earlier, Con O'Neill had offered me frequent hospitality.

But there was a fly in the ointment. Maura's recovery from meningitis was slow. She had little stamina. Such a move was bound to throw strain on her. We talked it through, and she nobly said we must accept the challenge. I told the Foreign Office the matter could not be hurried. I must have a month's leave before departure, and attend personally to both the packing and the unpacking, and to the letting of King's Walden. This was agreed. I handed over the Department to Ronald Arculus in the third week of January. We set off by car for Bonn on 23 March, travelling via Harwich and The Hook of Holland. In the meanwhile we had spent time at Ackenthwaite; found tenants for our house; and packed up. On arrival, I had five clear days – including the Easter weekend – to unpack and settle in, before going to my office in the Chancery on the 31st. After that, it was to be a hectic life for the next three years.

CHAPTER 13

Bonn and Berlin: Ostpolitik and the Four-Power Talks (1970-73)

Our home at Im Etzental 21

AS WE DROVE into the Etzental, in Bad Godesberg, on 24 March, a lovely sunny day, we found it much as it had been twenty years earlier. A quiet cul-de-sac, it contained a dozen large, elegant, white-painted houses, all occupied by senior staff of the British Embassy. There was a pleasing harmony of style, but each house was individually designed. The now mature front gardens were unfenced, giving a feeling of unity and openness. Behind the houses, each had its own, separate, garden. Our house, Number 21, was at the very end of the Etzental, on the east side. Its garden, of perhaps a quarter of a hectare, mainly grass with some trees, sloped gently down hill. There was a lovely view, from our main windows and from our large ground-floor balcony, across the Rhine Valley to the Siebengebirge, the vast and beautiful nature reserve of wooded hills which overlooks Bad Godesberg and provides a recreational lung for the whole Bonn conurbation. Opposite our front door, a discreet footpath led to the charming old village of Muffendorf.

When we arrived, on the Tuesday before Easter, Etzental was looking its best. Daffodils adorned the front gardens, and many flowering trees were out. Untimely snow fell on Easter Saturday, but soon thawed. The house was full of painters, who finished re-decorating three days later. We unpacked in peace. We attended Easter services at the nearby 'Old Catholic' German Church, which the Anglican Community was allowed to use. Several Embassy families offered friendly hospitality while we sorted ourselves out. Monday was a public holiday, so I did not start work in the Embassy until the Tuesday. By then, Im Etzental 21 was up and running. It was to provide our young family and ourselves with a delightful home – and a very necessary firm base – for the three eventful years to follow. Later in this chapter I shall have more to say about family life in Bonn, and about those who helped us with looking after both the family and the house. But first I turn to my professional activity.

General political background

Let us recall the political context when I reached Bonn. Over twenty years after the Berlin Blockade, the Cold War continued. In 1961, the Berlin Wall had divided the City in two. Movement between West Berlin and the surrounding GDR had virtually ceased. Subsequently, however, confrontation had somewhat reduced. The old United States doctrine of inflicting 'massive retaliation' if attacked by the USSR, had been followed, in the late 1960s when Soviet nuclear capability had developed, by Defence Secretary Robert McNamara's theory of ensuring that the two Super-Powers remained in a state of 'Mutual Assured Destruction' [MAD], which would prevent either of them from attempting a first nuclear strike.

The signature in 1963 – by the USA, the USSR and Britain – of the Nuclear Test Ban Treaty [NTBT], and in 1968 of the Nuclear Non-Proliferation Treaty [NPT], coupled with the fall of Kruschew in 1964, had lowered tensions. Nixon was by now a year into his first term as President of the United States. Brezhnew, the Soviet leader, troubled by China's growing assertiveness, was presenting a fairly conciliatory face to the West.

In the Federal Republic of Germany [FRG], two decades of post-war rule by CDU-led coalitions had recently ended: Chancellor Willy Brandt had come to power in 1969, leading an SPD/FDP Government. Brandt had committed the FRG to a totally new direction in foreign affairs: by his 'Ostpolitik' he sought to contribute to East-West détente in Europe, and in particular to bring about a more friendly relationship with the USSR, Poland and the German Democratic Republic [GDR]. His initiatives were causing anxiety in Washington, though his earlier, staunch record as the Governing Mayor of Berlin for nearly a decade, ending in 1966, spoke well for him. Five days before we reached Bonn, Brandt made a ground-breaking visit to the GDR.

The Russians had responded to the FRG's new orientation by beginning to develop what they later called a 'Westpolitik'. This included not only a generally positive response to Brandt, but also movement towards other measures of détente, notably the creation of a Conference on Security and Co-operation in Europe [CSCE] and agreement on Mutual and Balanced Force Reductions [MBFR].

None of these developments had induced NATO to lower its guard. The British were still honouring their 1950s commitment to WEU to keep the equivalent of four and a half Army Divisions, plus the 2nd Tactical Air

Force, stationed in Germany. They also had a significant military presence in West Berlin. (The Americans and French likewise maintained large military forces.)

On the European Community side, the resignation of General De Gaulle from the French Presidency in 1969 had allowed the Six Heads of Government to agree, at a meeting in The Hague that December, to launch a major process of 'completing, deepening and widening'. The following year saw the beginnings, between the Six, of a system of co-operation on foreign policy additional to and outside of the Community machinery: called at first 'The European Political Co-operation' [EPC], it was to develop, years later, into what today we call the 'Second Pillar' of European Union. When Ted Heath won the British elections in mid-1970, Accession negotiations were soon re-launched. They were to lead to signature of Accession Treaties by Britain, Ireland, Denmark and Norway in Brussels on 22nd January 1972. (Norway later failed to ratify.)

My role as Head of Chancery

This was the background to the work of the Embassy, and to my own role as Head of Chancery. As in Buenos Aires seven years earlier, that role involved (under the authority of the Ambassador) being in charge of the Embassy's political work; co-ordinating the activities of the different sections of the Chancery; and dealing with certain sensitive administrative and personnel matters. Now, however, the scale and importance of the whole operation was much greater.

Bonn was – as Berlin now is – one of the key British Embassies. There were about 150 UK-based staff, and a largish number of German staff as well, though happily their well-being was mainly in the hands of a UK-based, Administrative Officer. Their quality, as had been the case during my earlier posting to Bonn, was exceptional. A big proportion of the UK-based officers were 'high-flyers', people likely to go to the top of the Diplomatic Service.

Over and above the normal Head of Chancery rôle, in Bonn I had a unique, additional duty. I was titular British Representative in the Bonn Group, the informal Committee of Allied and FRG Counsellors charged with co-ordinating the work of all four Governments in the exercise of the Allies' powers in respect of *'Berlin and Germany as a whole'*: these were the residual powers retained by the Western Allies under the Bonn Conventions pending the negotiation of a final Peace Settlement for Germany. As we shall see, the progress of *Ostpolitik* required this Group to assume much wider responsibilities. For almost all the three years in Bonn of this posting, work in that context took up a huge proportion of my time. Consequently, although by great exertions I managed to keep tabs on the rest of the Embassy's political work, notably reporting on German domestic politics and keeping in touch with the Federal Government about progress in the Accession negotiations, other officials did almost all the work on matters outside the field of East-West relations.

The elements of Ostpolitik

By the time I got to Bonn, *Ostpolitik* had already acquired momentum. The Auswärtiges Amt, under Foreign Minister Walter Scheel (FDP), and State Secretary Paul Frank, had launched separate negotiations with the USSR and Poland, with a view to agreeing on Treaties of Friendship (the 'Eastern Treaties'). These had by now reached an advanced stage. The key ingredient was the formal acceptance by all parties of the Oder-Neisse line as constituting a frontier between Germany and Poland, which would not be challenged in any final peace settlement between the War-time Allies and Germany, despite the fact that extensive former German territories lay to the east of that line. Russians and Poles alike were very anxious to see this principle established.

The USSR and the GDR had also been made aware by the Allies of the FRG's wish to negotiate with the GDR for the solution of problems which had arisen concerning the use, for civilian purposes, of GDR roads, waterways, railways and postal services, notably between the FRG and West Berlin. (These negotiations became known in Bonn as the 'Inner-German negotiations', because the FRG had not at that stage recognised the existence of the GDR as a 'State'.)

After I left Bonn in 1952, the Status of the Western Sectors of Berlin [WSB] had been a permanent bone of contention between the Western Allies and the USSR. Although the Russians had made no further attempt to close the air corridors, Allied surface movement along the Autobahnen or the railways was another matter. Checks that Allied movements were *bona fide* became more tiresomely thorough.

As to civilian traffic, the Russians claimed that this had become a matter for the GDR authorities, and allowed or encouraged the latter to make all sorts of difficulties. By now, West Berliners felt that flying was the only safe way to get to the FRG. The City was an island, in a Communist sea. The USSR had been apprised of the FRG's readiness, in return for easements in this field, to accept limitations on the FRG presence in West Berlin, an element which greatly troubled the Russians and the GDR. There had not yet been much progress on these Inner-German negotiations, which, because of the GDR's status, were not handled by the Auswärtiges Amt but instead by the Bundeskanzleramt [BKA], Brandt's own office, under the leadership of its State-Secretary, Egon Bahr.

In May, 1970, Brandt committed himself, additionally, to the aim of negotiating a General Relations Treaty (GRT) – or *Grundlagenvertrag* – with the GDR. The underlying concept was that the 'two Germanies' would officially recognise each other, although there would be some kind of special relationship between them. For a long time the GDR did not accept this principle – maintaining that it already had full statehood which needed no confirmation. Only two years later, when the whole Ostpolitik package was at risk in the Bundestag, and USSR pressure for completion was strong, did the GDR agree to talk.

Although the negotiations for the Eastern Treaties, for the proposed Inner-German agreements, and for the GRT were quite rightly being undertaken by the FRG, there was an interface with the Allies' powers in respect of Berlin and Germany as a whole which required the Federal Government constantly to consult with the US, France and Britain. This was especially the case for the Inner-German negotiations.

Finally it had become clear that Brandt would not secure ratification of the Eastern Treaties by the Bundestag – where his majority was slender and declining – unless they were presented alongside of an Agreement between the Four Powers (the USA, Britain, France and the USSR) ensuring substantial improvement of the well-being of the beleaguered citizens of West Berlin. The Russians – besides trying to progress their own *détente* agenda of CSCE and MBFR – had reluctantly concluded that they would have to negotiate on this last point. The first Quadripartite meeting at Ambassadorial level had taken place in Berlin on 26 March. Like all its successors, it was held in the former Allied Control Authority Building in the British Sector: the only place where the Russian Ambassador was prepared to hold meetings with the Allies. This was just after I reached Bonn; but the Ambassador, Roger Jackling, had rightly assumed it would be formal and procedural, and considerately left me in Bonn to unpack.

The Bonn Group

Thus, a vast complex of separate East-West negotiations had now been launched: each on a different subject and with different participants, but all inter-connected and part of a wider East-West pattern. It made a lot of sense

Sir Roger Jackling and myself at the Berlin talks, 1970.

for the Foreign Ministers of the Allies and the FRG, who in any case had a long tradition of regular meetings, to recognise that they needed a group in which their Governments' views on <u>all</u> these matters, and on the balance and interfaces between them, could be co-ordinated. The Bonn Group was the obvious candidate. It had existed for years, as the forum for ongoing consultation between the Allies and the FRG on all matters relating to Berlin and Germany as a whole. It also had a reputation for effectiveness. In May 1970 the Foreign Ministers therefore commissioned the Bonn Group to take on the task, and in particular to prepare for them a Report reviewing comprehensively the prospects for Berlin, the Eastern Treaties, the Inner-German negotiations, the proposed GRT and consequential questions about the future entry of the two Germanies into the United Nations; as well as the relationship of all these to the preparations for CSCE and MBFR. This Report was completed in the space of a few weeks; was subsequently approved by the Allied/FRG Foreign Ministers; and provided the essential orientations for the action of all four Governments, and indeed for all NATO countries, in the various negotiating contexts.

The Bonn Group became the place in which these orientations were kept under constant review for the rest of my time in Bonn. The existence of this close co-ordination between the Allies and the FRG enabled them to operate consistently in all contexts, and also to use the leverage of any one of the negotiations to best advantage in relation to the others. While this Study, and its constant monitoring, represented a major commitment for the Bonn Group, over my three years in Bonn most of the Group's time was spent in co-ordinating Allied/FRG views on the conduct by the Allies of the various Quadripartite Talks in Berlin. We shall return to this. I am not trying to write history: that is for historians. The aim is far more limited: to give the flavour of my own work in Bonn.

One way of so doing is to recall what point had been reached on these various East-West initiatives by the time I left for Brussels in March 1973. A first-stage Quadripartite Agreement on Berlin had been signed; this had provided a framework for completion of various Inner-German agreements; a Final Quadripartite Protocol had been signed, providing for all the above Agreements to be inter-dependent and to enter into force at once; the lives of two million West Berliners had been hugely improved by these arrangements (which remained totally effective until the re-unification of Germany in 1990); the Eastern Treaties had been signed and ratified; the Allies and the Russians had agreed on the conditions in which they would support the applications of the 'Two Germanies' for membership of the United Nations (they in fact entered soon after); preparatory talks for the establishment of a CSCE had opened at Helsinki in November 1972; and, a month later, a General Relations Treaty (GRT) had been signed by the FRG and GDR, making clear that each recognised the other as a State but with special mutual relationships. (This summary of developments contains no reference to MBFR, because those particular negotiations proved very difficult and only produced a first Agreement in 1989.)

For those who wish to know in some detail how all this was done – and it should interest anyone interested in the history of East-West relations, or in how negotiations may be conducted – the next section, about the Quadripartite Talks, will supply the answer. Others can skip straight to the following section, about my remaining political work.

Looking back, I feel that the achievement of so much in so short a time was little short of a miracle: it certainly placed very heavy demands on the different groups of negotiators, and on none more than on the Bonn Group. For three years I operated at far greater pressure than ever before in my life.

As will be seen, however, that pressure was to remain for the rest of my professional career.

The Quadripartite Talks in Berlin (26/3/1970 to 5/11/1972)

On the very day the Berlin Wall came down, 9 November 1989, I completed a chapter I was contributing to a book, edited by Gerd Langguth, entitled *'Berlin: vom Brennpunkt der Teilung zur Brücke der Einheit'*[1]. This German title may be translated as *'Berlin: from Focus of Division to Bridge of Unity'*. My chapter was about the Quadripartite Talks in Berlin, and was headed *'Some reflections by a negotiator.'* It systematically reviewed the whole course of the negotiations. In so doing it dealt in turn with the inherent difficulties of the process (substance, terminology, confidence); the practical organisation of the negotiations (meetings at Ambassador and Counsellor level), and of the related briefing mechanisms on the Western side; and the different stages the negotiations went through.

There were four such stages: the first ended on 3 September 1971, with the signature of the initial Quadripartite Agreement, setting out key principles and inviting the German authorities on both sides to negotiate implementing arrangements; in the second, ending in December 1971, those Inner-German arrangements were agreed; the third ended, on 3 June 1972, with the signature of the Final Quadripartite Protocol, bringing the whole lot into force; the fourth and last culminated in the issuance by the Four Powers, on 9 November 1972, of a public Quadripartite Declaration, whose text had been agreed in Berlin four days before, making clear that the entry of the two Germanies into the United Nations would in no way affect Quadripartite Rights and Responsibilities. My chapter concluded with an analysis of the overall results, as contained in the various published agreements and arrangements. I put a lot of thought into what I wrote for Gerd Langguth, and the balance still seems sound. I shall not repeat all its content here. Instead, I shall add colour and personal touches to what was a deliberately factual text, drawing not only on it but also on my diaries.

Bonn Group work involved attending a seemingly endless round of meetings. Though wearing, they were never dull. In 1971, the busiest year, there were meetings of the Four-Power Ambassadors or Counsellors in Berlin (Counsellors attended both levels) on no less than 39 days. Rarely did they take place on consecutive days, so each usually involved a separate trip by air from Bonn to Berlin and back. The flight time was around an hour. But, allowing for check-in, and travel to and from airports, a one-way journey usually took around two. Occasionally I had to make two or even three such trips in a week. Before each Quadripartite Ambassadorial meeting, there was always a preparatory meeting of the Allied Ambassadors with their Counsellors. For convenience, these often took place in a US Air Force plane, provided for the American Ambassador, on the flight to Berlin.

In the same year, the Bonn Group itself met on at least 65 days – and sometimes twice or even three times in a single day. A meeting might last all day: at the other extreme, there might be a gathering of half an hour to sort out a specific, urgent problem. Meetings were no respecters of Saturdays, Sundays or Public holidays. They took place as, when and where they were needed – on one occasion in my house. When I joined the Embassy in 1970, it was standard practice for the Allied Counsellors to meet by themselves before each Bonn Group meeting. As pressure mounted, this was seen as a waste of time, and we only had such meetings if we knew a strong Allied/German argument was likely. On sensitive issues, the four Allied/ FRG Counsellors would sometimes meet by themselves; but the usual form was for each Counsellor to have two or three advisers present. Almost all the Group's meetings were in Bonn; but at crunch periods the FRG representatives would go to Berlin to be on hand for very rapid consultations.

When Allied/FRG consultations were needed at a level higher than Counsellor, the Allied Ambassadors and Counsellors would get together with one of the German State Secretaries concerned, usually Egon Bahr. These gatherings were rare until 1972, when there were some fifteen of them (including one in Washington). The top level for Allied/FRG consultation was that of the Foreign Ministers. They used to meet at occasional dinners, usually the night before a NATO Council Ministerial meeting, and these gatherings also were attended by the Bonn Group members (but not by our Ambassadors). Because of the NATO link, these events took us, over time, not only to Brussels, but also to Rome and Lisbon.

The Bonn Group was thus the hub of *Ostpolitik*. Though it is immodest to say so, the four Governments concerned had all staffed it at a high level of competence, and gave their teams an unusual level of flexibility. Apart from myself, the titular members were Günther Van Well (FRG), Jock Dean (US) and René Lustig (France). We got on very well together: indeed, given the amount we saw of each other, the Bonn Group would not have been able to deliver the goods otherwise. All were fluent in English, French and German; had extensive experience of Germany; and enjoyed the full confidence of our authorities.

It is sad to record that both Günther and René were to die young, René tragically. The former went from the Bonn Group to become German Ambassador in Washington, but later fell victim to cancer. The latter became French Ambassador to Chile. He was a man of strong personal convictions. He saw the President, General Pinochet, as evil, and was shocked by the policy of his then Government of selling arms to this Dictator. I was later told by a senior French diplomat that René had quietly but deliberately sabotaged these sales; and had for that reason been withdrawn prematurely and placed 'en disponibilité'. This preyed on René's mind. Some time later he committed suicide at his home at Chantemerle, near Samöens, in the French Alps. There, the Lustigs owned a chalet, with two 'dépendences', which René, during his holidays and retirement, had lovingly restored with his own hands. Jock Dean did not spend much more time in the US Foreign Service, but retired to his home in Virginia and devoted himself to writing.

The Allied Ambassadors, though they had very different personalities, likewise formed an effective group, well able to take on the experienced Russian, Abrasimow, then Soviet Ambassador in Berlin. The British Ambassador, Sir Roger Jackling, was an able and experienced diplomat who had served in Bonn before. He had seen me at work when he was in the Foreign Office in the late 1960s, and must I think have specifically asked to have me in Bonn. The American Ambassador, Ken Rush, was a businessman – former Chairman of Union Carbide – and a political appointee. His diplomatic skills were less highly developed; but he was shrewd and had the enormous asset of knowing President Nixon personally, and being able to telephone him direct when he did not like the State Department line. He and Roger Jackling shared a passion for golf. The French Ambassador, Jean Sauvagnargues, another experienced diplomat, was later to become French Foreign Minister and then Ambassador in London. Unlike many Frenchmen, he was not unduly bothered by having to deal with Anglo-Saxons.

The Allied Counsellors all had excellent support staff. In my case, all three of the First Secretaries who helped me – Nicholas Bayne, Nigel Broomfield and David Dain – later became senior British Ambassadors. Each could rely on the help of an able Research Assistant, Alex Mineeff. The two successive Embassy Legal Advisers – David Anderson and Frank Berman – were excellent. Indeed Frank, who had been my Legal Adviser in STD, and now followed me to Bonn (via a spell in Berlin), was to become the Foreign Office's Chief Legal Adviser for many years. Günther's team was equally star-studded. The American and French teams, though in my opinion not quite so good, were nevertheless very solid. In Berlin, the

Counsellors from Bonn all benefited from the advice of their respective Political Advisers, in my case Teddy Jackson. They would accompany us to the Counsellor level meetings with our Russian interlocutors. Teddy, a good friend and valued colleague, also came to Bonn for meetings of the Bonn Group more regularly than either of his colleagues: he thus acquired greater influence on events than them.

Our Russian opposite number was Yuri Kwitsinski, who later achieved fame in the MBFR negotiations in Geneva. His Political Adviser in Berlin was Khotulew.

The atmosphere in the different groups varied enormously. In the Bonn Group it was generally very relaxed. English and German were used indiscriminately: one usually replied in the language the interlocutor employed. There was a special German problem of how to address some individuals. From the time I arrived, the Counsellors called each other by Christian names and used the familiar '*du*' [thou] form. As they got to know the German supporting cast better, the Americans, British and French used the same arrangements with them too. This caused problems, since the Germans, by and large, did not '*dutzen*' each other or use each other's Christian names. We might, for example, ask a junior German, addressing him by his first name, some question in his field of expertise: and he might reply – '*Ich weiss nicht was Herr Dr Van Well davon denkt; aber Ich kann dir meine eigene Auffassung geben*'. *[I don't know what Dr Van Well thinks, but I can give 'thee' my own view]*. The end result was that the Germans became less formal themselves!

At the Quadripartite Ambassadorial level, things were at the opposite extreme. Christian names were not used there – although the Allied Ambassadors used them in tripartite or Allied/FRG meetings. There was no common language, so they always had interpretation – still tediously consecutive in those days. It made things very slow and stiff. This also meant that the Ambassadors could only talk to each other in relatively general terms: it was difficult for them to do any drafting together. So their usual practice was to discuss things, and then leave the Quadripartite Counsellors to convert their ideas into texts.

Abrasimow started a precedent, at an early meeting, by inviting the Allied Ambassadors to lunch at the Soviet Embassy afterwards, which they accepted. The Allied Ambassadors were not in fact keen on the lunch idea – partly because they wanted to return to their duties in Bonn, and partly because the interpretation problems rendered the lunches useless for informal negotiations. However, it would have been rude to refuse.

Not only did they go, but each then felt an obligation to lunch the others subsequently. They also started giving each lunch a 'national' flavour, for example Roger Jackling had a Scottish piper to play. At the last Allied-hosted lunch, Abrasimow said he hoped that, next time, when they came to <u>him</u>, they could stay on and enjoy his sauna. As it happened, none of the three cared for a sauna. On the US Air Force plane going to Bonn, they agreed to send Abrasimow a message to say that unexpected obligations would prevent them staying!

But they were not going to escape easily. Further invitations could be anticipated. The three agreed the sauna must somehow be avoided. The plane to Berlin was thereafter used by the Ambassadors, not only to receive briefing from the Counsellors on political matters, but also to devise a new excuse for sauna-avoidance. Finally the day came for yet another Abrasimow lunch. At the morning meeting, he confirmed his invitation, and added his hope that the colleagues would stay for a sauna. But the wily Sauvagnargues, in the Allied Chair, had a trick up his sleeve. He replied that he would love to accept, but feared it might not be appropriate because he had a new interpreter. (He had replaced his usual male interpreter by a very pretty girl!) The sauna was again deferred, and the Allies in the end completely escaped its clutches!

The Quadripartite Counsellors assisted by their Political Advisers in Berlin, found it easier than their Ambassadors to develop effective negotiating techniques. At their first meeting they agreed interpretation would waste time; and looked for a common language. This turned out to be German. So one had the strange situation of representatives of the Four Powers all negotiating in a tongue which was the official language of none. At first, nevertheless, this was a very practical solution. Only when it became necessary to start writing actual drafts was further procedural refinement necessary.

The problem did not at once arise, due to a legacy of over twenty years of mistrust between the Allies and the Russians. This had the result that, when the Allies tabled a first draft of a possible agreement, it was rejected out of hand by the other side. When the Russians tabled a counter-draft it was in such extreme language that we in turn refused to consider it. We feared Moscow was so suspicious of Allied motives that <u>any</u> revised text we advanced would be rejected <u>simply</u> because of its provenance! How was one to progress? We discussed tactics at length in the Bonn Group, and decided to try a different approach at our next meeting with Kwitsinski. This must have been in the spring of 1971.

We went to it armed with Allied texts on different issues, but did not say we had them. We arranged, as if by chance, for there to be a blackboard in the room. Next, we had a general discussion of a concept with Kwitsinski. Then I, as the Allied Chairman for the day, offered to suggest a form of words I had *'thought up during the conversation'*. We had already settled with Kwitsinski that, since the Quadripartite Agreement (hereinafter sometimes 'QA') was going to have official English, French and Russian texts – but no official German one – it made no sense to write drafts in German! Kwitsinski had agreed that English should be used for this purpose, as he had no French, and I no Russian.

I wrote on the board, therefore, in English. Kwitsinski reacted orally. But, as his spoken English was poor, he voiced his comments and suggestions for change in German, asking me to transpose his thought into English on the blackboard! Gradually a text was established – usually full of footnotes, reserves or alternative formulations – but a text we could put to our Ambassadors nevertheless. This procedure sounds clumsy; but it worked. It enabled Kwitsinski to report to his authorities, not that he had accepted an Allied text as a basis for negotiation, but that a compromise text had emerged from discussion! The device was almost invariably used from then to the end of the negotiations!

For the rest, our personal relations with Kwitsinski and Khotulew grew steadily closer as the negotiations progressed. Agreeing on substance was always tough. But we all respected each other, and knew that, for Kwitsinski as well as us, an *'aye was an aye, and a nay was a nay'*. Eating together soon became a habit, whether as a group of all eight Counsellors, or in a 'bilateral' occasion for two plus two [e.g. two Brits and two Russians].

In those circumstances we used to talk very freely off the record. Aware of the Russian penchant for Vodka, and not caring much for the stuff, I decided to plead health problems from the outset. The first time Vodka was offered, I explained that, having suffered from intestinal parasites in Buenos Aires and from jaundice in the UK, my liver could not stand hard licquors of any kind, though a little wine was OK. Thank goodness I stuck to my guns! René and Jock, though both held their drink well, suffered severely from being plied with Vodka in vast quantities in bilateral dinners, and in René's case on a weekend at Yuri's *'Dacha'* outside Berlin. But I am jumping ahead in talking of drafting exercises. Before we could undertake such things with Kwitsinski, we had to agree our negotiating position in the Bonn Group. That was done in the early autumn of 1970, in tandem with the preparation of the Bonn Group Study.

The Allies started the ball rolling by inviting Günther Van Well to put forward the FRG's wish-list for Berlin. When a German paper was tabled, the Allies told Van Well that, if our Governments were to take responsibility in Berlin, and before German public opinion, for the result of the negotiations, they would want to get something far more solid from the Russians. We tabled a muscular counter-paper. The Germans responded that they would be delighted if we could get what was in it: let us by all means try. But it was plain they expected us to fail, and thought we would be returning to propose fall-backs. We never did. We got the whole of our shopping list. And then, in summer, 1971, because the Federal Government's majority in the Bundestag was constantly falling, they asked us to go back and demand still more things from the Russians. At that stage we looked sad! But we agreed to do what was asked, so long as the FRG would itself make compensating concessions. We pulled it all off.

On 29 September 1970, the three Allied Ambassadors, with their Counsellors, were due to fly up to Berlin, leaving Köln-Bonn Airport at 1515 hours, for a meeting next day with Abrasimow. We had a preparatory Bonn Group meeting that morning. At around 1400 hours I was in the Chancery when a message came from Berlin. The Russians had just informed the Allies through the Berlin Air Traffic Control Centre – the only meaningful quadripartite organisation still operating in Berlin – that the Air Corridors to the FRG would be closed that night at 0130 hours. There was no provision for such closure in the relevant quadripartite agreements. At the same time, it was not Allied practice to use the corridors at those hours.

On the telephone I agreed with Jock and René that we would instruct our people in Berlin to protest; advise our Ambassadors that the Allies should fly military probing flights regardless; and ask our military to be ready to do so. I warned the Foreign Office on the secure phone that the Ambassadors were likely to make recommendations to their Governments accordingly, once they had talked to each other on the plane. This the airborne Ambassadors duly agreed to do. On arrival in Berlin, I cabled the Foreign Office, asking for the necessary authority. Just 32 minutes after my telegram was sent, the answer came on the secure phone. The Foreign Secretary (Alec Home), who had been alerted in advance, had walked to 10 Downing Street and secured Prime Minister Heath's instant agreement to our recommendation!

I phoned my colleagues. Jock was delighted. He had just heard from Washington that the US authorities thought it wiser not to fly. He believed news of British staunchness might induce a change of heart. I heard later Nixon had been away with the Sixth Fleet in the Mediterranean.

Washington had replied without checking with him. Rush now insisted that Nixon be asked; and Nixon promptly agreed. There was long delay in Paris, too. When orders were finally sent to waiting French Air Force planes at Strasbourg-Entzheim, as we were informally told later, the pilots could not be found, having got tired of waiting and gone to a bistro! The story may be apocryphal; but it is a fact that the French did not fly. At all events, British and US planes <u>did</u> fly; were not themselves molested; saw what appeared to be surface-to-air missiles at some distance; and concluded the Russians had wanted to practise without being observed!

At some point in the spring of 1971 the Allies had become worried about the behaviour of State Secretary Egon Bahr. It will be recalled that, in 1969, the Russians and the GDR had been informed of the FRG's wish to negotiate with the GDR for the solution of problems which had arisen concerning the use, for civilian purposes, of GDR waterways, railways and postal services, notably between the FRG and West Berlin. It was only later that the FRG asked the Allies to negotiate a Quadripartite Agreement with the Russians. By now, however, Bahr had got the Inner-German negotiations off the ground, and it soon became apparent that this suited the Russians' book all too well. It enabled them to argue with the Allies that there was no need for anything meaningful on the subject of 'transit traffic' in the QA, because the Bahr-Kohl negotiations were going swimmingly. For the Allies however, responsible as they were for the security of West Berlin, it was not sufficient for the FRG to get assurances from the GDR, which latter could always renege: we intended to have a proper commitment from the Russians to us.

We had told the Germans in the Bonn Group that we wanted Bahr to put his negotiations on hold until we had got what we wanted; but could obtain no satisfaction. The Allies privately used to call Bahr a 'compulsive negotiator', because we always felt he was more interested in concluding a negotiation than in getting the right content. Anyway, he went his way regardless. Roger Jackling therefore arranged a dinner one evening, at his Berlin Residence, to which were invited the other Allied Ambassadors, Bahr, and the Bonn Group Counsellors. During dinner, the Ambassadors made their point, firmly but politely, and asked for assurances. They could obtain none. Over coffee and cigars, Roger reopened discussion, but on a different tone. He had the impression, he said, that Bahr had failed to get the message. He was not being <u>asked</u> to stall; he was being <u>required</u> to. The Allies were convinced they would not get a good QA otherwise. Unless Bahr would, before leaving the house, promise to do what was asked, the

Ambassadors would see Brandt next day, and tell the Federal Chancellor they were not prepared to go on negotiating with the Russians on this basis. At this point, even the thick-skinned Bahr knew he was beaten! The promise was given and kept; the Russians were out-manoeuvred; and the Allies got what they wanted.

By now the Russians were beginning to feel the pressures building up. Suddenly, between Saturday 22 and Friday 28 May 1971, at a series of crunch quadripartite meetings in Berlin, more than half the QA was written. During the whole period I was Allied Chairman at Counsellor level.

The process began at a Quadripartite Counsellors meeting on Saturday the 22nd. The QA, when later fully agreed, had three parts: General Provisions; Provisions relating to the Western Sectors of Berlin (WSB); and Final Provisions, which laid down the conditions for actually bringing it into force. The second part in turn broke down into four sections, dealing respectively with transit traffic between the WSB and the FRG; ties [i.e. relationships] between the WSB and the FRG; travel by WSB residents to East Berlin and the GDR (as well as small exchanges of territory at the margins of the WSB); and representation abroad of the interests of the WSB, linked with Consular and other representation of the USSR in the WSB.

At this first crunch meeting, lasting all day, we emerged with a largely completed section on transit traffic, subject to Ambassadorial approval. My diary noted: *'If this sticks, it could be a turning point in the talks'*. And so it proved.

The break-through followed the presentation to Kwitsinski, at the meeting, of a carefully crafted Allied compromise on a matter of principle. Until then the Allies had been insisting that the only acceptable arrangements were ones on which the Four Powers formally agreed on everything together. The Soviet side had refused this, arguing, speciously but firmly, that they had long since handed over responsibility for this sort of thing to the GDR, whose capital was East Berlin. All such practical matters must therefore be settled between the FRG, the Berlin Senat and the GDR. The compromise was called the 'one-to-three and three-to-one' formula. It meant that the Russians would, in the QA, give specific but broad assurances to the Allies about the substance of the arrangements – and in appropriate cases the Allies would do the same to the Russians – while it would be left to the *'competent German authorities'* to agree on detailed arrangements consistent with them. To ensure that all this actually happened, the QA would come into force only after the detailed arrangements had been agreed, and the two sets of instruments would remain in force together.

I returned to Bonn on Sunday the 23rd; had a Bonn Group meeting on the Monday; and was back in Berlin that evening. On the Tuesday morning there was a meeting of the Allied Ambassadors; and then one between them and Abrasimow. The four Ambassadors instructed their four Counsellors to carry on. In the late afternoon the Bonn Group, meeting for the first time in Berlin, updated the positions the Allies were to take up. This meeting lasted from 1730 until after 0100, the only break being for a working dinner!

On Wednesday the 26th, the Bonn Group met again in the morning; the Quadripartite Counsellors in the afternoon; and the Bonn Group again from 2030 to 0100. On the Thursday, the Quadripartite Counsellors met for several hours: in the evening the Bonn Group met from 2030 to midnight. On the Friday, the Quadripartite Counsellors met, to finish their work, from 1000 to 2145, the only break being to lunch together.

I think it was at this series of meetings, though it could have been later, that the Allies made another move on an issue of principle. The Russians had always wanted any agreement to refer to 'the existing situation' [die bestehende Lage] in Berlin, and to say that it should not be changed by any unilateral action. The Allies had objected, on the grounds that the phrase was so vague as to be meaningless. The new Allied move was to tell the Russians that they would agree, if they could first get oral confirmation from the Russians about how they understood what the existing situation actually was on some key points. The Russians agreed to talk on this basis. Amongst our key points was the need to ensure the Russians would not challenge the fact that the Allies had extended the provisions of the European Community Treaties to cover the WSB. Because of my expertise about those Treaties, I acted as Allied spokesman during the discussion. I explained our perception of the existing situation on a number of points; *inter alia* took the Russians carefully through the application of the Treaties to Berlin; and obtained all the required assurances. Eight years later, as we shall see, when I had become the European Commission's co-ordinator for Berlin affairs, this was to have an interesting sequel.

Next morning, Saturday 29th, I flew back to Bonn. My diary records the following. In the preceding four days, Jock Dean, René Lustig and I had sat through 40 hours of talks, in either Quadripartite or Bonn Group meetings, as well as two working lunches. I was very tired indeed. But our Quadripartite output by now included not only the draft on transit, but also largely agreed sections on 'ties' and on travel by WSB residents into the east; a first shot at the section on 'representation'; and largely agreed Final Provisions.

Many problems still lay ahead; but the West Germans were absolutely delighted, and the chance of a full QA before the summer break had for the first time become significant. (On a more flippant note, I think it was in this period that the Counsellors between them added a vast new word to the German language: namely '*Aufenthaltsgenehmigungszulassungsschein*'. Only the *cognoscenti* would understand its significance[2]; but it was in fact an integral part of the deal!)

I recall, at the end of the Quadripartite meeting on the Friday, remarking to Kwitsinski that we had come a very long distance in a very short time. The Allied side were nevertheless confident that the results would be acceptable to our Governments and to 'our Germans'. (By now this terminology was regularly used by both Kwitsinski and ourselves.) Could he say the same? Kwitsinski thought hard before answering. Then he said: '*I have gone far beyond my instructions. I think it's a fair package. I shall do my very best to sell it in Moscow. But this time I cannot absolutely promise success.*' He told us later that he had been strongly criticised in some quarters. Indeed, some time was to pass before Abrasimow confirmed Moscow's approval. But confirm it he did, showing that Kwitsinski had been as good as his word.

Kwitsinski liked to relax during lunches with us. He would exchange jokes on all sorts of things. (Khotulew was very quiet by comparison.) We were struck by Kwitsinski's tendency to make critical remarks to us about the behaviour of the Russian military in Germany. He seemed to regard them as woodenheads! Our own military were the opposite: politically highly sophisticated. But one can always find some joke to tell at military expense. Jock, René and I used to do this, to keep Kwitsinski's flow of indiscretions going.

He was particularly indiscreet about 'his Germans'. It became clear that, while the Allies agreed to nothing without being sure in advance that it would be acceptable to the FRG and the Governing Mayor of [West] Berlin, the Russians decided their negotiating position first, and then just told 'their' Germans to like it or lump it. Equally they would make to us concessions which had clearly never been discussed with their Germans at all!

Kwitsinski was also indiscreet about some internal problems of the USSR. He felt himself very European. The Soviet Union was of course, for all its existence, controlled by its European elements, the Asians being kept in a position of subsidiarity. Kwitsinski gave vent on one occasion to open concern about the fact that the Asians were '*multiplying like rabbits*' and would soon outnumber the Europeans.

During many visits to Berlin I enjoyed the generous hospitality of old friends. On this particular occasion I stayed with Peter and Joyce Swain. More frequently I stayed with Teddy and Eve Jackson. My hostesses usually saw me only for breakfast! Nevertheless I hope they understood it was a huge benefit for me to be able to relax in real and delightful homes, instead of retiring to a hotel room. Teddy in turn often stayed with us, when he came for Bonn Group meetings, and was a favourite of our children. The Swains also visited.

Years later, in 1985, when Teddy Jackson was coming to the end of his time as British Ambassador to Belgium and I was at the Commission, we held a farewell dinner for them at our Brussels home on 29 May 1985. It proved ill-starred. The European Football Cup Final was taking place that evening, between Liverpool and Juventus, at the Heysel Stadium just outside Brussels. Hardly had Teddy and Eve arrived than the telephone rang for him. Fighting had broken out at the Heysel between the rival supporters. It all ended with 39 deaths and hundreds of injured. Teddy was barely off the phone all evening, and certainly could not have enjoyed his dinner!

I made earlier references to the mobilisation by the Allies/FRG of NATO support for their policies. We put much effort into this. At least three times in as many years the Bonn Group Counsellors attended meetings in Brussels of the NATO Council at Ambassadorial level. The first occasion, in January 1971, was to present and explain the Bonn Group Study, and seek general support from the Council. We decided all four Counsellors should speak, to show our unity, and we agreed who should talk about what. This worked well, and became our standard behaviour pattern. We called it our 'tumbling act'. Our visits paid off, in the sense that the NATO countries, throughout the *Ostpolitik* period, responded positively, even when asked to do things they might have preferred not to.

There was also a particularly important meeting of the NATO Council, this time at Ministerial level, in Lisbon on 3 and 4 June 1971; and, on 2 June, an Allied/FRG Ministerial dinner to prepare the ground. The British aim was to get language into the NATO communiqué making plain, at a crunch period of the negotiations in Berlin, that NATO fully supported the three Allies. (I was in luck: my parents were on holiday in Lisbon at the time; and I was able to go a day early and see them. It was a welcome change, coming immediately after the Berlin marathon week just described!)

On the afternoon of the 2nd, there was a meeting of Allied/FRG senior officials to prepare the dinner. In the evening I went to the British Embassy – where my one-time immediate boss in Washington, David Muirhead, was now Ambassador. There I had a glass of sherry with Alec Home, and briefed him for the after-dinner discussions at the US Embassy. His relaxed air hid a shrewd mind. The French Foreign Minister wanted, in the communiqué, not to state that the conclusion of the Berlin Talks was a pre-condition of progress towards a CSCE. (The French were always closer than we to the Russians on this linkage point.) Maurice Schumann had been to Bonn a few days earlier, and obtained Scheel's agreement to corresponding language. In Lisbon, the US Secretary of State (William Rogers) argued to the contrary, and was supported by Alec Home. Walter Scheel changed sides, and Schumann conceded: the communiqué was very tough on this point. This NATO Council, by the way, was the one at which Jo Luns was invited to take over as Secretary-General of the organisation (an invitation which he at once accepted). On the same evening I persuaded Home to support Scheel and Schumann in pressing Rogers to agree on much-needed Allied movement towards the Russians as regards Soviet interests in West Berlin.

After the marathon week in Berlin, and then the Lisbon communiqué, the Quadripartite Talks went into slow gear. The Allies felt the Russians were taking stock of the situation. Although there were several Quadripartite meetings in June, little further progress was made. In July, however, there was another sharp acceleration. During that month the Ambassadors met four times, and the Counsellors seven. The tempo was gruelling. The 6th of July was a not abnormal day. In the morning I flew to Berlin; chaired a Quadripartite Counsellors meeting most of the day; returned home late in the evening; climbed into a dinner-jacket; had a snack; and then joined Maura at the British Embassy Residence around 2230, and danced till 0200. I noted the dance as a 'most enjoyable affair'. But this sort of life takes its toll. By the middle of the month, my diary was recording serious fatigue.

There were several very long, crunch Counsellors meetings: on the 20th, for example, we worked from 1000 hours to 0130 next morning. By the 28th, the Allied Counsellors felt they could make no more progress with Kwitsinski unless the four Ambassadors could loosen things up. The latter had their last meeting of the month on the 30th. The day before, the British and French Ambassadors had been gloomy on prospects, but Rush, according to my diary, was 'unexplainedly optimistic' about the idea of holding a crunch Quadripartite Ambassadorial meeting on 10 August. In the event, Abrasimow agreed to this. (With benefit of hindsight I wonder whether this had been fixed up between the two Super-Powers through one of Henry Kissinger's famous 'back-channels'.)

Having for some time seen this August meeting as a likely development,

I had been worried that our long-planned family holiday in Bavaria, whither we were due to depart on the 4th, would be jeopardised. Roger Jackling, however, had seen I was close to exhaustion. On the 30th, he told me to go off on holiday regardless. It was a bothersome situation. On the one hand I would have liked to see things through. On the other, as my diary stated, I was feeling de-humanised by excessive concentration on one thing, for so long, with no time for anything else at all, even the family. I thanked Roger for his characteristic kindness, and obeyed his instructions.

In the event, the Ambassadors, in a series of tough meetings, finalised the text of the QA and its many associated documents on 18 August. (At their last meeting, the Quadripartite Counsellors – with Nicholas Bayne standing in for me – took time out to write me a postcard, still treasured in my papers, drafted on the famous blackboard and in the same style, conveying good wishes! It keeps company with a letter from Roger Jackling about my own role too flattering to be quoted.) The Ambassadors also agreed that, subject to confirmation in the quadripartite capitals, they would sign it on 2 September.

At this stage, however, the question of languages raised its head once more. As noted above, all the working texts on which the negotiations were conducted had been in English. Before signature, however, equally authentic French and Russian versions were going to be needed. There was no problem about the former, since the French had translated the English texts as they came along: a French version of the Agreement was soon available, and caused no problems.

The Russian version was quite another thing. No doubt Abrasimow had had translations made during the negotiations, but these had not been shown to the Allies. When they pressed for a Russian version, it was always about to arrive, but never did! Finally they were told that it must first be approved by the Presidium of the Supreme Soviet! More time passed. Then, on 31 August, the text arrived. It was found by the Allies/FRG to be full of distortions in favour of the Russians and GDR. In response to all suggestions for change, the Russians argued that they could not alter a text approved by the Presidium.

This made the Allies/FRG very dubious. There was to be no authentic German text. The Allies nevertheless demanded to see the unofficial one the GDR planned to work from. When this was received on the night of the 1st, it too was full of deliberate distortions. The French were ready to accept the situation. The British, Americans and West Germans were not. Signature was put off for 24 hours. The 'two German sides' got together, with Jock, René and Yuri as mediators, and worked all next day and part of the night to iron things out. However, although some amendments were agreed, important distortions remained. Meanwhile Rush fell ill with high blood pressure! This was the situation when I returned to the office [from my holiday] on 1 September, and at once flew to Berlin. On the 2nd, though uneasy, the Allies eventually agreed to sign next day. The result was that substantial discrepancies were to remain between the authentic English/ French and Russian official texts; and between the two unofficial German texts.

However, as Abrasimow was always saying, *'Ende gut, alles gut!'* All was ready for signature by the four Ambassadors on 3 September, in the Allied Control Authority Building. It is interesting to record that, in practice, the textual discrepancies did not give rise to any difficulties. Thus ended the first stage of the Quadripartite Talks.

The second stage of the Berlin process, as will be recalled, was to be the negotiation of implementing arrangements between the two German sides. They had of course already begun, in the shape of the Inner-German talks led by Bahr and Kohl, whose progress had earlier been suspended on Allied insistence. Now that these talks had been furnished with a quadripartite context, the Allies encouraged Bahr to move forward rapidly. This he did, and all were duly signed before Christmas of 1971. They fully conformed with the principles set by the QA itself. During most of this stage, the Bonn Group led a much quieter life, meeting less frequently, to monitor progress in applying the Bonn Group Study generally, and Bahr's negotiations in particular.

On 24 September, however, the world was startled by a British move, of which the public had no advance warning. Early that day, Sir Denis Greenhill, the Permanent Under-Secretary at the Foreign Office, summoned the Soviet Chargé; told him that 115 of the 500 Soviet officials in Britain were guilty of spying and must leave the country at once; and warned him that a press statement giving the full reasons would be issued 45 minutes later.

The British Security Services had reported these spying activities to British Ministers in May. They were considering what to do just as we reported from Berlin the major break-through in the Quadripartite Talks. Heath and Home then decided to hold up action against the Soviets to avoid prejudicing the chances for the QA. Instead, Home sent a tough written warning to Gromyko that, unless the Russians took corrective action themselves, British moves would follow. The Soviets did nothing. We were kept informed about all this in the Bonn Embassy. Once the QA was signed, there was no reason to delay. Hence the Greenhill *démarche*. The manoeuvre had been carefully calculated. On several previous occasions, Western countries had expelled Soviet Diplomats, resulting in tit-for-tat expulsions; and vice versa. But this behaviour was not open to the USSR because it would in practice have meant completely closing down the British Embassy in Moscow – where John Killick was by now the Ambassador. It became clear later that the Russians had not thought the British would have the courage to take such tough action. They protested the innocence of their own diplomats. But that availed nothing, and they had no effective counter-weapons in their armoury. In the end, to avoid total loss of face, they expelled 15 British diplomats and another 10 British citizens. The world saw that Britain had won a famous victory. And it made not a jot of difference to the *Ostpolitik* process.

One might have thought that, with the Inner-German implementing arrangements signed, there would be immediate movement to the third stage, signature of the Final Quadripartite Protocol (hereinafter sometimes 'FQP'): this was the instrument which was to tie the package together and bring everything into force. In fact, however, this did not happen until June 1972.

Why the delay? Because the Russians would not proceed until the Eastern Treaties were ratified by the FRG; and ratification required the prior approval of the Bundestag and Bundesrat. The SPD/FDP Bundestag majority had by now been whittled down to a handful of seats; and the Brandt Government had to proceed gently, to ensure the desired result. On 23 May, however, the Ratification Law was at last signed by President Heinemann, and the way was clear for simultaneous exchange of the instruments of ratification of both Treaties, and for signature of the FQP: the different ceremonies, in Bonn for the Treaties and in Berlin for the Protocol, were timed to take place on Saturday, 3 June.

Meanwhile, behind the scenes while all this had been going on, the Allies and the FRG had been preparing the next steps in the *Ostpolitik* game. The Bonn Group was again meeting more than once a week. The Allied Ambassadors were getting together regularly with Bahr.

The week of signature of the FQP was action-packed. It started on Sunday, 28 May, when the Allied/FRG Political Directors had an afternoon meeting in the '*Kanzlerbungalow*'. (This was a house, in the grounds of the Palais Schaumburg, built by Dr Erhard to live in when he was Chancellor, but now converted to a very agreeable centre for small conferences or medium-scale entertainment. It stands in a lovely park running down to the

Rhine.) The aim of the gathering, which was joined by Frank and Bahr, was to prepare for a working dinner of the Allied/FRG Foreign Ministers next day. Although we had had a warm-up meeting in Washington two weeks earlier, more time was needed: we continued working (and eating) till midnight. Even so, we had to meet again most of the following day, with a working lunch, this time at the British Embassy's Chancery building.

When all was finished there, we had agreed on a scenario, to follow the signature of the FQP, which would lead up to signature and ratification of the proposed GRT, Allied recognition of the GDR, the entry of the two Germanies into the UN, and a statement making clear that none of these developments in any way affected the continuing validity of the QA or of Quadripartite Rights and Responsibilities (QRR) for Germany as a whole and Berlin. It was agreed that this last point must be formally enshrined in a new Quadripartite Declaration. This package now had to be approved by the Allied/FGR Foreign Ministers, and then presented to the USSR. The Allied/FRG Ministers' dinner took place in the British Embassy, a charming white stucco 'Zuckerbaron' style villa on the banks of the Rhine at Bad Godesberg. The dinner itself was in the ballroom, seven-a-side, plus Roger Jackling as host. The actual discussions were in the drawing room, and lasted till 2300 hours: all our proposals were approved, and it was agreed that William Rogers would, on behalf of the Allies and the FRG, speak accordingly to Gromyko, the USSR Foreign Minister, after the FQP signing in Berlin.

The next two days (Tuesday and Wednesday) were occupied by a meeting of the NATO Ministerial Council, also in Bonn, when other members of the Alliance were updated on the *Ostpolitik* picture. The Thursday was a public holiday, and in the evening Maura and I attended a farewell dinner at the French Ambassador's lovely Residence at Schloss Ernich for the Jacklings, who were to leave Bonn a fortnight later.

On Friday 2 June, the three Allied Foreign Ministers flew back into Bonn to attend a celebratory, informal dinner offered to them by Brandt in the Bungalow. It was an intimate affair – the Allies were five-a-side (wives not invited) – but it included all the officials who had played a key role in the Berlin Talks. The Chancellor made a speech thanking the three Allied Ambassadors and their Counsellors for their *'tough and laborious work'*. He also thanked the Bonn Group in particular, describing it as a *'remarkable diplomatic instrument'*. The Foreign Ministers replied with speeches congratulating the Chancellor on his own role in inaugurating and driving through the Federal Government's *Ostpolitik*, and placing on record that the

Quadripartite Agreement could never have been negotiated at all except as a complement to *Ostpolitik*.

Although the Chancellor spoke quietly, it was an intensely emotional occasion for him. Here he was, a former Governing Mayor of Berlin, a former Federal Foreign Minister, the first Socialist Chancellor of the Federal Republic, at the successful climax of two and a half years of enormous personal effort to bring about a change in West Germany's entire relationship with the East, coupled with an improvement in the life of the people of Berlin. And here were the Foreign Ministers of the Federal Republic's three closest and most powerful Allies, who had assembled for the sole purpose of congratulating him personally.

On all four of the days just described, the Bonn Group teams were still hard at work, ensuring that the texts and other details of the Berlin ceremonies would be in order.

On Saturday the 3rd, the Allied Foreign Ministers, their Ambassadors, and their supporting staffs, arrived by air in Berlin. On the dot of mid-day, they and their Soviet opposite numbers entered the main Council Chamber of the ACA building, and sat down to sign four copies of the Final Quadripartite Protocol. Then, each Foreign Minister made a five-minute public speech, fortunately not translated, in his own language. The rest of us stood behind the Ministers. There were literally hundreds of press photographers and cameramen. There followed a lunch (four-a-side). The British team, besides the Foreign Secretary, consisted of Roger Jackling, Tom Brimelow and me. The American and Russian teams rightly included their former Ambassadors, Rush and Abrasimow, who had meanwhile been replaced in their respective Bonn and Berlin posts. Afterwards the four Foreign Ministers withdrew alone to talk over the matters the Allies and FRG had agreed to raise. Gromyko's response was very cautious.

When Gromyko had left, the Allied teams went on to Schloss Charlottenburg. There, in the mirror-room, under the dome of the Palace of the Kings of Prussia, they received the thanks of Governing Mayor Schütz, on behalf of the people of West Berlin. When later they had left for their planes I myself walked across the great forecourt – it was a lovely sunny day – to take another look at my favourite statue, the incredibly beautiful head of Queen Nefertiti, which is displayed in the Egyptology Museum, itself located in one of the old Guard-houses of the Palace.

Thus ended the third stage of the process: the fourth, as we have seen, was intended by the Allies to lead to agreement on a Declaration by the Four Powers concerning the continuance of their Rights and Responsibilities after

Signature of the Four-Power Agreement on Berlin, 3 September, 1971.
L to R: Ambassadors Sauvagnargues, Jackling, Abrasimow and Rush, with their four
Counsellors and others behind. (Photo: Ullstein Bild Berlin – Bundesbildstelle Berlin)

a GRT had been signed and ratified. Happily, there was to be a breathing space for the Allied teams. Our summer holidays were not this time under any threat. And time was needed for Bahr and Kohl to advance the negotiations of the GRT to a point where Allied concerns became actual.

For weeks, in the autumn, the Russians argued that no Quadripartite Declaration was necessary. But eventually they seem to have recognised that the negotiations for a GRT – in whose successful outcome they were much interested – would not be concluded unless they talked to the Allies. In the end, these talks, again held in Berlin, started on 23 October, and concluded successfully on 4 November. Because of the imminence of the US elections, which took place on 7 November, and of anticipated Elections in the FRG on 19 November, it was much harder to keep the Western side together than it had been in the earlier Quadripartite Talks. But the trick was managed. The fact that Jackling, Rush and Abrasimow had meanwhile been replaced – by Ambassadors Nico Henderson, Marty Hillenbrand and Yefremow respectively – was an added complication. On the British side, there was yet another twist to the story. Nico Henderson had only arrived after the FQP was signed, and, though a very skilled and experienced diplomat, by definition had no feel for the unique ambiance of the Berlin Talks. Moreover, for the first three of the nine Quadripartite Ambassadorial meetings, he was not available as he was required to accompany President Heinemann on his State visit to the UK: so I worked under the Minister, Reg Hibbert, who was not an easy colleague. It was a tough job to maintain continuity and a solid British performance. But that too was achieved.

In the first week there were only three Quadripartite Ambassadorial meetings, when both sides laid opening bids on the table and began discussing the issues. But from Monday 30 October to Sunday 5 November, the Conference was in continuous session. The Ambassadors met every day but Thursday: there were meetings at Quadripartite Counsellor level on the Monday, Tuesday, Wednesday, Thursday, Saturday and Sunday. In addition the Bonn Group met daily. The upshot, for me personally, was about 16 hours of work a day for 14 days. In the second week, many meals were missed: all those we did have were working meals. In parallel with all this, Bahr was in Berlin, negotiating with Kohl the final phase of the GRT negotiations. The Ambassadors met with him. At least once he came to the Bonn Group. On one occasion the Allies had to get Brandt to overrule Bahr's views.

At an early stage the Allies had warned the FRG that we might have to consider possible fall-backs. But the British, French and Germans were taken aback when, on Friday 27 October, the Americans circulated to us all what they called a 'minimal draft'. For the rest of us it was weak as water. The Germans even talked to me about *'another Vietnam'*. Sauvagnargues, exploiting his position as senior Allied Ambassador, took a lead in attacking it, but with strong support from us and the Germans. Bonn Group discussions in the end left it aside. This was another instance when we found an American initiative inexplicable. Once again, with benefit of hindsight, I wonder whether Henry Kissinger's 'back-channels' had led to an understanding between the Super-Powers to finish the Berlin Talks before the US Elections[3].

A helpful feature of the talks was that the Russians were still represented at Counsellor level by Kwitsinski. René Lustig was still there, and made a big contribution. But Jock Dean had been replaced. Consequently, since all the drafting work was again done in English, I became, in some respects, Kwitsinski's principal interlocutor. We again talked a lot outside meetings: indeed, one evening Teddy Jackson and I went to dine with him and Khotulew at the Soviet Embassy in East Berlin. This personal relationship with Kwitsinski was invaluable, enabling us to be much more direct and frank than would have been tactically wise in formal meetings.

By the night of Saturday 4 November, there was a general feeling around that, although much drafting remained to be done, the Four Ambassadors should be able to finish next day. And we knew that Bahr thought he could conclude his negotiations on the day after that. The heat was on. Meeting early on the Sunday, the three Allied Counsellors decided to play hard to get, with a view to obtaining maximal concessions from Kwitsinski in the last negotiating meeting. He was non-plussed. He must have been expecting us to be easy picking. He kept looking at his watch and saying we must not delay the Ambassadors' wrap-up meeting at 1500 hours. But we knew our own Ambassadors would prefer a wait to any unnecessary concessions, and sat tight. Kwitsinski blinked first. We got a good bargain. And the Ambassadors still got to meet at 1500; approved the text; and once again let in the press!

On 9 November the Quadripartite Declaration on Berlin was formally issued by the Four Governments in their respective capitals. It stated that they would support the applications for membership of the United Nations by the two Germanies which *'shall in no way affect the Rights and Responsibilities of the Four Powers and the corresponding, related quadripartite agreements, decisions and practices'*. Thus was the fourth stage of the Quadripartite Talks concluded.

We have already seen, from my account of the Brandt dinner, how positively the Allied Foreign Ministers regarded the outcome of *Ostpolitik*. Public opinion in the FRG and West Berlin, and in the Western World generally, was almost universally favourable, although at an earlier stage in the Ostpolitik process there had been a fair amount of scepticism.

In Berlin itself, during the final week of the Quadripartite Declaration talks, a West Berliner gave me a beneficiary's view of the QA, which had by then been in operation for 5 months. He was a German chauffeur with British Military Government, and had often driven me on my frequent visits to the City.

Late on 3 November, the day's work done, he asked me to have a drink, an invitation I was happy to accept. He said there was something he wanted to tell me. I cannot remember his exact words, but they went something like this. *'Throughout the negotiations you used to assure me that, though the going was tough, at the end of the day the Allies would get a good Agreement. I never commented, but frankly I did not share your optimism. Now I want to tell you that the Agreement has transformed my life. I have been 7 or 8 times to the GDR to visit relations I hadn't seen for over 10 years. At the beginning I found it was necessary to work very hard to re-establish normal links after so long a gap; but now we are back on the old terms.*

RAF Hastings at the heart of the 'Allied Museum', 1998.

Besides that, I can travel freely on the Autobahn to the FRG; and I can feel safe in doing so. Thank you very much.'

This man's story was deeply moving. One realised that he was in effect speaking for all the inhabitants of West Berlin. In my diplomatic career of nearly 40 years, all of which I enjoyed, my participation in the Four Power Talks on Berlin gave me satisfaction of a unique kind. Usually, in diplomacy, one is dealing with things, rather than people. One is negotiating about matters which are broadly speaking economic: about trade, taxation, technological co-operation, claims and counter-claims; and such-like. But on this occasion we were dealing with matters which directly affected the daily life of two million people. It was a profoundly worthwhile cause. It made the Allies determined to get the very best deal possible. And it sustained us in the long months when the Soviets initially tried to wear down the Allies into lowering our negotiating sights. In fact we did the opposite, and succeeded.

A quarter of a century later, after the re-unification of Germany, I was amongst some hundreds of Allied personnel who were invited to Berlin as guests, with all fares and expenses paid, to attend impressive ceremonies in the spring of 1998 marking both the 50th Anniversary of the start of the Berlin Airlift – a massive turning point of the Cold War – and the official

Signed portrait of Foreign Minister Walter Scheel.

opening of the Allied Museum. The latter was created by the Berliners themselves. They did so because they wanted to remember and honour the Allied protection of West Berlin, throughout the 45 years when the City found itself geographically isolated, and under continuing threat, in the heart of the GDR.

I will recall just one event from those memorable five days in Berlin. The programme called for a 'march of the Allied veterans' for a few hundred yards to the main gate of the Allied Museum. The march took us down the broad Clay-Allee. We were led by American, British, French and German military bands. Though it had been raining heavily, the Avenue was lined with Berliners. As we marched along, <u>each</u> Berliner said to <u>each</u> Allied marcher just one word: *'Danke!'*. The occasion was no less moving than that of the drink with my driver: indeed the fact that all this was happening so long after the period of drama had passed, made it perhaps even more so.

Many were the tributes paid to the Bonn Group and its members. In a feature article written by Rolf Breitenstein in July 1970, it had been strikingly described in the *Frankfurter Allgemeine Zeitung* as '*Das Scharnier an Brandts Tür zum Osten*' ['*The hinge of Brandt's door to the East*']. I have already mentioned Brandt's own warm and complimentary remarks about it to the Allied Foreign Ministers.

After the signing of the Quadripartite Agreement, the Auswärtiges Amt gave a dinner for the Group, when the titular members received a silver-framed, signed photo of Walter Scheel, inscribed in his own hand with the words '*in Erinnerung an die Berlin-Verhandlungen 1970/71*'. In June 1972, following signature of the FQP, State-Secretary Frank gave the Group a further dinner, this time at the Kanzlerbungalow, when the titular members received a fine silver salver, engraved with the signatures of Willy Brandt and Walter Scheel, and the words '*Zum Abschluss der Berlin-Verhandlungen 3 Juni 1972*'. Governing Mayor Schütz at some stage gave us each a silver cigarette box, engraved with a bear, the symbol of Berlin. Then, on the evening after the Quadripartite Declaration was agreed in Berlin, the entire British team, including its two secretarial staff, were invited by the Berlin Senat to the best seats in the Deutsche Oper for a delightful performance of Mozart's *Marriage of Figaro*. We felt thoroughly thanked!

Other political work

As already noted, although the Bonn Group work took up most of my working hours, I participated as much as possible in the Embassy's other political work.

I would normally be involved to some extent in visits by key British Ministers; in the many visits we received from senior British military officers (whether from BAOR or 2nd Tactical Air Force, from the Ministry of Defence, or from the Royal College of Defence Studies), although within the Embassy, the Minister traditionally took the lead role on military matters. There was also an annual Conference of British Consular officers from all over the FRG and Berlin, which lasted a couple of days. It frequently fell to me to give such visitors an overview of the political situation in Germany.

Each year we were also active in the context of the annual 'Koenigswinter Conference'. These conferences had been inaugurated in 1950, during my first tour in Bonn. The leading light was still Frau Lilo Milchsack. They were by now (and still are) an important feature of the Anglo-German calendar, bringing together for a long weekend, once a year, around 80 influential British and German personalities for off-the-record and always stimulating discussions: politicians, media people, bankers, businessmen, senior forces personnel, diplomats and academics. They are always fun, and generate their own special, social whirl! I last attended one, at Cambridge University, in 1990.

My Bonn Group work inevitably meant that German politicians – and also both German, British and other media people – were interested in talking with me. We got to know many Bundestag members, especially CDU/CSU leaders who wanted to hear about the Berlin Talks direct from the Allies; and also many interesting pressmen of many nationalities (there were few <u>women</u> on the press circuit in those days).

Maura and I were both impressed by the way in which German television handled the run-up to the Bundestag elections, which took place in November 1972. We despise the spineless practice of British politicians, who like to be interviewed singly by a presenter, and to avoid any face-to-face debate with spokesmen of other Parties. The four German Party Leaders (SPD/FDP/CDU and CSU), in complete contrast, took part in one or more long Round Table discussions, controlled by a firm moderator who made sure that all key issues were fully discussed, and that each leader got a fair proportion of the time. This seemed to me an infinitely more honest and informative way of helping the man-in-the-street understand what the election was all about. The format encouraged serious debate, and showed up leaders who tried to evade awkward questions. It was also good viewing.

Social life

Despite the pressures of work, we lived a very active social life. Not counting the times when I was away in Berlin, we found ourselves going out for meals or drinks on average two or three days a week; and at the same time entertaining at home on average once or twice a week, sometimes on a large scale. We held lunches, drinks parties, dinners, dinner-dances (with live bands), and even a wine-tasting. Hospitality was a very big commitment for Maura. To make matters worse, there were occasions when she did not know until the last moment whether I was going to get back in time from Berlin: and some when she had to act as both host and hostess because I failed to do so! She coped magnificently.

Our entertainment often had a specific aim. There were parties to introduce incoming British officials, or to help departing ones say their good-byes; others to enable 'visiting firemen' – British officials, senior officers of the Armed Forces, or British Consuls from the Länder – to meet Bonn contacts; others for the Bonn Group's 'extended family' (i.e. not only the 'titulaires' but also the back-up officials and their spouses); and others when we simply tried to put together a good mix of our enormous range of British and German friends. Finally, we took seriously the Head of Chancery's duty to know all the Embassy staff, and help them along: this involved many lunch or drinks events. Maura worked hard on the distaff side: on one occasion we held a wedding reception for a young lady on the Embassy staff!

Two occasions deserve particular mention. The first was a dinner dance, on 15 October 1970, to celebrate the completion of a quarter century of work for the Britain in Germany by Lance Pope[4] – an extraordinary, amusing and delightful personality. Lance had been partly educated before the War in München. He was virtually bilingual in German, speaking if he wanted with a strong Bavarian accent. During service with the British Army, he was captured and made a POW. He made several escape attempts, and more than once got out of his camp (on one occasion by masquerading as a Bavarian General), only to be re-captured. He ended up in Colditz.

After the War, Lance joined Military Government in the British Zone. He soon entered the Political Division of the Control Commission at Zonal Headquarters: working first in Berlin and then in Bonn. He moved on to the UK High Commission, and subsequently the British Embassy, always acting as chief contact man on German domestic politics – a task for which he was supremely suited. Married to Ilse, a charming Austrian, he loved parties; and was shrewd, quick-witted, and a good listener and talker. He also loved shooting, which opened many extra doors. By now, he had become a veritable Institution in Bonn – and also in Bavaria, where he had a second home, a hunting-lodge placed at his disposal by none other than the legendary Minister-President, Franz-Josef Strauss.

Such a record deserved a very special celebration. There was never going to be a problem about guests: everybody who was invited came. We must have been around 35 on the evening. These included Johnny Von Herwarth, a former German Ambassador to London (and later to Rome), leading German politicians and officials, the British Ambassador and Minister, and other British and German friends. We had planned that, between the dinner and the dance, there would be a surprise event. It was intended, not only as a tribute to Lance and Ilse, but also as a reminder, to many guests, of earlier days when Lance (with John Killick) had entertained so many in Bonn with satirical, topical songs of their own devising, in both English and German. Two new songs were written – one each in English and German.

The English one was to the tune of 'The Vicar of Bray'. It traced Lance's political career, verse by verse, under different bosses, ending with Roger Jackling himself. The chorus was:

> *Now this is law, that I'll maintain*
> *Until retirement time, sir;*
> *No matter who the boss may be,*
> <u>*I'll*</u> *be political adviser.*

The German song was to the tune *'In München steht ein Hofbräuhaus'*, one of Lance's favourites. The theme was similar, but presented with a strongly Bavarian flavour. And it focused more on Lance's extra-curricular activities like the *Schuhplattler*, his love of *'Underberg'* liqueur, his harmonica, his dachshund and his shooting. It ended with the thought that, when the time came for retirement from Bonn (as it did two years later), it would take Lance and Ilse a whole year simply to say goodbye to their army of friends all over Germany. Complete surprise was achieved, and everybody seemed much to enjoy the evening.

The second memorable party was a dinner for Roger and Joan Jackling, when he left the Embassy in June 1972. We had greatly liked them both; and both had been very kind, and most appreciative of what we had done under their aegis. When we offered to organise a farewell dinner, we were touched to learn that they would like to come to us for their very last night in Bonn. As it turned out, they had been lunched by Chancellor Brandt earlier in the day. By a happy coincidence my parents were staying in our house at the time, so could attend the dinner. The Jacklings' son – also Roger – was likewise present. Our dinner table took 16. The other guests were the State Secretaries of the President's Office (Fritz Caspari), of the Chancellor's Office (Egon Bahr), and of the Auswärtiges Amt (Paul Frank); my Deputy Head of Chancery (Robin O'Neill); and their respective wives. All these people knew and liked each other; all were good talkers; Maura laid on a superb dinner; and the evening flew by. It was perhaps the grandest party we were ever to give.

The social side of life included having a good many people to stay in the house. It was a particular pleasure twice to welcome Con O'Neill – by now the leader at official level of the UK Delegation to the negotiations for British Accession to the European Communities – to the house in which he had so kindly entertained me when my diplomatic career began more than 20 years earlier. Other senior British officials and military officers came to stay in fair numbers, for a night or two, whether from London, BAOR Headquarters in Rheindahlen, Berlin or elsewhere. But of course not all our visitors were of an official kind. Both our families came to stay, as well as a number of personal friends.

Maura and I obviously enjoyed much entertainment by others, both official and otherwise, whilst in Bonn. Two kinds of occasion stick much in mind: the first traditional, the other less so.

The traditional event was one of Foreign Minister Scheel's Diplomatic Receptions. Walter Scheel enjoyed parties and gave good ones. In 1970, his annual jamboree for the Diplomatic Corps co-incided with my birthday on 7 July, and took place at the elegant, baroque Schloss Brühl, between Bonn and Köln. The weather was perfect. There was a buffet supper on the terrace; a performance of ballet; and then dancing till all hours.

Less conventional events – in 1970 and 1971 – were the light-hearted Christmas Reviews put on by the British Embassy staff. They were the occasion for the latter to send up the top brass. The scripts were witty: and the acting and production, good. In 1971, it was time to take off the Bonn Group. There were four scenes in the Review, all about Bonn Group or Allied meetings, each introduced by a few couplets, modelled on one of A A Milne's famous rhyming verses, namely the following:

> *James, James, Morrison, Morrison,*
> *Weatherby, Charles Dupree,*
> *Took good care of his mother,*
> *Though he was only three.*
> *James, James, Morrison, Morrison,*
> *Said to his mother, said he:*
> *You must never go down to the end of the town*
> *If you don't go down with me.'*

The first scene of the Review had the narrator recite [emphasis supplied]:

> *'Rush, Rush,*
> *Saúvagnargues, Saúvagnargues,*
> *Jáckling – KCMG -*
> *Tóok great care of the Cháncellor,*
> *Thóugh they were only thrée.*
> *Rush, Rush,*
> *Jáckling and Saúvagnargues,*
> *Sáid to Herr Brandt: 'Don't cúss,*
> *But you'll néver get fár with the GDR*
> *Withóut consulting ús.'*

The concluding lines of the Review were these:

> 'Rush, Rush,
> Jáckling and Saúvagnargues,
> Fíxed old Abrásimów.
> Théy, thén,
> Sáid to the Chancellór:
> <u>Nów</u> you may tálk to Herr Stoph.
> Yóu, máy,
> Thínk our Agréement,
> Cánnot be worth all the fúss,
> But you'll néver get fár with the GDR
> Withóut consulting ús.'

[NB. Herr Stoph was Brandt's opposite number in the GDR.]

We took some of our American, French and German colleagues to see the Review. The Germans, in particular, were astonished to watch the British Ambassador, Minister and Head of Chancery being caricatured by their junior Embassy colleagues, and appearing to enjoy it!

The quality of family life

It is time to turn to the quality of our family life. It was not a bed of roses. The constraints were considerable; but we worked hard to overcome them, and ensure they impacted on our children as little as possible. When we went to Bonn, Rupert was boarding in the Pilgrims' School in England; and Claire soon went to Rookesbury Park at Wickham. Only William was with us all the time, soon attending local schools.

We did our best to visit the two boarders when we could (Maura far more than me); to have them home at half-terms; to take leave ourselves during their holidays; and to squeeze out as much time as we could with William, in my case especially at weekends. The garden was a great resource. Described earlier, it was for the children a marvellous and secure play area: tenting, tree-climbing, ski-ing and outdoor parties were amongst their activities. There was plenty of gardening for me, with some help from the next generation. Outside the front door, the Etzental, being a cul-de-sac, provided a safe place for cycling. We were only 200 metres walk from the public swimming pool of Bad Godesberg, where William was swimming by himself at four. Not much further away was the Heiderhof, an area of woods and downland we all liked.

The children enjoyed many local outings. There would be walks in the Siebengebirge; picnics in the lovely countryside of the Rhine, Ahr and Mosel valleys; steamer trips on the Rhine; ice shows and skating in Köln; and, for Rupert and Claire, visits to the opera there to see Humperdinck's *Hänsel und Gretel,* and also Rossini's *Cenerentola.* Each year, there was the Carnival Parade in Bad Godesberg on *Rosenmontag*: it never appealed greatly to our children, but they collected dozens of the cheap sweets thrown to the spectators. They had many friends, mainly British, and shared parties and outings with them.

At our first Christmas in Bonn, in 1970, there was a new addition to the family: Andy von der Rotter Höhe. The children had always wanted a dog. But Buenos Aires had been no place for one: rabies was common, and we could not have taken it home when we left. In England, a dog would have been an added complication when our children were small, and Maura overworked and later ill. Now, at Bonn, with both space and household support available, and with every likelihood of a further foreign posting to follow (obviating British quarantine), Maura and I felt the time had come. We were attracted to the idea of a rough-haired dachshund, a breed so beloved in Germany. And we arranged to acquire one, as a Christmas surprise.

On Christmas Eve we drove to nearby Siegburg to collect Andy, a little ball of brown velvet. We smuggled him into the house undetected. Then I sat in an armchair in our family sitting room, with Andy's tiny head looking out through the V of my sweater. Maura told the children there was a present for them hidden in the room, and they were to find it. Entering, they looked high and low, conscious I was watching them, but never dreaming the present was concealed on my person. At last he was spotted: delight was universal. Andy remained with us for over 15 years, first in Bonn and then in Brussels, where he fell ill and had to be put to sleep.

Andy was intelligent, sly and a born actor. When he was still very small, I accidentally trod on one of his paws. I believed he was not really hurt, as I was in slippers and we were on a thick pile carpet. But he held up his paw, whimpering in a heart-rending way. When we put him in his basket that night I felt sure he would have forgotten by morning. Not so. The same routine took place, so we felt he had better go to the vet. He was still complaining when put on the table for examination. The vet declared there was nothing wrong, and set him on the ground. At once he trotted off, wagging his tail, as much as to say *'Ha! Fooled you, didn't I!'*.

One evening, a year or so later, a German dinner guest asked an unexpected question: *'What is Andy's rank in the family?'* After some reflection I suggested he stood at no.4. In those days he would have accepted that Maura, myself and Rupert were senior to him. But he then had little respect for Claire, and he dominated William (by the simple expedient of nipping the latter's usually bare toes with his razor-sharp teeth!). As the years went by, he moved up the ladder, step by step. Long before he died, he was no. 1; and we did what <u>he</u> wanted!

With our official, social and family commitments, we needed a support team. Its composition varied. But in the end we settled down with two girls living in the house. Between them they somehow managed the cooking, the cleaning and helping with the children.

Holidays

In Bonn we started a pattern of holidays with the children which was to persist until, one-by-one, they left the parental home. There were three themes. The first, inspired by our own deep European commitment, was progressively to give the children a feel for a wide range of continental countries: the Iron Curtain, however, prevented visits to Central and East European countries. The second theme – mainly tackled at Davos-Laret in Switzerland (a hamlet where we came to acquire a great many good Swiss friends), with one holiday at Lech in Austria – was to give them a chance to become proficient skiers. In due course they all did, and came to love the sport. It is still a bond between us. The third was to keep them in touch with their grandparents and the latters' respective homes.

These holidays meant so much – to parents as well as children – that I have felt a strong temptation to write quite a lot about them. But it would have made the book too long. So it must suffice to say that, over the years from 1970 to 1986, when I retired, all or some of the family joined Maura and me on hugely enjoyable visits to Denmark (twice), Germany, France (three times), Norway, Switzerland and Spain (several times). We always travelled by car – and varied our itineraries to show the children as much as we could of beautiful and historic sites on the way out and back. Finally, in 1983, we took two of the children to the USA and Canada on a Camper holiday.

Destination Brussels

In the spring of 1972, by when I had been over two years in Bonn, the Foreign Office was beginning to think about my next posting. In July 1971, Roger Jackling had recommended to the Foreign Office that I should succeed Brooks Richards as Minister in the Bonn Embassy. I much appreciated his recommendation, which was a big compliment; but the Foreign Office seldom favours promotions at this level *sur place*, and I was not surprised when nothing came of it. Brooks was replaced by Reg Hibbert, who had served with the Special Operations Executive [SOE] in Yugoslavia and Albania in the War, and had later been Political Adviser to the C-in-C Far East. He had acquired a rather gruff, clipped way of speaking, and perhaps went down well with the military. But he always wanted to be right, and disliked anyone else getting credit: he came to be described by the staff as 'the Sergeant-Major', and did serious damage to Embassy morale. My shoulder was much in use as a weeping-post!

The Treaty for British Accession to the European Communities had been signed in Brussels at the beginning of 1972, and the UK was to become a Member State in the following January. Whitehall was concocting a list of British names to be proposed in Brussels for senior positions in the Community Institutions. It was natural, given my extensive European experience, that the Foreign Office should think of me in this context. I made it clear to top people that there was nothing I would like better.

On 13 January 1973, Michael Jenkins, Deputy Chef de Cabinet to George Thomson, one of Britain's first two European Commissioners, phoned from Brussels to say that the British Commissioners had proposed my appointment as a Deputy Secretary-General of the Commission: the proposal would soon be approved. Maura and I were delighted: not just because this would represent promotion to a very important job; but still more, because we would be contributing directly to a cause we had always strongly supported – the Community and Britain's entry into it. There were still points to be clarified: what exactly would be the nature of the job; when would the Commission want me to take it up; and where would we live on arrival. These were settled during various visits to Brussels in January.

The first question was soon disposed of, in discussion with Emile Noël, whom Maura and I had known in Strasbourg and again in the Heath negotiations, and who had been Secretary-General of the EEC (and then the merged Commission of the three Communities) since 1958. He was destined to hold that position for the first 30 years of the Communities' life.

Emile explained that the Commission had hitherto had only one Deputy Secretary-General (then Klaus Meyer from Germany). The latter was very fully occupied, assuring representation of the Commission in the Council instances, especially the Committee of Permanent Representatives [hereinafter usually 'Coreper'], and in the budding European Political

Co-operation [EPC]. There was a genuine need for a second Deputy, following the enlargement. The Commission was busier and bigger; whilst it had started in an informal way, suitable for a small and infant administration, it now needed to be modernised, better co-ordinated and better run; and it also needed to devote more resources to developing its relations with the European Parliament – which he correctly foresaw would soon be directly elected and thereby gain in authority and influence. Emile undertook to see that I played an important role in all this. Other tasks would arise naturally.

I fully trusted Emile from the start, and it is a pleasure now to record that we worked as good friends and close colleagues in a most enjoyable partnership until I retired in 1986. In conversations with François-Xavier Ortoli, Commission President, and Christopher Soames, the senior British Commissioner, I was urged to come at once. The operational reasons were for urgency were obvious, but personal considerations favoured a slower pace. There were many goodbyes to be said in Bonn. It seemed desirable to hand over properly to my successor, Peter Petrie, due in mid-March. And, last but certainly not least, we had already booked our family ski-ing holiday in Davos-Laret for a fortnight at the beginning of April. It was agreed that my appointment would run from 16 April. In the meanwhile the Foreign Office had appointed me to the rank of Under-Secretary.

Maura and I began looking for a house to rent, but took temporary accommodation at the 'Restaurant des Trois Tilleuls'. It was run by a delightful couple: Guy and Adrienne Vanderperre. He was a first-class chef: and, having served in the RAF in the War, was very pro-British. She was of Czech origin. We were made to feel very welcome. Not only did we use the Trois Tilleuls as our initial base, but we ate there on many occasions over subsequent years, and Maura later did a cookery course with Guy.

A few closing words more about leaving Bonn. We gave three large farewell drinks parties. Well over a dozen were also given for us, including by the Ambassador, the Minister, the Embassy Staff, the Van Wells and the Lustigs. There was also a Bonn Group lunch for me. These occasions provided a delightful conclusion for a memorable three years.

CHAPTER 14

Joint Deputy Secretary-General, European Commission 1973-76

Finding a home in Brussels

ON 19 MARCH, 1973, Maura and I left Im Etzental and drove to Brussels. William had flown to England to stay with his grandmother at Rose Garden Cottage [RGC] in Gerrards Cross; and our dachshund, Andy, had been lodged with kind Bonn Embassy friends. Installed at the Trois Tilleuls, we resumed the search for a house to rent. The very first we saw belonged to Madame Marguerite Lambin, and was at No 5 Avenue des Lauriers, in the Commune of Woluwe St Pierre. We liked it immediately. But the rent asked was large by British standards, and it took us time to adjust to the higher levels obtaining in Brussels. We saw many other houses, but none answered our needs nearly as well. A week later, we took a lease on No 5, effective from 1 July. This left us free for a break, before I took up my appointment. We drove to Switzerland; picked up all three children at Zürich Airport; had a fortnight's ski-ing at Davos; and drove them back to Brussels. All spent a night at the Trois Tilleuls. Next day Maura and the family flew to London, to stay at RGC: I remained in Brussels, to start work, taking a short lease of a flat near the Porte Louise. For a while, I lived a bachelor life, as Maura had an infection and stayed at RGC. She joined me, with William, in June; and the other two children came for their half terms.

Thereafter, life fell into a new pattern. William went every morning by bus to Uccle, where he had started at the European School; at the office, I began carving myself a role in the newly created job; and, in the flat, Maura had a relatively quiet time preparing to move to the Lauriers house. We were destined to buy it just over five years later, and it was our much-loved family home until I retired from professional life in 1986!

How delightful it was! Beautifully situated in a garden suburb; elegant within and without; large enough for the family, and for the amount of entertainment we wished to do; practical to run; and with a small but pleasant garden. The ground fell sharply from the front door to our road-side hedge, with a small terraced front garden. Opposite, rising ground closed the view, with a number of pleasant houses in large, well kept

Our House in Brussels – No. 5 Avenue des Lauriers.

gardens, with many trees. The vista from our front windows was very green, until autumn colours arrived. Behind, our small garden was quiet and private. At the back, a wicket gate led onto a footpath which, skirting a large field, led straight up into the Forêt de Soignes, the vast beech forest which flanks the south-east side of Brussels and stretches ten kilometres to Waterloo. It was a great recreational resource.

Inside, there were five bedrooms: one per child, plus a spare. Downstairs, the best feature was a large, square sitting-room, running the breadth of the house, with big picture windows facing front, and French windows to the rear. It was full of light. The location of the house was good too. Though it lay in the suburbs, access was easy. It seldom took as much as fifteen minutes to reach my office garage; and the timing to the airport, of which we became frequent users, was similar.

A change in career pattern

It is time to speak of the big change in our way of life which the move to Brussels implied; our approach to it; and the political context in which it developed.

Although we much welcomed the chance of a spell with the Community Institutions, for some time we kept an open mind on how long we would stay. We wanted to see how this different life-style would suit us and the family. We came to like it well. Five years later, I committed myself to spending the rest of my professional life with the Commission, and we stayed for a total of over thirteen years, a period more than three times as long as any normal posting I had with the Foreign Office.

On moving to Brussels, the Foreign Office placed me on 'indefinite special leave'. This meant my loyalty was no longer to the British Government, but entirely to the European Community. However, I had a right, after four years, to return to a Foreign Office career. By the time we had decided not to, and so informed the Foreign Office, I had found to my surprise that the position of being notionally on the latter's books gave me a degree of extra standing within the Community. Illogical as this may sound – because I never allowed it to influence in any way my loyalty to the Community – it led me to ask the Foreign Office to leave matters formally as they were, until I retired. I suspect that by then I must have held the record for length of time in the British Diplomatic Service spent on leave!

No less than four chapters of this book are devoted to my time with the Commission, reflecting the fact that I did four separate jobs. This one deals with the four years when I was one of two Deputy Secretaries-General, from early 1973 to early 1977; the next chapter deals with the following period, also of four years, when I was the sole Deputy Secretary-General, with larger responsibilities, continuing until early 1981; the third deals with my five years as Director-General for Energy of the European Commission; and the fourth – overlapping the third – deals with my period as the Commission's General Rapporteur for post-Chernobyl action. Each job was very different: each was fascinating.

Many British people have asked me, over the years, how I could reconcile working for the Community with my British nationality. The question is one I found difficult to understand, but merits a digression. Since we joined the Community in 1973, the UK has had essentially four levels of Government: the District, County, National and European levels. (To these has recently been added a new layer: the Regional one – at least for the Scots and the Welsh.) I see no incompatibility in being a South Lakelander, a Cumbrian, an Englishman, a Briton and a European: rather, there is valuable complementarity between all levels, each reinforcing the other, and adding depth and colour to one's personality. Logically, it is no more difficult to switch from a national to a European Community job, than to switch from a County to a Whitehall job, though there are some challenging practical problems. That is certainly how nationals in other Member States see things. I have never worked in the present Community of the Fifteen, only in those of the Nine, the Ten and the Twelve. But, even with the Twelve, I would say that the characteristically suspicious British approach was shared only by the Danes, and even then not to the same extent.

What is the reason for this difference? At bottom, it probably has to do with the decline in real importance of the House of Commons. In the early 20th century, to be an MP was a great thing. Britain saw herself as the principal Great Power; and the House was 'in charge' of much of the World. It was natural, indeed justifiable, for an MP to feel important. My Shepherd-Cross Grandfather, for 25 years a Member for Bolton, would certainly have done so.

The First World War should have shown us that the United States was taking over the lead role; but the British establishment chose not to recognise the fact. The aftermath of the Second World War, and the rise of the USSR, sharply reduced the power of the UK, and therefore of the House. Once again, MPs tried to pretend otherwise. And so it went on. The less real power the House has had, the more it has talked up the importance of its position. Joining the Community meant pooling a lot of sovereignty, and since 1973 Britain has approved the pooling of much more: all this has been done for good objective reasons, and approved by Parliament after long debates. Nevertheless, against all the evidence, many British politicians have tried to pretend that Parliament's own power is undiminished. In the process they have developed the 'them and us' syndrome, vis-à-vis the Community and its Institutions. 'Brussels' is constantly represented as having 'imposed' things on Britain.

'Brussels' is of course merely the place where the Institutions mainly meet. They are Institutions of a Community of which Britain has freely chosen to be a Member. In all these Institutions, the British have as large a place as the French, the Italians or – until reunification in 1990 – the Germans. The Council (of Ministers) is nonetheless represented as an Institution where a 'reasonable' Britain is constantly being out-voted by 'unreasonable' foreigners. And yet, for the first dozen or so years after British accession, there was very little voting in the Council at all. And one may wonder why, if the British position is always so reasonable, it should be possible to build a majority of two-thirds of the votes against it.

As the reality of the House of Commons' power has declined, so it has fought – ever more strongly – to defend the appearance. One sees this, not only in the way it has treated 'Brussels', but also in the way it has dealt with lower levels of Government in the UK. The post-war history of Britain has shown a continuing transfer of Governmental powers away from these lower levels, and upwards to Westminster and Whitehall. The creation by the present Labour Government of Regional Assemblies for Scotland and Wales is an honourable – though untidy – exception. The readiness of the same Government to 'take over' County or District Councils considered to be not performing to some Government norm, is nearer the rule.

Over the last twenty years, the anti-Brussels posturing of so many politicians has been compounded by the increasing concentration of media power in the hands of a small number of moguls – some of them not British – who support confrontational attitudes of narrow nationalism and jingoism.

Enough of 'them and us'. It is time to address some of the practical problems of working as an official of the European Community. By many, these officials are described as 'Eurocrats'. I avoid using the term: it is misleading, and often intended pejoratively. I prefer 'Community official', which is legally correct, or 'European Civil Servant'. After a quarter of a century as a British official, and then thirteen as a European Civil Servant, I am in no doubt that, as a general rule, the latter animal is much more open and less bureaucratic than the former: everybody I know who has substantial experience of dealing with both, agrees with this assessment. I am equally in no doubt that the European Civil Servant usually has a far more challenging job than his national counterpart.

Many think the multiplicity of languages must be the Community's biggest problem. Certainly there is a problem, but not as big as often supposed. And it is getting less as English becomes the *lingua franca* of all Europe.

When the first Community Treaty was negotiated – the Paris Treaty establishing the ECSC – it was intended that there would be only <u>one</u> official language, namely French. Then, at a late stage in the negotiations, a single Member State objected. Ironically, the objector was Belgium, then the <u>most</u> *communautaire* of all the Six. The explanation lay in Belgium's own Franco-Nederlands language problem. Paul-Henri Spaak felt obliged to tell his fellow negotiators that, if <u>either</u> of Belgium's official languages were to become an official language of the Community, then <u>both</u> would have to!

Once Nederlands was admitted, German, and Italian were bound to follow. (Happily Luxembourg did not press for its own variant of German!) Since then, each new Member State has insisted on adding its own official language(-s) to the list, raising the number to 11. The only exception was Ireland which, while insisting that there should be an authentic Gaelic version of the <u>Treaty texts</u>, did not insist on translation or interpretation in other respects. (The fact that not enough translators and interpreters could be found for this language had something to do with this generosity of spirit.)

Language is a problem wherever business has to be transacted by politicians – notably in meetings of the European Parliament, the Council or even the College of Commissioners. At the other extreme, there is no problem whatever in internal meetings between European Civil Servants. Nowadays, English or French are accepted as the Commission working languages, whether in discussion or in internal correspondence, and used without translation or interpretation. It was not always so. Before the first enlargement, all four Community languages were used to some extent, though French was dominant. Immediately after that, French was used as to about 65%, English as to about 30%, and the others hardly at all. Progressively one has moved to a position where the French/English ratio has been reversed; and, with further enlargement, the advance of English is likely to continue. For me, there was never a problem, since I spoke fluently in French, German and Spanish before joining the Commission; and soon acquired fluency in writing French as well.

The biggest problem for an incoming European Civil Servant is quite different. Most people are brought up, trained and work, in a very national ambiance. The language, education, history, traditions, ways of thought, and behaviour patterns of ordinary citizens, have a distinct national flavour. Each governmental 'establishment', moreover, works within its own constitutional and legal framework, and has its own rules, procedures and habits. In short, one operates within a protective cocoon. When I joined the Commission, I was leaving a particularly clear and well established national framework, and moving into a young, informal, rapidly developing, international structure.

There was one very helpful aspect. The Community operates on a strongly legal basis. The original Treaties, and various associated legal instruments, are the Constitution. The actions taken under them are usually based on specific Community laws – known as 'Secondary Legislation' by British lawyers – whereas in the UK much more would be done by administrative decision. Below the legal level, however, there is naturally still a lot of business. And it was at that point that the youth of the Community, and the lack of a great corpus of established practice, made life difficult for the newcomers.

When one looks at the complex Community of today, it is difficult to imagine the pioneering age of the 1950s and 60s. The whole Community concept was invented only in 1950. The first Executive, the High Authority of the ECSC, started work under President Jean Monnet in August 1952. Its original officials were appointed on an *ad hoc* basis. A Commissioner would ring up somebody he thought suitable and invite him to be a Director-General or Director. (They were virtually all male at those levels then!) Most of those approached were fired with enthusiasm for the enterprise; made no serious enquiries about salary or conditions; but simply came.

Much the same happened when the EEC and Euratom were established, six years later. The first Director-General of the EEC Budget – M Van Gronsveld – was still in that position when I arrived. He would tell how, in the early days, officials would come and ask him for their monthly salary. There were no salary scales for quite a time. So he would simply ask some questions about their urgent needs, and make them a corresponding advance! He claimed that, to begin with, there was no safe, and he took the Commission's cash reserves home at night, in a locked box strapped to his wrist!

The merger of the three Executives in the late 1960s, though eminently sensible, further delayed consolidation of the administration. Each Secretary-General, and also each Director-General, had developed administrative practices pragmatically. For the newcomer in 1973, it was bewildering. One would be faced with a simple problem, such as how to deal with an incoming letter, or address a message to a Member State. Each 'old' official from whom advice was sought would tend to have a different view, depending on which Directorate-General of which Executive he had worked with.

Last but not least, incoming European Civil Servants must enormously broaden their horizons and range of knowledge. At national level, Civil Servants will be expected to have a good grasp of national politics; but few will be expected to know much about 'abroad' unless they happen to be in the Foreign Office. In the Commission, things are completely different. A good official will have to understand, not only the Community system, but also the basic politics of each Member State, or at least those relating to his area of interest. He must be aware, for example, of the constitutional set-up; the political complexion of Parliament and Government; key personalities; burning issues; and upcoming election dates. He can of course brief himself by talking to other Commission officials from the countries concerned; but he must be alert and sensitive about political developments in the whole Community. It's a tall order!

General political background

In terms of international affairs, the focus of my last chapter was on *détente* in Europe, and more especially Ostpolitik. These developments were part of a wider pattern of stabilisation, and of stand-off between the two Super-Powers. They may be said to have reached their apogee with the establishment of the Conference on Security and Co-operation in Europe [CSCE], in Helsinki in August 1975.

The European Community was moving forward again. Agreement had been reached on a new régime for 'Own Resources' [direct Community financing, replacing unreliable, annual contributions from Member States]; and the initial principles for a Common Fisheries Policy were in place. Negotiations for enlargement of the Community had succeeded; there had been a first Summit of the Nine in October 1972, when the Heads of Government had committed themselves to agreeing many new Community policies and reforms; the UK, Denmark and Ireland had joined in January 1973, though a negative referendum had prevented Norway; and the European Political Co-operation machinery was beginning to make headway.

This first enlargement changed the Community's political chemistry. The Community of the Six had been marked by the circumstances of its establishment in the 1950s. At that time, the Benelux countries had some quite remarkable leaders – Paul-Henri Spaak, Jo Luns and Joseph Bech amongst them – and they had contributed enormously to the European Project. Partly for this reason, and partly to avoid creating an impression that the big countries would dominate the small, the three large ones – France, Italy and the FRG – had conceded to the Benelux countries a share of the votes in the Council far more than proportional to the size of their populations or economies. The Benelux countries together had as many votes as each of their larger partners.

This weighting was maintained in the Community of the Nine; but diluted by the addition of the newer Member States. Meanwhile, however, each of the Benelux countries had, for different reasons, lost political momentum. Italy had never had much. So the position of France and Germany became *de facto* more important. Increasingly, they had come to be seen as the motors of the Community. Britain could naturally have joined them in this role. Sadly, however, the reticence to deepening the Community she has ever since displayed, prevented this happening. She has remained a relatively marginal player. The main long-term effects of the enlargement – apart from giving the Community greater weight in world counsels – have, therefore, to be seen in the injection of doses of more northern traditions and behaviour patterns, and the establishment of the trend towards ever-increasing use of the English language.

In the wider world, President Nixon had visited Beijing early in 1972: this first visit to Communist China by an American President had eased tensions between China and the Free World. The so-called Cold War by surrogates – conflicts between friends of the USA and the USSR respectively – had also eased, particularly following a decision by President Anwar Sadat of Egypt to send home the 15,000 Russians who had been acting as 'Advisers' there. Overall, confrontational attitudes had waned. When I reached Brussels, the political sun was again shining. Nobody foresaw that 1973 would witness the outbreak of the Yom Kippur Arab-Israel War; the consequent explosion of oil prices and long-lasting depression of the World Economy; and the outbreak of Soviet-supported disturbances in Ethiopia and Angola. These last were soon to lead the World into the 'Second Cold War', and renew North-South tension.

The other main events serving as backdrop to the Community's work, during the four years covered by this chapter, may be briefly resumed. The political complexion of the Community was changed by the abrupt disappearance from office of three key Heads of Government: Pompidou, Brandt and Heath. Their successors, Giscard, Schmidt and Wilson were very different people. Wilson, whose party had opposed the terms of the Accession Treaty, though not the principle of membership, asked for its 're-negotiation'. This led to discussions between the Nine, and agreement on a number of vague formulae. They changed nothing of significance, and included no Treaty amendments. The package nevertheless enabled Wilson to 'sell' membership to his party. A referendum, in June 1975, confirmed British membership by 67.2% of votes cast.

In the same month Greece applied to join; and Spain and Portugal soon followed suit. Meanwhile the Heads of Government had decided to establish their hitherto occasional meetings on a regular basis, and to call themselves the 'European Council'. They had also commissioned Leo Tindemans, the Belgian Prime Minister, to write a Report on what would be involved in converting the Communities into a 'European Union'. Its submission, at the end of 1975, began the long-drawn-out and tortuous process which culminated in signature of the Maastricht Treaty, 16 years later. In 1976, agreement was reached to hold Direct Elections to the European Parliament (they took place three years later). And, at the beginning of 1977, Jimmy Carter had become President of the United States, and Roy Jenkins of the European Commission.

A different kind of office

In the Bonn Embassy job, I had enjoyed modest office facilities: two small rooms and one Secretary. For the new Deputy Secretary-General of the Commission in Brussels, provision was more generous. The main Commission offices were still in the Berlaymont building – that unique construction beloved by media people because at once recognisable to the public eye. There was a module size for offices, corresponding to the width of the standard segment of external glass cladding. Seniority was measured by the possession of a certain number of windows. A Commissioner had four; a Director-General, three; and a Deputy Director-General, two. Status was enhanced by the possession of office space on the top (or 13th) floor, because that was where the Commissioners themselves were housed. The phrase *'Ah, celui-là, il a un bureau de trois fenêtres au treizième'*, would be pronounced in tones of awe! In due course I was to graduate to two windows on the 13th, with two more rooms for my staff. However, on my first day, I was allotted more modest accommodation on the 11th.

I was to have two Secretaries – one fluent in French, the other in English. The choice of the former had been made. Emile Noël had suggested the name of Betty Muller; I had interviewed her before the Swiss holiday, and liked her; and she had agreed to come. Emile's recommendation was inspired. Betty had long worked in the Commission, most recently as Secretary to Daniel Cardon de Lichtbuer, Chef de Cabinet of the Belgian Commissioner, Albert Coppé: both Coppé and Cardon had left at the change of Commission. Betty knew everyone, and also how to get things done. From the start, we enjoyed working together. She stayed with me until my retirement, and was invaluable. We have remained good friends to this day.

When I walked into my new office, I found no furniture: only Betty, sitting on a packing case, equipped with a telephone, haranguing those responsible in the Administration for the surrounding chaos. The explanation was not far to seek: many officials from the new Member States were having to be housed rapidly, following the Community's enlargement. With Betty in charge, I soon had a fully furnished office. Later, we together recruited my first English mother-tongue Secretary. There was less stability here, and six girls worked under me in this capacity at different times. Overall, I was very fortunate. Thus equipped, I was ready to tackle the job. But what was it?

Emile Noël had prescribed two specific areas of activity: modernising the Commission's machinery, and developing its relations with the European Parliament. Let us look at each in turn; and then at others, later added. My first task, obviously, was to understand the Commission, and the people who worked in it.

Understanding the Commission

The Commission comprises, on the one hand, the Commissioners themselves, collectively known as the College; and, on the other, their Services. Many in the UK like to describe the Commissioners as officials; but they are not. Until recently they were appointed by simple, unanimous decision of the Member State Governments; but, from the very beginning of the Community, they were nonetheless subject to dismissal, at any time, by the European Parliament. (Since the Amsterdam Treaty took effect in 1999, moreover, their appointment has become dependent on a prior vote of approval by Parliament.) 'The Services' is the generic name for the different Directorates-General, and the other main Departments – like the Secretariat-General or the Legal Service. They indeed are staffed by Community officials: Directors-General, Directors, Heads of Division and so forth. A third category of Commission personnel consists of those in the different Commissioners' Cabinets – or Private Offices in Whitehall terminology. Cabinet members are appointed by the Commissioner himself. [NB. From now on in this book, whenever I use 'he' or 'him', the term should, where the context requires, be regarded as shorthand for 'he/she' or 'him/her'.] Cabinet members may be officials on secondment from the Services; or outsiders brought in on a temporary basis.

Clearly, I had to know all the Commissioners; all key players in Cabinets; and a wide range of officials in all the Services. Generally speaking, people in the Commission are more informal and approachable than those in Whitehall. And Emile's constant and obvious support for me opened many doors. Nevertheless, much effort had to be invested in building contacts.

I was authorised to attend all normal meetings of the Commission, usually held each Wednesday: a privilege then enjoyed by only seven Officials – namely the Secretary-General and his two Deputies, the Greffier (or Clerk to the Commission), the Legal Adviser (a very important post), the Commission's Press Spokesman, and the President's *Chef de Cabinet* [hereinafter 'Chefcab']. Attendance by the thirteen Commissioners was almost 100 %. If absent, they could be represented by their Chefcabs, but the latter could not vote. Other Officials could attend only if specifically authorised – for example a Director-General would usually be invited when a point for which his Commissioner was responsible was being discussed.

This situation offered a tremendous benefit. Not only was one almost uniquely placed to understand how and why the Commission came to particular decisions: one was also actively cultivated as a source of information by others, both Commission Officials and outsiders.

Likewise I could attend the regular Monday meetings of Chefcabs, when the Commission's own meeting was prepared; and also Emile's de-briefing session for all Directors-General each Thursday. On the rare occasions when Emile had to miss a Commission himself, I replaced him there; oversaw preparation of the Minutes by the Greffier; and briefed the Directors-General.

I soon built good contacts with all Directors-General and Cabinets. There was a particularly close relationship with the President's Cabinet, where the Chefcab, Philippe De Margerie [French], and his Deputy, Jean Degimbe [Belgian], were effective and thoroughly *sympathique*. The Secretariat-General worked under the President's authority. He relied on us to see that the Commission's work was well prepared; and that the College was well informed of what was going on in all parts of the Council machinery (the responsibility of Klaus Meyer), and of the European Parliament (my responsibility). We were also expected to ensure that Commission decisions were rapidly relayed to all concerned.

The tight restrictions on attendance at Commission meetings, the small number of Commissioners, and the fact that only French and English were usually spoken, gave the meetings an intimate character. In the early stages after my arrival, there was a good political climate. Almost every week the Commission had before it one or more proposals for a new policy line: many of them were inspired by the Paris Summit Communiqué of October 1972. There were long lunch hours. Lunch was then often taken by the Commissioners together; and I was not infrequently invited.

The first Commission after enlargement contained some interesting personalities. Its President, François-Xavier Ortoli (always 'Francís' to his friends) was experienced in Community affairs, intelligent, reflective, unassuming, very human, and quiet. More ebullient Members of the Commission were Christopher Soames and Henri Simonet [Belgian], both of whom enjoyed a good joke and also their liquor. On this point I permit myself another digression. There was an agreeable tradition that *digestifs* were served during the Commission meeting after lunch. After the first summer break, however, it transpired that Francís was concerned about putting on weight: he may also have noticed a certain torpor during the College's afternoon sessions. Francís instructed M Verpoorten, the Head *Huissier*, that in future there should be no service of *digestifs*. Colleagues were not told. At the next meeting, the order was implemented. Sitting near Christopher, I noted his surprise when no *framboise* appeared. He summoned M Verpoorten for a whispered conversation. Soon, a single glass of the *liqueur* was served to Christopher. Simonet, who had observed the whole *Theaterstück*, made a discreet sign to Verpoorten which ensured the same treatment for him. Every week thereafter, Christopher and Henri automatically had their *liqueur*: fellow Commissioners, less concerned or less determined, silently accepted the change.

Christopher, who had not impressed me when he was UK Minister of Agriculture during the Heath negotiations, but who had subsequently been British Ambassador in Paris, took to his role as Commissioner responsible for External Affairs with *panache* and effectiveness. He made a big personal input to the raising of the Community's profile throughout the world, which started with the first enlargement. Mary Soames was delightful and a great support. They entertained well, at their home on the edge of the Bois de la Cambre. On one occasion when Maura and I were invited, the Soames's Chef fell ill during the afternoon. Guests were all told that the party was being transferred to *'the pub around the corner'*. Closer enquiry revealed that the *'pub'* was in fact the Villa Lorraine, one of Brussels' very best restaurants.

The Commission runs to certain rhythms: that of its [then] four year term of office; an annual cycle; and a weekly cycle.

In its first year a Commission settles in, agrees priorities, and starts to present proposals to Parliament and Council for major initiatives. In its second, the emphasis begins to switch towards fighting the proposals through the other two Institutions. This trend strengthens in the third. In the fourth, the Commission progressively loses steam, and the Commissioners begin to prepare their futures. (Recently, the Member States have sensibly changed the Commission's term of office from four to five years, to coincide with that of the European Parliament, so the foregoing pattern has been stretched; but the principles of acceleration, cruising speed and deceleration remain.)

The annual cycle is similar to that of a British boarding school, with spring, summer and autumn terms. As in a good Public School, officials are required to work very hard in term-time, but get good holidays. The Institution virtually closes down for a week or so over Easter; for the whole month of August; and for some ten days at Christmas and New Year. Most people time their leave to fit round this pattern. Moreover there are so many public holidays in Brussels during May, it has become known as the month of Sundays. These arrangements suited the family well, since I could take time off to coincide with our childrens' holidays.

Parts of the weekly cycle of meetings have already been mentioned. But adaptations had to be made once a month, when the Commission trooped off to Plenary meetings of the European Parliament, in Luxembourg or Strasbourg. And meetings of the Council, in various formations, would demand the presence of one or more Commissioners about once a week.

Such was the background to my new job as a Deputy Secretary-General. I shall describe it under two broad headings: tasks within the Secretariat-General; and tasks in relation to the European Parliament. The work to be described was animated and controlled by myself. But of course many other people were involved. Three of the Secretariat-General's Divisions worked under my authority: one dealing with Internal Co-ordination; a second with the General Report and Monthly Bulletin (explained below); and a third with the European Parliament and the Economic and Social Committee. The other Divisions of the Secretariat-General were supervised by Klaus Meyer (those dealing with the Council) or by Emile himself; but their support for my work was freely given when needed.

Modernising and improving co-ordination of the Commission's machinery

Once I had gained an overall impression of the Commission's operations, I began trying to modernise, and improve internal co-ordination. This was a continuing task, in which I was to invest much effort over eight years – but especially the first four or five. It would be tedious to recount too much detail, or indicate a sequence, but the following paragraphs give the flavour by sketching principal activities. Since they cover a very wide range of matters, and I have had to concentrate much material into a short space, they are a demanding read; so I have inserted sub-headings to help the reader. The same applies to the following Section about the European Parliament.

From the start I worked closely on internal co-ordination with Emile. As he was much in demand, we soon began a useful and agreeable practice: namely to have a working dinner together at some good restaurant every now and then. Emile enjoyed fine cooking, even though he often went without proper food for long periods when needs must. These evenings gave us the opportunity to cover much ground in a relaxed way. Sometimes we would be joined by one or more of my Division Heads, particularly Nye Hughes who was responsible for internal co-ordination, and the late Andy Mulligan (succeeded by Yvo Dubois) who was responsible for publications. By July of 1973 I had secured approval to put a paper on internal co-ordination to the Commission, setting out some general lines of approach. It was approved, and furnished a launching-pad for many of the detailed measures discussed below.

Creating a manual of procedures

I remarked earlier that administrative practices in the Commission Services had grown up pragmatically. There were no standard procedures for doing routine tasks. Each Service had invented its own. Much depended on whether its origins lay with the ECSC, the EEC or Euratom. For recruits from the new Member States, the result was complete bafflement. I felt that a Manual of Procedures was the answer, but wondered whether such a suggestion would be seen by Emile as implied criticism. Not a bit. He replied that, although *'muddling through à l'anglaise'* had perhaps been right in the pioneering days, these were now over. Would I please write the Manual, basing myself on best practice, and the sooner the better! The Manual required much research, thought and discussion. But the Division of Internal Co-ordination kept at it, and completed the first edition by the summer of 1976. It found immediate, indeed universal, acceptance as a sort of bible, and has been constantly updated ever since. On a recent Brussels visit I found the latest edition had grown to 200 pages of A4.

The General Report and the Monthly Bulletin

Soon after my arrival, Emile gave me responsibility for the production of the Commission's General Report and Monthly Bulletin. The Commission is Treaty-bound to publish, by mid-February annually, a 'General Report on the Activities of the Community', taking account of events right up to 31 December. It must do this simultaneously in all official Community languages, which were, after the first enlargement, six in number (now eleven!).

Doing this properly at first appeared to represent quite a challenge. The Report is comprehensive, and my first one, covering 1973, ran to over 500 pages of A5 print. It was the job of the Secretariat-General to determine the structure of the Report, which varies as political and other circumstances change; itself to draft the general and institutional chapters; to secure drafts of the other chapters from the responsible Services towards the end of the year; to harmonise and edit the whole thing; to have the Services do a final revision of their chapters after the year-end; to have translations made into the different languages *pari passu*; and to get the whole thing approved by the Commission and sent to the Community's Office of Publications for printing in January.

I do not believe any other organisation, anywhere in the world, undertakes so ambitious a publishing activity to such tight deadlines. But Emile had long since set up a system capable of producing the desired result. For me, it turned out to be mainly a question of fine tuning the structure; good drafting and editing; and accommodating the two new official languages (English and Danish).

The Monthly Bulletin was quite another matter. This is a monthly record of Community events. Although the machinery for producing it was similar, it was nowhere near so effective, because there was less pressure. There is no legal requirement for the Bulletin: it is published simply because the Commission feels a duty to make such information readily available to the public. Things had slipped behind, and issues were appearing at different times in different languages, sometimes months in arrears. I applied my usual philosophy: do a job well or not at all. The principle was established that all versions would issue simultaneously, six weeks after the end of the month covered. The Division succeeded, after a while, in regularly hitting the target, though I believe there was some slippage after my time.

The legislative programme

In those days the General Report also contained the Commission's legislative programme for the year just begun, and this too was part of my remit. Of course I did not personally propose a programme. But the Secretariat-General was very heavily involved. We started by inviting all Services, under the authority of their respective Commissioners, to send us proposals for their respective sectors. On this basis, we created an overall structure; edited the proposals into it; and submitted the whole to the Commission. In the process we worked hand-in-hand with the President's Cabinet, since Ortoli was of course going to accept general responsibility for everything in the programme. There were always far too many legislative proposals. A key task, therefore, was to prune the material to reasonable proportions. There were tough negotiations with the Cabinets.

The Commission's internal decision-making

Work on the Manual led me to reflect about the Commission's internal decision-making process, where streamlining seemed imperative. The Treaty gives little guidance about Commission decisions. It does lay down that the Institution shall act by simple majority of the number of its Members. It also requires the Commission to adopt and publish Rules of Procedure, which should themselves prescribe the quorum required for a Commission meeting to be valid. But that is all. No doubt, in the earliest days of the Communities, all decisions were taken during the Commission's meetings. But the sheer number required would very soon have made this impractical. Some method had had to be found of getting minor or non-controversial decisions taken outside the meetings.

The device of the 'Written Procedure' had already been invented. Under this, a draft decision with explanatory memorandum was circulated by the Secretariat-General to all Commissioners. There was a deadline for comments or objections. If these could be accommodated, the decision would be considered as adopted: if not, the matter automatically went to a Commission meeting. By the time Britain joined the Community, most decisions were taken by the Written Procedure. It was time-consuming.

By early 1975 I concluded that more radical measures were needed. I proposed to Emile that the Commission consider the possibility, in the case of really minor matters, of quite simply delegating its corporate responsibility to the Commissioner responsible for the sector of activity involved. The rules for each such delegation – the French call it *habilitation* – should be strict. They should define the area covered very precisely. They should lay on the Commissioner concerned a duty to exercise his power only if he felt confident his colleagues would be happy; otherwise he must submit the proposal through the written procedure or in a meeting. He should also report to his colleagues in writing every decision so taken. The Secretariat-General should be mandated by the Commission to ensure full respect of the rules. Once again, Emile's reaction was favourable. He said that, in earlier days, such a procedure would have been impossible, because the necessary degree of mutual confidence between Commissioners had not developed. But now, we should try. We did: and it worked, greatly easing the conduct of routine business.

In this same field of decision-making, the wider legislative process of the Community was also creaking. The Commission was constantly making legislative proposals: often, however, these became blocked in the Council. One must remember that, at this stage of the Community's development, qualified majority voting was virtually never used, even when the Treaty prescribed it. The legacy of De Gaulle meant that the tradition of trying to find unanimity in the Council, regardless of the legal position, still obtained. As a result, Commission proposals lay on the Council table for years. A striking example was a draft Council Directive, providing for architects qualified in one Community country to be able to practise in all others: it had been proposed by the Commission thirteen years earlier, and was still stuck. All this was bringing the Community into disrepute. At my suggestion the Commission agreed to make a comprehensive review of its pending proposals; to withdraw any it considered to be without real prospect of success; and to make clear that responsibility lay with the Council. This happened. Many proposals were withdrawn. The Commission gained in credibility. The procedure became standard Commission practice.

Policing respect for Community legislation
The Commission was very active in proposing new laws, but did not systematically check to what extent they were being applied, nor act against Member States and others when they were not. The general attitude was one of timidity *vis-à-vis* the Member States.

This seemed wrong, and a dereliction of the Commission's fundamental duty under the Treaty to ensure that Community Law is properly applied. To change the mind-set, I was going to need the strong support, not just of Emile, but also of the Commission's Legal Adviser – Klaus Ehlermann, a good friend and an excellent official – and indeed of President Ortoli himself (responsible for both the Secretariat-General and the Legal Service). All these were forthcoming.

Progressively, a much tougher policy was set in place. Beginning in 1974, a machinery was established for checking the extent to which Member States correctly, and in a timely manner, transposed Council Directives into their national law. It became standard practice for the Commission, when Member States failed to proceed, and after one warning, to bring them before the Court of Justice. The Court itself welcomed this tougher line, and usually found for the Commission. Member States have on the whole been good about respecting Court judgements: indeed I do not think there is yet a case of long-term persistence in infringement after the Court has spoken. Nowadays, moreover, the Member States can be fined by the Court in case of mis-doing.

My positive view of the Court's position was shared by an outsider, particularly well qualified to hold an opinion. Warren Burger, Chief Justice of the US Supreme Court, informally visited the Community Institutions in September 1978. He lunched with the Commission, attended the

Parliament, and went to Luxembourg to see the Court of Justice. They also lunched him, and then sat him as a courtesy alongside the Court Members on the bench at a public session. Before his departure I asked his impressions. His response was strongly positive: he had been enormously struck by the extent to which Community law had been fully accepted by the Member States and the public in so short a time. (It was by then only twenty years since the Treaties of Rome had entered into force, yet nobody was seriously challenging the law.) He remarked that the position of the US Supreme Court, twenty years after <u>it</u> came into being, had been infinitely less secure and comfortable.

The Directives initiative was followed by others. On the basis of proposals from the Secretariat-General and the Legal Service, the Commission became much more active in the pursuit of <u>all</u> types of infringement of Community Law, whether by Member States or by juridical or natural persons.

Publications

Another task was that of bringing more order into the Commission's publishing activities generally. As in other fields, these activities had developed haphazardly: individual services had been free to publish what they pleased. There was waste and duplication. In 1974, it was decided to set up a Publications Committee to sort things out, and Emile asked me to chair it – which I did for nine years. In a large organisation like the Commission, there is probably only one way to ensure coherence: namely to have what Brussels calls 'un point de passage forcé' – a point through which all must pass. The Publications' Committee became one. No-one in the Commission could issue a publication without its approval. Once that rule was accepted, it was not too difficult to rationalise things.

The Community's archives

The Manual activity brought home to me, not only that a uniform procedure was needed for handling mail and current archives throughout the Commission's services, but also that no thought whatever had been given to the eventual opening to the public of the Community's historic archives. The British have a good record in handling historic archives, and I had grown up in this tradition. It seemed to me that the Commission not only needed to develop a policy, but that it had a duty to be at least as liberal as the most liberal of the Member States.

Eventually, we set about producing a draft Regulation which would apply to all Community historic archives, and <u>not only</u> those of the Commission. From the start I urged the adoption of a 30-year rule for opening of historic archives; and also the notion that they should be multiple photocopied, with at least one complete set of microfiches going to each Member State. At Emile's suggestion the principles were included that the originals of the Community archives should be deposited with the European University Institute [EUI] at Florence, where they would be exploited by real experts; and that the Institute could accept private archives for inclusion with them. Many years later, these decisions bore interesting fruit. Emile, who after his retirement was for some years President of the EUI, provided for his own private archives – a collection of enormous value – to be deposited there.

Our task now was to get the rules adopted. It was not difficult to obtain <u>Commission</u> agreement. But our aim of including the archives of the <u>other</u> Institutions in the arrangement meant that we had to persuade the Council, with the agreement of the European Parliament, and the consent of the Court of Justice, to adopt a formal Regulation. A lengthy procedure was needed. First, the Heads of all the National Archives of the Member States were invited to the Commission, and gave me their support. Then, the Commission adopted a formal proposal. This secured approval from Council, Parliament and Court; and the draft Regulation became law. Meanwhile we had recruited to the Commission Services a highly qualified person, Hans Hofmann from Germany, to advise on implementation. The historical archives of the European Communities were fully opened to researchers in December 1985. Their legislative history had been tortuous, and I have written an article about it, to be published soon. But no details are needed here.

Computerisation

Soon after my arrival, Emile asked me to join a new Committee of Officials, whose duty was to organise extensive computerisation of the Commission and its services, and to control the funds allotted for this purpose by the Commission's budget. At that time, large main-frame computers and batch-processing were in fashion. Our big machines were located in the main Computer Centre at Luxembourg, so our Committee was called the Computer Centre Management Committee [CCMC]. Later, as the trend towards devolved computing, local networks and intelligent work-stations took hold, our name was changed to *Comité Directeur de l'Informatique à la Commission [CDIC]*, a terminology I shall use from now on. I stayed on it for a dozen years. Before going to the Commission I had nothing whatever to do with computers, so I had to learn a lot fast. I never needed to know how computers <u>worked</u>: we had plenty of technicians for that. The challenge for me was to understand what they could or could not <u>do</u>, and how the Commission services could put their potential to best use. I left mathematical and economic uses to other people, and focused on two particular fields I knew well, documentation and translation.

The Secretariat-General soon set an example, within the Commission, for computerised documentation; and encouraged all other Directorates-General to follow suit. The Community moved to the forefront of developments, with rapid computerisation of its documents, of Community legislation, and of the jurisprudence of the Court of Justice.

My interest in the translation side was a response to operational needs. With its many official – and equally authentic – languages, the Community had an enormous translation requirement. It already had by far the biggest translation and interpretation services in the world; but they were under constant strain. It was obvious that, if translation work could be at least partly computerised, big staff savings could be made. By 1976, the Translation Services were already equipped with an automated dictionary of terminology [Eurodicautom], covering all the official languages. This was a valuable step, but I felt it should be followed by others. Machine translation had already been used for a single language pair – Russian and English – in the course of the joint Apollo space programme run by NASA and the USSR authorities. The CDIC wondered whether it could be used for the far more numerous language pairs we had to cope with? I supported the provision of funds to find out. In the event, large sums were spent; but the experts kept on reporting their programmes were not yet good enough for operational use. In the early 1980s, by which time I was Director-General for Energy, I felt they were being perfectionist. My Directorate-General needed to know the content of many publications on energy questions in different Community languages. I told the experts to machine-translate some of these, which they unwillingly did. My hunch proved correct. The machines could already provide a translation sufficiently good for my staff to tell whether they needed a more precise one. If they did, the existence of the machine product meant that the labour of high-class translation was greatly reduced.

The Commission's need for security and cypher facilities
In the 1970s, the European Political Co-operation [EPC], namely the mechanism for organising co-operation between the Member States on

foreign affairs, which has since been transformed into the 'Second Pillar' of European Union, was beginning to function. The Commission was represented, with the right to speak at all its formal meetings, but excluded from some informal ones. Certain Member States, notably Britain and France, were determined to keep foreign affairs as a national preserve, and for long took the line that the Commission was not an important partner. This was illogical, since they were constantly wanting to use the Community economic machinery, and the Community Budget, to support their political aims *vis-à-vis* third countries. However, it was a fact; and these same Member States supported their anti-Commission line with any argument which came to hand. One was that the Commission was insecure. Another, later, was that the Commission had no cypher capacity for the safe transmission of classified material; so its access to such material must be restricted.

The Commission instructed me to effect security improvements. The fact that I had gained relevant experience in the British Diplomatic Service was seen as an advantage: I would not only understand what was needed, but would also be considered by the Member States as an *'interlocuteur valable'*. It was not difficult to raise standards of security within the Commission Services. One just had to get the Commission to adopt tighter rules for the handling of sensitive information, and to ensure their application. This was soon done. Obtaining cypher facilities was more delicate. Clearly the Member States would only accept that the Commission had established a secure communication system if they had themselves been closely involved. So in 1975 I made a virtue of necessity, visiting top national cypher experts in several Member States (including Britain, Germany, the Netherlands and France), and securing their freely-given advice and help. It was obvious that they, or some of them, might end up with the ability to de-cypher the Commission's messages. But this did not seem important: we were in the game of ensuring that <u>other</u> countries could not read our messages, and had no business to have secrets from our own Member States. Our cypher capacity was soon installed.

Briefing President Ortoli

Six months after I joined the Commission, Francís Ortoli showed he had by now acquired solid confidence in me by agreeing that I, rather than the Secretary-General, should accompany him on some of his official visits to Member States. Such visits occur quite frequently. In particular, an incoming President will aim to make a courtesy visit to every Member State within months of taking office. My first visit was to The Hague. We drove there and back in a day. We met the Prime Minister and some of his colleagues, and reviewed Community affairs in the broad. My duty was to prepare the visit, through contacts with the Netherlands Permanent Representative and by ensuring that briefing was supplied to the President; to sit with him and advise in the meetings; and to circulate a report. Such visits were invaluable to me in terms of building personal contacts with senior officials of Member States, Ministers and even Prime Ministers.

Commission relations with the European Parliament, and related matters

The personality of the European Parliament
I turn now to my second main block of work: Commission relations with the European Parliament. In those days, the official name of the Institution was still 'the Assembly', as it had been since the beginning. But its Members had long felt this term suggested their Institution was no more than a talking shop.

In legal terms that was more or less true: only later did Parliament acquire real power in the legislative and budgetary processes of the Community. In 1973 the Treaties simply gave it a right to be consulted on all draft legislation, and to express an Opinion. The Commission and Council had a duty to consider such Opinions, but not necessarily to take any account of them. The Council virtually never did. The Commission had not hitherto done so, though this was soon to change. But it was more sensitive than the Council, if only because the Assembly held the power to dismiss it, by adopting a vote of censure. It was soon to start reminding the Commission of this. Even so, it was not until 16 June 1976 that Parliament first voted on such a motion. It did not pass; nor indeed has any passed to this day, although it was the imminent threat of this happening which caused the Commission to resign *en bloc* in 1999.

The Members had long since referred to their Institution as 'The European Parliament'. They could not do this in formal documents, for fear of these being held invalid; but they always did in less formal contexts, and were already pressing for the Treaty to be altered accordingly.

I told my Parliamentary friends this seemed to me a tactical mistake. Under the Treaty construction, it was clear that the Founding Fathers had intended to move to a bi-cameral legislature, with the Assembly acting as 'The House of the People', and the Council as 'The House of the States'. By calling themselves the European Parliament, the Assembly was playing into the hands of the Council in the Institutional power struggle. The Council was left free to regard itself as *sui generis*, and superior to the Assembly, which it has done ever since. The Parliamentarians would not listen to me, but I still think I was right! Nevertheless, from now on in this story, I refer to the Assembly as the European Parliament, and to its Members as MEPs.

Plenary sessions

In those days, Plenary Sessions took place on average once a month and lasted all or most of a week, with eight Sessions being held in Strasbourg and four in Luxembourg. I had to be often present; and usually attended from Tuesday to Thursday inclusive, and often on Monday and/or Friday also. I stayed, of course, in a hotel; and the Commission had a number of *bureaux de passage* in the Parliament Building. Commissioners came for shorter stays: both to attend that week's Commission meeting, usually held 'on location' and also to cover Plenary debates, or Question Time Questions, on subjects of their personal responsibility.

Although Parliament made some efforts to group business to suit individual Commissioners, these were only partially effective. Commissioners often had to hang around, awaiting their points; so Strasbourg and Luxembourg presented opportunities for relaxed conversations or meals with them which were not so easy to obtain in Brussels. Strasbourg is 450 kilometres from Brussels. The trains were slow. By car, the drive took four and a half hours. There were few scheduled flights. Commissioners soon got impatient with the journeys, which they saw as a waste of time. They started to take air-taxis, and I could often cadge a ride. It amused me to fly in small aircraft into the airfield where I had landed on my own flying test 20 years before. But the Commissioners overdid it. No real effort was made to co-ordinate air-taxis. Sometimes there would be two or three in the air simultaneously. The thing became a public scandal, and there was a sharp cut-back.

When I could go by car, Maura would sometimes come. Her preference was naturally for Strasbourg rather than Luxembourg. We both had sentimental memories of Alsace, and friends in the Council of Europe. And it was agreeable to return to old haunts. We specially enjoyed dinners in the *Bourse aux Vins*, where we had eaten on the evening we became engaged. (Once, in December 1975, when I was alone at Strasbourg, we arranged for Rupert to join me for a couple of days, to give him some feel for Community affairs.) Maura and I also appreciated Luxembourg restaurants, especially *Chez Bouzonviller,* at Fend near Capellen, famed for its '*feuillets de foie gras*'.

Committee meetings

Parliamentary Committee meetings were frequent. On average, there were two dozen a month. These would mostly take place in the Parliament's Brussels offices, grouped together in one week of each month, though a limited number were fitted into Plenary Session weeks in Strasbourg or Luxembourg. All were attended by officials of the Commission Secretariat-General. I went regularly to the Political Affairs Committee and the Committee on External Economic Relations, and showed my face occasionally in the others. Only Commissioners could represent their Institution in Plenary Sessions. Officials could do so in Committees – although Parliamentarians understandably preferred Commissioners. I often did this. I also frequently represented my Institution in the 'Enlarged Bureau', the Committee of senior Parliamentarians grouped around their President who organised the Institution's business.

It was vital that <u>all</u> Commissioners were well-informed about developments in Parliamentary Committees. It would have been dangerous to leave this information-giving rôle to individual Commissioners, or officials under their authority: should they have problems with Parliament, they might seek to hush them up, with possibly awkward fall-out for their colleagues. So I or my staff reported to the College direct. These reports, of course, had to be carefully written, particularly when they needed to make clear that a Commissioner or Commission representative had boobed!

Peter Kirk and the British Conservative Group

I came to know a huge range of the [then] 198 MEPs. I had good contacts in every political group. My best links, however, were with the British Conservatives. Being newcomers and needing to learn the ropes, they were attracted to a compatriot with long European experience. They carried disproportionate weight in the Parliament, for two reasons. First, because Harold Wilson's Labour opposition having withheld approval of the terms of British accession, his party sulkily refused to fill its allotted share of seats: the Conservatives filled most of the vacancies, and therefore came to be seen as the Parliamentary voice of Britain. Second, the Conservatives were people of high average quality.

This was particularly the case for their leader, Peter Kirk. Standing very close to Ted Heath politically, he had been a senior Tory Minister. He spoke good French and German, being one of the few British Parliamentarians of his generation prepared to debate in public or on TV in the latter language. He was deeply committed to the European cause. He was well respected by his Conservative colleagues. And he was much helped by his wife Elizabeth, who often came to Plenary Sessions with him. Maura and I came to know and like them both well, and we often ate together.

Unfortunately, in those days, MEPs had also to be members of their national Parliaments – the so-called 'dual mandate'. Elizabeth and I both feared that the strain of doing both jobs to the full would kill Peter. But he would not compromise; our fears, sadly, proved well founded; and he worked himself to an early death in 1977. He was so well liked that his family and friends decided to set up a Memorial Fund; a large collection was made; and the Fund has financed the sending of many young people each year to the continent on scholarships ever since.

The Ortoli Commission seeks to improve relations with the European Parliament
The Ortoli Commission decided to pay more respect to the Parliament than its predecessors. The likelihood of Governments agreeing soon to institute direct elections to Parliament, instead of continuing with a system under which National Parliaments appointed 'delegates', was casting shadows ahead. Moreover the new Member States had strong Parliamentary traditions. The Commission therefore broke new ground, by appointing one of its Members to have special responsibility for Commission/Parliament relations. The chosen Commissioner was Vice-President Carlo Scarascia Mugnozza of Italy. He was charming, but not a heavy-weight with his colleagues. However, Francís Ortoli also took a strong interest. I worked to both of them, and was assisted by Jean Schwed, an effective and dependable Commission official from Alsace, and his Division. Together, this group of people set about the task of improving relations with Parliament.

At the personal level, Ortoli took the initiative of instituting regular, informal, working lunches between the Presidents of the three political Institutions – Parliament, Council and Commission – sometimes joined by the President of the Court of Justice. These were backed by comparable lunches of the three Secretaries-General (and the Greffier of the Court of Justice). I attended them all. These were modest moves, but began to break down barriers and build bridges.

For the rest, the action of the Commission was three-pronged. It instituted a number of down-to-earth, practical measures to improve relations with Parliament; it proposed that Parliament be given real powers over the Community Budget; and it urged the Member States to honour their Treaty commitment to arrange elections to the Assembly *'by direct universal suffrage in accordance with a uniform procedure'* throughout the Community.

The 'practical measures' were proposed by the Schwed Division. We did much to ensure that Parliamentarians got better answers to their oral and written questions. We brought about the introduction of systematic arrangements for consideration by the Commission of all Parliament's Opinions on proposals for Community legislation: these arrangements resulted in a Commissioner reporting to Parliament, at every Session, on what follow-up would be given to each Opinion adopted at the previous one. Finally we pressed for wider involvement of Parliament in trade negotiations.

Formal proposals to give Parliament powers over the Budget were advanced by the Commission in 1973: just two years later, after a lot of hard work, they resulted in the signature of a Budgetary Powers Treaty by the Member States. Looking back today, the powers seem modest, compared with those now enjoyed by Parliament. The Commission nevertheless agonised before advancing its proposals. Many Community veterans believed it dangerous to propose <u>any</u> change in the inter-Institutional balance. They thought it would open a Pandora's box. How was one to prevent Member States from insisting on some kind of package deal, in which hard-won Community competences would be re-nationalised? Courage in the end prevailed; the proposals were put forward; and no serious effort was made to widen the field of discussion. This precedent was heartening for those who were quietly aiming at much bigger steps towards European Union.

The move to direct elections

Following pressure from Parliament and Commission, a Summit meeting of the Nine, in December 1974, agreed in principle that the Community should move to <u>Direct</u> <u>Elections</u> as soon as possible. Parliament had the right to initiate specific proposals in this particular field, and quickly did so. But it was for the Council, on that basis, *'to lay down the appropriate provisions'* and *'recommend them to Member States for adoption in accordance with their respective constitutional requirements'*. In the ensuing Council discussions, and in the 'trialogue' between Council, Parliament and Commission, I represented the last at official level. This brought me, for the first time, into the arcane world of Council, of Coreper and of Council Working Groups – a world

I was later to know very well. The move from the Summit decision of principle to concrete action was slow, with President Giscard d'Estaing of France dragging his feet. A formal Council decision was not reached until September 1976. However, ratification by the Member States did not give rise to serious difficulties, and the way was cleared for the first Direct Elections to the European Parliament in June 1979. It was good to have been involved in this historic development.

The Economic and Social Committee

My responsibility for representing the Commission at senior level in the European Parliament extended also to the Economic and Social Committee [ESC]. This, however, was not onerous. The ESC had little significance on the Community of the 1970s. No doubt it has still less today. It is not an Institution, but simply a consultative body set up by the Treaty. It consists of representatives of different categories of economic and social activity. Its members – then 144 in number – are appointed by the Council, in their personal capacity, but on the basis of proposals from each Member State. The Committee's sole power is the right to be consulted by the Council on legislation in many fields. However, while Parliament's Opinions were in those days given little enough weight by the Commission and still less by the Council, those of the ESC hardly seemed to carry any at all.

One may wonder why the ESC exists. The answer probably lies in history: I suspect that, when the Six were negotiating the Rome Treaties, they wanted to be sure the two new Executives would, from the start, be able to secure all the advice on specialist questions they needed. By 1973, however, the Commission had established its own extensive network of contacts, and did not really need the help of a formal consultative body. I discussed with Emile whether to suggest it be laid to rest. He agreed its value was minimal. But we concluded that such a proposal would expose the Commission to charges of trying to insulate itself from industry, trade unions, farmers and so forth.

The Committee's hemi-cycle on the Mont des Arts holds a place in Community folklore. It was once the home of the Council. At a certain meeting of Agriculture Ministers, there was the usual, annual controversy about price levels, with the farmers asking for more. Some Belgian *paysans* decided to create a stir. They marched through the streets of Brussels, leading a cow. Arriving at the Conference Building, the animal, which had been specially trained, was driven through the main entrance, ignoring the feeble attempts of officials to turn it back, and on up the grand staircase to the first floor hemi-cycle. A huissier closed the double door of the chamber in its face, and stood with his back arched against it. The noise inside the chamber was soon considerable. The President, determined to conclude a difficult debate, ignored the diversion and continued the meeting. The farmers, however, were determined. They drove the cow inexorably forward. The huissier held his ground. But in the end the doors were forced, the cow and the farmers moved in, and the Council had to be suspended. The story, sadly, ended in tears. The cow, though taught how to climb stairs, was not proficient in descent. It broke a leg going down, and had to be shot.

The Commission and National Parliaments of Member States
About the time of my arrival in Brussels, trouble had developed between the Commission and the British Parliament. As we have seen, the latter, despite its approval of British accession, wanted to feel some sense of control over the exercise of powers transferred by the UK to the Community. Select Committees, mainly of the Lords but also of the Commons, felt entitled directly to 'summon' individual Commissioners or Commission officials 'to give evidence', and started doing so. The initial reaction was one of astonishment – such a thing had never happened in the Community of the Six – and then of rejection. The view was advanced by many Commissioners that a strong response should be made. The British should be reminded that the Commission was responsible to the European Parliament, and also to the Council, but certainly not to any National Parliament. The two British Commissioners, however, with support notably from those of the other new Member States, argued that gratuitous confrontation would be unwise. They also felt it would be better for the British Parliamentary Committees to be informed about the Commission's actions by itself, rather than only by British Ministers and officials. A middle way was needed. The Commission agreed.

I was asked to make proposals. Once these had been approved, I was instructed to 'sell' them to the British Parliament: this involved me, during the late spring and summer of 1973, in a series of amicable talks with the Clerks to the two Houses – Sir David Stephens and Sir Barnett Cocks – and their staff. Michael Wheeler-Booth, whom I had known from Council of Europe days in the 1950s, was specially helpful. It did not take long to find a solution. The British Parliament would not 'summon' anyone from Brussels to 'give evidence'. It would request the Commission to send representatives – whether Commissioners or officials – to Committee 'Hearings'. The

Commission would respond sympathetically. Obviously, the College would also ensure that its representatives had Commission cover for their line. Honour was satisfied all round; the system worked well; and the Commission soon saw that better-informed reports from the Committees to the Lords and the Commons were the happy consequence.

Over the years I myself appeared before British Parliamentary Committees on many occasions. I particularly enjoyed those of the Lords, namely the Select Committee on the European Communities and its specialised Sub-Committees. One knew that they would always give serious consideration to whatever was said; and that, at every meeting, a number of Noble Lords would be real experts on the subject. Very soon it was generally recognised, amongst Community watchers throughout Europe, that the Lords' Reports would always be thorough, carefully reasoned, and educational. The Commons Committees had less expertise, and were more political.

As we have seen, I also appeared before many Committees of the European Parliament. Both they, and the British ones, required proper preparation. This could be relatively light with the Commons Committees, but had to be more thorough with those of the European Parliament, where there was less point-scoring and more serious questioning. But it was the Lords Committees which really put one most on one's mettle. I came to like them, and their civilised atmosphere, very much. So it gave me pleasure when, after retirement, I was invited by the Select Committee on the European Communities to act as one of its two Specialist Advisers in the preparation of its 1988 Report on the Staffing of the Community Institutions[1].

It is worth adding that, once the British Parliament had established these precedents, Parliaments in other Member States were not slow to follow the example.

A new Commission President takes over

In December 1976 the Member States formally appointed Roy Jenkins to succeed Francís Ortoli as President of the Commission. (They had agreed as early as July that this would happen, Roy having 'become available' when Harold Wilson unexpectedly resigned in March, and was succeeded by Jim Callaghan.) At an early stage it became clear I should be heavily engaged in the process of handover from Francís to Roy. Until then, Emile had kept such things in his own hands; but now he wanted me fully involved.

In late May, I was in London for a first contact with Roy, then still Home Secretary; and Hayden Phillips, his Private Secretary, who was to join his

Cabinet in Brussels. We reviewed the run-up to the Presidency: the preparation of all necessary briefing by the Secretariat-General; the problems Roy would have to deal with in the coming months; the programme of calls on Heads of Government he would have to make before and after taking office; and so forth. From then on, there was continuous interchange between Roy's staff and the Secretariat-General. The rest of his Cabinet gradually took shape: Crispin Tickell was designated as its head; other members included Michael Jenkins, Michael Emerson and David Marquand. All came, at different times, for working sessions with Emile and myself. Proposals were made by the two of us about a re-structuring of Directorates-General and their tasks; the allocation of portfolios between Commissioners; and changes of staff to be contemplated at the level of Directors-General. We also proposed a work programme for Roy's first few months of office.

Because of the Christmas and New Year holidays, a new Commission takes office, not on the first day of the year, but shortly after. In 1977, the Ortoli Commission held its final meeting on Wednesday, 5 January: Roy Jenkins arrived at the Berlaymont next morning, and his Commission met for the first time at 1500 hours that day. It had some formal business to transact, such as confirming arrangements for its first appearance before Parliament, and the date for taking the oath before the Court of Justice in Luxembourg. Next, Roy confirmed his proposed package deal on portfolios, already informally known to his colleagues. A number of comments were made. Then the session was suspended while Roy held 'confessionals' with individual Commissioners, to iron out any problems. This was to prove tricky.

The suspension continued until 0100 hours. Nobody could leave the building. Dinner was available in the Commission dining room for Commissioners and the very few senior officials and Chefcabs involved. The atmosphere was tense. Several Commissioners preferred sandwiches in their offices. The President never left his. Emile was with him throughout. The wise and experienced Danish Commissioner, Finn Gundelach, was a valued confidential adviser. Of course, there had been much preparation of the portfolio question. Roy and his incoming Cabinet members had been in touch for weeks with all the other Commissioners, following their appointment by the European Council in November. Roy's approach was known, and there was general support for it. But there remained some problems of interface, and of precise definition. Gradually, as the night wore on, these were solved.

Soon after dinner I was summoned to see Roy, Emile and Finn. They briefed me on the essence of the adjustments made to Roy's original scheme, and sent me away to draft the Commission's minutes on this agenda item. The confessionals continued in parallel; and changes were continuously being communicated whilst I dictated. Happily, the Commission's very experienced Greffier, Frans De Koster, was there to help. With his assistance I completed the draft [in English] just fourteen minutes after the last change was made.

At 0100, once the draft had been copied and circulated, the Commission re-convened; Roy explained the reasons for the changes; and Commissioners were asked whether they could agree. The Irish Commissioner, Dick Burke, alone had difficulties. He felt his portfolio, which focused on relations with the European Parliament, was too small. After four further hours of discussion, interrupted by frequent suspensions, formulae were eventually found which enabled him to accept. At 0510, Roy registered complete agreement, and the Session ended.

Twenty minutes later, using briefing notes I had meanwhile prepared, Roy presented the conclusions to the European media in the Commission's Press Room. The events were at once characterised as 'the night of the long knives'. I got to bed at 0630; rose at 0730; breakfasted; and with Emile briefed the Directors-General at 0900. That afternoon I had my first meeting with Dick Burke to discuss the handling of Parliamentary affairs. Four days later I was in Luxembourg, to attend Roy's presentation of the new Commission to Parliament, and to see the Commissioners give their solemn oath to the Court of Justice to serve always the interests of the Community.

It had been quite a week. I have described the events in some detail, because it is not given to many to play a significant rôle in the opening hours of a Commission's life. In the following chapter I shall be writing about other aspects of its early months, which were to include a complete change in the nature of my job, with big new challenges.

Social life

Social life in the Brussels circuit was very different from Bonn. Neither the European Parliament, nor the Council at Ministerial level, provided much in the way of hospitality. We had been broadly aware of the social picture before we left Bonn. Indeed, after our heavy social schedule there, we had seen the quieter social life as one among many attractions of going to Brussels. I therefore smiled when, a year after the move, Maura remarked that things had become <u>too</u> quiet. Perhaps in reaction, she became involved in *'Femmes d'Europe'*, an association of Community officials' wives; and in a small ladies' weekly lunch club. Whereas, in our Diplomatic Service postings, we had always had an obligation to undertake a certain level of official entertaining at home, the Community laid no such duties upon us. We could entertain as we wished. Fortunately, it was easy to hire staff. We tended to have a biggish reception about once a year; and occasional dinners or lunches, often linked to an arrival, a departure, or a visiting personality.

One rather special event took place in October 1974. I had been awarded a CMG in the New Year Honours List. It was not easy to take time off for visits to the UK; and, when we could, we liked to see our children, by now all at boarding school. The British Ambassador in Brussels was David Muirhead, who had been my immediate superior in Washington days. It was arranged that he would make the presentation; and he and Elspeth very kindly gave a lunch at the Embassy, then in the Parc Royal, and allowed us to choose the guests. As usual with David, it was all done with elegance and style. Rupert, home for half-term, attended.

We had rather more free evenings than in Bonn, and could take in more cultural events, notably ballet and opera. When we reached Brussels, Maurice Béjart was making a great name for himself: his ballets, even if sometimes rather *avant-garde* for our taste, were always exciting and of world class: some, like *Firebird*, were delightful. Opera at the *Théâtre Royale de la Monnaie*, on the other hand, had declined to poor, almost provincial standard. However, some time after our arrival, Gérard Mortier returned from Paris to take charge. We gambled on his turning things round, and bought an *abonnement* for two excellent stalls. In a single season he brought the company to good international standard, in the process sacking half the chorus and orchestra. It became increasingly difficult to get *abonnements*. But those who already held one enjoyed top priority. We retained the same places till we left Brussels, seeing a dozen operas a year: the Mortier productions were a constant joy.

Family affairs

For almost all of the four years covered by this chapter, our three children were at boarding school in England. Living at Brussels, it was much easier for us to get over to see them at School than it had been in Bonn. Maura went frequently, myself when I could. Also, they, being older, could travel unaccompanied, whether by air, or by bus and Hovercraft. One way and another, we almost always saw them at half-term. So we were well in touch.

It was a great resource, for them and for us, that Rupert, Claire and William were all fairly close to RGC. We were also able to see quite a lot of my parents in their later years. In 1973, we all attended their Golden Wedding Celebrations at Ackenthwaite. Next spring they came over by car ferry from Hull to Europoort, to stay with us for two weeks. It was their last trip abroad together. On the return journey my father made a *fausse manoeuvre*, which left the car with one wheel hanging over the edge of the ferry's loading-ramp. After that he stayed in the UK. In August 1975, we spent three weeks in Cumbria, two of them at Capple Rigg Farm, between Kendal and Crook, an idyllic spot, tucked away from any traffic at the end of a long *cul-de-sac*, and with stunning views in all directions. The remaining week, spent at Ackenthwaite, delighted the parents, and was a great family gathering. Of my father's three sisters, Marie had recently died; Freda was still in quite good form; and Joan came up from Cambridge to stay in Heversham, bringing her grandchildren, Jenny and Angus, with her. In October 1976, however, my father was killed by an attack of chickenpox. Maura, Rupert and I were at his funeral: we thought Claire and William too young. My mother joined us for Christmas in Brussels that year.

During these four years – 1973 to 1976 – we continued the pattern of family holidays begun in Bonn, visiting different parts of Europe. As to the Benelux, these three countries were amply covered on week-end expeditions. Over time, the children did all the obvious things: Amsterdam, for tulip fields and boat tours; The Hague and Madurodam; Antwerp and the Rubens House; Luxembourg and its battlements; canoe-ing on the Lesse; many rambles in the Ardennes; and so forth.

This section would be incomplete without some mention of the children's life at home, when not on the holidays outside Brussels. But they can be brief. They spent much time with Andy, and he was the reason for a great deal of walking in the Forêt de Soignes. There was riding to be had; and Rupert soon began to attend at a *Manège* known as 'La Métairie'. There was also tennis. The Olympic-sized swimming indoor pool of our Commune, only 300 metres away, was a great resource. (This was true also for me: I swam a kilometre regularly, several days a week, before breakfast, and this helped a lot in keeping me fit.) Ice shows were popular.

CHAPTER 15

Sole Deputy Secretary-General, European Commission 1977-1981

My job changes

IN THE LAST CHAPTER I described my work as one of two Deputy Secretaries-General, from 1973 to early 1977. With the advent of Roy Jenkins' Commission, my career took a new turn. Whilst my title was unaltered, my duties changed, and I assumed much larger responsibilities.

I had enjoyed my first job in the Commission. It taught me how the Community Institutions worked; gave me an overview of Community policies; afforded me deep insight into how the European Parliament was developing – from an essentially consultative Assembly into a political body with real teeth; and allowed me plenty of room for initiative in stimulating internal reform. But it was not something I wanted to do for ever: the administrative content was too high, and the operational too low. I let it be known to people who might help – including Emile Nöel, the two British Commissioners, the Foreign Office establishment and the Cabinet Office – that, if they wanted me to remain in Brussels instead of reverting to a Diplomatic Service career, I should need a change of job, and greater personal responsibilities.

One of the papers prepared by Emile and myself for the incoming President Jenkins concerned the re-structuring of Directorates-General and their tasks. This happens with every new Commission. Account has to be taken of fresh responsibilities continuously devolving on the Commission; of new external challenges for the Community; and of the shape of the incoming Commissioners' own portfolios. At an early stage, Emile told me that, since Klaus Meyer wanted to change jobs, becoming Director-General for Development, he wished me to take over Klaus's existing work, and serve as sole Deputy Secretary-General. He recognised some of my own responsibilities would have to be off-loaded. He felt that a lot had by now been done to modernise, and improve internal co-ordination; and that, in the next phase, relatively few new initiatives would be needed. As to relations with the European Parliament, he proposed to transfer this task to an able but less senior official of the Secretariat-General. I was delighted by his proposal, at once supported by Roy Jenkins and his Cabinet. But that was not the end of the story. The allocation of senior official posts – and notably those at Director-General and Deputy Director-General level – is a matter for the whole Commission.

In the year or so preceding a change of Commission, the Secretary-General starts preparing the ground for a package of appointments. Where a senior post falls vacant it is normally covered, not by a permanent appointment, but by an interim appointee. Other senior officials are encouraged to request early retirement; or to contemplate a move to another post. Room for manoeuvre is created; and the incoming Commission has a chance to adjust the complexion of the senior hierarchy. The President normally takes the initiative – on the advice of the Secretary-General – and complex negotiations then ensue between him and his colleagues until an acceptable package emerges. This in turn is normally approved by the Commission in two tranches: the first covers the Directors-General, and the second their Deputies. [This at any rate was the picture until 1999, when the incoming Prodi Commission indicated that changes would be made.]

It was not till mid-March of 1977 that Roy put to the Commission his proposal about me. Obviously I was not in attendance. I heard later from Emile that there had been broad support, but an objection from Vicomte Davignon – always known as Stevie – who had described me as 'too perfectionist'. Since Stevie did not know me, I was surprised; but Emile told me he was acting on the advice of the Belgian Permanent Representative, the late Joseph Van Der Meulen. When Emile asked Joseph for his reason – since Joseph hardly knew me either – he replied 'intuition'!

I took all this calmly – merely suggesting that the Belgians be advised to seek an opinion from personalities who knew my work well – like Ted Heath or Walter Scheel. A month later, the obstacles had faded away. It is a pleasure to record that both Joseph and Stevie later gave me their total confidence and indeed friendship. And so it was that, in mid-April of 1977, I assumed my new responsibilities. This chapter will give some feel for how they were exercised. But first it is necessary, once again, to recall the key developments in international and Community affairs which would take place in the four years ahead.

General political background

Internationally, the first two years of the new Commission's life were relatively quiet, though the world economy remained sickly. After that, however, big changes occurred. In 1979 came the nuclear accident at Three

Mile Island [TMI]: although damage was contained around the reactor, and there was no significant off-site release of radio-activity, grave concerns were roused. These were strongly felt throughout a Western World, then just beginning to turn seriously to nuclear energy, to reduce its dependence on Middle East oil. While these concerns soon eased, they at once revived after the Chernobyl disaster a few years later. Also in 1979, the Iranian Revolution triggered a second oil shock: the price again doubled, to reach $51 per barrel. Soon, the Middle East was in turmoil, as a result of the Iran-Iraq war.

There was also trouble with the Soviet Bloc. Although agreement was reached between the USSR and the USA, in June 1979, on a second Strategic Arms Limitation Treaty [SALT 2], this was never ratified because, at the year-end, the USSR invaded Afghanistan, ending *détente* and effectively starting the 'Second Cold War'. One can now see how subsequent Soviet misfortunes in Afghanistan were an important contributory factor to the USSR's decline, and ultimately to its collapse a decade later. Indeed, it was in 1980 that the Solidarity movement in Poland, which was likewise to contribute so much to that outcome, got seriously off the ground. At the time, however, one was conscious only of the negative aspect: a complete freeze of *détente*.

On a positive note, and in a different sector, the GATT Tokyo Round of Tariff reductions was in 1979 brought to a successful conclusion. Finally, in January 1981, Ronald Reagan succeeded Jimmy Carter as President of the United States: Cy Vance and Brzezinski became respectively his Secretary-of-State and Foreign Policy Adviser.

Within the Community, things were not easy, notably because of the wider economic situation. The steel, textile, oil-refinery and shipbuilding industries all had persistent structural problems. Nevertheless some real progress was made. In his opening speech to the European Parliament Roy Jenkins took as his theme that it was time for the Community to come out of the trenches. He foreshadowed the rebirth of European Monetary and Economic Union, launching the idea in a more concrete way in Florence in October 1977. Both Schmidt and Giscard liked the concept, and pushed it hard. In due course it took the shape of the European Monetary System [EMS], inaugurated in 1979, a precursor of the Single Currency provisions of the Maastricht Treaty of 1992.

On other fronts, the Member States extended their fishery limits to 200 miles at the beginning of the same year, and the development of the Common Fisheries Policy began, though it was to take effect only in 1983.

The 'Own Resources' system for financing the Community entered fully into force. The Commission made its first proposals for Community action on education. Negotiations started for agreements between the Community and other international, regional groupings of nations: first, with the Council for Mutual Economic Assistance [CMEA or COMECON], in other words the Soviet Bloc Trading System; second, with the Association of South-East Asian Nations [ASEAN]; and third, with the Andean Pact countries. The Community was gaining ground in the world economic arena, and played a major hand in the GATT negotiations.

In 1978, the Commission put forward an overall approach to the problems of enlargement, which led to Greek Accession three years later. Accession negotiations started with Portugal in 1978 and with Spain in 1979. In the latter year, Margaret Thatcher succeeded Jim Callaghan as British Prime Minister, and the subject of the British contribution to the Community Budget assumed prominence for some years.

Meanwhile the European Parliament was gaining status. The first direct elections of MEPs took place in June 1979: in the same year the Parliament blocked the Community Budget, and then wrung concessions from the Community Council before letting it through. And so to 1981, the year in which Mitterand succeeded Giscard as President of France; Germany proposed transforming the Community into a European Union; and the Jenkins Commission was replaced by a new one led by Gaston Thorn of Luxembourg.

The work menu

There is no need to say much about my work inside the Commission. After taking up my new remit, I continued to attend the weekly meetings of the Commission and the Chefcabs; no longer had any particular role to play vis-à-vis the European Parliament or the Economic and Social Committee; but still carried on with everything else I had done before. Most importantly, I succeeded Klaus Meyer as the Commission's senior representative, at official level, in the Council and the EPC machineries. My overall work-load substantially increased. But I now had four years' experience of the Community. I was also to benefit from the help of the able Renate Wolff, the research assistant I had inherited from Klaus, who stayed with me until I retired. So things remained manageable.

The new Commission was very different from its predecessor. Roy Jenkins, a distinguished former Chancellor of the Exchequer and Home Secretary, was more at ease with the political world and the media than

Francís Ortoli. The latter, now Vice-President for Economic and Financial affairs, was exemplary in the way he accepted and was totally loyal to his successor. Other strong figures were Finn Gundelach, now in charge of Agriculture and Fisheries (destined to die young, only four years later); and both Willi Haferkamp and Claude Cheysson, who shared External Affairs. All these had four years experience behind them. But the most flamboyant figure in the team was a newcomer, Stevie Davignon, whose flair and long European diplomatic experience equipped him to become, during the years ahead, a more effective Commissioner than any predecessor or successor. He was formally responsible for the Internal Market and Industry. But he stood very close to Roy, and his advice was sought on all politically sensitive matters. Christopher Tugendhat, the second British Commissioner, responsible for Budgetary Affairs and Administration, was quietly effective, but did not shine. After an early meeting of the Jenkins Commission I noted changes of style. Roy kept the discussion more focused than had his predecessor. There was concentration on key issues. Minor items went through on the nod or were settled after a short discussion. The level of debate rose.

In general there was less need for improving the Commission's internal co-ordination. Some of my earlier initiatives continued to bear fruit, however, and there was one big new change to be organised. Roy and his Chefcab, Crispin Tickell, complained about the kind of briefing being submitted by the Services to the President ahead of his meetings or official journeys. The tradition had been decidedly French. Although French *Énarques* can be <u>privately</u> critical or cynical about their political masters, they do not usually reflect any personal views in their <u>public</u> behaviour. There seems to be a tradition in the French Civil Service of avoiding anything which might suggest that a Minister needs <u>advice</u>. Rather, he is presented with *'éléments d'information'*, or background material, on the basis of which he is expected to see for himself what to do or say. If he doesn't, he is left to take the initiative and discuss further with officials. The British tradition, on the best *'Yes, Minister'* pattern, is quite different. Officials are expected to submit briefs which specifically suggest the line to be taken by the Minister; or which alternatively present specific options, weighing their merits. Often, they will be expected also to submit detailed speaking notes, for the Minister to draw upon. I was tasked to convert the Commission Services to follow this pattern in all submissions to the President. Its merits soon became obvious to others, and the habit spread.

More often than not, I was involved in Roy Jenkins' official visits to capitals of the Member States, usually very agreeable. One particularly sticks in mind. This was to Copenhagen in June 1977. Since it was Roy's first visit to Denmark after his assumption of office, we asked whether the President might, besides the official talks with the Prime Minister and others, pay his respects to Queen Margrethe. The whole of our team of four, including Roy's Secretary, were promptly invited to lunch with the Queen and Prince Henrik, the Prince Consort, at the charming Royal Country Palace of Fredensborg. The late Queen Ingrid, the Queen's mother, was one of the 26 guests, and I was placed on her right: we talked a good deal about the impact of the Second World War on Denmark and its Royal Family. The party also included the Prime Minister, other Ministers, and the Danish Permanent Representative. The whole event was delightfully easy and informal. Years afterwards, I was to have much to do with Prince Henrik, in a quite different context.

During the Jenkins Presidency, visits to the Commission by the great and good of the world multiplied. There was always a special Commission meeting, and usually a lunch, to which I would go. The visitors included the reigning monarchs of Belgium, the Netherlands and the United Kingdom; President Carter of the USA; the Grand Duke of Luxembourg; HRH Prince Charles; and the Prime Ministers of Britain, Greece, Turkey, India, Japan and Spain.

The Council

The Council worked at three levels. [If I put this passage in the past tense, it is to indicate that some details have changed in the meanwhile.] Apart from meetings at Ministerial level – the Council proper – the preparation of decisions was undertaken by the Committee of Permanent Representatives, [CRP: or *Coreper* – the French language acronym], and under them by Council Working Groups. My own involvement was mainly with the first two, although I attended occasional Working Group meetings for particular reasons.

The Council, like the Commission, had its own working methods and rhythm. Juridically, the Treaties recognise only one Council. But obviously, in a complex and wide-ranging Community, different Ministers deal with different subjects. So, though officially one talked of the Council coming together 'in different formations', in everyday usage one spoke of the Agriculture Council, the Energy Council, the Fisheries Council, the Research Council and so forth. *Primus inter pares*, however, was the General Affairs Council [hereinafter GAC], attended by Ministers of Foreign Affairs.

It dealt notably with External and Institutional Affairs, and with the preparation of meetings of the European Council [the Heads of State and of Government]. The latter function conferred on it an overall co-ordination role. In those days, the Council met in its various formations some 60 times a year; and in its GAC formation about once a month.

The CRP also met in more than one formation. Illogically, Coreper Two [CRP II] consisted of the Permanent Representatives, or Ambassadors to the Community, of the Member States, whilst CRP I consisted of their Deputies. It was in CRP II that I was the Commission's chief representative: a colleague, Henri Etienne, represented the Commission in the other body. We kept closely in touch. CRP II prepared the meetings of the GAC and certain other Councils; CRP I, those of the remainder. CRP II was very much a Club, and a good one too. If the Commission is the initiator of Community initiatives and legislation, the CRP is the marshalling yard – the place where, after Parliamentary consideration, proposals are sifted, refined and sorted; and thereafter given a final polish before Ministerial approval. A very high proportion of them are then approved by the Council 'on the nod'.

Given CRP's key position in the Community machinery, the Member States send officials of the very highest quality to represent them there. Most are senior and experienced civil servants, usually drawn from the Ministries of Foreign Affairs. The names of the Permanent Representatives whose time in CRP II most overlapped with my own, reads like a diplomatic roll of honour: Niels Ersbjøll and Gunnar Riberholdt for Denmark; Eugenio Plaja for Italy; Luc de Nanteuil for France; Jan Lubbers and Charles Rutten for the Netherlands; Helmut Sigrist, himself a former Commission Director-General, for the Federal Republic of Germany; Jean Dondelinger for Luxembourg; Brendan Dillon for Ireland; Donald Maitland, Michael Butler and David Hannay for the UK; and Joseph van der Meulen for Belgium. Their Deputies, in CRP I, were usually rising stars.

Meeting as a group for a whole day, at least once a week, the Permanent Representatives – or Ambassadors – got to know each other very well indeed. In the meeting room, they would have advisers and experts; and interpretation was available. However, at their weekly lunch, the Permanent Representatives were joined only by the Secretary-General of the Council and the Representative of the Commission, and were without interpreters. Only French and English were spoken. [I am not sure whether all this is true nowadays, with fifteen Member States; but that is how things were with nine in 1977.] It was indeed in the privacy of the dining room that compromises were usually sought and found on sensitive issues. All present reported on these lunches with discretion. There was no 'he said this' and 'I said that'. Rather, all reported to their principals that new ideas 'emerged in informal discussion'. And this enabled those who were immobilised by over-rigid instructions to seek new ones.

Great was my surprise to discover that my predecessor had been excluded from the lunches, where the Commission was represented only by Emile Nöel. I told Emile this placed me at a considerable disadvantage. He agreed to seek a better solution. Fortunately, the UK at that time held the Presidency of the Community. The British Permanent Representative, Donald Maitland, was an old friend. He soon obtained his colleagues' agreement that the Commission should be entitled to send two representatives to the lunches – Emile and myself.

Apart from these working gatherings, in the nature of things these very senior diplomats were constantly entertaining at home, often to enable distinguished visitors to make contacts; and their CRP colleagues were frequently among their guests. The same was true when the European Parliament, the Council and the Commission entertained, often in pleasing venues such as the Château de Val Duchesse, the Restaurant Rohmeyer or the Palais d'Egmont. Wives were invited to some, but certainly not all, of these occasions.

Being the Commission's chief representative in CRP II did not mean it was always for me to present the Commission's proposals and points of view. Usually, it was far better for the responsible Director-General, his Deputy, or an able Director, to present each dossier. I was the continuity and fail-safe person. One would warn a Director-General, coming in to present his file, of background problems he might not be aware of. If one sensed trouble, one would counsel prudence. But one always had to know in advance what line the Director-General was planning to take. Sometimes items were taken by the Chair in an unexpected order. Then, one had to pinch-hit. New issues would also arise unexpectedly, and one would have to respond.

Although, after a short while, I knew all the Permanent Representatives well, and indeed was a friend of them all, they were not above teasing me. This was no surprise. In the Community system, the Commission always has the initiative, which can be riling for the representatives of the Member States. The French Permanent Representative, Luc de Nanteuil, whom I had known when he was in the London Embassy in the 1960s, was much given to this game. It was his custom to scan the press in the hope of finding articles suggesting that the Commission was up to no good. Then he would choose a moment in CRP to cite the article and ask me to explain the behaviour of my Institution! Or else I would be asked for an instant Commission view on the latest international developments.

I soon learnt to skim the media; identify items likely to attract the interest of Luc or his colleagues; and brief myself!

When it came to Council meetings, only Commissioners could speak for the Commission. This made life difficult in the GAC, whose agendas were always wide-ranging. There might be a score of items for discussion, to be handled by perhaps half a dozen Commissioners. My task was to see that the right Commissioner was always there at the right time. But Commissioners were unwilling to leave their own offices – ten minutes walk away – until their item was due for debate. Moreover, Presidencies had a tiresome habit of switching the order of points. When, as happened not infrequently, I could see the Commissioner concerned was going to be late, my only resource was to whisper, or scribble notes, to the Commissioner dealing with the preceding item, asking him to stay and cover for his colleague, and indicating a line to take. This meant, of course, that I had to know, before the Council began, the official Commission position on every item.

On one such occasion, Stevie Davignon was in the Commission chair. He listened to my whisperings; nodded his head; and then plunged in, on behalf of his absent colleague. To my horror I found that, most uncharacteristically, he had misunderstood, and was making a presentation 180 degrees off course. Whilst he was in full flow I slipped him a note. Glimpsing at it without a pause, he went on to tell Ministers he would like to clarify a few points; and made a presentation that was a mere 90 degrees off course. Then, he told them he would close by summarising the message: and this time, he was bang on course. Stevie was such a bravura performer that most of his hearers would have assumed the summary was the nub; and ignored the rest. There were other Commissioners who did not achieve so happy an outcome.

Roy Jenkins seldom missed a GAC – they were good opportunities for corridor or lunchtime conversations with Foreign Ministers – and he usually stayed for almost the whole time. My duty was to ensure he was properly briefed on every agenda item, whether or not he was expected to intervene on it. This was tough: an agenda of 20 items was not unusual. The GAC normally met on Tuesdays. The meeting would be the subject of final preparation in CRP II on the previous Thursday, and for some items in CRP I on the Friday. Many of the Council papers would only be ready on the Friday or Saturday in final form, if then. But Roy liked to have his briefs on Sunday evening; absorb them overnight; and talk to Commissioners concerned and myself on Monday.

Once a month, this played havoc with my weekends. I would spend much of Saturday reading through the papers and checking background. My unfortunate Secretary would come in on Sunday morning, when the briefs – perhaps 20 pages of typed A4 – would be dictated. After typing and correction I would take them to Roy at his home in the evening. He was always most appreciative. (Word of this system gradually spread, and I was often asked by other Commissioners to let them see key parts of the brief. I know that sometimes they learnt from me things their own Services had not seen fit to tell them!)

Roy well understood the importance of CRP work. He lunched with the Permanent Representatives as a group every six weeks; and he had regular bilateral meetings with the President of CRP. Other Commissioners followed suit to some extent, holding occasional lunches or informal meetings with the Permanent Representatives. I was almost always involved.

My work in CRP was never boring. Moreover, every six months, by tradition, it was enlivened by some kind of jaunt in the Presidency country, again often with wives.

One such outing was a two-day visit arranged by the French Presidency to key French civil nuclear installations in the Lyon-Avignon area, in July 1980. This was of special interest to me, because I had visited comparable British installations whilst Head of the Foreign Office Science and Technology Department a dozen years earlier, and so was able to make valid comparisons. Needless to say, we were throughout lunched, wined, dined, and accommodated in style.

On the first day, we visited Bugey, a major nuclear power station with 5 reactors, and were shown the Training Centre for nuclear power station operators. In a huge simulator room, representing the control centre of a power station, we saw a series of operational tasks performed. Finally we were asked to postulate a scenario of our own choosing. My suggestion to simulate a major reactor accident, in which a massive coolant loss from the containment vessel was premised to have coincided with total failure of mains electrical supply from the grid, was accepted; and the corresponding scenario fed into the computers.

Immediately, in front of the trainee operators, hundreds of lights on the vast control panel, occupying a whole wall tens of metres long, started to flash. The reactor, being fail-safe, was seen to shut down at once. Following a well-honed drill, the operators rapidly identified the various causes of trouble; selected the remedial measures needed; and deployed the resources necessary to bring things under control. Coming within a year of the TMI accident, this demonstration gave me a great feeling of assurance that, in the industrialised world, though not in the then Soviet Bloc (as Tschernobyl was later dramatically to show), the level of safety of civil nuclear reactors is very high indeed. This feeling was re-inforced, later in the day, when we visited a reactor construction site, and saw the tiny tolerances (half a millimetre) to which the huge containment vessels are built.

On the second day, we visited the vast Eurodif plant at Pierrelatte, then still in construction, which was to enrich uranium, required for fuel elements, using the gaseous diffusion process. Its sheer scale was impressive, and its operation was expected to use most of the output of the adjacent 3,600 MW Tricastin nuclear power station. It has since worked perfectly well, but has not proved cost-effective by comparison with the Anglo/Dutch/German plant at Almelo, in the Netherlands, which uses the rival centrifuge enrichment method – with which I had been much concerned[1].

The next stop was the new vitrification plant for long-life, high-activity radioactive waste at Marcoule. We travelled from Pierrelatte by bus. As we drove, we were preceded by four *motards* [police motor-cyclists]. Their method was to keep some way ahead, using their sirens and waving traffic on both lanes into the sides, leaving our bus careering along the crown of the country roads. Observing the reactions of the motorists, I noted something curious. The victims' sentiments seemed to pass through a certain sequence: first, irritation at the delay; next, curiosity to see who were the VIPs with this privileged treatment; then, as the bus passed, manifest and stark amazement. The reason for this last only became apparent when we reached our destination. Then, one saw that our hired bus, which we had not been able to inspect on entry, was usually employed for other purposes. On its side was emblazoned the slogan: '*Pèlerinage à Lourdes – aller/retour seulement 20 Francs*'!

En route I heard a '*bon mot*' by M Villani, a senior Commission colleague concerned with the Joint European Torus [JET] at Culham in Oxfordshire, an experimental machine designed to explore the path towards use of nuclear fusion for electric power generation. I had asked him to explain what JET was, since the fate of the machine was a constant matter of CRP debate. His explanation was colourful: '*it's a snake of plasma, biting its own tail, and whizzing round in a vacuum-filled doughnut about 5 metres across, whilst giving off heat at 50 million degrees centigrade*'. He thought that JET would demonstrate fusion could be maintained and controlled, but that it would take 30-40 years to produce energy commercially.

At Marcoule, we marvelled at the vitrification processes. Foregathering at the end, on the metre thick concrete top of the repository for the canisters of vitrified waste, we had an opportunity to put questions. An Ambassador enquired what would happen if one of the canisters was left in the open countryside, and was told that anyone within 100 metres or even more would receive a lethal dose of radioactivity. Diplomats are trained to keep calm, and nobody seemed to bat an eyelid; but, a minute later, all had moved quietly on!

This visit left me in no doubt that the British, first in the field with a nuclear power station, namely Calder Hall in 1956, had been replaced by the French as world leaders in the civil nuclear field.

The European Political Co-operation

As already explained, my remit was to represent the Commission, not only in the Council instances, but also in those of the Political Co-operation. EPC, at that time, was not in any way Treaty-based – though it now is, constituting the Second Pillar of the Maastricht Treaty. It was grounded instead on a political understanding between the Member States, completely outside the Community framework, that they would try to co-operate, on a voluntary and purely Inter-Governmental basis, on questions of Foreign Affairs. For this purpose their representatives came together at three levels. The Commission was invited to attend, subject to some exceptions we shall come to later.

The three levels were those of the Foreign Ministers; of the Political Directors from the Ministries of Foreign Affairs, meeting as the 'Political Committee'; and of Working Groups (geographically or sectorially based) consisting of more junior diplomats. My personal involvement was with the first two levels only. My position there was different from my place in the Community machinery. The Commission had no particular right of initiative; only a right to comment and advise. At the Ministerial level, my Institution could speak only through the mouth of a Commissioner: my task was to be always at hand and brief him. At the Political Committee, however, I was normally the Commission's sole spokesman. At that time, EPC was very jealous of its separate status. Moreover, Political Directors had always had a tendency, within their own Ministries of Foreign Affairs, to look down their noses a bit at things economic: and, for most of those from the Member States, the Community was still seen as an essentially economic organisation. Likewise, Diplomats had a tendency to regard Community officials as having, *ex officio*, a lesser status.

All this explained why, in the Political Committee, there were certain discriminations. I was invited to the Political Directors lunches, but not their dinners: neither was I invited when, once in every Presidency, they had an 'informal' meeting. I never let these things bother me. Many of the Political Directors were old diplomatic colleagues from past postings. All knew I was from the diplomatic stable, and still on the books of the Foreign Office. I could easily find out from good friends what happened at gatherings from which I was absent. In any case it was clear that my acceptability within the group – it too was a good Club, though with a quite different style from CRP – would depend on the added value I could bring. This was not difficult. EPC had few instruments to deploy. Its main activity was to co-ordinate diplomatic reactions: often the result would be some kind of policy Declaration, without any legally binding force. The Community, however, had a number of instruments which could be used in support. It had a very large aid budget, enabling it to bestow or withhold favours. And it could also grant or withhold preferential trading arrangements, within certain limits. Once the Political Directors had been made to understand the value of these instruments, and the Commission's ability to deploy them, their attitude towards me warmed rapidly. Soon, I was accepted as a useful member of the Club – even if not admitted to all its rooms!

To mark its separateness from the Community, EPC at first always met in the capital of the Presidency country. For the Foreign Ministers this arrange-ment was so impractical as to be unsustainable. The break came during a Danish Presidency. The Foreign Ministers had arranged to have a GAC and an EPC meeting on the same day. The rules meant they all had to meet in Brussels for the Council in the morning, where they were advised by their Permanent Representatives; fly to Copenhagen during the lunch hour; and hold their EPC meeting there in the afternoon, advised by their Political Directors. Enough was enough. It was agreed that in future, wherever possible, the two kinds of meeting would take place in Brussels, on the same day!

The Political Directors, however, continued to hold their meetings in successive Presidency capitals. This suited me very well. It gave me opportunities for getting to know each Member State better. I could often manage things so as to have a little free time for culture and sightseeing. And my exclusion from the dinners gave me opportunities for other contacts:

perhaps to dine instead with the British Ambassador, often an old friend, or with the Head of the Commission's Delegation.

Less convenient, however, were the timings of the Political Committee meetings. The Political Directors had no need to co-ordinate them with those of CRP: nor did they. Occasionally there were clashes, and I had to decide when to go myself to EPC, and when to send my deputy for EPC matters, Jos Loeff from the Directorate-General of External Affairs. Not an easy choice, because continuity was important, in both cases. Moreover, the fact that I was the <u>only</u> individual to represent his country or Institution in <u>both</u> CRP and EPC, gave me a unique overview, which could often be turned to good account.

During my time on the Political Committee, there were many changes amongst the Political Directors: it would be pointless to list all those I knew. However, they included some interesting but disparate personalities. Many tales could be told about them. Here are a few.

Jean-Marie Mérillon was a very special case. I believe his career in the French Diplomatic Service had been chequered. He appeared to suffer from an inferiority complex; his pride in his country was unbounded; his command of English was moderate; and these factors together meant he was for ever taking offence, often when none was intended. With the first enlargement of the Community, the English language rapidly overtook French as the *lingua franca* of the Political Directors [there was no translation]. On one occasion, at the Palais Schaumburg in Bonn, under the Presidency of Klaus Blech in the second half of 1978, Charles Rutten of the Netherlands had been making an intervention in French when there was some interjection in English. Jean-Marie broke in to complain that far too much English was being spoken. When Charles was again given the floor he pointedly resumed his discourse using English. Jean-Marie exploded, and there was an interruption of the meeting. I heard later from Klaus that he had used the pause to tell Jean-Marie quietly that, if this sort of attitude were continued, he would have to demand equal rights for German!

I was myself the victim of one of Jean-Marie's tantrums. I had been making some intervention for the Commission – I no longer remember what about – when he rose to his feet; pushed back his chair; announced that the representative of the Commission had *'insulted the French Republic'*; and stormed out of the room. The remaining Political Directors and myself were non-plussed. We spent the next quarter of an hour trying hard to think what I had said which could possibly have given offence: our efforts were fruitless. We concluded he had misunderstood something. Eventually,

The Political Directors of the EU Member States, with the author,
at Villa Madama, Rome, 1980.[2]

Jean-Marie was persuaded to return to the table. The incident caused me concern. France was to hold the next Presidency of the Community; and I worried that Jean-Marie would take it out on me. To his credit he did nothing of the kind: indeed he was meticulous as President in ensuring that I had every opportunity to express Commission views.

The Italian Political Director was Walter Gardini, a very nice person but rather vague and rambling. He took the Chair for the first half of 1980. His Presidency was delightful in one respect: almost all the Committee meetings took place in the beautiful renaissance Villa Madama, on the hills northwest of Rome. But, on the operational side, it was far from ideal. This was a period of high and unusually productive activity by EPC. It had been decided to establish a common Community attitude on the Arab-Israël dispute. This was no mean challenge. The starting points of the Nine were very markedly different: it was never going to be easy to harmonise them. Yet Ministers had decided they wanted to agree a Common Declaration of Policy for publication at the European Council meeting at Venice in mid-June 1980. Under Walter's Presidency, progress was painfully slow. Despite the best efforts of his colleagues to help, he proved unable to move things forward. In the end, desperate measures were taken. Walter's colleagues hatched out a procedural plot amongst themselves.

One day they suggested to Walter that it might be easier for Political Directors to find the necessary flexibility if they talked informally, outside the actual meeting: could there not be an extended lunch-hour for this purpose? This was agreed. Of course there was no 'Chairman' at lunch, so all were free to discuss and propose formulae, instead of having to wait for Presidency Conclusions which never came. The trick worked. Things moved forward. Thereafter, formal meetings got shorter and shorter: lunches lasted longer and longer. The end-result was the adoption of the Venice Declaration on the Middle East – one of the most meaningful acts ever taken under the EPC flag – but one to which, sadly there has been no effective follow-up.

As to the other Political Directors, suffice it to say that they were usually, like the Permanent Representatives, particularly able diplomats.

The EPC work gave me a side-benefit: a reason for an annual visit to North America. The Political Directors were by now trying to harmonise the Nine's positions in the United Nations. So, at the beginning of each General Assembly, in late September, there were meetings in New York, first of the Directors, and then of the Foreign Ministers, with me attending.

The simplest way of giving the flavour of these North American trips is to recall the pattern of the first, in September 1978, and add briefer comments about those which followed. On that first occasion, I arrived in New York late on a Saturday, and found myself booked into the Waldorf Astoria. (I had asked for something more modest, but nothing could be found: for later visits, less fancy quarters were booked.) An early sky-scraper, the Hotel occupies a whole city block and contains Cole Porter's piano; 2,000 bedrooms; a reception hall like a small cathedral; a concourse of shops; several restaurants, each in different style; and a host of other facilities. It is remarkable, but devastatingly impersonal. This was my first visit to New York for 20 years, and much had changed. The skyscrapers had grown taller, with the arrival of the World Trade Centre, some 117 storeys high. The city's finances were poor: so the streets were dirty and in total disrepair, full of potholes, with steam from central heating systems escaping through them. The contrast between this public decay, and the private enterprise world of smart, modern, buildings and shops, was startling.

Most of Monday was spent with the Political Directors, who put together, from various contributions, including the Commission's, the remarks to be made to the General Assembly next day by Foreign Minister Genscher, representing the Community Presidency. On Tuesday I started by briefing the Commission Delegation on current developments in Brussels, before spending the rest of the day at the UN Headquarters. I happened to enter the General Assembly a few moments before Gromyko, the Soviet Foreign Minister, dramatically collapsed at the rostrum. After the confusion had subsided, his place was taken by Genscher, and I listened to his speech and several others.

My diary recorded impressions of this, my first, direct contact with the UN. Though written off the top of the head, the words seem worth recalling: both as an indication of the geo-political climate at the time, and as a yardstick of how far things have meanwhile progressed. '*A visit to the General Assembly is…very worthwhile… True, it's a talking shop. But it's right and valuable that there should be a place where all the nations air, confront and debate their views. It may not decide much. But it provides great opportunities for increasing mutual understanding, and therefore helping the world solve its problems more peacefully than in the past. When I called on several different UN officials, of different nationalities, all agreed that the growing unity of the Nine – as expressed for example in the Genscher speech – is seen by others as impressive, effective and valuable. An encouragement to people like me who have to work hard to bring it about.*'

On Wednesday, there was a working breakfast of the Nine Foreign Ministers, hosted by Genscher. It was by now customary for them to meet for a meal, in the margin of the General Assembly, joined by their Permanent Representatives to the UN, and their Political Directors. Topical international issues got an airing; but the meeting on this occasion was short, and I was able to fly on to Washington, where I was met by Andy Mulligan, now on the staff of the Commission Representation there, and whisked off to lunch with the President Bruce McLaury of the Brookings Institution, and various of his colleagues. Brookings ran the American end of the Commission/US Exchange Scheme: I was responsible for the European side. Each year, four Commission officials of middle rank spent a month in the US with an American counter-part, and then looked after the counter-part on his/her return visit to Brussels. The lunch was followed by visits to senior officials of the Library of Congress and the State Department.

Thursday morning started with another working breakfast: this time with Berndt Von Staden, an old friend who had been Hallstein's first Chefcab and was now West German Ambassador in Washington. There followed a visit to the Commission Delegation, on the New York pattern; a meeting with the President of the Marshall Fund, which financed the Exchange Scheme; and a quiet lunch with Patsy Sullivan. Then it was time to fly to Denver, to speak, at a dinner organised by the 'Denver Foreign Relations Committee', about '*Direct Elections to the European Parliament*', the first round of which had by now been fixed for the following year. Tiresomely, the flight was cancelled when we were already on the runway at Dulles Airport, due to a defective under-carriage. I was transferred by car to Baltimore, 50 miles away, to catch another. The Denver Committee dined by itself. I joined them afterwards to make the speech: not a good start! But the discussion went well.

Up early on Friday morning, I held a one-hour discussion with the Editor of the *Denver Post*, a key newspaper in the Rocky Mountain area. After a drive to Boulder, some 30 miles way, I gave a lunchtime talk to the city's 'Council for Foreign Relations'. Later, I flew back to New York, and spent the night at a JFK Airport Hotel.

Saturday was meant to be relaxed, flying to Brussels by Panam Boeing 747 in the comfort of an Executive Class seat, with stop-over at London. But fate intervened. No sooner had we taken off, and reached 2,000 feet, than the Captain announced that his undercarriage would not retract. (I seem to have had a malign effect on these structures!) We circled over the Atlantic for some time, while he pumped 6,500 gallons of fuel out through the wing-tip nozzles; and then landed at JFK, followed down the runway by an impressive array of 6 fire-trucks and 2 fire-chiefs. The aircraft had to be changed. Result: I reached Brussels at 0300 hours on Sunday, and my bed an hour later. *'Tiring but interesting',* said my diary.

In 1980, my last full year in the DSG job, a final visit took me out of Brussels for twelve days and included also Boston. By now, the Commission's Delegations at New York, Washington and Ottawa had worked out how my presence could best be exploited, and had between them devised a very intensive programme. It included briefings for all three Delegations, and at Ottawa for the assembled Ambassadors of the Nine. There were visits, with talks, to four US Universities: Columbia, Georgetown, American and Harvard. At the UN General Assembly I heard Gromyko deliver an uncompromising Second Cold War speech, on the very day, 23rd September, when the Iran/Iraq war broke out. In Washington, beside the usual State Department talks, I called at the National Security Council; and spent a lot of time on Capitol Hill, in discussions with Congressmen and Senatorial aides influential in terms of US/Community relations. I also visited old friends at the British Embassy. In all, I gave five set talks, on different aspects of Community affairs. My diary again recorded impressions. *'Trips of this kind give one a chance to see the Community as others see it: a valuable counter-part to my usual view from within. Preparations take time – speech-writing and briefing – but the experience makes all this worth while.'*

European Councils

It was not until the Single European Act entered into force in 1987 that the European Council acquired a legal status. That Treaty provided that it should bring together the Heads of State or of Government of the Member States and the President of the Commission; that they would be assisted by their Foreign Ministers and by a Member of the Commission; and that they should meet at least twice a year. The status of the European Council was enhanced, and its role clarified, by both the Maastricht and Amsterdam Treaties. Following Amsterdam, its role is defined as being *'to provide the European Union with the necessary impetus for its development'* and to *'define the general political guidelines thereof'*. Its meetings normally extended over two days, but could be longer.

In practice, the Heads of Government – only the French were represented by their Head of State – had been meeting frequently for many years on an informal basis: and they had called themselves 'The European Council' since 1974. As we have seen, that body's meetings were prepared partly by CRP and partly by the Political Directors, depending on the subject. It was therefore natural that, although Emile Nöel always went, I should have attended 10 of the 11 of the European Councils which took place between June 1977 and March 1981. (I was excused one, because it clashed with a family holiday!)

The notion of attendance needs closer definition. At the European Council itself, the only people then allowed in the <u>room</u> – apart from the interpreters in their booths – were the Heads of Government, accompanied by their Foreign Ministers, plus two note-takers furnished by the Council Secretariat-General. Others might enter with messages, or to take instructions, but must do so very discreetly and leave promptly. However, there were a good many other persons in the Conference <u>building</u>. It was necessary for both the Permanent Representatives and the Political Directors to be there, as they often had to meet, before, after, or in parallel with, the Heads of Government, to work up or finalise drafts of the so-called Presidency conclusions or related documents. On those occasions, the usual form was for Emile to 'cover' the CRP, while I attended the Political Committee. Delegations usually also have a Press Officer, and a number of other advisers. Outside the actual Conference area, the media are omni-present.

In a logical world, these events, like ordinary Council meetings, would take place in Brussels, where all the necessary facilities are readily available. But Heads of Government see things otherwise. They will tell you that they think it helps the Community's image in their country to be physically present there from time to time. But they are really more interested in the publicity value to themselves, both at home and abroad. So it has from the start been the custom for the European Council to meet, more frequently, in the Presidency country.

The first meeting I attended was at Lancaster House in London in June 1977, under Jim Callaghan's Presidency. I shall use this single European Council at London as an example, describe its flavour, and then comment more briefly on some of the others. The accent is on the word 'flavour'. No attempt is made to analyse the results of these meetings systematically. That would be laborious, and could in any case be better be done by a historian, ploughing through the Presidency Conclusions of each European Council.

At London, the Conference started in the afternoon, following separate lunches for the different levels of participants. The Heads of Government and Roy Jenkins were lunched at No 10 by the Prime Minister. They were meant to reach Lancaster House at 3.30 p.m.; but their discussions – which in those days, with only Nine Member States involved, were conducted using English only – were prolonged and, as we later learnt, heated.

Much time was spent in the Heads of Government telling their host, in no uncertain terms, that they thought recent British behaviour had been very *non-communautaire*. This was natural, since a number of 'anti-market' Ministers – notably Silkin, Foot and Benn – had been behaving in that way at Council meetings in Brussels. Callaghan learnt that, against this background, he could not expect a favourable decision that day on the proposal to locate the Joint European Torus [JET] at Culham. (In the event, agreement was withheld for 4 months.) Much time was also devoted to discussing the prospects of enlarging the Community to take in Greece, Spain and Portugal: certain Heads of Government who had initially declared themselves favourable were by now, having counted the cost, belatedly seeing difficulties. [This passage, originally written in the year 2000, prompts one to add, in 2002: *'plus ça change, plus c'est la même chose!*]

As a result, the Heads of Government arrived at Lancaster House 90 minutes late. The Foreign Ministers meanwhile had had nothing to do. Officials are used to hanging around, waiting for Ministers; but the latter aren't used to waiting at all, and soon became impatient. They were also anxious as to what their Prime Ministers were getting up to without them! Officials, however, were busy drafting two, not very meaningful, Declarations: on the Middle East, and on the state of the economy. These were discussed at the European Council that afternoon; re-worked overnight; and adopted at next morning's session. In short, a meagre output from much labour.

My next European Council took place, with much less fuss and bother, in Brussels in December 1977. The substance was far more solid. There was discussion of the Tindemans Report, which began a process leading eventually to the Maastricht Treaty establishing a European Union of 1992; of Economic and Monetary Union [EMU], re-launched by Roy Jenkins at Florence two months earlier; and of the run-up to the first direct elections to the European Parliament, by now set for 1979. But I have no special, personal memories of this European Council, nor of the next – since it was the one I missed.

In July 1978, however, when the European Council met in the lovely setting of the Rathaus at Bremen, there were two important innovations. The first was that the Heads of Government began talking seriously about a <u>Community</u> response – as opposed to unco-ordinated and indeed contradictory <u>national</u> responses – to the energy crisis which had begun when oil prices doubled after the Yom Kippur War. The response consisted of agreeing Community Energy Objectives for 1985, with the aims of saving energy and of cutting dependence on Middle East oil imports. The second innovation was this: the European Council was now, for the first time, used by the Nine to prepare a Community position for deployment by its representatives at a Western Economic Summit [WES]. Both innovations were repeated at Strasbourg, in June 1979: indeed the Iranian revolution in the previous month, and the resultant second doubling of the oil price, had so focused minds that much more precise energy aims were set.

Margaret Thatcher had become Prime Minister in May, so Bremen was the first of her many appearances at a European Council. She at once began demanding to *'have our money back'*; and at Dublin, five months later, she was swinging her handbag with a vengeance. She had a very good point. The Community's financial arrangements <u>did</u> place an inequitable share on British shoulders; her predecessors had been wrong to accept this; the other Eight knew that there should be changes, but naturally preferred to leave things alone as long as they could get away with it. Once they saw that this was no longer the case, an interim solution was found, only a year later, and a definitive one followed before long.

Of course, once it had been agreed with Margaret Thatcher that the British contribution would be opened up, the others began to open up other institutional questions; and all this ended, years later, with the Single European Act, the biggest amendment to the three Community Treaties ever undertaken up to that time, and the biggest concession of sovereignty to the supra-national institutions since the Treaties were written. Margaret Thatcher signed up to all this because she wanted a solution on the problem closest to her heart, and knew she would have to pay politically for what she wanted financially. And it was arrant nonsense for her to claim, later, that she didn't understand she was conceding so much sovereignty.

What view can one take of Margaret Thatcher in the broad European context? The trouble with her was that, having settled that particular package of issues, and not herself wanting anything else from the Community, she thereafter allowed her emotions to prevail. These had always been insular, not European. Later on, when the re-unification of Germany became a practical option, she immediately said: 'We must slow it down or block it'. This was a gut reaction. Intellectually she must have known that, for 45 years, Britain had been repeatedly signing Treaties and Agreements which said that Britain fully supported the notion of unification, as long as it was in a democratic context. But again, her emotions ran wild; and that did immense harm to Anglo-German relations. I think the later phase of Margaret Thatcher's tenure of office as Prime Minister had the same effect on wider Anglo-European relations.

The last European Council on which I comment took place at Venice in June 1980. The *venue* created considerable problems for the Italian Security Authorities, with dozens of VIP's in constant movement in the lagoon and through the canals! For the duration of the meeting – and for the Western Economic Summit a week later – Venice Airport was closed to public flights. The VIP's were <u>required</u> to arrive at Venice by air. The Heads of Government came in Air Force or requisitioned National Airline planes: the Commission Delegation in an air-taxi! Police divers inspected the underside of each launch before it took on board its passengers for the trip across the lagoon and up to the heavily guarded Hotel Danieli, where the Delegations were lodged. Police launches patrolled everywhere.

The meetings themselves all took place at the Fondazione Cini, on the Isola San Giorgio, and each Delegation had a launch to move them between Hotel and Island. The Heads of Government met in the beautiful baroque Library of the former Monastery. The Fondazione provided a wonderfully quiet and peaceful setting for the European Council's work, which was in fact productive. This was the occasion when, besides carrying forward the energy dossier, the Heads of Government ratified both the interim solution of the British budgetary problem, and the important Venice Declaration of the Nine on the Middle East discussed above.

*President Roy Jenkins and his Chef de Cabinet, Crispin Tickell (R),
at Venice Summit meeting, 1980.*

Western Economic Summits

I do not recall exactly when or how Western Economic Summits began and
developed. Initially, their appearance gave rise to friction within the
Community, for two reasons. First, Italy was excluded: the group consisted
only of Britain, France, Germany, Japan and the USA – at that time the five
largest economies of the Western World. And second, no specific provision
was made for representation of the Community as such. Italy was soon let
in. As to the Community, its Presidency happened for a while to be held by a
Member State which was itself in the 'magic circle': this then undertook to
express the Community voice. But such a procedure could not last. And, in
May 1977, a new arrangement was in force, under which the Community
was formally represented by the Prime Minister of its Presidency country –
whether or not that country was normally a member of the Summit group –
and by the Commission President. By then, Summits, like European
Councils, were extending over two days.

At first, these Summits were limited, as their name suggested, to
economic issues. But one cannot prevent persons of such eminence, when
they come together, from discussing whatever they like; and soon the
Summits extended their deliberations to purely political issues, like those of

the Cold War or the Middle East. The Community position was therefore prepared, partly in the Council and CRP, and partly in the EPC. The Summit meetings themselves were, and still are, prepared by officials who were described as 'Personal Representatives' of their principals, and who very soon acquired the unofficial title of 'Sherpas'. The Commission's Sherpa was the President's Chefcab, Crispin Tickell. Because of my overview of Community affairs, he arranged for me to be a regular member of the Commission's small team at the Summits themselves. This first happened at the Bonn Summit, which took place in the Palais Schaumburg during July 1978, 10 days after the Bremen European Council.

Attendance in the Summit Conference room was by now limited to the Principals, usually their Foreign Ministers, and one 'note-taker' each. The note-taker for the Commission was Crispin. However, other meetings would be taking place alongside. There would always be a main drafting group, and sometimes one or more specialised groups. I found myself at Bonn acting as the Commission's titular member of the drafting group, assisted as necessary by other Commission officials. Normally, the Sherpas would have prepared the first draft of the final communiqué before the Summit began, by formal meetings and exchanges of telegrams. The drafting group's task was to update it constantly, to take account of information emerging by dribs and drabs from the Principals' debates, and of external developments.

Thus, at Bonn, I spent almost the whole of the two days in the drafting group. It was a pattern which was to be repeated at the next two Summits, each of which closely followed a European Council: the first of these was at Tokyo in 1979; and the second, at Venice in 1980. There follow some notes about each of them.

I was excited by the prospect of Tokyo. This was to be my first excursion to the Far East. Moreover, Japanese civilisation had always aroused my curiosity. The main meetings were to take place on a Thursday and Friday, with some preparatory gatherings on the Wednesday. I left London Airport for Tokyo on the previous Sunday. It was amusing to find that, apart from a short stop-over at Anchorage, Alaska, our great circle route meant that the local time remained always the same: only the <u>day</u> changed, as we crossed the international date line in the North Pacific. Arriving in Tokyo at tea-time – after the longest day of my life! – I retired to bed in the New Otani Hotel, where Japanese standards of service never ceased to amaze me.

Tuesday was my rest day. I decided to join an organised group of English-speaking tourists visiting Nikko, a beautiful, wooded, mountainous area, with a collection of temples and shrines, an hour's train ride west of Tokyo. A charming Japanese lady was our guide. Wishing to learn as much as I could about her country, I contrived to be seated by her for the outward journey. She seemed to enjoy, as much as I did, exchanging information and thoughts about European and Japanese ways of life. In the course of conversation I learnt that her husband was a middle-level executive in a brewery, and she evidently came to understand that I was a Commission official attending the Summit.

A brief digression is now required. The Japanese economy was at this time very strong. There were concerns within the Community about the Europeans' ability to compete; and these were the subject of continuing debate in the Community Institutions. A working paper had been prepared for a Commission meeting by Roy Denman, as Director-General for External Relations. Roy is himself colourful, and has always used striking language. At one point, his paper had referred to the Japanese as *'workaholics living in rabbit-hutches'*. Inevitably, this had leaked to the press a few weeks before the Tokyo Summit. The Member States' Ambassadors in Japan were outraged, taking the line that it would set back European-Japanese relations by a quarter century, and just showed that Commission officials could not be trusted over foreign affairs. The Commission had tried to pour oil on the troubled waters by stressing that the document had been an internal one, not written for publication.

On the return journey, it was the Japanese lady who chose to sit by <u>me</u>; and our conversation continued in a lively and for me very educational way. When she enquired whether I was indeed a Commission official, I guessed I was in for some polite criticism. But it turned out not to be so.

When I assented, she replied on the following lines. *'Well, then I'm absolutely delighted to meet you. You're the people who described the Japanese as 'workaholics living in rabbit-hutches'.* I tried out the official line on her, but she brushed it aside and continued. *'I read it all, one day, in the* Asahi Shimbun. *That evening, when my husband came home, I sat him down in his chair; handed him his slippers; made sure he was comfortable; and brought him a beer. And then I said: 'We've been married for 30 years. But it's only today I've discovered what you are. You're a workaholic, and we're living in a rabbit-hutch. What are you going to do about it?'* I asked her about the result, and was relieved to hear that positive action had followed. Her husband had started coming home at a more reasonable hour; he had even – for the first time in their married life – taken the family on a holiday; and they were going to move into a larger house.

Next morning, when I opened the [English language version of the] *Asahi*

Shimbun, I was at once struck by a remarkable strip cartoon. It showed Roy Jenkins dozing on his flight towards Tokyo: in a 'thinks' balloon one saw him observing with interest a group of what were evidently Japanese *'workaholics living in rabbit-hutches'*. In the second picture he was shown being greeted at Narita Airport. In the third, where he was obviously being transported by car to his hotel, he was seen peering with amazement out of the window and observing – little birds with human Japanese faces jumping up and down in tiny bird-cages!

Taken together, these two images – my Japanese friend with her husband, and the strip-cartoon – left me with a warm feeling. They showed that, following their long post-war contact with the West, at least some Japanese had learnt not to take themselves too seriously, and even to question whether there should not be some limits to the work ethic. I concluded that Roy Denman might perhaps have a better feel for modern Japanese culture than the Community Ambassadors in Tokyo supposed. However, when I dined privately with the British Ambassador and his wife that night, and the workaholic matter was raised, it seemed polite simply to repeat the official line.

On a more serious note, another issue nearly raised diplomatic problems at Tokyo. It had to do with the position of the Commission President in the Summit pecking order. When Community attendance at the Summits was agreed, certain conventions had also been established. Tiresomely, these included a discrimination affecting the Commission President. He was to be included in all the Heads of Government lunches, but not dinners. The philosophical background, presumably, was to mark the sense of superiority which all these elected holders of high office felt over someone merely appointed, even though that appointment had itself been made by nine elected Heads of Government, acting unanimously. It was not a very practical arrangement, since Roy Jenkins missed out on possibly important parts of the overall picture of the two-day gathering. His Chefcab, Crispin Tickell, started looking for ways of improving matters.

The approach of the Tokyo Summit appeared to offer Crispin a good opening. It was the task of the host Government to make all practical arrangements for the event. Japan had never before hosted a Summit, and was less sensitive to the traditions than other participants. Crispin somehow left the Japanese Personal Representative with the impression that it would be normal for Roy Jenkins to attend all of the Heads of Government meals. And his name duly appeared on each guest list.

However, on the day of the official dinner, the Japanese Personal

Representative informed Crispin that another Delegation had told him that the Commission President was <u>not</u> normally at dinners, and that precedent <u>must</u> be observed. With enormous regret for any offence caused, therefore, the Japanese felt obliged to withdraw Roy's invitation. There was little doubt that France was behind all this: although Roy got on very well with Giscard, and the latter was, with Helmut Schmidt, the key supporter of Roy's re-launch of EMU, French Presidents have mostly suffered from *folie de grandeur*.

This last-minute rebuff deeply upset Roy. Though normally very philosophic, on this occasion he over-reacted. In a meeting with advisers, we were asked whether he should not mark his displeasure by flying home to Brussels that evening, instead of attending the second day's proceedings. The Delegation was unanimous in arguing this would be a mistake; and in the end their view prevailed. Roy stayed, and I believe it was not too long afterwards that the discrimination ceased.

It then remained to pass the vacant evening in a congenial way. Leslie Fielding, the Head of the Commission's Office in Tokyo, proposed we all dine at Tokyo's best Western-style restaurant. Roy had a great reputation as a connoisseur of claret. When we sat down, although still very grumpy, he undertook to choose the wine. A huge list of clarets was produced; Roy's pain eased visibly; and a bottle was chosen. The waiter duly poured a sample into Roy's glass. He smelt it, tasted it, wrinkled his nose, and demanded to see the bottle. Triumphantly, he pointed out that, although it was the right wine, it was the wrong year. The waiter humbly brought the correct vintage. We were able to taste both: it was chalk and cheese. From then on I felt safe in saying that Roy's reputation in this matter was soundly based!

The Venice Summit, as already remarked, followed ten days after the European Council. The same physical arrangements applied, *mutatis mutandis*. One particular incident sticks in my mind. It must be recalled that Venice took place some six months after the Soviet invasion of Afghanistan. The Americans had responded by announcing that no US athletes would participate in the Moscow Olympics that summer. On the second day, I was breakfasting at the Danieli with Berndt Von Staden, by now Secretary of State in the German Federal Chancellor's Office, in a position from which we could look out over the lagoon. Before our eyes, and by definition before those of President Jimmy Carter, a large steamer sailed in, to moor in full sight. On its side we read emblazoned the words 'Soviet Official Olympic Ship'. I never discovered whether this was happenstance or brilliant Soviet planning!

Berlin affairs

There was a further addition to my work portfolio. After the EEC was established, the question had arisen whether the Treaty should be applied to West Berlin. The City was not a part of the Federal Republic. But the three Allies who governed it had always ensured that its economy conformed to Federal Republic rules. Now, these in turn were going to be partly determined by the Community. The Allies had therefore agreed that relevant Community legislation would also be applied in the City. Thus, by a legal device, had West Berlin been *de facto* integrated into Community life. It had also been arranged that the Community would give various forms of economic assistance to the City. The Commission had decided that it would appoint, from amongst the ranks of its senior officials, a 'Berlin Co-ordinator'; and the task had been given to two successive Deputy Secretaries-General, ending with Klaus Meyer. But they had both been of German nationality.

Many expected that this function would now pass to a different German official. In the event, the Commission, aware of my own very special experience of Berlin, and complete fluency in the German language, determined that I would take over. It gave me enormous satisfaction to be able to serve the courageous people of the city for a third time, though modestly and in a quite different way. The work was not arduous. In essence, it involved being ready to see and assist Berlin visitors to Brussels; and myself making an annual visit to Berlin of three or four days, to show the Community flag and keep in touch.

Under the first head I received various visits from the Berlin Senator for Federal and Community affairs; Members of the Berlin House of Representatives; and editors of the Berlin newspapers. Under the second, it proved both practical and pleasant to visit Berlin in May: practical, because a plethora of public holidays in Belgium during that month slows down the tempo of Community business; and pleasant, because in May the great city looks its greenest. Better still, Maura was able to go too. We made a point of always including a weekend, to give ample time for culture, and for seeing friends, old and new. British friends kindly asked us to stay. For two years we refused, to mark the point that we were there to represent the Community, and no longer Britain. Instead, we patronised the simple, but comfortable Pension Belvedere, on the Seebergsteig in the Grünewald. Once our new role had been understood, however, we did on the last occasion stay with Francis MacGinnis, now the British Deputy

Commandant: Francis and Carolyn were old friends from Bonn days in the early 1970s.

These visits had some standard business elements: a briefing for the Commission Office staff; discussions with politicians and/or officials at the Berlin Senat, where Senatsrat Kunze was a much valued contact; public presentations on Community matters to University or other audiences; discussions with newspaper people; radio interviews; meetings with Allied authorities; and appearing at many official meals and receptions. There were also, however, two rather special days.

The first, in May 1979, began when we had a breakfast-time visitor at the Pension. We had known Richard Von Weizsäcker well, whilst in Bonn during the Berlin Talks period. He had been CDU spokesman on Ostpolitik and Berlin matters; and this had brought us much together. He now remained a leading figure in the party, and had a house in Berlin. In 1981 he was to be elected Governing Mayor of the City; and, three years after that, President of the Federal Republic. He was a truly impressive figure in both capacities, bringing to each a rare combination of wisdom, intelligence and great humanity. In those days we tried to meet when I came to Berlin.

On this occasion, we specially wished to do so, because the Russians were threatening dire consequences if the Allies and the Federal Republic maintained their plan to allow the election of Berlin MEPs, in the context of the first direct elections to the European Parliament, a month later. A working breakfast in our room in the Pension was the only possible venue. It was a strange place to entertain so distinguished a guest. (The hotelier told us afterwards that, if he had known who our visitor would be, he would have cleared the public dining room and made the other house-guests eat in <u>their</u> rooms!) The breakfast enabled me to tell Richard that I was convinced the Russians were bluffing. We had been through the whole matter with them during the Berlin talks [see passage in Chapter 13 on *'die bestehende lage'*]; and they had been aware, from then on, that the upcoming scenario was on the cards. They had no leg to stand on, and must know it; and they would not wish to renege on the Quadripartite Agreement. I added that I had invited Khotulew, one of the two Russians with whom I had negotiated in 1970-72, to a private lunch in West Berlin that day, and would remind him firmly of the position.

The lunch with Khotulew duly took place. We chatted of our shared experiences and of old friends. It was all very amicable. But towards the end I openly told him I thought the Russians were bluffing, and explained why.

He made no comment, but must certainly have reported to Moscow. In the event, the Russians did <u>not</u> attempt any reprisals.

As we parted, Khotulew asked me, in a social and friendly way, how I would be spending my afternoon. I replied that I had borrowed a car from the British authorities, and would be taking my wife with me to visit Potsdam, then in the German Democratic Republic, which was something time had never allowed during the negotiations for the Quadripartite Agreement. *'Why did you not warn me?'* he asked reproachfully, and I apologised for any unintended discourtesy. Soon after, he left, in evident haste.

Passing through the checkpoint into the GDR, we waited in line, and then found that our papers were painstakingly inspected; that mirrors were passed under our car to detect any smuggling; and that the process took quite some time. When we returned from Potsdam, two hours later, it was clear that Khotulew had set wheels in motion. Three Soviet officers were standing in the middle of the road, watching the oncoming traffic with binoculars. They spotted us from afar. We were waved out of the longish queue of cars; swept up to the front; smartly saluted; and sent on through the checkpoint with warm greetings.

A year later, I had a very different experience of Berlin life. Arrangements were made by the British authorities for me to take off from Gatow airfield – of Airlift fame – on an hour-long routine helicopter tour of the Berlin Wall around the British Sector, flown by Captain Southgate of the Army Air Corps. Although of course I had flown in and out of Berlin many times before, it was sobering to see, from low level and in every detail, the whole course of the wall, with the mined zone beyond, then a wire fence, and outside that, the dog patrols. It brought one up against Communist reality in a very direct way.

To close on a happier note, our visits to Berlin also enabled us to enjoy marvellous museums and beautiful music.

Helping to launch the Thorn Presidency

Towards the end of 1980 I was again involved in helping to prepare and launch a new Commission with a new President. If the choice of President four years earlier had been simple, this time it was not. A strong candidate was found, and gained the support of nine out of the ten Member States [Greece had joined the Community that January]; but Margaret Thatcher thought she did not want a strong President and imposed a veto. Hence the appointment, rather late in the day, of Gaston Thorn. His paper credentials were sound. He had been Prime Minister and/or Foreign Minister of one of the Member States – albeit the smallest – for many years. He was used to chairing Council and other Community meetings; and fully briefed on all Community issues. He was thoroughly likeable. As against all this, he was weak. Moreover, his Cabinet was not of the standard set by that of Roy Jenkins. The Commission soon tended to flounder. Even Margaret Thatcher came to see that a weak Commission was not in fact good for the Community, or therefore for Britain, and was frequently heard to refer to its President as *'poor little Gaston'*, or *'p.l.g'*. Four years later, she went along with the appointment of Jacques Delors, the strongest President the Commission ever had.

But the British often fail to learn from mistakes. Fifteen years after that, history repeated itself. John Major vetoed a strong candidate, acceptable to the other fourteen Member States; and another Luxembourger, Jacques Santer, was appointed in his place. Santer turned out to be hopeless; and the Commission was forced by the European Parliament to resign. Thus, to its shame, Britain alone bears responsibility for the appointment of the two least effective Presidents of the different Executives since the first Community was established in 1952!

At all events Emile Nöel and I prepared the ground for the new President's arrival in the same way as before. The new Commission met in the Berlaymont at 1600 hours on 6th January. But Thorn was not as well advanced on portfolio allocations as had been Jenkins. After he had made his initial proposals, the Commission was suspended for the customary bilateral talks between him and individual Commissioners. It emerged that many problems remained to be ironed out. Not until 2200 hours was the Commission reconvened. Thorn then said he did not see his way to a solution that day. The Commission was adjourned until 1030 hours next morning, giving rise to excited and critical media speculation overnight.

The whole of the second day was spent in bilateral consultations, interspersed with short formal Commission meetings. It was after midnight before Thorn could get his colleagues' agreement to a package. Again the media went to bed without hard news, being simply told that all would be revealed at a press conference at noon on the third day, 8th January! There was little excuse for all this delay. Half the new Commissioners were serving a second or third term, which should have made things easier.

After that, for three months, my work resumed its earlier pattern. In particular, Thorn found the briefing methods set up for his predecessor suited him well. And, as with Roy Jenkins, I accompanied the new President on some of his 'inaugural visits' to Member States' capitals. The visits to Paris and Athens proved dramatic, though for quite different reasons.

In Paris, on 23 February, 1981, there were the customary calls on President Giscard at the Elysée and on Prime Minister Barre at the Matignon, and the usual press briefing by Thorn afterwards at the Commission's Paris Office. Arrangements had also been made for Thorn to appear that evening on the regular TF1 Television news programme, whose presenter was the renowned Roger Gickell. When we reached the studios, however, there was complete turmoil. It was explained that, in Madrid, the dissident Colonel Tejero and his troops had just burst into the building of the Cortes, and were holding all the Members in it hostage at gunpoint. The democratic foundations of post-Franco Spain were in jeopardy.

This was high drama. It was going to occupy most of the time on the news programme. We would be lucky if Thorn appeared at all. We were asked to wait. Thorn was in the studio: myself in the control room. Thus it was that I had a ring-side view of how tricks can be played on TV audiences! TF1 had had a stroke of good fortune. Their reporter was the only one who had managed to escape from the Cortes, by jumping from a window. With 15 minutes to go before his programme started, we heard both sides of a telephone call between Roger Gickell and this reporter in Madrid. The reporter was overwrought and incoherent. Gickell had to halt him in mid-flow; and tell him to calm down and answer questions briefly and clearly. The effect was limited. Each time a question was put, words flowed back in a totally muddled sequence. There was no way they could be directly reproduced. But Gickell was a man of resource. He had his team drastically edit the transcript of the reporter's remarks, so that what remained was vaguely comprehensible. The remarks were then broken down further, so that each snippet sounded like the answer to a question. Then the script-writers typed out questions which would match the answers. With only seconds to spare, Gickell was ready. Once on air he informed his audience of the reporter's escape, and made out that he now had the man live on the telephone. Gickell then picked up his phone and read out the first scripted question; and the technicians played back the corresponding taped snippet. And so on for the whole of the 'live' interview. I found the whole affair impressive but scandalous. With such competition, Thorn thought himself fortunate to appear on the programme at all, however briefly!

In Athens, to which I thus returned after a 34-year gap, the excitements were of a different order. We flew there from Paris, next morning. After an official lunch with the Foreign Minister and two Ministerial colleagues, we called on Prime Minister Rallis. Then we were received by President Karamanlis, the charming, grand old man of Greek politics, in the former Royal Palace. He was impressive, both in terms of his record and also personally. Tall, distinguished looking, with bushy eyebrows over an inch long, he was immaculately dressed in a very English 3-piece tweed suit. He had a ready wit, a fund of anecdotes and a huge laugh. With him, we passed an hour or so, in a quiet, mellow library, discussing Europe in stratospheric language.

We had no evening engagements, so the Delegation went to dine quietly at a very pleasant Taverna, near the Olympic Stadium, with three men singing Greek songs and accompanying themselves on their mandolins. Suddenly, around 2200 hours, the tables and chairs shook, the building rocked, and all the lights went out. It was a powerful earthquake, which in fact measured 6.8 on the Richter scale at its epicentre some 70 kilometres away. In Greece, earthquakes are relatively common, so everyone knows what to do. In seconds, the waiters had pulled lighters from their pockets, lit numerous candles, and restored order. Many clients rushed to telephones, no doubt to exchange news with their near and dear. Fortunately our Taverna was a single-storey affair, and no serious damage had been done. Dinner over, we retired to our rooms in the Hotel Grande Bretagne. Mine was on the 6th floor. So, when a second and similar earthquake occurred, around 0330 hours, I could feel the whole building sway. I ran to stand in a doorway – the least dangerous place; but could do nothing else to help myself. Either the building would fall and I would die – or it would not. For a few seconds one felt suspended in time. But nothing happened. I went back to bed, but had some difficulty getting off to sleep again. I then overslept, and the Delegation nearly had to leave for the Airport without me.

Joining the Jet Set

This portfolio of activities meant massive travel. There were EPC meetings, at Ministerial or Political Director level, some 15 times a year; and European Councils away from Brussels, twice. I accompanied the President of the Commission on visits to Community or other European countries four or five times annually. There were GAC meetings at Luxembourg – the Council did not always meet then in Brussels – and visits to Strasbourg for Commission or Parliament affairs. There were also the visits to Berlin. All the foregoing trips were normally within the Community; but, once a year, EPC work took me to North America. And there was an annual meeting of the Western Economic Summit, usually in Europe but once in Japan. In some cases – Luxembourg, Strasbourg, The Hague, Bonn and Paris – the journeys were usually by train or car. But for the others I joined the Jet Set. From the start of my new job, I was certainly flying between 50 and 100 thousand miles a year. When I later became Director-General for Energy, still more travel was involved: in my last 12 months with the Commission, in 1985-86, I clocked up some 200,000 air miles.

Usually, I travelled on my British passport. Within the Community, however, I often used the *'laissez-passer'* issued by the Commission to establish the credentials of its officials in the Member States. On one occasion, I decided to see how this would go down in Britain! On arrival at Heathrow, keeping my passport in my wallet, I offered the *laissez-passer* to the Immigration Officer. He looked at it cautiously; scrutinised me; and then asked *'You do have a British passport, do you Sir?'* My answer was to enquire whether he was going to allow me in on the basis of the *laissez-passer*. His reply was exquisitely British: *'Of course we'll let you in, Sir, but we really prefer the British passports'.*

Although pretty fit for my years, it was obvious to me that a very heavy work-schedule, coupled with so much travel, required careful management. Besides taking my full allowance of leave – mostly to match the children's school or University holidays – I tried to ensure my journeys were not more tiring than they had to be. This involved developing a good ability to sleep on the plane; getting to the destination a bit ahead of time; perhaps adding a day's leave at the destination, or coupling the journey with a weekend; and – when it was going to interest her – sometimes taking Maura with me.

None of any 'extra time' was at official expense. From my first day in the Commission I left my Secretary to prepare my travel claims, with one very simple guideline: if there was ever any doubt about the justification for claiming a given item, it must be omitted. On one point I was, however, very firm – with the Commission, with myself and with my own officials. I felt strongly that an exhausted official would not perform well: so my officials had instructions that – when on a Trans-Atlantic or other very long distance mission – they should not participate in any important meeting until after a good night's rest. If that meant a day's extra subsistence, it was an investment it was right to make.

Social life and family affairs

Our social lifestyle was not greatly affected by my change of job, except that we were invited to many more receptions and dinners by Permanent Representatives.

The Sullivans' life at RGC continued in the established pattern, and we in turn continued to benefit from Layters Way as a UK base for ourselves and the children. At Ackenthwaite, however, there were great changes. After my father's death in 1976, my mother had stayed on in the house. It must have cost her a huge effort, although she did have some help, to keep home and garden in shape. Somehow she managed – despite inevitable falls in her last two years – until her final hospitalisation in Lancaster in March, 1981. She moved from there to a nursing home at Hollow Oak, Haverthwaite, where she died that May. After my father's death, we did what we could to see her as often as possible. She stayed with us twice in Brussels. There were quick trips by us to Ackenthwaite as occasion allowed. Our whole family attended her 80th birthday celebrations there in February, 1980; and she in turn came to our own Silver Wedding Celebration at the Club in London in November of the same year.

My father had left my mother a life interest in the house, but his will provided that it would thereafter go to Michael, as the eldest son. I inherited the Old Smithy; and Elizabeth, the three fields up Paradise Lane, which she sold to Teddy Tryon-Wilson. Maura and I saw no advantage in keeping the Smithy. Although it had strong connections with the family, it was not a house we would ever have been happy to live in, if only because it was bang on the side of a road much used by heavy traffic, and had no garden (nor at that time any prospect of getting one). Moreover, we had in 1978 finally decided that I would not return to the Foreign Office; and in October bought our home in Brussels from Madame Lambin. This had involved taking out a substantial loan, which we were anxious to pay off. We resolved, therefore, to dispose of the Smithy, and that same November it was sold to Roger Bingham, who has since greatly extended it.

Rupert finished at Bradfield College in summer, 1978. After working in a Bank in Gerrards Cross, he joined an English family in setting up a riding school in Javea, Spain. Soon, he began breeding Andalusian horses. Later, the horses became a hobby, and he acquired and developed his own publishing company. Claire returned to live at home, in the spring of 1980, to study for her A levels at the British School of Brussels, in Tervueren. William stayed at Boarding School in England, transferring from The Pilgrims' to Winchester College in 1980. We continued to use our family holidays to explore different parts of Europe: ski-ing took an even larger part in our lives, when we started to go regularly at Christmas, as well as Easter. My self-denying ordinance as regards writing about holidays should not be seen as indicating that their importance to the whole family had in the least declined.

CHAPTER 16

Director-General for Energy, European Commission 1981-1986

The last job of my professional life

WHILST I HAD greatly relished my four years as the Commission's sole Deputy Secretary-General, with the vast widening of horizons and experience the job had entailed, by 1981 and at age 54, I wanted, for the first time in my life, to be in sole charge of a big outfit – in Commission terms, the boss of a major Directorate-General. Following the two oil-shocks, energy policy had become very important, and the British Director-General for Energy, Len Williams, was due to retire in the re-shuffle following the arrival of the Thorn Commission. I indicated my wish to be considered for the succession: to Emile Nöel and Michael Butler (the UK Permanent Representative), and finally to President Thorn. An understanding was reached in the Commission that a British candidate would be appropriate. The choice of appointee would essentially be made by the Commissioner concerned.

Stevie Davignon had enormously enlarged his empire in the portfolio allocation exercise: it now covered Industry, Energy, the Euratom Supply Agency, Research and Science, and the Community's Joint Research Centre. His earlier reservations about me had disappeared, so the prospects seemed good. But then came a nasty surprise. Over the years, several senior Foreign Office people had said they would like me to get a Director-General job. But the Foreign Office does not alone decide such things: the broader Whitehall establishment takes over. The message delivered to Stevie by the latter was that their preferred candidate was an Under-Secretary at the Department of Energy; however, if the Commissioner really wanted an internal candidate, then I was their second choice! The other candidate, Chris Herzig, was at that time unknown to me. Later, I came to know him professionally, and to respect and like him. Fortunately, Stevie's reaction was favourable. He told me he would at once propose my name to the Commission, and the appointment was approved at its next meeting on 1st April. It was meant to take effect that day. My last act as Deputy Secretary-General, however, was

297

to change the Commission minutes so that the effective date was 2 April: I did not wish to be taken as a joke!

None of this surprised Len Williams. I had asked him, some time before, whether somebody not an energy specialist would be able to make a good job of the succession. He had told me firmly that I would be supported by very good specialist officials, as indeed turned out to be the case, and that I would bring them a breadth of experience in operating in all the Community Institutions and associated bodies which they would find very helpful: I should have no qualms.

I had for long made a point of attending meetings of the Energy Council; and seen them being prepared in CRP 2. I spent much of the next two days with Len and his staff, in the Directorate-General's then offices at 10, Rue Guimard; and with my new Commissioner and his Cabinet in the Berlaymont building. Happily, Stevie's able Chefcab, Hugo Paemen, was someone I knew and liked. From then on, I was left to get on with things. We will look shortly at the shape of the Directorate-General, and how I began running it. But first I must record Maura's reaction to these developments; and then, for the last time in this narrative, review the international and Community scene, over the years 1981-86.

Maura was of course fully abreast of developments, and offered her congratulations. She enquired what this appointment would do to my salary. When I said it would not be changed, she was surprised, and asked whether added pay did not usually go with added responsibility. When told that I was already at the top of the salary range, she was mollified, but perhaps not convinced. On my first day in my new office, however, I learned of an economic benefit, when the Head of the Commission car pool telephoned to ask which type of car from the Commission's pool, should be assigned to me. I had completely overlooked this point when answering Maura. A Mercedes was selected, and placed at my disposal, together with a very nice official driver, Roger Schroeder. It soon troubled me to find that, although Roger could also be used by my staff, he was frequently at a loose end. It transpired that I could have the best of both worlds: I should normally drive the car myself, but a chauffeur would be supplied when needed – for example for long journeys on which I wanted to work. It was usually Roger!

General political background

Turning now to the international background, when Ronald Reagan became President of the United States in January 1981, the world's economy was still in a poor way, with widespread inflation and unemployment. Not until

1983 did a slow and hesitant upturn begin. The key challenges for advanced economies were the continued effects of the oil-price rises, the huge surpluses accruing to the oil-producing countries, and the rising competition from Japan and the newly industrialised countries [NIC]. Dialogue with Japan progressed, but slowly. Developing countries continued to complain about lack of help over their economic problems from the industrialised world. Attempts at a broad 'North-South Dialogue' were not fruitful. However, the Community succeeded in negotiating a third Lomé Convention, granting substantial aid and preferential trading arrangements to over 60 African, Caribbean and Pacific countries. The industrialised world's economic difficulties were reflected in a series of trade disputes between the USA and the Community. Fortunately, these were handled by both sides with a certain sensitivity. The cause of free trade did not go under. And, in 1985, consensus was reached to launch within GATT a major new round of multilateral trade negotiations, which became known as 'The Uruguay Round'. The economic outlook began to perk up.

Politically, East-West relations remained chilly. In late 1981, Marshal Jaruselski declared martial law in Poland, and banned the Solidarity Movement. Its leader, Lech Walesa, prophetically told the arresting officer: 'This is the moment of your defeat'. The truth of this became apparent much later. Meanwhile, Brezhnew died in 1982. His immediate successors, Andropow and Czernyenko, made no real changes of direction. Only when Gorbachew came to power in 1985 – and started the twin processes of *Glasnost* [Openness] and *Perestroika* [Restructuring] – did things begin to change for the better. And, in October 1986, at the Second [Reykjavik] Summit meeting between Reagan and Gorbachew, the Second Cold War was put to bed. In the Middle East the Arab-Israel dispute rumbled on: and the 1982 assassination of Anwar Sadat, the peace-promoting Egyptian President, further damaged the atmosphere. In the same year, the Argentine invasion of the Falkland Islands, and the resultant war with Britain, led to problems within the Community, and between it and other countries, particularly those of Latin America. One final event of world significance must be mentioned: the explosion of a Soviet nuclear reactor at Chernobyl in April 1986.

In the Community, a sharp distinction can be made between the years of the Thorn Commission [1981-84] and those of the first Delors Commission, which took office in January, 1985. The Thorn years were the most discouraging for the Community idea, up to that time, since De Gaulle's original challenge to its key concepts in the mid-1960s. Things had started positively, with Greece becoming the tenth Member State in January 1981. But the Community was under constant threat, from outside and within. The external economic problems have already been summarised. And, in 1984, there were twelve million unemployed in the Community. The Member States tended to respond by unilateral, national action, and the Commission's main concern became the preservation of the Common Market. Somehow this was achieved.

Meanwhile, however, the Community's Institutions were wrestling with a whole range of difficult and inter-connected problems about its future development. It was accepted that the Common Agricultural Policy and the Structural Funds needed substantial reform; that more encouragement must be given to introducing new technologies, notably in the information technology [IT] sector; that the Community's own financial resources must be expanded; and that a long-term solution must be found to the problem – of special concern to Britain – of an inequitable budgetary burden falling on different Member States. Gradually also, pressures were building up for making the now creaking Community more efficient, and linking it constitutionally to the Political Co-operation machinery. The idea of transforming the two bodies into a 'European Union' had emerged. Solutions to all these questions must, it was felt by the Ten Member States, be found before they could safely admit the two candidate countries, Portugal and Spain, with which accession negotiations had been in progress since 1978 and 1979 respectively. Faced with such strong economic pressures, the Community Institutions found it difficult to summon up the political will to confront these wide-ranging, strategic issues. Thorn was not the man to give the lead Member States were entitled to expect from the Commission President. Progress was painfully slow. It was not until mid-1984 that the first clear orientations were taken, at a European Council meeting in Fontainebleau.

The arrival of the Delors Commission in 1985 heralded a dramatic increase in tempo. Jacques Delors was – and to this day remains – the strongest and most effective President the Commission has ever had. His other Commissioners were probably not on average better than their immediate predecessors: indeed, the departure of Stevie Davignon constituted a weakening. The difference was that the Commission as a whole was led by Delors with tremendous imagination, verve, political nous and determination. He gained the respect of the Heads of Government in a way no predecessor or successor has ever done. By the end of his first year of office, solutions had been found to all the problems just described. Most important of all, the text had been agreed of the Single European Act, the most important set of amendments to the Community Treaties since the EEC and Euratom had been set up in 1958. This in turn enabled Spain and Portugal to join the Community in January 1986. These momentous developments had, in the space of little over a year, raised the morale of the Community Institutions from very low to very high.

If energy has not been highlighted above, this is not because of doubts about its importance. The lessons of 1973, when the Yom Kippur War had triggered a doubling of the oil price, to reach $25 a barrel, had not been forgotten. The Iranian revolution of 1979, followed by the outbreak of the Iran-Iraq War, when the oil price re-doubled to reach $51, had rammed them home. Energy had thus become an ongoing and major international pre-occupation, and so remained throughout the six years now being reviewed. It was constantly on the agendas of the Commission, Parliament, the Council, the European Council and the Western Economic Summits. The determination to reduce Community dependence on Middle East oil – on which it had relied for around 50% of its total energy consumption in 1973 – was as great as ever. Important moves had been made in this direction. A new international body – the International Energy Agency [IEA] – had been set up in 1974, as an autonomous authority within the framework of the OECD in Paris. There, the energy policies of the European Community were co-ordinated with those of the rest of the industrialised world.

Within the Community, the first oil shock had gravely strained solidarity, with individual Member States even trying to secure bilateral assurances of supply from individual oil-producing countries. But, over the years, wiser counsels had gradually prevailed. Len Williams had laboured steadily to help the Community get its act together. And in mid-1980 the Council had finally adopted a Resolution containing Community specific energy objectives for 1990: their main aims were to replace oil by alternative sources, especially coal or nuclear; and to dissociate economic growth from energy consumption, notably by energy saving measures. The Resolution had no binding legal force. But the Commission was mandated to monitor, and report to the Council, on how the Member States were performing in relation to these; and this created a political pressure on each of them to deliver.

Len had been handicapped by working under a Commissioner, Guido Brunner, who carried little weight with Energy Ministers. Now, however, that Stevie Davignon had succeeded Guido, it was clear that he would want the Commission to play a much more prominent role; that he would engage his own authority; and that he would look to his new Director-General for strong support. It was a challenge I liked. But the task was not easy. For historical reasons the status of energy in the basic Treaties was uneven. The Paris Treaty, which established the ECSC, dated from 1951. At that time, coal and steel were still regarded as key strategic raw materials, and so the Treaty gave the Community Institutions extensive powers of intervention. By the same token, when the Rome Treaty establishing the European Atomic Energy Community [or Euratom] was signed, some six years later, the peaceful use of nuclear materials, a process in its infancy, was seen as needing close control: here, too, the Community Institutions received extensive powers. By contrast, the other Rome Treaty, establishing the European Economic Community, had nothing to say about general energy policy. This reflected the fact that, although the Community's dependence on oil from the Persian Gulf had been steadily growing, the area had then been seen as generally stable. Thus, whereas there was to be, for example, a Common Agricultural Policy and a Common Transport Policy, there was no suggestion of a Common Energy Policy. The energy sector was dealt with only indirectly, in the sense that it was covered by the horizontal provisions of the EEC Treaty – for example on the internal market, on free movement, on competition and on social questions.

Nor were the Member States, in 1981, in a mood to grant major new powers to the Institutions. When, therefore, we needed a legal base for Community action in energy sectors not covered by the first two Treaties, we had to resort to Article 235 of the EEC Treaty – the so-called evolutive Article. Although this allowed the Council to authorise measures whenever necessary, its use was subject to the unanimity rule, and unanimity amongst the 10 Member States was not easy to secure. That, then, was the energy picture in the Community when I became Director-General. During my tenure of that office – a period of five and a half years – there were to be major developments. These are now summarised, but only briefly because we shall return to most of them – and cover other issues too – as the story unfolds.

Higher oil prices – coupled with the perceived need to diversify sources of supply – had provoked much greater efforts of exploration for hydrocarbon resources. These progressively brought on stream new oil and gas fields, most notably in the North Sea. Pipelines were built, to carry gas from these, and also from Algeria and the USSR. Oil used for electricity production was substantially replaced by coal, and later by the coming on

The new Director-General for Energy at his desk, 1981.

stream of numerous nuclear power plants in Europe and the United States. Thanks to energy saving, the 'energy intensity' of the industrialised world – in other words the amount of energy needed to support a given level of economic activity – fell sharply. Strategic stocks of oil were built up in Europe, North America and Japan, and could be used, not only in case of a supply crisis, but also to moderate the scale of oil-price movements.

All these factors combined to reduce the ability of OPEC, and in particular the oil-producing countries around the Persian Gulf, to control the price of oil. On the positive side, these countries and the industrialised world both came to accept that dialogue would be more productive than confrontation. Gradually the oil price stabilised; and from 1983 onwards, it began to fall. It became clear that the Community's 1990 energy objectives were likely to be met; and the Commission persuaded the Council to adopt fresh objectives for 1995. In a word, energy policy seemed to be progressing well until, in April 1986, the Chernobyl explosion raised big new questions in the public mind about the wisdom of reliance on nuclear power. This was so important that I have devoted the whole of the following chapter to my involvement in it.

The Directorate-General for Energy

The Directorate-General for Energy – usually known in those days as DG XVII – was both complex and large. It was complex for three reasons: it covered a wide range of subjects, many of which had a high technical content; they were handled under three different Treaties; and the staff of 400 were equally divided between Brussels and Luxembourg.

An early task for an incoming Director-General was to review human resources, and the way they were organised. I found that the average quality of the staff was very high; and that the structure was generally practical. A few changes nevertheless seemed desirable. These were quickly made. And, with my Commissioner's active support, it also proved possible to bring in additional high-flyers from other services. Thereafter, an excellent structure and team were in place, and few organisational changes were made until I left. The Directorate-General now had six Directorates. To help paint a picture of my own workload, it will be useful to recall briefly the duties of each, and also the names of some of those who were key staff members of the Directorate-General for most of my time.

Directorate A, led by Clive Jones and Robert De Bauw, dealt with horizontal questions: most importantly with energy policy as a whole; but also with energy relations with non-Community countries; with analysis and forecasting; and with ensuring that our budgetary expenditures, even if delegated in many cases to other Directorates, were subject to horizontal disciplines. Directorate B, led by Karl-Heinz [Charlie] Reichert, dealt with solid fuels: coal, lignite and peat. Directorate C, led by Georges Brondel, dealt with hydrocarbons: oil and gas. Directorate D, led by Fabrizio Caccia-Dominioni, dealt with policy on Nuclear Energy; and also with the important matter of negotiations with other countries, notably the United States, Canada and Australia, to settle the conditions on which they would supply to the Community's Member States their needs of nuclear materials for peaceful purposes. These were known as Euratom Supply Agreements. Directorate D also acquired, over time, a *de facto* position as co-ordinator, throughout <u>all</u> the Commission Services, of the application of the Euratom Treaty. And it shared with Directorate F responsibility for the Community's relations with the IAEA in Vienna. Directorate E, led by Michael Davis, dealt with energy saving, alternative sources of energy, and electricity.

Finally, Directorate F, led by Wilhelm [Willem] Gmelin, was responsible for the application, throughout the Community, of the Euratom Safeguards system, designed to ensure that nuclear materials were not diverted from peaceful purposes. This system was in turn 'verified' by IAEA Inspectors, under an agreement between Euratom and the Agency. The meaning of this opaque terminology will be explained later.

Initially, I had the support of an able Deputy Director-General [DDG], in the person of Michel Carpentier. For two or three years, this arrangement continued, and we worked happily in tandem. But then, when Stevie needed someone to run the expanding Commission IT programmes being developed under his authority, Michel was taken away for the purpose, and not replaced till after I left.

A Director-General in the Commission always has an 'Assistant'. This is a key position. The Assistant is a sort of Chief of Staff, or Adjutant. He must act as the eyes and ears of the boss, in many ways; advise on questions of personnel and administration; and always know what the boss thinks on everything. My first assistant was Rolf Meijer, succeeded later by Alberto Hasson. Both served me well. My Private Office – Betty, Renate and Helen James – were able to move with me from the Secretariat-General, providing marvellous continuity of support.

On my first Monday as Director-General I set a pattern maintained until my retirement. Having spent much of the weekend reading a mass of material collected by my Assistant and my Private Office, I held a meeting with my six Directors. Each was asked to outline his Directorate's topical issues, and make recommendations. Each received the clearest guidance I could offer. Once the pattern was established, and the Directors had got used to it, I aimed to finish these weekly meetings within 60 minutes, getting through perhaps 20 points, and usually succeeded. Obviously, if issues came up which needed deeper study, a special meeting with officials concerned was set up for later. The system worked well. It meant that, at the beginning of each week, I could form a clear and up-to-date overview of the Directorate-General's affairs.

Another point on which I insisted was the importance of considering, at all times, the wider pattern within which our energy work must be handled. First and foremost, we needed to relate to other Directorates-General of the Commission, looking always for interfaces, and trying to use them for mutual support, never competitively. Beyond that, we needed to relate well to other Community Institutions, to all the Member States, to Third Countries and to other International Organisations. For me, after a career spent mainly in multilateral diplomacy, all this was obvious. But many officials had been allowed to think in narrower terms. I sought always to broaden horizons.

For four years my relations with my Commissioner, Stevie Davignon, were close, confident and productive. His work pattern included a regular weekly meeting with his Directors-General, attended by his Chefcab. Besides the latter and myself, those present were Fernand Braun [Industry], Paolo Fasella [Research and Science], and Michel Carpentier [at first along with me, later in his new IT capacity]. Not infrequently, Stevie kept us waiting. But, once one <u>did</u> get to see him, it was rewarding. We got through so much business so fast. With his retentive memory there was never a need to repeat things. He was incisive and had many flashes of inspiration. And he was an expert at lateral thinking and on political tactics. These weekly meetings were not of course my only encounters with the Commissioner. He was readily accessible. It was wise, also, to keep a weather eye on his appointments diary. Not infrequently one would see two or three over-lapping engagements. This simply meant Stevie was keeping his options open to the last minute. His Director-General concerned might be required to 'cover' for any of these engagements at minimal notice: 'be prepared' was the order of the day. Needless to say, working for Stevie was both challenging and enriching. As he had a keen sense of humour, it was also good fun.

But, in January 1985, the pattern dramatically changed. Stevie left the Commission to become President of the vast Société-Général de Belgique. Under the incoming Delors Commission the energy portfolio was allocated to Nic Mosar, the Commissioner from Luxembourg. After working for the most brilliant Commissioner of all time, I now had to operate under the authority of the dullest! As an individual, Nic was kind and absolutely charming. But his mind moved very slowly; his memory was poor; and he had no political judgement.

Outwardly, nothing changed. I and my Directors probably met with our Commissioner and his Cabinet as often as before. But it was chalk and cheese. We went there to explain. He simply listened. It was clear that, often, he did not understand. Particularly trying were those occasions when I had to get his approval for matters arising under the Euratom Treaty, usually to do with safeguards. The Treaty is highly technical and complex, and he could never remember the first thing about it. I would have to start with the opening gambit: '*Commissioner, you recall the Euratom Treaty?*' Re-assured on this point, I would then need to remind him that it contained, for example, a Chapter about Safeguards. It would take some time before I could even approach the specific matter in hand. And so it went on: time after time, for all the twenty-one months he was my Commissioner.

Commissioner Stevie Davignon says goodbye to the
Directorate General for Energy, 1984.

Outsiders could see the situation. I was actually taking almost all the decisions. If I felt political cover was necessary, it had to be obtained by other methods. One was for me to inform Jacques Delors' very able Chefcab, Pascal Lamy [now himself a Commissioner], of what I was proposing to Nic, knowing he would tell me if the President was likely to see a problem. Another was to advise Nic that the matter was so important he should put it to the full Commission. Such situations are embarrassing, and difficult to manage. It was lucky that, when the problem arose, I had such a range of Community experience behind me. A consolation was that, when others perceive such a situation, they usually do their best to help the hapless Director-General.

A Director-General must feel answerable for everything done under his authority. He must know what is going on. But he should feel confident – and I was – that most of the work can safely be delegated to his staff. He should reserve his own main efforts for areas of activity where his personal involvement is most necessary, and/or will give the best return. The reader will not therefore be burdened with any detailed or comprehensive account of the Directorate-General's work during my time. Anyone wishing for that should refer to the energy and associated chapters of the annual 'General Report on the Activities of the European Communities', as published by the Commission, for the years 1981-86. Instead, this narrative will try to give a feel for this part of my own life by commenting on a selection of energy matters with which I had a particularly strong personal involvement.

To be of value, a Director-General must have or develop close relations with an enormous number of people. Before moving to energy I already knew many who would continue to be useful, such as Permanent Representatives; MEPs; Senior Officials of other Institutions; and a wide variety of people of influence in all the Member States. Over time, I was now to build up an additional range of specifically energy contacts. They included the Energy Ministers of the Twelve Member States, and their most senior supporting officials; top dogs in UNICE and ETUC; leading figures in several international organisations, notably the IEA, the IAEA, OPEC, OAPEC and the Gulf Co-operation Council [GCC]; key energy personalities in the Administrations of third countries, whether from the industrialised or developing worlds; top dogs in every branch of European energy industries; and media people concerned with energy. These categories are not exhaustive. Reviewing the hundreds of names of those I met, has shown me how very extensive the list became.

Amongst these different groups, there was one of special importance: the Senior Officials of Member States who represented their country in the High-Level Energy Group [HLEG], the body which did most of the preparatory work for meetings of the Energy Council. With all these people, I was on first-name and friendly terms, and could discuss anything, frankly and with mutual confidence. The same was true with the top people in all the international organisations just mentioned.

Running the Community's energy policy involved frequent attendance at meetings of Chefcabs, the Commission, the HLEG, CRP 2 and the Energy Council. It was also to involve attendance at occasional European Councils or Western Economic Summits. The normal pattern was that each six-month Presidency would chair one Energy Council, which in turn would be prepared by one or two meetings of the HLEG. Often, there would also be an 'Informal Meeting of Energy Ministers', in the Presidency country. Before each Presidency began, there would be energy meetings with it, at Commissioner level and at my level: these would be repeated just before an

Energy Council or an HLEG. There were also occasional, informal meetings with members of the Energy Working Group of the Council, where the Commission was always represented by one or more of my Directors. There was frequent attendance at Parliament's Committee on Energy, Research and Technology. When dealing with things that were specifically nuclear, however, one was usually faced with a rather different behaviour pattern.

There was much speechifying to be done: here I relied heavily on the support of two excellent ghost-writers – David McGlue and Martin Power. Finally the running of the Directorate-General, and co-operation with other Directorate-Generals, involved me in a wide range of Inter-Divisional and Inter-Departmental meetings. So much then, by way of introduction. I now turn to the promised selection of energy matters with which I had a strong personal involvement.

Conventional energy issues

There was a lot going on in my 'horizontal Directorate' [Directorate A]. But most of the work took place in the Council Working Group, so did not very directly involve me. It will be recalled that the Council had adopted a Resolution laying down targets for 1990, and calling on the Commission to monitor performance by the individual Member States. This was a continuing commitment, and required a lot of work from the officials concerned. It was on the basis of their observations under this head, and their analysis and forecasting, moreover, that they proceeded to work out, with the other Directorates, new proposals for developing the 'Community's Energy Strategy', which went forward to the Council in the autumn of 1981. The term was carefully chosen, so as to avoid any objection that we were trying to introduce a 'Common Energy Policy' by the back door, though in fact we were. There were five priorities: investment in alternatives to oil and energy saving; developing a common approach to energy pricing and taxation; establishing Community solidarity to avoid oil market instability; reinforcing common policies on R & D and technological demonstration; and, finally, further developing common approaches in external energy relations. This communication was broadly approved. Later, it was followed by a series of more specific communications, dealing with individual aspects of energy policy. In 1985, the Commission proposed new Energy Objectives for ten years ahead. As finally approved, after some tergiversation in the Council, the primary objectives were to limit reliance on oil to around 40% of energy consumption; to keep Community net oil imports at less than one-third of total energy consumption; to improve energy efficiency by at least 20%; to reduce the proportion of electricity generated from oil to less than 15%; to increase the share of solid fuels in the energy balance, and maintain the share of natural gas; and substantially to increase the contribution made by new and renewable sources in place of conventional fuels. These objectives were finally adopted by the Council during September 1986, my last month of office, representing a major achievement by the Directorate-General.

The various demonstration and technology projects being run by the Directorate-General gradually grew, in terms both of size and scope. They had to be monitored and held together. Our budget, mainly used to finance these projects, moved from 100 MECUs in 1980 to 160 MECUs in 1986. By the time I joined the Directorate-General the projects covered energy saving and alternative energies. The last heading included solar; geothermy; and liquefaction and gasification of solid fuels: wind-turbines were added in 1983. I took occasions to see some of these.

Perhaps it is worth saying, in this connection, that I was personally much involved in trying to get greater continuity in all these demonstration projects. But we were always up against the opposition of the Netherlands, British and German Delegations, on budgetary grounds. Gradually we wore them down. In the end, the Germans stood alone. Finally, they caved in. Next time there was a tendering exercise, my Services came to me with the news that over 40% of the best projects were German! What should they do? I felt my Commissioner should be alerted. He had only one question: 'Are you sure these are the best projects?' When I said 'Yes!', that was the end of the matter. The Germans got all their projects.

Then, in 1983 and 1984, in the context of wider budgetary adjustments in favour of the United Kingdom & the Federal Republic of Germany, the Commission granted aid of 1,240 MECUs for energy projects in the two countries: mainly for nuclear reactors, but also for gas and coal projects. All this money passed through the Directorate-General. Fortunately, however, we were not expected to exercise any direct control over how the money was used: just as well, since we were given no extra staff!

My first external involvement, on behalf of the Commission, was not in a Community body at all, but rather in the so-called High-Level Monitoring Group [HLMG], which was to meet at the beautifully situated Banff Springs Hotel in Canada on 25 May, 1981. This Group had been established by the WES, and its purpose was to monitor the extent to which the different members, by now including the Community as such, were reacting to the challenges posed by the energy situation and thus meeting the 'Venice Energy Objectives' of May 1980. I flew to Calgary the day before. The Group passed off quietly. It was a good occasion to meet informally with Ulf Lantzke, Executive Director of the IEA, and other colleagues in the same body. The latter included Rodric Braithwaite, who had been Head of Chancery in the UK Delegation to the European Communities but had now moved to become Head of my old Department in the Foreign Office, by then called Energy, Science and Space Department.

Maura rang me that evening to say my mother had died. This was very sad, but no surprise. When I had seen her a month before, I felt it unlikely we should greet each other in this world again. I now wrote in my diary: *'I could not wish it otherwise. Michael and Elizabeth had both told me in the last few days that she was desperately weak and unable to recognise anyone. It's very much the end of an era. I see no way of keeping Ackenthwaite in the family.'* How wrong can one be? The funeral, which I attended, was five days later. Before we came together for it, Michael, to whom the house had been left by my father, had made clear he wanted to sell it. After consulting our three children, Maura and I had agreed to buy it. Michael was generous over the sale. And, on 4 August, 1981, the family home passed into my hands.

My next Community exposure was to the Energy Council. Almost my first act as Director-General had been to visit the Dutch Chairman of the HLEG in The Hague, Tieleman. Now followed a meeting of the Group. This was prepared, first with Stevie, and then with Tieleman. The Commission representative – myself – was expected to take a lead on all points. Soon after that, came an Energy Council in Luxembourg.

It was not until November that year that I first attended a meeting of the IEA Governing Board in Paris. A personal *rapport* had by now been established with Ulf Lantzke: after Banff, I had twice been to the IEA for talks on oil matters. The normal IEA Board meeting held to a clear pattern. It met about three times a year. I went up the evening before, and attended a dinner of the Heads of Delegation. Next morning there was a Community co-ordination meeting; then the Board meeting; and then a train home. In addition to these standard meetings, there were also occasionally more informal gatherings, known as 'Dourdan-type' because the first had been at Dourdan, a Château near Paris. Finally, once a year, there was a Board meeting at Ministerial level, to which I accompanied the Commissioner.

Sitting in CRP, I had seen nothing directly of the IEA. But, as I became used to it, I realised how it could be used as a means of extending the Community's influence to a wider world. Thereafter the HLEG lunches proved a useful means of preparing the Community's position at the IEA, the membership having a lot of commonality. As the years went by, the Community operated more and more together in the IEA. Indeed I was touched when, at my last Governing Board meeting, Helga Steeg, who had succeeded Ulf as Executive Director, commented warmly on my ability to co-ordinate and 'deliver' the Community on key issues, where Community competence was usually limited. It is time to consider what some of those issues were.

Solid fuels gave me much work, chiefly as regards projects for the liquefaction and gasification of coal; and also as regards state aids for coal, which we were trying to reduce. My chief recollections in this sector are of visits made to various industrial installations. These included the Kellingley colliery in Yorkshire, then one of Britain's most modern; the Rheinbraun open-cast lignite mine near Cologne – so deep that Cologne Cathedral could have stood in it without its spire being visible; and a Bord na Mona peat extraction site in Ireland, where peat was being stripped out at a phenomenal rate.

The visit to Kellingley was made in summer, 1981, when we were on holiday at Ackenthwaite. William went with me; and was entertained by the miners having clearly decided to take the micky. When we went to change, I first discovered two left boots in my bag of clothes. Once that 'error' had been rectified, the changing started. Next, I found a pair of underpants big enough for an elephant – with no draw-string. These were exchanged for a pair of Y-fronts about right for a twelve-year old! Somehow I struggled in, and our walk-about started. Underground, I found little had altered since my visit to a deep Saar coal-mine in the 1950s – except that the extraction machinery had become a lot noisier.

Looking back on my time working with solid fuels, I am chiefly struck by the fact that, right until I left in the autumn of 1986, the Commission was still pushing coal use to the maximum, on grounds of diversification of energy supplies. There was no mention by the Directorate-General for the Environment of global warming. Its attention was still focused on things like drinking water standards and exhaust emissions from motor vehicles. Times change!

On hydrocarbons I recall chiefly the growing importance of gas in Community energy supplies. When I arrived it was still being treated as a scarce resource, to be carefully husbanded. The Directorate-General was constantly arguing that it should not therefore be used in electricity generation. As it was by now clear that new gas resources were coming on stream, both abroad and at home, I used to question this with my officials.

But it got me nowhere. Our position remained essentially unchanged throughout my time, although in 1986 the Commission was publicly recognising the importance of the new Norwegian fields. It amuses me to see today that, since recognition of the threat from greenhouse gases, half of all the electricity in the UK which formerly came from oil, comes from gas. And we are now beginning to import gas from overseas.

A principal action of the Community as regards hydrocarbons was the hydrocarbon technology projects scheme. Here, the *pièce de résistance* was Community support for the technology needed for construction of the Trans-Mediterranean pipeline to carry gas from Algeria to the European continent.

I was able to visit the BP Forties Oilfield in August 1981. As things turned out, there had been fatal helicopter crashes in the North Sea on each of the two preceding days. The BP staff were nervous. Fog descended, and we were held on shore till 1700 hours. But we finally made it; I sat by the pilot for the approach; and the visit was instructive. *Inter alia* I learnt that, even then, there were more than 10,000 staff on the British North Sea platforms at any one time.

Another principal action – indeed it took more and more of my time – was to build bridges towards the Middle East oil producers, and notably those of the Gulf. Although the Western Governments were beginning to pay lip service to the idea, none were willing to act. It seemed to us in the Commission that there was a disharmony, and that perhaps the Commission could do something to improve matters.

Soon after assuming office I was invited to one of the regular meetings of the 'Oxford Energy Policy Club', organised by Robert Mabro at St Anthony's College. (Later, the Club effectively spawned the Oxford Energy Institute, a free-standing Institute whose Governing Board contained nine non-British members, including the Commission.) These Policy Club meetings proved invaluable. They brought together, in a completely informal way, people with influence from both oil-producing and oil-consuming parts of the world.

The most striking performer was Ali Attiga, the Secretary-General of the Organisation of Arab Oil Producing Countries [OAPEC], based in Kuwait. From the start, I found Ali to be both moderate and trustworthy: he appeared to see me in the same light. By 1982, our Directorate-General had started holding informal bilateral talks with OAPEC, the venues alternating between Kuwait and Brussels. Meanwhile the Commission's Deputy Director-General for External Relations, Jean Durieux, had started informal talks with the Gulf Co-operation Council [GCC]; and these too acquired an energy component. I became a fairly frequent visitor to the Persian Gulf or, as I soon learned to call it when speaking to Arabs, the Arabian Gulf.

My first, exploratory visit was in November 1982, and took me to Cairo, Ryadh and Kuwait. Cairo was included simply because there were then no Saudia flights from Brussels. I was accompanied by Georges Brondel, my Hydrocarbons Director. We spent a Saturday sightseeing in Cairo before flying on to Ryadh. Although upwards of 40 years had passed since my last visit, and Cairo had grown enormously, it was not much altered in character. My diary noted: *'Countryside little changed…Donkey carts, camels and ibis. Teeming kids. Primitive houses. Days short. In the office, it's 8 a.m. till 2 p.m. People retire at 60. There are 2 or 3 people per real job. Our dragoman grumbles he gets more money, but it goes no farther.'*

That evening we flew on to Ryadh. There we found a surge of vitality, reflecting the wealth which two oil-price hikes had injected into the economy. *'The Hotel is brand new, like most things here. Thirty years ago, Ryadh was a small township. Today, who knows? Some say 1 million inhabitants. A grid of roads extends huge distances. Water is brought for hundreds of miles by pipe-line. Buildings spring up to fill empty spaces at colossal speed. Everything appears to be done by foreign labour. Saudis seem to be mainly businessmen or officials. The streets are swept [beautifully] by a Korean Company. We are served in the Hotel by Thais, Filipinos and so forth.'* It was a modern 'Arabian Nights'.

We were looked after by James Craig, the then British Ambassador, whom I had helped induct into the ways of the Foreign Office, years before in African Department, and the Danish [Presidency] Ambassador. We saw Farouk al Husseini, Director-General of Economics at the Petroleum Ministry; and Abdullah El-Kuwaiz, Associate Secretary-General for Economic Affairs of the Gulf Co-operation Council [GCC]. We formed the impression that the recently formed GCC was getting its act together.

Then we were off to Kuwait. We had all been given seat allocations; but much time was lost while the passengers were re-arranged so that no veiled lady was sitting next to a man other than her husband! Why Saudia allow their air hostesses to wear body-hugging Western-style uniforms remained a mystery. In Kuwait, where we were under the wing of Ali Attiga, things went smoothly. In particular, our talks at OAPEC Headquarters were frank and direct. We also fitted in a visit to Shuaiba Oil Refinery. We closed with a briefing for Community Ambassadors: they were happy, but it was painful for us to see how little they knew about oil, let alone about energy policy.

My diary noted: *'Kuwait is certainly an unusual country. Climate-wise it's super*

EEC-OAPEC talks: Ali Attiga, OAPEC Secretary-General,
with the author, Georges Brondel and Robert De Bauw, Brussels, 1983.

in winter. Grasses spring up. But in summer temperatures rise to 50 degrees centigrade and there's just sand. Till 1937, when they found oil, the country was peopled by Bedouin, and Kuwait City was a handful of houses. Now, the population is over 1 million, mostly in the City, and 60% of them are foreign. Kuwaitis keep lots of privileges: cheap land, a right to a University education, and so forth – but for how long?… Virtually nothing is produced, except oil and its derivatives: all else is imported at fiercely competitive prices. But land is at a premium. A plot like mine [in Brussels], would cost £1 million in Kuwait. You can retire after 20 years, on a pension equal to 80% of salary. Buildings are replaced after only 20 years, as maintenance is poor. Because the sand used was too saline for the mortar, they now import sand! As in Ryadh, architects have marvellous opportunities. The Kuwait Towers [with bulges like golf balls] are an example. After they were built, the Scenic Tower could not be used for a year, as the Emir decided he didn't want people to see into his garden!' More 'Arabian Nights'!

This first visit had convinced me that it was worth while to spend time in the Gulf. In the autumn of 1983, however, it was the turn of OAPEC to come to Brussels; so my second visit to the Gulf was in December 1984. This time I had three companions: Robert De Bauw to advise on general policy, Jacques Michaux covering hydrocarbons, and Bob Hull covering the

GCC angle. We had good talks with two of the Executive Managing Directors of Kuwait Petroleum Company [KPC]. Then there was a fascinating hour with the Minister of Oil, Sheikh Ali al Khalifa al Sabah, who was also Minister of Finance and President of KPC, a man with very wide experience, a quick mind and a sense of humour. He was fearful of a collapse in the price of oil. We talked of the Community's aim of reaching a Co-operation Agreement with the GCC, when he emphasised the problems for Gulf producers of exporting petro-chemicals. I was able to respond that the Community was relatively liberal, Japan much less so. This time our talks with OAPEC were followed by a press conference. Questions flew thick and fast for 90 minutes. Why was the Community protectionist on imports of petro-chemicals? Why were we pro-Israel? Why were we boosting our oil production? Why were we trying to reduce our oil imports? The press conference attracted much coverage throughout the Middle East.

It was by now the Arab weekend. So we flew to Jeddah, where I spent the Friday with Sir Patrick Wright [the new British Ambassador[1]] and his wife Virginia, looking at coral reefs from a friend's boat; and then flew on to Ryadh. My diary takes over again. *'Visiting this part of the world can be compared with the Muslim Haj, or pilgrimage. You must set out in faith; you must press through to your destination; but only Allah knows what will happen during the journey. Thus, at breakfast, we had no word from Abdullah El-Kuwaiz of the GCC, who had said he wanted to see me. It turned out he had asked his Secretary to arrange things, but somehow this had not happened. When we rang at 0900 hours we were told the only chance was to come at once. We did – and were rewarded by a friendly reception, a useful talk and an invitation to dinner. Our next meeting, with Farouk al Husseini of the Petroleum Ministry, was similarly haphazard. He explained he had gone to the Airport to meet us the previous evening; but Saudia without warning landed at the other terminal! Our meeting was meant to last an hour and a half, but overshot by an hour! It was all friendly and useful.'*

Later we reported to the Member States' representatives at the British Embassy. I told them our experience showed there was a big need for more Commission contact with this part of the world. There was so much to explain and discuss; and so many are willing to listen. Bob Hull and I then joined Abdullah El-Kuwaiz for dinner at the Equestrian Club, where he talked a lot. *'The GCC was going slower than he'd hoped. But it was definitely moving. Countries were now really working together, which was not easy to achieve in the Arab World: Arab diversity made it hard to convert Pan-Arabism into anything practical. Perhaps that was why the GCC was now 'accepted' by the other Arabs, even Arab media, and was not the subject of complaints. In reply to a chance question it* emerged – complete news to the Directorate-General for External Relations – that the US had suggested a free trade relationship; that the Secretariat did not favour the idea, partly because it had been offered to Israel and partly because of doubt as to whether the Administration could 'deliver' Congress; and that all this had been reported to the GCC Council.'

On the way back to Brussels, I stopped in Amman and signed an Agreement with the Minister for Planning under which the Commission would, over three years, provide technical assistance to help the Jordanians build up their new Energy Ministry. This gave me an opportunity to fulfil an ambition of thirty-five years, by getting to see Petra.

My final visit to the Middle East as Director-General took place in April 1986. I travelled out, this time, with Jean Durieux, who was leading the European Community team for official talks with the GCC, and Robert De Bauw. We flew from Paris to Ryadh; lost half an hour through having to discharge a VIP at the Royal Terminal before being decanted ourselves at the International one; and then another 45 minutes clearing customs. It was hoped by both sides that the GCC talks would be seminal, and so it turned out. The Community side wanted to be able, at the end, to prepare a request to the Council for a mandate to negotiate a Co-operation Agreement. My personal aim was to convince the GCC people that regular exchanges of view on energy would really be useful.

We must have had 14 hours of talks over two consecutive days. (It was during the first day that we heard of the Chernobyl explosion.) From the Commission, there was a team of nine; on the other side we had not only the GCC Secretariat people, led by Ma'moon Kurdi and Sulaiman Jassir al Harbash, but also representatives of all six GCC States. I was impressed by the extent to which the GCC side had honed their act. Their arguments displayed a shrewd knowledge of international trade principles and precedents which had been totally lacking before. On the energy front I tackled head-on the reasons why we had been buying massively less oil from the Gulf; why people in Europe don't usually see the Gulf Countries as reliable suppliers; and whether new import duties on oil could be headed off. We ended by adopting a very brief communiqué, but also a three-page agreed summary record of discussions. The latter set out a common understanding of what the proposed Agreement should say on energy. It also recorded that we would initiate at once, without waiting for the Agreement, regular exchanges of view on energy issues. Gratifyingly, this had been suggested by the GCC. And the first such meeting took place in Brussels that September.

Then, on to Kuwait. My diary records a great sense of contrast. *'At Riyadh, a Westerner can go for days and see no woman without a chador. There are virtually no entertainments, apart from eating; no worthwhile shops; and no real culture. At Kuwait, it is the opposite. Almost all women are dressed western-style; have bright-coloured clothes; and can be very elegant. There are smart boutiques, beautiful shops, and various tourist attractions. Besides, you're on the sea. People are smiling and vivacious, while at Riyadh they're mostly solemn and serious.'*

This visit to Kuwait was short. There was a 90-minute meeting with Ali Attiga and his staff. I said it was a day both sad and happy: sad because I should not come again as Director-General; and happy because I felt that, with Ali and OAPEC, we had done much to improve relations between the European Community and the Arab World. Ali, after a generous reply, gave me a surprise by presenting a beautiful Arab coffee jug and cups. He also invited me to lecture in Kuwait after retirement. We called on Sheikh Ali Khalifa al Sabah. There was straight talking for half an hour. The Sheikh amazed my colleagues by spending much of the time with one bare foot on the sofa, massaging his big toe! That night, at 0200 hours, I left Kuwait Airport for Amsterdam, seen off by Usameh Jamali and Ajwad Hamad.

To complete the picture of the relationship I established with the Oil Producers I should add that there also contacts with OPEC. Nuclear questions took me not infrequently to Vienna. I used these occasions also to meet Fadhil Al Chalabi, Director-General of the Organisation. These contacts were informal: it had to be so, since not all OPEC countries favoured talking with the Community. But they were nevertheless of great value. Conversely, although we followed the work of the Euro-Arab Dialogue, we soon found there was no serious place for energy in it.

My considerable, direct involvement in hydrocarbons also had to do with oil refineries and the Japanese. After the first oil crisis, the Middle East oil producers had felt they would like to increase their own profits by undertaking downstream refining activities, instead of simply exporting crude oil. They had therefore constructed a number of refineries. The oil majors, who had until then had refining to themselves, felt threatened. They at first urged Western Governments to discourage the Middle East producers. But this had no effect. Indeed the Gulf countries in particular, as we have seen, were demanding free entry for their refined products to the Community; or at the least the avoidance by the industrialised countries of any increase in tariffs.

Things came to a head in 1985. In March that year the Commission proposed to the Council guidelines on refineries and the import of petroleum products. In particular, it suggested that the European Community should make room for such imports from the Gulf countries, which would involve some rationalisation (down-sizing) of domestic refineries. The Council accepted this approach on condition that the Americans and Japanese agreed to act similarly. The Americans, though unenthusiastic, confirmed that they were in a broadly similar position. I was instructed by the Commission, supported by the Member States, to try and get the Japanese on board. This was a tall order. However, I departed for Japan at end-May.

There was time for a weekend of sightseeing *en route* for Tokyo, and my small party was able to gain impressions of Kyoto and Nara. This time I was accompanied by Robert De Bauw. We were unexpectedly invited by Mr Yamada, the Manager of the Nippon Oil Company, to a geisha evening at the Tsuruya Restaurant in Kyoto, which took place in the room where The Queen and the Duke of Edinburgh had been received at an earlier date.

When I mentioned this event, some time later, to a German Diplomat, he told me that Helmut Kohl, when Federal Chancellor, had visited Japan and been invited by the Government to a similar Tsuruya occasion. He had wanted to refuse, but then accepted *Auswärtiges Amt* advice that this would give offence. Next he had been affronted to learn his wife was not included; but had again accepted advice that a request on her behalf would be ill-received. On arrival in Tokyo, he had asked for more details about the entertainment. When told it would involve his sitting on the floor, he flatly refused, and could not be budged. Finally his hosts agreed that those at the Kohl party should sit up at a Western-style table for the evening. This caused the utmost confusion. Geishas kneel when serving guests. This convention was observed; but the poor girls were at their wits' end trying to help guests who were sitting above their heads!

The weekend behind us, we plunged into a dense series of talks. Most of the first day was with MITI, where we worked through a huge agenda under the chairmanship of Director-General Shibata. I was putting over the idea that there was much on which we could both benefit by exchanging views. The message got across. On the other hand, on refineries and the need for Japan to take some of the extra petroleum products from the Middle East, there were sympathetic noises, but no bankable assurances. After leaving MITI, and at their suggestion, meetings had been arranged with, first, the President and Vice-Presidents of the Petroleum Association of Japan; and, second, the Japanese National Oil Corporation [JNOC]. It was chalk and cheese.

The meeting with the Association was rough. I was accompanied by

Robert De Bauw and Laurens-Jan Brinkhorst, the Commission's experienced representative in Tokyo. He had advised me to call a spade a spade; but we had agreed that he would pluck my sleeve if I went too far. He never did. On the Japanese side, the Chairman was a very old gentleman, hard as nails. The Vice-Presidents were similar. I made a moderate presentation of my message on petroleum products. The President replied by an extremely aggressive statement: his association thought opening up the market would not be in the Japanese national interest. There was a Japanese law which provided that the country should be self-sufficient in refinery capacity. This should not be changed. This provoked me into some sharp criticisms. I remarked *inter alia* that Japan had no domestic oil production; that 90% of Japanese imports of crude oil came from the Persian Gulf; and that the Community and the United States were prepared to accept imports of refined products. I asked where Japan would expect to get the crude for its domestic refineries if there were again to be an oil shortage. These remarks provoked no response. It was clear that prolonging the meeting would bring no benefits, so I left.

The meeting with the JNOC was completely different. They had interesting things to tell us about the operation of their Government's oil stock policy, and they wanted to hear about our Hydrocarbon Technology Project Scheme, which the Japanese were copying.

Next morning, Laurens-Jan had arranged a working breakfast with leading Members of the Diet and the Deputy Chief Cabinet Secretary. Then came talks at the Science and Technology Agency; an interview with the *Nihon Keizai Shimbun*, the leading economic newspaper, which later ran it prominently; lunch and a meeting with the Federation of Electric Power Companies; a half-hour speech on Community energy policy to the prestigious Committee for Energy Policy Promotion; and finally a dinner organised by Dr Ikuta, President of the Institute of Energy Economics and a colleague in the Oxford Energy Policy Club, which was attended by some twenty industrialists, including oil industry top dogs. This last was a robust but friendly gathering. After all this, I told Laurens-Jan that, while it had all been of great interest, the pace had been rather too hot! The next day, after a working breakfast with the Director-General of MITI's Petroleum Department, a meeting with Community Ambassadors, a one-hour press Conference, and a final working lunch at Laurens-Jan's home, I was off to more meetings in Washington.

It is never easy to say what effect such encounters have. Certainly there was no instant movement in the Japanese official position. However,

I suspect that MITI had promoted the idea of a discussion with the Petroleum Association partly in order to expose me directly to the industry, but also to expose the industry to hearing directly the European side of the argument. At all events, things moved. At the IEA Ministerial meeting in July, only four months later, __all__ participating countries undertook to maintain or provide freedom of access to their markets for oil products, particularly for those from new refineries in the Middle East. There is no doubt that the Community had played a leading role in procuring this undertaking. It may be worth adding that the Japanese Government later had the refineries law altered to give effect to its commitment.

I cannot close this passage about 'conventional' energy without some mention of a trip made to China in the autumn of 1985. It lasted eight days, and was fascinating but very tiring. It took place, by chance, at a peculiarly favourable moment of China's evolution: nearly a decade after the 'Cultural Revolution' had been brought to an end by Mr Deng driving out the 'Gang of Four', and four years before the shootings at Tiananmen Square.

Why did I go? I had not previously had strong, personal involvement in 'energy co-operation' with less-developed countries. Until he left us, this sector had been primarily in the hands of Michel Carpentier. He had made a strong start, and the work had been carried on by Hans-Eiche Von Scholz. By now, however, we were spending about 750,000 ECUs a year on China alone; the following year's budget had to be decided; and I felt a need to know more about our operation on the ground. Besides, anybody concerned with energy must be interested in a country which then consumed 8% of the world's energy, and whose proportion was rising fast, in line with phenomenal economic growth. The Chinese planned to quadruple their income over the next 15 years: this implied doubling their energy production – and their energy efficiency. Finally, I had been specifically invited to go by the State Science and Technology Commission.

Who were we? Because the co-operation programme was by now wide-ranging, I took other Commission officials with me. There was also a film-crew of two, as a film was being made about our energy co-operation programmes generally. At least two Chinese conducting officials went everywhere with us. So the party – and still more its baggage – was substantial.

Where did we go? Starting from Hong Kong, we flew to Beijing, where three full days were passed. Though they were busy, the first day was a Sunday, and we had the morning free to see the Great Wall and the Ming Tombs. On the third day we were also able to pay brief visits to the

Forbidden City and the Temple of Heaven. Thence we flew to Shanghai for a day, where we snatched an hour in the unforgettable National Museum. Then on by train to Nanjing for two nights. The following day was spent largely on a train journey to Hangzhou, where again two nights were spent. Hangzhou, called by Marco Polo the most beautiful city in the world, still has much charm, and is a frequent choice for Chinese honeymoons: we were able to enjoy a short boat trip on the Lake and visit the 'Valley of the Buddhas', of which there are over 160 cut in rock faces. Early next morning we left for Hong Kong and London.

What did we do, apart from the snippets of sightseeing? We saw a vast number of officials, especially in Beijing. First meetings were typically around 0800 hours. There were working lunches daily. There was also an official banquet for us on every night but one (when we were travelling by train). As a matter of courtesy, we ate everything put in front of us, excepting only 'sea-cucumber', which is a giant, translucent sea-slug! I signed a new Co-operation Agreement with the Head of the State Scientific and Technical Commission. We participated in an EC-China Workshop on rural energy planning in Asia, attended the closing ceremony of a Seminar at an EC-China Energy Training Centre, and inaugurated a new EC-China Energy Bus. We also visited a town running a bio-gas installation. It may not sound much when summarised. But in fact it kept us very busy. I was left in no doubt about the value of the operation as a whole.

A few impressions I gathered in China may be worth recalling. It was in an amazingly rapid state of evolution. For a decade before 1976, the Cultural Revolution had created chaos. Higher education was stopped completely. The Professors were sent to work in the ricefields. Religious observance was forbidden. Production fell. Thought was regimented. Clothing was uniform and drab. Then suddenly Mr Deng, at the age of around 75, set the country on a new course. By the time I was there, output had doubled; the army had been reduced and downgraded; the peasants – constituting four-fifths of the population – had been de-collectivised; the Party had been taken out of industrial management; the notions of economic pricing and cost-effectiveness had been introduced; foreigners had been invited in on a large scale to help build the economy; religion was permitted; discussion was free; people could spend their money as they liked; and so forth. Result: quite literally, a smiling population. Of course, life remained far from perfect. There was minimal space in the home. There was a six-day week, with no holidays apart from official ones. Nobody had a private car; buses were crowded; and trains scarce. But income had risen dramatically; and there was an overall sense of upswing. I hope all that was not too much set back by Tiananmen.

Nuclear issues

I turn now to the nuclear sector of the Directorate-General's work. Once more, I must recall the framework: very different from that of the EEC. We were operating within the rules of the Euratom Treaty. Soon after this had entered into force in the late 1950s, Euratom had contracted Agreements with the US and Canada [Supply Agreements], defining the terms under which these latter would supply nuclear materials to the Community. The agreements provided that such materials could be used only for peaceful purposes and that verification of this commitment would be undertaken by the Euratom Safeguards system.

Later, when the Non-Proliferation Treaty [NPT] was concluded, it was agreed that the safeguards to be applied by the newly-established IAEA, within the Community, should be the subject of an agreement between the latter organisation and Euratom. This in due course provided for 'verification' by IAEA Inspectors of Euratom Safeguards. Later still, when the 'Nuclear Suppliers' Group' was established, and determined rules going beyond those of the NPT, and when Euratom and its Member States signed the Treaty on the Physical Protection of Nuclear Materials, it was agreed to establish, within the European Political Co-operation, a 'Working Group on Nuclear Non-Proliferation'. To make matters more complex, the Euratom Treaty had always distinguished within the Community between Nuclear Weapon States [NWS] – namely Britain and France – and Non-Nuclear Weapon States [NNWS].

Euratom Safeguards were the responsibility of a Directorate which, for almost all of my time, was led by Willem Gmelin. Because it consisted mainly of Inspectors, it was large, numbering some 200 individuals. Moreover, unlike the others, it was based in Luxembourg. It seemed essential that it should nevertheless be fully integrated. Two new principles were therefore established from the start: first, the Directorate would always be represented at my regular, weekly meetings with Directors; and second, I would spend at least one full day a month at Luxembourg. Initially, my visits were more frequent, as this was an area of the Directorate-General's activity of which I was largely ignorant, and it was important to catch up.

As time went by, I also learnt much by visiting a variety of nuclear installations in the Community: such as the Almelo and Capenhurst Centrifuge plants; the Alkem fuel element fabrication plant; the

Schmehausen High Temperature Reactor; the Cap de la Hague reprocessing facility; the Biblis and Heysham nuclear power stations; and – though not relevant to normal Safeguards – the Joint European Torus [JET] nuclear fusion installation at Culham.

It is important to understand that the NWS are free under the Euratom Treaty, subject to any particular safeguarding obligations assumed by the Community under an agreement with a third State or an international organisation being respected, to withdraw materials from safeguarding to meet defence requirements [Article 84]. The NWS had however accepted that their non-defence operations were subject to Euratom Inspections. There remained a problem about 'mixed installations', in other words ones where defence and peaceful materials were both present. We gave this priority attention; and it was a source of satisfaction that the arrangements for the key mixed British installation, the centrifuge plant at Capenhurst, were agreed shortly before I left. Finally, one must also be aware that the Commission has power, in case of infringements of safeguarding obligations, effectively to close down any peaceful nuclear installation [Article 83].

It soon became clear that we were short of Euratom Inspectors. Over the years there was a constant fight to redress the balance, which made good progress. In my last full year as Director-General, the number of man-days of Safeguarding operations had risen to 7,600, nearly double the figure of four years earlier. This was just as well: the system had to know where to find, at any given time, every kilogramme of 'peaceful' natural uranium, and every gramme of 'peaceful' plutonium, or highly enriched uranium, wherever it was within the Community. The task of Safeguarding nuclear materials is sophisticated. Moreover, the technology of the nuclear industry is always changing, and Safeguarding procedures have to keep up to date. Euratom was constantly engaged on this process, not only using its own research resources, but also co-operating with various Member and Third States, and also with the IAEA.

Because of the Safeguards Directorate I was hauled in person before the Community's Court of Justice in Luxembourg! Under its Director, there were four Heads of Division. Together, these five persons made up the Directorate's senior management team. One of the Division Heads, of French nationality, was due to leave. A recruitment competition was arranged. Two candidates emerged. Of these, one was an internal Belgian, while the other was an external Frenchman from the French national nuclear services. I considered them of equal professional quality. It was, however, evident that, if I appointed the Belgian, there would be no person of French nationality in the senior management team. I chose the Frenchman, who was appointed. In those days – though this is no longer the case – European Community officials with a grievance against an administrative decision could complain direct to the Court of Justice. The Belgian did just that, arguing that he had been the victim of discrimination on grounds of nationality.

The case came before a Panel of three Justices on 6 June, 1985. Although the Commission, as appointing authority, was represented by a member of its Legal Service, my attendance was also required. The plaintiff's lawyer made his case; and the Commission's lawyer replied. Then I was asked by the President to explain my choice. After running over the facts, I told the Court that France held more than half of all the 'peaceful' nuclear materials in the entire Community. I felt that, if there were no person of French nationality in the Directorate's senior management team, France's confidence in the system might suffer. This was something I could not risk; and that fact had influenced my decision.

The President found the point interesting. I was arguing not for a French 'hat' to be placed permanently over a post – a procedure which the Court had already declared to be contrary to Community law – but rather that, in the particular circumstances, the absence of any French national from a sensitive team could be contrary to the public interest. He asked the plaintiff's lawyer to comment. The latter replied that this was not a point which had emerged in the written proceedings: he had not therefore had time to study it, and requested an adjournment. The President's riposte was scathing. He remarked that the lawyer was a trained barrister, and that barristers were taught to think on their feet. 'The Court will therefore grant you an adjournment – for five minutes.' At the end of that time, the lawyer gave some kind of reply; and the President declared that the Court's judgement would be announced later. When the judgement emerged, it became clear that I had lost the case, but won the argument! The Court recorded that some purely formal mistake had been made by the Commission in the appointing procedure, and annulled the appointment on that ground alone. We then re-ran the whole procedure – carefully avoiding the mistake – and the Belgian official decided not to pursue his case.

In 2001 a postscript was added to this passage about Safeguards. In February of that year, one of my former colleagues, Christian Waeterloos, telephoned to ask if I would agree to serve on an Expert Consultative Group being set up to advise the Commission on a new mission statement and methodology for Euratom Safeguards. It would be chaired by the former Commissioner, Henning Christoffersen, and include Fabrizio Caccia-Dominioni; the last Head of Safeguards at the Vienna Agency; a man from Asea Brown Boveri; and hopefully myself. On hearing that it would need to work in both Brussels and Luxembourg for a week a month until the summer, I declined. During our conversation, however, Christian confirmed my suspicion that, up till then, no Director-General has given as much effort to Safeguards as I did, at least since the Merger Treaty of 1965.

After a while, the suggestion was made by one of my officials that we should conduct a review of the implementation of the Euratom Treaty, something which had not been done for many years. A number of other Commission Services were involved, including the Legal Service; the Joint Research Centre; and the Directorates-General for Research and Development; for the Environment; for Industry; for Employment, Social Affairs and Education; and for External Affairs. We set up an Inter-Service Group [ISG], under my Chairmanship, and started work. It was apparent that the level of implementation was very varied. We made recommendations to the Commission. Their content no longer comes to mind; but perhaps the most important thing was simply that we made people aware of the problems, and that we had set up a machinery – the ISG – for processing them. This was to prove invaluable after the Chernobyl explosion.

I turn now to the Commission's relations with the IAEA. Watching in CRP, as Len Williams had sought to implement the Safeguards provisions of our Agreement with the Vienna Agency, I had felt some perplexity. The Agreement itself was clear: it provided that Euratom Safeguards would be verified by the Agency. But in practice the Agency was constantly pressing to duplicate our Inspections. This was understandable, to the extent that most Agency Member States had no understanding of the Community or the Euratom system; saw the Agreement as a kind of fig-leaf, behind which the Community countries would do what they wanted; and therefore sought to circumvent its provisions. The situation was not, to my mind, acceptable; but it was one to approach with care.

The first task was to establish a range of contacts with the Agency. Nobody advised me to attend the Agency's Annual General Conference in September, 1981. So, my first visit was that December, when I flew to Vienna for the sole purpose of lunching with the Director-General, Hans Blix [Swedish]. This was very much an exploratory event; but I immediately felt a rapport with Hans, who was quick-thinking, practical and wise. The next contact came the following autumn, with attendance at the General Conference. When first advised to go, I asked my officials what to say at the Conference. The question surprised them. They explained that the Commission had only observer status, and my predecessor had not spoken. When the point was pressed, they warned that reactions were uncertain. Much would depend on the attitude of the Soviet Delegation: given the fact that the Second Cold War was in full swing, this was unpredictable. It was therefore decided to prepare a draft speech, but keep it anodyne. The idea was to establish a precedent which could be exploited later.

At Vienna I found that there were not one, but two, co-ordination meetings: in addition to the usual Community affair, there was also a 'Western European & Others Group' [WEOG], which more or less corresponded to the OECD countries. I used these meetings, and bilateral talks with Blix (who had meanwhile recruited Chris Herzig to his staff), the British and the Germans, to warn friendly countries of my planned intervention and discuss how to handle any Soviet counter-move. Fortunately, attention was diverted by talk of an Arab motion to suspend the membership of Israel. I was billed as the last speaker in the three-day general debate. My predecessor, the Iranian Delegate, made a Koran-thumping speech of half an hour. My remarks were, by comparison, short and tame, but perhaps more to the point. The Soviet dog did not bark.

By now, Hans had become interested in relations with the Commission, and a few weeks later came to Brussels to visit Stevie, myself and the Directorate-General. After that, our contacts were regular and fruitful. I was able to explain openly to Hans my concerns about duplication of Safe-guarding operations. He reacted characteristically. The IAEA Governments were not giving him the Inspectors he needed. Euratom controls were good. Resources should not be wasted. After that, safeguards problems with the Agency eased sharply.

Another sector of nuclear activity which produced a lot of work was that of Nuclear Supply Agreements, where the principal ones were with Canada, the United States and Australia.

The aim, in the Canadian case, was to update the existing bilateral Agreement, so that it took account of the various changes in circumstances already mentioned. In this we succeeded. An Australian Agreement had already been negotiated, under my predecessor.

With the Americans, it was different. President Carter had altered American policy in such a way that he wanted our existing Agreement to be re-negotiated. As it was more favourable than anything we could have obtained in its place, we were determined not to re-open things. To avoid so doing we had to 'give evidence of activity' which the State Department could report to Congress, thus allowing matters to go on as before. The evidence consisted of 'talks about talks'.

It is amazing how much work was involved, with both the Canadians and the Americans. Because of the sensitive nature of the issues, and the number of parties who had to be satisfied on our side, things went very slowly. We started pre-negotiations with the Canadians in early 1982, and did not sign a new agreement until some four years later. The Treaty provisions did not make things easy. At first blush they did not appear difficult, because it was for the Commission to negotiate, a task which fell to me, and then for the Council to approve by qualified majority vote; but there was also provision that the Commission must negotiate 'in accordance with the directives of the Council'. We sought to keep these simple. However, there was a constant tug-of-war, with each Member State seeking to inject complex requirements, and the Commission having to compromise to rally approval. We sometimes had to accept conditions we knew the Canadians would reject. At the final meeting, we derogated from instructions on certain points in order to conclude. We trusted, as it turned out correctly, that the Member States would swallow the result.

I recall an incident following the negotiations in Ottawa, late in 1983. After briefing the Community Ambassadors about the talks, we left that evening for Montreal, where we were to dine at Meribel Airport before flying to Schiphol. The menus settled, I called for the wine list. My colleagues were from Italy and Belgium. When I enquired whether they would like a Canadian wine, there were predictable looks of shock. Pressed to be open-minded, they agreed to try. I studied the list. Not one Canadian wine was to be found! The wine-waiter was asked how it could be that at Meribel, then known as the gateway to Canada, the list contained no Canadian wines. *'Mieux vaut que non, Monsieur'* was his laconic reply! We were in Quebec, and all Canadian wines come from English-speaking parts of the country!

From 1984 onwards, the Commission had to keep up an appearance of negotiating a new Supply Agreement with the United States. There were plenty of opportunities for talking to them. We met them also over Safeguards philosophy; and in the context of the IAEA. I was frequently in Washington for different reasons. I soon developed a personal rapport with the charming and very intelligent US Roving Ambassador for nuclear questions, Dick Kennedy. A lot of goodwill was built up, and some years later, when the existing Agreement was approaching its term, Fabrizio was successful in negotiating a new one. Meanwhile, however, the relationship with Kennedy was invaluable in the IAEA context, and later in that of Chernobyl.

My contacts with Dick produced a memorable side-benefit, in the shape of a visit to the Villa Stoclet at Brussels, built early in the 20th century and the finest surviving achievement of Joseph Hoffmann's *Wiener Werkstatt*. It was almost opposite my office on the Avenue de Tervueren; and Michel Berryer, a member of the Directorate-General's staff was related to the Baronne Stoclet. When Dick came to Brussels for talks with us, it was arranged that he, the Berryers, Maura and myself would call at the Villa on a Saturday morning, when Madame Stoclet would receive us. Dick asked whether Mr Middendorf, the US Ambassador to the Community, with whom he was staying, could join the party. This was agreed, but proved unfortunate.

Middendorf was appallingly late: so much so that, after half an hour, the rest of us started our tour of this fascinating house. It had been in the family since it was built. Its main contents – down to the furniture and the tableware – had all been designed by the architect, and were still there. During the last war, they had been removed to a family house in the country, and not found by the Germans. We began to go round. Then I heard the bell ring: it was Middendorf. It turned out that he was himself a considerable collector. He made a number of comments about the objects he saw which Madame Stoclet clearly felt to be disparaging. She was looking for revenge. We came to a part of the house where she had herself put together an important collection of mediaeval European paintings. When Middendorf admired one of these, she asked if he knew its provenance. *'Oh yes'* came the reply, *'it's from a village near Gerona [which he named] and was painted by so and so between the years…'*. Madame Stoclet unwisely persisted. *'Do you have one in your collection?'* she asked. *'Yes, I've got two'* came the reply. That was the end of the conversation!

It only remains to say a few words about our relations with our third main supplier of nuclear materials, namely Australia. We never needed further negotiations with them. But we did a lot of talking. The Australian Ambassador Fernandez was a frequent caller at my office. He was also a good host, and the first person to introduce me to the excellence of Australian wines, long before they hit the supermarket shelves. Teams came from Australia to talk about Safeguards, or supplies of uranium. There was plenty of contact at the IAEA General Conference. There were also more general energy contacts at the IEA. By 1985, I had decided it was time for me to see more of a country which had the world's biggest uranium mine, at Ranger, near Darwin, as well as very large resources of coal; and also to take the temperature of Australian Ministers and Senior Officials, and grasp the opportunity to influence public opinion in a modest way. I took with me two of my own staff, Martin Power and Derek Taylor, the latter being a uranium specialist. Our first official stop was to be Ranger. We timed it, however, so as to arrive at Darwin on a Saturday night, and have a day off to visit Kakadu National Park on the Sunday. It was a never-to-be-forgotten experience. Some 30,000 square kilometres in size, the Park contains a rich jumble of forest, rivers, billabongs, termite hills, dingos, wild pig, cicadas, water-buffaloes, wallabies, crocodiles, iguanas, python and fish. Everywhere, there was the sound of birds: many of these were very large, like the Jabiru, a black and white stork with red legs; all sorts of geese; sea-eagles and kites. We were also fascinated by a charming, long-legged, red-headed bird, with bright plumage, which walked on the water-lily leaves. We saw one with four chicks: when frightened, they all climbed up inside its wings, leaving four pairs of little legs dangling outside. We experienced a willy-whilly [whirlwind] and forest fires; and saw aboriginal paintings perhaps 20,000 years old.

Next day we visited Ranger, an impressive undertaking. On to Melbourne, where I addressed Australia's Business Council, making the point that the Community needs supplies of coal and uranium from Australia: I knew the latter to be a delicate affair, as there was an ongoing political movement within the Australian Labour Party against such exports. Then on to Canberra, for two days of go, go, go. We met with members of the Senate Committee on Natural Resources, and various Ministers and Officials. There was also a Round Table, chaired by Alan Woods, the Secretary at the Department of Resources and Energy whom I knew from many IEA contacts. This enabled me to address a good audience, with representatives of five Ministries. The visit ended with a meeting with Community Ambassadors and a press conference. The main message I tried to put across was that we would like to take a lot of Australian uranium, which would greatly help Australia's then rocky balance of payments; but we needed more assurance that Government policy would permit such exports to continue. All this was well reflected in the press next morning. Meanwhile we had moved on to Sydney for our last day in the country. It included seeing *The Mikado* in the Opera House; talks with coal and uranium producers; and a fascinating tour of the Harbour in a large and comfortable launch belonging to the Harbour Master, kindly arranged by Alan Woods.

We shall return to a particular, massive part of the nuclear *dossier* – Chernobyl – in the following chapter.

Social life & Family affairs

Life at RGC continued as before. However when, after my mother's death in May 1981, the family house at Ackenthwaite passed into my hands, it could not be left empty and uncared for. So we sealed off the east end of the attic, leaving in it all the furniture and other items we had acquired before or at the sale, and leased the house to a Mr and Mrs Williams. I found ways and means of visiting from time to time. Initially the Williams looked after house and garden quite well. However, after a while he seemed to fall into some financial difficulties. At all events, he ceased to look after the garden properly. As a result it was in a deplorable state by the time we retired, and we had to put enormous efforts into setting it to rights in summer, 1986.

Rupert was by now living in Javea. Claire continued attending the British School of Brussels until 1982, when she obtained a place at Southlands College, in the Roehampton Institute of Higher Education. William was at Winchester College until the end of 1984, after which he had a gap year before taking up a place at Queen's College, Oxford. His gap year was spent partly with a Portuguese family at Cascais, doing a crash course in the Portuguese language; and partly as a *gaucho* on *estancias* in Uruguay and Paraguay, under arrangements kindly made by his godfather, Charles Wallace, then the British Ambassador in Montevideo. He was able also to visit his birth-place, Buenos Aires.

Our faithful dachshund, Andy, passed away in May, 1986, leaving a large gap in the family. He was well over 15 years old; and had been a tremendous character. Until his last few months he had remained fit; but then liver troubles began, and eventually he was put to sleep. Burying him under his favourite rhododendron bush in the garden left us all in tears, and the house seemed suddenly much emptier. The only consolation was that we did not have to put him into quarantine, or give him away, when we left Brussels soon after: either course would have been tantamount to a death sentence.

CHAPTER 17

Chernobyl Rapporteur-General, and leaving the Commission

THE CHERNOBYL explosion occurred at 0124 hours on 26 April, 1986, when I was in the Middle East. Chernobyl is near Kiev, in the Ukraine, then still part of the USSR. The implications of this event were to dominate my professional life until the summer holidays, and resulted in my term of office being extended by the Commission for a month to 30 September. The following notes about Chernobyl are based on my diary, and Commission documents.

For several days after the accident, the Soviet Authorities gave out no information, or alternatively information of little value or reliability. The first clear news came when, from 28 April onwards, radio-activity levels started to rise sharply in surrounding countries – notably Sweden, Denmark and Poland; and US satellites focused their cameras on the area. Next day, Commission officials requested Member States to provide rapid and continuing information about radio-activity levels, as required in the Euratom Treaty. It took some time before any reasonable appreciation of the position could be made. But it did soon emerge that one of the four RBMK type reactors at Chernobyl had blown up, and the others had then been shut down. The RBMK is a Soviet design, about which Western experts had always had some doubts. When this became clear, many industrialised countries were faced with a big problem. Since the first oil-shock in 1973, they had invested heavily in diversification of energy supplies – and especially in building nuclear power-stations. By now, no less than one-third of the European Community's electricity was obtained from nuclear power. But three Member States – Denmark, Greece and Ireland – had decided not to follow the nuclear path. There was clearly going to be a strengthening of public doubts about safety.

From the moment of the explosion, the nuclear staff of my Directorate-General set to work, first to gather facts and analyse them; next to keep in touch with the Permanent Representations in Brussels; and last, to try and develop some guidelines for a Community reaction. They were in contact throughout with the other interested Directorates-General of the Commission.

Arriving back on Wednesday, 30 April, I was at once told by Pascal Lamy that President Delors wanted me to join the Delegation for the Tokyo meeting of the Western Economic Summit, due to begin four days later. I quickly shortened plans for a long-arranged working visit to London, and deferred arrangements for a farewell visit to Italy. I also had two telephone conversations with Hans Blix: he had told the USSR he was ready to act as a channel for any technical assistance the Soviets might need, and for the passage of any information about the accident to other countries. These were the first of many such exchanges with Hans over the following weeks, when the mutual confidence and friendship built up over several years were to prove invaluable.

I also gathered briefing material, and discussed the position with the staff, before driving that same evening to London. The lack of time for preparation was not so serious as might be thought. This was because, as Chernobyl showed, very little work had been openly done – whether at international, Community or national levels – on how to cope with a nuclear accident of such magnitude. Emergency planning had taken place in some countries. But there had been reticence on the part of the authorities about releasing information on the subject.

Why? Part of the answer is obvious. The authorities, aware of the potential scale of damage from a major reactor accident, had preferred to keep quiet and hope none would occur; rather than publicise facts which could have fed opposition to nuclear power. I believe another factor, though less evident, also played a role. Nuclear fission was originally exploited, first and foremost, to make the bomb. Everything to do with nuclear military programmes was secret. In a second phase, the world began to harness nuclear fission to make electricity. Initially, this work was done by public authorities – such as the Atomic Energy Authority and the Central Electricity Generating Board, or the Commission à l'Energie Atomique and Electricité de France. The habit of secrecy spilled over from military to civil side. A third factor derived from the danger of diversion of nuclear materials from civil to military cycles: for this reason, the civil cycles were placed under severe security restrictions. These took the form of safeguards on the use and movement of the materials; controls on exports of materials and technology; and international rules on the physical protection of installations and materials. All these factors meant that, even when the nuclear power industry in many cases moved outside the public sector and into private hands, the habit of secrecy persisted. Following Chernobyl, it became clear this had not been wise. It had aroused suspicion that there was something to hide. From now on, open-ness became fashionable.

For the Commission, the Euratom Treaty was a starting point. But radio-activity flows over frontiers, so it was from the start obvious to me that measures to deal with fall-out would need to be taken, generally speaking, in the widest international forum. That forum would be, for the most part, the IAEA [which from now on may be called 'the Agency']; but other international organisations like the World Health Organisation [WHO], the Food and Agriculture Organisation [FAO] and the Nuclear Energy Agency [NEA] – an offshoot of the OECD in Paris – would have lesser roles. Following my talks with Hans, I had reached some preliminary conclusions. We needed the best possible information about just what had happened. Nothing – as far as we knew – called in question the safety of reactors used in the industrialised world outside the USSR. On the positive side, the accident might well stimulate greater co-operation at world level – in an IAEA Context – about safety standards for reactors. There would not be a lead role for the Community to play in this context. The Euratom Treaty did not give the Commission specific powers, and the Member States had jealously guarded their independence in fixing the rules in this field. We did however have a major Community Research Programme as regards nuclear safety. Hans had recalled having suggested to the IAEA Annual General Conference, some two years previously, that there was a need to strengthen reactor safety standards. Cold water had been poured on the idea by many Delegations. It had only been possible to set up a small Committee of Experts – known as the International Nuclear Safety Advisory Group [INSAG], and this had made little headway.

What written briefing material did I therefore take with me when I left Brussels *en route* for London and then Tokyo on 30 April? There were two Agency documents and one publication of the Commission. The first of the former was entitled 'Agency Guidelines on Reportable Events, Integrated Planning and Information Exchange in the Transboundary Release of Nuclear Materials'[1]. The second was entitled 'Agency Guidelines for Mutual Emergency Assistance Arrangements in Connection with a Nuclear Accident or Radiological Emergency'[2]. Before Chernobyl, few outside the charmed circle of IAEA devotees would have known what an Agency Guideline was. Technically, they were no more than information documents. But they were based on the careful work of a Committee of Experts, and were subsequently circulated for the information and use of

Member States, They had, on at least one previous occasion, subsequently been converted, at a Conference, into an International Convention[3]. The Commission publication was a brochure on 'Nuclear Safety in the European Community' of 1985. The Commission is sometimes accused of producing inadequate publications. This one was a mine of authoritative and extremely valuable information. It surveyed, in some 60 pages, the whole history of nuclear safety in the Community.

Next day, Thursday, 1 May, I spent two hours in discussion with the Energy Sub-Committee of the House of Lords, about a Report they were writing on the use of nuclear energy in the Member States – starting from the Commission's relevant documents. Then I lunched with the Chairman, Lord Torrington; had afternoon meetings with top officials of the Department of Energy; and finally dined and saw a show with Maura. In my talks that day, my initial thinking about Chernobyl had stood up well to cross-examination.

Next day, Friday 2nd May, Maura dropped me at Heathrow in the morning, whence I flew to Paris, to join Delors on a 10,400km non-stop flight over Northern Europe, Leningrad [now St Petersburg], and Siberia, to Tokyo. Having been much on the move by then for a week, I was particularly pleased that travelling with the President entitled me to a first-class seat! Moreover, Air France served 'Dom Perignon' Champagne to its First Class passengers!

Saturday in Tokyo was meant to be a rest day. It is customary for participants at Summits to arrive a day or two before the meetings, and use the intervening time for bilateral talks with Summit colleagues. This happened at Tokyo. The 7,000 accredited media correspondents and photographers saw to it that almost everything said during the bilateral talks was rapidly communicated to the outside world!.

For me it was 'all systems go'. First, I sat down and drafted, on lines discussed with Delors in the plane, some 'elements for inclusion in the Declaration on the post-Chernobyl situation' we now assumed the Summit would be making. Next, at 1730 hours, there was a de-briefing by Delors to his Delegation about his afternoon talk with the Summit Chairman, Prime Minister Nakasone. Finally, I attended a dinner, offered by the MITI Minister, Watanabe, for Delors and Declercq (the Commissioner responsible for External Relations), where Chernobyl was a prime subject of conversation, and where the MITI Director-General for Energy, Nonouchi, and myself, were required to make the running in the discussions.

Sunday the 4th was the first day of the Summit. At a working breakfast in the hotel with Togo of the Gaimusho [Ministry of Foreign Affairs], I received my first information about Japanese ideas for the Declaration, and responded with ours. An hour later, I was visited in my bedroom by Ogawa, the MITI Deputy Director-General for Energy, and a small team, for further discussions about the Japanese draft. In mid-morning, there was a Delegation meeting with Delors. In the afternoon, I did further work with the Japanese. Later, they circulated to Delegations a letter containing their thoughts. This gave rise to many contacts and discussions. It is interesting to remark that – apart from the Japanese – none of the other Delegations to the Summit were as well prepared as the Commission; nor did any of them seem to be in direct touch with Hans at the IAEA.

At 1830 hours, there was a social interlude, in the shape of a Japanese Reception in the Hotel's Garden Lounge, when I found myself brushing shoulders with Reagan, Kohl, Mitterand and Thatcher, whilst talking to the Netherlands Prime Minister Lubbers, who as the Prime Minister of the Presidency Country was, with Delors, representing the Community. The more serious work began at 2000 hours, when I participated in a Summit Working Group under the Chairmanship of Matsuda [Gaimusho]. Four and a half hours later, we had produced a reasonable text. We passed our text to the Sherpas, who were due to work overnight on the preparation of the overall Summit conclusions, and went to bed. Later that night, news came through on the agency tapes that Hans had received and accepted an invitation from the USSR to go to Moscow for discussions next day.

On Monday the 5th, we found the Sherpas had changed little of what the Group had done. However, the Heads of Government spent 45 minutes that morning making a few revisions: in particular they added language welcoming the Soviet Government's just-announced decision to receive Hans Blix.

It is perhaps worth saying that, by now, the physical arrangements for Summit meetings had become very sophisticated. Whilst those actually present are normally limited to the Heads of Government, their Foreign Ministers, the Prime Minister of the Community Presidency, the President of the Commission – and the Sherpas of all these – it is easy for other members of Delegations to follow the proceedings. The Sherpas can scribble messages to their Delegation by telewriter, and get instant replies. They also take manuscript notes of everything said, and these notes can be telefaxed instantly to the Delegation, page by page.

The Summit Declaration was so important it is worth recalling below the full text [my underlining].

'The Heads of State or Government of [the] seven major industrial nations and the Representatives of the European Community remain ready to extend assistance as and when requested. <u>Nuclear power is and, properly managed, will continue to be an increasingly widely used source of energy.</u> For each country, the maintenance of safety and security is an international responsibility, and each country engaged in nuclear power generation bears full responsibility for the safety of the design, manufacture, operation and maintenance of its installations.

Each of our countries meets exacting standards. Each country, furthermore, is responsible for prompt provision of detailed and complete information on nuclear emergencies and accidents, in particular those with potential trans-boundary consequences. Each of our countries accepts that responsibility, and we urge the Government of the Soviet Union, which did not do so in the case of Chernobyl, to provide urgently such information, as our and other countries have requested.

We note with satisfaction the Soviet Union's willingness to undertake discussions this week with the Director-General of the IAEA. We expect that these discussions will lead to the Soviet Union's participation in the desired post-accident analysis.

We welcome & encourage the work of the IAEA in seeking to improve international co-operation on the safety of nuclear installations, the handling of nuclear accidents and their consequences, and the provision of mutual emergency assistance. Moving forward from the relevant IAEA guidelines, we urge the early elaboration of an international convention committing the parties to report and exchange information in the event of nuclear emergencies or accidents. This should be done with the least possible delay.'

It was a fortunate chance that the Summit had been fixed to take place just nine days after the Chernobyl accident. The intervening time was just sufficient for the Summiteers to make a first useful assessment of its significance, and to react in a way which was measured with regard to the Soviet Union; insistent on the need for nuclear electricity to play a major role in energy supply, but also of the need for the highest safety standards; and positive on the need for specific IAEA actions. It undoubtedly had a calmative effect on world public opinion. At the press briefing that morning by Hugo Paemen, now President Delors' Spokesman, I answered most of the questions. It was well-attended, as the media had by then realised that the Commission and the Japanese were best able to explain. Then, in the afternoon – when it was 0600 hours Vienna time – I telephoned Hans to read over, and comment on, the draft Declaration. This was welcomed, since nobody else was keeping him briefed, prior to his departure for Moscow three hours later.

On Tuesday the 6th, the Summit ended. Meanwhile, the game-plan had changed for Delors and his Delegation, since we had been invited by Prime

Minister Chirac to join him on his Concorde for the return trip to Paris next morning. I was pleased Delors accepted, because, although I knew the flight would be much less comfortable than the Air France Jumbo, this might be my only opportunity to fly at twice the speed of sound.

And so, on Wednesday 7th, we returned to Paris. We left Tokyo at 0930 hours. After a one-hour fuelling stop at Novosibirsk – the only time until 2001 I ever set foot in Russia – we reached our Paris destination in a total elapsed time of 9 hours. My hunch was right. I would never fly Concorde for convenience. It is cramped and noisy. But it was interesting, nevertheless, to pass through the sound barrier; and also to see clearly the curvature of the earth from the cruising height of 70,000 feet. Returning to Brussels from Paris by car, I reported events to my Commissioner, and so to bed.

Now, there was a switch in mode. It was time to move towards a more specific Community reaction to events. This was not made easier by the fact that May is known in Community circles as 'a month of Sundays' – no less than four weekends being extended by Public Holidays! Of course, for senior people in the Commission concerned with Chernobyl, these were honoured in the breach. To add to my personal pressures, I had seen the months of May and June as a period when I would visit a number of other countries to carry forward bits of important business before retirement – and to say good-bye to key colleagues. I contrived, despite huge work pressures, to maintain these commitments.

When I returned from Tokyo, the Commission had already made proposals on one matter of great urgency: namely the levels of radio-activity to be permitted in different types of foodstuff if they were to be sold in the Community. These limits were based on discussions within a Committee of Experts. However, the Experts could agree only on a range of figures, and in the end the Commission had to adjudicate as best it might. For some foodstuffs, these proposals needed only qualified majority voting in the Council; but for others, unanimity was the rule. For the latter – despite the obvious urgency – it took six days of argument in Coreper to reach agreement. The debate became known as 'the battle of the becquerels' – after the name of the unit of measurement used for radio-activity. The rules were to be valid for a month. They were later extended.

Friday 9 May was rich in developments. A *communiqué* was issued in Moscow at the end of Hans Blix's visit. It marked a clear shift in the Soviet authorities' attitude. Until then, they had been in denial. This was regrettable but predictable. Chernobyl had confronted the Soviet system with a problem, with which it was ill-equipped to deal. For decades, information had been manipulated by Party and State authorities. When things went wrong, they were hushed up. Here, things had gone very wrong indeed, and in a field where Soviet prestige would be most affected. For years the USSR had been trying to promote its reputation as a technological power, on a par with the USA. But the initial reaction of the Soviet authorities was untenable. There were radio-active clouds spreading far and wide in Europe. It was also very relevant that Gorbachew had come to power the year before, and instituted his policy of *Glasnost* [open-ness].

The Moscow *communiqué* showed the Soviets were now willing to come clean – at least to a certain extent. They had given Hans and his team far more information than had been released before, and promised a further supply; they had taken him and his team to visit Chernobyl; they had agreed everything should be discussed openly in the IAEA; and they had encouraged the Agency to put much more effort into the handling of accidents.

On the same day, a number of Community Heads of Government began to make public declarations *en ordre dispersé*. Chancellor Kohl's office announced that the Federal Republic of Germany planned to call an inter-Governmental Conference on nuclear safety in Bonn, making no reference to the IAEA. The Greek Prime Minister proposed to the UN Secretary-General that all reactors world-wide should be made subject to safety controls of the Vienna Agency and the WHO; and also that construction of Fast Breeder Reactors should cease. Neither Prime Minister consulted the Community or any of its Member States before taking these steps. Less controversially – but not helpfully – the Netherlands Government announced that it would review its recent decision to build two new reactors. The need for the Community to get its act together was apparent.

On 12 May I recommended to President Delors and his colleagues that the Commission should work towards the early production of a Framework Communication to the European Parliament and the Council; and that we should try as much as possible to move forward on a world-wide basis, using the Vienna Agency. Measures at Community level should be supportive, or a *pis-aller*. This was the line also followed at all meetings of the nuclear inter-service group [ISG], which was, for the rest of my time with the Commission, to meet frequently and at two levels: the normal one, plus a higher-level gathering of Directors-General. My Directorate-General chaired and serviced both: the Secretary was a quietly efficient member of my staff, Yvan Capouet. No less than nine Directorates-General were involved. Meanwhile, the President established a Special Chefcabs

Committee, chaired by Günther Burghard, an able member of his Cabinet. There was also an informal group of Commissioners, which met from time to time with Delors in the Chair. Through these mechanisms, we prepared the deliberations regarding Chernobyl of the full Commission; the European Parliament and its relevant Committees; Coreper 2; the Energy Council and its the High-Level Energy Group; formal and informal meetings of the General Affairs Council; and the European Council's meeting on 26-27 June.

What were we preparing? First, there was the Framework Communication to the Council, covering the post-Chernobyl situation generally, prepared by my Directorate-General in continuous consultation with others, and in the end running to some 20 pages: it was to foreshadow more detailed proposals in different fields. Because of its importance and complexity, it was not ready for submission to the Commission until its meeting in Strasbourg on 10 June. A first, outline document was, however, approved by the Commission as early as 14 May. And thereafter, short, indicative documents, based upon the current state of its preparation, were distributed to meetings of Parliament and Council bodies.

There was to be a first debate in the European Parliament plenary on Thursday 15 May. It was to be prepared, the day before, by a meeting of the Parliamentary Committee concerned with Energy. However, it was agreed to convert this into a joint meeting between that Committee and the one dealing with the Environment. The Commission was to be represented by three of the Commissioners with relevant responsibilities – MM Mosar, Clinton-Davis and Narjes. The former was to lead off; the second to make a follow-up statement; and the third to be in reserve.

The main aim of Nic Mosar's intervention was to argue that two extreme reactions should be avoided. One would be to place in question the whole nuclear industry and the Community's Energy Strategy: this would be unrealistic and dangerous. The other would be to try and minimise the significance of Chernobyl, even if Western reactor types were different. Another purpose of the intervention would be to explain to the MEPs – many of whom had been making statements arguing that all should be done by the Community – that the wider international level should be given high priority. Tony Clinton-Davis's remarks were aimed at valorising the work done by the Commission on nuclear safety in the past.

The rules of the game were that, after the Commissioners had made their statements, the MEPs would ask questions, and the Commissioners would then reply. These rules, however, were almost entirely ignored. Instead of questions, the MEPs made a series of long and often polemic interventions, with the odd question interspersed. The great majority of speakers were persons known for their anti-nuclear views. The clock ticked on. In the end the Chairman of the Committee due to use the room next, kicked up a stink, and the meeting stopped. There was thus no time for the Commissioners to answer the debate at all! In closing the session, the Energy Committee President, M Poniatowski of France, a political heavyweight, said that Parliament must devote a lot of time to the consequences of Chernobyl. One of the things to be looked at was the possibility of the Community establishing norms for reactor safety. (I later told him it seemed extremely unlikely that, in his own country, the national authorities would ever consider such a thing. He agreed; but felt it was necessary to be seen as having examined the possibility.)

The overall picture which an objective observer of the Committees' debate would have gained – namely that a strong majority in the European Parliament thought Chernobyl was a reason for slowing or stopping existing nuclear power programmes – was false. This was bound to be the case, because the composition of the two Committees together was not representative. In the European Parliament as a whole there had always been a rather even split between those favouring and those opposed to nuclear power. As a result it had never been possible for Parliament to take a very clear view. This pattern was reflected in the composition of the Energy Committee. But a distortion took place, due to the adjunction of the Environment Committee, which had a heavy anti-nuclear bias. The outcome had nonetheless rattled Nic – never a very confident man. I advised him that a key tactical consideration was to avoid getting into a position, as a result of next day's Plenary session debate, which would prevent the Commission from arguing strongly in the Energy Council, just under three weeks ahead, for the adoption of the proposed new Community energy objectives for 1995. Recent big falls in the price of oil – coupled with uncertainties arising from Chernobyl – made this more necessary than ever. Later that day – at a meeting I attended between the three Commissioners and President Delors – this view was accepted, though the President felt one should *'ouvrir une petite fenêtre, mais pas plus'* as regards possible changes in nuclear policy. It was decided that the nuclear debate would again be handled by the three Commissioners; but the President would remain in Strasbourg, listen to the debate from his office, and be on hand in case of need.

The Plenary debate was to be presided by Madame Péry – not a particularly strong personality. A procedure was agreed between her and all concerned. The debate was in principle to take place on the basis of rules applying to 'urgency motions'. Under these, the presenter of a motion speaks first; other Parliamentarians speak next; and a Commissioner winds up. But the situation was extra-ordinary. No less than eleven separate Resolutions had been presented; and it had not been possible to re-group them into a more manageable form. The Commissioners felt that, unless they got into the act early on, the debate might be very unstructured. President Péry, therefore, agreed that they could speak immediately after the presenters of motions.

This tidy scenario was disrupted. No sooner had Nic Mosar begun his remarks than he was interrupted by a demonstration. A number of people – who were quite illegally standing <u>in</u> the hemi-cycle, immediately behind the back rank of MEPs – suddenly hoisted banners saying 'radio-activity knows no frontiers'. A number of right-wing MEPs called on Madame Péry to interrupt the debate and restore order. She replied that she had already told *huissiers* to remove the demonstrators, so the debate should continue. The right-wingers shouted all the louder. Finally she used her microphone to shout, louder still: *'taisez-vous'*. The right-wingers subsided: the banners disappeared. All this while, Nic Mosar, though instructed by the President to continue, had stood perplexed. But eventually he recovered his nerve, and finished what he had to say.

Monsieur Pflimlin, the distinguished, elderly, President of the European Parliament, informed of the incident, had by now replaced the session President. The debate was of high quality. The presenters of motions spoke clearly; went to the heart of many issues; and were moderate. The debate – apart from the incident – was conducted in a dignified and well-controlled way. The two Resolutions adopted at the end were well-balanced and far from extreme. Often in Britain, the European Parliament is wrongly criticised for being incompetent or irrelevant. On many occasions – and certainly on this one – the quality of debate was a good deal higher than that of the House of Commons. I suspect that the Committee debate of the previous day had helped achieve this satisfactory result. It had enabled anti-nuclear MEPs to let off a lot of steam, and they were less excitable in Plenary. Others – who supported the use of nuclear – had perhaps been frightened by the excesses of their colleagues in the Committees. At all events, they came out fighting their corner solidly.

In the following week, the Governing Board of the Vienna Agency held a special post-Chernobyl session. This was important in setting the tone for the IAEA's subsequent work. In the run-up, the Netherlands Presidency of the Community had made valiant efforts to co-ordinate a Community position in Vienna. But these efforts had failed. Why? After all, the Governments of the Community's Member States were fully committed to the principle of speaking in international organisations with a single voice. This is easiest when dealing with matters solely of Community competence, where the Community machinery works adequately. For other matters, the principle is one of co-ordination within the EPC. This too could work well. (The most striking example of its success was the detailed and solid statement on a huge range of issues, made annually by the Presidency country on behalf of the Community, at the autumn meeting of the UN General Assembly.)

But nuclear is a special case. The reasons are complex. Perhaps most importantly, the international nuclear establishment is a world of its own, jealous of its position. Only countries with substantial nuclear assets can pretend to membership – for example the United States, the UK, France and the Federal Republic of Germany. Within these countries, there is a charmed circle of nuclear specialists, enjoying great authority. At international level, they know each other well. They try to fix things in the Club. They are not therefore amenable to the notion of Community co-ordination. Fortunately I knew many of the club members. This went right back to the early 1970s when I had negotiated with several of them about the Almelo Agreement on Uranium Enrichment[4]. My current responsibilities, as the Commission's Director-General chiefly responsible for the Euratom Treaty, had re-inforced these early contacts. But all this helped only up to a point.

Nonetheless, the meeting of the Governing Board on 21 May – which I could not attend because of a Commission meeting in Brussels – went well. Agreement was reached that the Director-General of the Agency should proceed on four fronts. First, he should urgently convene a post-accident review meeting. Second, he should organise the drafting of International Conventions on information exchange about nuclear accidents with possible trans-boundary effects, and on co-ordination of emergency assistance after such accidents. Third, he should, over a longer time-scale, consider additional measures to improve co-operation in the field of nuclear energy, including ways and means to further refine nuclear safety standards. And fourth, he should convene an early Conference of Governmental Representatives on the full range of nuclear safety issues. The Director-General was also asked to report progress at the next regular Board meeting in mid-June.

The meeting of the Energy Council in Luxembourg on 3 June was presided by the Netherlands Minister, M Van Ardenne. I had spent six hours, the day before, briefing my Commissioner; but he was lost, and I had to chip in – disregarding protocol – throughout the day. There were two specially difficult items: the definition of 'Energy Objectives 1995' so soon after Chernobyl; and a new system for aids to the coal industry. On both, the Council debate was of course based on Commission proposals. In a preparatory meeting, Nic Mosar had agreed with the Chair on tactics for whittling away the numerous reserves, so that we would be left only with profound Danish hesitations on nuclear electricity, and French on coal. The basic approach was to go once round both files before lunch, when the heavyweight Ministers – Peter Walker and Bangemann – would arrive; and then leave it to Ministers over lunch to wheel and deal. It worked. The lunch lasted four hours; and the Council ended at 2130. But the goal was achieved. Nic also used the occasion to distribute an updating paper on Chernobyl.

Two days later I participated in a 'European Nuclear Conference – 1986' in Geneva, organised by the ENEA. I had agreed to speak about nuclear co-operation within the European Community a long time before. I had done so largely as a matter of courtesy, but obviously the value of the occasion had now completely changed. There were several hundred more participants than usual. Many members of the nuclear establishment were there. It was possible to take the political temperature.

The nuclear power industry had been shaken by Chernobyl. The view predominantly held was that the situation would never be the same again; and that, if the public were to continue to accept nuclear, the industry would have to put much more effort into persuading people that it was sufficiently safe. Only the French spokesmen were arguing that safety in West European power stations was already adequate.

On 10 June, the Commission was to meet in the evening in Strasbourg – as it was a Parliamentary week – to finalise its Framework Communication. The draft essentially reviewed developments so far, and foreshadowed upcoming, more detailed proposals. My presence was required for this point. It was not reached until 2300 hours. In the event, there was no debate. The paper had by now been so well prepared by the ISG and the Chefcabs, that it was rubber-stamped[5]. Uncharacteristically, Delors offered me warm congratulations. My diary commented that these were not entirely unmerited. '*I have had to pilot the paper through umpteen meetings of the… Directorates-General concerned, as well as of the Special Chefcabs.*' The Commission also approved various practical recommendations, one of which was that I should remain as its Rapporteur-General on Chernobyl affairs. It was after this meeting that I was also asked to stay on into the autumn as a Special Adviser on Nuclear Questions, instead of retiring completely.

Two days later, I set off on a tour which was to take me, breathlessly over the following nine days, to destinations on both sides of the Atlantic. First, I went to The Hague, to discuss with the Netherlands Presidency, at official and Deputy Foreign Minister level, the preparation of the Chernobyl item at the General Affairs Council four days later, and at the European Council ten days after that. Next, I flew to Vienna, for a farewell dinner with Hans Blix, when I learnt about the detailed forward planning agreed by the Governing Board earlier that day. This was a delightful evening at the Römischer Kaiser, where we were each accompanied by two close colleagues.

Then I was off to Ottawa, for energy and nuclear talks with Deputy Energy Minister De Montigny Marchand, Parliamentarians and officials. I also appeared two mornings running on nation-wide TV, and underwent a two-hour, taped, on-the-record, lunch-time discussion with journalists on all aspects of energy policy. (The text of one of the interviews for Canadian TV – with CBC on 17 June – still in my files – has stood up well to the test of time.) The tour continued to Washington, for a final round of talks with officials. It ended at Oxford, where I went to say goodbye to the Energy Institute Governing Board as the time to relinquish my membership approached.

Less than a week later, I was in Scheveningen for the European Council meeting of 26-27 June. The first day was devoted to other issues, Chernobyl being left to the second. On the second morning I made the mistake of leaving my bedroom in the Hotel without putting on my Conference badge. I was at once apprehended, and escorted back to fetch it by two 'gorillas'! Then to breakfast with Delors, Pascal Lamy, and Günther Burghard. By then the Netherlands Presidency had produced their draft conclusions: they were remarkably like those I had suggested to them, during my visit two weeks earlier, only shorter. Despite this, Delors showed an uncharacteristic nervousness, which the rest of us sought to calm.

At the European Council there was a debate, in the course of which several Heads of Government played down the importance of Community action, and stressed the importance of action by the Vienna Agency. The Commission's thesis was that, while the Agency had a key and essential role, the Community could in some cases move farther and faster. At all events, the Netherlands text was approved, with small changes only.

After that, the pace of events mercifully slackened for the month of July. Work was still continuing internally on a follow-up Communication, dealing with the application of the Euratom Treaty provisions on Health and Safety, which was approved by the Commission – after a lot of argument and debate – at the end of the month[6]. It showed, *inter alia*, that no less than six out of the Twelve Member States stood in breach of their Treaty obligations, and had only not been hauled before the Court of Justice because of shortage of staff in the Commission Services concerned. The Directorate-General for Research and Development was working up another Communication on reactor safety. There were Community preparations for a Special General Conference of the IAEA at end-September to consider the consequences of Chernobyl. Two international nuclear conventions were being prepared by the IAEA. Finally, Peter Walker, the British Minister for Energy, visited Brussels to discuss his plans for the British Presidency of the Energy Council just beginning.

Towards the end of July, the Soviet Union published the conclusions of the Politburo of the Central Committee of the Communist Party concerning a Report by the Soviet Commission of Enquiry into the causes of the Chernobyl accident, and the measures taken to overcome its consequences and ensure the safety of nuclear power. Basing itself on this Report, the Politburo placed all the blame for the accident on gross violations of operating rules by the staff of the power station. This suggested that the Soviet Union was not going to admit any criticism of the reactor's design.

At last, August arrived. The first few days of the month were spent packing up our Brussels house, which we had agreed to hand over to the new owners, the Bregentzers, on the 11th. Next day we set off for Ackenthwaite, which had been reclaimed from our tenants.

I returned alone to Brussels in early September, living in a flat lent by a kind friend. Chernobyl work continued at a more moderate pace. This enabled me to prepare the hand-over to my Greek successor as Director-General, Dinos Maniatopoulos, who was retiring at the end of the month after two years as Chairman and Managing-Director of EKO – the State-owned Greek Petroleum and Chemicals Company. First, however, I accompanied Nic Mosar to the IAEA Special General Conference from 24-26 September, where he spoke for the Commission. My very last act as Director-General was to attend a meeting of the IEA Governing Board in Paris on 30 September. From there I flew on, in my new role as Special Adviser to the Commission, to Vienna, to represent my Institution at the

Annual General Conference of the Agency. As the last speaker in the General Debate on 2 October, I offered some valedictory remarks, stressing the steady improvement of Euratom/IAEA co-operation over the last five years, and addressing the problems of Nuclear Safeguards and the merits of Safeguards Inspectors.

I cannot leave the subject of Chernobyl without commenting that – serious though the accident certainly was – the anti-nuclear lobby have exaggerated the damage done to human life to an unbelievable extent. As recently as 2002, for example, the BBC gave prominence to a report that 45,000 people had died as a result of the accident. The figure of Chernobyl related deaths has in fact been kept under review, ever since the event, by the UN Scientific Committee on the Effects of Atomic Radiation [UNSCEAR]: by 2002, their figure was 48! The BBC subsequently undertook to brief their editors about the UNSCEAR report; but the damage to public opinion was already done.

On 5 October I left Brussels for Ackenthwaite to begin my 'real' retirement, only returning as Adviser on two further occasions. By now the ISG had checked out a further Communication – on Technological Problems of Nuclear Safety – for the Commission to send to the Council and Parliament[7]. The first trip was a flying visit of twenty-four hours in November. The second was longer. It started with a journey to Oxford, where I met Dinos Maniatopoulos and inducted him into the mysteries of the Energy Policy Club and Institute. From there we flew to Brussels, where on 25 November I effectively handed over Chairmanship of the Nuclear ISG to my friend Laurens-Jan Brinkhorst, who had now become Director-General for the Environment and Nuclear Safety. The Group had meanwhile processed two further Communications: a general update[8], and another on the Control of Radio-active Contamination of Products[9]. I also attended a farewell dinner offered by Emile Nöel for outgoing colleagues; and said some other goodbyes. Thus, in practice, ended my time as Special Adviser and my employment with the Commission.

Leaving the Commission

How did I feel about the past, as I left the Commission after more than 13 years within it, and the Diplomatic Service after over 36? And in what mood did I approach the future?

As to the past, I felt profoundly grateful for all the opportunities life had offered. Every job – whether national or European – had proved rewarding, and each had helped me in the later ones. I felt particular gratitude to the

Commission for having entrusted me with three successive senior posts – plus the Chernobyl dossier for the crucial months after the catastrophe – to conclude my professional career. All the time I was in Brussels, the Commission was going through a period of generally intense activity. It very effectively performed its rôle as the true motor – and the conscience – of the Community. The College of Commissioners had been generally of high quality, although we have noted one or two points of weakness. The Services, already very effective when I arrived, were still more so when I left, despite two more enlargements and the need to cope with a far wider range of problems.

The leadership of President Delors – for the decade beginning in 1985 – was to raise the Commission's standing much further. But now, with hindsight, it is clear that his departure marked the start of a long decline in the effectiveness of the Commission, and its position within the Community generally. The appointment, as successive Presidents, of Santer and Prodi, have both turned out to be mistakes. The resignation of the former, and the attendant circumstances, set off a sharp decline in the morale of the Services. The behaviour of Prodi has not restored the position. There have been one or two scandals in the Services. However the tendency of the British media to suggest that the entire staff of the Commission are corrupt is absurd. The high quality I knew must still be there: it needs simply to be well led again. Nevertheless the Institution as a whole is in poor shape to face up to the impending enlargement of the EU to 25 Member States. One can now see that I served the Commission during thirteen of the best years of its history. I feel privileged and proud to have done so.

Throughout my professional life I had always been primarily concerned with getting things done, and cared little about receiving public credit. I had benefited enormously from the help of colleagues, and had always greatly valued this. So, when I left Brussels, my last three acts, on 1 October, 1986, were to send warm, circular letters of thanks to all my fellow Directors-General, and all members of my staff; to write individually to some 300 personalities outside the Commission with whom I had worked closely; and finally to ask Betty Muller, my faithful Secretary for all the time I was in the Institution, to move onto Christian name terms! (She would have regarded it as *lèse-majesté* to do so earlier!)

To the Directors-General I expressed thanks for their friendship and support, and a feeling of privilege at having belonged to this unique European Club.

To my staff I was happy to say that I was leaving a Directorate-General which was very highly regarded throughout the Commission and in the Member States. I felt we had done many useful things together. The energy challenges had changed enormously, but we had risen to them. Our methods of operation had been modernised. Informatics had come in with a bang. In 1981 we had had five work-stations and nothing else: now we had 95, as well as two main-frame computers of our own. We were among the guinea-pigs in the Commission for using computerised translation and e-mail. There was now much higher output per person throughout the Directorate-General.

My letter to those outside the Commission was a standard one, announcing my departure and giving details about my successor; but I added personal touches in most cases. Over 100 of the recipients replied, from all parts of the world. Their kind tributes should perhaps have prepared my mind for the award of a KCMG in the New Year's Honours List for 1987. In fact, the preliminary approach from the Palace came as a complete surprise. Somehow I had contrived to forget that my predecessor, Len Williams, had been knighted after retirement. And I had tacitly assumed that Margaret Thatcher, who was Prime Minister at the time, would not approve of honours for someone she must have regarded as a 'Euro-fanatic'. I was wrong.

Turning to the last question, namely what of the future, I answer more briefly. As I flew from Paris to Vienna, on the morning after my retirement, it suddenly struck me that, literally for the first time in my life, I was in a position in which nobody – except my wife and children – could give me orders. This seemed very satisfactory. But I had no intention of doing nothing; nor, on the other hand, of filling up my time without careful thought.

CHAPTER 18

An active retirement begins

A ND SO, in the autumn of 1986, Maura and I changed gear. We entered a retirement period with only a very few clear ideas about how we would pass our time. The purpose of this chapter is to give a general impression of how things turned out. It will cover the period to the end of 2002. The aim will be to reflect the true, overall balance of our retirement. Because of its multi-faceted nature, the task is not easy.

The early days were complicated by an accident. I was run over by a car in Milnthorpe in early December, 1986, just a few days after my last visit to Brussels as a Special Adviser to the Commission. It was ironic that this accident occurred in my village – after a lifetime of living in capital cities! I was crossing the road on foot on a dark night, in pouring rain and with awful visibility. Responsibility must be shared between the driver and myself, though the matter never went to Court. I was struck on the left knee; rolled over the top of the car; and landed head first on the kerbside, floating in and out of consciousness. My skull and left leg were fractured, and there were nasty abrasions of the right one. I was lucky to be alive. Kind people picked up the bits; and saw me despatched by ambulance to Lancaster Infirmary. The Police advised Maura, who followed hot foot. When I woke, in the Accident and Emergency Department, an Indian Doctor leant over me and asked: *'How do you feel?'*. He was somewhat surprised by my reply: *'Shall I be able to ski at Easter?'*. However, after a moment's reflection, he replied: *'At the moment I do not see why not.'* He was right. The following Easter I ski-ed at Davos, with Maura and all three children.

Occupations

How did retirement look otherwise? Ahead lay just one clear prospect: I was committed to teach regularly at Edinburgh University about European Union Institutions. Otherwise there was a blank slate, except that I had written to Dame Jennifer Jenkins to offer my services to the National Trust if they could be of use. Chernobyl had left no time for thinking about the future. We wanted to feel out a new path, unhurriedly. One or two things

Our three children before William's wedding, Rome, June, 1994.

went without saying. We should want to see the most we could of our children. We should want to re-fashion house, garden and paddock. Maura and Claire wanted Andy replaced. And we should wish to travel quite a lot, both at home and abroad. Over time, all these modest aims were attained. I also saw retirement as an opportunity to catch up with literature, something for which a busy professional life had left little opportunity. But, from the start, I wanted to take on other interesting activities; and these became so time-consuming that literature took a back seat. As time went by, I gradually built up a large portfolio of different interests. They changed in composition over the years. But together they kept me occupied a great deal. Not until I retired from being Pro-Chancellor of Lancaster University, in 1997, did the total work-load begin to decrease.

Enhancing house, garden and paddock has been a constant concern for both of us. As to the house, we did not touch the exterior left by my parents, except to add bits here and there, and restore some attractive, old architectural details. Indoors, however, we were radical. Floors, plumbing and heating were replaced. The front rooms were made into a continuous

The Old House at Ackenthwaite after alteration, 2001.

suite. A new kitchen was built. The attic was converted to give a bedroom and a study. For months, while this was going on, we largely lived in a mobile home in the drive, though Maura and I always slept in the house, even with no windows and few floors! These works were a major preoccupation for three years.

As to the garden, it was completely re-shaped. We acquired extra land and built a greenhouse. Then we set to work creating a vista from the front of the house, right down the garden, and looking out on the fields of our neighbours' farm. A ramshackle shed in the orchard was replaced by a smart new one, with local stone facing, which houses our tractors. Every other kind of machinery which would save labour has been acquired.

Once the main work was done, we began opening the garden to the public in aid of charities. We have also held several parties there. The most memorable took place on 29 July, 2000. Organised for Maura's 70th birthday, it was held in summer, so as to honour also Rupert's 40th and Julie's 80th birthdays. Maura's approach, which delighted me, was to invite every living descendant of my grand-father – Edward Audland – and their spouses, a total of twenty-seven: with Julie and Patsy. All accepted, and all came. We had a marquee on the lawn opposite the front door. The weather was perfect. The guests were with us from lunch until tea. All could wander in house or garden, or play croquet. Many had made a huge effort to come to this event. But all thought it worthwhile, and there was much bonding between three generations of Edward Audland's clan.

As to the paddock across the road, it was completely transformed in the mid-nineties. My father had bought the southern part in the 1930s, and left it to me. But the northern part then went with the nearby house, 'The Homestead'. This house was built in 1934 by the then blacksmith of Ackenthwaite, Willie Douthwaite. Unfortunately he also constructed, on its paddock and immediately opposite our front gate, a new Smithy, clad in corrugated iron, on a timber frame. Although aged only eight at the time, I always considered this an eyesore. In 1994, the whole property – house and paddock – came on the market. We managed to get it. The house, its curtail, and a small part of the paddock were sold on. But we retained that part of the latter which faced our house. The paddocks were united. Shortly after, to our huge satisfaction, contractors bulldozed away the Smithy and garage. New stone walls were built where needed. This was done by Kevin Bateman and Edward Waller, then respectively the senior and junior champion stone wall builders of Britain: the walls are a model of their kind. We then progressively turned our enlarged paddock into an amenity area, with ornamental trees and flowering shrubs. Thus the land opposite almost the whole length of our property is safe from unwanted development and pleasing to the eye.

Changes in garden and paddock involved me personally in much hard labour. My diary is filled with references to getting up at 0500 hours in summer, and gardening for hours and hours. But I was not alone. Mike Singleton, who had helped my mother in the garden, returned to work with me when we came home, and is a tower of strength. By 1996, however, ten years after my retirement, I was physically slowing down. A turning point had come. So we gradually shifted gardening activities away from development, towards care and maintenance.

I contributed thoughts to various books by other people on European affairs, including notably to the chapter in Ted Heath's autobiography *The Course of my Life* about the Accession Negotiations with the European Community Member States of 1961-63; and more generally to Hugo Young's fascinating book *This Blessed Plot* about Britain and Europe. I advised extensively on two television series on the same theme: a three-part series broadcast on Channel 4 in 1995 under the title 'The Last Europeans', in which I appeared personally; and a four-part series, devised by Hugo Young, produced by John Bridcut and presented by Michael Elliott, which was broadcast on BBC 2 in 1996 under the title 'The Poisoned Chalice'. My knowledge of Europe was also to involve me in the creation of a Cumbrian and North Lancashire Branch of the European Movement. Finally, not long after retirement, I was asked by Lady (Elizabeth) Kirk to join the Selection Committee of the Peter Kirk Memorial Fund, a charity set up in memory of her late husband, Peter, which sends young people on scholarships to the continent.

All these were things which came to <u>me</u>, rather than commissions I <u>sought</u>. Fortunately, my Commission pension was sufficient to let us live as we wished, without my having to seek other paid employment. My post-retirement activities were made *pro bono publico*, with as a maximum expenses paid by the beneficiary. The only exception came in 1988, when I became a member of the ICL European Strategy Board, a post held until 1996.

Michael Butler had telephoned out of the blue, to ask whether I would consider joining the Board, then in formation, of which he was to be Chairman. The Board's task was to advise ICL's Chairman and Managing Director, Sir Peter Bonfield, about political and economic developments in Europe. The aim was to help ICL operate effectively in the EU's Internal Market, due for completion by 1992, and in Europe outwith the Community. Michael explained that the work would involve attending monthly, half-day meetings in London; and undertaking some information-gathering and lobbying activity in Brussels, Strasbourg and Luxembourg. ICL would pay me a few thousand pounds a year; and of course my expenses. I was immediately attracted: not because of the emoluments, but because the job offered a reason for regular visits to London, Brussels and the other Community locations on an expenses paid basis. (In the event, I went to the continent on ICL business two or three times a year, usually for two or three days.) These arrangements enabled me to keep up to date on EU affairs. This was helpful in many ways, and especially with regard to my teaching activities at Edinburgh, my involvement as European Adviser to the National Trust, and my activities in Europa Nostra and the International Castles Institute, to which we shall come. So, after a conversation with Peter Bonfield, I accepted; and took up my duties in May. My contract was for one year only, but was regularly renewed until I decided not to continue.

The European Strategy Board [ESB] was an agreeable body. It was small, and informal. Peter attended personally almost every time. He has a friendly and open personality. He enjoyed the atmosphere, and was prepared to discuss anything with us freely. Every now and then he had to be reminded that we were talking of things outside our remit, and that he would have to *'run them in front of his full Board'* later! I got to like and respect him.

The ESB was serviced by George Hall, an able former member of the Diplomatic Service, who ensured all was well prepared. Its outside membership varied over time, and it would serve no purpose to give full details. But we were joined, in 1994, by another former FCO colleague, Sir Rodric Braithwaite, who had by then served in the UK Permanent Representation in Brussels; as British Ambassador in Moscow; and as Adviser on International Affairs to the Prime Minister. My own role was to advise about European developments generally, and also more particularly about IT progress and prospects within the EU Institutions. It was useful to have been, for a dozen years, a member of the *Comité Directeur de l'Informatique à la Commission'* [CDIC]. As a result I still knew most of the people who counted in the Commission's IT and Telecoms sectors.

Soon after we were set up, *détente* re-started with Gorbachew; the USSR fell to pieces; first Hungary, then Poland, took charge of their own affairs; *Die Wende* took place in Germany; and the face of the European Continent changed completely. When these things began to happen, the ESB assumed an additional role, that of analysing and predicting the likely course of change in Central and Eastern Europe. Over the years, the Board gave consistently sound advice on this front, offering ICL the best chance to exploit the newly developing markets.

I much enjoyed my time with ICL. But I decided that, on reaching the age of 70, I should cut down on travel. So I resigned, attending my last meeting in July 1996. The ESB presented me with a nice watercolour of the Thames in Putney, which hangs at home. It represents the view from the top floor of the ICL building, where most of our meetings had been held.

My offer of services to the National Trust also bore fruit. My approach to Jennifer Jenkins led to my becoming a member of the Trust's Northwest Regional Committee; and also its Representative to two European-level heritage organisations, Europa Nostra and the International Castles Institute. It also indirectly led to my appointment by the Secretary of State as one of his nominated representatives on the Lake District National Park Authority. And these in turn resulted in my becoming interested in Planning Policy in the South Lakeland District Council. Taken together, my 'heritage jobs' gave me a great deal of work over a number of years. And other things flowed from them.

The next specific addition to my portfolio came when I joined the Council of Lancaster University, and subsequently became its Pro-Chancellor for seven years. My position in the University in turn led to my close involvement in the setting up of the Ruskin Foundation, the building of the new Ruskin Library on the University Campus, and the transfer to it of the Whitehouse Collection of Ruskiniana from Bembridge on the Isle of Wight.

Another field was music. Things started in a small way after the death, in 1989, of my friend and neighbour, Leslie Powell, who had been Music Director of the locally based Eversley Choral Union for over forty years, and then its President. I was asked to succeed him in the latter capacity. Though a keen listener, I have no musical training, and knew I could bring the Choir nothing musically. But Leslie's widow Edith, a lifelong friend, urged me to accept, so it would have been hard to refuse. Usually, little work was involved, though I did some fund-raising when the Choir celebrated their centenary in 2000-2001: in that season, there were some particularly ambitious and successful concerts, and the publication of a history of the Choir entitled 'Eversley's Century of Song' by Donald Pringle. The Presidency, however, brought me into a close relationship with an important local Institution. I was pleased to be able, this year, to see Hal Bagot of Levens Hall elected to succeed me, in the steps of his father.

Secondly, through a shared association with Lancaster University, I came much into contact with the Royal Northern College of Music at Manchester, and notably its first Principal Sir John Manduell. John, then approaching retirement, had observed that, whilst Britain is well provided, most European countries do not have adequate facilities for the high level training young people need to move from being Conservatoire *alumni* to the performance of solo roles in opera. He proposed the establishment of a European Opera Centre with EU funding, and sought my assistance. Almost miraculously, the proposal has been realised, though its assurances of continued EU funding – without which it would collapse – are fragile. Until 2002, it involved much work for me.

Another point to mention is that, in 1999, I agreed to become Secretary of the Parochial Church Council of St Peter's Church, Heversham. This too has meant much work. The three subsequent years have seen the considerable enhancement of the Churchyard; the floodlighting of the whole Church; a major refurbishment of the Church Interior; and a big upgrade of the Old School [the Church Hall]. Arrangements have now been made for a complete repair and renovation of the Church Clock. None of these changes have been easy to achieve.

Finally, in the Millennium year, I agreed to establish, and for two years chair, a new non-governmental organisation, to be known as Friends of

*Our <u>whole</u> Family, including William, Antonella and their children,
in London, July 2002.*

Eden, Lakeland and Lunesdale Scenery, or FELLS, to fight against the
building of wind-turbines in unsuitable places in the named area.

Family affairs

Obviously, we wanted to see as much as possible of our own family. The
adaptation of the house made it convenient for them to come and stay.

Rupert has remained in Spain. Claire, after obtaining her Degree in
Education at Southlands, taught in State Schools in London for a while. In
1990, she worked for a year with the St Stephen's Society in Hong Kong,
which helps rescue drug addicts from their addiction. Back in England, she
took a further Degree at Birmingham to enable her to teach blind children,
which she has done, mainly in Oxfordshire, since 1994. William, after
obtaining a Degree in Spanish and Portuguese, undertook a stage in the
European Commission, and worked for a while in the Europa Nostra
Secretariat. In 1990-91, however, he took a Diploma in Law in City
University, and was later called to the Bar, working in a London Chambers.
In 1994, he married Antonella Bonetti from Rome: they had a boy, Edwin,
in 1997; and a girl, Esmé, in 1999. All our children and grandchildren have
been regular visitors.

At the beginning of this chapter I mentioned our plan that Andy should have a successor. Maura and Claire were very attracted by Alsatians. Their views prevailed. At last we had a garden large enough to house a big dog, and of course endless countryside to walk in. In the end, we had two, whose lives overlapped. First came 'Sasha'. She had a black and sable double-coat, and beautiful proportions. She was the most intelligent dog we ever owned, and highly possessive about her territory. Anyone entering the property for the first time, without a proper greeting by us at the gate, was received with ferocity, though nobody was bitten! Once she realised the family accepted them, they were her friends too, and she would become very calm. With all the comings and goings of builders in her early years, this was important. She adored looking at distant views. She loved all the family, and was marvellous with small children. At the crawling stage, our grandchildren were treated like puppies, and on the lawns were 'nosed' away from flowerbeds. All her senses were acute, and fully used, and she was a good watchdog. She was also very wise. She died suddenly, in 1999, as a result of a disease of the nervous system, which made her lose control of her legs. She had to be put to sleep.

By then we had acquired her successor, Penny, born in 1993. We feared Sasha might be jealous. She never was, although Penny got a nip when she occasionally forgot who was top dog. Penny's character was very different. With humans she was always amiable; but she was aggressive with other dogs, which sometimes gave their owners a different impression. She was not particularly intelligent, and basically only wanted people to play ball, or throw sticks, for her. She used mainly her nose, and seldom saw a rabbit unless it got up a yard ahead! Sadly, she too came to suffer from the same disease and had to be put to sleep in 2002. The graves of both dogs in the paddock are marked by a memorial stone. So long as they were alive, dog-walking was a daily commitment.

Another point mentioned at the beginning of this chapter was our wish to travel. Apart from ski-ing, we have in fact had motoring holidays on several occasions, both in the UK and abroad. But we have also travelled enormously in connection with some of our activities, as will emerge later.

Between 1993 and 1995 we helped Julie and Elizabeth to move from their respective homes, in Gerrards Cross and Gatehouse of Fleet, to new ones in Sandside and at Ackenthwaite. These seem to have suited them well, and we have enjoyed having them nearby.

I cannot close this short chapter without mentioning Maura's position. She would perhaps have preferred it if less had fallen on my shoulders. On the other hand she could see that these activities were worthwhile, and did not discourage me from proceeding. In many cases – perhaps especially in relation to the Europa Institute, Lancaster University, Europa Nostra and the International Castles Institute – she has joined me at events, and given unfailingly strong moral support.

She also developed a substantial portfolio of her own activities, all of a local character, which she has now largely passed on to others. Its key components have been work for the Mothers' Union, at various levels; work for the NSPCC; the establishment and operation of a Child Contact Centre at Kendal; and helping to run a *crèche* for the children of people visiting inmates of HM Prison at Haverigg, near Barrow. Above all, of course, she has run the house, with much less help than I had wished, and done much in the garden. And she has always sprung into action whenever any of our children have asked us for help. She, in short, has been the rock on which our family life firmly rests. I cannot say more, because I promised not to write about her! But I hope she understands the immeasurable depth of my gratitude.

When I look back over the last fifteen years, they show me very much as my father's son. He too, after retirement, developed a wide range of *pro bono* activities. He too worked hard to improve house and garden so long as his strength lasted. We both perhaps tried to do more than was good for us – but also enjoyed what we were doing. And we probably both hope to be remembered as having achieved some things of value to others. We both, along the way, were made Deputy-Lieutenants of Cumbria.

Many of the activities mentioned above are described in more detail in the following chapters: they are arranged sectorially, not chronologically, making an approach quite different from that followed hitherto. They vary considerably in length, partly because they differ intrinsically in interest, and partly because some of the sectors are well covered by other publications I have produced.

This brief itemisation of our activities gives only limited clues to the amount of my time they consumed. For a number of years in the 1990s I kept a record of the days spent attending meetings connected with my *pro bono* activities. By 1994, the total had risen to 125; and in 1995 and 1996 was probably higher, because of the financial crisis at Lancaster University. These figures cover only the time needed for the meetings themselves, and associated travel. But probably work at home on preparation and follow-up was not much less. All this was on top of work connected with house, garden and paddock – and with dog-walking! There was never any secretarial assistance; but I had by now, perforce, trained myself to make good use of a personal computer.

CHAPTER 19

Presenting the European Union to other people

WHEN I LEFT the Commission I had accepted only one job. One of the many Brits who used to come and pick my brains on Institutional matters when I was Deputy Secretary-General was David Edward. He had become President of the Consultative Committee of Bars and Law Societies of the European Communities, and as such a frequent visitor to Brussels. Before my retirement, he had succeeded to the Chair of Salvesen Professor of European Institutions at Edinburgh University. His 'Europa Institute' – formerly the Centre of European Governmental Studies – was one of the best Institutes for the study of European Community Law and Institutions in the British University system. Before leaving Brussels I had written to ask whether there might be room, within it, for someone without a Law Degree – or indeed any Degree at all – who would like to teach about European Institutions. His response was so immediate and positive that there could be no going back. Because my retirement had been slated for end-September I in fact began teaching at Edinburgh before I had left the Commission! This chapter is largely concerned with what that commitment meant, but deals also with my other activities in the general field of presenting the European Union [EU] to different groups of people in Britain.

Lectures in The Europa Institute in Edinburgh, and elsewhere

In the Institute, I participated for four academic years in two kinds of teaching: a course of lectures for under-graduates, and a series of seminars for students working for a taught Master's Degree. Both were concerned with European Community Law and Institutions. The Institute was a very agreeable place to work: in terms both of its location, and of the people involved. It occupied several rooms in the Courtyard of Old College, conveniently adjacent to the University Library. It was by now a part of the Law Faculty, of which I was elected an Honorary Fellow.

David Edward lived with his wife, Elizabeth, and family on Heriot Row, in Edinburgh's New Town, where Maura and I frequently enjoyed hospitality. A distinguished practising Advocate at the Scottish Bar, and a specialist in European Community Law, he held the position of Director, with great distinction, from 1985 until, just four years later, he was appointed as the UK's first Judge in the newly-created Court of First Instance of the European Community at Luxembourg. Three years after that, on the retirement of Jack Mackenzie-Stuart, he moved up to the main Court. Thus, when I arrived, David had been teaching for only a year. But he had taken to that – and also to the administrative duties of a Head of Department – like a duck to water. I was again joining an excellent ship.

David had inherited from his predecessor – Professor John Mitchell, Founder of the Institute – one of those top-class Personal Assistants who are at the heart of most successful Institutions. Margaret Ainslie was perfection. She knew everything about the Institute, and everybody who might be useful to her throughout the University. She was efficient, quiet, discreet and universally popular. When John had died of a heart attack, whilst in office, it was she more than anyone who had kept the wheels turning during the interregnum. David's Deputy was Bob Lane, a Canadian Lecturer who had likewise become a specialist in Community Law. There were also one or two Assistant Lecturers, including the French-born Christine Boch.

This was the setting into which I stepped in autumn, 1986. There now began a regular rhythm of term-time visits, which took me to Edinburgh a dozen times in the autumn and spring terms. Usually I travelled up on a Wednesday; spent the night at the New Club on Princes Street, which was happy to accommodate members of my own Oxford and Cambridge Club; lectured the undergraduates next morning; participated in a seminar for the post-graduates with David and Bob in the afternoon; then returned home that evening. The trip was often made by car – a beautiful run going over the spectacular Beef-tub Pass – especially if Maura was going with me; but also often by train. The system gave me plenty of time in Edinburgh, for shopping, theatre, concerts, exhibitions, and so forth; and forced me to keep fully up to date on Brussels affairs. In this, the European Commission Office in Edinburgh – under Stanley Budd and later Kenneth Munro – was a great help. There were soon other reasons for keeping up with Brussels, notably ICL. Moreover, my sister Elizabeth, then living at Gatehouse-of-Fleet, would sometimes see me on her visits to Edinburgh

Our undergraduates were for the most part British, and came largely, though not entirely, from the Law Faculty. The Scottish educational system had soon understood that, following British entry into the Community, Community law was an integral part of British law. All law students had to pass a basic course in the former. (England had still not caught up.) The students were generally of good quality. Our course covered not only the law of the Community, but also the way its Institutions worked. My lectures were on the latter subject. They covered the origins, development and prospects of the Communities; the broad legislative processes; the workings of all the Institutions – except the Court of Justice which I left to my colleagues; the workings of the European Council and the Western Economic Summits; the workings of the European Political Co-operation; the External Relations of the Community proper; and the Community's Finances. It was a large field for a dozen lectures.

My practice was to leave ten minutes for questions at the end of the hour. But none were asked. This was due to what I perceived as the 'Dominie syndrome' of Scottish education. Teachers in Scotland are held in higher regard than in England. Students assume the Dominie will teach them all they need to know; and see it as disrespectful to ask questions, since this implies the teacher has not done his job. When students move from school to University, they seem to carry this approach with them.

I made one or two attempts to force them out of the habit, pointing out that they were probably unique in the UK in having such lectures from somebody who had participated actively in the work of <u>all</u> the bodies just mentioned. It seemed impossible that they should understand everything I said so clearly that that they never wanted to ask a question. If they did not, they were wasting my time and their own. Being polite, for the next couple of lectures they put up some 'fig-leaf' undergraduates to ask questions. But the habit did not stick.

The seminars with the post-graduates were completely different. They were a very dissimilar group. Only those of particularly high quality had a chance of being on the course. There was, and still is, a tradition that a post-graduate student in European Community affairs goes abroad for his second degree. As a result, the great majority of the post-graduates came from other countries: in some years, it was the whole lot. At Edinburgh we always had students from other Community countries, but also from the United States and Canada. The set-up was also quite different. The main preparation for a two-hour seminar was done by two nominated students. The subject was announced a fortnight ahead. And each of the two was expected, at the outset, to make a presentation. The sessions were normally chaired by David, who would thereafter lead the discussion. He was brilliant, always raising questions which forced students to go the heart of the matter.

The Director of the Institute had always made a practice of arranging, from time to time, special seminars for an invited, informed public. They took place, normally, in the 'Raeburn Room' of Old College, a charming hall, easily capable of sitting 50 or 60 people, and decorated by splendid Raeburn paintings. At night, when the proceedings might be by candle-light, there was a warm glow to the place. There was a presentation by a visiting speaker, followed by an always animated period of questions and answers. I spoke at these on occasion. But usually the speakers came from Brussels or London. The gatherings might be followed by a dinner for the speaker.

Soon after I started teaching in Edinburgh, David and I were invited to act as Specialist Advisers to the House of Lords Select Sub-Committee on the European Communities, chaired by Lady Serota. We were to advise on the preparation and conduct of an Enquiry the Committee was making into the 'Staffing of Community Institutions', and also on the preparation of the resultant Report. The Committee had two main objectives: to assess whether current practices enabled the Institutions to recruit high quality staff from all Member States; and to consider whether Community policy was being hampered by present staffing levels. We accompanied them on a visit they made to Brussels to talk directly to people in the Institutions. We went to all meetings of the Committee. We advised who should be included amongst the witnesses. We met many interesting people in the process. We ourselves answered many questions from Members of the Committee. And we assisted the House of Lords staffer concerned – Mary De Groose – in the preparation of the final Report. It was – as is usually the case with Committee Reports of the House of Lords – a solid piece of work. There is no need to recall the conclusions, since a summary is contained in the Report[1].

In an earlier chapter I mentioned my involvement with the preparation of the Council Regulation providing for the care, and eventually the opening to the public, of the Community's Historic Archives. As a result of working at the Institute, and getting to know Scotland far better at first hand, it struck me that it would be valuable if a set of the photocopies being made for Member States could be made available in Edinburgh. With David, I called on Dennis Roberts, the Librarian of the National Library of Scotland, and established that he would be happy to hold the Archives in his Institution if this could be arranged. I sought the help of a former Commissioner, George Thomson, now Lord Thomson of Moniefieth. Together, we convinced Emile Nöel that, the UK being made up of four countries, it should be entitled to four sets of the Archives. This was formally agreed. And Hans Hofmann, the Historic Archivist of the

Commission, came over for the opening of the Edinburgh copy, at the National Library in October, 1987.

All good things come to an end. I was elected Pro-Chancellor of Lancaster University with effect from October, 1990. These new duties meant I had to end my teaching at Edinburgh after the 1989/90 academic year. By now, however, Maura and I had become very attached to the city, and we have continued visiting it for social and cultural reasons.

Though lecturing in this regular and structured way, was now at an end, I continued the activity on a more occasional basis for as long as I felt sufficiently up to date. After my departure from Brussels, the main developments in following years were the successive entry into force of the Single European Act, and the Maastricht and Amsterdam Treaties. All these developments, each of which was positive, I followed closely. So I felt able to lecture with authority into the new Millennium. During the first fourteen years of my retirement, therefore, there were occasional lectures in other Universities: Lancaster, Manchester, Leeds and Dundee Abertay. And also talks in unexpected venues such as the Isle of Man and Cornwall.

The Oral History Project

The Manchester talk had an unexpected consequence. In 1998, I was approached by Professor Ruggiero Ranieri, Jean Monnet Lecturer at Manchester University, for whom I had lectured. He told me that the European University Institute in Florence was co-ordinating an 'Oral History Project' on the development of the European Union. The concept was that a large range of people now in retirement *'who have been most centrally involved in the European experience, either within their own country or in the European Community Institutions'* should be approached and asked to participate. Participation simply meant readiness to be interviewed by serious academics. Only one interview would be needed. The interviews would eventually be placed in the Historic Archives of the Community. It sounded simple enough, so I accepted. It was agreed that I would be interviewed at home by Ruggiero himself, and Charles Turner, one of his Research Students.

As so often, things proved less simple than expected. In a run-up phase, I was sent an extensive list of questions which the team would wish to raise with me. Reflecting how to answer these inevitably meant delving into my extensive documentation. Then the day came – in July, 1998. The team arrived at my home at 11 o'clock. We spent two full hours discussing the precise structure and subject matter of the interview proper. Maura then offered them lunch. But they politely declined, saying they would need their lunch-time to mull over what had been said, and prepare their detailed questions. On return, they taped an interview lasting 140 minutes. It covered the whole of my official involvement in European affairs, including my time in Germany. That was far from being the end. After a while, I received an edited, written version of the interview, with a request for any comments, additions or subtractions. I gave the matter further thought, and sent extensive emendations. Some time later, the amended version came back. It was accompanied by a letter which commented that the team had found the interview particularly interesting; that my comments had greatly enriched it; and that they would be very grateful if I could give it a final read, to see whether still further improvements were possible.

My immediate reaction was one of considerable irritation: had I not done enough already? But then I applied my usual principle: do a job properly or not at all. A careful re-read prompted further inputs from me. It was an action I never regretted. When the final version of the interview arrived, I concluded that – independently of any historic interest it might have for researchers – it represented a compendium of much of my diplomatic career which would be valuable for me to have. It may be consulted amongst the Historical Archives of the Community at the Florence Institute[2].

Forward in Europe: the local European Movement Branch

In 1994 I was invited to attend an informal meeting – which took place round John Ruskin's dining room table at Brantwood – to see whether there was sufficient support for a small group to establish a Cumbria and North Lancashire affiliate of the European Movement. We decided there was. It was officially founded in Kendal on 27 March 1995, under the name of 'Forward in Europe', and addressed by our then MEP, Mr Tony Cunningham. Five Patrons were appointed: the Lords-Lieutenant of Cumbria and Lancashire; our two successive local MEPs; and myself. An excellent Committee of volunteers was established, which I have until now regularly attended as a guest, and with which it is a pleasure to work.

Forward in Europe's principal activity has been the organisation of an annual series of four or five presentations on EU affairs by authoritative speakers. My contacts in Brussels have been shamelessly used. Largely as a result, we have had a remarkable collection of talks, given by present or former MEPs and MPs; present or former Directors-General of the Commission; David Edward from the Court of Justice; a former

Commissioner, Leon Brittan; Shirley Williams; and other well-qualified individuals. I have myself given talks.

All those who have come from afar to speak, have been gratifyingly surprised at the extent of knowledge and enthusiasm about Europe which exists among the 100 or so members of our organisation. It contrasts starkly with the steadily anti-European line of most of the media. Forward in Europe has not limited itself to the series of talks. Another key activity has been the organisation of an annual inter-schools quiz on European affairs. This has proved very popular. The children have shown, also, a surprising degree of knowledge about Europe.

The Peter Kirk Memorial Fund

I mentioned earlier how, after my retirement, I was asked by Elizabeth Kirk to join the Selection Committee of the Peter Kirk Memorial Fund, a charity set up in memory of her late husband, Peter, whom Maura and I had known when he was leader of the first group of British MEPs to go to Strasbourg and Brussels after the UK joined the European Community. We had contributed financially to the creation of the Fund, and I was delighted to help practically. For several years I took part in the annual meeting of the Selection Committee, which chose from a field of strong candidates those few who would benefit from a scholarship: its purpose was to enable beneficiaries to increase their understanding of modern Europe by undertaking a study project on the European Continent. They were then given a lot of help, in terms of practical advice and useful contacts. This involved me in a few days hard work each year, but was enormously rewarding.

I was very pleased, in October 2002, to be asked to move the vote of thanks to Elizabeth, when she ceased to be Chair and was elected Honorary Life President, at a Reception in London. It gave me an occasion to recall Peter's own life. Though taken from the world when only 48, he had already achieved a great deal. The fact that part of his education was at Zürich University must have helped develop his deep commitment to the European cause. He actually heard Churchill deliver his famous speech in that city, in 1946, when Winston said that *'the first step in the re-creation of the European family must be a partnership between France and Germany'*, and then personally proposed the creation of the Council of Europe.

Peter's European commitment was apparent throughout his life: first as President of the Oxford Union; and then as a journalist; a Conservative MP; a Government Minister; a Representative of Britain in the Assemblies of the

Council of Europe and the WEU; and finally, as an MEP. In this last capacity, he fought hard for the enlargement of the European Parliament's responsibilities, particularly in the budgetary field, and for the improvement of its procedures. Parliament was a field where British entry made a very real, positive difference to the European Community. It was sad that Peter's deep commitment to his labours as leader of the Conservative MEPs, and simultaneously as an MP, had contributed to his early death. In thanking Elizabeth, I observed that Peter would have been delighted to think that, now for almost a quarter of a century, a number of young people had each year been helped to spend time studying their chosen subject in a European context.

Conclusion

Over the years, this business of educating people – from the old to the very young – in European affairs, has given me much work but also much pleasure. Clearly, I have been talking mostly to people disposed to give me a good hearing. But students are not always an easy audience. And many of the Forward in Europe lectures have been fully open to the public. Over time, lots of questions have been asked. Not everyone will have been persuaded to share my European views. But I have never been attacked for any of them. And the most common reaction has been to accept that my explanations are sincere, and to ask *'Why don't our media and politicians tell us these things?'*.

CHAPTER 20

Helping conserve the Cumbrian heritage

The National Trust Northwest Regional Committee

AT THE AGE OF TEN, I already had an ingrained love for the beauty of Cumbria's natural heritage – its outstanding scenery of fells, rivers, becks, lakes, tarns, glacial valleys, forests, woods, limestone pavements, and varied shoreline. By the time I was fifteen, prolonged exposure to the architectural wonders of Salisbury and Winchester had imbued a similar love of historic and beautiful buildings. This attachment to the natural and built heritage has steadily grown, throughout my life.

I aimed to use part of my retirement to help conserve Cumbria's heritage. The value of the National Trust's work was obvious. Maura and I had long been members. Jennifer Jenkins responded positively to the approach made to her. Soon after, the Regional Chairman for the Northwest, Spencer Crookenden, and the Regional Director, Laurence Harwood, got in touch. By January 1987, I had been appointed a Member of the Trust's Northwest Regional Committee. My approach to Jennifer was to have other consequences, to which we come later.

The broad aims of the Trust are to acquire heritage properties – whether natural or built – and then manage them in the long-term interests of the Nation, making them as accessible as may be to the general public. Regional Committees are responsible for all matters in their Regions except those specifically reserved to the Council, or to Head Office Committees. The Regional Director and his staff must implement the principles and policies of management laid down by the Regional Committee. The Committee is also responsible for negotiations with Local Authorities, local organisations and local branches of national organisations. The senior staff of the Region are appointed by the Director, after consulting the Committee Chairman.

The Committee, during my time, was chaired first by Spencer Crookenden of Staveley, and then, from 1989, by Peter Sharp of Borwick. It had 10 or 11 members, including at different times people with practical experience of farming, gardening, business, museums, art, fabrics, art history, geology, vegetation science, the law – and in my case Europe. All but one lived inside the Region. They had been carefully chosen; were constructive; and got on well together and with the staff. It was a nice group. It met formally only once a quarter, though there were many other informal get-togethers.

The 300 or so permanent or temporary staff in the Region were generally excellent. National Trust personnel are not well paid. They take their jobs more because they believe in the value of the work than because of the money. The Regional staff are assisted by over 2,000 volunteers. It is a great attribute of the Trust that it is able to attract, and then retain, the loyalty of so many willing helpers. The Regional Headquarters was initially in Ambleside, but moved in 1990 to Grasmere.

The National Trust's Cumbrian properties are mostly land, although there are a few historic buildings, like Sizergh Castle; Hilltop, the Sawrey home of Beatrix Potter; and Wordsworth's childhood home at Cockermouth. Almost all the Central Fell Area of the Lake District is owned, or held on long lease, by the Trust. It is thus responsible for the conservation and management of around one quarter of the area of the Lake District National Park, including England's highest mountain, Scafell Pike; her deepest Lake, Wastwater; twenty-four other Lakes or Tarns; and over ninety farms. The acquisition of this vast estate, pieced together over the first century of the Trust's existence, is one of its finest achievements. It constitutes about 25% of the Trust's total land holdings. Its continued care, and protection against the pressures of changing agricultural policies and mass tourism, is one of the Trust's greatest challenges. The Regional Committee's key function, therefore, was to ensure that this great holding was well conserved and managed. This is important, not only for the properties themselves, but also because the Trust sets an example of good behaviour for others in the Region to follow.

The Committee spent much time discussing proposals for acquisitions. These tended to start with offers of gifts or legacies. The Trust had a general policy only to accept property if it would be economically self-sustaining. If not, the gift or legacy must be accompanied by sufficient capital to fund the balance of its upkeep. Of course, exceptions would be made, in the case of properties of special interest to the Trust. In some cases, the Trust would itself purchase property as it came on the market. The Committee also had to take a view as to whether a property should be declared by the Trust as 'inalienable', which meant that it could not later be sold without a special Act of Parliament. The Committee's recommendations on all these matters went to Headquarters in London, where the final decision lay.

A particularly interesting case arose in 1994. Appleby Castle came on the market, and the question was whether the Trust should aim to buy. Appleby is one of Cumbria's principal and most historic mediaeval Castles. Peter Sharp took me on a reconnaissance. We visited the Castle itself, to see exactly what was on offer. We were aware that the Trust's criteria required that a property, to be a potential acquisition, must be of national importance and under threat: we felt both criteria were met. Then we called on Lord and Lady Hothfield – Anthony and Luly – whose family had sold the Castle in 1962. Anthony has a major collection of works of art, miniatures, archives and so forth, which came from the Castle. He and his wife were prepared, if the Trust bought the Castle, to rent a part of it, and re-install the collection there. Peter and I felt the Trust should see it as a duty to acquire the property. Apart from its intrinsic importance, there was the general point that the Trust owns few stately homes in Cumbria. Five days later, the Regional Committee unanimously agreed a recommendation in this sense to the Trust's Headquarters. I personally pressed the case on Roger [Lord] Chorley, who had by now succeeded Jennifer Jenkins as the Trust's Chairman. But it was of no avail. The National Heritage Memorial Fund had taken the view that Appleby was not of sufficient importance to merit a grant from its coffers. And the Chairman and Director-General of the Trust had in turn advised the Executive Committee against a purchase, which would have involved a total investment of over £5 million. The Committee 'reluctantly' agreed. And that was that.

The Castle was bought by an *entrepreneur*, who had many ideas for making money from it. They all came to nothing, because planning permission could not be obtained. So the purchaser has now put the Castle back on the market. Sadly, I cannot hope that National Trust interest can be more successfully aroused.

It would be tedious to look in detail at all the issues which came before the Committee during my nine years as a member. I shall just list the more important ones.

We had many debates on agricultural and forestry policy. We were helped by the grant of 'environmentally sensitive area status' to the National Park. We agreed to express serious reservations to the authorities about proposals to build a barrage across the Duddon Estuary. We created the Beatrix Potter Visitor Centre in Keswick. We completely re-vamped the National Trust Park at Fell Foot, on Windermere, doing away with the caravans and chalets we had inherited, and restoring it to its original status as a landscaped garden. We agreed – over-ruling a more cautious approach by the staff – to support the proposal of the Lake District National Park Authority to impose a 10 mph speed limit on motor-boats on Windermere. And finally, in 1995, we organised some very good celebrations, in the whole of the Northwest, of the Centenary of the National Trust.

I was present at a big celebratory Lunch in London, in the Great Room of Grosvenor House, on 12 January 1995, a hundred years to the day since the Trust's founding. On that very spot, Octavia Hill, Canon Rawlings and Sir Robert Hunter – under the *aegis* of the Duke of Westminster – had met together to start the whole thing. The Centenary lunch was impeccably organised: a fine balance was struck between recording achievement and a sense of purpose. Excellent speeches were made by the Director-General, Angus Stirling; HRH The Prince of Wales; and the present Duke of Westminster. Well-devised entertainment was provided by representative members of the Trust's staff, with the involvement of many school-children. The guests – some 400 in number – were a congenial mix of the great and the good with those who had given good service to the Trust, whether as professionals or as volunteers. It was moving.

The bare facts related above do less than justice to the important role which membership of the Regional Committee had in my life. It made me many new local contacts. Above all, it forced me to get around to every corner of the Lake District, and to many in Lancashire. And the Committee gave me hands-on experience of the running of farms, fells, forests, historic buildings and so forth. This was to be a great help in other activities with which I became engaged in parallel, notably as a Member of the Lake District National Park Authority and with Europa Nostra (both recorded later).

I close this section with an account of a typical site visit, in June 1990. We had held a meeting of the Committee in Eskdale in the morning. In the afternoon, we went to visit a local, valley farm owned by the Trust. Trust farms are not leased on a fully commercial basis. An arrangement is reached more or less in the following way. The rent is set by negotiation. In the course of this, the farmer indicates how he proposes to run the farm. The Trust in return indicates to what extent this is acceptable, and to what extent changes are needed to make the tenancy compatible with the Trust's policies – for example in terms of stock numbers, fertilisers, hedge-cutting or the use of buildings. These will often involve loss of potential earnings – or additional work – by the tenant. A commercially calculated rent is reduced to take account of these.

On the Eskdale visit, we were shown round by the delightful farmer. He gave us many details about the running of his 60 hectare farm. These naturally included the number of sheep maintained. The visit over, the Committee sat down to a delicious *al fresco* tea, provided by the farmer's wife. One of our members – a considerable farmer himself – opened up a conversation with the tenant about the economics of his farm. It turned out that he had an income of around £7,000; that his rent was £1,600; that he had the new and hated Thatcher poll-tax to pay – for himself, his wife and their two children; that he must also pay a business rate if he continued with his B & B sideline; and that, at the end of the day, he was at best breaking even. The farmer was asked why he thought it sensible to go on farming in such adverse economic circumstances. The reply was revealing. *'You're perfectly right on the figures. I only just keep my head above water. If a major piece of farm equipment had to be replaced, I should have to borrow. Why do I do it? The answer is simple. Look around you. We live in one of the most beautiful and peaceful situations in the whole of England. We would not leave it for all the world.'*

The Lake District National Park Authority

I do not know how my name was suggested to the Secretary of State for the Environment, for appointment as a Member of the Lake District National Park Authority (henceforward sometimes abbreviated to NPA). The first hint came in 1987, when Robin Dower of the Countryside Commission called to discuss the possibility. A year later, I was called to the Headquarters of the NPA for preliminary discussions. Finally, in January 1989, the Minister for the Environment, Virginia Bottomley, wrote to ask whether I would be willing to serve for a three-year initial appointment. I sent an immediate, positive response, and the appointment was confirmed. My first attendance at a meeting of the NPA Board was that April. I continued in office for six years.

The NPA's Board then had 30 Members. Sixteen appointed by the Cumbria County Council; four District Councillors; and the remaining ten Secretary of State appointees. This last group were made up of people living locally, but who were politically independent: they were meant to ensure that the national interest in the Park was given proper expression.

This composition of the Board had an interesting result. The first two groups were made up of individuals from political parties. However, the balance between them was such that no one party could have a majority in the Board. A split on party lines would always mean handing the real power of decision to the appointed Members. In consequence, party politics were abandoned on issues of substance. Items were considered by all Members on their individual merits.

In 1997, after I left the Board, the Government legislated to change the balance. The Board was reduced to 26 Members. But the number of appointed, independent Members was cut to seven; another seven were County Councillors; another seven were District Councillors; and the remaining five were Parish Councillors. In short, the representation of the national interest declined; and that of local interests increased. Party politics had a freer run. I cannot believe this has been beneficial, and there is now talk of putting the process into reverse.

The Board's main duty is to conserve the Lake District's natural beauty, wildlife and cultural heritage. It must also promote opportunities for the public's enjoyment and understanding of the area. In pursuing these purposes, it seeks to foster the economic and social well-being of the local community. To these ends it is the unitary Planning Authority for the whole of the National Park – the County Council and the respective District Councils being only consultees.

From my second meeting on, the Board had an excellent Chairman, in the person of Steele Addison, a County Councillor from near Penrith. All Members lived in Cumbria. They were on the whole well chosen by the different appointing authorities. And they tended to be mutually tolerant and to work well together. The National Park Officer, John Toothill, was top class. And he had very good staff. It was a real pleasure to work in such an ambiance.

The full Board usually met four times a year, though there were occasional extra meetings. In between, each of the five Committees met once, except for Development Control, which controlled all development in the Park, and met three times. All meetings were in the National Park Offices. These were initially split between Busher Walk, in Kendal, and Brockhole, on Lake Windermere: later, they were almost completely united at Murley Moss in Kendal. There were also a good many informal site meetings. These meetings and their preparation, coupled with those of the National Trust, took up a lot of time. There was also much associated travel round the Lake District. It was fascinating.

Taking a long view, our most important work was on Planning Policy. This was primarily handled in the competent Committee. Here one learnt how the whole of the country's town and country planning arrangements work – all new to me.

We used to be consulted by the Government on a range of Green Papers, whose subjects included such heterogeneous matters as the environment, agriculture, forestry, traffic signs, noise nuisance, waste disposal, sport, recreation and tourism. The end-product of this consultation often took the form of Planning Policy Guidance notes [PPG] issued by the Government to Planning Authorities. These were meant to guide County Councils and National Parks in the preparation of their Structure Plans [SP]. The latter in turn guided District Councils in the preparation of their Local Plans [LP]. And these together guided Development Control Committees in determining applications for planning permission, although a Planning Authority is not forced by law to apply all these instruments to the letter if it sees compelling reasons – usually local ones – for making exceptions.

As already noted, the NPA was technically a Unitary Authority. This meant it was responsible for producing both an SP and an LP for the Lake District National Park. In practice, however, there was close co-operation between Cumbria County Council and the NPA, so the SP was a shared document, though with very special conditions attaching to the Park.

During my term of office, we formulated both a new SP (with the County Council); and a new LP. Each had a time span of a decade, ending in 2006. I learnt from scratch how these things take shape, going through a consultation phase, a deposit phase, and then usually a public enquiry, before reaching final approval. For the SP, a Joint Member Steering Group established with the County Council, included me. Throughout its development, the Board's general approach was to insist on the principle that the National Park was there for quiet enjoyment; and also on high levels of landscape protection for the County as a whole and the Park in particular.

For the LP, a special Panel of Board Members was established, again including me. Here, and also in the National Trust Regional Committee, I caused something of a stir in the preparation phase by questioning the need, as stated by the Government, to create more 'affordable housing'. This is received wisdom amongst Local Authorities. But I do not personally think it makes sense in the Lake District. The underlying problem here is the low level of local wages. This means that house prices are determined essentially by incomers from better paid areas, whether as long range commuters or as retirement home seekers. The moral seems to be that, over time, the level of local wages should be ratcheted up. Building cheap houses for rent, and then allocating them to 'local people', seems to me a flawed option. After the Thatcher Government, in my view foolishly, gave individual tenants a right to buy their rented Council housing on the cheap, there was always a danger of further Government interference of this sort. The definition of local occupancy is open to abuse.

I also argued against the system of 'generic consents' granted for agricultural buildings. There seemed to me no reason why farmers – who have chosen to turn agriculture into an industry driven by subsidies alone – should not be subject to the same sort of planning permissions as other industries: indeed, since their buildings are put up in open countryside, there is all the more reason why they should be tightly controlled. But agricultural buildings are substantially exempt from controls.

Unfortunately, farmers – who claim to be 'the guardians of our countryside' – have since the War collectively done more than anyone else to harm it. In addition to putting up vast, cheap and tasteless buildings, and themselves having poor standards of maintenance on existing ones, they have flailed our hedges to death, and allowed our traditional dry stone walls to fall down, replacing both with posts and wire. There are honourable exceptions. But all too few farmers seem to have any feel for the built and natural heritage.

On both these matters, I felt I was striking blows for common sense, but never expected my efforts to have big effects – and they didn't!

Whilst Planning Policy may have been our most important activity, the most high profile was certainly the Authority's handling of the management of the Lakes, and in particular its decision to impose a speed limit for navigation on Lake Windermere.

The NPA has a general power to control navigation on the lakes and tarns in the Park. This is exercised through bye-laws, and case by case. On some lakes, no boats are permitted; on others, rowing boats only; on others sailing boats also; on others, power boats also; and so forth. In the 1970s, byelaws had been issued, with the approval of the Secretary of State, forbidding the use of power boats on 20 of the smaller lakes and tarns. Later, the NPA had proposed a 10 mph speed limit for three of the Park's four largest Lakes – Coniston, Ullswater and Derwentwater. In 1976, a public enquiry was held, known as 'The Three-Lakes Enquiry'. The Inspector concluded that fast power boat use was, generally speaking, incompatible with the National Park concept. At that time, however, the Board had regarded the level of use of Windermere for fast power boating and associated water-skiing as tolerable. Indeed, it had argued that those involved in such activities on the three Lakes could transfer them to Windermere. Now, this chicken came home to roost.

The NPA had instituted a system of compulsory registration for powered boats on Windermere. By 1989, this showed that 16,000 vessels were so registered. By no means all of these were permanently on the Lake: many owners lived far away, and only came by the day, or for holidays. The figure was nevertheless alarming. Applications had been made – and refused – for parascending and the landing of seaplanes on the Lake. Dangerous incidents involving power boats and water-skiers had occurred. Moreover the principle of 'quiet enjoyment' was now making headway at national level.

It was felt something must be done. The question was what. Officers put forward three options: the promotion of a Bill forbidding all navigation; byelaws providing for an overall 10 mph speed limit; or a mix of lesser measures. The first option did not receive serious consideration. It was noted that the second would arouse strong opposition from the power boaters and water skiers. But it had been supported at a Seminar the NPA had organised that year at Brockhole, attended by a wide range of other organisations with interests on the Lake. From the start, it had my own enthusiastic support. In July 1991 – after long debates in Committee and at the Board – it was decided, subject to the views of the Countryside Commission, to promote a byelaw for an overall 10 mph limit. The Commission in due course supported it, though the Sports Council objected.

Meanwhile a Windermere Commercial User Group had been formed to fight the proposal. After considering its objections, the Board nonetheless decided to proceed. Its key decision, taken in 1992 by a majority of 22 to 6 votes, was to propose that a 10 mph limit be instituted, coming into effect five years after confirmation of the Byelaw by the Secretary of State. The latter ordered a Public Enquiry. From now on, the Windermere Commercial User Group was fighting the authority tooth and nail, arguing against it at the Enquiry, stirring up opposition amongst the media, and lobbying politicians at every level.

The Enquiry closed early in 1995, and the Inspector's Report was published. Mr Alesbury found persuasive evidence that significant numbers of people were deterred from using the Lake for recreation because of the 'hostile' conditions encountered. He judged that neither the 'Alternative Management Plan', nor any readily conceivable variant, represented a satisfactory way of addressing the problems. His final conclusion was that there would be a marked improvement in conditions if the speed limit were confirmed, which would still leave intact an enormous range of recreational activities.

The then Secretary of State for the Environment agreed that conflict existed on the Lake. However, he did not consider that the only solution was a general speed limit, which would effectively ban major and long-established users from the Lake. He believed it would be 'unreasonable' to deny a substantial number of users the full use of so important a stretch of water, over which there is a public right of navigation. He refused to confirm the byelaws, and expressed the wish that the parties concerned should explore ways in which management arrangements might be worked up to enable the various activities on the Lake to continue to co-exist.

The power-boat lobby and the water-skiers were cock-a-hoop. But their joy was short-lived. The Board was advised by Counsel that the Secretary of State's decision letter was manifestly defective in law, being 'perverse and irrational'; and judicial review was recommended. Many members felt that the Secretary of State did not seem to have given any consideration to the Inspector's findings, and was proposing negotiations about a Management Plan which the Inspector had found to be impracticable as a means of solving the Lake's problems. In my diary, I referred to the Secretary of State's decision as 'arrogant'. The Board, in September 1996, made an application to the High Court for Judicial Review.

Whilst this was pending, John Major's Government was replaced by the Labour Government of Tony Blair. The new Secretary of State for the Environment announced that he would himself review his predecessor's decision. The process took an inordinate amount of time. However, in the millennium year, the decision was effectively overturned, and the bye-laws approved. They are thus due to enter into force in March 2005. It had been a long battle, but had ended in a famous victory for the National Park Authority.

All sorts of questions about the use of vehicles in the National Park arose. One, inevitably, was the question of road improvements. The NPA had a very simple, basic approach: there should be none in the Park unless absolutely necessary. There was wide consensus to apply this principle rigorously. A good illustration was the consideration of a proposal from the Highways Authority to provide for a series of new passing places on the mainly single-track road which skirts the eastern shore of Ullswater. This road is a *cul de sac*, leading only to the remote and beautiful valley of Martindale. We saw every reason not to encourage its use. Many of us opposed any improvement, but some were more flexible. I suggested a compromise – to approve the provision of just one more passing place! This was approved.

More contentious for the media has been the Authority's continuing opposition to the building of a by-pass for Ambleside. The town is not only a major cross-roads for important Lake District routes, but also one of its principle 'honeypots' for tourists; and there can at times be considerable traffic congestion. There has been a lot of pressure from many people, over the years, to relieve the situation by constructing a by-pass. The obvious solution would be the one adopted in so many other mountainous, continental countries in Europe – or in North America – namely to bore a tunnel: this could easily go under the fells east of the town. Nothing could be technically simpler, as I pointed out in the Board. But in England, such an obvious solution is almost invariably ruled out by the Highways Authority, on grounds of cost. The only route thus far advanced has therefore involved a by-pass through the stunningly beautiful Rothay Meadows north-west of the town. This has been consistently opposed by the NPA because of the damage it would do to the scenery. The Authority has also made the point that the congestion is limited to only a few days in the year: most of the time, there is none. So far, the by-pass has been opposed with success.

We were also very reluctant to increase car parking facilities, especially in open countryside, holding that visitors to the Park should be encouraged to get out of their cars, use steamers, buses or 'mountain goats' – the name given to the local mini-buses – and walk. We did, however, accept the case for keeping coaches out of Grasmere: the concomitant was to approve a big increase in the car park just east of the village.

We looked very closely at all quarrying issues, and I mention, by way of illustration, two particular cases: namely that of the prominent Pink Quarry near Shap, and of the still more prominent Pett's Quarry on the Kirkstone Pass.

The starting point, in all quarrying cases, was a request for planning permission to open or extend a working. Any such permissions are accompanied by close definition of the area covered, and are time limited. Government policy makes clear that proposals for the development of new mines or quarries in National Parks will not normally be permitted. Expansion of existing facilities will only be permitted where it is clear that the development can be achieved without adverse impacts on the landscape or surrounding area, and there are demonstrable benefits to the Park arising from continued working.

The Board always took a tough line. In many cases, quarrying simply ceased. But in both the cases mentioned above, after full site visits had been made, the Board felt that it should move – as the US Supreme Court once famously said – 'with all deliberate speed'. In both cases, the quarry provided important employment for local people. In 1990, approval was given for a final extension of planning permission at Shap Pink Quarry, but subject to stringent conditions. The 'tipping area' was to be restricted. Worked-out areas were to be graded and restored. A band of trees was to be planted, to screen the workings from the main A6 road. And, by the end of 2015, all quarrying plant would have to be removed from the area, and the ground restored to a defined condition. In 1995, similar arrangements were made with regard to Pett's Quarry, at the Head of the Kirkstone Pass. This scar on the landscape can be seen for many miles around. The Board again granted a final extension, with analogous conditions; but this time final closure was to be by the end of 2005. For both these eyesores, therefore, the end is now in sight.

The only renewable energy proposals we had to consider in the Park Authority related to wind-farms. Nobody has yet applied to build a wind-farm in any National Park. There is nothing in law to prevent this, but fortunately the planning instruments mean that the grant of planning permission would be very unlikely. The two cases which came before us during my time therefore related to applications for wind-farms sufficiently near to the Park as to have a visual impact on it. Both were dealt with by the Development Control Committee, of which I was not a member.

The first application was for a wind-farm at Haverigg, on the sea-shore some way to the south-west of the Park: the Committee decided not to raise any objection. The second application, for a wind-farm on Kirkby Moor, to the south of Coniston Water, and right on the edge of the Park, was more contentious. The SLDC – with the support of the Park Authority – turned it down. An appeal was made, and the Inspector upheld the SLDC. The responsible Government Minister, however, ignored the Inspector, and gave planning permission with remarkably little explanation of his decision. National Park Officers launched proceedings for a judicial review. The Development Control Committee ordered that the case be dropped. The wind-farm was built, and has ever since had a very negative visual impact on a vast area of the Park lying to its north. I thought the Committee's decision not to refer these key issues of principle to the full Board was in both cases unfortunate.

In the Planning Policy Committee, we were far less complaisant towards wind-farms near the Park, and supported a Report by the Council for the National Parks entitled 'Power and the Parks' which argued that wind-farms should be off-shore and that the Government should put much more effort into energy saving. Although these matters did not then take much of my time, they were relevant to much subsequent activity on my part aimed at keeping wind-turbines off the Cumbrian and Lunesdale fells.

The last issue to be discussed in any detail had to do with the siting of the National Park Offices and the use of the Brockhole Visitor Centre. It arose in the first place because, in 1999, the County Council advised the Board that it was not prepared to renew the lease of the premises rented by the latter at Busher Walk, Kendal. Other accommodation must therefore be found. This gave rise to lengthy debates over a long period. In the end, the choice fell on Murley Moss, a green-field site, lying on the Kendal to Oxenholme road, which had just been authorised by the South Lakeland District Council for development. It had many merits, including being close to Oxenholme Station and having lots of parking space. The elegant new building was opened in April by our then MP, Michael Jopling. He made a very inappropriate speech, criticising the Authority for the way it worked. One felt that, if he could not mark the occasion in a more friendly manner, he should have declined the invitation.

The question now remained – how to use Brockhole. Money had recently been spent to improve its facilities as a Visitor Centre. Although the option of sale was examined in Committee, there was never any real likelihood of its adoption. Instead the Board decided to continue the process of improvement, and locate its expanded Education Department in offices there. As a result, Cumbrian children can now use Brockhole's magnificent setting as an all-year-round classroom for lessons on the environment. The Field Studies Council also helps deliver the NPA's education programme both at Brockhole, and at the Blencathra residential centre near Keswick.

To round off this account of my involvement with the National Park Authority, I will just mention, without substantial comment, a few other issues to which we gave attention. There were planning issues, like footpath policy and upland path erosion; barn conversion in the open countryside, or the use of artificial slates on traditional buildings. Orders were made for the protection of limestone pavement areas. Grants were approved for farm conservation; woodland re-generation; countryside conservation; the enhancement of conservation areas in towns and villages; the restoration of historic buildings, and archaeological work. Forest Enterprise submitted Design Plans for forests for our approval, with or without changes. With the then Ministry of Agriculture, Fisheries and Food [now DEFRA], we promoted the idea of extensification in farming. Last, but not least, we received regular reports on the work of the large number of Voluntary Wardens, who did an immense amount to help maintain the good state of the National Park.

In 1995, I heard from the Secretary of State that my term of office would not be renewed for a second time. And so, on 31 March of that year, I left the Board. It had been an active and most interesting six years.

Friends of Eden, Lakeland and Lunesdale Scenery (FELLS)

Over time I gradually became involved with wind energy issues, first in the National Park Authority, and then when participating in the Public Enquiry about the development of the South Lakeland District Council [SLDC] Local Plan. But, in 1998, events took place which led me to become a leading actor on wind energy issues in the Northwest, and especially in Cumbria and North Lancashire.

In that year applications were made to SLDC for planning permission for three wind-farms to be constructed locally: at Barkin House Farm, on the Kendal to Kirkby Lonsdale road; at Firbank Fell near Sedbergh; and at Lambrigg Fell, north of the Kendal to Sedbergh road. SLDC officers recommended that the first two be refused; and they were. However, the officers recommended approval of the third. They were unwilling to turn the application down, for fear that the Secretary of State should see them as systematically opposed to wind-farms; call in the application; and determine it himself.

There were many written objections from the public, including me. At a first meeting, the Development Control Committee [DCC] nevertheless voted in favour; but the vote was very close, and there had been coming and going of Councillors during the debate. Advice was given by Counsel that a determination made on this basis would not be safe. So it was decided to hold a further meeting. The DCC allows members of the public to express views before a decision is taken. I was amongst several who exercised this right, giving many reasons why we thought the application ought to fail. However, this would have involved loss of face for Councillors. Many had clearly taken a personal decision before the debate began. The result was approval – after another very close vote. Several of the objectors decided to have lunch together, after the meeting, to review the position. We all felt something must be done, to stiffen the fight against wind-turbines in beautiful open countryside.

Three weeks later, nine of the objectors met together at Rigmaden, the lovely home of Daphne Wilson. We agreed to set up a group to fight inappropriate wind-turbines in our area. A Firbank resident was to chair it, and Belinda Lancing undertook to be Secretary. Although she was already Country Guardian's local representative, it was agreed that the two positions should be quite separate. The Group itself would not be affiliated to the other body – which was widely perceived as being opposed to wind-turbines in all circumstances – since we did not wish to be seen in this light. For a while, our gathering was known simply as 'the Rigmaden Group'. Some six months later, however, it had acquired a more formal existence: it now became known as the Organising Committee of FELLS, the acronym of the organisation we were in process of establishing. These letters stood for 'Friends of Eden, Lakeland and Lunesdale Scenery', and the short title quickly caught the public imagination. Its creation was publicised in local newspapers, and announced to Regional and Local Authorities, on whom we later called.

Contact was made with two other Lakeland NGOs, with a similar outlook, in Barrow and Allerdale; and later with a third, in the Crake Valley area of South Lakeland. Preparations were set in train to recruit members of the organisation and to hold an Inaugural Meeting. A draft Constitution was drawn up, as well as publicity material to explain who we were, what we thought and what we planned to do. A slate of candidates for office was proposed to the Committee by the Chairman – with him in that position – and accepted. I agreed to run for the Presidency – a chiefly honorific position. There was even a date set – in March 2000 – for the Inaugural Meeting, and a plan for its conduct.

It is perhaps worthwhile resuming the key publicity document – 'Our point of view' – which has meanwhile changed little. It explained that FELLS was an association set up to fight wind-turbines wherever they would damage our beautiful countryside – whose inspirational qualities must be defended from harm. Britain's inhabitants needed places where they could still enjoy unspoilt beauty, peace and quiet. Moreover, tourism was a key industry locally: ruining the countryside would wreck it. For decades, planning legislation had largely safeguarded the countryside. We should not today allow wind-turbines – huge, aggressive, noisy, industrial structures – to spoil it. The Government had no clear energy policy. While it saw 'renewable sources', and especially wind-turbines, as a means of reducing 'greenhouse gases', its own figures showed their contribution could at best be small. And it would not say what were to be the roles of coal, gas or nuclear in energy supply.

In conclusion, we recalled that all Planning Instruments recognised wind-turbines could have damaging visual impact. In Lancashire and Cumbria, Planning Authorities had under-valued this consideration, and been persuaded by the flawed arguments of developers, or environmental lobbying organisations, who exaggerated the benefits of wind-turbines and ignored their limitations (which we described). FELLS was not opposing wind-turbines everywhere. In a more industrial scene, or offshore, they could be acceptable. But they must not wreck our beautiful countryside.

On this basis, we were moving steadily towards our Inaugural Meeting. And then, in mid-February, the whole picture changed. The Chairman informed the Committee of his resignation. Now that he could see the organisation was going to be substantial, with a corresponding load on the Chair, he felt unable to give the job the time and effort required. We faced a crisis. Several other Committee members strongly urged me to take on the task. I was more than loath to do so. Well into my seventies, I was progressively pulling out of *pro bono* activities, and also trying to complete this book. Chairmanship would run counter to both processes.

At the same time, no-one else on the Committee had the kind of experience – in terms of planning matters, energy policy, and dealing with authorities at different levels – that was mine. Moreover, without ever encroaching on the prerogatives of the Chair, I had made a substantial input to the development of the Committee's thinking. There was a real danger of the infant organisation being still-born. I ended by reluctantly agreeing that my name be placed before the Committee. My only stipulation was that my term of office be limited to two years: this would be long enough to get the organisation up and running, and to allow it to find a good successor. All this was agreed.

Momentum had of course been lost. It was impossible to hold to the date for the Inaugural Meeting. It was re-scheduled for June. There were, in fact, to be two successive meetings on the same evening: a General Meeting, for the formal business, open only to people who had by then joined the organisation; and a Public Meeting, to inform a wider audience of our aims and purposes. The Committee launched vigorously into the process of attracting individuals to the two of them.

One day in mid-April, when this process was in full swing, Belinda Lancing came to see me to discuss various issues. Late that evening, I was telephoned by the Lancaster Infirmary to say that she had been admitted following a car accident. She had been struck by another car, and had suffered very severe injuries. I would have to do her job as Secretary as well as my own for the two months before the Inaugural Meetings! This meant preparing, and organising the despatch, of all the send-outs; and sorting out all the queries and answers from the public. Not a good beginning!

Despite these happenings, the Inaugural Meetings were a considerable success. Over 60 people attended the Public Meeting. I addressed it: and a good discussion followed. It was made clear we planned to operate on two levels: on the ground, by opposing unsuitable proposals for planning permission; and strategically, by seeking to influence political thinking about wind-turbines at the level of Local, County, Regional and even – in a modest way – National Authorities. To help us at the local level, we wanted to recruit Parish Representatives in as many Parishes as possible. By the end of that evening, we had acquired over 100 members – a figure which soon rose to 140.

Thereafter, the Executive Committee met every two months or so. From the start it was a good Committee. Over time, we added new members: whether because we started below the statutory ceiling, and filled the spaces; or because old hands fell out and were replaced. In the process, the quality of the Committee steadily improved. Progressively, it built up a shared philosophy, which enabled FELLS to speak on all occasions with an informed and single voice. By the time I left, there was an excellent group of twelve, including the President [super-numerary] and a solid, new Chairman.

Below the level of the Executive Committee, we built up a group of Parish Representatives. The idea was that these individuals would act as eyes and ears in individual Parishes, and be prepared to motivate people when need arose. We held briefing meetings for them, and agreed a drill for dealing with any planning applications which came in. We also used them as a channel of communication, on occasions when we wanted to promote letter-writing campaigns. As to the general membership, they attended our Annual General Meetings, and also received a newsletter twice a year. This was in addition to the website we opened.

From the start we launched into a campaign of writing to the local newspapers in Cumbria and North Lancashire. This was very necessary because, until then, the Friends of the Earth [FOE] and other supposedly 'Green' individuals, had largely dominated the correspondence columns as regards wind-farms. We had much in common with FOE. We agreed on the need to reduce greenhouse gases [GHG]; and on the importance of energy saving. But we emphatically did not agree with their approach to the matter of visual impact. They never had a good word to say about the natural beauty of the countryside. They openly stated that, even in National Parks or AONBs, they did not necessarily object to turbines – unless they were in a 'large' wind-farm. But it turned out that even 10 turbines – each 50 metres high at blade tip -were not seen as meriting this description. In short they seemed to have no scruples whatever about turbines anywhere.

Our line was to salute FOE's concern for the biosphere, but to argue that they had no consideration at all for Cumbria's and Lancashire's natural landscape heritage. They never tried to answer such comments, though we made them frequently in the newspapers, on the radio or in the many Conferences we both attended.

I cannot describe in detail our operations regarding planning applications over the two years of my Chairmanship. Suffice it to say that we objected to new applications for a single, vast wind-turbine at Lowick Beacon, and for eight at Wharrels Hill in Allerdale. We also supported the efforts of another NGO to secure removal of wind-turbines from a wind-farm near Barrow, on the grounds that they were not located in the places designated in the planning permission, and were causing major noise, flicker and visual intrusion nuisances to local people. At an early stage we decided we should be too stretched if we tried to intervene in planning applications 'out of area', except where special considerations applied. One such case was Nympsfield in Gloucestershire, where we objected to four wind-turbines, because it was proposed to locate them in an AONB. We also objected – along with a vast number of others – to a proposed decision by the Secretary of State for Trade and Industry to authorise 39 large wind-turbines at Cefn Croes, in Wales, who had refused even to hold a Public Enquiry; but she went ahead regardless.

So far as on-shore wind-turbines were concerned, our biggest worry, during all the time of my Chairmanship, was that planning applications would be submitted for the Shap Fells area. The Non-Fossil Fuels Office a long time ago gave contracts to developers in relation to the Whinfell and Whinash ridges. The former has so far led to nothing. But the latter became a horrendous proposal to locate 27 wind-turbines, each some 115 metres high to blade tip (4 metres higher than St Paul's Cathedral!), along the length of the ridge between the A6 and the M6. We organised a public meeting in Tebay to alert the population to what was planned, and a considerable, local resistance movement has now built up.

At an early stage of our existence, the Government became increasingly interested in off-shore wind-farms. From the start we considered that wind-turbines were more acceptable offshore than on our fells. We argued, however, that they should be well out to sea, and that the way they were placed in relation to each other was visually important.

As regards seeking to influence political thinking at different levels of Government, we injected thoughts in writing about the revisions of the Local Plans of South Lakeland and Eden; and of the Joint Structure Plan for

Cumbria and the Lake District National Park. We commented to the Regional Assembly about the draft Regional Planning Guidance. We also submitted comments to Government Departments. These included critical observations on a Government Green Paper on Planning, one of whose aims was largely to eliminate Public Enquiries. We also made submissions to the Government's Review of Energy Policy, led by the Performance and Innovation Unit of the Cabinet Office. This Blairite think-tank produced a Report of a quality lower than I would ever have tolerated from my Directorate-General of Energy in the European Commission. It was very pro-renewables and in practice anti-nuclear. It showed no understanding of the concept of security of energy supplies; or of what was going on abroad – where the Scandinavian countries were moving away from wind energy – their first love, and the Californians were suffering power-cuts as a result, *inter alia*, of excessive reliance on wind. The Report was no doubt 'politically correct', but did not begin to propose a comprehensive energy policy. It was badly mauled in public, and the Government undertook to produce a new White Paper.

In order to make serious inputs to all these Authorities, we had to keep ourselves well-informed, involving much research and a lot of hard work. In the process, I naturally made good use of my own long association with the Energy Directorate-General of the Commission, and with the International Energy Agency.

As an example of this kind of research I recall that the Government, in 2001, completely changed the electricity supply system throughout the country, introducing something called the New Electricity Trading Arrangements – or NETA. It was necessary to understand these, so that we could see how renewable energy was being accommodated. We talked to United Utilities, and to the Office of Gas and Electricity Markets [Ofgem]. It became quite clear that the whole purpose of NETA was to increase competition between the big generators, with a view to reducing prices. Prices have indeed come down markedly, at wholesale level; but the benefits to end-consumers have been minimal. No thought whatever appears to have been given to security of supply. NETA – coupled with the stupid Government decision to apply the Climate Change Levy to nuclear generators, though they produce <u>no</u> greenhouse gases – is one of the main reasons why British Energy, the big nuclear supplier, is teetering on the edge of bankruptcy. Meanwhile, renewable energy generators have privileged access to the grid, and a guaranteed share of the electricity market. If things go on like this, we shall soon either become largely dependent on foreign gas from unstable countries, or face electricity blackouts like California, or both!

The attitude to be taken by FELLS as regards nuclear power was sensitive. Personally, I feel certain, as do many professional associations with profound knowledge of energy issues, that a major nuclear component is essential to any energy policy which hopes to meet the Kyoto targets for reduction of greenhouse gases. On the other hand, politicians and the media are generally anti-nuclear, or at best keep quiet about the need for it. Ordinary people – left in the dark about the facts – are therefore easily persuaded by 'Greens' that nuclear is dangerous. Some of our Committee members feared we should be accused of being apologists for nuclear, and would therefore have liked us to express no opinions. Others argued that we must have a public position. At an early stage, therefore, the Committee agreed to take a confident but not aggressive line. We decided to say that we shared the view of Government and many NGOs that greenhouse gas emissions must be reduced, and saw energy saving as a top priority; but that nuclear should be preferred over coal and gas, as it does not produce CO_2 and has a good safety record.

As my term of office approached its end, in the early summer of 2002, I made it clear to the Committee that my insistence on a two year limit was unchanged. Once this was accepted, the Committee rapidly agreed to propose the experienced Tim Kimber for election as my successor at the Annual General Meeting. This took place in Kendal on 7 June. After the elections were over, I gave a valedictory report on my stewardship. I was able to say that, during my tenure of office, not a single wind-turbine had been authorised in our area. But there was no room for a false sense of security. (Indeed, ten days later, an Inspector – scandalously in our view – allowed an appeal by NWP against the refusal of planning permission by Allerdale District Council for the wind-farm at Brocklebank.) I also said that the Government's Green Paper on Planning had been awful; and that one could not expect any good to come out of its White Paper on Energy Policy[1]. There would be plenty to fight about.

As I handed over to Tim, I reflected that, in two years, the Committee had managed to create a strong and effective organisation for him to lead. It had been a hard row to hoe, and taken up an enormous amount of my time and energies. But the game had been worth the candle.

CHAPTER 21

Europa Nostra and the
International Castles Institute (IBI)

My initial remit and briefing

IN 1987, Jennifer Jenkins and Angus Stirling, respectively Chairman and Director-General of the National Trust, asked me to succeed Sir Evelyn Shuckburgh as the Trust's Honorary Representative to Europa Nostra and to the International Castles Institute. The latter's acronym of 'IBI', as used below, derives from the German terminology for the Institute. Europa Nostra is the European Federation of Heritage NGOs at National, Regional and Local level. I knew Evelyn well from Diplomatic Service days[1]. Ending his career as Ambassador in Rome, his hobby was cabinet-making, and he had constructed a dozen clavichords. Over an extended tea at his home, he gave me an initial briefing about the two organisations: their aims and purposes; their working methods; and their leading personalities. It sounded interesting: I accepted the invitation.

Later, I advised Jennifer and Angus, that the Trust had not paid sufficient attention to the work of the EU, which could offer it greater benefits than they seemed to think. When they asked me to advise on that also, my role broadened to became that of Honorary Adviser to the Trust on European affairs. I held this position for nearly a decade. It was to prove fascinating, lead me on to greater things, and ultimately take up a great deal of my time.

The merger of the International Castles Institute and Europa Nostra

The most important event for the two organisations, Europa Nostra and IBI, during the early 1990s, was their merger. It was so important, and cost me so much effort, that I begin this account of my work for the Trust in Europe by telling its story. It is always difficult to know where such bold and imaginative concepts begin their life, and who first proposes them. But few would question that the key agents in bringing the process to fruition were Hans De Koster, Caroline Fuchs and myself. Let us begin, therefore with a few words about the two former.

Hans had been a leading light in European politics for many years. As Deputy Foreign Minister of the Netherlands, he had helped draft the Rome

Treaties at Val Duchesse in the late 1950s, and later had much experience of the Council of the EU. Subsequently he became President of the Parliamentary Assembly of the Council of Europe. On retirement from that position, he was elected to succeed Lord Duncan Sandys as President of Europa Nostra, which had a staff of two in a London office. Alongside all this, he had had a successful business career. He and his delightful and immensely dependable wife, Dineke, lived at Wassenaar, just north of The Hague. Hans had an unrivalled politician's sense of European affairs. He was wise, *simpático*, active and far-sighted. We got on well, and there was always complete openness and mutual confidence.

Caroline Fuchs is English, married to a German Professor of Archaeology. They had both worked in Rome and Athens. When we first met, he was teaching at Münster University. There, Caroline had been recruited to be Secretary-General of IBI, whose President lived not far away. IBI had its Headquarters at Rosendael Castle, near Arnhem, where the only staff member was the ever-efficient Els Quarles van Ufford. Caroline, like Hans, is a gifted linguist. She is articulate, perceptive, imaginative, and practical. She had a feel for international organisations from working in the FAO, and contacts with the Council of Europe; but she had little understanding of EU Institutions. Her impact, as Evelyn had predicted, was as positive as that of Hans.

It was at once apparent that both organisations contained excellent people, that there was plenty of goodwill, but that neither was as effective as they could be. When I got to know them better, it struck me forcibly that both, in different ways, needed to be updated and professionalised; but also that there was a lot of overlap in their activities, which suggested the merit of a merger. When this second idea was aired, it aroused keen interest, and later full support, from Hans and Caroline. It began to gather strength in early 1989: the move from concept to reality was unusually rapid. How did it happen?

IBI had been set up, in 1949, primarily as an association of private owners of castles. Over time, it had developed in many ways. It had extended its interests beyond castles – in the strict sense of *'Châteaux forts'* – so as to include progressively *'ancient fortified works and buildings, castles and dwellings having a historic character, or their ruins, and associated parks and gardens'*. It had accepted for membership organisations as well as individuals. It had gradually come to focus on the conservation of the historic buildings themselves, without regard for the nature of their ownership. And it had developed a strong academic arm – the Scientific Council.

Europa Nostra had been set up, in 1963, as an indirect result of the dangers threatening the survival of Venice. These had heightened Italian awareness of the wider threat to the whole built heritage. Italia Nostra and the Italian Castles Institute – the latter's creation had itself been inspired by IBI – became increasingly active. But influential Italians felt that the scale of the conservation problems confronted by their country – both generally and still more in the case of Venice – could not be effectively tackled without a measure of international solidarity. That was the context in which Prince Filippo Carraciolo, on retiring from being Deputy Secretary-General of the Council of Europe for many years, launched the idea of a European-level conservation organisation: this was duly set up as Europa Nostra. Unlike IBI, its membership was made up entirely of organisations, and not of individuals. Later, in the 1970s and 1980s, Europa Nostra grew strongly, under the succeeding Presidencies of two distinguished European personalities – Duncan Sandys and Hans de Koster.

Like IBI, Europa Nostra had progressively extended its scope. Its original focus on the built heritage had broadened. Its Statute, as amended not long before the merger, declared its aims as being to encourage the protection and enhancement of the European cultural and natural heritage; high standards of town and country planning and architecture; and the improvement of the European environment. It also incorporated a new provision for 'patrons and friends', which for the first time gave individuals a right to attend and speak at some meetings, but no right to vote.

This, broadly was the picture in 1987, when I succeeded Evelyn in both organisations. The National Trust had, for long, been actively participating in each; and each in turn now appointed me to their respective managing committees, and later to be a Vice-President. (No-one else enjoyed these privileges in both bodies.)

The Presidents of the two organisations were then Baron Wessel von Landsberg-Velen, for IBI; and Hans de Koster, for Europa Nostra. (The notion of having both a President and an Executive President in Europa Nostra only came to fruition in 1989: at that stage, HRH Prince Henrik, Prince Consort of Denmark, became President, while Hans became Executive President.) Within IBI, I was myself elected to succeed Wessel in 1990. The experience of Hans and Wessel was very different, though complementary. Wessel was the private owner of a moated castle in Germany, a delightful person, but not accustomed to the work of international organisations; Hans, as we have seen, was a major European statesman and businessman.

In April 1989, IBI's Management Committee, meeting in the lovely home of the Marquis Olivier de Trazegnies, the mediaeval Château de Corroy in Belgium, after a thorough review of the organisation's activities proposed and led by myself, reached two key conclusions: it would develop internally on lines which the Committee defined, and enter into exploratory discussions with three other organisations – ICOMOS, Europa Nostra and the Union of European Historic Houses Associations [UEHHA] – about *'all possibilities for developing co-operation and/or joining forces to mutual benefit'*. I was asked by Wessel to undertake these discussions, and duly talked with the Presidents of all three organisations. These talks were based on an identical letter I sent them, in December 1989, making clear that IBI was willing to discuss anything from (a) co-operation on individual activities; through (b) a certain pooling of resources; right on to (c) the concept of complete amalgamation.

The ICOMOS response was sympathetic, but made clear that the organisation could contemplate only option (a). The UEHHA response was on the lines that they saw no merit in options (a) or (b). They put forward some ideas about option (c); but these were complex and appeared to IBI difficult to realise. The response of Europa Nostra, which came in the form of a letter from Hans de Koster to me, dated 5 February 1990, could not have been more positive or enthusiastic. (It had in fact been drafted by me after a private talk with Hans!)

It followed a discussion of the issues in Europa Nostra's Executive Committee. The letter warmly welcomed the IBI approach. It saw complementarity, and no conflict, between the activities of the two organisations. It favoured immediate discussion of option (c). It suggested that the aim of any eventual amalgamation should be to retain the best features of both organisations; that things should be so handled that the members of each felt thoroughly at home in the enlarged body; and that the result should be an operation which was not only combined but also strengthened.

Hans de Koster's letter also made precise and practical suggestions about further procedure. He said that, if IBI were willing to take option (c) further, nothing would be gained by delay. Each organisation might therefore wish to name a small team. The teams would be mandated, *ad referendum* to their parent organisation, to prepare outline proposals for amalgamation. These would provide a basis sufficient for both organisations to consult their members, perhaps in the course of their respective General Assemblies later that year. If the outline proposals were well received, then negotiations for a definitive agreement could follow.

Amazingly, not only did all this happen, but the subsequent negotiations led to the merger of the two organisations at a Joint Meeting in the beautiful and historic setting of Dublin Castle, on 14 September 1991, a little over two years after I had formally launched the idea. I recorded the full history of the merger process in a historical note originally written for the merged organisation at the time of its Tenth Anniversary[2]. No attempt, therefore, is made to go into a lot of detail in the following paragraphs, which are confined to essentials.

Both organisations agreed, without too much difficulty, to set up the Joint Team. This included the two Presidents and Secretaries-General, myself, and a number of others. In August 1990, the teams finalised a *Joint Memorandum for submission to IBI and Europa Nostra'* proposing merger, and agreed to submit it to their respective General Assemblies. It reflected the basic approach suggested in Hans de Koster's letter; and it advanced two further key concepts, namely that any merged organisation should launch a big drive for more members and supporters; and that it should try hard to assist Central and East European countries – just emerging from the constraints of 45 years in the former Soviet Bloc – in confronting their vast inherited problems of conservation. This last was a concept specially close to the heart of Hans. Finally, it recommended the establishment of a Joint Preparatory Committee (which became known as Prepcom) to propose all the details. All this, too, was approved by the two organisations.

It may help, at this stage, to identify the most interesting and sensitive of the issues of substance which emerged in the preparation of the Joint Memorandum, and in the subsequent work of Prepcom; and to indicate the key elements of the careful debate and reflection which took place on each.

The Statute of Europa Nostra had limited the organisation's aims and membership to Europe, whereas that of IBI had described the organisation as 'international' with no geographical limitation. In debate, some argued that the merged organisation should have the broadest geographical span. Others pointed out that the action of IBI had <u>in practice</u> been almost entirely Europe-orientated; and that the merged organisation would be fully stretched to provide a meaningful service, even for Europe, now that the possibility of effective coverage of the Central and East European countries was real. These latter, practical arguments prevailed.

The Statute of Europa Nostra had defined its aims in terms of the whole of the 'cultural and natural heritage', whereas that of IBI was limited to the built and a small part of the natural heritage: in other words the heritage was widely defined in the former, while the latter completely excluded such aspects of culture as art-works, painting and literature. On this issue, many felt that a narrowing of the field addressed by either of the organisations would be a mistake in the context of merger; and that any separation of the different sectors of the cultural heritage would be arbitrary. But it was argued that Europa Nostra had in practice hitherto focused almost exclusively on the built and natural heritage; that it would be difficult to couple with the problems of merger a meaningful entry into other heritage fields; and that it would be wiser to limit the merged organisation's ambitions but ensure that it did well anything it claimed to be doing. Once again the practical arguments prevailed, and the first Statute of the merged organisation was to speak of the 'architectural and natural heritage'.

There was much discussion about the balance between collective and individual members. Europa Nostra's Statute had described it as a 'federation of organisations'; and 'friends' had had no vote. IBI's Statute had recently been revised so as to give a stronger position than before to its collective members, but the individual members nevertheless retained full voting rights. It was clear that, in the much larger organisation which merger was creating, there had to be effective decision-making processes, with voting rights apportioned carefully. The end-result was to give individual members one vote each at the General Assembly, but at the same time to give certain categories of collective members (organisations) 2 to 5 votes each.

There was much discussion about the central institutions of the merged organisation: the General Assembly, the Council and the Management Committee. The General Assembly was from the start seen as the sovereign body of the organisation. However, it could not normally meet more than once a year. This meant its powers must be confined to strategic issues: the Statute; the Annual Report on the activities of the organisation; finances; and key elections. The Council was therefore seen as responsible for broad policy questions, and for selecting those officers and committee members not elected by the General Assembly. It was clear, however, that this body, though substantially smaller than the General Assembly, would still have to be quite large if it were adequately to represent the many different interests and regions of the merged organisation. Practicality and expense suggested twice-yearly meetings should be the rule. This meant there was a need for a small, well-balanced, hard-working Management Committee, to ensure the effective day-to-day running of a corporate body of the scale and sophistication of the merged organisation. In proposing the creation of this Committee, they spoke of it as 'the work-horse and continuity body'. It was expected to meet four times a year.

One other point covered in the Joint Memorandum must be recalled, namely the choice of a Title for the merged organisation. It was agreed that the full statutory name was to be 'Europa Nostra united with the International Castles Institute'; but, since such a title would be unwieldy, it could be shortened to 'Europa Nostra' for everyday use.

The two Secretariats were combined, though for a while retaining offices in Rosendael as well as The Hague.

Prepcom met several times, always in a very positive atmosphere. It approved, for submission to the Institutions of both Europa Nostra and IBI, three key documents: a full Report on its work; a draft Statute for the merged organisation; and a draft Initial Programme of Activities. It also recommended that the whole process of merger be completed in a Joint Meeting of the two General Assemblies in Dublin Castle, to be immediately followed by the first meetings of the General Assembly and Council of the merged organisation.

It was always clear that a successful merger would only be assured if, at the first meetings of the new organisation, agreement could be smoothly reached on a balanced slate of the individuals from the two organisations who would assume the various offices and committee positions in the new Institutions. It was felt by Hans and myself that this matter should not be covered in the Prepcom Report. Instead, we held extensive, confidential and delicate consultations within our respective organisations: out of these a slate emerged which both felt able to submit to our respective Institutions. A key point, on which Hans and I were unshakeable, was that those proposed for the Management Committee included <u>no</u> passengers! It is interesting to note that, apart from the proposed President of the merged organisation (HRH The Prince Consort of Denmark), the slate comprised 24 names, of which just half came from each organisation.

One might suppose that, after such careful preparation, the meetings at Dublin Castle would present no problems. Indeed, as at a good play or opera, those who were present, but had not been involved in the run-up, may perhaps have had that impression. The stage managers, on the other hand, could not relax for an instant. We had two very full days ahead of us, with a complex sequence of meetings, each one with a different cast of characters, and with few real precedents to guide us. Moreover, most unfortunately, Hans de Koster, who was to be the first Executive President of the merged organisation, was taken ill just before it began, and could not be active. Characteristically, his illness had been precipitated by heavy travel in pursuit of his Central and East European aims. Nevertheless, all went well. All the documents – and the slate – were approved. And our Irish hosts had arranged some very agreeable celebratory events.

This backward look at the merger process, completed so long ago, has led me to certain personal reflections.

When the process was launched, all concerned knew it would be difficult. People are usually hesitant about change, especially when it relates to long-established habits and structures. So it is hard to achieve, even when dealing with efficient governmental or professional organisations. It is harder still in a context of non-governmental organisations, which, important though they are, have slender infra-structures and cannot pretend to the same level of efficiency. Individuals play a larger role in them; and very often they are individuals who are busy and have many fish to fry.

In this case, we were fortunate to have, in the key positions in both organisations, people of goodwill and determination, who developed a relation of mutual confidence, first between themselves, and then between their respective organisations. That was why, first the exploratory talks, and then the negotiations proper, moved so fast. There were some very real problems of substance in the exchanges. Finding solutions was not easy. It required patience, forbearance and imagination: all were forthcoming. Ambiance also counts for much. The fact that the crunch meetings on both sides, and the meetings between the two organisations, almost invariably took place in highly agreeable surroundings, helped things forward.

As to the substance of the merger arrangements, the outcome of the key debates discussed above has stood up well to the test of time. I have already quoted Hans de Koster's letter of February 1990, which suggested that the aim of any eventual amalgamation should be to retain the best features of both organisations; that things should be so handled that the members of each felt thoroughly at home in the enlarged body; and that the result would be an operation which was not only combined but also strengthened. Those clear and noble aims have been amply achieved, not just because the merger process itself went well, but also, and still more importantly, because those who have led and served the merged organisation since then, have done so with tact, good sense, conviction, persistence, fortitude and imagination.

It is gratifying to be able to write in this way, because the challenge of merger had forced me to do an _enormous_ amount of work. At each meeting – whether of Europa Nostra, or of IBI, or of the two together – I had drafted the agendas and written all the key papers. Later I had written the complex briefs for the President – Prince Henrik – at the Inaugural Meetings. Of course I had a lot of help. This came especially from Hans and Caroline.

But there were many others, far too numerous to mention individually, who gave assistance and advice: I hope they will see this phrase as an expression of my sincere gratitude.

In the play 'Julius Caesar', William Shakespeare put into the mouth of Brutus seven famous lines which may serve to conclude these comments on the merger:

> *'There is a tide in the affairs of men,*
> *Which, taken at the flood, leads on to fortune;*
> *Omitted, all the voyage of their life*
> *Is bound in shallows and in miseries.*
> *On such a full sea are we now afloat;*
> *And we must take the current when it serves,*
> *Or lose our ventures.'*

The current has served us well.

A backward look: some pre-merger developments

I have chosen to run the merger story without interruption. But let it not be thought that, during those four years, from 1987 to 1991, nothing else happened in either organisation. Both were in a process of internal reform and improvement. Both devised and adopted new Constitutions, bringing themselves up to date. Being in both Committees, I was constantly suggesting how one could benefit from the experience of the other. I was the author of the IBI Constitution; whilst Costa Carras from Greece was responsible for Europa Nostra's. We worked hand in hand: so, as the merger process progressed, the two Constitutions grew together. This made the writing of the Constitution for the merged organisation a lot easier.

Before merger, each organisation had two or three meetings a year. In those days, each had a General Assembly and a Committee, with no Council. In each case the bigger meetings were accompanied by some kind of cultural expedition, usually of considerable interest. They took place in a variety of attractive places.

Throughout this period, the Headquarters of IBI remained at Rosendael. But its Europa Nostra counterpart faced a move. When I arrived, it was housed in Buckingham Gate, London, where the staff consisted of two girls. Hans came over from the Netherlands as necessary; and the Secretary-General was Maurice Lindsay of the Scottish Civic Trust, who came down from Glasgow. However, the landlords decided to raise our rent. We could ill afford this, and Hans, who had a business office he no longer really needed, in a very desirable location – the Lange Voorhout in The Hague – generously decided, after wide consultation, to move Europa Nostra's Headquarters into it rent-free.

In January 1990, both the London girls – Charmian Marshall and Marianne Huhtala [a Belgian] – announced, a few weeks before the move, that neither wished to go to the Netherlands. This was awkward. To make matters worse, I had raised some commercial sponsorship with which to launch the first Europa Nostra Magazine, due out just before the move! I asked Hans whether, if my son William were interested, his temporary assistance would be appreciated. This suited everybody. William, therefore, arrived at once in the London office; picked up all the tips he could from the two girls there; packed up the files; assured the timely issuance of the Magazine; transferred the office to The Hague; and stayed on for quite a number of weeks, helping the two Dutch girls recruited by Hans and Dineke – Meta Gemert and Margot Dijkgraf – to find their feet.

The Europa Nostra Awards Scheme was and remains so important in the work of Europa Nostra that it must have a special mention. It had been started by Duncan Sandys in 1979. He had presided the British Civic Trust, and was used to its Awards Scheme. He felt it could be transposed to European level. When I appeared on the scene, however, it was poorly run, and open to abuse. Each applicant sent in a file, corresponding to only the vaguest of parameters. Before and after photographs of the restoration work were a requirement. But there was no system of neutral inspection, to make sure that these truly reflected the state of the project.

Each year, 100 or so files, from all over Europe, were submitted to a full-day, special meeting of the Europa Nostra Committee. I suppose this comprised upwards of thirty people, many of them without any specialised knowledge. Several of them, moreover, were mainly concerned to ensure the success of applicants from their own country! It was a miracle that, by then, there had been no scandals. The system had to be put on a more solid basis. Merger offered the perfect occasion. And the corrective work was done by the distinguished architect Sir James Dunbar-Nasmith – a Scottish contemporary of mine at Winchester College – who raised the standard of the whole scheme to exemplary levels. In this he was much helped by a new staff member, Marijnke De Jongh, a former Keeper of Prints of the Rijksmuseum at Amsterdam, who with Professor Marcel Van Jole, has produced a splendidly illustrated book 'The Power of Example', covering the first twenty-four years of the scheme's existence[3].

Six Europa Nostra Awards presented in Glasgow, 1990.

My relations with the National Trust

How were my relations with the National Trust proceeding? Let us look at the period of our active co-operation on European affairs, from 1987 to 1996. During the early years, I cannot speak too highly of their co-operation. My acceptance of Jennifer's invitation had been based on the understanding that the Trust would pay my direct travel and subsistence costs when working for them, though it was often possible to keep these low by combining the trips I was making for ICL with some Trust business. They fully honoured this commitment for the whole decade. I had also insisted on having a personal contact amongst the senior staff at the Trust's Head-quarters in Queen Anne's Gate; and it was agreed that Leslie McCracken would fulfil that role, which he did with great skill until his retirement in 1992. After that the co-operation was less easy.

Angus Stirling made clear from the start that he was under continuing pressure from certain heritage NGOs on the continent to set up a European Federation of National Trusts and like-minded organisations. He was not willing to do this. The National Trust co-operated with like-minded organisations all over the world. Insofar as European NGOs wanted something closer, he always advised them to join Europa Nostra, or IBI, or both.

In all this, Angus was backed by Jennifer Jenkins, as Chairman, and by Lord (Roger) Chorley, her successor; and underpinned by Leslie McCracken. The National Trust was constantly supportive of the Europa Nostra and IBI, lending pleasant venues for meetings – such as Polesden Lacey, Chirk Castle and Hatchlands – and providing speakers. They helped me, too, to meet other British NGO's or similar, including English Heritage. They also supplied me with briefing, whenever needed, for particular meetings.

Both Jennifer and Roger took teams, at my suggestion and including myself, to visit the European Commission and the European Parliament. Before the first such visit, Jennifer and Angus enquired what they should be asking for. *'Nothing'*, I said. *'Do not go as demandeurs, but as people with a great deal to offer to the Community Institutions. The National Trust is very highly regarded throughout Europe. Tell them you would like to place your expertise and experience at their disposal. They will be delighted. At a later stage, when you start to apply more systematically for aid from the Structural Funds, they will be only too pleased to help you'.* My advice was followed, and it worked. Later, the National Trust obtained millions of Ecus and Euros from Brussels.

Getting the merged organisation off the ground

It had always been clear that, while it would be gratifying to bring the two organisations together, it would be tough ensuring they were well run. I had told Hans that he could count on my continuing support. However, as we have seen, his health was already a worry at the time of merger. Indeed, though he rallied for a while after Dublin, he never recovered his full vigour. Both he and Caroline Fuchs had made clear that, while prepared to exercise the functions of Executive President and Secretary-General for a year, others must then take over. The first problem, therefore, was to identify a successor to Hans.

He and other Council colleagues urged me to stand. But I had no such wish. The strain would have been too great: after I had joined the two parent organisations in 1987, I had become Pro-Chancellor of Lancaster University. Hans had got to the point of suggesting some names to me – including that of Daniel Cardon de Lichtbuer from Belgium, whom I knew – when suddenly his health worsened. In March, 1992, he felt obliged to ask me to take over as interim Executive President pending the appointment of a proper successor. Having come so far together, I felt unable to refuse. Late that month, Prince Henrik wrote to all Council members saying that he had appointed me *ad interim*, and on the understanding that

Prince Henrik of Denmark, President of Europa Nostra,
at Istanbul, with the Mayor, 1992.

I did not wish to continue after the Annual General Meeting in September at Istanbul.

Within days, I had approached Daniel Cardon in Brussels. He was due to retire from his position on the Board of the Banque de Bruxelles Lambert that December, and was pleased to be asked. By end-April, he had agreed; the Prince had approved; and I had written to Council members proposing his candidacy. The Council liked the idea. And, in September, the General Assembly, meeting in Istanbul, elected Daniel as the new Executive President. There was, however, one condition. The appointment was not to take effect immediately. It should co-incide with Daniel's retirement from the Board; and I must continue to serve until end-December, 1992.

But the story was not yet over. Late in November Hans died. Chancing to be in Brussels, I was driven to the funeral near Leiden by Daniel. On the way, he told me that there had been a Palace Revolution in his Bank, and that he had agreed to take over as President and Managing Director. He much regretted the inconvenience this would cause for Europa Nostra, and suggested that he should resign from his post as Executive President.

I asked whether there was any alternative. He replied that, as Bank President, he was allowed to hold one external *pro bono* job. He was quite willing that this should be the Executive Presidency of Europa Nostra, but

Daniel Cardon and Els Quarles at Istanbul, 1992.

he could only promise to give us an average of half a day a week. He would participate fully in all Council and General Assembly meetings, and preside all Management Committee meetings.

It was an awkward moment. As Bank President, Daniel could place many facilities at the disposal of Europa Nostra, and would have a stronger personal position. He would also have plenty of administrative support. Half a day a week of his time would be worth a day or more a week of most people's. Nevertheless, it was obvious that he could not always give Europa Nostra affairs priority. To be an effective Executive President in the new circumstances, he would need me to give a lot of time too. I would have to become – not an ordinary Vice-President as I had planned – but a very active first Vice-President, ready to support and substitute for him. This was the basis on which we agreed to proceed. The picture did not change until the end of 1996, when Daniel ceased to be Bank President. The partnership appeared to me to operate well. Both of us had both worked for long periods in the European Commission; and were deeply committed both to the European cause, and to the cause of culture. Our temperaments were complementary: he was a centre-stage man; I liked to remain back-stage so long as the right results were achieved. We saw a great deal of each other; and I think we always knew what the other thought on Europa Nostra matters.

Daniel, for all the years I was there, fulfilled my hopes that he would offer practical help in many ways. His flat on the Avenue Franklin Roosevelt was always available for smaller meetings, and the Bank's offices on the Place Royale were often used for larger gatherings. He also fully respected his undertaking to participate fully in Council and General Assembly meetings, and preside Management Committee meetings. There were exceptions – when I took his place – but they were rare.

I cannot allow Hans De Koster's name to disappear from these pages without some last thoughts about him. To all the causes he adopted, he gave with a very warm heart. This was true of the European Union, of the Council of Europe, of Europa Nostra, and finally of the re-integration of the Central and East European countries into the historic European family of nations. As for Europa Nostra, he not only presided it well, chose its staff with care and perception, and worked devotedly for merger with IBI, but was also immensely generous. During the merger talks he privately advised me that a job should be found within the organisation for Dineke: this would be good, not only for the organisation, but also for her. The job we created, that of Deputy Treasurer, she performed for years with devotion, distinction and enormous efficiency. In 2002, she moved up to become Treasurer, following the premature death of the incumbent, Dino Leventis of Cyprus, a man of great quality. A mere six months before Hans died, he told me that he and Dineke had decided to prolong the rent-free period of five years for the Europa Nostra Office, originally given in 1990, to count from 1992. The Headquarters is still there – only occupying a much larger part of the same building.

Hans's funeral at Oegstgeest, near Leiden, was immensely moving. Although held in a lovely, red-brick, barrel-vaulted Church, it had no religious content, Hans having been agnostic. But it was sincere and profound. It included interventions about Hans's career from four people who had known him well; remarks by two of his children; and finally closing comments by Dineke, very composed, who said Hans had died smiling, and listening to the Beethoven Piano Concerto of which excerpts had been played to us earlier. It was at once decided to set up a Fund in his memory. It was easily agreed that it should be used to help people from Central and East European countries participate in the work of Europa Nostra. Substantial sums were subscribed at the time, and money still comes in. The Hans De Koster Fund continues to contribute to its declared purpose.

The next task was to find a successor for Caroline Fuchs, who had done

Hans De Koster.

so much to put new life into IBI; to promote merger; and then to inspire the mainly new staff of the merged organisation to get the business off to a flying start. Lester Borley was an obvious candidate. As Director of the Scottish National Trust, he had long been an active member of the Council. And he was due to retire. Fortunately he was willing to stand, and acceptable to Daniel, and he too was elected in Istanbul.

At this point I shall jump ahead to talk about all of the merged organisation's Secretaries-General. Lester served four years, but then resigned. He contributed much professionalism to the organisation, and substantially increased its involvement in Central and East European countries. At my suggestion, Daniel then invited Antonio Marchini Camia to succeed, and he in turn served four years. He had been in the Commission for decades, and ended his time as its standing representative in CRP I, and then as Chef de Cabinet of a Commissioner. His contributions lay in enormously improving – in tandem with Daniel – relations with the EU Institutions; in promoting harmony in the Council of the organisation; in further professionalisation of the whole outfit; in raising the sights of the staff; and in a substantial update of the Statute. During his time, the annual subsidy received by the organisation from the EU – which had started at my initiative some years earlier – had risen to 80,000 Euros.

On his departure, the Council decided to appoint a professional as Secretary-General. It gave the job to a staff member, Sneska Quaedvlieg Mihaelovic. The name, translated from Serbian and Dutch, means literally *'Snow-white buzzing fly, son of Michael!'*. She had been recruited in 1991, and was already Deputy Secretary-General. Before joining Europa Nostra, she had done two *stages* with the Community Institutions, and then served in the Commission Delegation Office in Belgrade. A Serb, she had met her Dutch husband at Nancy University, and was now living in the Netherlands. On her appointment she came to meet me at a 'working breakfast' in my London Club: my diary records that it lasted for over four hours – the responsibility being perhaps equally divided! She is determined to keep raising the standards of the organisation.

From merger until the end of 1996, when Daniel ceased to be Bank President, and let me resign from the position of Vice-President, my activities on behalf of Europa Nostra gradually acquired a pattern. I attended all meetings of the General Assembly, Council and Management Committee. These were grouped so as to involve four occasions a year, but for periods ranging between a day and a week. Half the meetings were in Brussels: the rest, all over Europe. I also attended the annual meetings of the Scientific Council – to be described later – and the Awards Panel; as well as occasional meetings of something called the European Heritage Group, and of certain Europa Nostra Committees. Not infrequently, I lobbied the EU Institutions, though always when I was in Brussels anyway. And occasionally I was in contact with the Council of Europe – although our Members gradually came to see that the EU was far more important to us, since over the years it became a major source of subsidies. Finally I continued, when asked by Daniel, to make presentations 'on location' of Europa Nostra Awards in many parts of Europe.

Key activities of the merged organisation

The scene is now set for a brisk review of what the newly merged organisation was in fact doing. This will be almost entirely factual, but some human colour will follow.

Let us dispose briskly of the European Heritage Group. Although Europa Nostra always thought of itself as *primus inter pares* amongst the European level heritage NGOs, it had to face the fact that there were others, including the UEHHA, the European Forum for Arts and the Heritage (EFAH), and the European Branch of ICOMOS. There were many points on which we held shared or similar views. Daniel encouraged the idea of our talking to these different bodies; and we began this in 1994. But gradually he cooled to the process. He would not commit himself to chairing the meetings of another group, and asked me to do this. Things went well. We soon had common views we wanted to share with the Commission and the European Parliament. Meetings were arranged, notably with the then Commissioner for Culture, Marcelino Oreja. Our Delegation to these was led by Daniel. But he never got into the habit of distinguishing clearly between Europa Nostra and the EHG. Finally, after I left, he switched back to representing Europa Nostra as the true voice of European culture, and allowed the EHG to die. I was sorry to see a body I had spent some time in shaping treated in this way. I feel there is still a need for it.

I turn next to the work of the Scientific Council. It had been created in 1959, within IBI, by a remarkable Italian, Piero Gazzola, its President for 19 years. He was also co-founder of ICOMOS. His strong leadership led to a rapid flowering. As the Scientific Council's name indicates, this was a completely different body from the more political Institutions of IBI. The latter comprised top dogs of various heritage NGOs, castle owners and interested lay people. The members of the Scientific Council, however, were scholars of various disciplines relevant to conservation.

There were regular Conferences. Some of the themes covered are mentioned in the next section. Many excellent papers were presented. And these were published in the former 'IBI Bulletin' – since merger renamed as the 'Europa Nostra Bulletin'. In 1999, when in his 80s, and with steadily failing eyesight, a distinguished Spanish member of the Scientific Council, Don Leonardo Villena, published a *'Prontuario'* of the Bulletin[4]. This word does not translate into English: we have to use the Latin word *Compendium* to give its sense. The *Prontuario* contains a full index, by theme, by geographical area, and by author, of all the 600 or so articles which had appeared in the first 50 numbers of the Bulletin. It was also, I believe, the Scientific Council which coined the word 'Castellólogy' to define the field of its activity.

Following Gazzola's death in 1979, there was a period of instability in the Scientific Council, leading to loss of momentum. It became detached from the General Assembly and the Committee. Both problems were put right when Gianni Perbellini was elected President in 1988. The fact that his election took place at a meeting in Marienburg Castle, Poland, reminds us of another characteristic of the Scientific Council. Its scientific *rôle* enabled it to maintain contacts in Central and East European countries, even during the worst of the Cold War, which were impossible for other bodies. It met in Warsaw and Cracow (in 1972), and in Budapest (in 1970).

On taking office, Gianni felt that a number of Scientific Council members had lost some of their fire with age. They were gracefully persuaded to accept a retirement age of 70 for <u>regular</u> members, who enjoy certain privileges: on condition that those <u>over</u> 70 could remain as <u>honorary</u> members, though without the privileges. This manoeuvre, worthy of his compatriot Machiavelli, enabled Gianni to recruit a host of active, younger members, many from Central and Eastern Europe. The Scientific Council was rejuvenated just as I was assuming the Presidency of IBI. At the same time, the process of merger helped bring about a much closer co-operation between the Scientific Council and the central institutions, with mutual benefit. This was something I strongly encouraged, setting an example by attending the Scientific Conferences regularly, sometimes with Maura, and encouraging other Council members to do likewise.

I have already explained how, in the merger context, James Dunbar-Nasmith reformed the Awards Scheme. From 1991, I became a member of his Judging Panel. James was an excellent Chairman. He had brought Gianni Perbellini and some other knowledgeable people into the Panel; eliminated all 'nationalistic' considerations from the discussions; started serious debates on conservation technology, often of great interest; and led the Panel to reasoned, measured conclusions. By a year later, the situation was still more solid. Marijnke De Jongh having joined the staff, everything was better prepared. The Panel had grown in size, and in quality. Participating was very hard work, as the meetings lasted several days, but enormously worth while. The Panel finally attained a total of twelve members, and now includes architects, landscape architects, art historians, practising conservationists, professors, and senior employees of national cultural institutions.

Under these new arrangements, the Awards rapidly assumed much greater significance. They are keenly contested. The annual announcement of the results of the Panel's work is eagerly awaited. The application of very testing criteria means that – for the whole of Europe – only seven or eight Medals are awarded, and a further thirty or so Diplomas. Winners are entitled to consider themselves as belonging to a very select group. The Europa Nostra Scheme is now recognised as the most important competition, at European level, in the different fields it covers: churches;

historic houses; the industrial heritage; public buildings; gardens and landscape; and fortifications. Furthermore, it enjoys the Patronage and financial support of the EU. Indeed, beginning in 2003, the Commission decided to authorise six money prizes – one for the best award in each category.

Prior to the merger, while Europa Nostra had its Awards for objects, IBI had a Medals of Honour Scheme, whose aim was to recognise the merit of individuals who had undertaken exemplary work in favour of the heritage. The concept was excellent; but the procedure and criteria for awarding the Medals were ill-defined. Merger again provided the occasion for review and tightening. An upper limit of three Medals a year was adopted. They are awarded by the Management Committee, and no Medal may be given unless two thirds of the members present vote in favour. Since then, the Medals' stature has progressively grown; and in recent years some very distinguished people have been happy to receive them. They have included, for example, HRH the Prince of Wales and the principal Restorers of Warsaw Castle and the Sistine Chapel.

Prior to the merger, IBI had a small Restoration Fund, which is now run by the merged organisation. Its initiator had hoped that substantial capital would be raised for this purpose. But this did not happen. Instead, IBI received an annual donation of $10,000, which has been made by an individual, anonymous donor for many years. That donation was matched by an equal amount from a sponsor. Any beneficiary, to qualify for a grant, must find counterpart funds from another source of a further $20,000. The combined, resultant sum of $40,000 can make an essential contribution to smaller-scale restoration projects, and the Fund has enabled many such restorations to take place, which would not otherwise have been possible. Each year, it announces a limited theme for the grant, and applications are received accordingly. In a recent year, for example, the theme was *A decorated or ornamented ceiling, originally executed before 1914, in a residential historic building, owned by an individual or a foundation'*.

From the earliest days, both organisations had developed a habit of adopting Resolutions. These used to get sent regularly to the Council of Europe, but not necessarily to others concerned. Moreover, they were at times adopted on the spur of the moment, without proper consideration of the background or implications. Once again, merger was the spur to reforms. Resolutions used to deal indiscriminately with horizontal issues – such as the need to exempt restoration work from the incidence of VAT – or with very specific matters, such as a threat to a particular heritage property.

Nowadays, Declarations or Resolutions address the former category, or issues of clearly international concern, while the latter are usually handled by means of a letter to very specific addressees from the Executive President.

Declarations and Resolutions are also given a much wider distribution, including for example the Institutions of the EU and the Council of Europe, National Governments, and Regional or Local Authorities. All these papers are the subject of mature reflection and debate before they issue. They quite often achieve surprisingly positive responses, if only because none of the bodies addressed likes to be the object of criticism by such a broad-based, European-level NGO as Europa Nostra.

It is customary for Europa Nostra to organise, alongside one of its regular Council or General Assembly meetings, some kind of themed Conference. These events also originated with IBI, where they were known as Open Days or later Forums. After merger they have been variously called Conferences and Round Tables. Initially, the events were informal and indeed haphazard. But four successive Secretaries-General have devoted much time and effort to raising them to a high level of professionalism and quality. Today, they attract wide participation, both of Europa Nostra members and of others.

Another IBI activity subsumed by the merged organisation was the Study Tours programme. Started decades ago, the basic idea was to offer to members of our organisation a cultural excursion with good creature comforts, privileged access to many private houses, and good tour leadership, usually by a knowledgeable fellow-member. They are now very popular, and earn money for Europa Nostra. I was tour leader myself on one occasion.

Over the years, Europa Nostra's publications have steadily improved. We have already taken note of the Bulletin and the 'Prontuario', recording the work of the Scientific Council; and also of 'The Power of Example' about the Awards Scheme. In addition, there is an internal newsletter for members, prepared by the Secretariat. And finally there is an excellent Review, looking at issues of European interest in the whole field of the built and natural heritage. Enormous credit must go to Olivier De Trazegnies for this last creation. The linear descendant of the Europa Nostra Magazine, which I established when the Europa Nostra Headquarters was moving to The Hague in 1990, it is as different in quality as chalk from cheese.

The Human Touch

This chapter has so far represented an attempt to explain, in straightforward and largely factual terms, how Europa Nostra and IBI merged, and what the effects of that merger have been. Inevitably it has been somewhat dry. But my long association with Europa Nostra involved me in much travel; put me in touch with hundreds of fascinating people of almost every European nationality; and allowed me privileged access to many fascinating places. To conclude the Chapter I shall try and convey some of what I experienced, but preface it all with a general remark.

I had spent most of my professional life dealing with European affairs – but from an essentially <u>political</u> and <u>legal</u> standpoint. Now, Europe was to assume an additional dimension. My knowledge of the <u>cultural</u> side was hugely enriched. I became far more aware of artistic, religious, historical and racial aspects. This helped me understand, to a far deeper level, what makes Europe tick. Moreover, geographically, I was for the first time able to visit Central and East European countries. All this was an enormous pleasure. I shall however avoid presenting a cultural travelogue, and focus instead on a few occasions and events of wider interest.

The rest of this chapter is arranged in three sections. The first recalls points from some of the Europa Nostra Conferences and key meetings I attended between 1990 and 2002. The second describes a number of striking Award Ceremonies. And the third recounts just one of the several journeys Maura and I undertook in response to invitations from our many Europa Nostra friends.

Europa Nostra Conferences and key meetings

Celle was the place where the IBI General Assembly in 1990 agreed that negotiations for merger with Europa Nostra should take place, and elected me as IBI President. The 17th century Schloss and 16th century *Rathaus* were both used for our meetings. In the Castle, we had an *'IBI Day'*, of far higher quality than its predecessors, thanks to Caroline Fuchs. The theme was *'The Castle and the People'*. I also used my time at Celle getting to know as many IBI members as possible; planning my brief Presidency; and talking to Gianni Perbellini and Caroline about bringing the Scientific Council back into the mainstream of IBI affairs.

The Italian members of IBI told me that some of the four Italian conservation NGOs were doubtful about merger, and asked me to see them. They agreed to send representatives to a gathering in Milan, early in 1991. We foregathered in the beautiful apartment of Count Alessandro Cicogna, part of a 16th century *Palazzo*, near the City Centre, filled with lovely paintings, porcelain and furniture. We sat round a table, and I made the case for merger. Those present, besides Caroline and me, included the Presidents of the Italian Castles Institute, of Italia Nostra and of the *Fondo per l'Ambiente Italiano* (FAI); plus a representative of the President of *Dimore Storiche*.

The most unusual personality was Giuglia Maria Mozzoni Crespi, President of FAI. The Crespi family had made money in the 19th century out of textiles. In the 20th, they moved away from textiles, and became proprietors of the *Corriere della Sera*. This too was later sold. Giuglia Maria now lived in a large *Palazzo* on the Corso Venezia inherited from her parents, with her husband, the quiet but charming Guglielmo Mozzoni. Unsurprisingly, given the beauty of her own home, Giuglia Maria was very interested in the conservation of her country's treasures. She felt Italy deserved a National Trust, on the British model, and encouraged the foundation of such a body. At first it did not take off. She became persuaded that stronger leadership was required, and accepted to become President of the FAI, founded in 1975. Then she firmly and persistently twisted arms to obtain donations for the purchase of castles, stately homes and beautiful countryside.

From the start Giuglia Maria was determined <u>not</u> to re-invent the wheel. She took it for granted that, as problems arose, the first thing to do was to see whether the National Trust had confronted them. Unless there was some special reason to the contrary, she then followed its lead. Her visits to Queen Anne's Gate aroused both delight and anxiety: delight, because the Trust was happy with the creation and work of the FAI; but anxiety, because she was going to need advice and help – and therefore precious time! The result is an amazing success story. The first 15 years of FAI's life are chronicled in '*Il libro del FAI*⁵', a superb book, filled with illustrations of lovely properties now owned by the FAI. It shows that, while the idea of creating such a Foundation was that of another lady – Elena Croce – Giuglia Maria was the person who got it going, and had ever since presided it.

At our meeting, Giuglia Maria took charge. After a few questions and answers, she intervened to say she assumed all agreed with my presentation. Taking silence for consent, she then proceeded to allocate to different individuals tasks which needed to be tackled to see the merger properly on its way. Later, I was very happy when she agreed to serve on the Europa Nostra Council for a number of years. Her contributions were always admirably concise and to the point. A spade, to her, was always a spade!

In May 1991, the Europa Nostra Council was to meet in the home of its new President, Prince Henrik, to recommend the merger to its General Assembly. The meeting was in the Amalienborg Palace in Copenhagen. For two days, out of the window, we could see the Royal Guards march up and down in their busbies, dark blue jackets and light blue trousers. On the second day, after business was over, we were invited to dinner at Fredensborg Palace, where I had last been with Roy Jenkins fourteen years before. Driven by a friend, we arrived early and had drinks with the Prince and his dogs on a terrace overlooking the fine park. The dinner was in the Cupola Room – a graceful, airy space, with marble floor, light stucco decoration, and original 18th century Danish pictures. Afterwards we could stroll in the adjacent, delightful private apartments. The Palace is enormously liveable and friendly.

The merger meetings at Dublin have already been covered. At the next Council of the merged organisation, at Milan in early May, 1992, I was interim Executive President. It lasted a day and a half, there being much to do following merger, and went well. The two sets of people were getting used to each other: the quality of the excursions had helped in the process.

In September 1992, we went to Istanbul – a first for both Europa Nostra and me. There was a Council, an Open Day (or Forum) and a General Assembly. In addition, Europa Nostra attended the inauguration, by a Turkish personality, of Turkish Monuments Day. The Prince and I also attended the opening of a 'European Symposium of Historic Towns', sponsored by the Council of Europe. Istanbul had been chosen as the venue before the merger. I felt anxiety at running such a full series of meetings in a place I did not know. But comfort was at hand. Caroline was still in office. And there was strong local support, in the persons of Ilhan Nebioglu, a Turkish Banker who represented the Turkish Conservation NGO, Patria Nostra; and of Costa Carras. The latter, a leading light of Elliniki Itairia (the Greek National Trust), assured me that he had excellent relations with Ilhan, and that all would be well. He was right.

The excursions included a choral concert in the underground Basilica Cistern built by the Emperor Justinian in the 6th century A.D. to supply the city with water. There were two dinners at splendid Palaces. There was a delightful boat-trip up the Bosphorus. We also took tea with the Nebioglus at their 'Yali', again on the southern side. The steadily growing professionalism of Europa Nostra in its post-merger formation was widely noted.

Our last day was remarkable. It was a Tuesday, the weekly closure day for the Topkapi Museum. This was opened, for us alone, all morning; and we even had lunch there, by ourselves, on a terrace overlooking the Bosphorus. We saw the whole Museum. What a formidable place it is. The objects are superb. But for me, the best feature was the beauty of the Palace complex as a whole: courtyards, cool arcades, flowers, fountains. Then we moved on to visit Hagia Sofia and the Blue Mosque.

Only a month later, Maura and I visited Cyprus for a meeting of the Scientific Council, coupled with a week's holiday. (The 'we' included not only Maura, but also Julie and Elizabeth.) The game plan was to fly to Paphos; stay for a week at the excellent Amathus Beach Hotel, sightseeing and participating in the meetings; move with the Scientific Council to the Ledra Hotel at Nicosia; cross the 'Green Line' dividing Turkish-controlled Cyprus from the rest of the Island, and visit the Castle of St Hilarion and the walled City of Famagusta. Then our little group of four would separate from the others and tour the Troodos Mountains until it was time to fly home. We were much helped by the loan of an air-conditioned Discovery Landrover for our stay. Cyprus is a cross-roads of history. Settlements exist from as early as 7,000 B.C. The Myceneans from Greece reached the Island in 1,400 B.C. Others, who were there at different times, included Phoenicians, Assyrians, Egyptians, Persians, Romans, Crusaders, Venetians, Ottomans and British. A visit to the Archaeological Museum in Nicosia showed one clearly why, for Cypriot children, history begins 9,000 years ago, and the Middle Ages are relativised!

Thursday 15 October was the day devoted to the visit to North Eastern Cyprus. From the moment Gianni Perbellini told me he wanted this, I knew we were handling a hot potato. Before reaching Cyprus I was in touch with the UK High Commissioner, who fortunately was David Dain, a close colleague and friend during my Bonn Embassy days in the 1970s. I explained to him, in view of the political sensitivities on both sides of the Green Line, that the Scientific Council was absolutely <u>not</u> a political body, but concerned only with the academic study of antiquities. A visit by its members could carry no political overtones. Since the Turkish Cypriot authorities were touchy about nationalities, we were excluding from our group any members of Greek or Greek-Cypriot origin! David put a member of his staff, Andrew Patrick, on to the delicate task of explaining this to the Cypriots on either side. David felt we had an 80% chance of carrying through the visit without incident. It was not to be quite so simple! At the check-point, a lady in the group was taken aside by the Turkish Cypriot authorities, who accused her of being Greek, and subjected her to close interrogation. She was, in fact an Italian, but came from near Ravenna, an area where Greeks had settled in the great days of Venice! So she had a name of distantly Greek origin. After an hour, she decided to leave our party, and the rest of us were allowed to proceed. We had a fascinating day.

Next day we spent largely with the Dino Leventis. Dino was a Cypriot. He lived in London, where he and his wife, Mema, were pillars of the Greek Orthodox Church. He was in charge of the Leventis Trading organisation, which operates largely in West Africa. But he was also President of the Leventis Foundation, a Trust which makes grants to cultural initiatives. It had been generous to Europa Nostra on many occasions, and Dino was our Treasurer. Sadly, Dino himself was to die – very prematurely from cancer – in 2002.

Finally, our little party of four set off on our own for four nights based on Pano Platres in the Troodos Mountains. From there we toured the monasteries and painted churches. The painted <u>interiors</u> of these churches are unique – though the Orthodox churches in Transylvania are similarly painted on the <u>outside</u>. The visit to Cyprus was altogether memorable.

In May, 1993, I had organised a major series of Europa Nostra events in Hungary, at which however Daniel Cardon was now Executive President. Although 'Die Wende' was now four years in the past, and Hungary had previously benefited from a fairly relaxed Communist régime, the economy was still very much in transition to capitalism. I wondered what the level of organisation would be, and how Hungaria Nostra, formed some years earlier, would underpin the arrival of upwards of 200 people – the scale on which Europa Nostra was now operating. Much effort therefore went into good preparation. Caroline Fuchs was on her way out as Secretary-General, and Lester Borley not yet in.

Sneska and I spent three days in Budapest a year before the event. Our main aim was to 'present' Europa Nostra; fly the flag; arouse interest; sketch out a programme; and obtain promises of support. We stressed that this would be the first visit by the main Institutions of Europa Nostra (though not of the Scientific Council of IBI) to any Central or East European country, and our hope that it would draw in also people from neighbouring lands, such as Czechs, Slovaks and Poles. We were well cared for by Laszlo Hegedús, President of Hungaria Nostra, and many others. We settled venues, hotels and other practical matters. So far, so good. But I looked in again on my way to Istanbul in September, 1992. Things were moving steadily forward. I also spent time with Istvan Feld, the Hungarian member of the Scientific Council. We had timed the latter's annual meeting to take place at Sarospaták, in Eastern Hungary, immediately after the other meetings in Budapest, so its members could participate in both. By now I felt real confidence. The Hungarians had wanted us to hold a General Assembly in Budapest. This would not have been timely; but we had set up an overall programme more ambitious than any ever attempted by the new Europa Nostra, or either of its parent organisations. And, in May 1993, it worked like a dream!

Lester Borley and I arrived early. The Prince held a press conference, and opened an exhibition illustrating the first fifteen years of the Awards Scheme, in a set of rooms on Buda Hill. On our second working day, there was a Council meeting in the splendid Hall of the Budapest Municipal Council, where we were joined by twenty or so guests from Hungary and other Central and East European countries.

The next day, a Sunday, we bused out to Visegrad Castle, passing the extensive remains of the fortified town of Aquineum, which for four centuries was Rome's outpost against the barbarians across the Danube. Visegrad Castle, now a ruin, was once the Palace of Hungary's great 15th century King, Matthias Corvinas, and dominates the deep wooded gorge through which the Danube runs before debouching into the Great Hungarian Plain. Then we returned by steamer the 40 kilometres to the Gellert Hotel. I reflected that, after boat trips on the Bosphorus and the Danube, our members would assume that navigation was part of each gathering! Next day was the Europa Nostra 'Open Day on the Urban Environment', held in the fine, Ceremonial Hall of the Hungarian Academy of Sciences on Buda Hill. It lasted all day; heard fascinating lectures; broke up into workshops; and closed with a final plenary. It was a big success. Afterwards, Mayor Demszky – the former principal 'Samizdat' publisher – gave a Reception in the Gothic Hall of the Imperial Castle, restored by a Hungarian member of our Scientific Council.

On the day after the various meetings, according to my diary 'I covered most of Hungary'! In the morning there was again an excursion to visit Székésféhervar, a township near Lake Balaton which had earlier received a Europa Nostra Medal for the restoration of its Serbian Quarter. Then a small party, led by the Prince, took off by car to present a Medal to the village of Magyarpolány, given for the restoration of a large group of peasant houses. On entering the village we were received by a Delegation in national costume, who gave us the traditional gifts of salt, bread and water. In the village itself, the entire population had turned out. There was a band, and much singing of Swabian songs by girls and men in traditional costume. The Medal was presented to the Mayor by the Prince. Then came the roasting of a pig, and the broaching of a wine-barrel. By now, our hosts had discovered that Prince Henrik grows wine in France. He undertook the broaching, entering into the spirit of the thing by standing by the barrel and handing out wine. There followed an open-air meal for the whole village. It was huge fun; it got much media attention; went out on national TV; and served to underline the value of conservation work throughout the country.

From Magyarpolány, I was driven many kilometres east to the Castle of Sarospaták, where the Scientific Council had started its seminar on 'The Transformation of the *Château Fort* into the *Château de Plaisance*'. It was gratifying to find that the quality of the Scientific Council, under Gianni, and now with Johanna Steriotou as its able Secretary, continued to improve; and also fascinating to learn that the theme of *Plaisance* had been introduced at least as early as the 12th century!

The second Council in 1993 was at Cardiff. This time, Daniel Cardon and Lester, especially the latter, had done all the preparation, and I was expecting just to watch it happen. But, two days ahead, Daniel trapped a nerve between two vertebrae and couldn't move, so I stood in. Our Council and General Assembly, in the University of Wales Council Chamber, went well. My diary recorded it as *'our best...so far in terms of substance'*. Prince Henrik had found a good style of Chairmanship. Excellent agenda papers, written by Lester, provoked a good, quick-fire discussion. The chemistry of the group was improving. Good new members were joining, and passengers were disappearing. Emotions about merger had dissolved. The Council – of about 50 people – was shaking down into a team.

We had long been anxious to encourage interest in Europa Nostra by younger people, given that Council members tend to be mid-career professionals or *pro bono* oldies! We devoted our Open Day to Youth and the Heritage. Lester had brought in a dozen young persons, involved in a conservation workshop nearby. The morning comprised a plenary session, where four keynote speakers of different nationalities kicked things off. For the afternoon, we divided into three workshops, for more detailed discussion. The young were hesitant to speak at first, but warmed up. By the end, there was a real exchange of current. We closed with a plenary, chaired by me, which saw the adoption of *'The Cardiff Declaration on Youth and Heritage'*. This precedent – of involving young people – has been followed meanwhile on several occasions.

In April 1994, Maura went with me to our former home city of Strasbourg – for a Council, General Assembly and Open Day. We enjoyed visiting old haunts. This time, the Council considered three Resolutions. One – to be sent to the EU and its Member States – called for a lifting of VAT on repairs of old buildings. Another – addressed to all European Governments – called for better protection of the Cultural Landscape of

River Valleys. A third, far more specific, called on the Italian authorities to be more responsive to heritage protection in Ticino. The Open Day was here renamed as a Forum, and no less than 260 people came to it. Its theme, naturally, was the Landscape of River Valleys. The Social Programme was excellent. However, on our last night, a buffet supper at the lovely Chambre de Commerce in Strasbourg was spoilt by the President of that Institution making an appalling 40-minute speech while we all <u>stood,</u> waiting to eat. But there was immediate compensation – in the shape of a magical Organ and Trumpet Recital in the Cathedral to follow!

I went alone to a Europa Nostra meeting in Berlin that September. It was strange to be, for the first time, staying in the former Soviet Sector – in fact on the Friedrichstrasse, only 100 metres from the Unter den Linden. The Capital of the Federal Republic was still in Bonn; but Britain had a Minister in Berlin – Rosemary Spencer – with special responsibility for 'Die Neue Bundesländer'. By now I was beginning to get the hang of the geography of the former East Berlin, and how it related to the former Western Sectors I knew so well. I could understand how West Berliners must have felt, with the Sectoral Division and the erection of the Wall, that their great City had lost its administrative and monumental heart. There are some fine buildings in East Berlin, notably the twin Cathedrals, and the *Schauspielhaus* on the *Gendarmenplatz*.

There was another good Council meeting, which discussed changes in the Statute; the range of activities to be pursued by the organisation; and Europa Nostra's attitude to the EU's emerging Cultural Policy. There was also a Forum – this time on *'Restoring and adapting Historic Buildings: the public and private partnership'*. The speakers included the Managing-Director of Schloss Schönbrunn in Vienna; the restorer of the Münchener Residenz; and Wilhelm von Boddien, who was plugging the idea of rebuilding the Berliner Schloss, deliberately destroyed by the GDR regime. Herr von Boddien had, at enormous personal expense, constructed a simulation of the building on its original site, using painted canvas stretched over a tubular steel structure, which covered a whole city block. It was still up when we arrived in Berlin, and disappeared overnight, while we were there! The effect was electric. Interest in the Forum was so great we had to move the event to the *'Aula Maxima'* of the Humboldt University, where some 300 people listened to six and a half hours of presentations. I had rashly agreed to act as Rapporteur, so had the challenging task of orally summing up the debate as soon as the last speaker closed his remarks!

There followed two days of optional excursions into two of '*Die Neue*

Bundesländer' – Brandenburg and Sachsen-Anhalt. The programme was attractive, and some 70 people rode in our two buses. As Daniel and Lester did not join, I made the speeches required on such occasions. On the return journey, I conducted a public debate, on the bus, in English, French and German, about the profile of Europa Nostra excursions for members. Their planning had always raised problems. The host country organisers usually wanted to show the visitors as many of their treasures as they possibly could. But there was a danger of giving them cultural indigestion, and tiring them out, with counter-productive effect. The debate was lively, and left me in no doubt that we should always err on the side of less rather than more!

These five days in Berlin and its surroundings gave me a personal feel for the re-unified Germany. The former East Germany, and most especially East Berlin, was a colossal building site. One could feel the power of the German work-ethic – just as I had felt it in West Germany nearly 50 years earlier. True, the state of many cities, towns, villages and houses was still desolate. But – only four years after the Wall came down – the rate of improvement was very rapid. I felt that East Germany would have largely caught up with the West in <u>material</u> terms in another decade or so. But it would take at least a generation to bring about mental and cultural re-unification.

May 1995 was to take Maura and me to Poland. We flew to Warsaw for four nights, trained on to Cracow, spent three nights there, and flew home. There was to be a Council in Warsaw, and a General Assembly and Forum in Cracow. The Prince was ill, and could not come. But all was well organised; Daniel and Lester were both present. We also had very effective Polish Council and Scientific Council members to help. For the very first time at a major Europa Nostra event, I had no official duties, and could thoroughly relax! The Polish visit was an experience not to be missed. Numbers were still rising: as many as 350 people were inscribed for the meetings, in both places. No less than 135 were from Central and East European countries. Hans De Koster would have been thrilled!

As in Budapest, our eyes were opened to many things I had never understood about the country. We realised that Poles had, for hundreds of years, regarded themselves, culturally and politically, as part of <u>Western</u> Europe. Though the country had all too often been torn apart by its large neighbours, and the Poles had just suffered fifty years of German and Soviet occupation, they did not think of Poland as 'joining' Western Europe, but rather as being re-united with it.

It was also clear that the Polish Communist authorities had not been very effective in terms of thought-control. The young Polish girl who acted as guide for Maura and me in Cracow told us – over a quiet dinner – that most Poles had secretly rejected the whole system. Her father, a physicist, had made no secret of these political views to her or her siblings, and the family had systematically – but illegally – listened to the BBC. At school, they had known who were the informers – mostly children of *Apparatchiks* – and been discreet when talking to them. It was all news to us.

The highlight of Warsaw was a delightful, private, evening tour of the Royal Castle. The tour starts with a photograph of the state of the Castle at the end of World War II. Of the whole enormous structure, only a few feet of one wall were left standing. Most of the money for reconstruction came from *emigré* Poles. As the destruction was going on, ordinary Poles went and salvaged bits and pieces: a picture, a door, a cupboard, even a moulding. When it was decided to restore, these people brought their bits and pieces back, so the work of restoration was enormously helped. The famous Bellotto paintings of the Castle were also invaluable to the restorers. We ended our tour in the 20-chandelier baroque ball-room, overlooking the Vistula. And there, Europa Nostra Medals of Honour were presented to Professor Gieystor, the chief Restorer, and also to Ruth Riis Hansen, the retired Founder of Dania Nostra.

We went by train to Cracow, and were greeted on arrival by a music group from the Nova Huta steelworks, in national costume! Cracow, the former Capital, is a delightful city, largely mediaeval, with a fine central square. The highlight, again, was a delightful, private, evening tour of the Wavel Royal Castle, which has the best series of Flemish tapestries I've seen anywhere. On the work side, the Forum – on *'Threats to the Wooden Architecture of Europe'* was excellent.

At Manchester, that September, Lester had again organised a good programme, including an excellent Forum on *'Conserving Europe's Industrial Heritage'*; and I could again sit back. The Social Programme – prepared with the help of the National Trust, English Heritage and the Duchess of Devonshire, was outstanding. At a Trust Dinner at Dunham Massey, Angus Stirling gave a very reflective talk about the challenges facing the Trust in the 21st century. A Reception at the Space Gallery of the Manchester Museum of Science and Technology allowed us to ride in a simulator and experience the thrills of taking part, first, in a ski-race, and then in a low-level flight in a Tornado through the Lake District! It was amusing to see some of our oldest members taking to this like ducks to water!

On a first day's excursion we visited the fascinating Quarry Bank Mill, a 'Working Museum' with demonstrations of hand and machine processes for carding, spinning and weaving. It is seen by 250,000 visitors a year, of whom a quarter are school-children. Then on we went, to present a Europa Nostra Award to Tatton Park for restoration of the Orangery. On the second day, we visited both Lyme Park and Chatsworth.

Only a week later, I was on my way to Trujillo, in Extremadura, for a meeting of the Scientific Council. Another memorable occasion. Carmen de Salas, now well advanced in years, had been trying for ages to have the Council or General Assembly of Europa Nostra meet in her home town. The sheer scale of these meetings made this a difficult concept. I had helped Gianni Perbellini persuade her to accept a visit by the Scientific Council instead. Her agreement was undoubtedly reluctant, but by the time the visit was over she was delighted.

Carmen had for long been widowed. We must digress about both herself and her husband – two truly remarkable people. An illustrious art historian, Don Xavier de Salas was appointed by General Franco, after the Second World War, as Cultural Attaché in the Spanish Embassy to the Court of St James. Although the Embassy staff were in general coolly received by the British establishment, Xavier contrived to break down all constraints. He was so well respected in his own field, and took such care not to talk politics, that he was fully accepted by London's artistic world. Indeed, he was one of those very rare foreigners to be made a Fellow of the Royal Society! The De Salas lived – like Ted Heath in those days – in The Albany.

Xavier left London to become Director of the Prado at Madrid – a post he filled with distinction for a considerable period. On retirement, his friends told him he could not slow down. He must undertake another important task. Why not, said some, 'rescue' Trujillo from the desperate state into which it had fallen? The old city, built on a rocky hill, had gradually fallen down; and a new, modern city had risen outside the walls. Xavier accepted the challenge. The idea appealed not only to him but equally to Carmen. Whilst in Britain, they had both been impressed by the attention given there to the conservation of the architectural and natural heritage, and this much influenced the later course of their lives. In 1970, with a small group of friends, they formed an association, *'Los Amigos de Trujillo'*, under the auspices of which, over the following quarter of a century, an amazing transformation of the old city was effected. Some twenty historic buildings were taken over, one by one; previous occupiers re-housed; and sound legal title established from a complex structure of sub-divided property rights. The houses were then restored, or adapted in harmony with their environment, by the new owners. Today, Trujillo attracts a stream of cultural tourists, and its example has encouraged the restoration of other small European cities.

In the same year, Xavier and Carmen themselves personally set about the study and later the restoration of a historic building in Trujillo, namely the former Convent of San Francisco el Real, known locally as the 'Convento de la Coria', with a view to establishing there a Cultural Foundation whose aims would include notably the study of the historical ties between Latin America and the Region of Extremadura, a Region from which some of the greatest of the Conquistadores had come. Following Xavier's death, in 1982, Carmen not only continued this work, but also took on further large heritage tasks at local, regional and national level. Her friendship with Duncan Sandys, for many years President of the English Civic Trust, and then of Europa Nostra, led Carmen to take an active part in the European Heritage Year of 1975, and this in turn prompted her to become President of the Spanish heritage conservation organisation, Hispania Nostra. Her contribution to its high standing in Spain today has been enormous. Only those who have been members of the Europa Nostra Awards Panel, and who have seen what Carmen has done in her own country, can appreciate it to the full. Carmen has promoted the Awards Scheme tirelessly, through Hispania Nostra, to the point where it is seen in Spain as unquestionably the heritage award scheme. Such Awards are often rendered still more prestigious through being presented by HM Queen Fabiola of Spain. Carmen encouraged the submission of Spanish applications to the point where, starting from scratch, Spain eventually overtook Britain in terms of the number of applications. The average quality of the Spanish applications is second to none. Carmen travelled all over Spain to ensure these things.

At Trujillo, we found ourselves comfortably settled into the Parador – the 16th century Convent of Santa Clara – which looks north to the Sierra de Gredos. The Scientific Council met in the Coria for two days and deliberated on Urban Fortified Houses, a very suitable theme for the venue.

In April 1996, Maura and I spent a week with Europa Nostra in Vienna. With Daniel due to retire from his Presidency of the BBL in December, I was steadily winding down my role supporting in Europa Nostra. I spoke little in the meetings: my retirement from the Awards Panel was announced. The Forum, this time, was on the *Jugendstil*. Gabor Winkler, who had been so helpful in Budapest, and also in the Council, had brought a good group of his students from Hungary. And the content was good, with well-chosen speakers from seven countries. Two or three memories of Austria stand out. An evening reception at Schönbrunn Palace closed with a performance by the Wiener Sängerknaben. We were also treated to a performance of *The Magic Flute* by the Schönbrunn Schloss-Marionettentheater, a new group on the model of Salzburg. Finally there was a visit to the Esterhazy Schloss at Eisenstadt, where Haydn lived for thirty years, and where we enjoyed a concert by the Haydn Quartet in the Haydn Saal.

That September was to see my last Council meeting in the capacity of Vice-President. It was again in Denmark. Happily, Daniel was in a new mode, following the nomination of a successor to the Presidency of the BBL to take over in January 1997. Although he told me his totally unexpected four years at the helm of the Bank had been the most interesting time of his life, and he was leaving the Bank in good shape, they had also been very exacting. Now, he was planning his future, and making clear that Europa Nostra would lie at its heart. Happily, also, the Council elected Antonio Marchini Camia to succeed Lester Borley as Secretary-General.

In January, 1997, I resigned the Vice-Presidency. Martin Drury, who had succeeded Angus at the helm of the National Trust, and his wife Liz, had shortly before offered Maura and me a very farewell dinner, when I ceased to be the National Trust's European Adviser. I resigned also my membership of the Council and Management Committee of Europa Nostra. At this stage Daniel made clear that I would continue to be a welcome guest at any meetings of these bodies. But attendance was now completely voluntary. In practice the occasions are sufficiently interesting – and there are so many friends among the participants – that I have attended several times.

Indeed I went, with Maura and Claire, to the clutch of gatherings in Madrid in April 1997. We arrived early; rented a car; and first visited Rupert in Javea. (He was by now in effective charge of publishing a Satellite TV Guide for expats.) In Madrid the Council was marked by the presence of Marcelino Oreja, the European Commissioner responsible for Culture, for a good debate on *'The Cultural Heritage and Employment'*. Next came a joint meeting of Europa Nostra with Hispania Nostra. The Commissioner gave a talk about EU Cultural Policy: then the Prince presented a number of Awards. Carmen de Salas, having now retired from the Council, had become eligible to be nominated – and been enthusiastically elected – to receive a Europa Nostra Medal of Honour, which made her very happy. Next day started with the General Assembly. The Prince made a nice speech about me: gracious in content, and delivered with charm. Next, on the proposal of Daniel, the Assembly elected me to be Honorary President. This was a new, non-Statutory, honorific position. Finally, the Prince presented me with a pleasing picture of Rosendael Castle, for so long the home of IBI, with a kind inscription by him on the back. I had not expected <u>any</u> of these things until told just before, so responded with a short speech from the heart.

My labours were not yet over. Antonio Marchini Camia had organised his first Forum, which was to be on the subject of *'Educational Activities relating to Protected Areas in Europe'*. He had gone to great trouble. So, when he had asked me to act as Rapporteur, I felt unable to refuse. It was tough. There were seven scheduled speakers, all of whom fortunately submitted their remarks to me ahead of time; and an excellent Question and Answer session. Then it fell to me to present at once – as at Berlin – a summary of main points, and to procure the adoption of some conclusions. The whole affair had lasted six and a half hours: quite long enough for me!

Over two years later, in October 1999, Maura joined me in a sentimental trip to Rosendael, when the 50th Anniversary of the creation of IBI was celebrated in style. We went by car. On the journey, we stopped briefly to see the deeply moving Arnhem Airborne Cemetery where, on <u>every</u> Anniversary of the landing of 30,000 Airborne soldiers in 1944, Dutch schoolchildren still make a pilgrimage and ensure that flowers are laid on <u>every</u> grave. I also saw the impressive Airborne Museum, housed in a building which was General Urquhart's Headquarters during Operation 'Market Garden'. Both these places are enormously worth a visit.

There had by now been a change of Secretaries-General. Sneska had succeeded Antonio. The IBI anniversary celebrations had been organised by Els Quarles and me, and went well. There was first a visit to the Castle, where a Reception was offered by the Gelderland Trust. The Prince commented on IBI's long association with the Castle, and then invited me, as IBI's last President, to hand a belated surprise present to the President of the Trust. It was an antique musket, which had been in the possession of IBI for so long that none of us knew its origins.

There was then a Gala Dinner in honour of IBI's 50th birthday, at the *Résidence* Restaurant, just up the hill. Over coffee Prince Henrik announced that the Troika of former IBI Presidents there present – Henk Tuyll, Wessel von Landsberg-Velen and me – had held a conclave. At its conclusion, smoke signals had revealed that the task of speaking about the origins and achievements of IBI, had been allocated to their most junior member: the two senior ones had undertaken to correct him if he made mistakes. I spoke in light-hearted vein, but sought to underline what IBI had achieved, and who had been the movers and shakers. I expressed conviction that these

Rosendael Castle, with Maura and Els Quarles, 1998.

achievements had been continued, and further developed, by our merged organisation; and that merger had amounted to a happy marriage.

My next connection with a Europa Nostra was at Lucerne in May 2001. I attended the Management Committee, Council and General Assembly. The question of succession to Daniel Cardon was to be discussed, although his term did not expire for two further years. It was agreed that the Management Committee was not an ideal forum: first, because it was rather small, and second because there was a preference for a group of which Daniel was not a member! So it was agreed, outside all the official meetings, to hold a meeting of an Ad Hoc Group, consisting of all the other Management Committee members, the Vice-Presidents and myself. There it was agreed to place the matter formally on the agenda of the next Council meeting; to have it thoroughly prepared by a group of four wise men, none of whom would wish to be considered as a possible Executive President – led by Costa Carras – and then to have it considered at a Special Meeting of the Council chaired neither by the President nor by the Executive President. Clearly this job was going to come my way!

Our next trip together was to Europa Nostra gatherings in Riga in September 2001. We decided that, if going so far east, we must carry on afterwards to St Petersburg, even though time was short. Both places were new to us. The trip lasted eight days. We flew to Riga via Copenhagen; took an overnight train to St Petersburg four days later; and flew back to Manchester another four days after that. Thus, we were ourselves in the air at the very moment the hijacked jets were crashing into the Twin Towers in New York, and the Pentagon.

We loved Riga, where we stayed in the Grand Hotel, on the edge of the pedestrianised old city. It has a number of mediaeval buildings, but also many in the *art nouveau* style. The city is prosperous to look at, and huge amounts of restoration have been done. The people are happy with their re-found independence, and we were struck by the number of smiling faces – very different from London! Many of the girls are long-legged and tall, so that I frequently found myself looking up at them!

At the Council meeting, I gave a 15-minute talk about the day of merger with the International Castles Institute, just ten years before in Dublin – in which I contrived to recall that it was our son, William, who had shortly before moved the Europa Nostra Headquarters to The Hague! I also chaired a special session of the Council, from which both Prince Henrik and Daniel Cardon were absent, to set up a procedure to look for someone to succeed the latter in 2003. Fortunately the Prince had meanwhile been persuaded that he should not himself retire until the new Executive President had found his feet. A lot of work had been done by the Ad Hoc Group set up in Lucerne. Nevertheless there remained a good deal of wheeling and dealing before the meeting. It all passed off peacefully, and the outcome was the establishment of a strong, broadly-based Search Committee, which later agreed on a single candidate, Otto von der Gablentz, who was duly elected.

Much could be said about Riga, but one thing in particular must be said. It possesses a remarkable 'Museum of the Occupation'. This deals with Latvia's successive occupation by Russians, then Germans, then Russians again – between 1941 and 1991. The Museum is largely photographic and literary, with few artefacts. But it is marvellously displayed, in a modern structure; and it brings home to you, in a way that no amount of book reading could, what the Latvians – and the other Baltic countries – suffered during that dreadful half-century. In that period – and especially during the war – the country's population was reduced from over 2 million to under 1.4 million: the remainder were killed, sent to Gulags, or deported for political reasons to Germany or Russia.

Our overall impression of Riga was very positive, and we were not surprised to learn that, in the 19th century, it was called 'The Paris of the North'. Today it is a most friendly place. The whole Riga programme had been effectively devised by our very efficient Danish Vice-President, Catherina Collet. She had been determined that we should again meet in a Central or East European country, and she made it her business to ensure that it went well and that plenty of people from the whole Region attended.

One evening, Maura and I boarded our train for St Petersburg. Of course, this had nothing to do with Europa Nostra, but I cannot resist the temptation to write about it! Two strapping, young female attendants watched idly as I staggered to get our two heavy cases up four high steps from ground level to the sleeper corridor. Then we had a miserable supper in a squalid restaurant car, as the train rolled slowly along for fourteen hours to St Petersburg. Crossing the Russian frontier at 0200 hours we were woken to have our passports inspected by four successive Russians! Then a security man came; signalled us to get up; and raised the base of each bed to make sure we were not smuggling anyone or anything into Russia! You can't buy roubles <u>outside</u> the country, so we were counting on changing money at the Baltic Station on arrival. The exchange office was shut!

Maura haggled a taxi-driver down from 25 to 15 roubles for the journey – you always have to haggle over taxis in St Petersburg – explaining he would be paid at the hotel! On arrival, we found we were sharing the Astoria Hotel with the Prime Minister of China, Mr Zhu Rongji, and a vast retinue. So the approach road was shut to all other traffic! We had to park 100 metres away and walk. After that it all got simpler! Happily the Astoria is a first-class hotel, only 400 metres walk from the Winter Palace and Hermitage complex.

When it comes to describing the latter, words fail. It must surely be the world's finest art collection. The key impressions left on us were: the scale and splendour of the Palace; the marvellous, decorated, ceilings and wooden floors; the luxurious elegance of the State rooms; the masses of gold ornamentation; the numerous, fine chandeliers; the lack of any feeling of crowding – despite the 2 million visitors a year – due to the sheer size of the place; the large numbers of well-behaved, well-dressed school parties; and of course the range and quality of the many collections. There are also a lot of seats: on one occasion Maura sat in a bay occupied otherwise solely by superb Rembrandts – seven in all – and no people! We saw many other sights, besides the Hermitage, but I resist the temptation to write about them.

A few things struck us particularly about St Petersburg. It is a city of 2 million: as in Latvia over a far longer period, more than a third of the population disappeared during the 4-year German siege, here mostly dying of starvation, though the population is now back to normal. The city is full of canals, and is often known as 'The Venice of the North'. Apart from the main avenues, there is remarkably little traffic. The people are on the whole well-dressed, except for the fairly numerous beggars. They are polite and well-behaved, and we never felt under any threat. Unfortunately, there seemed to be no restrictions on the use of microphones in public places, and our ears were constantly assailed by declamations all round the Hermitage. There were large numbers of idle, hands-in-pockets, smoking, police, everywhere. Only some of the younger people speak any European language but Russian. In the Hermitage, many inscriptions are in English as well as Russian, though not all: in the other Museums we saw, virtually none are translated. We ate well, including delicious Borscht and Beef Stroganov. And, in the main Museums, there are cafeterias at reasonable prices. This, of course, is to suit the Russian pocket: when it comes to entrance fees, foreign visitors pay about seven times as much as Russians!

Maura has added some personal observations to all this. She noted that both St Petersburg and Riga were spotless. There is no litter or even a dropped sweet-wrapper. <u>No-one</u> eats or drinks walking in the street. In Riga, no-one was raucous: all spoke quietly. We saw one old Russian woman wiping a telephone kiosk with a wet floor-cloth on a pole, from the roof down. We heard only one tired child cry in eight days. All the others, even those clearly bored in the Hermitage, followed their parents obediently round, listening to their explanations. Everyone in Latvia was thin: in Russia a few of the over-50s were more rotund. Weight is no problem there.

In short, it was all a great adventure. It took us further east in mainland Europe than we had ever been before. Apart from the train, the whole thing was done in great comfort.

Awards Ceremonies

I have explained earlier how the Europa Nostra Awards Scheme is run, and how Medals and Diplomas are awarded. Until a few years ago, it was customary for each Award to be presented to the recipient on his home ground. I made a few presentations myself, and assisted at some others. In this section I record <u>four</u> such events, each of which had a particular interest. Procedures have now changed. All recipients are now invited to a single venue, when the Awards can be given by a very distinguished personality. For example, in 2002, they were presented at the Amalienborg Palace in Copenhagen. However, those who so wish can still opt for a presentation 'on location'.

In May, 1992, I travelled to Oberoderwitz, which had received a Medal

One of the windmills at Oberoderwitz, Germany,
to receive a Europa Nostra Medal for restoration, 1992.

for the restoration of three old windmills. The story was unusual. Oberoderwitz is a small village in the Lausitzerland, in Saxony, a region to the east of Dresden, near the Czech and Polish borders. The windmills had always dominated the village. During the days of the GDR, however, they fell into a poor state. The Mayor and the inhabitants wanted them repaired. But they would need permission from the Land authorities.

There was a problem. If this was requested in a straightforward way, it would be refused, on the ground that an all-seeing and all-wise Communist authority was of course aware of the problem and intended to repair the mills shortly. Nothing would then have been done. So the Mayor made his approach guilefully. He put it to the authorities that they were certainly aware of the problem, and equally certainly preparing to do something about it. If it would help, the local people would be happy to do some of the simple work, under supervision, in their spare time. Amazingly, the trick succeeded. The authorities named an architect. And all the work was then done by the local people, on a voluntary basis, and to a very high standard. It was only when it was well-advanced that the Re-unification of Germany occurred.

As Executive President, I agreed to make the presentation. Arriving at Dresden, I was joined by a Vice-President of Europa Nostra, Peter Oltmanns. He had been a Federal Civil Servant in Bonn; had recently retired; and was now hired by the Dresden authorities as a Special Adviser on the City's development. We drove to Oberoderwitz, where there was an unofficial public holiday – and perfect weather! We toured the three mills. At the third, a veritable *Volksfest* had been organised by the Mayor and the President of the '*Mühlenaktiv*', Herr Herbst. An excellent local choir sang for us. Then came speeches by the Mayor, myself, Peter Oltmanns and Herr Herbst. The Medal was handed over. Then, schoolchildren performed a cultural programme, with dancing, singing, and playlets ('The miller and his wife'). All around were stalls for sausages, cakes and drinks. People had come from the neighbouring villages: there were around 500 all told. We had to leave at tea-time; but we were told the celebrations would continue late into the night, with the local band, the choir again, horse rides, a '*Fackelzug*' (procession with torches) round the mills, and fireworks. One felt that the Medal had not only been well-deserved, but had also had a powerful impact on that part of Germany.

On the same basis, I flew to Norway a month later, to give a Europa Nostra Medal to the City of Arendal. Catherina Collet, President of Dania Nostra, had kindly agreed to join me. My flight took me through Copenhagen, so we joined up there. Eivind Vesterkjaer, then our most active Norwegian member, met us at Kristiansand, with his wife, Lilliane, and drove us to Arendal. There was a story attaching to this Medal also. Arendal, once a major port, had much declined. At its heart, on a small island, lay the old City, with characteristic south Norwegian, wooden architecture. This had become degraded. The majority party leadership in the City Government was all for bulldozing the lot, and replacing the buildings with featureless, concrete structures. A citizens' movement against this lamentable initiative developed and grew. In the end the motion for destruction was defeated by a single vote in the City Government! And then, once the die was cast, people set too with a will to restore the wooden buildings, and the old part of the City was declared a conservation area. A walk-about convinced me the Panel had been absolutely right to give the Medal for restoration of a group of wooden buildings. But, equally clearly, much more work would be needed before the whole of the Old City would deserve to be called a conservation area.

The presentation itself was colourful, with an excellent wind band of over 50 players. When the time came to present the Award, I gave my remarks a triple theme: first, my admiration for the decision of principle, and for the buildings already restored; second, an emphasis on the rarity and importance of a Europa Nostra Medal; and third, my hope that the City Fathers would carry on the good work until it was complete. During the day I repeated these themes at a press conference and in radio interviews. It was pleasing to find that the event filled half the front page of southern Norway's principal newspaper next day.

That evening, our Norwegian hosts organised a boat trip out to one of the islands for a barbecue supper. En route, we saw some large stone cairns. A question elicited that these were the tombs of ancient Norwegian kings of the 10th century AD. When I asked about their religion, the answer was: 'Christians of course – you should know.' When I put the idiot child question 'Why?', I got a history lesson. I was told that the Norwegian warriors who went to the British Isles, in the course of keeping order, had been obliged to execute a number of British tribesmen. They had noticed that some, who wore a particular kind of robe, seemed not to mind being killed. This was because they were priests of the local religion (Christianity), and held the view that death would bring them at once to heaven. The Vikings found this interesting; decided that it would be 'good for their women to be informed'; and 'volunteered' a number of priests to come to Norway. Thus, apparently, was Norway converted! Another slice of cultural history had slotted into place for me!

For sentimental reasons, I took care to be present when, in November 1992, Prince Henrik presented a Medal to Douglas Hurd for what the citation called 'the magnificent and meticulous restoration to the original design of one of the finest examples of Victorian architecture in the United Kingdom': more particularly the Main Staircase and Locarno Room Suite of the Foreign and Commonwealth Office. It was not only that Douglas and I had been at school together, and then worked in the building years earlier, as fellow-members of the Diplomatic Service, but also to mark my personal appreciation of the battle Douglas had fought to get the Treasury to fork up the restoration costs!

Finally, Maura and I were delighted to be invited to the Ceremony at Windsor Castle in May, 2000, when a Medal was presented by Daniel Cardon for the marvellous restoration of the Castle after the great fire eight years earlier, in the presence of the Duke of Edinburgh. On the same occasion, a number of Diplomas were presented to other British project owners. A splendid book by Adam Nicholson – *Restoration: the Re-building of Windsor Castle*[6] tells the story. Most interesting is the extent to which the Duke controlled the whole process himself, every important decision being taken by a Committee he presided. It was therefore a great pleasure for the visiting party to hear him speak, personally and informally, about his role. We had drinks with him in the Crimson Drawing Room. And then we broke into groups of a dozen, for delightful conducted tours of the whole restoration, led by the very top people in the team.

Holidays with Europa Nostra friends

I cannot close this chapter about Europa Nostra without mentioning several continental holidays which would never have occurred – at least in that form – but for the friends we made over the many years of my involvement with the organisation. They took place in the 1990s, and we saw many wonderful things in privileged conditions. But I will describe only one – particularly unusual – event.

It resulted from an invitation from Andrea Schuler, long-time President of the Awards Panel and a good friend, to attend the *Landesgemeinde* of Canton Glarus in Switzerland – the Glärnerland – on 3rd May 1998. We were to stay three nights. Andrea and Amrose live in the Gerichtsstrasse. Their house is large and stands in a park near the City Centre. Inside, it is spacious, with collections of everything, especially furniture, rugs, pictures and porcelain. Andrea was then a leading lawyer in Zürich; a Colonel in the Swiss Army; and a Vice-President of the *Stadtrat* of Glarus. On our first day, we accompanied him to Zürich. Our main aim was to meet Catherina Collet and her husband Bernt, at the Airport. They too had been invited to see the *Landesgemeinde*. But Andrea also gave us an interesting walking tour, including a visit to the '*Zunfthaus zur Meisen*' where Winston Churchill made his famous speech in favour of a European Community in 1948.

Next day was the *Landesgemeinde*. This is the annual gathering of the electors of a Canton. It takes place outdoors, and citizens are called on to vote by show of hands on all questions affecting the Canton. (The *Landesgemeinde* can be deferred for a short time in case of bad weather.) The practice has been in decline in the Cantons for a long time – other more practical methods of exercising the Swiss tradition of direct democracy, such as referenda, having replaced it. It now survives only in Appenzell and Glarus, where the population is small. In each case, the citizens vote, but only in Glarus can they also speak before the vote is taken – a right which is exercised.

The 'Landesgemeinde' at Glarus, 1998.

Andrea had arranged for his twelve visitors to be installed at windows on the south side of the great Main Square of Glarus. We had a perfect view of the proceedings. The whole town is ringed by high, precipitous mountains. It was grey, but with only a few light showers. At 0930 hours the Church bell was the signal for a procession to move into the Square, led by the Cantonal Band. Behind came a contingent of the Swiss Army. Then two officials in red – the Cantonal Sword-bearer and the outgoing *Landamann* – the Senior Officer of the Cantonal Government. Then, other dignitaries. By now the Square was fairly full of voters – perhaps 3,000 out of a Cantonal population of 35,000. They stood for the entire proceedings, leaving a space around the dais from which the business was conducted. Only senior citizens were allowed chairs. Small children were permitted to sit on the steps of the dais, or on the ground nearby, to get a good view. A rope separated voters from non-voters. People could – and did – drift in and out of the resultant enclosure. Surrounding cafés did a good trade! When we asked whether this could not give rise to improper voting, we were told there was no danger: the voters all stood by their fellow villagers, or by their fellows from a particular part of a town. Any impostor would have been at once detected.

The proceedings began with a speech by the outgoing *Landamann*. Next came the election of a new *Landamann*, a new *Landesstathalter*, and other Officers. Then came consideration of each of the 11 items on the agenda. I do not remember them all; but one, for example, was to consider authorising the opening of a new railway station. Some of the votes were close. In those cases the *Landamann* called on all voters to raise hands to signal 'aye' or 'nay', and then had four Councillors to help him count. On this occasion, all was over in about four hours; but Andrea told us that there had been years when six or seven thousand electors had attended, and the proceedings had lasted for eight hours. After this impressive event was over, we returned to Andrea's home for an excellent lunch, where we also enjoyed the company of his three children – Hans, Martina and Karin.

Closing thoughts

In bringing to an end these thoughts and reminiscences about Europa Nostra, I close with a single observation. Such organisations will always rest on bases which are less than solid. But the position of Europa Nostra has immeasurably improved since the merger of 1991. And I am happy to have had something to do with that situation. I am also grateful to Europa Nostra – and the International Castles Institute – for the value it has added to my own life over, now, more than fifteen years.

CHAPTER 22

Lancaster University: Pro-Chancellor

How it all began

SOON AFTER RETIREMENT, I was invited by the Vice-Chancellor of Lancaster University, Professor Harry Hanham – henceforward Harry – to visit the Campus. Long afterwards, I learnt that my Commission friend and colleague, Hywel Jones, in charge of Higher Education at European level, had given him my name. The visit led to my becoming a lay member of the University Council from the autumn term of 1988. I had little idea what to expect, having never studied at a University. But my time at Edinburgh had given me some feel for academic life; the Vice-Chancellor felt my experience could be of service; the University was an important feature of public life in Lancashire and South Cumbria; and it therefore seemed right to respond positively. The decision was to involve me, over the next nine years, in a lot of work, and also in some important University developments, both positive and negative.

To understand what follows, one must first know how Lancaster University is run. The Council is its Governing Body. It controls, manages and administers all University revenue and property. It must take into consideration any comments or representations made to it by Court or Senate. The Senate – an internal body comprising mainly staff but also students – is responsible for the academic work of the University, and for the education, living conditions and discipline of its students. The Court – a very much larger body than Council or Senate, with wide representation from inside and outside the University – meets annually. It can discuss anything; but its powers are limited to appointing the Chancellor, the Pro-Chancellor and the latter's Deputies. The appointment of the Pro-Chancellor must, however, be made on the recommendation of Council. There is a Vice-Chancellor – hereinafter the VC – who is appointed by Council on the advice of a joint Committee of Council and Senate. He is the Chief Academic and Administrative Officer of the University, and the Accounting Officer; has a general responsibility for maintaining and promoting the University's effective working and good order; and chairs the Senate. Finally – and Lancaster is one of a very small number of post-1950 Universities which have this arrangement – there is a system of Colleges, based on the Oxbridge system but sadly lacking any significant endowments.

All this sounds complicated. An analogy with the governance of the UK might help to explain. The VC is essentially the Prime Minister. Council and Senate are his Parliament – the bodies to which he must present his policies for approval. Council alone has power to dismiss him.

How is Council constituted? It has just over forty members. They include eight senior officers of the University; a similar number of members appointed by the Senate; half a dozen lay persons appointed by Court, usually from the region; four members appointed by local authorities; a small number appointed by the assistant staff, students or graduates; and up to eight other lay persons co-opted by Council itself. There are thus, broadly speaking, four constituencies: the officers; the academic and other staff; the students; and the lay members. The last category amount to around half of the total; but they never forget that the University's purpose is educational, and therefore give great weight to the views of the others. Council's complexity, and the sensitivity of the issues it must decide, makes it a difficult body to preside. The Chancellor is *ex officio* Chair of both Court and Council. The present Chancellor – HRH Princess Alexandra – has, however, chosen never to exercise these duties; so Council is normally chaired by the Pro-Chancellor, and Court by one of his/her Deputies.

The Development Campaign

For my first two years or so in Council, my main work lay in the setting up and running of a brand-new University Development Campaign. The proposal came from consultants. Council agreed to set up a Development Campaign Committee (DCC), including academics, administrators and lay Council members, with me in the Chair. In 1989, a Development Director was appointed – Ms Jo James. Departments were asked to submit projects for which Development funding would be valuable. The Committee chose the three or four best; helped the project owners work them up; and set about raising money. For fund-raising, it was assisted by a Development Campaign Board (DCB), led by Lord Shuttleworth (Charlie). The University was totally unused to this sort of activity. My wide range of outside contacts, or those I could make, were handy. There were visits to London and other centres to meet potential providers. When needed, Charlie was asked to help.

It was soon clear that one project – the Ruskin Project – had a far higher profile than the others, and offered greater potential returns. It came to occupy a large part of my time. Its successful completion amounted to a modern fairy story. The whole of the next chapter therefore devoted to it, so it receives only incidental attention here.

The DCC itself remained active until 'laid down' – a University euphemism for abolished – in March 1992. This was on the proposal of the VC. His initial approach was – not only to abolish the Development Office and part company with its Director – but also to put an end to the Development Campaign as such. I did not favour any of these ideas, but was told that Jo had offended a number of academics. In the end, the VC conceded that the Development Office should be incorporated within the Office of External Relations, under its Director, Stephen Lamley, but insisted on the *démise* of the DCC. The DCB struggled on for a while. But the concession was more apparent than real. Stephen gave some help to the Ruskin Project, but did little else to promote development. Eighteen months later the Council formally discontinued the Development Campaign. Years afterwards, Harry agreed with me privately he should have given development more attention. And Jo James, applying the same methodology, raised a lot of money for St Catherine's College and later the Radcliffe Infirmary, at Oxford.

Elected Pro-Chancellor (1989)

Meanwhile, the Pro-Chancellor, Sir Alastair Pilkington, had decided not to seek re-election at the end of his second five-year term in September 1990. Though I did not know it, both he and Harry, after putting out some feelers, had decided I would be a suitable successor. But they could not move without an assurance that Princess Alexandra would be happy. Maura and I were asked to attend a Degree Ceremony and meet her. We seemed to pass muster. Next day, Harry revealed the plot, and asked me to reflect. The decision was not easy. I was heavily engaged on my conservation ploys. And, once again, I felt short of relevant experience. But Alastair and Harry were insistent, and I agreed my name could go forward. In the end it was the only one to be presented to Council; and was submitted by the latter to Court, which in December unanimously elected me to succeed Alastair on 1 October 1990 for a five-year term of office.

Some three years later the VC asked whether I would in principle be willing to serve a second term. He thought this would help continuity when he himself reached retirement in 1995. The University at that time appeared to be in calm waters. I was dubious about serving much beyond my 70th birthday. But I could see his point. So I declared a readiness to serve two extra years until 1997, but not a full five years. At the end of 1993, Council and Court approved.

Two seminal figures: HRH Princess Alexandra and Sir Alastair Pilkington

It is time for a few words about Princess Alexandra and Alastair. The former had been Chancellor of the University from the day its doors opened in 1964. She has an extraordinary combination of intelligence, charm, dignity and simplicity. Soon after my election, Alastair and I were asked to lunch with her and her Assistant at her apartment in St James's Palace. The atmosphere was completely informal. There was soup and a cold buffet. I was asked 'would you mind serving the wine please?'. The Princess warned me then that she wanted to retire within four years; and meanwhile find ways of lightening the load. Happily, the first event has still to materialise. But we did lighten the load by proposing that, whereas HRH had until then presided every Degree Ceremony of the University, now that there were around sixteen a year, she should share this duty with the only other two people authorised to act – the Pro-Chancellor or the VC.

On the last occasion when it fell to me to address her at such a Ceremony – in July 1997 – I took the occasion to say this: *'I want to express, on behalf of the whole University…our enormous gratitude for the generosity and graciousness with which, for thirty-three years, you have bestowed so much time, effort, and indeed love on this Institution.'* It is a remarkable record. She was not accompanied, on her many visits to the University, by her husband, Sir Angus Ogilvy; but he was fully supportive behind the scenes.

Alastair Pilkington, who sadly died of a brain tumour in 1995, is the only individual I ever knew who literally changed the world in his lifetime. Though not himself a member of the famous family of glass-makers, he worked for them; and his invention of the revolutionary float-glass process in the 1950s permitted them to move from being a small firm in Lancashire to becoming the most important glass-maker in the world. It was developed by him and a small team, in total secrecy, over a period of seven years, to the point where Pilkingtons could burst from scratch into mass production, taking the world of glass by surprise – something which would now be inconceivable. Long before he died, over 90% of all flat glass throughout the world was being made, using the new process, by or under licence from Pilkington's, a firm of which he became the President. A visit to the production line at St Helens is an experience I shall never forget.

And yet Alastair remained what he had always been: a delightful, straightforward, wise, kind and supremely modest man. When he left the University, he never proffered gratuitous advice to me, but his invaluable knowledge and experience was always available when requested. He made a parting gift of £250,000 to the Development Campaign. His memory is prominently recorded at the University. The fine reading room in the Main Library extension is named for him: and he is publicly listed as a major donor to the Ruskin Library.

Overview of my term of office (1990-1997)

How can one best encapsulate my seven years as Pro-Chancellor in a few pages? There were three quite different periods. The first ran from 1990 to August 1995: the University throughout appeared to be in a period of rapid and successful expansion, in terms both of student numbers and of the necessary buildings. The second began with the dramatic and abrupt discovery, in August 1995, that major financial mistakes had been made and the University was in a state of financial crisis. The third started at the end of 1996, when we began to bottom out financially, and continued till I ended my second term of office in September 1997.

The role of the Pro-Chancellor

What were the duties I had by now assumed, and how did I approach them? We have already seen that the Pro-Chancellor's most important task is to preside the Council. He is also an *ex officio* member of all Council Committees. My practice was to attend regularly a few key Committees, notably that on Finance and General Purposes; to chair one or two others, notably those concerned with remuneration of senior staff, and premature retirements; to chair some with specific short-term remits, such as those set up to select a new VC and a new University Secretary, or to alter the Committee structure, or later those involved in the University's launch of Debentures on the Stock Exchange; to attend some dealing with matters in which I had a particular interest, notably the Colleges and Student Support Board, the Peter Scott Gallery Committee, and the Campus Enhancement Committee; and to attend some others on a 'taster' basis. The Pro-Chancellor is not a member of the Senate; but I attended that body two or three times by invitation.

The Pro-Chancellor also represents the University at outside functions and events. Most important, he alone can attend the influential Committee of University Chairmen (CUC) from all over the UK, which used to meet twice a year, for one or two days. I also made a practice of visiting other Universities and Colleges, especially those with which Lancaster had a special relationship, such as Leeds University, the University College of St Martin's (also at Lancaster), Charlotte Mason College at Ambleside, Edge Hill College near Liverpool, and Blackpool and the Fylde College.

All these activities involved much preparatory reading. I am by nature a 'doer' and was told I devoted more time to the role than any other Pro-Chancellor in the University's history. In the early stages I was on campus for over forty days per annum on University business. In 1996, after the crisis had broken, the figure rose to sixty — plus a few other days on Ruskin Foundation business. To this total must be added days for University business in other venues. My diary is again peppered with phrases like 'Up early (0500 hours) and worked all morning in study.' For each business day, there was probably much of a day's preparation at home, with many, many telephone calls. There was little time for leisure activities during term! As my work-load in other sectors of activity decreased — for example Europa Nostra and ICL — so it expanded at Lancaster!

An independent authority, namely the CRILL Committee to which we shall come later, has commented as follows on the Pro-Chancellor's role at Lancaster. *As the most senior lay officer at operational level, the Pro-Chancellor has considerable influence with the members of the Council and with senior officers, especially the Vice-Chancellor of the day. The way in which the Council is guided, and new initiatives welcomed or questioned, gives the post-holder a wider influence than within the single domain of the Council chamber.'* This is fair comment.

Lancaster University expands

The early 1990s were a period of rapid growth, and led the University to an eminence it had not previously enjoyed. Student numbers increased by over 1,400 'full-time equivalent students' — the strange units by which academe measures these things. For both the Government's two main indicators of academic quality — research and teaching — Lancaster was consistently in the top ten Universities in the UK.

Many of the staff had been recruited when the University was born, and had now reached maturity in their careers, whilst excellent new staff were being attracted. Harry told me he regarded Lancaster as the 'Oxbridge of the Northwest': it was a reasonable thing to say. A welter of new buildings were going up on the campus. These included a lot of student accommodation; the new Peter Scott Art Gallery; a large new teaching and lecturing building — the George Fox Building; a massive extension to the Main Library; a separate, new Ruskin Library, to house the Whitehouse collection (described in the next Chapter); a Graduate Management School, a Graduate College; and a range of administrative and other smaller buildings beside.

The task of chairing Council meetings was nevertheless sometimes tricky. My first Council, in October 1990, passed off quietly, with the students actually accepting a rent rise of 13.75%! At my second Council, in November 1990, however, there was a substantial row. Its origins may seem strange. The students were complaining that the standard of the new accommodation to be built was too high! They argued that, rather than building *en suite* student accommodation, the University should provide the more traditional style, with shared toilet facilities. Otherwise, there would be discrimination between undergraduates, some being better housed than others. Any money saved should be used to improve the older accommodation. The administration, however, favoured the *en suite* type because this could be let for conferences and other events during vacations, thus bringing in income, whereas the traditional style was increasingly difficult to let.

The Presidents of the eight College Junior Common Rooms (JCRs) wished to attend the Council debate, in addition to the normal student representatives. I met them before Council began, and ruled that the question of their admittance must be decided by Council itself, when the agenda item was reached. Meanwhile a crowd of students started demonstrating noisily in Alexandra Square, just below the windows of the Senate Room where the meetings were held. Once the meeting began, the demonstrators started pelting the windows with eggs and tomatoes. The noise was distracting, but we ploughed on.

When the procedural point was raised, a motion that the Presidents be admitted with the right to speak was rejected; another, that the right to speak be limited to those of them so invited by the Chair, was accepted. There then followed a relatively good-humoured, two-hour debate, where the students' case was put by the President of the Union. I invited one JCR President to speak also. The outcome was approval for the *en suite* accommodation, subject to an agreement to review the quality of existing stock, and an assurance that in future the students would be more fully consulted.

I retired to the Vice-Chancellor's office for a *post mortem* with his Deputy (the VC himself having been away). The demonstrators, discontented with the debate's outcome, burst into University House through a side door, and blockaded us in the office. When I sought to leave, I was accused of assault! We were on the point of calling the police when the President of the Union,

Stuart Crawford, asked for five minutes to 'talk me out'. He succeeded, and I went home. The experience taught me some lessons, and perhaps particularly the value of keeping on good personal terms with the Union leadership. It is not easy to be a good Students Union President. There is always a balance to be struck between arguing strongly but reasonably for student views, and pushing so far as to become counter-productive. During my time as Pro-Chancellor, the Presidency of the Union was usually very sound. The duty carries its own rewards. Incumbents learn negotiating skills which stand them in good stead later in life. The present Foreign Secretary, Jack Straw, is a former President of the Lancaster University Students Union (hereinafter LUSU).

Over the next few years, with Governments of both political complexions, Universities saw enormous change. Governments called for an ever higher percentage of young people to enter University. By mid-1996, the rate of participation in higher education, at national level, had risen in one decade from 13% to over 30%. [Today it is 40%.] But at the same time, the Government were making it more difficult for the Universities to meet demand. Government funding of the system was steadily reduced. And students were increasingly expected to fund their own accommodation and fees, with a Government run system of student loans to help them.

In parallel with this, the Universities were being re-grouped. Until then there had been four different groups: the 'older Universities' dating from the middle ages; the 19th century Universities; the 'new Universities', like Lancaster, formed in the 1960s; and the 'Polytechnics and Colleges', founded still later. The last group had originally been set up to provide an essentially 'technical' education, and to a large extent still did. But many of its Institutions had also been offering more traditional University courses. It was argued that the time had come to give the fourth group full University status. This happened in 1992.

The first of these developments – the Government's downward pressure on public funding – was soon to have consequences for the University. The National Union of Students (NUS) mounted a campaign to draw attention to the financial hardship suffered by students throughout the country. The University authorities were in full sympathy with the aims of the campaign. However, the NUS now decided to hold a demonstration, on the campus at Lancaster, on the date of a Council meeting, namely 29 November 1991.

Meanwhile the subject of rents had again reared its head, following a new rise of 13% decided by Council in July. This had a substantial proportion of students to withhold their rent payments from the beginning of term.

Moreover, on 14 November, a group of students had occupied the Senate Room and the main offices of the Administration in University House. There they remained, until removed without violence by bailiffs and police on the 23rd. The threat of the NUS demonstration, coupled with the unsettled rents issue, led us to hold the Council meeting, not on the campus at all, but in the more secure Lancaster Town Hall. There, Council refused to bow to pressure on rent levels, and moreover decided that LUSU must pay for restoring the occupied rooms to order. It did, however, agree that a Review Panel, composed of equal numbers of staff and students, should consider the relationship between the University and the student body and report back.

A year later, following this review, the Council approved the establishment of a Student Hardship Fund. A key figure in this drama, whose calm, sympathetic and sustained approach did much to reconcile students to these decisions, and later did much else to help them, was the Provost of Colleges, Vernon Pratt. He remarked that LUSU validation for the occupation had been reached at an open, public meeting of a limited number of students – the students claimed up to 1,000 – without any balloting of the membership at large. It was obvious that hotheads had gained control and that the President of the Union was unhappy with the turn of events. Fortunately, relations with students thereafter improved markedly, and no further trouble with them arose until the crisis period.

There would no merit in systematically reviewing the other main business of Council during this period of growth and expansion. But a few unusual points deserve a mention. First amongst these is the acquisition of two important collections for the Peter Scott Gallery – one of pictures and prints, and one of ceramics.

In its first twenty years, the University had built up a small collection of prints, paintings and sculptures, mainly including works by British contemporary artists. In 1988, Harry brought about the construction of a custom-built home for it, in the Great Hall Arts Complex. It was named the Peter Scott Gallery, after its principal benefactor, and the opening was celebrated by an exhibition. It was decided that the Manton Collection would make an important contribution to the exhibition. Professor Irene Manton had been a Professor of Botany at Leeds University, but had also taught at Lancaster where she received an Honorary Doctorate. Unmarried, she had built up a substantial collection of prints, and some pictures. On her retirement at Leeds, she had expected to be allowed to use laboratories there for research. Leeds, however, had not agreed. Lancaster, on hearing this, were pleased to make Professor Manton an Honorary Research Fellow, and she could thus pursue her work. This was done purely in appreciation of her research activity, but was to have unexpected consequences.

Mary Gavagan, Curator of the Peter Scott Gallery, asked Professor Manton whether some pictures and prints could be borrowed. Receiving a positive reply, she now visited the Manton Collection at Leeds, and selected many of the finest items. The exhibition took place. All this gave Professor Manton much pleasure. Sadly, she died while it was still open. When her will was read, there was a provision that her whole Collection was bequeathed to Leeds University. However, later on, she had added a codicil to say that if, at the time of her death, any part of the Collection was on loan to another Institute of Learning, then that part was bequeathed to that Institute!

Leeds were unhappy. They spoke of going to Court; but legally their position was untenable. This was the situation when I became Pro-Chancellor. Council now decided to offer Leeds full co-operation. In 1991, we suggested that ownership of the Collection should remain where the will put it, split half and half; but that the two Universities should manage the whole collection jointly, with items moving between them. Leeds now decided to drop any idea of legal challenge. But they confronted a further difficulty, which was that the original will required of them an assurance that there would be a permanent display of any works they inherited: Leeds was short of Gallery space. In the end, they decided that, since the best items belonged to Lancaster, it was not worth their while to accept the rest. They offered us their share as a gift, which in 1993 our Council was very pleased to accept.

In 1994, Council was approached by the owner of the John Chambers Collection of Pilkington's Royal Lancastrian Ware. The Pilkington Tile and Pottery Company had been set up near Manchester in the late 19th century. Though its initial product was high-quality tiles, by 1903 it was also producing ornamental pottery. John Chambers was for long its chief designer, and he built up over his lifetime an important collection of both tiles and pottery, produced by the Company. This later became the property of his daughter, Miss Mary Chambers, who offered it to the University on condition that it could be properly housed and displayed.

The offer was accepted; money was raised; and a special 'John Chambers Ceramics Gallery' was built, being opened in 1997 by Eric Knowles, of *Antiques Roadshow* fame. The acquisition of these two Collections moved the Peter Scott Gallery up from being a purely regional Art Museum to one of some renown.

An unexpected development was a decision by the Governors of Charlotte Mason College at Ambleside, in June 1991, to approach Lancaster University to see whether the College could become a constituent part of the University. They made it clear they would like to move fast. Council appointed a Working Party of Council and Senate, chaired by me, to discuss and report. I was pleased to be involved. Charlotte Mason herself had been both a local and a national figure, and had set up the Parents National Educational Union (PNEU). Her College had long been an important feature of Ambleside life. There appeared to be complementarities. The College's main focus was teacher training, an area not covered by the University itself, whilst Educational Research was one of the University's strengths. Moreover it was thought that Lancaster would do well to establish a foothold in the Lake District.

The Working Party encountered no difficulties. With hindsight it is now clear that we should have dug deeper on some points. Be that as it may, we reported favourably. Council approved the principle of full incorporation in the summer of 1992, which was the College's Centenary year. The National bodies concerned agreed. Soon after merger, a Council Committee was established to keep an eye on developments at the College. Though I did not chair it, the Lake District Campus Advisory Committee (LDCAC) was amongst those I regularly attended. We shall hear more about Charlotte Mason College. But it is perhaps relevant just to note that, in 1994, the University accepted the resignation of Professor John Thorley as Chief Executive of the College, and appointed in his place a member of its Lancaster staff.

In 1993, following some irregularities in one of the Colleges, the Council decided to organise a thorough-going review of the College System, to take account of the many changes in the University since it was first established. Some time earlier I had told the VC it was hard to understand how the System worked. He now turned the tables by suggesting I chair the Review Committee in order to find out! It proved a fascinating experience. The Committee had a wide remit and a good membership, including two students among its nine members. It also had an excellent Secretary, in the person of Paul Graves.

It took the best part of a year to prepare the Report. During this time the Committee met frequently. It organised a survey of student attitudes on the College System, interviewing 400 students; and also a number of focus groups. It visited comparator Universities, namely Durham, York and Kent; and some members went to see a University of similar vintage relying on

Halls of Residence, namely Nottingham. Once produced, the Report was widely circulated in draft, and a great many of the comments received were taken into account. The final version was approved by both Senate and Council, and remained official University policy on the College System until I retired.

The main conclusions reached were not revolutionary, but constituted a package welcomed by academics, administrators and staff alike. They were that the University needed to put the same effort into student care as it had done to improving the quality of teaching and research; that it must re-affirm the importance of the College System and make clear what was expected from Colleges; and that it must place value on service to Colleges by its members, and also clarify the tutorial system, in which there was a place for both Colleges and Academic Departments. To ensure all this really happened, a Colleges and Student Support Board (CSSB) should be set up. And some new money must be found to help the Colleges respond.

This approach reflected a near unanimous agreement amongst those giving evidence that for students the Colleges do a great deal. In a University with (then) 8,600 students they provide smaller, more human-scale communities, to which students can have a sense of belonging; and a framework for sporting activities which allows participation at all levels of ability. They give students a sense of identity, and of control over their affairs. And they play a key role in providing pastoral care for students. We argued that no College should be larger than 900 students in size. The Report was approved by Council in March 1994.

In May 1993, George Cockburn resigned his post as University Secretary. This left a vacuum, with several additional officers reporting directly to the VC. He asked me to chair a Search Committee for a replacement. The Committee was composed of Harry, three other lay members of Council, three other academics appointed by the Senate, the President of the Students' Union (Sarah Carpenter) and an external assessor from Durham University. Following a public announcement, over 100 candidatures were received from outside, with very varied qualifications. It was agreed to call for interview the three internal, and three of the external, candidates. The final choice fell on an insider, Stephen Lamley. As we shall see, he later faced a very difficult situation in the University: in the end his health was strained and he took early retirement. But the choice had been a good one, and Stephen served the University well when crisis struck.

Meanwhile, in December 1993, the Council had approved a procedure to find also a successor to Harry. It had been proposed by me, after extensive consultation about precedent with Alastair Pilkington, and also with the two most senior officers of the University below the VC, namely Joe Shennan, Deputy Vice-Chancellor and Janet Finch, Pro-Vice-Chancellor. It involved establishing a Joint Committee of Council and Senate to conduct a search. Though Harry still had upwards of two years in office, it was desirable for his successor to be appointed well ahead of time so as to prepare for the task. This procedure was also confirmed by the Senate. I chaired the Committee. This time there were six others – three appointed from amongst the lay members of Council, and three academics appointed by the Senate. The President of the Students' Union (Sarah Carpenter) was again invited to join. It was a varied but well-balanced group.

First, the Committee set criteria for the appointment. Then, it advertised widely and by a variety of means, receiving over 170 candidatures. A 'long' short-list was prepared, and those selected made brief visits to the University in the Summer Term, where they were seen by a number of key players. Finally three candidates – all men – were called for interview by the whole Committee.

One of the unsuccessful candidates eliminated himself. Instead of being interviewed by the Committee, he preferred to reverse the roles! He also displayed impatience when subjected to questioning. When we got round to discussing merits, after the last candidate had left, there was immediate unanimity against his candidature. He must have sensed the effect he had made. He telephoned me next morning to say he had decided to withdraw his name. As between the other two, there was much to be said for each. However, the Committee, after careful debate, unanimously agreed to propose the name of Professor William Ritchie, Senior Vice-Principal of Aberdeen University, for appointment. After discussion of alternatives, it was decided to offer him a seven-year term of office. The Council approved the proposal in October 1994. Although, just before Bill took office, Lancaster suffered a total reverse of fortune, he accepted this philosophically, and will I think long be remembered as the man who saw the University through its worst crisis.

Meanwhile the ongoing programme of new building had led to a growth of short-term debt. The VC told the Council he felt the University should 'rationalise its borrowing policy and place loans for a substantial sum on a long-term fixed-interest basis.' He no doubt did so on the advice of Chris Savory, the Finance Officer, who had taken post some two years earlier, and who was under pressure from Harry to find ways of financing a huge building programme. In May 1994 the Council agreed that Barclays de

Zoette Wedd Ltd should advise the University on modalities. Their advice was to float a large Debenture Issue on the London International Stock Exchange.

This was novel. No University had attempted this method of funding. Others were thinking of it, but I believe no other University brought such a scheme to fruition. Though the Government was broadly supportive, it was clear that, if we proceeded, we should be guinea-pigs, and there were dangers. With no direct experience of such an operation, I felt a need for great caution. At the crunch meeting of the important Finance and General Purposes Committee of the Council in June, the pros and cons were exhaustively discussed. Both Chris Savory, and the external advisers, gave full and seemingly convincing justifications at every stage. The VC supported them. Gradually, the Committee was convinced, and it agreed to put a formal proposal to the Council, in July, to approve the launch of £50 million of long-term Debenture Stock for a period of up to 30 years, secured against a high proportion of the University's real estate. Associated with this was a proposal for new buildings which would bring the total capital cost up to the same figure.

As it happened – most unusually, and because I was in Rome for my son William's wedding to Antonella – I could not be present at the July Council, so it was chaired by the VC. But the Treasurer reported that *'the Pro-Chancellor, after some initial uncertainty, had come to welcome and support the proposals'*. They were of course extensively discussed. Members were warned that, if the matter went ahead, all would have to approve the detailed 'offering particulars'; and it was agreed that a totally independent legal adviser would be appointed, at University expense, to offer Council members advice. In the end, the proposals were agreed. Later, however, it was decided to stretch out the building programme over a longer period, and therefore to reduce the Stock Issue to £35 million.

Over the summer a great deal of work was done to take things forward, and the Council had a further long debate in October. Some members had shown reluctance to sign the listing particulars. It was, however, explained that the Stock Exchange regarded the Council as the body most closely resembling a Company Board of Directors, and would exempt <u>only</u> Princess Alexandra from the signature requirement. It was also explained that members would be insured by the University in respect of any consequences. After a debate of over two hours, the Council finally resolved, on a unanimous vote, that members 'were in principle prepared to sign, subject to their being satisfied with the content of the listing particulars at the final stage'.

The Council also set up a Working Party, chaired by me, with full powers to determine, on its behalf, the timing and price of the stock, though the price should not exceed 10%. (Interest rates were at that time very high.) The Working Party would agree the documents, which would be sent for ratification and signature by all members, together with a paper for them to sign, containing an irrevocable undertaking to ratify the actions of the Working Party at the Council meeting following Issue.

The documents which had to be prepared were voluminous, and went into an enormous level of detail. Finally, however, they were despatched by the Working Party to members. All but one signed. I persuaded the recalcitrant that his duty was to resign. I could thus tell the Council, in December, that all current members had signed. The Charity Commissioners had 'sealed an order', authorising the University to proceed. Myself and others had visited the Chairman and Chief Executive of the Higher Education Funding Council for England, who had required to be convinced that the scheme offered clear financial advantage to Lancaster University, and had eventually accepted this was so. Its approval was imminently expected. (It was soon after received.) The Council again debated at length. In the end it agreed to reduce the Working Party to five persons, and empower it to decide all outstanding matters. I remained its Chairman.

By the end of January every last detail was ready for the float, and I had the authority of the Working Party to proceed whenever our external advisers recommended, so long as our conditions were met. The nervous state of the market now imposed a longish waiting period. The Funding Council had stipulated the rate must not exceed 9.75%, and the market stood higher. Finally, on 24 March, Barclays de Zoette Wedd telephoned to say that the Stock could be successfully issued at that rate; and I told them to proceed. The Stock was successfully floated. On 5 April an amount of £35 million was received by the University.

Now for a complete change of theme. In 1995, The Queen decided to award Prizes for good performance in Higher Education. There were different categories. Lancaster won one of the 21 Prizes – for the quality of our work in integrating disabled or handicapped students. The prizes were presented by Her Majesty personally, at a Ceremony in Buckingham Palace; and in the evening there was a dinner at the Guildhall, with the Princess Royal and the Prime Minister as guests of Honour. Each winning University had been asked to send a Delegation of seven. I led our team, which included the VC, and the Special Needs Officer. There were also two student members, of whom one was Liz Matthews: blind from birth, she had already secured her BA in History, and was working for an MA.

The twenty-one Delegations assembled in the Picture Gallery of Buckingham Palace in mid-morning. It was colourful – all Chancellors, Pro-Chancellors, Chairmen and Vice-Chancellors being robed. There was a tremendous buzz of conversation. The Princess Royal, Chancellor of London University, entered quietly through a door next to where I stood, and asked me what was the collective term for such a gathering of University Dignitaries. I suggested 'a gaggle'. We processed to the Ballroom, where The Queen and The Duke of Edinburgh presented a handsome medal and diploma to each VC. Then back to the Picture Gallery, where we were grouped in two lines of Delegations, and Their Royal Highnesses walked round separately, in opposite directions, talking to each Delegation.

The Duke was the first to reach Lancaster, and I presented our Delegation. He naturally addressed Liz, whose blindness was evident, asking her what she was studying. When she replied *'The history of ice-cream, Sir'* he burst out laughing. He asked her when ice-cream had first been served at the Palace, and was impressed to be told the exact date and occasion. When The Queen reached us, the initial question to Liz, and the answer, were the same. Standing by The Queen, and watching her closely, it seemed to me that she at first suspected a joke. If so, she recovered instantly, but limited her response to an expression of interest!

That evening, at the Guildhall, there were robes and black ties. There were many great and good people. We started with drinks in the Library, and then processed through for dinner. Ordinary Delegates went first; then Chancellors and Pro-Chancellors; and finally Vice-Chancellors.

A master of ceremonies called out the name of the University and the person as each dignitary entered. Unfortunately he had been wrongly briefed, and called out – for the Chancellors and Pro-Chancellors – in each case the name, not of the correct person, but of the University's VC! This caused merriment, as many of those whose names were theoretically being called were well-known figures! The MC was clearly puzzled by the constant laughter. Eventually, somebody pulled his sleeve and enlightened him. He at once made a handsome apology: first for having boobed, and second for having to use the same list again for the following procession of VCs!

I also learnt a lot from Liz, as the day went on, about how the blind-from-birth cope with their disability. During the initial wait in the Picture Gallery I thought she might like me to tell her something about the room. She was delighted. After I had done so, she asked me to describe my favourite picture. Next, I was amazed when she enquired about the **_colour_** of the wall-paper. I told her it was red; but also that it was not paper, but a raised velvet material, which I encouraged her to feel. Seeing what was going on, a Chamberlain approached and asked if Liz would like to feel also the statue of Mrs Fitzherbert with her child, which of course she did. By the end of the day, I had come to understand better how blind people can make up, with their other senses heightened, and with imagination, for much of their deprivation.

A few months later, I was delighted when Liz was elected President of the Students' Union, a post she was to fill with wisdom and distinction through a very difficult period of the University's history. Her blindness never seemed to slow her down, and she was very quick to detect changes of mood and atmosphere. Later still, when Liz came to spend a weekend with us at home in the Lake District, it was a joy to see how well she could appreciate the mystery of places like the Hazelrigg Stone Circle near Keswick, or the homes of Wordsworth and Ruskin, at Dove Cottage and Brantwood respectively. It is a temptation to speak of her achievements after Lancaster, but space does not permit.

And so, as the summer term of 1995 ended, Lancaster seemed to be riding the crest of a wave. Teaching and research standards continued high. A huge building programme was on course. We had raised £35 million on the Stock Market to finance it. The University's annual budgets had continued to show small surpluses. Harry was to retire at the end of September, after ten years during which the University had moved up, in the perception of academe, from being of good regional standing to a position near the top of the national league. And Bill Ritchie, a man with a strong record of achievement, was to take his place.

The University enters a period of financial crisis

Sadly, we were soon to learn that the giant had feet of clay. On 22 August I was invited to a meeting at the University with the outgoing VC, the Treasurer (Peter Browning) and the University Secretary (Stephen Lamley). It became clear that the Finance Office was in a state of total disarray.

Although the Finance Officer (Chris Savory) had – with a lot of help from others – brought the Debenture Stock Issue to a successful conclusion, it had seemed to us at times that he was something of a loner, that he did not always undertake sufficient reconnaissance, that he had tended to ignore guidance from the Funding Council, and that his paperwork could be slap-dash. He had also completely fallen out with his Deputy. Now, it had suddenly emerged that there were two other causes of concern: we faced a major cash-flow crisis, of which he had given no warning; and the promised 'break-even' in the 1994/95 budget was under threat. Chris was recalled from holiday to explain. Soon after this, the VC agreed to commission a Special Investigation by the University's External Auditors, KPMG, on the extent of the cash-flow problem and on how it had arisen. The results were not received until end-October; but it was already clear that the University faced grave and unexpected financial difficulties. This was the situation at the end of September, when Harry was succeeded as VC by Bill Ritchie.

Harry was given a big farewell party in the Great Hall of the University. Princess Alexandra had come up specially for it, and we used the earlier part of the day to take her to visit Brantwood and Dove Cottage, both of which were new to her. How do I now assess Harry's ten years in the position of Vice-Chancellor? A New Zealander by birth, and educated there and at Cambridge University, he had come to Lancaster after teaching at Manchester, Edinburgh and Harvard. He had been in most ways an excellent VC. From the day he arrived he had started a process of urging academics to raise their sights. He saw that the staff had enormous potential, which had not yet been fully brought out. He was always confronting them with new challenges. He thought big for the University. His door was open to academics who wanted guidance or help. He was a great lateral thinker, and people tended to emerge from his office with completely revised aims and ideas. He usually chose staff well for particular tasks. And he brought Lancaster University forward, as already remarked, from being an essentially regional Institution to being one which was recognised as being top-class nationally in many disciplines, and internationally in several. It is very sad that the end of his Vice-Chancellorship was marred by the emergence of what turned out to be a massive financial crisis. He must bear his share of the responsibility for this, since it was the scale of his building ambitions, coupled with errors of the Finance Officer he had appointed, which were key contributors. The University, as we shall see, took two years to turn the financial corner. Yet, all in all, I am convinced that Harry was a great Vice-Chancellor of Lancaster University, and left a legacy of which he may be proud.

None of this was of much comfort to Bill Ritchie, his successor. Bill had been told a year earlier that he would be taking over a University with finances in good shape. Things were now very different. His first year was spent trying to gain control of an extra-ordinarily difficult situation, as one blow followed another. He confronted the task soberly, but with enormous determination and stamina. Tough and courageous decisions were needed, and were forthcoming. Although he felt it fair to give the Finance Officer a second chance for a year – against the repeated advice of myself, the Treasurer, and other senior lay members of Council – he seemed to make no other mistakes. When the Finance Officer did eventually leave, an excellent successor was found, in the person of Euan McGregor. The fact that a solid financial situation in the end emerged, is largely due to the way Bill and Euan managed things.

But the effort involved was vast. It was no surprise to me when, six years later, Bill decided he did not wish for the renewal of his contract, which would doubtless have been approved. Before ever the financial crisis broke, Bill had told me how delighted he was that the Ruskin Library was to be built, and how he hoped that another flagship project – but this one in the scientific field – could be engineered during his Vice-Chancellorship. In fact, two have been. In 2001 it was agreed to build a large new Lancaster Environmental Centre on the campus, incorporating the Institute of Terrestrial Ecology from Merlewood in Cumbria – a unit of the National Environment Research Centre – and thus ensuring that Lancaster has one of the largest groups of environmental researchers and teachers in Europe. It is now also agreed that the University will create 'Infolab', a new Computing Centre of European significance to develop future internet technology. These developments, for which the funding has been raised, should give Bill cause for much satisfaction.

I shall not describe all the problems faced by the University during the remaining two years of my term of office, but simply highlight some of them. Contracts had been let, during the summer vacation of 1995, for the building of the Main Library Extension, the Ruskin Library and the new accommodation for the Graduate College. The first was later the subject of big cost over-runs, and also suffered a major fire during construction. The Finance Office was declared by KPMG to have been unprofessional.

In March 1996, and out of a blue sky, we learnt that Charlotte Mason College was not carrying out teacher training to the standards required by the Teacher Training Agency. It later turned out that a much earlier negative report by Her Majesty's Inspectors in 1992 had been submitted to the Senate, but not followed up; and the Council had not been told! It was eventually agreed to transfer control of Charlotte Mason College to St Martin's College in Lancaster, which had more expertise than the University in the teacher training field, with effect from September of the same year. It was a sad decision for the University to take.

By May 1996 the University's overdraft. which had stood at around £1 M over the past two years, was expected to rise to £4.5 million by July: in the event it rose to nearly £9 million by the end of the University's financial year. Then the Government made a wholly unexpected cut of 31% in the provision of capital funding and equipment for Universities, whilst continuing to demand cumulative 'efficiency cuts' on current expenditures. Moreover, the University's Bankers now demanded a radical Recovery Plan, which would clear the core overdraft problem by 1999-2000. The Plan, once negotiated to meet the Bank's desiderata, in turn went though Council, which at the end of 1996 approved a target of a 5% surplus on current account in each of the four years 1996-00.

The financial crisis bottoms out & LU moves forward again

The adoption of this Recovery Plan, and its firm implementation by Euan McGregor, proved to be the turning point. The financial picture steadily improved.

This position was not reached without much difficulty. The six Council meetings in 1996 were all more or less uphill struggles. Members were rightly afraid that the University was on the brink of ruin. Academics and students were hard hit by the economies the situation required. In particular they reacted strongly against a proposal from the VC that provision should be made for some compulsory redundancies to be declared: in the end, Bill withdrew this, saying he would manage with the voluntary arrangements for premature retirement.

At the May meeting in 1996, we arrived at the Council Chamber to find it occupied by a large group of students – some of them from other Universities! The protest was about staff cuts proposed in order to cut costs. Eventually it was agreed that ten Lancaster students might remain as observers for discussion of this item, which would be taken first, but without the right to speak. We started an hour late. Soon, one of the ten started speaking, and would not shut up. I suspended the meeting. His fellow-students began to pressure him. He was clearly under the influence of alcohol. In the end he promised to leave if I would allow one student to speak. This was agreed, and at last we were able to get on with the meeting, which lasted five hours instead of the more usual two! By December we were up to six hours, and Members asked me to reflect with the Council Secretary on how to cut back! We later made some suggestions, which were accepted. But fortunately, this request coincided with the turn of the financial tide, so things returned to more normal conditions for the rest of my time.

In July 1996 the Students Union had requested the organisation of an independent enquiry about the reasons for the University's problems. The VC had opposed any witch-hunt, but accepted the need for the University to learn lessons. He proposed the establishment of a *'Committee to Review the Institutional Lessons to be Learned'*, and this was very effectively chaired by Professor Peter Rowe of the Law Department: given the University's penchant for acronyms, its conclusions inevitably became known as the CRILL Report[1]. Completed in May 1997, it was the subject of two debates that July: first, on 4 July, in a unique Joint Meeting of Council and Senate, chaired by myself; and then, later on the same day, in my own last Council meeting. Both were attended by my successor elect, Mr Brian Heron, as an invited guest.

The CRILL Report covered four main themes: cost overruns on the capital expenditure programme; the costs of disposing of Charlotte Mason College; the high interest payable on the Debenture Stock; and the one-off costs of the Premature Retirement Programme. It summarised its conclusions in the following terms: *'the Committee has identified issues of loss of control, lack of appraisal, inadequate and misleading information, lack of objectivity and of clarity in terms of accountability, inadequate accounting systems, and insufficient consideration given to safeguarding academic interests'.*

I had, of course, given a lot of thought to the Report. I opened the Joint Meeting by explaining the rules for the discussion, and then left it to the VC to offer the views of his Senior Management Team.

Then I intervened again. Given the importance of the occasion, and the role I had played in all these matters, I began by suggesting things which might, at the end of the debate, be included in Council's conclusions. The CRILL report was of very high quality. The Committee should be thanked for it. We should specifically recognise that, on the key points covered by the Report, the Council, between July 1994 and October 1995, took certain decisions which, though made in good faith, had turned out to be mistaken, and to be damaging to the Institution we were trying to serve, something we all deeply regretted. Those who were members of Council from the beginning of that period – that is to say myself and 12 other persons – must accept our full share of the responsibility. Council should also give broad endorsement to the CRILL analysis of how these errors came to be made, which had included a careful assessment of the then ambient climate of opinion, within and outside the Institution; a recognition that the figures laid before Council as the basis for the proposals approved were badly flawed; and the lack or inadequacy of option appraisals and of independent, outside advice. Officers should submit relevant parts of the Report to appropriate Committees for consideration, and for report back to Council and Senate on actions taken in consequence. This would make clear that we gave a strong general endorsement to the CRILL recommendations. The VC should be asked to submit to Council, in a year's time, an overview of the follow-up.

Continuing, I then offered a few personal comments of my own. I felt that, if the figures presented to Council had been consistently solid, the latter's decisions would have been different. Also, we should recall how Council took all the key decisions. There had always been a tradition that Council should seek to decide by consensus. This had the advantage that decisions taken were likely to enjoy maximum support. The key decisions, on the capital build programme and the debenture stock issue, were made between July 1994 and October 1995. The relevant Council minutes revealed an interesting picture. On every matter (except the Ruskin Project which had effectively been settled some time previously) there was extensive debate, with a wide range of views expressed, whose main points were fully recorded. However, with only two exceptions, the decisions were then taken by consensus. The exceptions were these. The basic decisions of July 1994, when Council resolved to approve the capital expenditure programme, and also took the decision of principle to launch the debenture stock issue, were made 'on a show of hands'. And the decisions in October 1994, when Council settled the details of the debenture stock issue, were specified as having been agreed unanimously. In all the other cases, even where doubts or anxieties had been expressed in debate, in the end no member of Council asked for a vote.

A very long debate ensued at the Joint Meeting of Council and Senate, followed by a shorter one at the Council, where perhaps the *leitmotif* was the damage done by the decisions to the staff and students of the University generally. Suggestions were made that senior Council members, and responsible officials, should have resigned. (Both the Treasurer and I had considered doing so in the summer of 1995, and I had again reflected when the University decided to pull out of Charlotte Mason College. On both occasions I was urged by the VC not to leave. It had seemed to me that, given his own recent arrival on the scene, and my experience as chair of the Council for five years, my departure would be more likely to hinder than to help recovery.) The Senior Management Team was also the subject of criticism. The VC responded by comparing the situation since the end of 1995 with a well-ordered military retreat.

At the end of the Council debate it was agreed – again by consensus! – to adopt the conclusions I had proposed, adding an admonition to the Senior Management Team to pay more attention to Audit Committee Reports. I was sad that my last Council should end on such a gloomy note; but I also felt, when my term of office ended on 31 July, that the University's financial problems had bottomed out and that it was beginning to move forward again.

Leaving the University

As this chapter about my nine years of close involvement with Lancaster University affairs draws to a close, it is timely to recall some elements which have not fitted easily into the narrative, but nevertheless form part of the wider picture.

Lancaster Degree Ceremonies are special. The University has always felt they marked a right of passage, and should be celebrated with real dignity. I have attended Degree Ceremonies elsewhere, including at the Bodleian in Oxford and at Guildford Cathedral (for Surrey University), but none so impressive. Many elements lend them stature. The fact that a Royal Chancellor – Princess Alexandra – presided them all for so long, and still conducts many, has set the tone.

In what way are they special? The Great Hall, with its fine organ, makes a dignified venue. It seats several hundred students, plus friends or relations. The Academic Procession is impressive. The University takes trouble to ensure a good turn-out of academic staff, duly robed. The scarlet gowns warn by the Chancellor and Senior Officers match the occasion. The Procession includes both a mace-bearer and halberdiers. The smart trumpeters of the Lancaster Constabulary play a fanfare.

The great personal interest of Princess Alexandra adds its own lustre. She is generous with her time. Each graduand in turn stands before the Princess, bows, and shakes her hand. Each has her total attention. She detains a random selection of students for a few words. After each group has passed, she formally pronounces conferment of the Degrees. And so things go on till all the groups are through.

Then it is the turn of those presented for Honorary Degrees. Lancaster has long been sparing with these. By 1980 a pattern had developed: numbers rarely exceed five in a year, and names are not normally considered without a clear regional connection. All must have real distinction. The University's Public Orator, Colin Lyas, 'presents' each Honorary Graduand to the Princess, making a witty and elegant address. The Honorary Degree is conferred.

Degree Ceremony at Lancaster University: platform party, 1995.

Then, the whole Ceremony ends. After these Ceremonies the Princess usually does walk-about outdoors among the new graduates, with much photography, and also attends a lunch for a representative group of graduands, families and staff. These Ceremonies take place twice a year: in July for the First Degree students, when the Ceremonies now stretch over four days, involving 3-4,000 students; and in December, when there is a single day for Higher Degrees and Doctorates.

As already indicated, I began to preside some Ceremonies myself, in 1994. It was at once apparent how demanding the Princess's behaviour pattern is. I took care to focus on each individual, look straight into their eyes, and say at least *'Congratulations: well done'*. The answers of those with whom there was time for a few extra words were listened to with care. They could at times be amusing. By the end of 300 students, in an hour's Ceremony, one felt drained, and in need of a rest.

One particular Degree Ceremony – in July of 1991 – sticks particularly in my mind. Honorary Degrees were being conferred on Barbara Castle and Christy Nolan. Christy, from Ireland, was a rare exception from the local connections rule. The Honorary Degrees Committee had felt his qualities so exceptional that an offer should nonetheless be made. In his autobiography *Under the Eye of the Clock*, Christy tells how, born without speech and paralysed from the neck down, declared by doctors to be effectively a vegetable, but with the support of a mother who would never give up, he gradually fought his way out of virtual prison, and became a best-selling author. When we wrote to offer Christy the Degree, we had no idea whether he would accept an Honour from a University which could claim no direct connection; or whether, if he did, he would feel able to come in person to receive it. In the event, we were the first University to make such an offer, and he was delighted to accept. He also insisted on coming in person. This Ceremony was deeply moving. Barbara Castle made the acceptance speech for both: when the moment came she read out remarks by Christy. On reflecting that he had typed them on a computer, with a headstick, often missing the correct key and having to job back, one saw at once the level of courage which had made him what he was. There were tears in many eyes by the end of the Ceremony.

I went next day to see Christy at the Post House Hotel, where he was staying with three helpers: his mother, his sister Yvonne, and his carer Tom. I wondered how to handle such a conversation, and decided to address Christy like anyone else, trusting in the team to sort things out. I asked his reactions. His mother provided answers, which were enthusiastic: but it was obvious from his eyes that he agreed with every word. With his mother, this largely reflected telepathy and long association. But it was clear that, with his regular carers, he could converse quite easily, having developed a code by which movements of his eyes – the only part of him under his full physical control – could be used to give coded messages which they understood. I felt my talk with Christy had given me a real personal contact.

A truly exceptional Degree Congregation of Lancaster University took place in Kuala Lumpur in April 1997 for 95 part-time students of St Martin's College from Malaysia – with some from Saba and Sarawak – who had followed courses in their own country. They came from all over the Federation. They included a high percentage of the Principals of Malaysia's 22 Nursing Colleges, who had taken a Nursing Studies Teaching Degree. Other students had followed a course in Health Studies, being Medical Assistants – almost Doctors – in remote locations all over the country. Their studies had been accomplished whilst they held down their normal jobs. They were directed by St Martin's staff, partly by going to a central venue at Ipoh, where the students came for short bursts of intensive teaching; and partly by supporting distance learning, at or near their places of work. St Martin's College wanted to mark its recent entry into the educational field of Malaysia. And the Principal, Professor Ian Edynbry, asked me to help

After a Degree Ceremony at Lancaster University. L to R: Peter Browning, Harry Hanham, HRH Princess Alexandra, myself, Joe Shennan.

by travelling out to make the conferments, instead of having the Degrees sent by post. I agreed, on condition that the Ceremony should as closely as possible resemble what we did at Lancaster. The St Martin's staff played the game to the full.

We were in a hired hall, and there were no trumpeters or organ. But the Lancaster organ music had been taped, and was played. There was a small, but genuine, academic procession. All graduands were in gown and hood. I had taken my normal robes and mortarboard. Knowing Malaysian habits, we had forbidden individual photography during the Ceremony, though an official video of the entire proceedings was made and sold, as we always did at Lancaster. A vast number of private photographs were also taken afterwards. I opened the Congregation. Ian made a short speech of welcome. I gave an address, explaining the accreditation of St Martin's College by the University, and stressing the academic value of Lancaster Degrees. I also made clear this was the first time the University had <u>ever</u> conferred Degrees away from Lancaster. The conferments then took place; and there was time for a few words with <u>each</u> graduand. The students lustily sang the Malaysian National Anthem. And then we processed out.

There followed an extensive walk-about, and a buffet lunch. Thanks to a compulsory walk-through by the Graduands the day before, there no glitches. In addition to the Graduands themselves, there were around 250 guests. It was striking that all the students came, in some cases with four or five family or friends, though many had to travel very long distances. All were smart. The men wore dark suits under their gowns. The ladies wore long, silk dresses of Malay silk, in rich and varied hues. Never has a Lancaster Degree Ceremony been so colourful. The whole affair excited much local media attention, and was very helpful to the image in Malaysia of both St Martin's College and the University. The trip took me six days, as I was determined not to travel so far without at least having a good look at Kuala Lumpur. The game had certainly been worth the candle.

Maura almost invariably lent me her support at Degree Congregations – though she did not feel able to travel to Kuala Lumpur. She also came to a host of other official functions. Indeed I could not have carried out the duties of the Pro-Chancellor without a huge amount of her support in a thousand ways.

A very agreeable feature at Lancaster University is the annual season of Concerts in the Great Hall, then organised by Professor Denis McCaldin, who was not only the Director of Music but also President of the Haydn Society of Great Britain. He managed to attract to Lancaster many excellent performers, of whom perhaps the BBC Philharmonic and the Manchester Camerata Orchestras were the most striking.

Another agreeable feature is the convenience and beautiful setting of the hill-top campus. There had been overall campus architects – Shepherd, Epstein – from when the first buildings rose in the 1960s, who were still acting in the same capacity when I left the University. They were not responsible for all the individual buildings; but their task was to ensure that an overall pattern was respected, and that all new buildings were compatible with it. Their concept was based on that of an Italian Hill Village. A perimeter road ran round the summit; all the buildings were initially placed within it (though there is now some overspill); there was a central square, served by an underground bus station; no building was meant to be more than five minutes walk from it (though here again there has been some slippage to cope with University growth); and Colleges were built round courtyards. The whole complex stands in extensive grounds, well planted with trees, and containing a range of sports fields.

Where the University is approached from the main A6 road, the road winds past a group of agricultural buildings, beside a duck-pond. When leaving the University I would offer lifts to students waiting at one of the bus-stops, and often ask them as we went along why they had chosen Lancaster. One day I put this question to three girls who had hitched a ride. The first two gave predictable answers. One had wanted to read a subject for which Lancaster had a high reputation; and another had wanted to study under a particular professor. But the third gave a more unusual response. *"Ee, 'twas because o' the doocks',* she said – in a Lancastrian and distinctly rural accent. It turned out she was a local farmer's daughter. When she came to inspect Lancaster, the first thing she saw was the pond and the ducks: her heart was won!

A small cultural contribution was also made by the University to the cultural life of South Lakeland. The Armitt Trust of Ambleside, holder of an important collection of works by Ruskin, Beatrix Potter, Harriet Martineau and others, had never had space to display the artefacts adequately. In the short time Lancaster University was in charge at Charlotte Mason College, this deficiency was addressed. The Treasurer of the University, Peter Browning, was also then the Chairman of the Trust. The idea was conceived of securing money from the Heritage Lottery Fund, and taking a long-term lease of part of the Charlotte Mason premises, in order to create a proper museum. Peter, being in charge of the Trust's operations, always declared an interest and left the University's Council Chamber when the lease was debated. Fortunately it was agreed shortly before Lancaster left the College. And in 1998, as a result, the Armitt Trust was able to open a fine home for its property.

My last month at the University was busy. There were four days of Degree Congregations. As so often in the previous seven years, these included my birthday! During the second day, Princess Alexandra was able officially to open the Main Library Extension, and to name the splendid Main Reading Room after Alastair Pilkington. His widow, Kathleen, was there, and was deeply moved. The Secretary of Manchester University, a visitor, told me he thought the time for such large Library reading rooms was over. I was more inclined to accept the view expressed by some of the new Graduates that they would never have obtained such high Degree ratings if they had not been able to study quietly in such congenial and well-equipped surroundings. That evening the Bill and Elspeth Ritchie gave an intimate dinner in their home, The Croft, attended by The Princess and her Lady-in-Waiting, Lady Mary Mumford: Kathleen Pilkington; as well as some old and trusted Council members, namely Kathleen Ollerenshaw; Joe Shennan, the Deputy Vice-Chancellor, with his wife Margaret; two or three others; and Maura and myself.

CHAPTER 23

The Creation of the Ruskin
Foundation and Ruskin Library

LIKE SO MANY things in life, the whole Ruskin Project began with a chance
encounter. Harry Hanham has told me how, when he happened to meet
Lord Lloyd of Kilgerran at a Royal Society event in 1986, and had explained
that he was Vice-Chancellor of Lancaster, Lord Lloyd had responded with
the sentence: *'Oh, I have this house in the Lake District'*. It was a reference to
Brantwood, John Ruskin's home on Coniston Water. And Lord Lloyd –
Gerran Lloyd – was Chairman of the Trusts which controlled the property.

A year or so later, there was a further chance meeting. By now Harry had
a general picture of Gerran Lloyd's connections with Brantwood. Ruskin
had spent the last twenty years of his life there. On arrival he was already
acknowledged as a great Victorian sage and polymath. A considerable artist,
and Oxford University's first Slade Professor of Art, he was seen as the
world's leading art critic. But he was also much else besides: a tremendous
traveller; a distinguished author; a pioneer environmentalist; a geologist; a
social reformer, rebelling against the excesses of the industrial revolution; a
political thinker; the man who first propounded the notion of the National
Trust; and one whose writings touched the lives of many, including
expressly Gandhi and Tolstoy.

He was also wealthy. The only son of a successful wine-merchant, his
failed marriage had left him with no family to support. He owned a large art
collection. At one time he and his father between them possessed no fewer
than 250 works by Turner; and he had later given away fifty to the
Ashmolean Museum at Oxford and twenty-five to the Fitzwilliam at
Cambridge. At Brantwood, his cousin, Joan Severn, was his housekeeper;
she and her husband, Arthur, lived in the house, and indeed Ruskin built on
a studio so that Arthur could indulge his artistic talents.

When Ruskin died in 1900, he left the house and all his effects to the
Severns. He had, however, expressed a wish that the house be open to the
public. Sadly, things went downhill. The Severns maintained the Ruskinian
living style, but without the income to support it. Gradually things were sold
off. In the end, everything went, including the house. Ruskin's many

disciples were distraught. Fortunately, they included a man of action, determined to save whatever could be rescued: John Howard Whitehouse (1873-1955). Whitehouse was initially a Liberal MP, but turned to education and authorship. Within the limit of his means, and over many years, he bought everything as it came on the market, including, in 1933, Brantwood itself, with 250 acres around it. A year later, he opened it to the public, as a National Memorial to Ruskin.

Whitehouse could not afford any Turners – Ruskin had died with eight looking down on his bed! But the Whitehouse Collection – as it came to be known – in the end included over 400 works of art on paper by Ruskin; 125 daguerreotypes; over 2,000 drawings by Ruskin and his associates; more than 8,000 manuscripts, including 29 volumes of Ruskin's diaries; several hundred historic photographs (Ruskin was a very early user of photography); and a uniquely comprehensive holding of books by and about Ruskin. It was the largest Collection of Ruskiniana in the world. About one-fifth of the Collection was returned to the house, which was at last opened to the public. The remainder was kept at Bembridge on the Isle of Wight, in a boys' Public School, established by Whitehouse in 1919, and run 'on Ruskinian principles'. The full story of how Whitehouse contrived to put together this vast and unique collection has been told by its Curator for almost 40 years, Dr James Dearden[1].

When Whitehouse himself died, in 1955, he left Brantwood and the Collection – and also Bembridge School – in Trust. Gerran Lloyd found that Whitehouse had expressed the wish that he be sole executor of the will. He became Chairman of Trustees. Gerran was by then practising as a Barrister, specialising in patent law. But at an earlier stage in his career he had been a master at Bembridge School, and Whitehouse had taken a liking to him. It was a considerable challenge; but Gerran rose to it. The Collection was catalogued. Some scholars made the pilgrimage to Bembridge, and items were loaned for exhibitions elsewhere. Jim Dearden wrote extensively about it. But in general the Collection remained largely inaccessible. From then until his death in 1991, Gerran was to remain Chairman of Trustees.

When Harry Hanham came into contact with Gerran, there were two Trusts. The first, Education Trust Ltd (ETL), held direct responsibility for the School and the Collection. The second, the Brantwood Trust, was responsible for Brantwood only. A High Court order of 1951 appointed Education Trust as sole Trustee of Brantwood, and required it to appoint 'Management Trustees'. Harry was aware that Gerran had long been concerned by the inaccessibility of the Collection to researchers and the wider public. It needed to be re-housed in purpose-built accommodation. Gerran had, many years before, approached Oxford University, whose connections with Ruskin were strong. The University had expressed itself very interested in providing a suitable permanent home for the Collection, but nothing had actually happened.

Harry's lateral thought processes began to work. Lancaster University had good English, Art and History Departments, all with a strong focus on Victorian studies. It was also the closest University to Brantwood. Harry arranged for a Lancaster team to visit Bembridge and inspect the Collection. Professor Keith Hanley of the English Department and Mr John Illingworth, a University Librarian, were commissioned to undertake this task: they were accompanied by Tony Cann, whose position will be clarified later; and they duly reported. The importance of the Collection, its need for greater accessibility, its requirement for conservation work to be done, and its value as a research resource, were at once clear.

In 1988 and 1989, several significant events took place. Harry had decided that it would be good, both for the Collection and for the University, if somehow it could be brought to Lancaster. He placed Professor Michael Wheeler, a Victorianist, and a senior member of the English Department, in charge of what soon became known as the Ruskin Project. Gradually the Project took concrete shape. The essence was that Gerran be asked whether, if the University would construct a purpose-built Ruskin Library on its Campus, ETL would be prepared to transfer the Collection to it. The next move was that Gerran Lloyd and his wife, Phyllis were invited to visit the University, where they lunched with the Pro-Chancellor, Sir Alastair Pilkington, and Harry.

Meanwhile the University had started its Development Campaign, with me as Chair of the responsible Committee (see preceding Chapter). In September, 1989, we received presentations of a number of projects, including Ruskin. Michael Wheeler was told that, if he wanted the Development Campaign to take the Ruskin Project under its wing, this could only happen if and when Gerran had agreed to the principle of transfer. I also sought an assurance, which he readily gave, that he would run the Project for a minimum of five years. In the event, he was to stay for ten! In December of the same year I was elected to become Pro-Chancellor from October 1990. This assured the Project a lot of additional support and protection from a high level within the University.

1990 was another seminal year. Michael had realised that, if the

University wished to be considered as a serious contender to house the Collection, it must contribute seriously to Ruskinian studies. In January of that year, he inaugurated a new Ruskin Programme, based on a series of weekly research seminars, with twenty participants every week. These brought leading Ruskinian scholars from all over the country – and some from abroad – to high-level Ruskin discussions. Over the years, the themes were to include, *inter alia*, Ruskin and Environment; Modern Painters; Ruskin's Northern France; and Ruskin, Turner and the Pre-Raphaelites. Out of all these themes, books emerged, and were published: and the last-named made a big input to the exhibition at the Tate, to which we come later. The Programme was also awarded a four-year Research Grant, worth £140,000, for the compilation of an electronic edition of *Modern Painters*; and continues in operation to this day. While initially the Programme was run by the Director, Ruskin's very nature meant that it became strongly multi-disciplinary, and a feeling grew up that it should rest on a broader base. A Management Committee was established in 1996, chaired by Professor Jeffrey Richards of the History Department.

Michael could not have undertaken all the work involved in both the Project and the Programme without strong underpinning. Starting on a part-time basis, Ruth Hutchison in 1994 became Michael's full-time – and inspired – Assistant. She served Project and Programme devotedly – and later had a major role in the co-ordination of *Ruskin Today* – the year-long, international, centenary programme in the year 2000, which commemorated Ruskin's death. After that, she took on different employment in the University, but those concerned will always recall her unique contribution to the Ruskinian cause for over six years.

In 1990 it was time to put the key question to Gerran Lloyd. He was again invited to the University, this time for most of a day. On 2nd February, he came with Phyllis. They were shown round the University. (I had met Gerran, six years earlier, at a gathering of the 'All Party Group for Energy Studies' in London.) They were assured by me that the Development Campaign was prepared to make the Project its flagship activity, and that we believed we could raise the money needed to build a high quality Ruskin Library. And, at the end of the day, over a dinner at The Croft involving the Hanhams and the Wheelers, Gerran said: *'I think the Collection should come to Lancaster'*. Later that month, a public statement was released by the University and ETL saying they intended to collaborate on the Project.

The Development Campaign immediately began to raise money for it. Alongside this activity, we devoted much effort to building up a network of key supporters. These included the Northwest Museums Service; the Royal Commission on Historic Monuments; the National Arts Collection Fund; the Fine Arts Society; the National Trust; the Wordsworth Trust; the National Heritage Memorial Fund; the Victoria and Albert Museum; and the Public Records Office. The two first were soon advising the University on a design brief for the proposed Ruskin Library; and were followed in this later by the Bodleian Library, the Ashmolean Museum and the Tate Gallery. Moreover, the Northwest Museums Service joined the University in commissioning and funding a Conservation Survey of the Whitehouse Collection.

It was at this crucial stage, in February 1991, that Gerran Lloyd suddenly died. A great deal of work had been done on the Project; but all had been based on mutual trust. There was as yet nothing in the way of a legally binding commitment by ETL that the Collection would be transferred to the Ruskin Library. It is a quite extra-ordinary fact that, on the very day of Gerran's death, his eldest daughter, The Honourable Mrs Elizabeth Robins, telephoned Michael Wheeler at the University and said: *'You will have heard of my Father's death – my Mother and I wish you to know that it was my Father's wish that the Collection should come to Lancaster, and so it will'*. We in the University were deeply moved by this spontaneous initiative, and encouraged thereby to redouble our efforts.

Elizabeth had for long been a Trustee of ETL, and we had already had a good many meetings with her. But she had certainly not anticipated having to take over as Chairman so soon. Moreover she had, only three months before her father's death, lost her husband as a result of a sudden illness. We were enormously impressed by the way in which, despite all this, she immediately took the reins at ETL and drove the enterprise forward. She was greatly helped in this by her fellow Trustees: namely her sister, the Honourable Mrs Catherine Edwards, and a family friend, Michael Prince.

Meanwhile the Fine Arts Society had given us great help in promoting and popularising the Project. That March they displayed Jim Dearden's exhibition *'Ruskin and the Alps'*, based on the Whitehouse Collection. The Development Campaign funded two private viewings. At the first, Princess Alexandra, and her husband the Honourable Sir Angus Ogilvy, were the guests of honour. On each occasion the guests – including many of the great and the good – were fully briefed about the Project.

The viewings were accompanied by working lunches and dinners between the University and ETL teams, at each of which the Project acquired sharper definition. At the second dinner, agreement was reached that we must have some kind of agreement on paper; and the idea was born that we should jointly write a Memorandum of Understanding. This dinner was also attended by Phyllis Lloyd; and by Sir Richard Parsons, a former Diplomatic Service colleague and friend of mine, who was both a Bembridge alumnus and a friend of the Lloyd family. Enjoying the full confidence of both parties, he was soon to play an important role in the Project.

That journey to London also brought me into closer contact with another key player, namely Tony Cann. Tony is a successful Lancashire businessman, who has always supported good causes, and done so in an extra-ordinarily discreet and unassuming way. He and his wife Ruth, having five children, had in the 1970s acquired a holiday home on the west shore of Coniston Water. Each summer the family visited Brantwood, across the Lake. One day, Tony bought a copy of Ruskin's book, *Unto This Last*, and was impressed. He took an increasing interest.

Tony's connection with Brantwood was initially mainly through the then Director, Bruce Hanson. He heard that a refurbishment of the Stables Block was being considered, and offered financial help from the Bowland Trust, a charity he controls. This was accepted by Gerran, and later Tony continued to finance improvements at Brantwood in the same way. Tony wanted to see Brantwood develop, and Gerran was happy that this should happen if the Trust was willing to pay. It was clear that his attitude to our Project would be of great importance. Fortunately, he was overjoyed to hear of it, because he felt that Ruskin would never receive proper appreciation unless he was the subject of solid research.

The National Heritage Memorial Fund (NHMF) now came on the scene. Georgina Nayler, its then Director, was to prove a staunch ally. She already knew all about the Collection, and its need for greater accessibility. She was delighted with the notion of its being housed in a first-class University with good Ruskinian connections. And, at our very first meeting, she made clear the NHMF would do its best to help things forward. Thereafter, many of the key meetings between the parties, for some years, took place in the NHMF Boardroom in St James's Street, and Georgina often attended part of them. This meant, not only that the NHMF were fully informed at all times, but also that we benefited from their most helpful advice.

Particularly important was a meeting there on 11 June 1991, where the aim was to determine the substance of the Memorandum of Understanding. Georgina came to this, accompanied by Sir Matthew Farrer, the Fund's

Legal Adviser. The University and ETL were struggling to find a mutually acceptable formula to cover the ownership and the management of both the Collection and the Ruskin Library. Matthew's advice was simple and clear. Leave all matters of ownership aside. The Collection should remain in the possession of ETL; and the Library in that of the University. Set up a new organisation. Arrange for that organisation to have effective management and control over both elements, for a pre-determined but lengthy period. None of this would be legally difficult. Changes of ownership would create vast complications. This approach appealed immediately to both Parties. We jointly decided that this was the basis on which we would try to agree. And that, in the end, is exactly what happened.

And then, unexpectedly, a new question was raised by ETL. How was Brantwood to be brought into the structure? It had been obvious to all of us in the University, that there was a strong *de facto* connection. Both the Collection and Brantwood were under the ultimate control of the same organisation, ETL. The Collection was physically split between Bembridge, which housed about four fifths, and Brantwood, which housed the remainder. Problems of physical communication meant that it was difficult to organise any regular interchange between the two parts. Visitors to Brantwood almost always saw the same artefacts, and many of these were being over-exposed to the light.

We had not, however, thought it sensible for the University to raise the matter. Our overriding aim was, and remained, to procure the Bembridge part of the Collection to come to the Ruskin Library. It did not seem wise to put questions about Brantwood. Apart from the fact that their discussion would complicate the picture, we had formed the impression, rightly or wrongly, that the Lloyd family was sensitive on the subject of Brantwood. They had always had a flat there, where their holidays were often passed. And, although the house and grounds were open to the public, we felt that, after half a century of guardianship over this priceless asset, they might not wish control to pass out of their hands. Now that the family themselves had raised the issue, however, it did not take long for the University and ETL to agree that Brantwood should somehow be covered in the arrangements to be made.

And so, by the end of 1991, we had moved a long way forward. The Memorandum of Understanding had been agreed between the Parties and approved by the University Council. It provided that ETL and the University would create a Ruskin Foundation, which would include among its Trustees not only a number appointed by each of them, but also certain independent persons chosen for their relevant experience, and which would have an independent Chairman. The Foundation would be responsible for the care and maintenance of Brantwood, of the Collection, and of the Ruskin Library to be built at the University. The policies of the Trustees would be enacted by a Management Committee made up of those responsible for the day-to-day running of the Library, of Brantwood, and of the academic Ruskin Programme, again with an independent Chairman.

The year 1992 was to see the disappearance of the Development Campaign as such (see previous Chapter), and with it of Jo James, its Director; but fund-raising for the Ruskin Project continued. By May a total of £300,000 had been raised, over and above the £250,000 donated by Alastair Pilkington. By then also, the University had finalised its design brief for the Ruskin Library, and sent it to four selected architects with a request for preliminary drawings. In the same month the University mounted an Exhibition, in the Peter Scott Gallery, entitled 'Ruskin, Tradition and Architecture'. And the first fruits of the Ruskin Programme appeared, in the shape of a scholarly book on the same subject: *The Lamp of Memory*. Later that year Princess Alexandra kindly agreed to become Patron of the Ruskin Project – a patronage which was transferred to the Ruskin Foundation after its establishment.

In 1993, the Memorandum and Articles of Association of the Ruskin Foundation were formally approved, and an agreement of principle was reached about the Trustees to be appointed. Meanwhile a Preparatory Committee, chaired by me, was working up the more detailed arrangements. By now, there were frequent meetings between the Parties. The University side was normally represented by myself and Michael Wheeler. The ETL side usually contained Elizabeth Robins; her sister, Catherine Edwards; and Michael Prince. On the University side we gave much thought to the preparation of each meeting. We felt a need to move gently. ETL were clearly committed to the principles of the scheme. But they were also, understandably, cautious. They knew it was right to bring the Collection into the public domain; yet each move in that direction involved some abandonment of a control the Lloyd family had effectively maintained for thirty-five years. We wanted them to feel comfortable and confident at every stage. I therefore encouraged Michael Wheeler to take the lead in advancing ideas from the University side, while I sought to maintain a certain level of detachment.

The University Council now approved the design for the Ruskin Library submitted by Richard MacCormac, at that time President of the Royal

*The Ruskin Foundation Trustees' inaugural meeting: photographed on
Lancaster University Bowling Green, 3 May, 1994[2].*

Institute of British Architects, and later knighted. All sides in the University
had been impressed with the quality of Richard's plans. Like his work in
other universities, there was enormous innovation, but at the same time the
maintenance of harmony with the context. The Ruskin Library guidebook
explains his thinking, which clearly had a Ruskinian inspiration. When the
building was finally completed it was to win prestigious architectural awards.

The Council also agreed that outline planning permission be sought.
Whereas fund-raising had hitherto been conducted quietly, the Council now
launched a big public appeal for funds. This was followed by a generous
conditional offer from Tony Cann's Bowland Trust to donate £500,000 – if
the University was prepared to make a matching offer. The Council
responded by agreeing to make available up to £600,000 for capital
expenditure, and £75,000 a year to cover the Library's running costs.

In 1994, the tempo quickened. The Foundation was registered as a
Charity, and in May the newly appointed Trustees held their inaugural
meetings, at the University and Brantwood. ETL and the University had
each appointed three; they had agreed on the appointment of six
independent Trustees; and the Trustees collectively, at their first meeting,
elected Richard Parsons as the independent Chairman. Dr Ken Kitchen, just

retired from being Secretary to the University of Manchester, became Honorary Secretary, a position of real importance in the Foundation's early years, which he filled with great aplomb. The Trustees also agreed that one of their independent members, namely Tony Cann, should chair the Management Committee. During the year, the Trustees worked hard to agree with both ETL and the University the more detailed legal agreements between them and the Foundation.

Fund-raising by the University continued steadily. It was again helped by the Fine Arts Society which hosted two further exhibitions. Michael Wheeler also gave a fascinating lecture at the National Gallery on 'Ruskin's Museums and Galleries'. By now it had become clear, however, that normal fund-raising would not easily attain the cost of the Ruskin Library, for which the lowest tender had come in at £2,300,000. This proved, in the event, not to be tragic. The Government was establishing the National Lottery. The proceeds were to be partly used to create a Heritage Lottery Fund. This Fund, scheduled to begin operations in January of the following year, was to be controlled by the NHMF. They had for some time been encouraging the University to apply early for Ruskin Library funding. For this we would need matching funds of only one-third: a target we could now easily meet. The University therefore persuaded the Bowland Trust to agree that the £500,000 it had decided to grant towards capital expenditures, should instead be used to create an endowment to help cover the future running costs of the Library.

Meanwhile there had been an important new appointment. The Ruskin Library staff and budget, once established, would be coming under the administrative control of the University Librarian. Mrs Jacqueline Whiteside now assumed this post. She was delighted to do so just as the University was committing itself to a large extension of its Main Library and the building of the Ruskin Library. She was from the start a whole-hearted supporter of the Ruskin Project. Over the next six or seven years, both Projects were to leave her wrestling with huge difficulties, compounded by the University's financial disasters, described in the preceding Chapter. She also suffered severe health problems. But she never wavered. And the Ruskin Library, in particular, was always protected within the Librarian's total budget.

In January 1995 the Ruskin Library proposal was the thirteenth application received by the HLF. The documentation required was complex and very extensive. Fortunately Michael Wheeler was by now very used to dealing with Whitehall, and had been working on it for a considerable time. We requested a contribution of £1.5 million towards the building costs.

Between 1993 and 1995, all the remaining Legal Agreements between ETL, the University and the Ruskin Foundation were signed.

Perhaps I had better briefly describe the pattern established by these Agreements. The Ruskin Foundation itself had been established by a Memorandum of Association, dated 11 May 1993. The Foundation's principal aim was the advancement of education in the life and work of John Ruskin. To this end it was to acquire, either outright by purchase or gift, or on loan, any property associated with Ruskin, particularly the Ruskin Collection, the Ruskin Diaries, and Brantwood. It was to ensure that such property was housed either at Brantwood or at the new Ruskin Library at Lancaster University. And it was to care for, maintain, conserve, repair and enhance such property and make it available to the general public and scholars.

On 12 April 1995, Bailment Agreements were signed between ETL and the Ruskin Foundation. These provided for the lease by ETL to the Foundation, for twenty-five years, of the Collection and Diaries, on certain conditions. There was an informal understanding that, if both sides were happy at the end of that time, the lease would be extended. On the same day a Deed of Agreement was signed between Lancaster University, the Ruskin Foundation and ETL. This committed the University to provide a permanent home for these 'chattels', and associated staffing. The staff would include a Curator, whose responsibilities would include the care of all the chattels, whether at Lancaster University or at Brantwood. In a separate letter ETL gave an assurance that, for the duration of the lease, the Brantwood Management Trustees would all be drawn from amongst the Ruskin Foundation Trustees who were themselves members of the Foundation Management Committee.

In July the Ruskin Foundation Management Committee[3] met for the first time, with Tony Cann in the Chair, and began to address many practical issues.

Now, another threat hove into sight. ETL explained to us that Bembridge School, in common with many other small Public Schools, had become uneconomic. They had therefore negotiated a deal in which it would be taken over by the nearby Ryde School. A group of *alumni* opposed the whole plan. They went so far as to suggest that the Collection be sold off, to salvage the School. In the end, however, nothing came of this, and the deal went though.

In June 1995, the HLF Trustees had approved our application in principle, but were not yet ready to agree details. They promised a decision in late

July; but continued seeking clarifications. Then they said they must first visit the site of the Library, which could not be done until August. The University Council was therefore unable to give the go-ahead to build the Library at its last meeting before the summer holidays, but – on my birthday! – authorised a named 'Approvals Group' of officials under the Vice-Chancellor to do so in August, if the HLF granted our application in such a way that the University would not itself need to commit more money than already agreed.

The HLF had meanwhile been multiplying their detailed questions: we counted sixty-eight in all! At this stage, moreover, they told us that, because they wished the Ruskin Library to be a prestige project, they wanted us to enhance it in various ways. We replied that this could be done if they would pay the whole bill for the extras: our capital input could not be increased. To our surprise and delight, they accepted! Finally, in August, they sent us a contract, in which they undertook to furnish £2,300,000 out of the increased total cost of £3 million. As I noted in my diary at the time, this represented 'the culmination of six years of excellent work by Michael [Wheeler], not without considerable advice and support from me. We've hit the jackpot for Lancaster University'.

However, the timing could hardly have been more awkward. On 22 August I had learnt from the Vice-Chancellor that the University faced a completely unexpected cash-flow crisis, the scale of which was large but still uncertain (see preceding Chapter). Nevertheless, it seemed to the Approvals Group, and to me, that there could be no going back on the Ruskin Project at this stage, when the University was at last in a position to receive a massive subsidy and arrange the transfer to the campus of a unique literary and artistic collection of national and indeed international importance. And so the contract was signed and the building authorised. We had passed a point of no-return. At the end of September, moreover, Harry Hanham concluded his term of office, and was succeeded as VC by Bill Ritchie.

In October, 1995, Laing's Northwest began construction of the Ruskin Library, under the firm control of Richard MacCormac and our newly appointed University Buildings Officer, Michael Haslam. Thirteen months had been allowed for completion. But the complexities of the building seem to have been underestimated. By July 1996, Laing's were seven weeks behind schedule. Although they claimed to have completed work in January 1997, the University refused to accept the building because water was leaking in through roof and walls. Some of the roof had to be replaced; and, in the walls, the solution was to remove the cavity lining material and re-grout between the facing blocks. The builders and the architect argued as to who was responsible. Fortunately, the University was not involved. However, we suffered the delays!

It was not until November 1997 that formal acceptance was possible; and the internal fitting meant that the Collection could not move in for two further months. This period included the installation of the purpose-built furniture made by the specialist cabinet-makers, Peter Hall and Son of Staveley. (It had been seen as important to involve a skilled, local maker, in accord with Ruskinian principles.) Meanwhile, of course, the Collection had had to be removed from Bembridge and temporarily stored, first in London and then in the Main Library at the University, where limited access could be arranged for scholars. A sorry story.

Now, however, better times began. In 1996 three important appointments were made. The University, with the full support of the Ruskin Foundation, appointed Stephen Wildman as Curator of the Ruskin Library as from the end of the year, following the retirement of Jim Dearden from his position as Curator of the Ruskin Galleries (at Bembridge) and of Brantwood. Stephen had previously been Curator of Prints and Drawings at the Birmingham Museum and Art Gallery, and also Professor of the History of Art to the Royal Birmingham Society of Artists. An internationally renowned expert on the Pre-Raphaelites, his acceptance of the Lancaster appointment reflected on his part a wish to take up the challenge of bringing this previously inaccessible Collection into the light of day.

A few months later, a Deputy Curator was appointed, in the person of Rebecca Finnerty. The academic and artistic staff of the Library was thus complete before it was officially opened. At around the same time the University set up a Ruskin Library Board, including some of the Foundation Trustees, to whom the Curator was to report.

Meanwhile an unexpected vacancy occurred when the Brantwood Manager, Bruce Hanson, took early retirement. The situation was temporarily covered by Gordon Hall, the former Northwest Regional Land Agent of the National Trust. A search for a permanent successor resulted in the appointment of Howard Hull at the end of 1996. He proved to have qualities of a high order in terms both of imagination and management.

In that year also, another generous gift of the Bowland Trust bore fruit. Cambridge University Press was enabled to publish and sell a CD-ROM version of the Library Edition of the Complete Works of John Ruskin: 39 Volumes, involving the input of 60 million keystrokes. This made the nine million words of text rapidly searchable.

The completed Ruskin Library.

The year 1997 brought an uncovenanted benefit. The University had paid VAT on the construction of the Ruskin Library. But later the question was raised whether, as a Charity, we could not be exempted for expenditures on new buildings. Customs and Excise conceded the point. We got our VAT payments back. Of course, we had to share the benefit with the Lottery Fund. But much remained. And this was used as seed funding, which in 2001 attracted a further grant from the Heritage Lottery Fund of £181,500 to conserve parts of the Collection.

1997 also brought further changes of actors on the stage. Michael Wheeler, after nine years as Director of the Ruskin Project and the Ruskin Programme, took a year's research leave, with British Academy funding, to complete his book, *Ruskin's God*. During that year, his place as Director of the Programme was taken by Professor Robert Hewison, a brilliant Ruskinian, author and journalist. Robert had been a regular attender at the Programme's seminars. He was a Founder Trustee of the Foundation. Michael, nevertheless, found time to help the Project forward. He was always injecting good ideas at all levels. At the end of his leave he returned to his academic duties for a year; but in September 1999 he left the University for another post.

Michael had excellent entrepreneurial skills. Of course, he was not new to administration when he started the Project, having been Head of his Department and Chairman of a Board of Studies for a number of years. But those challenges were as nothing compared with the demands now made upon him. He had to learn, first and foremost, how to think in terms of high-level strategy; how to handle some very important people; how to get to grips with whole new worlds, like museums and galleries, curators, and fund-raising; and how to defend a multi-disciplinary Project in a University, where people tend to think too much in Departmental terms and seldom give real thought to the standing of the Institution as a whole. He had to assess sensitive situations, and be always two jumps ahead of the game. He had to undertake good reconnaissance, and also have potentially useful drafts in his pocket at all times. He had to be a good ambassador for his Project, abroad as well as at home. Besides operating effectively in Whitehall, he spread the word, and gathered intelligence, in other countries: notably the United States, Japan, France, Switzerland and Italy. All these tasks he mastered. It was a great pleasure for me personally to work with such an effective operator. When he left, the Chairman of Trustees made direct representations to the VC about a full-time replacement, but his advice, sadly in my view, was not followed.

It was also in 1997 that my own time as Pro-Chancellor ended. At the University's request I continued to serve as one of its Trustees on the Foundation, but no longer held any other University position.

In May 1998 Princess Alexandra made a special visit to Lancaster in order officially to open the Ruskin Library. This was a tremendous occasion for Ruskinians world-wide, but of course especially for those who had laboured so long to bring this event about. Stephen Wildman had mounted the first of his thrice-yearly Exhibitions in the Library: it was on 'Ruskin and the Lake District', and designed by Mrs Claire Wordsworth. There had been three days of previews for particular guests, including one for the media which resulted in heavy coverage of this great achievement.

The 9th of May sticks in my mind. *Mirabile dictu*, it was fine. Some forty-five guests gathered in the Senate Room by lunch-time. Amongst them, happily, was Kathleen Pilkington. She had come by train and taxi – despite being run over by a taxi on a zebra crossing in London five days before! We took her round by wheel-chair; and later she inaugurated the special wheel-chair lift in the Ruskin Library! The Princess entered the Senate Room, and a buffet lunch was served. Thence to the Library, where another two dozen people joined our throng! After short speeches, the Princess unveiled a plaque. All toured the Exhibition.

*Dinner for those granted Honorary Doctorates for service
to the Ruskin Foundation, 9 May, 1998[4].*

Thence to the George Fox Building for a unique Degree Ceremony. Honorary Doctorates were conferred by the Princess on three of those who had done most to help the Project succeed: Tony Cann, Jim Dearden and Elizabeth Robins. The scene was full of colour. In addition to the academic robes, Charlie Shuttleworth – by now Lord Lieutenant of Lancashire – appeared in full fig and with sword! He made a speech about the Project. Then the University Orator made another, presenting the Graduands. Both made kind references to my part in developing the Project, bringing the two main Parties to agreement, and keeping Lancaster University's support constant. Later that day the Vice-Chancellor offered a dinner at his home, attended by the Princess and Lady Mary Mumford, the Pro-Chancellor and Margaret Heron, the three new Honorary Doctors with their spouses or partners, the Wheelers, Maura and myself.

Finally it is worth recording that, towards the end of that year, the Guild of St George, a Society founded by Ruskin, held its Annual General Meeting at the Ruskin Library.

These events marked the end of the Ruskin Project as such. From now on, the Ruskin Library and Brantwood worked closely together, whilst the Ruskin Programme kept in touch. One might have expected a period of calmness and consolidation. But this was not to be. All had long been conscious that the year 2000 was the Centenary of Ruskin's death, and must be appropriately marked. As early as 1996, a Committee had been set up. Chaired throughout by David Barrie, Director of the National Arts Collection Fund [NACF] and a Trustee of the Ruskin Foundation, it received inputs from many sides, including from the Foundation itself and from the Ruskin Programme. Particularly important was the contribution of Robert Hewison. It was he who had the idea of mounting a major Ruskin Exhibition at the Tate, and sold it to that institution's Trustees. Again, Tony was prepared, through the Bowland Trust, to provide sponsorship. This was to be the centre piece of a world-wide programme of celebrations, which was given the name 'Ruskin Today'. From now on, much of the energy of the Foundation, and of the Curatorial Staff of the Ruskin Library, was devoted to the input they would need to make – not only at Lancaster and Brantwood – but to other events in many parts of the world.

Let us recall the key manifestations. There were three exhibitions at the Ruskin Library, and another at Yale. Robert Hewison, the new Slade Professor of Art at Oxford University, the post initiated by Ruskin, gave brilliant lectures about him. More dramatically, the date of the sage's death – 20 January – was marked by ceremonies at Coniston and Brantwood described below; and by the world première at Lancaster University of a new musical work *The King of the Golden River*. In February, the Ruskin Foundation hosted, with the Ruskin Society of London, a magnificent dinner at the Tallow Chandlers Hall in London. In March, the Tate – now renamed Tate Britain – opened the Exhibition, curated by Robert Hewison and Ian Warrell, entitled *Ruskin, Turner and the Pre-Raphaelites*, where the Whitehouse Collection provided the largest number of exhibits.

In April, the Fitzwilliam Museum, Cambridge exhibited *Ruskin's Turners*, showing the Turner pictures donated by Ruskin himself. There was also an International Conference on *Prophetic Ruskin* at Christ Church College, Oxford. James Dearden's touring exhibition, commissioned by the Sheffield Galleries and Museums Trust, and entitled *The Portraits of John Ruskin*, toured the country. There was an International Symposium on 'The Brantwood Years' at Lancaster University. There were Ruskin exhibitions at the Mikimoto Hall in Tokyo; at the Pierpont Morgan Library in New York; at the Birmingham Museum and Art Gallery; and at the Ashmolean Museum at Oxford. The BBC did an Omnibus programme on Ruskin; and the University's Television Unit made a good video entitled *Ruskin's Journey*, written and presented by Michael Wheeler. The title was a play on words.

The film followed routes which Ruskin had taken on his travels; but it also described the intellectual side of his journey through life.

The ceremony at Coniston and Brantwood in January had been arranged by Howard Hull, the Brantwood Manager, with great imagination. There was first a service in St Andrew's Church, filled to overflowing. A welcome by John Dawson, Chairman of the Friends of Ruskin's Brantwood, was anecdotal, warm and delightful. Dorothy Reilly (soprano) gave a beautiful rendering of Canon Rawnsley's 'Evening and Morning', which had been sung at the funeral by the renowned Mary Wakefield. The children of Coniston Primary School offered a charming cameo of 'Ruskin Today'. There was a brilliant address by Robert Hewison. And prayers were said by Ian Harland, the Bishop of Carlisle. As we emerged from the Church, a lamp was lit at Ruskin's grave. A procession was formed, led by Ruskin's coach with outriders, and conveyed the lamp to the jetty. Then a lone rower, in Victorian costume, rowed it in Ruskin's boat, the *Jumping Jenny*, to Ruskin's harbour at Brantwood. Participants had meanwhile driven round the head of the Lake, and escorted it to the House, where *Glühwein* and cakes were served. The whole event took place in perfect, sunny, still, crisp, January weather, and was unforgettable.

The dinner in February, at the Tallow Chandlers' Hall, on the occasion of Ruskin's birthday, was attended by ninety people with Ruskinian interests, of three successive generations. The host was Richard Parsons, Chairman of the Ruskin Foundation. The guests of honour were Princess Alexandra and Sir Angus Ogilvy. Some of the guests were moved around after the main course, so as to give the guests of honour a change of interlocutor. Michael Wheeler thus found himself next to the Princess for coffee, when an amusing address was given by Sir Nicholas Serota, Director of the Tate Gallery; and a reply made by Robert Hewison. In a surprise move, the Princess then presented to Michael, on behalf of the Foundation, a first edition of Ruskin's *Arrows of the Chace*. The evening ended soon after. As we were leaving Phyllis Lloyd said to me: *'I think I must be the only person present who attended the last Ruskin birthday celebration, organised by Whitehouse in the 1950s'*.

I had meanwhile told my fellow Trustees that I felt the completion of the *Ruskin Today* Programme represented a good moment for me to leave. In May 2001, Elizabeth Robins gave a nice farewell dinner for Maura and me at Lancaster, and also for Ruth Hutchison, with whom I was delighted to be associated. It was attended by the Trustees and the VC. And, on my 75th birthday in the same year, I resigned my position as a Trustee with the

Ruskin's coach at the Centenary Commemorations of his death, Coniston, January, 2000.

Ruskin Foundation, and thus severed my last official connection with the University. On that day I wrote my fellow Trustees a letter, the end of which I now quote.

'*While…no longer…a Trustee, I leave your ranks happy in the knowledge that the ship is sailing steadily forward, and also that a younger generation of Trustees is taking an increasingly active interest in setting new horizons for the Foundation. I shall not forget our work together for a moment. The kind gift of 'Master Drawings by John Ruskin', with its generous inscription, presented to me at my last Trustees meeting in May, will help keep it in mind. The accidental discovery, during genealogical research some time ago, that one of my great-great-grandfathers (the Reverend John Heslop) died at Brantwood in 1850, added a sentimental element to my attachment to our enterprise. And you may be amused to hear that, for my birthday dinner tonight, Maura and I will dine with Howard Hull at the Jumping Jenny Restaurant [Brantwood], and then hear a lecture from Professor Keith Hanley [Director of the Ruskin Programme] to the Friends of Brantwood about Ruskin and Europe. I thank you for your friendship, your co-operation and your many kindnesses, and wish you all well for the future. I also warmly commend to you my successor as University Trustee, Lord Judd of Portsea.'*

CHAPTER 24

The European Opera Centre:
a remarkable venture

IN AUTUMN, September 1990, Sir John Manduell asked me – is there any chance of the European Union subsidising an advanced Opera Training Centre organised at European level? I said that the idea was interesting; that it was worth exploring with the EU; but that it would be hard to sell. This all proved right. Nevertheless, the idea prospered. The European Opera Centre was established; has enjoyed continued EU financial support since 1996; and has succeeded to an extent few would have dared predict.

John was approaching retirement from the post of Principal of the Royal Northern College of Music [RNCM] in Manchester, and therefore also from that of President of the European Association of Conservatoires [known by its French acronym – AEC]. In this dual capacity, he had observed a shortage of specialist opera schools in Europe, capable of helping young people to move from graduation at conservatoire level to professional, solo operatic roles. In consequence, a high proportion of opera soloists in European Houses were coming from the United States, where the situation was more favourable. It would be absurd for each European country to set up an advanced Opera School. It would make more economic sense – as well as being artistically better – to set up a School at European level. John had tried out this idea within the European musical world, and it had aroused interest.

Lancaster University had brought me into contact with him. A Deputy Pro-Chancellor, Dame Kathleen Ollerenshaw, had invited Maura and me to the performance of an opera at the RNCM, when we had dined with John. Later, the Lord-Lieutenant of Lancashire, Simon Towneley, who also knew me through the University, and was aware of my work as Chairman of its Development Committee, had invited me to join the comparable body of the RNCM. His invitation was accepted. I was soon meeting John regularly. Once he had registered my EU background, it was natural he should put his question to me.

I agreed to take the occasion of visits to Brussels for other reasons to cast a fly over the then Director-General of Culture, Colette Flesch of

Luxembourg, whom I knew well. She responded at a meeting that December. She drew my attention to five operatic projects which had been considered at EU level, and advised that we consider how our ideas related to any of these. Only one of them proved relevant: we shall come to it later. I advised John to reflect on next steps; on how to develop his Project; and on whether it should be free-standing or linked to one of the others. Once those matters were clear, we could consider how to progress matters in Brussels.

John spent two years refining the project, in consultation with the Executive Committee of the AEC, and with individual Opera Houses. In January 1993, however, there was an important development at EU level. The Maastricht Treaty entered into force, bringing Culture, Education, Training and Youth for the first time within the ambit of the European Community. The Community Institutions had for some time been thinking how to give practical expression to these new aims. In the same year, the RNCM obtained funding from the European Regional Development Fund to organise a feasibility study for the establishment of a European Centre for Advanced Opera Studies at the College.

Things now moved fast. In July 1994, I received a letter from the newly appointed Managing Director of the European Opera Centre [EOC], which was at this stage within the RNCM but enjoyed a high degree of autonomy. The Managing Director was Kenneth Baird, who had previously been House Manager at English National Opera, General Manager of the Aldeburgh Foundation, and Music Director of the Arts Council. The Project Development Team already included, besides John and Kenneth, such prestigious personalities as Kent Nagano, Music Director of the Hallé Orchestra; Jean-Pierre Brosmann, Artistic Director of the Lyon Opera; Brigitte Fassbänder, Opera Singer and Producer; Stefan Janski, Director of Opera Studies at the RNCM; Elaine Padmore, Director of Royal Danish Opera; and Nicholas Payne, Director of the Royal Opera at Covent Garden.

The basic concept was this: to provide a bridge between opera training courses and professional employment in opera, by offering further training to a standard not currently available at the European level. Participants would be selected by auditions throughout Europe, entirely on merit. No fees would be charged. Participants would receive a stipend to cover living costs. The principle would be that of training through doing. Each year, following a period of vocal study, rôle coaching, stagecraft and language tuition, productions would be prepared at the Centre, and toured to as many Member States of the EU as could be arranged. The running costs were to be met, in part, by sponsorship, box office income, support from Foundations, and collaboration with partner Opera Houses; but important financial support from the EU would be essential.

John and Kenneth now sought advice about how to approach the European Community Institutions. I suggested a high-level team of professionals be formed, willing to go to Brussels for a few days and talk to as many as possible of the key people in the Commission and Parliament. We should go first to the former, since under the Treaties it had the sole power of formal initiative within the Community. But, in my judgement, we should be told that – whatever the Commission thought about the merits of the Project – the funds available for Culture in the Community Budget would not be sufficient to allow a major contribution. For that reason we should also talk to MEPs – with priority to those in the Culture Committee, but also those in the Budget Committee – because they had significant powers to add money to the Budget.

It was too late to start trying to impact on the Budget for 1995, but we should nevertheless visit Brussels that spring, with a view to influencing the Budget for the following year. It would help if we could produce a statement of likely needs for EU support over a five-year period. We should also seek support from the UK Permanent Representative to the Community, then Sir John Kerr, in making the necessary arrangements. The latter, when approached, warned against undue optimism, but was nevertheless very helpful. It should be added that his two successors – Sir Stephen Wall and Sir Nigel Sheinwald – were equally so. Against this background, planning and preparatory work continued in Manchester, on the hypothesis that our first full year of operation would be 1997, but finance must be provided for a preparatory year in 1996.

Thus, in April 1995, a team of professionals set off for Brussels. It consisted of John Manduell, in his dual capacity at the RNCM and AEC; Jeremy Isaacs, General Director of Covent Garden; Michael Christiansen, General Director of the Royal Danish Opera, accompanied by Elaine Padmore; Jean-Pierre Brosmann; Colin Beeson, from the RNCM; myself as the team's 'guide-dog'; and Kenneth Baird. In the Commission, we saw Commissioners, the Secretary-General, Cabinet members, and senior officials. Their response, broadly speaking was as expected. But we had also arranged to hold a Reception by the EOC – described as representing Covent Garden, the Opéra de Lyon, Royal Danish Opera and the RNCM – in the Building of the European Parliament itself, to which we invited over fifty MEPs, of whom a substantial majority came.

We had rehearsed this event with some care beforehand, at a meeting held in the Brussels Office of the City of Manchester. A full written brief, prepared by Kenneth with my advice, was available. Four points from it deserve special mention. First, the EOC, though still to operate from Manchester, was to be independent of the RNCM, and be effectively led by the three above-named Opera Houses – Covent Garden, Copenhagen and Lyon – with the addition of other major Houses shortly. (Soon after, both Madrid and Genoa joined the group.) Second, there was strong expectation that, once the Project was in full operation, it would attract substantial income, so the request to the EU was largely justified as launching aid. Third, the aim was to present two fully staged productions a year, to be toured to a number of European countries, requiring substantial course preparation time. Fourth, the competition for places on each course would be entirely on merit, and open to individuals from all EU countries, and from European countries with which the EU had a Cultural Agreement. This last point was at that time seen as very positive by the Commission, though later it ill-advisedly wanted to limit coverage to the EU and countries which were candidates for membership. In the end we also considered, exceptionally, applications from citizens of third countries who had been based in the EU for at least two years.

The general idea was to hold an initial presentation for the MEPs; then take questions and give replies. I had advised the Team what kind of questions they were likely to get; and we discussed the best answers and who should give them. The presentation made no bones about the subsidy we were going to need from the EU in order to carry out our programme: it ran from the preparatory year of 1996, at 690 KECUs [thousands of ECUs]; up to much larger sums by 1999; with a modest, degressive move in 2000.

Our event in the European Parliament was seminal. There was a positive response. There were the anticipated questions, to which good answers were given. One of them was whether opera was not *'élitist'*. *Inter alia* Michael Christiansen was able to respond that the biggest single public event in Denmark during the year – exceeding the best attended football match – had been an open air opera performance! We had by now made an important friend, in the person of Roy Perry, MEP for Wight and Hampshire South, a well-respected member of the Culture Committee who was that year its Budget Co-ordinator. Since then, his continuing sympathy for and advocacy of our cause have been invaluable.

We had also, however, stirred some old bones. One of the initiatives mentioned by Colette Flesch had been a European Parliament Resolution, adopted seven years previously (1988) on the proposal of Lady Elles MEP, supporting the establishment by the European Community Youth Orchestra of a European Community Youth Opera. (The Youth Opera was to change its name more than once in its short history: for convenience it will be hereafter be known by that short title.) No action had followed, and we had assumed the protagonists had become discouraged. In July, 1995, however, they told us the initiative was being revived! As it happened, Lady Elles, now retired, had an important ally in the European Parliament's Budget Committee. This was to have consequences.

The 1996 <u>Draft</u> Budget had contained a lump sum of 750 KECUs for the EOC. By the time the Budget was finally adopted, however, thanks to manoeuvrings in the Budget Committee, it turned out to contain the same figure – but qualified as intended to cover both the EOC <u>and</u> the Youth Opera, leaving the Commission to divide the total. When the Commission's final decision was made, as late as August 1996, it turned out that the EOC had obtained just over 400 KECUs of the funding, the rest going to the Youth Opera. Our allocation was far less than we had defined as necessary for our programme, which had to be down-sized. Each year since then we have obtained a cultural subsidy of approximately the same amount.

It is now necessary to digress from strictly EOC affairs, and follow those of the Youth Opera to their unfortunate conclusion, just two years later. Despite the fall-out on the EOC's own subsidies, our management, throughout the whole period, remained on friendly terms with that of the Youth Opera. We did however seek to explain to the EU Institutions that the two initiatives were different in kind. Ours, intended to be run by a partnership of European Opera Houses, was geared to giving high-level professional training. That of the Youth Opera was focused on giving some practical experience of opera to young people.

The Youth Opera arranged to give a number of performances in the context of the Baden-Baden Festival of 1998. They obtained important promises of sponsorship and support – besides their EU subsidy. Unfortunately these promises were not properly honoured. As a result, the Youth Opera made a substantial loss; and their Trustees decided in 1999 that their operations must cease. Thus, during three years, over 1,000 KECUs – which might well have come to the EOC – was instead devoted to an initiative which came to nothing. It was a sad story.

Meanwhile, armed at last with a first EU funding commitment, the EOC's plans for gradual build-up in 1996 and the following year progressed. Our first public performance was given on 10 December, 1997. The name of Kent Nagano now comes centre stage. He had been a supporter of John Manduell's initiative from the start. The EOC had originally planned to tour our first production – a fully staged version of Mozart's *Lucio Silla* – from the beginning of 1998. But Kent insisted on presiding over our public *début*. He arranged for a concert version of *Tosca* to be performed by our singers in the Bridgewater Hall at Manchester, with the Hallé Orchestra and Choir, and the Manchester Boys' Choir, the *ensemble* being conducted by him: these performances were followed by a short tour in the north of England.

During our first year of operations 400 singers were auditioned, for *Tosca* and *Lucio Silla*, in twenty European *venues* with a view to selecting a double cast for each of the two Operas. Forty candidates were chosen, from fifteen different countries. Nick Winter was recruited as our very efficient Auditions Manager, later becoming Artistic Administrator. He had previously worked at Aldeburgh, and then as a Concert Agent in St Petersburg for six years before and after the collapse of the Soviet Union. The audition panel had a central core, chaired by John Manduell himself, and was re-inforced at each venue abroad by local experts. Meanwhile, a lease was taken on premises for our administrative and training operations at 68, Grosvenor Street, Manchester. The selected singers each received a personal monthly grant, in return for an exclusive arrangement: in other words, they could not, while working with us, undertake any other work without our permission. The EOC also recruited its own Orchestra for *Lucio Silla* in 1998, drawing on young players from the north of England.

At the administrative level, the need to obtain continued EU funding was a constant concern. Life is bound to be difficult for cultural organisations which rely on the EU as their principal source of funds. In our case, the story was particularly complex. A first misadventure was caused by the President of the European Parliament, who in 1995 for some time withheld final signature of the whole Community Budget for the following year – and this for abstruse reasons which had nothing to do with us. When that obstacle had disappeared, there were long delays while the responsible Directorate-General ruminated how to divide the money. Much valuable time was lost; and we had to make commitments on assumptions which proved too optimistic. In the preparation of the two following EU Budgets, we continued to ask for increased sums of money. It is received wisdom in the Community that *'les absents ont toujours tort'*. We made it a rule, therefore, that either Kenneth Baird or I, or both of us, would be present every time either the Culture Committee or the Budget Committee of Parliament was to discuss the cultural part of the EU Budget. We also made many other visits to MEPs, and also to Commission officials, as did John Manduell. When we started, Kenneth came completely fresh to Community procedures, which are very difficult for newcomers to understand. He learnt this special skill with extra-ordinary speed; and, as time went by, needed less and less help.

In parallel to the budgetary action in Brussels, we set up a management structure. Various options for legal personality were considered. It was finally decided that, although the Centre was to have strong European artistic leadership, since it was based in Manchester, it would be sensible to establish it as a Charitable Trust under English Law. On John's proposal, Sir Jeremy Isaacs and I agreed to join him as the sole founder Trustees. The Trust Deed, dated 27 September, 1996, was drafted in rather general terms, leaving the Trustees much discretion. The aim was stated simply as being to apply the Trust *'for advancing the education of the public in the arts of opera and music-theatre and in particular…to establish and maintain…a centre providing training through practical experience for talented singers, conductors, repetiteurs, technicians, producers, designers, arts administrators, and others'.*

The first meeting of Trustees took place that November. John was elected Chairman until the next meeting, and this arrangement has been repeated at each meeting until now. Kenneth was elected Secretary. Various appointments in the Centre were confirmed, including notably that of Kenneth as Managing Director. In giving my agreement to Trusteeship I had stipulated that the EOC should seek a high quality Finance Officer who would maintain our finances in full respect of all funding or other contracts with the Commission. Caron Chalmers was appointed to this demanding post, and has given sterling service ever since. We, meanwhile, had found it difficult to raise the expected sponsorship. Commercial sponsorship is very hard to acquire for activities organised at European level. We had reduced our original programme from two operas a year to one. We also cut staff and production costs, as well as the touring schedule.

However, these cutbacks did not affect the first season, which began with the Concert Performances of *Tosca* at the Bridgewater Hall and elsewhere; continued with an extensive tour of the staged production of *Lucio Silla* through England, Ireland, Scotland and Denmark; and also featured EOC participation in recitals for the Foreign and then the Culture and Audio-Visual Ministers of the EU when they met in the UK during the British Presidency in 1998. The operas were – and still are – given under the Centre's performing name of 'Opera Europe'.

A strange tale is associated with the *Tosca* production. A charming young

After Opera Europe's production of 'Lucio Silla', at the Royal Opera House,
Copenhagen, 1998. Kenneth Baird & Hega Gustava Tjøhn.

lady from Moldova, Lada Biriucov, who had been studying at the Moscow
Conservatoire, attended the audition at Lyon. The panel was immensely
impressed, and at once saw her in the title role. But, since auditions were
not over, they could only tell her she had sung well and would be hearing
from them after her return to Moscow. She became upset, and explained she
had spent her last rouble buying a return ticket to Lyon, and had no money
left. This was naturally advanced to her. She went back to Moscow. There,
she was advised that she was wanted for the title role, and asked to appear in
Manchester for the preparatory course. On 13 November, 1997, I was told
by the Manchester staff that the Visa Section of the British Embassy in
Moscow had – without any reference to us – refused Lada a visa to visit
England. This was less than a month before the opening night.

On asking the Foreign and Commonwealth Office for an explanation
I was told that Lada's passport had suggested to the authorities that she was
of a vagrant disposition. Travel is of course a feature of the singing world!
The decision was idiotic. But, once bureaucracy has decided something, it is
hard to get the decision changed. I raised the level of approach in the FCO.
Finally, the decision was reversed, and Lada arrived in Manchester just
thirteen days before the event at the Bridgewater Hall. The situation was

dramatic. Lada, at that time, had never sung with an Orchestra in her life. She was given a crash course. Kent Nagano provided her with thirteen hours of his personal tuition. She learnt fast!

And so, on 10 December, 1997, Maura and I went to Manchester for the opening night. We knew there was an excellent cast. But we also knew of Lada's problems. Besides, this was, for me, the moment of truth. Would this initiative, launched over seven years earlier, meet with success? All were on tenterhooks, as we, the Orchestra and the two Choirs, waited for Kent Nagano to lead in the soloists. Lada walked on like a Queen, in a stunning red and black velvet dress. Kent raised his baton. And we were off. No sooner had Lada started singing than we sat back with relief. Hers was a fabulous performance. And the other soloists all did well. That night, at a Reception in the Manchester City Hall, Kent opened his remarks with the words: 'Tonight a star is born'. And so she was. Within months, the girl who had arrived at Lyon without a rouble was performing leading roles of different operas with Scottish and Welsh Opera, and North Opera; and was certainly capable of earning over £1,000 a night. Similar progress was made by several of the other *alumni*, such as Bulent Bezdüz from Turkey, and Anke Vondung from Germany. (Several other star singers were also to emerge in our subsequent productions.) Here was proof positive of the value of our Project!

The *Lucio Silla* production opened in February, 1998, at the Shaftesbury Theatre, London, the temporary home of the Royal Opera House. A large number of Community bigwigs came, including Spyros Pappas who had succeeded Colette Flesch as Director-General for Culture. The production was relatively expensive, having been commissioned before our financial constraints were apparent. Musical direction was by Fabrizio Ventura, then about to take up a position as First Conductor to the Nürnberg Opera. The Director was the great Lieder and Opera Singer, Brigitte Fassbänder. The Orchestra was recruited largely from the National Youth Orchestra of England. Solo singers doubled as Chorus members when the alternative cast was performing, keeping the Chorus proper quite small. The critics commented favourably on the concept of the EOC; and on the whole musical side; but were more divided on the Production.

When the season was over, we found that a new role had developed quite naturally for our staff. Our *alumni* had quickly realised that the EOC staff were an invaluable, and completely unbiased and independent, source of advice on the further development of their professional careers, whereas even the best agents have their own interests to consider. We decided to provide this service free of charge, and have done so ever since. It is greatly appreciated.

Meanwhile the Court of Justice of the EU had thrown a spanner into the EU funding works by a judgement that the Commission could only lawfully make expenditures under its operational Budget where the action was supported, not <u>only</u> by a Budget Line – as in our case – but <u>also</u> by a specific piece of Community legislation. The Institutions were, during 1998, moving towards agreement on such legislation in the form of a Framework Programme for Cultural Action – later known as Culture 2000 – and it looked as though the impending legislation would in future have to be used as the legal base for any payments to us.

On the plus side, however, the EOC had so far delivered exactly what it had promised in its various contracts with the Commission; and the quality of the product had been seen as excellent.

There was another reason for optimism. In 1998, a new Project had begun to see the light of day. It derived from a series of discussions between Kent, Kenneth and John. Its aim was to produce an animated version of an opera, which could attract the interest of a wider audience towards opera generally. The choice fell on Janáček's *The Cunning Little Vixen* [*CLV*]. The story of this opera had in fact emerged from a strip cartoon; and it was all about animals. It was felt that such a Project fell well within the Trust's aim of *'advancing the education of the public in the arts of opera and music-theatre'.* It could also reach out to new audiences for opera.

Kent Nagano has meanwhile told the story of how this idea came to life. When a young lad – at school in California with no interest in classical music – he had been taken to a touring performance by the San Francisco Symphony Orchestra in a village barn. He had been bowled over by hearing Beethoven for the first time. The experience had changed his life. Thereafter, he had always wanted other young people to have similar opportunities to learn. One day he was invited to talk to the Chair of the Seaver Foundation. She wanted to put some money into a project for doing just that, and sought ideas. He had put up the concept of an animated opera. She had indicated a willingness to provide sponsorship if he could realise it. Kent began talking the idea round with his musical contacts. Without exception, they all poured cold water on it. Then, one day, he had put it to the EOC Managers. They responded with unqualified enthusiasm. And so the idea found a home. What was needed was a feasibility study.

We knew the whole concept would need careful selling in Brussels. We felt we should present it as an <u>up-grade</u> of EOC activity, timed to come to fruition in the Millennium year. This would imply a 'quiet year' in 1999. We should make it clear that 1997-98 had proved the validity of the 'academic year approach' for bringing forward new lead opera singers; and that we would revert to it after the *CLV* had been completed. In the meanwhile, the training of singers in the special skills needed to perform in an animated opera would itself represent a unique service to the musical world. There was a very obvious danger that our friends in the European Parliament and the Commission would be upset at an apparent change of direction. And Kenneth and I therefore spent much time and effort in preparing them for the new line.

It was just the time when the Commission needed to agree with us how our 1999 subsidy should be spent. They were viewing cultural actions that year as a run-up to the adoption of 'Culture 2000'. There were to be three pilot programmes, and this year our application for funds must respond to one of them. None really catered for our core activity – support for the production of a conventional opera. Advised by the Commission Services, we therefore selected a programme called 'Connect', which had to do with *'preparatory actions linking culture and new technologies'*. The main aim of the Project we now proposed was to produce a pilot video of the *CLV* animation: the rest of the money was to be spent on enhancing our networks and computer systems. The Project was approved, and carried out. We had also secured a grant of $ 88,000 for the *CLV* Project from the Seaver Foundation.

The work on the pilot video was highly rewarding. The definitive recording would require production of four separate tracks: one for the orchestral part; one for the vocal; one for other sound-effects; and the last for the animation – in other words pictures. We selected Rodney Wilson as the Producer. For animation, we relied at this stage on a Czech artist. We recruited and trained our own voices, insisting that they convey all performing rights to us. We were able to use the RNCM Symphony Orchestra, conducted by Kent. The practical outcome was a video of excerpts, lasting only a few minutes. But the video was sufficient to demonstrate what could be done, and aroused much interest. In particular it proved attractive to the BBC, who saw a developed version as potentially suitable for showing at peak family viewing time. From May 2000 onwards, we were entitled to say that the final version of the *CLV* was to be produced in a partnership between us and BBC TV. And the BBC, which would provide the core finance, had itself committed hundreds of thousands of pounds to the venture.

One of the two casts of Opera Europe's production of 'La Scala di Seta' at Sierre, Switzerland, 2000, with Conductor, Giovanni Pacor[1].

During the summer of 2000, Peter Maniura, Head of BBC Television Classical Music and Performance, worked with Kent Nagano, and his Assistant, the late Christophe Durrant, in the margins of the Salzburg Festival, to edit the opera score down to a television hour. It had meanwhile been concluded that, for the definitive version, a different animator should be used. Geoff Dunbar produced initial drawings, which admirably blended the desired animal and human characteristics of the animals; and started making test animations. These led to a series of interim videos, known as 'Work in Progress', which proved invaluable tools in presenting the whole Project to different audiences. Later, it was decided that the Orchestral track would be recorded by the Deutsches Symphonie Orchester Berlin, now conducted by Kent Nagano. This recording was completed in Berlin during July 2001. My best 75th birthday present, on 7 July of that year, was a telegram from Berlin – signed by Kent, Christophe, Kenneth, Nick and Rodney – to say the work had been completed. In a gesture typical of those who have so long supported the EOC in material ways from the start, the Deutsches Symphonie Orchester generously made no charge to us or the BBC for its services. Meanwhile the animations had progressed well, and Kent considered we had reached the point of no-return.

While all this had been happening, various changes were taking place in the management of the EOC's activities. The first was entirely positive. We had begun at an early stage to build up a Council of Honour. We agreed right away that we were not looking for high-level personalities who would simply allow us to use their names on our notepaper. We wanted individuals who would be pro-active, feed in ideas and give practical help. We would seek to get a good geographic spread of members, but not feel obliged to have one in every Community Member State. Our current notepaper shows that we have made good progress – most strikingly by the readiness of Kent Nagano to become the Council's President. There has never been an intention to hold regular meetings of all the members; but we have kept them steadily informed of progress and plans, and looked to them for advice on an individual basis.

Another change was perhaps less positive. We found by experience that our original idea of leadership by a standing group of Opera Houses was difficult to operate, due to the relatively high movement of senior opera staff between Houses and jobs. Whilst, therefore, we have very close contacts with many Houses, and often seek their advice, we have progressively abandoned the idea of giving our relationship with them a formal status.

A third change was the addition of new Trustees. Michael Kennedy, the opera critic, came on board quite soon; and more recently the Trustees have been joined by Dame Gwyneth Jones, the opera singer, and Roger Beetham, a former British Diplomat with much experience of European Institutions.

A final change was the creation of a Manchester fan club. The EOC was, is and will remain, determinedly European. But our home base is Manchester. It seemed to us that influential local people would be willing to lend us support. On different occasions, we have held open evenings at the Centre or nearby. The aim has been to 'sell' ourselves pro-actively. The general pattern has been to make a formal presentation about the EOC, and its current activities and plans; arrange for the guests to see and hear the young artists at work; and end with an informal reception when they could talk to artists and staff. The idea emerged to persuade some of these people to form an independent Charitable Trust – 'The Medlock Educational Trust' – which would seek to help the EOC, but would also draw side-benefits from its work for the benefit of the local community. It enjoys Charitable Trust status. Its Chairman is Andrew Thomson, a retired Manchester businessman.

1999 had been an extra-ordinarily difficult year for people depending heavily on the European Commission. There were accusations of fraud and nepotism by several Commissioners, and notably by Edith Cresson, responsible for Education and Training. President Santer's Commission, threatened with a vote of censure by Parliament, resigned as a body in March. Under the Treaty, it continued in office, on a caretaker basis, until Parliament confirmed the appointment of a successor Commission, under Romano Prodi, in mid-September, to hold office till 2005. The new Commissioner appointed responsible for Education, Culture and Training, Madame Viviane Reding from Luxembourg, presented herself at the preliminary hearings by the Culture Committee that September. All these changes, of course, caused chaos and loss of morale amongst the Commission Services.

Meanwhile, as we worked on the *CLV* Project, we were telling Roy Perry, fortunately once again the Culture Committee's Budget Co-ordinator, that we saw the 2000 Budget as crucial for our future. We hoped that, with the Youth Opera now defunct, we could get both more money and a greater assurance of continuity. In the latter respect we thought our position would be far safer if we could follow a precedent set by some other cultural organisations in 1999, namely to have our support carried, no longer on the unpredictable 'Culture 2000' lines of the operational Budget, but instead on the administrative Budget of the Commission – an 'A' line in EU jargon. Kenneth Baird and I went to Brussels in August-September 1999 to spread this message in Parliament and Commission.

In the event, we received only the now customary 400 KECUs [now converted into Euros]: however, they were on an 'A-line' of the Budget. This meant we only had to submit a programme of activities to the Commission in order to obtain the money. In June, 1999, during a visit by Kenneth and me to Brussels, the new UK Permanent Representative, Stephen Wall, invited us to a lunch at his home attended by Klaus van der Pas, the third Director-General for Culture with whom we had had to deal in nine years. The only other guests were Arlene McCarthy, an MEP from Manchester, and Alison Rose – Stephen's Culture expert. They were all deeply impressed by the success of the *CLV* Project, for which of course EU financing could claim a significant part of the credit.

By the time of the 2001 and 2002 Budget exercises it had become clear that, as a result of its achievements, the EOC had become accepted by Parliament, and perhaps even by the Council; but also that, in the uncertain situation created by impending enlargement of the EU and all that went with it, we could not expect any larger amounts. We must live within these modest means, with any other outside income we could acquire. And in fact we have meanwhile received 400K Euros from the Commission each year. This means that – after the EUYO – we are in receipt of the largest subsidy from the EU in the musical sector. Here you have the EU wearing a very human face.

In 2000, we based our request to the Commission for funds on a return to the presentation of a staged opera. We avoided any request for help with the *CLV*, because it was too early to believe the definitive version would be completed that year. Fortunately the Tibor Varga Music Festival, based on Sion, in the Valais area of Switzerland, had invited us to present an Opera – Rossini's *La Scala di Seta* – as part of their summer season. We focused our plan primarily on preparing this opera, presenting it as a staged production outdoors at the Château Mercier in Sierre, and thereafter taking it to perform at the EXPO 2000 Exhibition, at Hannover, in the EU Pavilion. *La Scala di Seta* was conducted by Giovanni Pacor, the Artistic Vice-Director of the Teatro Communale Giuseppe Verdi Trieste; and directed by Elaine Kidd. There were two casts of EOC singers, performing on alternate nights. The Opera has no chorus, helping to keep costs down. The orchestra was formed from strings provided by Tibor Varga's excellent Festival Orchestra; and winds recruited individually. The first group was at first pained to be asked to take part in an opera performance, a medium of which they had no experience. But Giovanni soon had everyone pulling together.

At Sierre there were four performances, of which I attended the last two. All were out of doors, with the fine walls of the Château Mercier as backdrop, and clear views to the high Alps all around. There was a huge storm the night before the first performance; and the weather broke again just after the last. In short, we were very lucky. The opera, deservedly, was well received, and played to capacity audiences each night. Besides the opera, our singers also gave a concert one afternoon at the Church in Hérémence – a nearby mountain village at an altitude of 1500 metres – the main pieces being two lovely Bach cantatas.

On the return journey by bus I sat near the conductor. As we approached Sion, where the strings were to say goodbye and leave us for good, their leader – a nice girl from St Petersburg – came over for a final word with Giovanni. '*Maestro*' – she said – '*I would like you to know that the strings had some concerns about playing in opera before we started. But it has been a marvellous experience, and we have all learnt an immense amount from you*'. The singers and the wind-players lived together in the castle, and had a very jolly time. On this last night, when we had parted from the strings, we repaired to the Château to enjoy an *al fresco* barbecue. The Conductor was the Chef, and one of the two top sopranos – Yvette Tannenberger from Slovakia – was his assistant cook! While waiting for the barbecue to be ready, the other young people were amusing themselves. Some were in the drawing room, where they were singing Johann Strauss tunes round the piano: others were playing 'snap' in the dining room, under instruction from the British members!

I found time, whilst in Sierre, to make an excursion to the great glacier of Plaine Morte. Ben Holland, the Repetiteur and Assistant Conductor, and Jo Morton, the Stage Director, joined me. There was much talk about the production. Over the years, I had found a side-benefit of my involvement with the EOC was to learn a lot about the preparation of opera: including, notably, the respective rôles of the producer, musical director, repetiteur, director, singing coach, designer, and so forth. It was highly educational and amusing.

In 2001, we took a production of Britten's *The Rape of Lucretia* to Hungary, where the work was premièred in Budapest, and staged also in Szeged. We attracted financial help from the Britten-Pears Foundation, and local sponsors. The conductor, this time, was Peter Selwyn, House Conductor from the Nürnberg State Opera. The Director was Brian Brady, with Designer Conor Murphy. The soloists, as usual, were double cast. The orchestra was custom-built: with a string section of Hungarians, a wind section based in the Netherlands, and an Irish harpist. All were young. I joined the tour on its last night in Szeged, where the performance was in the fine 19th century Opera House, seating upwards of 1000. Earlier, the British Council had supported an associated Study Day on Britten at the University, animated by Professor Donald Mitchell – a musicologist with profound and personal knowledge of the Composer.

Next day we went by train with the whole company to Budapest for our last performance there. It was staged in an *Art Nouveau* theatre which had received a Europa Nostra Award for its restoration, when I was on the Judging Panel. In Budapest, there were also associated Concerts in the historic building of the present British Embassy, from which Raul Wallenberg had conducted his war-time operations to save Jews from Hitler when it was the Swedish Legation; and in the equally historic Metropolitan Ervin Szabó Library – the former Wenkheim Palace. All the Opera performances, and the Concerts, were well received.

By the beginning of 2002, the BBC was planning to show the final version of the *CLV* on television at Christmas, though later they re-scheduled it for peak family viewing time on Easter Day 2003. So we put the major part of our 2002 EU funding into work connected with bringing the film to fruition. The Seaver Institute had by now agreed, that, after the initial English language version had been produced, it would provide a further $ 200,000 towards making a Spanish version, in 2003 – with the vocal track being recorded at Barcelona, alongside a Catalán version – the voice training again being provided by the EOC.

Not wishing, however, to abandon our commitment to a staged performance of Opera for a second year, we revived *The Rape of Lucretia* with a different cast, and took it to performances in the Studio Theatre of the Latvian National Opera in Riga; and then in the prestigious Hermitage Theatre in St Petersburg, in autumn, 2002. It was to be presented, not only as an example of the EU's interest in culture, but also as an advance contribution by the partner city of Manchester to St Petersburg's Tercentenary Celebrations.

For some time now, I had been telling Trustees that I could not continue much longer. A few weeks before the Seventeenth Meeting of Trustees, which took place on 25th July 2002, I wrote to tell my colleagues I wished to take the occasion to resign. I was 76. Since retirement from professional employment sixteen years earlier, I had devoted myself largely to working for good causes – of which the EOC was but one. This had left little space for private affairs. Now, I needed to attend to them – before becoming senile! For the benefit of the newer Trustees, I then recalled key developments in the life of the EOC. Soon, the *CLV* would be broadcast. Roger Beetham had demonstrated that he enjoyed the same sort of privileged access to the EU Institutions as myself. My resignation could take place in positive circumstances. I had immensely enjoyed my time on the Board of the EOC. The organisation had been fortunate in its tiny band of professional staff. It had achieved a great deal in a short time. Many of its *alumni* had gone on to great things. It would surely continue to prosper.

The meeting was held, by my invitation, in the Oxford and Cambridge Club. Meanwhile Roger, Kenneth and I had made visits to Brussels. From these it had emerged that EU funding at an unchanged level, and on an A-line, seemed secure for 2003 and probably 2004. There also now appeared to be a much greater awareness in the Community Institutions of the benefits of large-scale projects like Opera Europe. Moreover, a formal, very recent evaluation of the EOC, conducted by a Commission expert, had proved favourable.

My colleagues, besides thanking me warmly for my labours on behalf of the EOC, over a period of nearly twelve years, bestowed on me the honorific title of 'Trustee Emeritus'. They also made me an imaginative presentation, in the shape of some of Geoff Dunbar's original drawings for the *CLV*, signed by him. I was delighted with both these tokens of esteem and affection.

There was to be a postscript. Maura and I decided to go to St Petersburg and see *The Rape of Lucretia* there. Our production represented the first showing of the Opera in the 'Venice of the North' since 1965, when Britten had himself conducted it there. Although it was a restaging of the one we had taken to Hungary, there were significant changes. The conductor (Christophe Durrant), the Stage Director (Elaine Kidd), all but one of the members of the Orchestra, and all the male voices, were new.

Sadly, the lorry bringing the props and costumes from Riga was blocked at the Russian border by Customs Officials until very early on the day of the first performance – and then only released following a direct approach to the Deputy Head of Customs for the whole of Russia! It was blocked again by the St Petersburg authorities at the gates of the City. And it reached the Hermitage 75 minutes before curtain up! The Director, having feared the worst, had rehearsed the company to perform without any scenery – apart from three wooden cases. It was too late to change, so that was how both performances were done! Incidentally, the Hermitage authorities had by now shut their gates, so the lorry was imprisoned for the night. Such are the hazards of doing business in Russia! Despite these unfavourable circumstances, the Company put on a very good show. On both nights they were very well received by attentive audiences.

As a postscript to all this, it is worth adding that the EOC has been given to understand by Liverpool – Cultural Capital of Europe for 2008 – that, for five years, it will receive sponsorship in return for performing the *première* of its annual production each year, beginning in 2004. This is very good news.

CHAPTER 25

Closing thoughts on the future
of the European Union

WHEN I CAME TO choose a final chapter heading I had no pre-conceived views about content. Perhaps it would consider the state of my family; of the nation; of Europe; or of the world. Having written the book, it is apparent that – while my life has had many facets – my most important work has been concerned with the construction of that 'ever closer union among the peoples of Europe' which, since 1957, has been the declared and noble aim of the European Community, and more recently of the European Union. I have been engaged in its workings for over 50 years. So I shall close with a few reflections on where that Union stands today.

Emile Noël

I begin with a backward look. It is a pleasant duty to recall something of the role played in the Union's development, for more than thirty years, by one of its chief architects – the one I knew longest and best: Emile Nöel, a great personal friend. He retired as Secretary-General of the Commission in 1987; served for several years as President of the European University Institute at Florence; and died in 1996 at the age of only 73. A year later, a special 'Day of Tributes' to him was organised, at the European Commission Offices in London. With former British Commissioners, other Senior Officials of the Commission, and Emile's daughter, I was pleased to take part. There were some twenty interventions, but little repetition. Though I had known Emile for nearly forty years, and could have addressed many aspects of his personality, I focused instead on how he had worked when I was closest to him – from 1973 to 1981. I set the scene, however, by saying that Emile had been regarded as outstanding, already at the age of 30, when in Strasbourg; and, by the time of the Heath negotiations in 1961-63, had become an incipient legend.

Emile lived for his work, with no time for other active pursuits. Yet somehow, he kept himself extraordinarily well informed, at generalist level, on a huge range of subjects: whether scientific, academic or cultural. People

Emile Nöel, ca. 1973.

thought him ascetic: even called him 'the monk'. True, he regularly worked non-stop through the lunch hour, taking only a glass of water. But when he <u>did</u> lunch or dine, usually officially, he was something of a *gourmet*. He had a fabulous memory, and a great sense of the appropriate. He was absolutely truthful, and absolutely incorruptible. He was a perceptive judge of character. He had an old-world courtesy, and preferred backstage to limelight. As Secretary-General, his loyalty was always to the Institution and to the European Community. His country of origin was never privileged, in his thoughts or in his work.

Many officials, not only in the Commission but also outside, saw Emile as remote and awesome. Many were frightened to approach him on that account. They were wrong. However busy, he was always willing to see people, regardless of rank or station. As his Secretary was heard to say, '*Il était à la disposition de tout le monde*'. He listened carefully, and gave straight answers. His responses were brief, never over-stated, always well considered. They were based on a vast fund of experience. And they were often spiced by his quiet, but strong, sense of humour. This openness to people was a great strength. To quote his Secretary again, it meant that '*il était au courant de tout*'.

In concluding that memorable day's discussions, Professor Helen Wallace, the Rapporteur, rightly remarked that two key conclusions could be drawn: namely that Emile was one of the great Europeans, to be placed alongside Monnet, Schuman, Adenauer, Spaak and Luns; and that he inspired huge respect and affection amongst very many different people.

British attitudes to the EU

How does the EU stand today? Before addressing that broad issue, some closing thoughts on British attitudes are in order. I have considered earlier why so many politicians, and many of the media, are anti-European. They would mostly prefer to be called Euro-sceptic; but that is another word for the same thing. They choose to ignore the fact that, in 1975, Harold Wilson's Labour Government organised a referendum on whether the UK should remain in the Community, which it had entered just two years earlier. All three major parties argued for a 'yes'. And over 67% of the votes cast were in favour. Twenty years later, in 1996, at a time when most of the Tory Party had gone into a strongly anti-European mode, an opinion poll showed 51% of mainland Brits nevertheless believed the UK should 'share more sovereignty with the other Member States'. These facts are difficult to reconcile with the claims made by politicians and media that everyone in Britain would like to see the powers of the EU reduced – or even that we should withdraw from the organisation completely! But, because they are made, let us briefly consider the reasons why the EU is a good thing, and why Britain should play a positive part in it.

On the first point, let us recall the seven main reasons advanced by the Founding Fathers in the 1950s for establishing the Communities. First, two devastating World Wars had shown beyond doubt the need for constraints on the unbridled nation state. Second, there was no faith that the United Nations could make nation states conform to rules of civilised conduct. Third, there was a need to confront Stalin's aggressive empire: a monolith which embraced all the then Communist world, including China. Fourth, there was a need for Europe to come together if she wanted to count for anything in the world. Fifth, it was essential for Europe to put an end to protectionism, to achieve economic health. Sixth, Germany must be anchored in a democratic framework. Seventh, inter-governmentalism was seen as an inadequate response to these challenges: elements of supra-nationality were essential.

All but one of the Founding Fathers' reasons are just as valid today. The only exception is that Stalin's Empire has gone. But there remain many major threats to peace in Europe and the World. These include uncertainties about the future of Russia, which could still develop in very different ways, and about China; permanent tension in the Indian sub-continent, rendered infinitely more dangerous by successful Indian and Pakistani nuclear tests; the likely emergence of 'rogue' States armed with nuclear weapons; the unresolved Arab-Israeli question; fundamentalism in Islam, with consequent threats to one third of Europe's energy supplies; grave instability in Africa; and the terrorist threat.

Let us also recall that the existence of the Union has contributed hugely to our prosperity. With NATO, it has ensured that Europe survived the Cold War, and that Russia, after forty-five years of unrelenting aggression, has retired behind her old borders. Sadly, and to their shame, most British political leaders say little about these achievements; but they are recognised, and appreciated at their true worth, elsewhere. The EU counts in the world. Its population, with 15 Member States, is smaller than China's or India's; but bigger than those of either the US or the Russian Federation. Its GDP in 2002 was not far off that of the US; and nearly twice that of Japan. It is far the largest trading group in the world. It is also, and few realise this, the biggest provider of public development aid to the Third World. So why do people say the Union cannot afford to do this or that? What nonsense! It is big enough and strong enough to do anything America can do. The limiting factor is not size or riches: it is a lack of ambition, self-confidence and political will, and of the necessary political structure. In Britain, it's fashionable to say the Union should not become a Federation. This is a case of nobody daring to notice the emperor is naked. The Union is a Federation, even if only a partial one; has been since before we joined in 1973; and ironically moved a lot farther down the federal road under, successively, Margaret Thatcher, John Major and Tony Blair. Moreover twelve of its fifteen Member States have a single currency. It is a family of European peoples which deserves our support, and our active participation. Instead, British Prime Ministers in practice keep us as marginal players. Too often they seem to prefer that the UK should be an extra State of the USA – with duties but no rights!

What is the alternative to membership? As long ago as 1979, Sir Nicholas Henderson, ending his distinguished spell as British Ambassador in Paris, deliberately leaked his valedictory despatch to the Foreign Office, in which he proclaimed that Britain, far from being the World Power of its politicians' pretensions, was no longer even in the first rank of the European Powers! How true! Britain outside the Union would have no serious voice in world affairs. As Tony Blair said in 2001[1], 'the tragedy for British politics – for Britain –

has been that politicians of both parties have consistently failed, not just in the 1950s but on up to the present day, to appreciate the emerging reality of European integration. And in doing so, they have failed Britain's interest'.

And yet the Prime Minister, whilst thus paying lip-service to the importance of the EU's role, does nothing effective to advance its cause. Was his first thought, when the present crisis over Iraq arose, to fulfil Britain's absolute duty, under the Treaty on European Union, to *'inform and consult [the other Member States] within the Council on any matter of Foreign and Security Policy of general interest, in order to ensure that the Union's influence is exerted as effectively as possible by means of concerted and convergent action'?* Hardly. He unilaterally offered support, including military support, to the United States in any confrontation with Iraq.

The Conservatives, as Blair pointed out, are completely split on EU issues: only the Liberal Democrats are firmly in favour.

The European Union today

In 1986, when I left the Commission, the EU had been up-beat. The Community was moving to adoption of the Maastricht Treaty. The Commissioners were a strong bunch; led by Jacques Delors, an extraordinarily able and inspiring President. And Community officials were generally of high quality. How come that, sixteen years later, the EU was in the doldrums; the Commission had been forced to resign as a body, in 1999; and many officials were demoralised?

The answer lies in a massive failure of leadership. Delors came to the end of his second and last term in January, 1995. His nine years in office had seen the signature and entry into force of the Single European Act and the Maastricht Treaty: the biggest steps towards ever closer union since British entry in 1973. His departure began a long period of decline. He was succeeded by the weakest Commission President ever: Jacques Santer. This followed the solitary and regrettable refusal by John Major to accept a much stronger Belgian candidate, Jean-Luc Dehaene. Santer, under pressure from President Chirac, then allowed his entire Commission to resign, rather than insisting on the departure of a French Commissioner, Madame Cresson, which would have averted Parliament's censure motion. One of his Commissioners put to him the sensible idea that, if Madame Cresson refused to go, she should be deprived of all her responsibilities. This would have required no more than a simple majority vote in the Commission. But Santer was frightened by Chirac and did not have the courage. These and other factors combined to produce a collapse of morale within the

Commission. The subsequent assumption of office by the Prodi Commission has done nothing to restore it.

But the failure of leadership is not limited to the Commission. At top, national level, Mitterand was replaced by Chirac in 1994; Major by Blair in 1997; and Kohl by Schröder in 1998. Mitterand and Kohl had their faults domestically, but they had ambitious aims for Europe. Their successors gave no serious leadership in the period of negotiation of the Amsterdam and Nice Treaties which followed, from 1996 to 2000. Neither Major nor Blair have been relevant.

For over a decade it has been clear that the opportunity existed massively to enlarge the EU, bringing in Central and East European countries formerly part of the Soviet Bloc. Three things were needed to achieve this in favourable circumstances: enlargement negotiations with all serious applicant countries; a financial settlement giving generous support for countries recovering from half a century of Soviet Bloc mis-management; and a complete adaptation of the EU Institutions to take account of enlargement from fifteen to twenty-five Member States and more. The enlargement negotiations have been completed; the financial settlement is sadly ungenerous; the applicant countries have nevertheless agreed to massive internal reforms; but the adaptation of the EU Institutions has got virtually nowhere.

Last month, the Heads of Government agreed to admit ten new Member States to the EU as early as 1 May 2004: the Czech Republic, Cyprus, Estonia, Hungary, Latvia, Lithuania, Malta, Poland, Slovakia and Slovenia. Many things could meanwhile go awry. Some – either of the old or the proposed new Member States – could fail to ratify the Accession Treaties. Or there could be slippage in timing. But there is much momentum; so my guess is that all will probably join, and we shall have an EU of twenty-five Member States. In other words, we shall be on the way to creating a zone of freedom, human rights, democracy, peace and prosperity stretching from the Atlantic to the borders of Russia. It is something we should all heartily welcome.

Let me, *en passant*, dispel a British Euro-myth. Our people are constantly told that the Founding Fathers of the Community, in the 1950s, deliberately wanted to keep it small; that they would have opposed its enlargement to the present fifteen Member States; and that they would have opposed still more adding another ten. Nothing could be further from the truth. Way back in 1947, when the Marshall Plan was launched, the USSR forbade the Soviet Bloc countries of Central and East Europe to participate. Thereafter these countries were virtually isolated from Western Europe, until *'Die Wende'* in 1989. When Robert Schuman launched his Declaration proposing a European Coal and Steel Community, on 9 May 1950, the invitation went to all the other countries of Europe. When the EEC Treaty was signed by the Six in 1957, it deliberately included a clause calling on 'the other peoples of Europe who share their ideal to join in their efforts'. There was never a wish to exclude any European country. Indeed, anybody who knew Monnet – as I did – or has read his memoirs, knows that he was always favourable to a broader Europe. He, and the other Founding Fathers, would have been overjoyed to see the coming together of virtually the whole of Europe.

We must now ask whether – given that the Heads of Government have signally failed to prepare the Institutions for the enlargement to which they have rightly committed us – it can in fact work? The first enlargement – when Denmark, Ireland and Britain joined – was feasible by simply increasing numbers of individuals in the different Institutions: Parliament, the Council, the Court of Justice and the Commission. The second enlargement – when Greece joined – followed the same course. But by now, with Ten Member States in place of the original Six, the machinery was creaking.

Everybody realised that, when Spain and Portugal joined, there would have to be big changes in the Council. Accordingly, just before their Accession, the Single European Act was agreed, enabling many important decisions to be taken by qualified majority voting [QMV] in the Council, instead of by unanimity. Similarly, ahead of the enlargement which took in Austria, Finland and Sweden, the Maastricht Treaty substantially increased the areas of QMV. However the composition of the Commission was not changed by either instrument: so it remained the case that two Commissioners would come from each large Member State, and one from each of the rest. Thus, by 1995, the number of the Commissioners had progressively risen from the initial nine to no less than twenty. It has never worked properly since then, and neither has the EU for which it is meant to provide the initiative.

Ahead of the latest enlargement, the Heads of Government agreed in principle that further Institutional reform was again essential. The Amsterdam Treaty of 1997 represented a first attempt. Realising this was not enough, they moved on to sign the Nice Treaty in 2001. Taken together, these two Treaties effected some modest progress. What did they do – and fail to do? Usefully, they provided a ceiling on the number of MEPs, namely 720: this is meant to apply no matter how many new Member States join.

There are also further extensions of QMV; but these are of modest importance.

But what about the sins of omission? The Heads of Government, as always, passed over in silence the fact that, where unanimity remains the rule, as most notably with regard to the Common Foreign and Security Policy, in an enlarged Community there are unlikely to be any decisions at all in areas of controversy. They should have had the courage to say honestly to their peoples: *'Where there is no QMV, we cannot pretend to have serious policies at all, and such matters should in future be defined only as aspirations'*. They preferred silence.

But the worst decisions taken by the Heads of Government have to do with the Commission. Following the impending entry into force of the Nice Treaty in February 2002, and the recent Copenhagen Summit, they may be summarised as follows. When the Ten new Member States join, the Commission will be enlarged by one per country, making thirty Commissioners – a patently absurd concept. After the first subsequent elections to the European Parliament, the College will be reduced to one Commissioner per Member State. The number will thus fall to twenty-five: a figure almost equally absurd. Thereafter – though the number of Commissioners <u>can</u> in theory be changed by unanimous decision of the Council – there is no <u>requirement</u> for change until two <u>further</u> Member States have joined! Then, the number of Commissioners is to be less than the number of Member States. The Members are to be chosen on a rotation system, based on the principle of equality. The implementing arrangements are to be adopted by the Council, again acting unanimously. After that time, each successive College is to be so composed as to reflect satisfactorily the demographic and geographical range of all Member States of the Union.

In addition, under the Nice Treaty, the position of the President of the Commission is enormously strengthened. The Commission is to work under his political guidance. He will decide on its internal organisation, and allocate portfolios as and when he wishes. The Members of the Commission act under the Authority of the President. A Member shall resign if the President so requests, after obtaining the approval of the College.

All this is complete nonsense. In the Community – and especially when there are twenty-five Member States – there must be a really strong Commission. That means it must be small. My experience of working for nine years as Deputy Secretary-General of that Institution – a period when I attended some 300 Commission meetings – leads me to the view that the best number of Commissioners would be thirteen, and an absolute maximum would be fifteen. Experience of a Commission of 20, since the last enlargement, has demonstrated that it does not work: a Commission of 25 would be a disaster.

It is quite clear that, if the Heads of Government had been serious, the Treaty rule that the Commission must include at least one national of each Member State should have been changed now – before enlargement. And why not? Commissioners are not there to 'represent' their country. Their sole responsibility is *'to act in the general interest of the Community and be completely independent in the performance of their duties.'* There is no reason why the whole area of the EU should not be broken up into thirteen (or fifteen) groups of countries, with a Commissioner coming from each.

The strong Commission must of course have a strong President. But it is not right that so large a share of the Commission's power as is now arranged, should be vested in its President. Historically, the Heads of Government have been very fallible in their choice of incumbent. For different reasons, Gaston Thorn and Romano Prodi have both been relatively poor Presidents; and Jacques Santer's hopelessness led to resignation of the whole College. Jacques Delors showed, on the other hand, that a strong President can lead the Commission very effectively without extra powers. With a small Commission, every Member should be capable of making a serious, personal contribution to the working of the College. The relationship between President and Members should be one of trust and co-operation. The President should remain, as he has always been up to now *'primus inter pares'*. If not, the Commission will not enjoy public confidence. It will be seen as a one-man show.

In short, the Heads of Government have left an appalling mess. They have, however, also set up a Convention, under the Presidency of Valéry Giscard d'Estaing, former President of the French Republic, to elaborate proposals for the content of a 'Constitutional Treaty' for the EU. It is requested to report ahead of the European Council in June, 2003. This is then to form the basis of an Inter-Governmental Conference, to which all the new Member States are also to be invited, to elaborate a Treaty to be signed after their accession.

The idea of a Constitution is sound. The European Parliament put forward a draft text as long ago as 1984; and it is incredible that it took the European Council upwards of twenty years to pick up the ball. Having done so, however, they should have concluded a draft Treaty early enough for it to be adopted, in both existing and new Member States, as an integral part of the process of Accession. It will be infinitely harder afterwards.

It is impossible for one who has spent a lifetime working for European unity, and is optimistic by nature, to end on a note of total discouragement. My last word, therefore, is an expression of hope that Giscard d'Estaing's Convention will produce a draft which not only remedies the flaws here identified, but is so persuasive that it can be adopted rapidly despite the obvious difficulties. I hope too that a new generation of European statesmen will emerge, comparable in stature to the Founding Fathers of the 50s and 60s; that they will see both the challenge and the dangers of today; and that they will take an imaginative and courageous line with public opinion radically different from that of Europe's present political leaders. If they did so, my belief is that their peoples, disenchanted with a generation of so-called leaders who talk only about a cushy life, would respond well to a new lot who talked instead about great and noble causes.

Notes to the text

Introduction to the Notes

*T*HESE NOTES *need an introduction, to explain where things came from. Whilst I have done little research, I have an armoury of factual material. When The Old House was acquired from my brother, in 1981, all the valuable family papers and photographs at Ackenthwaite became my property. Our attics are a Treasure House.*

Amongst the papers was the original text of a book 'The Audland Family', researched and written by my father, Brigadier Audland, after his retirement in 1951: although not formally published, a copy of this was deposited in the County Record Office, County Offices, Kendal, and is open for consultation. Initially limited to the Audlands, it was extended to my mother's – Shepherd-Cross – family. The original text – with family trees – is signed, and dated March 1973.

Many diaries are also in The Old House. They include those of my father, going back to October 1911, and then right through the First World War. They cover also the whole of the Second World War and on to 1946. Also present are the diaries of my mother, almost continuous from September 1939 to the same date; of my wife, Maura; and of myself.

My own diaries, going back to 1967, have in general the character of appointment books, with few records of what I thought. But there are exceptions: after attending some important event, I would occasionally record impressions in detail. Alternatively I would record them in separate notes, or copies of letters to the family. For checking essential dates in earlier days, I have my passports going back to 1947: how useful it was, until the 1970s, to have the passport stamped with a date each time one crossed a frontier. One's passport became a permanent record of all international movements. I likewise have my school reports; and, for my first 18 months in the Army, my Pay Book, in which all sorts of things were recorded.

There is a large array of official publications and other papers, for example Treaties; official records of conferences, such as those of the Heath negotiations for British entry into the European Community; and similar. All these have been kept, on matters where I was personally involved in the affairs they covered.

There is a particularly rich series of photo collections, going back for 130 years.

In short, there was an enormous amount of material available before I started to write. I followed the advice on authorship of Giles Andreae: 'Don't get it right, get it written'.

Nevertheless, a lot had to be checked through before starting, so as to think myself back into a given period before trying to write it up. It has been hard work, but evocative. Patrick Davis wrote the following, in A Child at Arms *(ISBN 0-907675-54-9.) 'Probably it is not possible to recall with accuracy how one thought 25 years ago…There are certain recorded facts, chartered landmarks among the deceiving mists…Surviving documents, letters, notes in diaries, prove these… The rest is inference and reconstruction, for after 25 years what are we left with but the memory of memories, random, illusive, doubtfully authentic?' In my case, however, the time-span is not 25 years, but nearly three times as long! I hope memory has not played too many tricks on me.*

Chapter 1: Family Origins and Parents

1. The following is a summary of the Audland Family History. On my father's side, the family was traced back accurately to the first half of the sixteenth century at Ackenthwaite. (Indeed, if one could assume that the Audland or Adeland family are the lineal descendants of the De Astentwayt or De Astenthwaite family, who lived previously at Ackenthwaite – and there is circumstantial evidence for this – then the line goes back to the mid-thirteenth century.) My Audland ancestors were yeomen, owning houses at Ackenthwaite and Woodhouse, and fields in the locality, and often serving as churchwardens at Heversham and as jurors. ('Owning' is here used in the 16th/17th century sense of Customary Hold or Freehold: under either tenure, the leaseholder had the absolute right to will or sell the property as he/she wished, so long as the manor rental and fines were paid.) From the early seventeenth century at least, the family were blacksmiths, and in the eighteenth century whitesmiths. The present house – then known as 'Ackenthwaite House' – was 'restored' in 1735, and parts of it are probably of sixteenth century origin. It has, in the 20th century, been extended and restored by my parents and by us.

   In the early nineteenth century the family moved into the professional classes, and became more mobile. William Fisher Audland (1803-1861), educated at Kendal Grammar School, Sedbergh School and Queen's College, Oxford, was ordained; and then remained at his College, where he ended as Bursar and Senior Fellow. His brother John (1813-1892), my great-grandfather, likewise educated at Kendal, studied at Guy's and St Thomas's Hospitals, and became a General Practitioner at Tintern. He set the pattern of moving back to Ackenthwaite on retirement, which has since become something of a habit in the family. My great-uncle, John Audland, was educated at Magdalen College, Oxford, and became a country clergyman, retiring to Ackenthwaite after 36 years as Rector of Dinton, Wiltshire. His younger brother Edward (my grandfather) studied medicine at Guy's Hospital, London; and became a General Practitioner in Wellingborough. Both rode to hounds. On the death of their father's widow, in 1892, the house passed to my Grandfather, although my great-uncle was the older: perhaps because the former had four surviving children, and the latter was not married. My great-uncle lived there till his death in 1931. It then became a holiday house for my grandfather, who also died there.

My grandfather acquired a Coat of Arms on 7th October 1929. These are described as *'Argent on a bend between two owls Sable a caduceus Proper'*; the crest as *'On a wreath of colours (Argent and Sable), in front of a wing Sable a sprig of oak fructed Proper'*; and the motto as *'Firmus et intrepidus'*.

The Family History also shows that, at various times, there were other groups of Audlands in Westmorland and Lancashire, the name being usually traceable back to the sixteenth century. Such groups existed at Preston Patrick, Crooklands, Endmoor, Holmescales, Gatebeck, Old and New Hutton, Firbank, Lambrigg, Kendal, Crosthwaite, Holme, Burton, Kirkby Lonsdale, Preston, Bolton and even Liverpool. (From the Old Hutton group came the redoubtable John Audland of Old Hutton (1630-1664), and his wife Anne, who were converted to Quakerism by George Fox personally in 1652. John was a major figure amongst the Quakers in their earliest days. He preached throughout England; he and his wife suffered imprisonment for the faith; and he died of pneumonia contracted in prison.) It seems probable that all these different groups of Audlands were in some way related to each other: those at Preston, Bolton and Liverpool were indeed related to those at Preston Patrick. But, although my father made extended efforts to prove connections between these groups and the Audlands of Ackenthwaite and Woodhouse, he never succeeded.

The Shepherd-Cross family is also covered in the Family History, though my father could not trace its origins back so far. The picture, since the early eighteenth century, is of a line of successful businessmen, initially with legal qualifications, based in Bolton, Lancashire. It starts with Hamer Cross (1734-1805), who was an Attorney. His son James (1771-1850) was apprenticed to an Attorney: whether he became one is unclear. The family was well off, thanks mainly to the industrial revolution and the growth of the cotton industry in Lancashire. James was owner of the Mortfield Bleaching Mill, and other mills. In 1818, he and three other men founded the Hardcastle, Cross and Company Bank (which later became William Deacon's Bank). James's son, Thomas Cross JP (1805-1879), kept these same businesses going. They must have done well: he ended up owning three estates, in Lancashire, Cumberland and Nottingham. Thomas was father of my maternal Grandfather, Herbert Cross (1847-1916), who was destined to complicate the family tree by marrying twice, and changing his surname to Shepherd-Cross in the process. His first wife was Lucy Mary Shepherd-Birley, of Bolton. She was an only child, and her clergyman father provided in his will that she would inherit his estate only if her husband added either Birley or Shepherd to his surname. Herbert's second wife, Patty Penelope Horter, had been governess to Lucy's children.

Herbert Shepherd-Cross must have been impressive. Though he studied for the Bar, he was forced to abandon that pursuit *'due to rheumatic gout'*, so he ran the family Bleaching Mill, which by now had an international reputation; and became the first Chairman of the Bleachers' Association of Manchester. He undertook numerous public duties. He and his brother built St Thomas's Church, Bolton. He was Bolton's senior MP from 1885 to 1906, when ill-health forced retirement. By then he was living in Hamels Park, Hertfordshire, which he had bought in 1884; and he also bought a town house in Queen's Gate Gardens. In Hertfordshire, too, he undertook many public duties; and largely financed the restoration of the Parish Church at Braughing. He died at Hamels in 1916.

2. The term 'DA and QMG' means that my father was 'Deputy Adjutant and Quarter-Master General' for the Corps. During the Second World War, the Fifth Corps in Italy would have comprised around 50,000 men; the two senior and co-equal officers below the Corps Commander, a Lieutenant-General, were the Brigadier General Staff (BGS) and the DA and QMG. The latter was responsible for all administrative and logistical matters. My father's BGS, for part of the time, was Toby Lowe, subsequently Lord Aldington of Cossack fame.

3. My father was, at different times in retirement, a Deputy-Lieutenant; a Justice of the Peace; a member of the Planning Committee, and later the Development Control Committee, of the Westmorland County Council; Chairman of the South Westmorland Section of the General Commissioners of Income Tax; Chairman of various Hospital Committees; Chairman of the Board of Visitors of the then Open Prison at Hang Bridge on the Milnthorpe to Burton Road (to which he was appointed after conducting a strong campaign against the Prison's creation!); and Churchwarden at Milnthorpe.

4. *Inter alia*, he bought the (south) paddock at Ackenthwaite in 1933 for £133; bought Smithy Cottage – now The Old Smithy – in 1943 for £540 (which later passed to me); and re-roofed, restored and enlarged the House itself for £4,000 (1951-1953).

5. Major-General Sir John Winterton KCB, KCMG, CBE (1898-1987).

Chapter 2: Childhood and Twyford

1. Here are further details about The Old House in the 1930s. The front [south] door led into a passage, with drawing room on right and dining room on left, both very small. At the end, a door with glass panels opened into a short transverse passage, with kitchen on right, and pantry on left. Stairs ahead led upwards to the first floor and down to the cellar. Upstairs, there were two (double) front bedrooms; a single room left rear; and a bathroom right rear. The

bathroom contained a huge Victorian bath, large enough for two boys easily to
bath in together, one at each end.

2. *Shades of the Prison-House* by the Rev R G Wickham, published in 1986 by
Foxbury Press, Winchester (ISBN 0 946053 01 4).

3. 'Memories of Twyford School 1932-36', written by G M Audland in 1987, not
published.

4. See Wickham Op cit p 94.

5. See Wickham Op cit p. 115. Those masters who principally taught me were
Major Christopher Bull (who taught for 54 years); Lesley Davies; Charles
Mason (who taught for 51 years); Desmond Hill (killed as a fighter pilot in
World War II); and Maurice Taylor.

Chapter 4: Army Service in Britain and the Middle East

1. See Chapter 1.
2. ISBN 0 213 16554 6.

Chapter 5: Entering the British Diplomatic Service

1. See Chapter 2, page 26.
2. Photo of the Forest Divonne Family. Those shown are [L to R] Monsieur and
Madame; Louis, Anne-Marie (Mimi) and Amédée.

Chapter 6: Berlin and Bonn – the Federal Republic joins the Free World (1949-52)

1. Although most Germans suppose the airlift was a US invention, in fact it was
devised by an RAF Officer, Air-Commodore Waite. His idea was sold by the
British Military Governor, General Sir Brian Robertson, to the American,
General Lucius Clay. If President Truman had not then agreed the plan, the
airlift could not have happened. When the operation got going, the Americans
became the senior partners. But the British share was a good deal larger than
most Germans think. Of the 550,000 sorties flown in 11 months, 32% were
British. And the British had the heaviest casualties. However the US planes
were on average larger: so, of the 2.3 million short tons of supplies carried to
Berlin, only 23% were carried by the British. The French did not play any
significant role in the air, since they were heavily engaged in Vietnam; but they
helped by extending Tegel Airport in their Sector in a mere 85 days. In this way
a City of two million people was completely supplied by air for nine months. By
the end of the operation, aircraft were flying into West Berlin at the rate of one
every 65 seconds. In a single day, 12,941 tons of supplies were brought in, on
1,400 flights. Overall, there were 300,000 flights.

2. The Occupation Statute was published by HMSO as Cmd 7677 (Annex 1)
under the Title 'Germany No.1 (1949)'.

3. André François-Poncet was one of France's most senior Ambassadors. Many years later, his son, Jean, was to become French Foreign Minister.
4. The Bonn Conventions were printed by HMSO as Cmd. 9368 under the title 'Germany No 1: Documents relating to the Termination of the Occupation Régime in the Federal Republic of Germany'. They entered into force in 1955.
5. I suspect it was M. Jacques Patey.
6. General Heusinger (1897-1982) was on the General Staff of the German Army from 1931-1944, rising to the rank of General in 1943, when he was Chief of Military Operations in the Army High Command. Arrested by the Gestapo following the failed assassination attempt on Hitler on 20 July 1944, he was released four months later as not having been involved. Following the establishment of the Federal German Republic, he and General Speidel were in 1950 called out of retirement to prepare for the establishment of a German Federal Army. Heusinger subsequently became Inspector-General of the Bundeswehr, and then Chairman of the Military Committee of NATO.
7. Later, Sir John Killick GCMG.

Chapter 7: Strasbourg: Maura and the Council of Europe (1952-55)

1. Later Sir Peter Scarlett.
2. Book of Addresses by the Rev J d'E E Firth, published by OUP in 1938.

Chapter 10: The Heath Negotiations for Accession to the European Communities (1961-63)

1. ISBN 0 333 57992 5.
2. 'Narrative Reports by the UK Delegations to the Conferences at Brussels and Luxembourg for British Accession to the three European Communities: 1961-1963'. Available from HMSO.
3. General Agreement on Tariffs and Trade.
4. See Chapter 2 and Chapter 5 above esp. pages 66-68.
5. ISBN: 0 340 70852 2.
6. Some might argue that Margaret Thatcher also merited this description. Certainly she may be considered a national statesman. But in my view she was too insular and 'Britain centred' – and did not trouble to understand other peoples of the world and their problems sufficiently – to allow her to be regarded as a statesman of world class.
7. See Chapter 6 above, page 90.

Chapter 11: Argentina, the Falkland Islands, and completing the family (1963-67)

1. For more details see Sir Eugen's book *The Drama of the Graf Spee and the Battle of the River Plate*.

Chapter 12: The Foreign Office: Rhodesian Sanctions; Science and Technology

1. See Chapter 3 above.
2. See Chapter 6 above.

Chapter 13: Bonn & Berlin: Ostpolitik and the Four-Power Talks (1970-73)

1. ISBN 3-8046-8755-5
2. The word *Aufenthaltsgenehmigungszulassungsschein* meant, literally, 'a coupon for acquiring a residence permit'. It was invented by the Allies to avoid their having to admit the concept that the GDR was a sovereign Government with power to issue visas. Its spelling – since it is not in any German dictionary – gave rise to a recent correspondence between myself and Klaus Blech – once the German Delegate to the Bonn Group – which students of what Mark Twain called 'the awful German language' might find amusing. I had originally spelt it with two less -s's- [*Aufenthaltsgenehmigungzulassungschein*] but checked with him. He commented as follows. 'You drove me to look up my German grammar for such 'word-worms'. I thought the -s- indicated a logical genitive connection; the *certificate* of the *grant* of an *authorisation* of *residence*. Wrong. We are not that logical. We do as you do: we line up the various words as they are, but we write and speak them together, and we use what my grammar calls 'joining elements'. Basically they are euphonic, and have very little to do with the gender of the word. So you may have an -s- at the end of a female noun where it would never occur if used independently. If two people have problems in their marriage, they might go to the '*Eheberatung*' [*Ehe* is feminine]. If this does not help, they see their lawyers for '*Scheidungsberatung*' [*Scheidung* is feminine as well, but with with -s-]. You simply have to learn it by ear, <u>our</u> ear.'
3. This incident throws light on Kissinger's memoirs touching Germany, where he claims a lot of credit for the outcome of the Four-Power Talks.
4. See Chapter 6, page 88.

Chapter 14: Joint Deputy-Secretary-General, European Commission (1973-1977)

1. Session 1987-8, HL Paper 66.

Chapter 15: Sole Deputy-Secretary-General, European Commission (1977-81)

1. See Chapter 12.
2. Photo of the Political Directors. Those shown are [L to R]: Caspar Reyninck [NL]; Alfred Cahen [BEL]; Noel Dorr [IRE]; Peter Dywig [DK]; Julian Bullard [UK]; Paul Merz [LUX]; Walter Gardini [I]; Klaus Blech [FRG]; Christopher Audland [Commission]; and Jacques Dupont [F].

Chapter 16: Director General for Energy (1981-86)

1. Later Permanent Under Secretary F.C.O. Now Lord Wright of Richmond, GCMG.

Chapter 17: Chernobyl Rapporteur-General, and leaving the Commission

1. INFCIRC 321 of January 1985.
2. INFCIRC 310 of January 1984.
3. The Convention on the Physical Protection of Nuclear Materials.
4. See Chapter 12.
5. COM (86) 327 Final.
6. COM (86) 434 Final.
7. This communication was delayed, but eventually issued as COM (87) 96 Final.
8. COM (86) 607 Final.
9. COM (86) 667/6 Final.

Chapter 19: Presenting the European Union to the wider public

1. The Report was published as HL Paper 66 on 29 March 1988.
2. The reference is: 'Collection "Oral History" INT 564 – Sir AUDLAND Christopher.

Chapter 20: Helping Conserve the East Cumbrian Heritage

1. The White Paper, published in February 2003, was in fact no better than the predecessor green version.

Chapter 21: Europa Nostra and the International Castles Institute (IBI)

1. For Sir Evelyn Shuckburgh, see Chapter 10.
2. See 'The merger of Europa Nostra and the International Castles Institute, a historical note by Sir Christopher Audland' dated 16 August 2001, copies of which may be obtained from the Europa Nostra Secretariat at 35 Lange Voorhout, 2514 The Hague, Netherlands.
3. The latest edition, produced to mark the 40th Anniversary of Europa Nostra's creation, was published in 2003 as ISBN 90-75463-24-3.
4. This was published in 2000 as Europa Nostra Bulletin no 52. Copies may be requested from the Europa Nostra Secretariat, Lange Voorhout 35, 2514 EC The Hague, Netherlands.
5. ISBN 88-435-3345-2
6. ISBN 07181 4192 X

Chapter 22: Lancaster University – Pro-Chancellor

1. The CRILL Report was published as ISBN 1-86220-027-1

Chapter 23: The Creation of the Ruskin Foundation and the Ruskin Library

1. *Ruskin, Bembridge and Brantwood* – paperpack edition ISBN 1 85331 099 9.
2. Photo of persons involved in the inaugural meeting of the Ruskin Foundation. Those shown are the following. Back row, L to R: Tony Cann; Michael Prince; Robert Hewison; Michael Wheeler; Professor John Mackenzie; Arthur Davies; and Sir Nicholas Pearson. Front row, L to R: Christopher Audland; Catherine Edwards; Sir Richard Parsons; Elizabeth Robins; Vice-Chancellor Harry Hanham; Timothy Wilson; and Brian Pilkington.
3. Technically this Committee was not only the Ruskin Foundation Management Committee, but also a meeting of the Brantwood Management Trustees. However, the same people were members of each body. So it was usually known simply as the Management Committee, a title used from now on.
4. Photo of those at the Dinner for those receiving Honorary Doctorates connected with the creation of the Ruskin Foundation. Those in the photo were the following. Back row, L to R: Margaret Heron; Viv Wheeler; Christopher Audland; HRH Princess Alexandra; Dr Jim Dearden; Elspeth Ritchie [Hostess]; Dr Elizabeth Robins; Jill Dearden; and Michael Prince. Front row, L to R: Maura Audland; Michael Wheeler; Dr Tony Cann; Brian Heron [Pro-Chancellor]; Ruth Cann; the Hon Mary Mumford; and Professor Bill Ritchie [Vice-Chancellor and Host].

Chapter 24: The European Opera Centre: a remarkable venture

1. Those appearing on photo of one of the casts of Opera Europe's production of *La Scala di Seta* at Sierre, Switzerland, 2000, include Conductor Giovanni Pacor (Italy), 4th from L.
2. It was to receive many favourable reviews, except from one critic who was opposed to any cutting of opera scores. The EOC – at the Preview and in the credits – received public credit for its extensive contribution in terms of devising and developing the project; obtaining the support of Kent Nagano with the German Symphony Orchestra; and selecting and training the voices.

Chapter 25: Closing thoughts on the future of the European Union

1. Speech by Mr Tony Blair on 'Britain's Role in Europe' at the European Research Institute in Birmingham on 23 November 2001.

List of abbreviations used in text

ACA	Allied Control Authority
AEC	European Assocation of Conservatories
AGR	Advanced Gas-cooled Reactor
AHC	Allied High Commission for Germany
AQWG	Atomic Questions Working Group [of the Council of the Community]
ASEAN	Association of South-East Asian Nations
BAOR	British Army of the Rhine
BEPS	British Embassy Preparatory School
BIM	British Institute of Management
BJU	Bob Jones University
BKA	Bundeskanzleramt [Office of the German Federal Chancellor]
BSB	British School of Brussels
BTO	Brussels Treaty Organisation
CAP	Common Agricultural Policy
CBC	Canadian Broadcasting Corporation
CCG (BE)	Control Commission for Germany (British Element)
CDIC	Comité Directeur de l'Informatique à la Commission
CDU	Christian Democratic Union (of Germany)
CMEA	The Council for Mutual Economic Assistance
COMECON	The Council for Mutual Economic Assistance
	[Both the above acronyms refer to the Soviet Bloc Trading System]
COREPER	Comité des Réprésantants Permanents [also known as CRP]
CRILL	Committee to Review the Institutional Lessons to be Learned [of LU]
CRO	Commonwealth Relations Office
CRP	*See* COREPER
CSCE	Conference on Security and Co-operation in Europe
CSSB	Colleges and Student Support Board
CUC	Committee of University Chairmen
DAQMG	Deputy Assistant Quarter-Master General
DCB	Development Control Board [of LU]
DCC	Development Control Committee [of LU]

DDG	Deputy Director-General
DG	Director-General or Directorate-General
EAEC	European Atomic Energy Community (or Euratom)
ECSC	European Coal and Steel Community
ECU	European Currency Unit
EDC	European Defence Community
EEC	European Economic Community
EEID	European Economic Integration Department (FCO)
EEOD	The European Economic Organisations Department (FCO)
EFAH	European Forum for Arts and Heritage
EFTA	European Free Trade Association
ELDO	The European Launcher Development Organisation
EMS	European Monetary System
EOC	European Opera Centre
EPC	European Political Co-operation
ESA	The European Space Agency
ESB	European Strategy Board [of ICL]
ESC	Economic and Social Committee
ESRO	The European Space Research Organisation (ESRO)
ETL	Education Trust Ltd.
ETUC	European Trades Union Congress
EU	European Union
EURO	European Currency
EUYO	European Union Youth Orchestra
FAI	Fondo per l'Ambiente Italiano
FAO	Food and Agriculture Organisation
FDP	Free Democratic Party (of Germany)
FO	Foreign Office
FCO	Foreign and Commonwealth Office
FQT	Final Quadripartite Protocol on Berlin [brought QA into force]
FRG	Federal Republic of Germany
GAC	General Affairs Council [of the EU]
GATT	General Agreement on Tariffs and Trade
GCC	Gulf Co-operation Council
GCHQ	Government Communications Headquarters
GDR	German Democratic Republic
GRT	General Relations Treaty [between FRG & GDR]
HLEG	High-Level Energy Group [of the Community]
HLF	Heritage Lottery Fund
HLLC	High-Level Liaison Committee [IAEA-Euratom]
IAEA	International Atomic Energy Agency [HQ in Vienna]

ICL	International Computers Ltd.
ICOMOS	International Council on Monuments and Sites
IEA	International Energy Agency [HQ in Paris]
IMF	International Monetary Fund
ISG	Inter-Service Group
IT	Information Technology
JCR	Junior Common Room
JET	Joint European Torus [at Culham in Oxfordshire]
JNOC	Japanese National Oil Company
KECU	Thousands of European Currency Units
LDCAC	Lake District Campus Advisory Committee [of LU]
LLLC	Low-Level Liaison Committee [IAEA-Euratom]
LUSU	Lancaster University Students Union
MAD	Mutual Assured Destruction
MAFF	Ministry of Agriculture, Fisheries and Food
MBFR	Mutual and Balanced Force Reductions
MEP	Member of the European Parliament
MI5	The British Security Service
MI6	The British Secret Intelligence Service
MITI	Ministry for International Trade and Industry [Japanese]
NATO	North Atlantic Treaty Organisation
NEA	Nuclear Energy Agency [under OECD auspices]
NHMF	National Heritage Memorial Fund
NIC	Newly Industrialised Countries
NNWS	Non Nuclear Weapon States
NWS	Nuclear Weapon States
NPT	Nuclear Non-Proliferation Treaty
NTBT	Nuclear Test Ban Treaty
NUS	National Union of Students
NWS	Nuclear Weapon States
OAPEC	Organisation of Arab Petroleum Exporting Countries
OECD	Organisation for Economic Co-operation and Development
OPEC	Organisation of Petroleum Exporting Countries
PINC	Programme Indicatif Nucléaire de la Communité
PNEU	Parents National Educational Union
QA	Quadripartite Agreement on Berlin
QMV	Qualified Majority Voting [in the Council of the EU]
QRR	Quadripartite Rights and Responsibilities
RGC	Rose Garden Cottage
RMC	Royal Military College [Sandhurst]
RNCM	Royal Northern College of Music

RSU	Rhodesian Sanctions Unit [of the Foreign Office]
SALT	Strategic Arms Limitation Treaty
SOE	Special Operations Executive
SPD	Sozialistische Partei Deutschlands
STD	Science and Technology Department
TMI	Three Mile Island [US Reactor site]
UDI	Unilateral Declaration of Independence [Rhodesia]
UEHHA	Union of European Historic Houses Associations
UKAEA	UK Atomic Energy Authority
UN	United Nations
UNGA	UN General Assembly
UNICE	Union of the Industries of the European Community
UNSCEAR	UN Scientific Committee on Environmental Atomic Radiation
URENCO	Uranium Enrichment Company
USIS	United States Information Services
USSR	Union of Soviet Socialist Republics
VAT	Value Added Tax
VC	Vice-Chancellor
WEOG	Western European & Others Group [in UN bodies]
WES	Western Economic Summit
WEU	Western European Union
WHO	World Health Organisation
WSB	Western Sectors of Berlin
WTO	World Trade Organisation

Index

521